Structured Document
Image Analysis

H. S. Baird H. Bunke K. Yamamoto (Eds.)

Structured Document Image Analysis

With 230 Figures and 34 Tables

Springer-Verlag
Berlin Heidelberg New York
London Paris Tokyo
Hong Kong Barcelona
Budapest

Editors

Henry S. Baird

AT&T Bell Laboratories
Computing Science Research Center
600 Mountain Avenue, Room 2C-322
P. O. Box 636
Murray Hill, NJ 07974-0636, USA

Horst Bunke

Institut für Informatik und angewandte Mathematik
Universität Bern
Länggass-Str. 51, CH-3012 Bern

Kazuhiko Yamamoto

Machine Understanding Division
Electrotechnical Laboratory
1-1-4, Umezono, Tsukuba Science City
Ibaraki 305, Japan

ISBN-13:978-3-642-77283-2   e-ISBN-13:978-3-642-77281-8
DOI: 10.1007/978-3-642-77281-8

Library of Congress Cataloging-in-Publication Data.
Structured document image analysis / H.S. Baird, H. Bunke, K. Yamamoto, eds.   p.   cm.
Includes bibliographical references and index.
ISBN-13:978-3-642-77283-2 (alk. paper : U.S.)
1. Image processing.   2. Computer vision.   I. Baird, Henry S.   II. Bunke, Horst.   III.
Yamamoto, K. (Kazuhiko)   TA1632.S852   1992   621.36'7–dc20   92-27386   CIP

© Springer-Verlag Berlin Heidelberg 1992
Softcover reprint of the hardcover 1st edition 1992

Cover Design: H. Lopka, Ilvesheim
Typesetting: Camera ready by the editors
45/3140 - 5 4 3 2 1 0 - Printed on acid-free paper

To H. Clark Maziuk

Preface

Document image analysis is concerned with the automatic interpretation of images of printed and handwritten documents, including text, engineering drawings, maps, music scores, etc. Research in this field descends in an unbroken tradition from the earliest experiments in computer vision, and remains distinguished by close and productive ties between the academic and industrial communities. While the difficulty of its characteristic problems continues to stimulate basic research, general agreement on quantifiable performance standards has encouraged the evolution of sound engineering methods. As a result, research in this area supports a rapidly growing industry.

We are pleased to offer a collection of state-of-the-art papers touching on virtually every topic of current research interest: printed documents; character and symbol recognition; handwriting; graphics, maps, and technical drawings; music notation; and methodology. Among these are several authoritative critical surveys of the literature. We have singled out music notation for special emphasis since it offers an ideal vehicle for sharing basic research internationally: identical scores are available, and are unambiguously understood, in every country.

Document images offer computer vision researchers unique opportunities. The early stages of processing such as feature extraction are relatively tractable, allowing rapid access to extraordinarily challenging later stages requiring the construction of full interpretations of complex scenes. As a result, a major focus of research is the architecture of complete, integrated vision systems, often exhibiting extremely high competency. We have included several parallel studies of this kind.

All but four of these papers were first presented at the International Association for Pattern Recognition workshop on Syntactic and Structural Pattern Recognition (SSPR'90), held at Murray Hill, New Jersey USA, June 13-15, 1990. At that time, they were reviewed by three referees, and in many cases revised; since then, most have been expanded or extensively reworked for publication here. For improved balance, we have also invited four new contributions.

In the closing section of the book, we report briefly on the SSPR'90 workshop and several of its working groups. These groups, consisting of experts interested in a common topic, drew up lists of open problems and proven methods; their debates provide a fascinating perspective on the field.

Murray Hill, New Jersey, USA   Henry S. Baird

Bern, Switzerland   Horst Bunke

Tsukuba, Japan   Kazuhiko Yamamoto

July 1991

Table of Contents

Printed Documents

Character and Symbol Recognition

Handwriting

Graphics, Maps, and Technical Drawings

Music Notation

Methodology

IAPR 1990 Workshop on SSPR

Printed Documents

Towards the Understanding of Printed Documents

Thomas Bayer, Jürgen Franke, Ulrich Kressel,
Eberhard Mandler, Matthias Oberländer,
and Jürgen Schürmann

Daimler–Benz AG, Research Center Ulm,
Wilhelm–Runge–Str. 11, D–7900 Ulm, Germany

1 Introduction

Document analysis aims at the transformation of data presented on paper and addressed to human comprehension into a computer-revisable form. The pixel representation of a scanned document must be converted into a structured set of symbolic entities, which are appropriate for the intended kind of computerized information processing. It can be argued that the achieved symbolic description level resembles the degree of understanding acquired by a document analysis system. This interpretation of the term 'understanding' shall be explained a little more deeply. An attempt shall be made to clarify the important question: "Up to what level can a machine really understand a given document?" Looking at the many problems still unsolved, this is indeed questionable.

Is it acceptable to use the term understanding, if the internal data structure merely describes geometric properties? Or is it necessary, at least, to be on the level of word meanings, or even more, to have knowledge about the topics being addressed in a given letter?

In answering these questions, it is helpful to consider a particular document model, for example, the Office Document Architecture (ODA, see [Horak 85]). ODA provides a general concept for describing office documents. It allows for standardized access by all kind of text processing programs, like editors or print formatters. It also specifies an interchange format (called ODIF) not only for final, but also for revisable document formats. Though originally conceived for document generation, it gives some insight into the reverse task: document analysis.

The central idea of ODA is the distinction between layout structure and logical structure of a document. The layout structure deals with the appearance of a document, whereas the logical structure speaks about its logical constituents (*e.g.* headline, paragraph, captions, references, etc), completely disregarding any geometric properties. Obviously, the logical objects are much closer to semantics, and hence to understanding. But it would be a precipitate conclusion that layout data has nothing to do with understanding.

When trying to understand a document, the layout structure, the logical structure, or both, may be considered. A very simple processing scheme for a document understanding system might be: the document is treated as an entity and is assigned a class label according to its content type. For instance, it may be a business letter, a bill, a check, etc. Though the system tells nothing about the internal structure, it is likely to have privately gathered at least some sort of geometric information in order to have a basis for its decision.

It is a very nice experiment to render the image of a letter by only drawing the surrounding boxes of the connected components. Not only does a human observer get the immediate impression of 'text', but he may also associate categories of meaning, like 'This is the recipient, that's the date!', and so on. It is not necessary to read even a single letter. Hence, it seems possible to devise a computer program, that attaches labels to text blocks denoting their semantic category, doing so without any access to text content. On a letter, we do not know who is the recipient, and on a check we may know where the amount is printed but not how much it is.

A lot of document analysis can be done without treating character classification at all. What we get are blocks of text, each consisting of one or more lines, which themselves consist of at least one character box. The image content of the character boxes can then be delivered to a character recognizer module. After that, each character box has an associated ASCII character code. A plain string of ASCII characters can now be sent to a text editor, neglecting all information about the higher level objects. A system producing output on the letter level only accomplishes the task of a typist. The symbolic description that remains holds the same information as an ASCII file that was keyed in manually. One may have the feeling, that in many cases this is exactly what was desired: a letter by letter transformation into an ASCII string. But there is a peculiarity of reading systems to be noticed: Even though only spelling capabilities are intended, a much higher level of understanding is necessary in order to gain high accuracy on the letter level. This is proven by the fact that also human typists have a significant increase in error rate, if they do not understand the language the text was written in.

The symbolic description then contains the character content of the When no specific logical labels are attached to

Text comprehension, rather than text understanding (according to the definition given in the first paragraph), implies much more than only correct letter spelling. It is the highest level of understanding. Not only the semantic category of text portions has been perceived, but also all connotations and associations with respect to common sense knowledge must have been established at this stage.

For example, analyzing this page in front of you, a system would have to realize it as the introduction of a paper, which discusses different levels of understanding. It might remember that ODA has been mentioned to introduce the distinction between layout and logic content. And, after all, it might conclude, that document analysis really is an intricate problem.

Probably, this utopia will not come true in the near future, since many fundamental problems of pattern analysis and natural language processing are still waiting to be solved. However, specific subgoals of text comprehension could be reached. For instance the full interpretation of postal addresses for automated letter sorting. This does not only include city name and zip code, but also street name, building and floor number. Up to a certain degree this is already carried out by some commercially available products. Specific subsets of natural language, and also certain two–dimensional layout schemes, can be described using formal grammars or any other grammar–like formalism.

Consider, for example, the first page of a publication in an IEEE journal as shown in Figure 6. They all obey to a prescribed format. Thus, the layout and the logical information of such pages can be described by an appropriate formal language. Parsing such documents into their semantic constituents according to the underlying grammar appears as a rudimentary kind of comprehension. But if text content is not restricted to a very small sublanguage, or if the pages (like those of this article), are not structured according to strict layout rules, understanding must end with trivial labeling, for instance 'text block' as a layout label and 'paragraph' as a logical one. Both do in no way reflect the meaning of the document.

Besides unrestricted semantics, there is still another obstacle on the way to document understanding and comprehension. The implicit assumption was made that the document has been cleanly rendered without any distortions and errors. In this case, the necessary primitive objects for constructing higher entities can be extracted very easily and in an accurate manner. However, this assumption only holds true in the academic world, but the real world looks very much different. A reading system has to cope with varying document quality: skewed text, ink spots, merged characters, cursive script, etc. Thus, it is necessary to develop — besides structural techniques for understanding documents — appropriate preprocessing algorithms on the iconic level. They should at least partly compensate for the different sorts of noise. What is needed in practice are tools that transform a pixel representation step by step into meaningful objects. Those tools should also be efficient and reliable.

The main body of this paper will focus on some selected topics, which should elucidate the minimum requirements, if planning to build a document analysis system. But it is not a comprehensive treatment on "How to build a document analysis system," nor is it a study of the innumerable approaches in the literature. Instead, these requirements are more of a conceptual nature, in contrast to functional building blocks written in some programming language. Conceptual modules are the prerequisite for implementing functional modules, and functional modules are the prerequisite for configuring application systems.

The following sections shall discuss some of these conceptual modules more deeply. However, the software aspects, especially the data model, have been omitted completely for space reasons.

Figure 1 exhibits the set of real software building blocks which are part of an experimental system at the Daimler–Benz Research Institute. The algorithms process iconic data, generate simple symbolic primitives, (like connected components), create more structured ones (like words, lines and text–blocks), and deduce the meaning of primitives (as the character classifier does). This toolbox is alive. It grows, it is going to be improved and adapted to new problems.

The figure also includes links between different tools, specifying their dependencies: tool A can be performed only when tool B has been carried out before. Thus, functional modules can be applied and interwoven in many ways to form a specialized document analysis system. The documents considered in this paper are assumed to contain printed text, although many of the tools of the experimental system deal with handwritten patterns, graphics and photographic data.

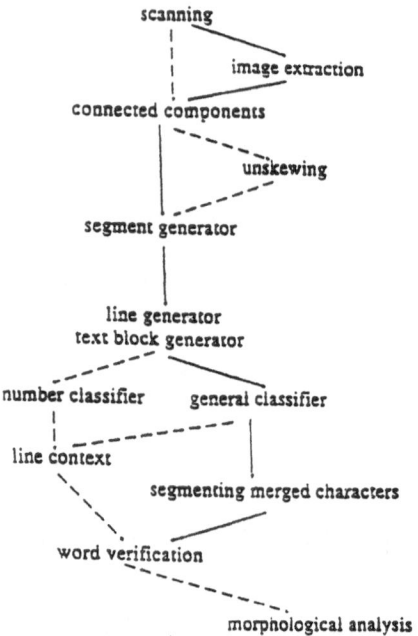

Fig. 1. Tools for building a dedicated document analysis system — the lines denote the dependencies between the algorithms. The tools composed by the path of the straight lines represent an analysis of standard documents.

The dependencies between modules may suggest a hierarchically organized system. So there arises a question, which is likely to reveal a difference between researchers, the technical attitude on the one hand, and the psychological one on the other. "Is it at all possible to design and implement a document analysis system in a strict hierarchical manner, split into separate modules with a pure bottom–up control principle?" — An example of such a partition could be: i) binary image acquisition, ii) layout analysis, iii) character classification, iv) word recognition, and finally v) text interpretation.

The answer to this question can be both "yes" and "no." It is indeed possible to build up a straightforward system. It will work very nicely — at least for the set of demo examples. But the program will comprise a lot of special rules for handling exceptions of the fundamental rules that was begun with. There only was the limited test environment. And finally the human designer has adapted himself to the test set. His original plan, of course, was to let the system adapt on his own. There is a deeper reason for all the exceptional rules, which are characteristic for systems in practice. It is a fatal assumption that so called low level processing (like character segmentation) can be done independently from higher recognition levels. People are often unaware of this assumption, but are nonetheless aiming at a 100% performance in unrestricted environments. But if this should actually be achieved, the answer to the above question must be a clear "no."

Each document analysis system needs at least two major ingredients: analysis of layout structure and classification of individual characters. Therefore, Section 2 starts with layout analysis. No specific method is proposed claiming it to be the best. The discussion should rather develop a feeling for the inherent difficulties and traps. The approach is based on primary objects which are obtained by connectivity analysis. Algorithms are available today that can do this task very efficiently.

Section 3 contains a very important subject, since it explains a sound method with respect to both theory and practice: the design and generation of polynomial classifiers together with its predominant — but not sole — application to character recognition.

A theme vividly discussed today is the combination of votes from different 'experts'. However, this field is still in its infancy. But as systems become more and more hybrid, this is a burning problem. Section 4 presents our experience with the Dempster/Shafer theory in particular.

Section 5 shows a kind of a case study. It exemplifies the integration of different knowledge sources and techniques in order to attack the merged characters problem.

Section 6 deals with higher knowledge representation, namely with modeling the structure of specialized documents, like business letters. A document representation scheme is presented along with a processing algorithm allowing for understanding structured documents.

Finally, this paper concludes with a few summarizing remarks on where we are and where we want to go.

2 Layout Analysis

2.1 Obtaining Primitive Objects

The first major algorithmic step after binary raster image acquisition is the analysis of connected components. It is important to note that this is a mere transformation into another, but still equivalent, image representation. The picture is described now not in terms of single pixels, but in terms of pixel sets — the so called connected components. For usual text documents this leads to a tremendous reduction of items. To give an impression: If a DIN A4 page is scanned with 230 dpi, this yields $2275 \times 1278 = 2{,}907{,}460$ pixels. If the page is type written with 35 lines per page, it may contain approximately 1700 characters. This roughly corresponds to 2,600 connected components. (Note, that a letter 'P' comprises two components: a black one and a white one.) It is a lucky case with character recognition, that the objects of interests so often directly correspond to connected components. But this is not always true. The case of merged characters reveals that the problem of segmentation for general vision tasks has not been solved at all. In document analysis it can be simply bypassed for a good time. The segmentation itself, that is the distinction between object and background, has been accomplished by the binary thresholding. Connected component analysis is just a clever data structure transformation helping to locate and describe these objects. The method we employ has been described in [Bartneck 89, Mandler 90a, Mandler 90b]. Here is a summary of its characteristics:

- 4×4 neighborhood is used to define connectivity of pixels. Black and white diagonals are treated asymmetrically. It is a parameter of the algorithm to regard either black diagonal pixels connected or white ones.
- The contours (*i.e.* the borders between black and white regions) are described by a chain code with four directions.
- Each contour corresponds to a connected component, which is either black or white, and *vice versa*.
- Each contour corresponds either to a black or a white region.
- All contours form a hierarchical structure representing the nesting relations:
  - Each contour (except the root) has a unique surrounding contour.
  - A contour may or may not have inner contours.
  - A contour may or may not have "brothers," which are contours with the same surrounding contour.
- From the contour code it is easy to compute features like area, circumference, center of gravity, surrounding rectangle, etc.
- The original image can be reconstructed without loss from the contour code. The reconstruction can be confined to parts of the image by selecting appropriate subsets of contours.
- The complete description of a connected component (image primitive) consists of three parts:
  - the contour code
  - the hierarchy (or nesting) information (topological features)
  - geometric features.

The detection and encoding of these image primitives can be carried out very fast using a sequential algorithm. It may operate in parallel with the raster scan process. Only two scan lines must be stored at one time in a buffer. The output of the algorithm, in particular the geometric features, is the basis of the now starting document analysis, beginning with its layout. It is worth noting, that all typical image operations like cut, rotation, size normalization and so on can be performed on a representation very close to the contour code, which we call corner sets (a corner may be regarded as the transition of a vertical edge into a horizontal edge, or *vice versa*). Since on normal documents corners are very much less in number than pixels, switching from raster image space to corner space turns out to be of great computational advantage.

2.2 Line Finding Principles

The many variations of line finding algorithms can be roughly discriminated into two categories: global and local approaches. The principle of local methods is to start with some seed object and then jump from one object to the next. For this technique a distance measures is needed plus some threshold values in order to define in geometrical terms what the next right neighbor should be.

In contrast to the local approach, global methods can do without the notion of closely related objects. They are based on features common to a group or cluster of objects. For instance, the 'y' coordinate of the object's center is a feature that is very similar for all objects within the same line.

The drawback of the local methods is that a specific metric has to be chosen first and must then be completely relied on. This works well in some, but not in all cases. The plain euclidean distance measure would fail, because the vertical line offset if often smaller than the horizontal character spacing. Consequently, a kind of weighting must be introduced. Also punctuation or diacritical marks within the text may easily mislead the local algorithm. Many further heuristics are necessary to get the method working in a reliable way.

An advantage of the local, distance based method is the preciseness of specifying mathematically what the notion "line" means. For this purpose we define the predicate SameLine(x, y) (say: 'x belongs to same line as y') by the help of the predicate RightNeighbor(x,y) (say: 'x is rightmost neighbor of y'), which is based on the chosen distance measure:

$$SameLine(x, y) ::= (x = y) \vee RightNeighbor(x, y)$$
$$\vee RightNeighbor(y, x)$$
$$\vee \exists z (SameLine(x, z) \wedge SameLine(z, y))$$

Recalling algebra, SameLine is an equivalence relation. The "lines" are the elements of the quotient set induced by the equivalence relation. Now where is the hitch? It's the predicate RightNeighbor which we assume to be context independent and hence decidable on a pure local basis. Though this technical concept of a "line" is very precise, it cannot really resemble our "common sense notion" of a text line.

A very well-known global method for line finding is the Hough transform (see [Rastogi 86]). The principal idea is that each individual pixel may be part of many potential (geometrical) lines, which have different slopes, but have this particular point in common. Since on a digital computer always a discrete resolution is used, only a limited number of different slope values are possible. This leads to a finite two dimensional parameter space with a form similar to a raster image. Peaks in this parameter space correspond to lines in the original image. But the constituents of these lines need not be all connected. Dashed lines can be recognized in the same manner as solid lines. It is also possible, to regard the individual, well separated character objects as the basic constituents of a (text) line.

A special case of the Hough transform is the projection of the whole image onto the vertical axis. The parameter space reduces to one dimension. This is applicable if we assume the document to be well aligned, that is, the slope of all text lines is zero. As long a the ratio between line spacing and line skew is such that the peaks on the projection axis do not overlap, this method is feasible.

A third approach to line finding might be expected from morphology, *e.g.* by dilatation and thinning methods. But the objections are the same as with the local methods. The meaning of gaps, for instance, are context specific. How far shall a region grow?

The next section introduces a novel approach to line finding, which incorporates a specific knowledge source in this early stage of analysis. According to the above, criteria, it stands between local and global methods. It was inspired when looking at plots showing only the surrounding boxes of the connected components. Though it is impossible to read the text, a human can tell something about the possible character values for each box. The reason behind is the typographical knowledge about the western writing style we all have assimilated. In the next section an attempt will be made to express this knowledge algorithmically.

2.3 Line Finding and Typographical Knowledge

Setting up types is an art. The final outcome of professional typesetting has been carefully adapted to human perceptive and cognitive capabilities, and last but not least, to human aesthetics. Nevertheless there exist common rules for combining letters to words, and words to lines. Although humans are able to accept a broad variety of styles, most of today's text is produced in a rather simple fashion. For conventional text it is possible to imagine five horizontal lines, controlling the horizontal alignment of letters. For explanatory purposes, they were given the following names:

- top-line
- top-line of lower-case letters
- middle-line
- base-line
- under-line

2.3.1 Different typographical classes. For European letter alphabets and character sets it is sufficient to distinguish eight typographical classes, which may be generalized into two superclasses: "symbol"- and "satellite"-class. The "satellite "-class comprises all non-letter characters.

The "symbol"-class is partitioned into:

- "**x**"-class: lower-case letters; *e.g.* m, n, o; but not: l, f, g;
- "**H**"-class: upper-case letters; *e.g.* A, B, P, l, f;
- "**q**"-class: lower-case with descenders; *e.g.* p, g, q;
- "**|**"-class: full range symbols; *e.g.* (,),{, };

The "satellite"-class can be specialized according to the sign's center of gravity position:

- "_"-class: symbol below the base-line; *e.g.* _;
- ","-class: symbol at the base-line; *e.g.* ., ,;
- "+"-class: symbol around the middle-line; *e.g.* ·, -, =;
- "~"-class: symbol above the top-line of lower-case letters; *e.g.* ", ", ~;

All symbols occurring in regular text can be related to one of the above classes or disjunctive combinations of them. However, this scheme is not sufficient for mathematical or other types of text, including subscripts and special symbols. For these an analogous extension has to be provided.

2.3.2 Alignment of the typographical classes. The following example illustrates the alignment of letters within the word "Typography". Each letter belongs to exactly one of of the above typographical classes.

In the right illustration the individual characters have been substituted by their surrounding rectangles. The determination of these coordinate values is one of the basic operations performed by the extraction of connected components in the first step of document analysis. But at this stage it is not evident which objects are characters. These may consist of more than only one connected component. So there are three different tasks to be solved:

- Determining the set of connected components of exactly one line
- Assigning a typographical label to each component
- Building letters from connected components

2.3.3 Building a line and assigning typo-labels. There is only little reliable knowledge available in the starting phase of the algorithm. Even height and width of the letters are unknown as well as special measures like baseline skip. Therefore, the height values of all connected components within a window of appropriate dimensions are collected in a histogram. Using this histogram a classification into the two typographical superclasses for each connected component can be performed. Components with the typographical label "satellite" are temporarily set aside. The remaining are used for constructing a skeleton line.

To begin with, membership to any of the typographical classes is hypothesized for each component. Similar to the relaxation approach in pattern recognition, it is the task of an algorithm to let only the correct ones survive. It turned out that the well known Viterbi algorithm can be adopted for this purpose [Forney 73, Bayer 86].

The components are sorted according to their left side coordinates. A local measurement between adjacent components evaluates the compatibility of two hypotheses. Theoretically $8 \times 8 = 64$ combinations have to be evaluated for each pair of components. Since the "satellite" objects are neglected first, only $4 \times 4 = 16$ values have to be calculated. On the whole sequence level, the Viterbi algorithm avoids the combinatorial explosion.

Since no information about the line structure is available, the situation may arise, that a component is considered, that does not belong to that line at all. Hence, the algorithm should eventually leave out such an object completely. This becomes possible by modifying the Viterbi algorithm to allow for skipping a trellis column. For the application here this was restricted to at most three adjacent objects. Each skip causes a penalty given by a heuristically determined function, taking into account the length of the skip. In the same manner components are handled which have been assigned the wrong superclass after histogram analysis, and hence cannot fit.

When the Viterbi algorithm reaches the rightmost component in the analysis window, the best path (or combination) has been determined. Unfortunately, in exceptional situations, *e.g.* on test sheets, there might be several combinations with very similar overall plausibility values. This problem is handled by evaluating the first three best paths. This further enhancement of the Viterbi algorithm does not significantly increase its time complexity.

It is assumed that the objects of a solution path constitute a line in a correct way. Objects belonging to the line above or below should have been omitted by the algorithm. This components of the solution path also fit into the writing line model. After constructing this way a skeleton line from "full-size" objects only, the remaining objects of the "satellite"-class are inserted, simultaneously attaching a typographical label derived from their relative position. The primitive objects (*i.e.* the connected components), have now been made into characters (*i.e.* letters, digits or punctuation marks). The typographical class for a character object is given by the disjunction of the different typographical classes of the primitive objects involved.

The character images, together with their typographical class labels, are now ready to be fed into the character classification module. By use of this technique it is possible to handle also slightly wavy lines, as well as lines with varying interword space. Only the rare cases of lines with characters of only one typographical class, or with to few objects, cause serious difficulties. A fall back position has been provided, constructing the line with some heuristics, but producing no typographical information at all.

However, if the character recognizer can be included, it could provide the line finding algorithm with information it urgently needs but cannot get within its limited knowledge. This could enable the algorithm to finish its job with the same performance as described above. Consequently, the simple forward structure must be abandoned.

3 Classifier Design

3.1 Mathematical Analysis

The task of the classifier is assigning class labels to isolated objects, obtained by the layout analysis. For mathematical treatment, a N–dimensional euclidean pattern space $\mathcal{X}$ is introduced and each object is described by a feature vector $\mathbf{x}$. These features are usually either the grey–values of the raster image pixels (often after some normalization procedure), or transformed values thereof (*e.g.* by Karhunen–Loève transformation), or any set of suitable features gained from the original raster image by heuristic rules. The decision on the K class labels (including confidence values) is best represented by a K–dimensional euclidean decision space $\mathcal{D}$. The K orthonormal basis vectors spanning the decision space are taken as representatives (or target vectors) for the K classes. They have each one single component with value 'one' indicating membership to the corresponding class and $K - 1$ values 'zero' indicating the contrary. The problem of classifying objects can now be viewed as mapping the N–dimensional pattern space $\mathcal{X}$ into the K–dimensional decision space $\mathcal{D}$:

$$ \boldsymbol{f}: \quad \mathcal{X} \rightarrow \mathcal{D} \qquad \mathcal{X} = \mathbb{R}^N, \ \mathcal{D} = \mathbb{R}^K \ . $$

This concept is general enough to embrace almost any of the known recognition schemes (even those based on topological features) and allows for a sound mathematical analysis of the classification process.

The task of classifier adaptation is therefore equivalent to find the best function $\boldsymbol{f}$ according to a suitable optimization criterion. Common mean–square–optimization leads to

$$ \mathrm{E}\left\{|\mathbf{y}(\mathbf{x}) - \mathbf{d}(\mathbf{x})|^2\right\} \ \overset{!}{=} \ \min_{\boldsymbol{f}} \ , \tag{1} $$

where $\mathrm{E}\{\cdots\}$ stands for the expectation operator, $\mathbf{d}(\mathbf{x})$ is the result of the classifier function $\boldsymbol{f}$ and $\mathbf{y}(\mathbf{x})$ is the desired output for the feature vector $\mathbf{x}$.

Since the pattern generation can be viewed as a stochastic process, the optimum decision function is uniquely determined. Applying variation techniques to the optimization problem above leads to the regression function [Schürmann 77], [Schürmann 78], [Lee 90], [Watanabe 72], [Meisel 68]:

$$ \boldsymbol{f}: \quad \mathbf{d}_{opt}(\mathbf{x}) \ = \ \mathrm{E}\left\{\mathbf{y}|\mathbf{x}\right\} \ . $$

Due to the definition of $\mathbf{y}$ as one of the K orthonormal basis vectors of $\mathcal{D}$, the optimum decision function $\mathbf{d}_{opt}(\mathbf{x})$ comes out as the vector of *a posteriori* probabilities

$$ \mathbf{d}_{opt}^{T} \ = \ \Big(p(\text{class-1}|\mathbf{x}) \ , \ \ p(\text{class-2}|\mathbf{x}) \ , \ \ \cdots \ p(\text{class-}K|\mathbf{x})\Big) \ , $$

which obviously is the optimum susceptible class membership estimator having the properties of

$$ 0 \leq \text{component}_k\left[\mathbf{d}_{opt}\right] \leq 1 \quad \text{and} \quad \sum_k \text{component}_k\left[\mathbf{d}_{opt}\right] = 1 \ . $$

However, since the *a posteriori* probabilities $p(\mathbf{y}|\mathbf{x})$ are usually not known nor can they be modeled by simple distributions, approximations of the vector function $\boldsymbol{f}$ are required. The approximations are gained from a given training set consisting of a list of pairs $(\mathbf{x}, \mathbf{y})$, each describing the feature vector $\mathbf{x}$ and the associated desired outcome $\mathbf{y}$. In the following we will compare two approaches of approximating the vector function $\boldsymbol{f}$, respectively polynomial classifier and multilayer perceptron.

3.2 Polynomial Classifier Versus Multilayer Perceptron

Common to both approaches is the restriction to certain families of possible discriminant functions $\boldsymbol{f}$, which owe their adaptability and flexibility to a, normally, large number of parameters, which are adjusted under the control of the optimization criterion (Equation 1) based on the training set.

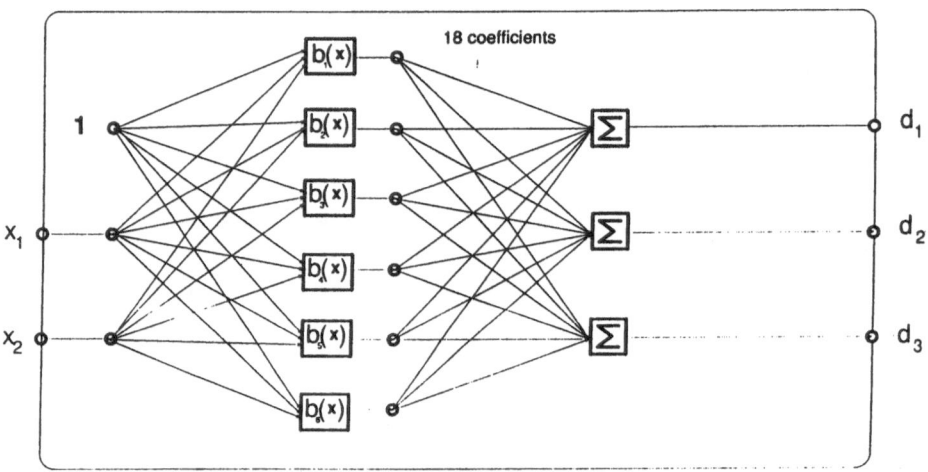

Fig. 2. Polynomial Classifier.

For the **polynomial classifier** the decision functions are restricted to be linear combinations of arbitrary (including any nonlinear) functions of the given features (see Figure 2):

$$d_i(\mathbf{x}) = \sum_j a_{ji} \cdot b_j(\mathbf{x}) = \mathbf{a}_i^T \cdot \boldsymbol{b}(\mathbf{x}) \qquad \text{or} \qquad \mathbf{d}(\mathbf{x}) = \mathbf{A}^T \, \boldsymbol{b}(\mathbf{x}) \,.$$

The functions b_j may be viewed as enhancements of the original features $\mathbf{x}$. Frequently the given features by themselves plus their quadratic (and higher order) combinations are used for the functions b_j, resulting in the name 'polynomial' classifier.

The advantage of the polynomial (or more general: functional) classifier approach is that the coefficients of **A** can be computed from the training set by simply solving a set of linear equations:

$$\mathrm{E}\left\{\boldsymbol{b}(\mathbf{x})\,\boldsymbol{b}^T(\mathbf{x})\right\} \cdot \mathbf{A} \;=\; \mathrm{E}\left\{\boldsymbol{b}(\mathbf{x})\,\mathbf{y}^T\right\}. \tag{2}$$

It is sufficient to compute the cross-correlation matrix $\mathrm{E}\{\boldsymbol{b}(\mathbf{x})\,\mathbf{y}^T\}$ and the moment matrix of the enhanced features $\mathrm{E}\{\boldsymbol{b}(\mathbf{x})\,\boldsymbol{b}^T(\mathbf{x})\}$ from the training set and to apply a proper matrix inversion procedure, which takes care of linear dependencies in $\mathrm{E}\{\boldsymbol{b}(\mathbf{x})\,\boldsymbol{b}^T(\mathbf{x})\}$. Beyond that the solution can just as well be found by applying a steepest descent gradient algorithm as it is the case with the adaptation of neural nets.

In the **multilayer perceptron** approach the family of potential discriminant functions is given by those functions which can be represented by arrangements of artificial neurons connected in a feedforward structure (see Figure 3). Each single artificial neuron is defined by: $o \;=\; s\left(\sum_j a_j\,i_j\right)$, where s is the sigmoid function $(s(u) = \frac{1}{1+e^{-u}})$, i_j are the inputs and o is the output of the neuron.

Since there is no analytical solution known for adapting the set of coefficients for the multilayer perceptron, a gradient descent algorithm has to be used. This method is called error back-propagation and yields the following equations for updating the weights:

$$a_{ij}(I) = a_{ij}(I-1) + \alpha \cdot o_i \cdot o_j \cdot (1-o_j) \cdot \delta_j$$

$$\delta_j = y_j - o_j \qquad\qquad \text{for the output variables}$$

$$\delta_j = \sum_k \delta_k \cdot a_{jk} \qquad\qquad \text{for the hidden variables .}$$

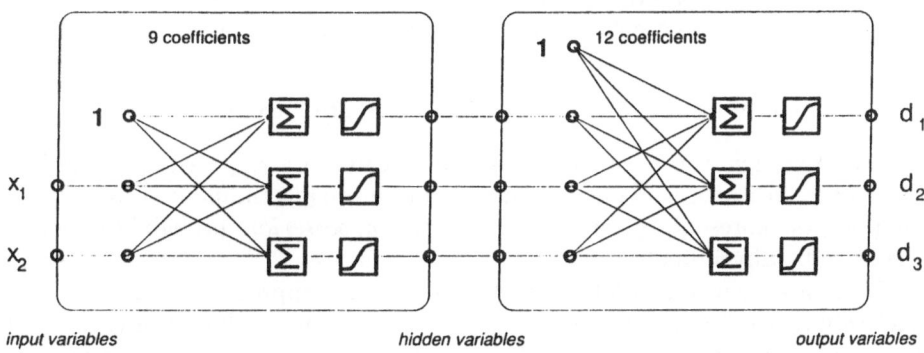

Fig. 3. Multilayer Perceptron.

Theoretical comparisons show [Hornik 89] that the polynomial classifier as well as the multilayer perceptron with at least one hidden layer are universal approximators, provided that either the polynomial degree or the number of hidden neurons are sufficiently large. From this point of view there seems to be no fundamental difference in their discriminative power [Kressel 90]. The XOR–problem, for example, can either be solved by a polynomial classifier using only one enhancement function $x_1 \cdot x_2$ (by solving a set of linear equations with 4 unknowns) or by the multilayer perceptron with two hidden nodes in one hidden layer, but with a comparably long gradient–search training procedure.

For practical purposes the direct solution for the polynomial classifier is very much preferable compared to the time consuming iterative training procedure for the multilayer perceptron. Beyond that, the analytical solution has some further advantages as it provides feature ranking and early elimination of linear dependent and thus redundant features.

The polynomial classifier can also be viewed as a perceptron–like neural network with $\prod$ (product) and $\sum$ (sum) units in a strict order of first a layer of $\prod$–units followed by one layer of $\sum$–units — see Figure 2. The advantages of forming nonlinear combinations from the given input variables are also discussed in a paper on functional link nets [Pao 89] mainly from the viewpoint of removing hidden layers. It is shown that — by inserting a layer of predefined nonlinearities directly behind the input nodes — flat nets may be constructed with equal discriminative power as multilayer perceptrons, but much better convergence behavior.

The paper also addresses the question of computing the coefficients of those higher order neural nets by solving a system of linear equations. The set of linear equations in this case is established directly by the given table of desired input output relations as defined by the training set. Doing so, the number of training samples must equal the number of unknowns within the linear equations, which inevitably will lead to overfitting. Increasing, however, the number of training samples sufficiently over the number of unknowns the problem of overfitting can be completely removed. This leads to a mean square solution of the system of linear equations — pseudo–inverse solution — with stable generalization properties. It is exactly that solution what is provided by Equation (2).

3.3 Improvements by Designing Classifier Hierarchies

The classification approach as just sketched leads to a single–stage procedure. The feature vector **x** is in one step mapped into the discriminant vector **d**, with components representing estimations for the a posteriori probabilities for all classes to be discriminated.

There are, however, a lot of different structural approaches to improve distinctively the performance of the system. By partitioning the set of class labels into subsets, a hierarchy of classifiers can be constructed which operates very similar to a decision tree. The main difference is, that no hard decisions are forwarded along the tree branches but rather conditional probabilities, repeatedly multiplied until at the tree leaves estimations for the a posteriori probabilities are gained [Schürmann 84]. Would it be possible to compute the true a posteriori probabilities at the different nodes the order of hierarchy would have no influence on performance at all. But, because that is impossible in practice, there is a potential for improving recognition performance by partitioning the overall problem into subproblems and designing suitable hierarchical structures. This is due to the fact that the majority of node classifiers within the classifier tree operate on small subsets of the set of class labels and improve recognition accuracy by specialization. This kind of classifier architecture has the additional advantage of allowing to direct the computing effort to those branches of the classifier tree which most probably will generate the relevant results and, thus, to save redundant operations.

A close look at the operations of the hierarchical classifier shows further that multiplying the estimations along the pathes is equivalent to multiplying the individual discriminant functions. This results in overall polynomial discriminant functions of much higher degree than those from which the classifier tree was composed. Since, however, the optimization of coefficients is executed separately at each node, the multiplied polynomial has not necessarily the overall-optimal coefficients. This again emphasizes the importance of proper structuring the classifier hierarchy. Arbitrary partition of the overall problem into subproblems may even worsen recognition performance. A good classifier hierarchy is usually gained from clustering procedures.

Individual classifiers are the building blocks of classifier hierarchies. There exist a number of additional approaches to arrange classifiers (and classifier hierarchies) to more powerful systems. The most obvious way is that of organizing the cooperation of different classifier systems, which due to different architectural properties exhibit different strengths and weaknesses. Combining their outputs, in the same way as the votes of human experts are merged can improve the performance of the whole system (see Section 4).

Another special design is the classifier net, constructed from as many individual classifiers as there are pairs of class labels. Each of them is trained on the class specific subsets of the overall training set in order just to separate the two corresponding classes. The estimations of the individual classifiers are mathematically combined in order to yield again estimations for the *a posteriori* probabilities as with all of the other architectural concepts. Since the number of pairwise classifiers grows quadratic $\binom{k}{2}$, redundant pairs must be detected and removed before the whole net is calculated.

3.4 Database for Classifier Adaptation

Whatever classification technology is applied classifier development is based on learning from examples. Since classifier adaptation in one sense or another is based on optimization with respect to the training set the resulting classifier simply reflects what was taught it during training. Therefore, collection and selection of training sets is the task carrying most of the responsibility for success or failure of the whole design. Thousands of labeled patterns must be prepared per class. In the case of printed character recognition, with about hundred classes to be discriminated, data sets with some hundred thousands of raster images are needed. Similar numbers are needed for independent test sets. A classifier adapted to smaller data sets normally suffers from overfitting, *i.e.* is good on the training set but fails on life material.

The data sets must be labeled carefully. Wrong labels can lead the training into the wrong direction. Typical datasets have millions of characters, often more than 10 000 characters per class. To speed up the labeling process already existing classifiers are employed to generate default labels which need only be accepted or rejected by human operators.

Collection, labeling, and handling of training sets is expensive and time--consuming. The same dataset should therefore be usable for several classifier adaptations — different subsets of fonts, of classes, and of document sources. This necessitates to organize the collection of training data in form of a training data base, with sufficient structure and easy access by adequate keys.

The concept of the polynomial classifier reduces the task of classifier adaptation to solving a set of linear equations (see Equation 2) composed of matrices of statistical moments extracted from the training set. The training set, on the other hand, is a mixture of partial training sets each corresponding to a certain triple of font, class and document source. The mixing rule is given by the specification according to which the classifier has to be built. Since there exists an equivalence between mixing sets of samples and mixing the corresponding moment matrices by linear combination with weights given by the mixing rule, all mixing processes can be moved to the level of moment matrices. Computing the moment matrices is the most time consuming part of the adaptation procedure. Therefore parallel to the database of raster images of the learning samples a corresponding database of moment matrices is established from which with little effort the matrices for Equation 2 can be derived.

3.5 Further Refinements

The performance of the hierarchical classifier strongly depends on the chosen partition of the set of classes into subsets. Similar classes (in the sense of being easily mixed up with each other) should lie on the same branch of the classifier tree as long as possible. This leads to the idea of subdividing classes into subclasses in cases where characters of the one class are likely to appear with distinctly different shapes. The digit 0 class for example will thus be split into two subclasses $(0, \emptyset)$. On the other hand it may happen that identical shapes appear for different character classes (*e.g.*: digit 1, lower-case l, and body of i). Considerations of this kind lead to defining the set of class labels more closely oriented towards character shapes than character meanings. In such a case the classification module must be followed by a corresponding mechanism translating shape classes back to the normal meaning classes. The definition of the suitable shape classes is supported by clustering procedures.

The use of quadratic polynomial discriminant functions yields a remarkable increase in classifier performance compared to linear ones. Since size–normalized characters have a resolution of some hundred pixels it is not reasonable to realize complete quadratic polynomials with some 10000 coefficients per class on this level of representation. This problem is removed if a sufficiently small number of features can be extracted from the pixel representation without sacrificing relevant information. A well–known powerful method is to apply the principal axis transformation — *i.e.* Karhunen–Loève transformation. Doing so, the feature vector dimension can be drastically reduced from some hundreds down to 30 to 50 without loosing the power of reconstructing the image from the transformed measurements. This leads to classifier systems with about 500 to 1300 coefficients per class. A competing approach is to use the original pixel representation and to select a smaller number of the most 'relevant' quadratic terms from the complete quadratic polynomial. The selection can be effectively supported by exploiting the feature ranking result of the regression analysis.

The back-propagation training procedure for neural nets repeatedly passes the training set through the net until the required performance is reached. Weight adjustment is proportional to the deviation between actual and desired outcome and can be totally skipped if the estimation error is below a certain threshold. A similar recursive adaptation scheme is applicable to polynomial classifiers to increase their performance. The procedure starts with a polynomial classifier derived in the traditional way. It is confronted first with the training set, whereby all misclassified or poorly classified samples are separated and collected in a problem set. (Because there is the risk of containing incorrectly labeled samples the problem set must be carefully inspected.) Statistical moment matrices are then calculated from the problem set and mixed with the original ones with suitably chosen weights. Classifier recalculation generates a version with significantly improved recognition performance. Classifier iteration is then repeated with newly collected training sets of preferably much larger size. Classifier iteration is a way of efficiently generating powerful classifiers from extremely large training sets starting with distinctly smaller extracted subsets.

4 Combining the Results of Recognition Experts

4.1 Recognition Experts

Recognition can be regarded as a mapping of patterns onto class labels. The actual mapping is based on the descriptive features of patterns. The class labels represent the application specific abstract view of the world. If the labels form a class/subclass (or generalization/specialization) hierarchy, the set of labels may be also called the application's taxonomy.

In a restricted sense, a recognition system resembles the capabilities of a human expert in a well defined problem domain. Of course, the inevitable use of background or common sense knowledge by human experts still makes a big difference. Nevertheless, we use the term expert for such a dedicated technical system. We refer to an expert as a specialist, if it a) operates only on a feature subset or b) only discriminates between a subset of all classes.

The complexity of real recognition tasks even requires splitting of the overall task into smaller subtasks. Compound patterns may be decomposed into subpatterns, each to be classified on his own. Clearly, several recognition specialists must evolve from this decomposition, performing independently from each other.

Finally, however, a superior specialist has to combine the individual results, taking into account the relational data of the subpatterns, which makes the whole pattern more than only the sum of its parts.

From a specialist we expect statements of the form "This pattern is of kind A with plausibility p." It is imaginable that kind A might also imply kind B. The most specialized statement is desired, since it contains the most detailed information. But this is at the risk of increased error. On the contrary, if someone replies in general terms, he is unlikely to fail, but he would be of little help. Reliability and preciseness are the two criteria that must be outbalanced: "Be as special as possible, but as general as necessary!"

Restricting the view of a specialist to specific aspects, *i.e.* to subsets of the original classes, reduces the variability and the number of distinct classes drastically. On the other hand two different classes from the original taxonomy may be undistinguishable when projected onto the feature subspace selected for the specialist.

It is not sensible to force a specialist to discriminate between classes which are homogeneous in the given feature space. In this case, incidental and insignificant differences might be the cause for discrimination. This can be avoided, if classes too special with respect to a certain feature representation are taken out of consideration, and replaced by the most special common superclass.

Better classification results can be achieved by adapting the feature space and classification method to the actual needs. But the division into subtasks leads to the problem of evaluating and combining the individual results. These may vary in: output value range, in the dynamic behavior and in the global order of its votes. Therefore, a common representation for all votes is needed to make them comparable and finally combinable.

One common representation framework for uncertainty is Probability Theory. In this particular case of pattern recognition, its semantics correspond to a model where a random noise process disturbs observations. Each observed value is the superposition of a true and distinct state value and a random value.

Unfortunately, Probability Theory provides no means to represent what might be called ignorance, uncertainty or incompetence. An expert might wish to express: "I can't neither say yes nor no." In many applications this situation is handled by giving equal probability mass to all of the given classes. But as the number of distinguishable classes varies, this value changes, too. Hence, the degree of ignorance cannot be seen from an individual class vote, but only from the equal distribution of votes over all classes.

4.2 Evidence Theory as a Generalization of Probability Theory

A more general approach for modeling the uncertainty inherent in every nontrivial recognition task is the Evidence Theory [Shafer 76]. This theory can be seen as a generalization of Probability Theory towards handling sets of propositions. The belief functions *Bel* has some characteristics comparable to the probability function P. Both theories are based on three basic axioms:

Probability Theory		Evidence Theory	
$P(\emptyset) = 0$	$(1.a)$	$Bel(\emptyset) = 0$	$(1.b)$
$P(\Omega) = 1$	$(2.a)$	$Bel(\Theta) = 1$	$(2.b)$
$P(A \cup B) = P(A) + P(B)$	$(3.a)$	$Bel(A \cup B) \geq Bel(A) + Bel(B)$	$(3.b)$

given that the events A and B are disjoint.

The belief of a disjunction of events $Bel(A \cup B)$ may be higher than the sum of the beliefs of the two constituents $Bel(\cdot)$. This offers the opportunity to distribute the probability mass of a vote to the disjunction of events rather than the singletons (basic classes) itself. In contrast, Probability Theory always demands the distribution of the whole probability mass to the singletons, $i.e.$ the distinct and mutually exclusive events. A probability function can be seen as a belief function having all of the probability mass distributed on singletons. In this case the belief function is made into a probability function. Hence, Evidence Theory is a generalization of Probability Theory.

If the whole probability mass is set to the superset Θ, then this corresponds to total ignorance. Therefore, in Evidence Theory it is easy to distinguish between ignorance and equal chance of each event. An expert without any knowledge can represent his state of being helpless by setting the whole probability mass to Θ. However, the model makes use of the closed world assumption. To handle the problem of undefined or unknown classes, it is necessary to introduce a special class *"everything else"*.

4.3 Adaptation of Evidence Theory to Practical Restrictions

There is one essential obstacle in the application of Evidence Theory: the cardinality of the possible Bel-functions, which is prohibitively large in all real situations. Theoretically the number of votes to be evaluated by the belief is $|Bel| = 2^{|\Theta|}$, which corresponds to the cardinality of the power set over Θ. Thus, for applicability reasons special cases must be derived. One such case is the restriction of the Bel-function to *separable support functions* [Barnett 81]. A *separable support function* is the orthogonal sum of two or more *simple support functions*. A *simple support function* is a belief function having only two basic probability assignments greater than zero. One of the basic probability assignments is in the focus of the Bel-function and the other one is in Θ. The practically relevant cardinality of such a Bel-function is only two! So for a *simple support functions* holds: $m(A) = s, m(\Theta) = 1 - s$, and $m = 0$ elsewhere. These specialization offers the opportunity to evaluate a belief function from clearly arranged votes in an efficient manner. Further specializations are possible to achieve special forms of the final belief function.

4.4 Achieving the Probability Measurements

The belief values needed in the combination phase must be derived from the votes of the different specialists. It is possible to use the experience from Probability Theory to estimate belief functions [Mandler 88]. The class membership of an entity can be estimated in a conventional way. All of the classes distinguished by a specialist i form the space $\Omega_i = \{\omega_{i,1}, \omega_{i,2}, \ldots, \omega_{i,m}\}$. There is a probability measure P_i defined on Ω_i [Kohlas 90]. This probability measure can be estimated by means of common statistics. The system designer must define a mapping function Γ_i from Ω_i to Θ specifying the relation between the different class sets. Θ is called the *frame of discernment*. The belief function Bel is defined on Θ. Using this scheme it is possible to use conventional statistics to estimate belief functions.

Every nontrivial classifier incorporates a nonlinear mapping function from feature space to class space. A classifier is not forced to vote for a single class only. Since if each classifier was restricted to vote for exactly one class, this decision would dominate during all further processing steps and would also be the final decision! A "soft" classifier can be interpreted as a system which estimates for a pattern a similarity or distance with respect to several different classes. So the output of a classifier usually comprises some alternative votes.

Conventional classifiers may vary in

- their ability to discriminate
- the amount of samples needed for adaptation
- their ability to integrate additional samples
- the order of their votes (similarity or distance)

To come to a common base for all classifiers the output of each classifier is analyzed for its own in a statistical manner. One obvious approach is to have specialists each responsible only for one class — class means here one ω_i. Each specialist is modeled for its own. Therefore, the output of the specialist is put into a histogram distinguishing between samples belonging to the specialists class domain and all other ones. Depending on the type of classifier and the features used the form of the observed histograms varies. For *nearest neighbor classifiers* the *gamma distribution* or certain specializations of it are often appropriate. For *polynomial classifiers normal distributions* may be appropriate. Nevertheless, the form of distribution selected should be careful examined by the system designer. Main criteria are:

- exactness of the matching between the estimated distribution function and the observed histogram
- number of parameters of the distribution function.
- computational effort for evaluating the distribution function.
- statistical characteristics of the distribution.

For an on-line script recognizer it was necessary to devise a fast adaptable classifier. In this case it was feasible to choose an exponential model for the intra-class distances [Mandler 88]. The exponential density is a special case of the Gamma density and is determined by only one parameter: the mean value. The inter-class distribution of the distances is only interesting in the range where the intra-class distance has non-zero probability. Therefore it was sufficient to model the distribution of the inter-class distances in the range of small values.

From these observations a probability measure is defined in a conventional way. Thus each observed distance $d_{i,k}$ in the subsystem i — specialist — is transformed into a probability measurement $P_i(\omega_{i,k}) = P_i(\omega_{i,k}|d_{i,k})$ estimating the class membership in $\omega_{i,k}$.

This probability measurement $P_i(\omega_k|d_{i,k})$ for each $\omega_{i,k}$ is transferred to the *frame of discernment* Θ by means of the transfer function $\Gamma_i(\omega_{i,k}) = \theta_{i,k}$. θ is the focus of the classifier in the aspired space Θ. The probability measure $P_i(\omega_{i,k}) = m(\Gamma_i(\omega_{i,k}))$ is transformed to the basic probability assignment of the set of propositions in the frame of discernment Θ corresponding to the $\omega_{i,k}$. For each specialists' vote a *Bel*-function on the common frame of discernment is constructed.

4.5 Applying Dempster's Rule of Combination

In Evidence Theory there is one central theorem discussed in a controversial manner: *Dempster's Rule of Combination* [Dempster 67]. This rule is also called orthogonal sum. The combination of two *Bel*-functions defined on the same frame of discernment Θ is performed by setting the product of two basic probability assignments $m_1(A) \cdot m_2(B) = m(A \cap B)$ to the conjunction of the two propositions A and B. This is done for all combinations of nonzero probability masses. The rule has got the advantage of being commutative and associative. In the case that all conjunctions are not empty the rule is undisputed. In this case the output of the sum as well as the input meet the condition $\sum_{A \in \Theta} m(A) = 1$. But this is a rather rare case. Normally there are conjunctions yielding the empty set. This corresponds to a contradiction in the specialists' votes. Since the above conditions must be met, the results have to be standardized such that the overall sum equals one again. This is the most controversial point of the debate. The fact of contradiction is hidden by the standardization procedure. From a formal point of view this is correct due to the closed world assumption. Nevertheless, in many cases it would be fine to record the fact of contradiction, detected while combining the votes.

Another crucial point is that the votes combined should be independent in order to justify the application of Dempster's rule. This is often neglected in practical situations, though it is not clear how it should be examined whether this condition holds true or not. Unfortunately, it is often easier to show that the condition is not fulfilled, than to prove the contrary.

In the case that two votes are of Bayesian kind — all probability masses are in gathered in propositions with cardinality one — Dempster's Rule corresponds to the Bayesian combination rule.

In a pragmatic view Dempster's Rule of combination is in the case of two votes a unit square having the votes of the two specialist at the two axes. These axes cut the square in $n \times m$ rectangles. The area of the rectangles is set to the conjunction of the foci of the two parts. The mass remaining in the empty set is proportionally distributed to all remaining sets — this is the standardization. Having more than two votes, the square becomes a hypercube, but the procedure is still the same. The result of such a combination does not depend on normalization after each step of the procedure. Therefore, it is sufficient to normalize the final result to $\sum m(A) = 1$.

4.6 Common Strategy for Combining Intermediate Results

In the pure form Dempster's Rule of combination requires to many calculations. But in restricted cases the numerical effort can be drastically reduced. In the already mentioned example of on-line script recognition a very special form was chosen such that the combination became trivial.

We construct binary specialists responsible only for one class. Thus the votes are of the form "Pro" or "Contra". Contra means that all other classes are in the focus of the vote. Therefore, for every defined class and for every subset of the features there exists one specialist.

For each such specialist an individual adaptation is performed. Depending on the intra- and inter-class distance histograms the parameters for the probabilistic vote function of the specialist are determined. This corresponds to the regular probability space Ω. From Bayes theorem we get the probability measure.

$$P_{pro} = P_i(k|d_{i,k}) = \frac{P_i(d_{i,k}|k) \cdot P(k)}{P_i(d_{i,k})}$$

Assuming equal *a priori* probability $P(k) = const.$ for each of the K classes this simplifies to:

$$P_{pro_i}(k) = \frac{1}{1 + (K-1) \cdot \frac{P_i(d_{i,k}|\neg k)}{P_i(d_{i,k}|k)}}$$

For adaptation only the likelihood ratio of the two distance distributions is needed weighted with the number of defined classes. Correspondingly the contra vote is given by:

$$P_{contra_i}(k) = 1 - P_{pro_i}(k)$$

So for each such specialist two mapping function $\Gamma_{i,1}(k)$ and $\Gamma_{i,2}(\neg k)$ are needed for defining the relation between Ω and Θ. The two functions have the properties: $\Gamma_{i,1}(k) \cup \Gamma_{i,2}(\neg k) = \Theta$ and $\Gamma_{i,1}(k) \cap \Gamma_{i,2}(\neg k) = \emptyset$. The two probabilities are transformed to basic probability assignments: $m(\Gamma_i(k)) = P_{pro_i}(k)$ and $m(\Gamma_i(\neg k)) = P_{contra_i}(k)$.

The combination rule can be drastically simplified — keeping in mind that for each class and subset one specialist with such special characteristics exists. The final pro vote is the product of all pro votes and all contra votes with the class in the focus.

$$Bel(k) = m(k) = C \cdot \prod_i P_{pro_i}(k) \cdot \prod_i \prod_{\neg k} P_{contra_i}(k)$$

This can be further simplified by using the constant C as a general normalizer:

$$Bel(k) = C' \cdot \prod_i \frac{P_{pro_i}(k)}{(1 - P_{pro_i}(k))}$$

This is a rather simple expression which can be efficiently evaluated.

4.7 Remarks

Experimental results [Mandler 88] confirm the way given in the previous section. Compared to conventional approaches of computing the combined estimation of different classifiers by linear combination with suitably chosen weights, the approach described here is clearly superior. The questionable assumption of independency may be regarded justified by the success of the above strategy.

Restricting Evidence Theory to special forms makes its intrinsic problem of computational effort disappear. The overall design must carried out in a careful manner. For applications with ample statistical information, the construction of the combination procedure could be refined.

5 Segmenting Merged Characters

Merged characters represent a major problem in document analysis. Since by default such a pattern is assumed to be an isolated single character, it is misclassified. Merged character patterns may occur if the characters already stick together on the document sheet or are merged due to insufficient scanner resolution. In order to obtain correct recognition results these patterns must be separated and reclassified.

If the text is printed with proportional spacing, segmentation is difficult, since it is not known beforehand how many characters are enclosed and where the positions for cutting are located. In contrast to this, minor problems arise when the text is typed with fixed character spacing: the width can be deduced from the characters correctly segmented and the pattern can be cut at these equidistant positions. The following only deals with patterns containing characters typed in proportional font.

Segmenting merged character patterns involves three steps. First, among the sequence of potential character images candidates sticking together must be extracted. Second, cut positions must be identified and third, the segmented character images must be classified. Since the character classifier deals with characters of nearly any font and size, one objective for the segmentation algorithm presented here is to behave the same way. Furthermore, the algorithm shall cope with patterns consisting of an arbitrary number of characters and shall segment efficiently and with a high recognition rate.

In principle, merged characters can already be separated when the pixel image is segmented into characters. Such approaches are based on the geometrical and even structural properties of the shape and on primitives extracted from the pattern. The disadvantage of these methods is that distortions in the pixel representation may mislead the preprocessing when the primitives are extracted. Furthermore, this approach is not well suited for multi–font applications, since the kind of join between two characters may vary largely from one font to the other. Moreover, it is very difficult to detect merged patterns in the text; the criterion to consider a connected component as representing a merged character pattern can only be based on geometric and structural properties of the object. If, for example, two 'r' merge, it becomes very hard to detect it, since its width seems reasonable as well as its structure. Therefore, segmentation of merged character patterns after the classification seems to be more promising. The information that is available at this level of processing helps to achieve good segmentation results.

In the first step potential merged character patterns are extracted. Since the segmentation is applied after the character classification the classification result as well as geometric features are used. All character patterns that exceed the maximum width of the character of the surrounding text are considered as merged patterns. However, these patterns do not comprise the total set: if two small characters merge, they are still smaller than the widest one, but this pattern is normally classified with low confidence value. Therefore, a pattern is also hypothesized as merged when the confidence of the recognition remains below a certain threshold.

The next two processing steps — finding the position and reclassification — are combined in a single procedure and follow the lines reported in [Bayer 87]. The multi–font classifier is applied to accomplish both tasks: a cut position is tested by classifying the pixel region cut. The basic segmentation idea is to cut the image several times with fixed left border and various right borders. When starting the first pixel column in the pattern represents the left border. Several candidates are extracted by cutting rectangular regions out of the pattern with increasing widths. Every candidate is submitted to the classifier and evaluated by the resulting confidence score. At the first leftmost character position that candidate is selected with the most reliable confidence value. In the following step the left border is set the to the beginning of the remaining pattern, and the cutting process is continued from left to right, until the end of the pattern is reached. During processing all segmentation alternatives are held in the underlying data structure.

The system accomplishing the segmentation has a blackboard structure; it contains a set of knowledge sources that evaluate each decision for cutting whether it represents a true character. These knowledge sources comprise the character classifier and a set of algorithms for context processing. The blackboard structure enables a processing that involves backtracking rather than a straight forward processing: previously taken decisions can be canceled and alternative segmentation results can be pursued. Thus, the process of segmentation is a search process looking for the correct solution in an efficient manner by applying as much knowledge sources as necessary. The search space is illustrated in Figure 4.

The whole system is controlled by a best–first graph search method known as the A* algorithm (see [Nilsson 82], [Pearl 84]). It searches for a path from an initial state to a final state with minimal costs. It tries to reduce the theoretically exponential growth of the search space as much as possible by using heuristic information. It leaves no state unexplored and examines no state more than once and allows switching between several possible solution paths and therefore, canceling decisions previously made. In this application we use certainty scores that vary from 0 to 1, rather than costs. If a path optimally fits to the input pattern, it is associated with the score 1, and, if it does not fit at all, with

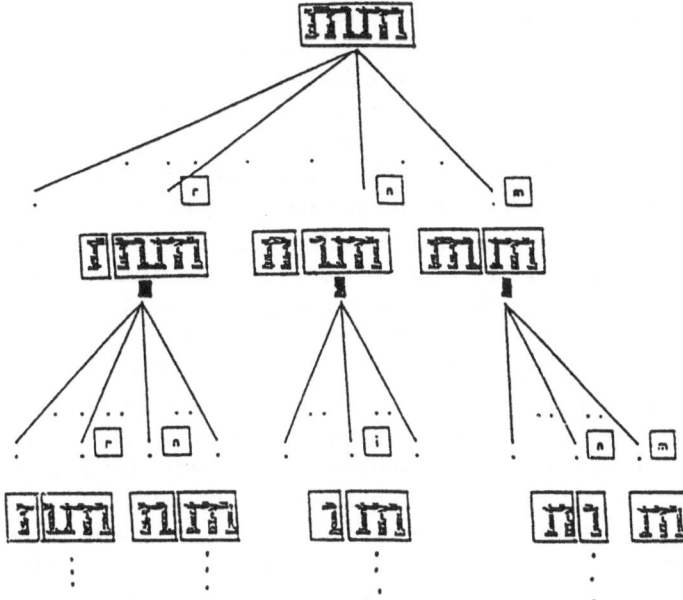

Fig. 4. The search space: each state represents a character candidate and the remaining pattern. A path from the root to a node constitutes an attempt for a segmentation.

the value 0. Additionally, it proposes more than one alternatives for segmenting a pattern along with certainty scores, when a flag is set: not only best best segmentation result is returned, but also the following best ones.

The ultimate objective of the segmentation algorithm is to obtain the positions for cutting without search and with minimum computational effort. The algorithm using the classifier as the only knowledge source works sufficiently successful and fulfills most of the objectives stated. However, it is rather inefficient; for example, it takes 57 steps — and therefore as much classifications — to obtain the correct solution for the merged characters of the pattern 'po' (see Figure 5). Therefore, different improvements are introduced that on the one hand decrease the number of search states significantly and on the other hand increase the power of the algorithm.

The additional knowledge sources refer mainly to context information obtained by the text portions of the document. In order to evaluate a search state the geometric properties of the character are tested, both matching local geometric features and matching its position in the word containing the merged characters. Beside the geometric properties the recognition results of the characters cut are checked for plausibility by applying a dictionary: a character candidate is kept in the search space, if the (partial) word that is built of the characters correctly segmented and the characters extracted from the pattern can be found in a dictionary — otherwise, this state is removed from the search space.

A very valuable method to decrease the size of the search space is to generate only few character hypotheses by selecting specific cut positions rather than cutting at every pixel position. Two methods have been developed and tested. The first method is adopted from the work described in [Baird 86]. Let P denote the number of black pixels in a column; then the second discrete derivative $\triangle P(x)$ is calculated and divided by the number of P at each position. The position with the maximum value points to the cut position. In the second method the upper contour Q_u as well as the lower contour Q_l of the merged pattern are investigated. However, when selecting only one position and leaving pixel positions untested, it is very important to keep the correct ones to be able to find the correct segmentation. To ensure this property, the two methods proposed suggest not only one, but three to four positions for cutting.

In Figure 5 examples of merged characters along with the segmentation results are shown. They are selected from a sample set of more than 400 merged character patterns collected from different documents in different font styles.

All knowledge sources except the dictionary (since the patterns are contained in documents of more than one language) are applied to obtain the results. Patterns containing two merged characters need about 7 to 15 classifications, if the positions for cutting are selected by investigating either the function P or $Q_{l,u}$. The overall computation time is then below one second. If three characters are contained the number of steps rises from 10 to 20 classifications. If more than five characters are merged into one single object, the search tree becomes rather large, but the number of classifications does not increase exponentially as it does in theory. The certainty scores obtained by the knowledge sources shrink the search space significantly. However, for patterns containing even more characters it is recommended to execute the best–first search in a modified mode: prevent backtracking after two or three characters have been cut from the pattern; thus, the problem is reduced to smaller partial problems, however loosing a bit of its generality and possibly the correct solution.

In conclusion the algorithm works very successful for patterns consisting of two to four characters, which represent the majority of merged character patterns. Approximately 80% of the 400 examples are segmented correctly investigating very few states compared to the number theoretically possible. Thus, the efficiency conditions are met, as well as the objective coping with different fonts and styles of nearly any size.

6 Modeling Structured Documents

In the previous sections concepts and tools were presented which are essential when analyzing printed documents. The layout structure of the document has been generated and the single characters have been classified. However, as it was argued in the introduction, the results obtained by these tools represent a rather weak form of understanding, since the symbolic representation contains logical objects only on the (low) character level: the textual information is interpreted as a stream of single characters structured by some layout control information.

When aiming at understanding documents on a higher level, more abstract logical concepts must be attached to objects of the document rather than a sim-

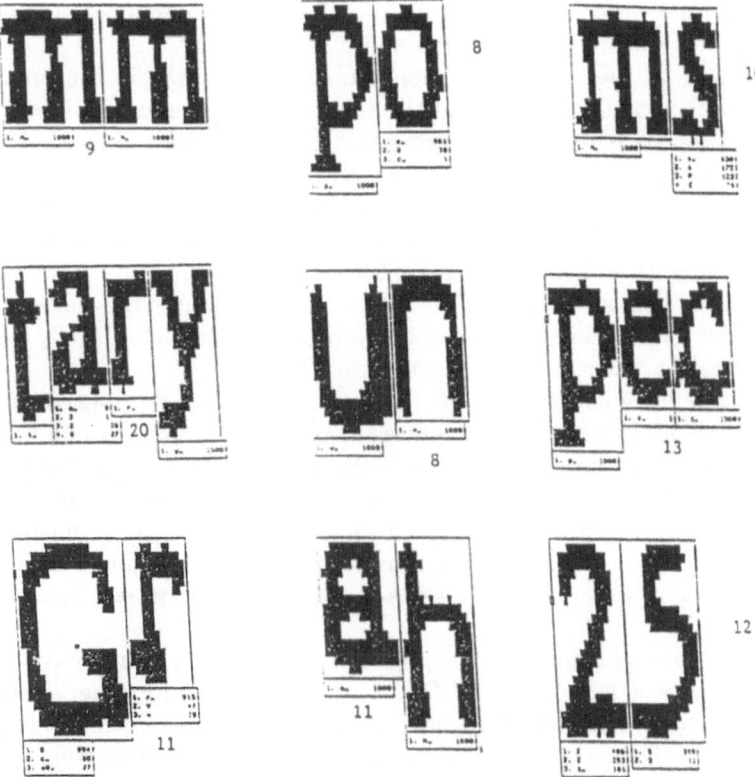

Fig. 5. Examples of merged characters segmented. The numbers annotated specify the number of states of the search space and thus, the number of classifications necessary during the search..

ple character content. These logical objects must be introduced into the analysis system as conceptual entities to define the problem domain in which a document can be understood. The concepts are linked by a set of relations so that different hierarchies arise. When attempting to understand document portions on a very abstract level, a complex structure of conceptual entities must be designed.

The title page of an IEEE scientific publication, here the Transactions on Computers, serves as an example and is illustrated in Figure 6. The set of papers published in this journal shall be read automatically in such a way that the author, the title and the page is known for each paper. Having extracted this information, the references may be inserted into a data base keeping all information of IEEE publications. The main conceptual entities specify the blocks that denote the reference of the publication. Further concepts are the three constituents of this concept, the title of the contribution, the authors and the page where the paper can be found. The analysis system that knows these concepts generates the symbolic description step by step guided by the description of the document. The result of the analysis is denoted in Figure 6: Understanding of this document means interpretation of the constituents of the document within these concepts — the IEEE document contains a specific number of papers each consisting of a list of authors, a title and a page number.

Compared to the notions of understanding mentioned in the introduction this approach is not able to fulfill the highest level of understanding, the full comprehension of arbitrary text portions. Rather, portions of those documents can be understood in which the layout structure is directly connected to the logical structure. This close neighborhood between content and layout enables the analysis system to deduce the logical content from the layout content without deeper investigation of logical structures.

In the following a representation language, which makes the conceptual entities available to the analysis system, and a processing model is briefly presented. A more detailed discussion can be found in [Bayer 90].

When modeling conceptual entities of documents the representation scheme ODA as a standard proposed by different organizations (see [Horak 85]) has to be considered. This language separates the objects into a set of layout objects and in a set of logical ones which are linked by certain relations. However, ODA provides a data structure that aims at a general representation of documents and at interchange of documents rather than for purposes of document analysis. For example, there is no possibility in ODA to represent alternatives in an adequate way.

Hence, a specific language for representing concepts of structured documents has been developed named FRESCO — Frame representation language for structured documents. Conceptual entities are represented in an object–oriented style; each concept defines a class which is is described by three properties (which are represented as classes as well):

- a set of attributes
- a set of relationships between concepts
- a set of constraints

Examples of concepts are *character* and *word* (layout objects) and *title* and *address* (logical objects). Attributes describe the internal state of a concept, like the font or the extent of the surrounding rectangle of a character. Two relationships *has–part* and *is–subclass* link the concepts and generate two orthogonal hierarchies useful for subsequent processing. Constraints between attributes and components express certain relationships which must be satisfied, *e.g.*, that the objects in Figure 6 are left–justified.

Fresco is specifically designed for modeling entities of structured documents. Geometric properties, like left–justified, and content properties, are predefined and a constituent of the language. Along with the attribute and relationship classes these objects represent the language primitives of Fresco.

As it is usual in object–oriented systems, Fresco provides an inheritance mechanism along the relation subclass. This means that the properties enumerated above and the values of the properties of a concept are passed to a concept that is a subclass of it. For example, the concept sender inherits all properties of the concept address. Thus, this mechanism facilitates the definition of new document classes, since the descriptional information must be specified only once

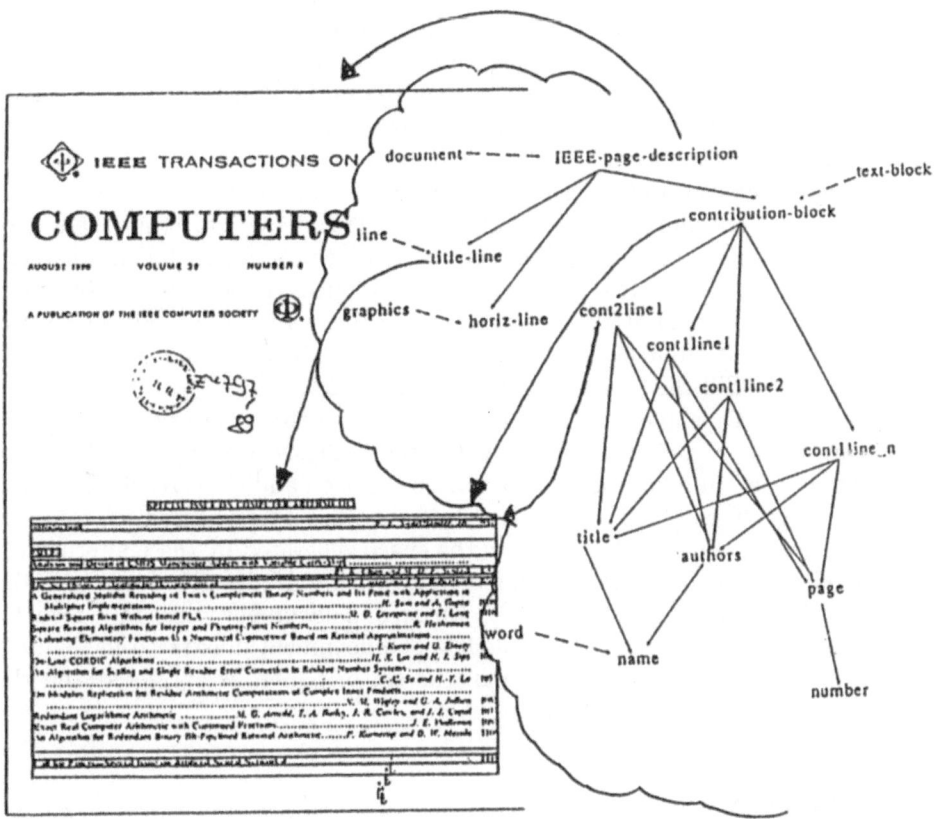

Fig. 6. Title page of the IEEE Journal of Computing. The concepts outline the model of this document. The dashed lines denote the subclass relationship, the straight lines the part relationship. For reasons of simplicity no attributes and constraints are illustrated..

in the more general classes. Fresco models the conceptual entities of structured documents from the very low level of connected components (layout object) to high level logical objects, like the document class IEEE–Journal.

Processing models guided by a syntactic description of objects are generally divided in a preprocessing part and in the interpretation part: symbols are extracted by preprocessing and passed as primitives to an interpreter matching these primitives with conceptual entities and constraints of the model. However, when the preprocessing step extracts symbols not matching with the model, the interpretation will finally fail. One reason is that backtracking — a common technique during interpretation — does not pass the control back to the preprocessing phase in order to change the set of symbols and restart with the new set.

In the processing model proposed here an attempt is made to bridge this gap between structural approaches and the preprocessing by using a blackboard architecture containing the document model, a set of knowledge sources and the blackboard itself. The knowledge sources (KS) comprise all algorithms needed in the domain of document image analysis; it ranges from image algorithms up to algorithms using linguistic information (cp. Figure 1). This architecture allows backtracking to each processing step so that no distinction between preprocessing and interpretation is made.

A KS contains a set of descriptional information about its properties and the procedure that accomplishes the required task. The knowledge about the way of solving a problem is contained in the code of a procedure rather than represented in a declarative manner like in Fresco. When applied, it returns a set of values interpreted as values of attributes in Fresco; to these attributes and to concepts related to these attributes instances are generated, added to the blackboard and tested if they fulfill the various tests and constraints.

The document is analyzed automatically; due to the descriptions of the KS, the sequence of algorithms necessary for the analysis is composed. Different alternatives arise, if more than one KS can be applied and if the results obtained by the algorithms can be interpreted in different ways dependent on the concepts in the document model. The search in the space generated by these alternatives is controlled by the best–first graph search algorithm A* described briefly in the previous section. Currently, the interpretation of a document works top–down by specifying a document class of the model. The document illustrated in Figure 6 is interpreted then as a IEEE journal; the set of papers is extracted and the authors, titles and page numbers are known.

7 Conclusion

This paper has presented some specialized tools being essential for analyzing and understanding documents rather than mentioning the nearly innumerable attempts for solving the whole problem. The layout generation has been discussed briefly; it provides the character objects — apart from further layout information — that are classified by a single character classifier or by further experts that are combined by techniques of the evidence theory. An application involving votes of different experts is the segmentation of merged characters. The last section deals with document modeling and aims at understanding of documents which are strictly structured, like forms or the page of IEEE publications in Figure 6. No remarks have been made in this contribution about the following topics, although they play an important role and have been attacked in our group: graphic recognition, decreasing noise, separation of background against information, extraction of half-tone images, hand-written characters, etc.

In the following, two questions are answered briefly: The first one is: "How powerful is a dedicated document analysis system consisting of these tools?"

If the document to be analyzed contains few distortions and the text of the document is typed in a rather common font (an example is this page), the characters of the text are recognized with nearly 100% certainty. The reasons are that the single characters can be completely obtained by the process generating the layout structure and the character recognition classifies these characters with very high performance. The system even copes with slight distortions, like skewing of text or merged characters (see Section 6). Then, the result is an ASCII file containing the characters of the text that seem to be keyed in manually. When involving knowledge about the structure and the content of certain documents, the system is even able to interpret portions of the document by converting these parts into a symbolic representation being more abstract than simple characters. Entities of this representation may denote a date and the full information of an address. They can be attached to the text objects since the entities can be described by a formal language and, hence, can be parsed. An example is the document in Figure 6: the structure obviously follows a formal grammar. It must be pointed out, however, that this kind of understanding is only a weak form of document comprehension and does not at all reflect text comprehension as it is explained in the introduction.

When claiming a nearly 100% performance, it is clear that many assumption are involved in the analysis. These assumptions are hidden in the previous paragraph in the phrases "few distortions" and "common font." Considering distortions some prerequisites are that the characters are well separated, that the lines are set parallel, that the characters correspond each to one connected component, that no annotations in cursive script are contained in the text and many more. Each of these events let the recognition rate drop dramatically. It is no pure chance that these distortions refer to the processing step that determines the layout structure of the document. If this algorithm fails, further steps will carry the burden of its errors and will not be relieved later. On the other hand, if it works successful, there is good chance to obtain a correct character sequence or a symbolic description reflecting a reasonable level of understanding.

These deliberations about the many remaining problems lead to the second question: "Where we want to go to?" or "What are we aiming at?."

As it was already outlined in the introduction the processing steps executed during analysis cannot be performed sequentially in a straight forward manner. For example, the objects generated in the layout step are only hypothesized as lines, words and characters. These objects must be verified or falsified in following processing steps.

In order to verify hypotheses knowledge about the structural properties of the document as well as knowledge about content portions must be provided. This knowledge is integrated in a document model; it helps to focus on constituents of the document and to select the proper tools for the analysis: when expecting numbers, why using a general purpose classifier rather than the expert responsible for numbers? Moreover, the document model enables the analysis system to interpret — to understand — the data in terms of its conceptual entities. Without them, the result would comprise only character meanings. A further advantage of integrating knowledge into a document analysis system is that the processing strategy may work in a bottom–up manner as well as in a top–down manner. In the latter case knowledge about document structures guides the analysis.

But, does knowledge about the document solve all problems? The answer is no! Knowledge diminishes the scope what to expect in certain situations and is necessary to understand documents. However, knowledge about specific text portions does not help at all, for example, to eliminate a stroke going through a whole text block. Thus, apart from modeling the structure of documents, specialized tools must be improved, new powerful tools trying to obtain *e.g.* a specific layout structure or to eliminate distortions, must be developed.

Furthermore, the strategy of processing must be changed to be more flexible and to leave the straightforward sequence of algorithms as it is described in the previous section. In this tentative processing model backtracking is involved to return to a specific stage in the analysis, if the current processing sequence has led to a dead end.

Presently, we have gained some promising results in document analysis. Integrating knowledge, improving the algorithms of the preprocessing stage and turning to a flexible processing strategy will be the major steps in the near future. Actually, we are on the way to understand documents in some sense automatically. Nevertheless, we are still far away from document comprehension in general; and we are even far away from the much weaker objective of document understanding when considering the documents that real life presents — the documents that humans deal with, unconsciously, perfectly!

References

[Baird 86]   H. S. Baird, S. Kahan, and T. Pavlidis, "Components of an Omnifont Page Reader," *Proc. 8th ICPR*, Paris, 1986.

[Barnett 81]   J. A. Barnett, "Computational Methods for a Mathematical Theory of Evidence," *Proc. 7th Int'l Joint Conf. on AI*, Vancouver, BC, 1981.

[Bartneck 89]   N. Bartneck, "A general data structure for image analysis based on a description of connected components," *Computing* 42, pp. 17–34, 1989.

[Bayer 86]   T. Bayer and M. Oberländer, "Ein erweiterter Viterbi Algorithmus zur Berechnung der n–besten Wege in zyklenfreien Modellgraphen," In G. Hartmann (ed.), *Proc. 8th DAGM–Symposium Mustererkennung*, Springer–Verlag, Berlin, 1986.

[Bayer 87]   T. Bayer, "Segmentation of Merged Character Patterns with AI–Techniques," In *Proc. 5th Scandinavian Conf. on Image Analysis*, Stockholm, 1987.

[Bayer 90]   T. Bayer, "Representation of Structured Documents in a Frame System," In H. Baird (ed.), *Pre–Proc. IAPR Workshop on SSPR*, Murray Hill, NJ, 1990.

[Dempster 67]   A. P. Dempster, "Upper and Lower Probabilities Induced by a Multivalued Mapping," *Annals of Mathematical Statistics*, 38, pp. 325–339, 1967.

[Forney 73]   G. D. Forney, "The Viterbi Algorithm," *Proc. IEEE*, Vol. 61, No.3, March 1973.

[Horak 85]   W. Horak, "Office Document Architecture and Office Document Interchange Format, Current Status of International Standardization," *IEEE Computer*, October 1985.

[Hornik 89]   K. Hornik, M. Stinchcombe, and H. White, "Multilayer feedforward networks are universal approximators," *Neural Networks*, Vol. 2, pp. 359–366, 1989.

[Kressel 90]   U. Kressel, J. Franke, and J. Schürmann, "Polynomklassifikator versus Multilayer–Perzeptron," In R.E. Grosskopf (ed.), *Proc. 12th DAGM–Symposium Mustererkennung*, Springer–Verlag, Berlin, pp. 75–80, 1990.

[Kohlas 90]   J. Kohlas, "A Mathematical Theory of Hints: Preliminary Version of the Paper," Univ. Fribourg, Fribourg, CH, 1990.

[Lee 90]   D.-S. Lee, S. N. Srihari, and R. Gaborski, "Experiments in Handwritten Character Recognition with Pattern Recognition and Neural Network Approaches," *Fourth Advanced Technology Conf.*, Vol. 2, pp. 1013–1027, 1990.

[Mandler 88]   E. Mandler and J. Schürmann, "Combining the Classification Results of Independent Classifiers based on the Dempster/Shafer Theory of Evidence," *Pattern Recognition in Practice*, Amsterdam, 1988.

[Mandler 90a]   E. Mandler and M. Oberländer, "Ein single–pass Algorithmus für die schnelle Konturkodierung von Binärbildern," In R.E. Grosskopf (ed.), *Proc. 12th DAGM–Symposium Mustererkennung*, Springer–Verlag, Berlin, 1990.

[Mandler 90b]   E. Mandler and M. Oberländer, "One–Pass Encoding of Connected Components in Multi–Valued Images," *Proc. 10th ICPR*, Atlantic City, 1990.

[Meisel 68]   W. S. Meisel, "Least–Square Methods in Abstract Pattern Recognition," *Information Sciences* 1, pp. 43–54, 1968.

[Nilsson 82]   J. N. Nilsson, *Principles of Artificial Intelligence*, Springer–Verlag, Berlin, 1982.

[Pao 89]   Y. H. Pao, *Adaptive Pattern Recognition and Neural Networks*, Addison–Wesley, Reading, MA, pp. 197–222, 1989.

[Pearl 84]   J. Pearl, *Heuristics, Intelligent Search Strategies For Computer Problem Solving*, Addison–Wesley, Reading, MA, 1984.

[Rastogi 86]   A. Rastogi and S.N. Srihari, "Recognizing Textual Blocks in Document Images Using the Hough Transform," TR 86–01, Dept of Computer Science, SUNY at Buffalo, 1986.

[Schürmann 77]   J. Schürmann, "Polynomklassifikatoren für die Zeichenerkennung," *Oldenbourg Verlag*, München Wien, 1977.

[Schürmann 78]   J. Schürmann, "A Multi–Font Word Recognition System for Postal Address Readings," *IEEE Trans.*, G27, 1978 3, pp. 359–369, 1984.

[Schürmann 84]   J. Schürmann and W. Doster, "A Decision Theoretic Approach to Hierarchical Classifier Design," *Pattern Recognition*, Vol. 17, No. 3, pp. 359–369, 1984.

[Shafer 76]   G. Shafer, *A Mathematical Theory of Evidence*, Princeton Univ. Press, Princeton, 1976.

[Watanabe 72]   S. Watanabe, *Frontiers of Pattern Recognition*, Academic Press, New York, 1972.

An Experimental Implementation of a Document Recognition System for Papers Containing Mathematical Expressions

Masayuki Okamoto and Akira Miyazawa

Department of Information Engineering, Faculty of Engineering,
Shinshu University, 500 Wakasato Nagano 380, Japan

This paper describes the current state of an experimental document recognition system for scientific papers. A scientific paper contains not only text but also tables, pictures, graphics, and mathematical expressions. This system can convert character or symbol strings in text as well as mathematical expressions and tables into coded data. Out of all the functions required for the entire process from document scanning through recognition, these have been investigated and implemented: skew detection and correction, region (block) segmentation, and mathematical expression recognition. The algorithms have been designed for high speed as much as possible. This experimental system is implemented entirely in software on a work station under X-windows. Some experimental results on each stage of the document recognition process are presented.

1 Introduction

To realize a document analysis or "understanding" system [1, 2], many algorithms or techniques related to each stage of analysis, from scanning documents through understanding them, must be developed and tested. The principal stages of processing are: (1) image digitization and if necessary, skew detection and correction, (2) region (block) segmentation, (3) region classification, (4) character segmentation and classification, and (5) document analysis which includes various steps from simple spelling correction to natural language understanding. Except for stage (4), each of these is a rather new research field and needs intensive studies for dealing with many types of complex printed documents.

This paper describes experimental implementation of a recognition system for scientific papers. A scientific paper page consists of many components, such as text, mathematical expressions, pictures or graphics, tables, and so on. Constructing a complete system is our long-term goal: at the moment, we have assembled several of the essential functions into a prototype system. We feel that recent increases in work station hardware performance are rapidly making such integrated systems feasible.

In our system, new algorithms have been developed and tested for the stages (1) and (2). They are based on coded data which are generated by the segmented block (SB) coding scheme [3] we proposed for document images. These algorithms are designed to avoid time consuming pixel-by-pixel processing. For task (2), several region segmentation methods have already been proposed [1, 4, 5, 6, 7, 8]. However many of them are very restrictive in the layout styles and document components (text, tables, etc) they can process. Though scientific papers have rather simple page layout styles in general, it is desirable to develop a new region segmentation method which can be uniformly applied to many types of documents. Our method has exhibited good performance in terms of effectiveness and computational efficiency.

For stage (3), this system has only a simple function which is to classify the regions segmented into text or expressions, tables, and pictures. Even though some methods of further classification which specify title, abstract, header, paragraph, etc have been proposed, this problem seems to be closely related to stage (5) which involves complete document structure understanding, so this remains for future work.

For stage (4), a simple template matching technique similar to [1, 12] is used. The main reason for selecting a simple template matching is that at the current state of character recognition, the discrimination of font styles such as italic, slanted, bold and so on is very difficult. In mathematical papers, this discrimination is a very important task. Another reason is to avoid the requirement of enormous CPU power in order to implement this system on a conventional work station. In this stage, our system also recognizes mathematical expressions. For classification of many sizes of mathematical symbols, part of the method based on [10] is used.

This paper is organized into five sections. Section 1 describes the segmented block coding scheme; Section 2, skew detection and correction; Section 3, region segmentation; Section 4, text and mathematical expression recognition; and Section 5, implementation and experimental results.

2 Segmented Block Coding Scheme

This section describes the segmented block (SB) coding scheme briefly. Our methods for detection and correction of skew and region (block) segmentation of scanned documents are based on the blocks of SB code. The SB coding scheme is proposed for the following reasons:

(1) Efficient data compression of document images

(2) Easy image processing on coded data

In the SB coding scheme, a contiguous black pixel area is represented by its position and simple shape. Therefore some kind of later image processing can be carried out efficiently on coded data.

The encoding of a document image is carried out as follows. First, the document page image is partitioned into small rectangular areas which are called segments and in each segment, contiguous black pixel areas are divided into blocks which have slopes in their left or right edges. For example, block B can be represented by a combination the following codeword elements:

$$B = (I, HP, VP, HL, VL, GL, GR)$$

where:

I : additional information about the codeword elements

HP : the relative horizontal position of the block in a segment

VP : the relative vertical position of the block in a segment

HL : the horizontal length of the starting run of the block

VL : the vertical length of the block

GL : the slope of the left-hand side of the block

GR : the slope of the right-hand side of the block

Figure 1(a) shows an example of a block partition. Figure 1(b) shows the representation of a block in the SB coding format.

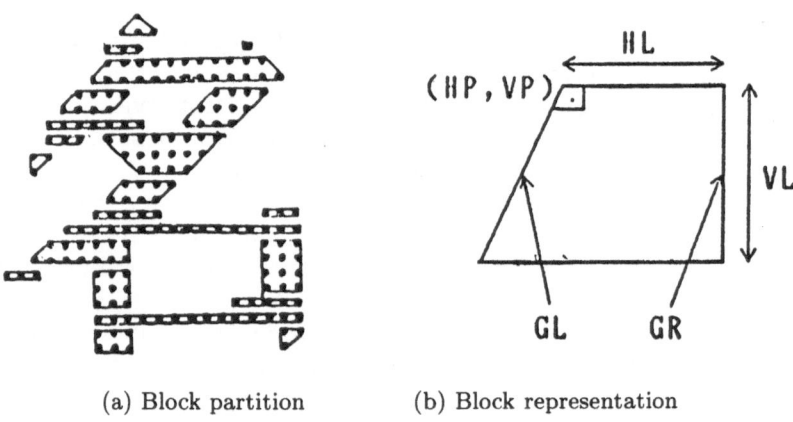

(a) Block partition   (b) Block representation

Fig. 1. Representation of SB coded data.

3 Detection and Correction of Skew

Our method for detection and correction of skewed documents is based on the blocks of SB coding. The SB blocks are grouped into rectangles which correspond approximately to one character per rectangle. The baseline of these rectangles are used to detect skew in text areas of documents. Skew correction is performed by rotating each block according to the detected skew angle. These two procedures can be omitted when a scanned document has a very small skew angle.

3.1 Detection of Skew

The skew of a document can be estimated from the base lines of text. In the rectangle representation of a document image obtained in step (3) of the region segmentation procedure, character candidate rectangles (*CCR*) correspond approximately to each character in the text areas. Therefore, if we can find series of *CCR's* corresponding to single text lines, the skew angle can be estimated. Our skew detection method is carried out as follows.

Grouping of *CCR's*. We group *CCR's* into classes such that the *CCR's* in the same class correspond to a single text line. Rectangles R_i and R_j are classified to be in the same class if they satisfy the following conditions:

$$rx_j - rx_i < \theta_1, |ry_j - ry_i| < \theta_2, \theta_1 = 3 \cdot R_h^f, \theta_2 = 0.5 \cdot R_v^f,$$

where (rx_i, ry_i) and (rx_j, ry_j) are the bottom left points of neighboring rectangles R_i, R_j. R_h^f, R_v^f are defined in step (2) of region segmentation in the next section.

Estimation of Base Lines. We estimate the base line corresponding to each text line by using the least square method on the sequence of bottom left points of grouped rectangles.

We determine the skew angle of a document by averaging the base line slope values obtained in step (2). In step (1), θ_1 is determined from R_h^f to prevent merging of text lines which are located on either side of a multi-column document. θ_2 is determined from R_v^f to prevent merging of each pair of adjacent text lines. Table 1 shows the results of skew detections. As shown in Table 1, the number of extracted text lines is sometimes greater than that of the actual number of text lines in scanned document. This is caused by grouping errors in step (1). For the example, a group of *CCR's* corresponding to a single text line can be divided into or two more groups. But, the average number of rectangles which are contained in the extracted text lines is greater than 35. So the angles of base lines can be estimated with sufficient accuracy.

Table 1. Results of skew detection.

Document No.	Text Lines in Document	Extracted Text Lines	Detected Skew Values (deg.)	Measured Skew Values (deg.)
1	66	66	1.70	1.80
2	66	82	0.50	0.56
3	85	105	−0.80	−0.78
4	92	99	1.40	1.43
5	92	92	3.00	2.95
6	84	84	1.90	1.82

3.2 Correction of Skew

The pixel by pixel skew correction procedure requires considerable processing time. Our procedure corrects skewed documents by rotating blocks in order to reduce processing time. First, the relative coordinates (HP, VP) of the starting point of the block in a segment are transformed into absolute coordinates (HP_c, VP_c) relative to an origin located at the center of the document. Then, the starting point of each block is rotated by the following formulas:

$$x = HP_c \cdot \cos\theta - VP_c \cdot \sin\theta, y = HP_c \cdot \sin\theta + VP_c \cdot \cos\theta,$$

where θ is the angle of skew.

This rotation causes some separation or overlapping of blocks which are adjacent to each other in the original document. This decreases the quality of rotated images so separated or overlapped blocks are moved in order to maintain the adjacency relation of blocks before rotation.

Figure 2 shows a comparison of skew correction quality. The scanned document has a skew of 1.7 degree. It is difficult to compare the qualities of rotated images by these methods, but as far as our experiments are concerned, both methods are regarded as having nearly the same qualities. The right hand image of Figure 2(a) has a 3.0 degree skew. This example shows that our method tends to maintain global original shapes and reduces the jagged edges on characters more than the pixel by pixel method.

The skew correction by our method can be carried out more efficiently than that of the pixel by pixel method. In ordinal documents, the number of blocks of SB code is one-tenth the total number of black pixels, so theoretically the processing time for the rotation of blocks is one-tenth that of the pixel by pixel rotation. However, our method needs an extra procedure of improving the rotated image, so the actual total processing time is equal to one-fifth that of the pixel by pixel method.

4 Segmentation of Documents

Region (block) segmentation of a document determines the layout structure of the document from its binary image. In region segmentation, it is very important to distinguish the regions which correspond exactly to each component of a document. For this reason, the simple recursive projection profile cuts or run length smoothing algorithms are not enough to deal with the complex layouts and numerous components of a document. Since the feedback from the classification or analysis stage to the segmentation process seems to be essential to perform complete segmentation, this needs intensive studies in many fields and remains for future work.

The main purposes of our algorithm are (1) to handle uniformly as many layout styles and document components as possible without using document dependent parameters such as pre-determined character sizes or width of line

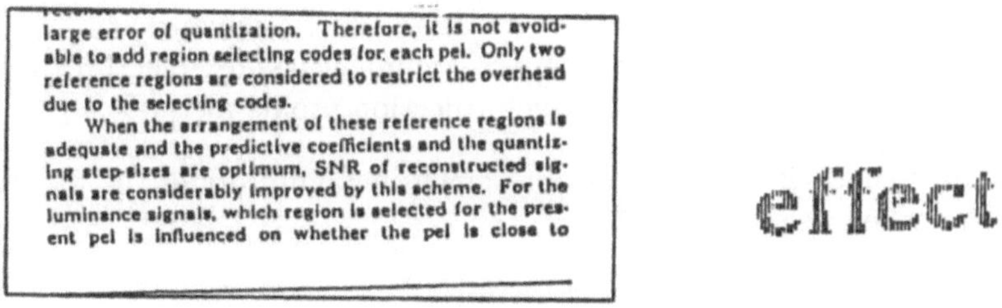
large error of quantization. Therefore, it is not avoidable to add region selecting codes for each pel. Only two reference regions are considered to restrict the overhead due to the selecting codes.

When the arrangement of these reference regions is adequate and the predictive coefficients and the quantizing step-sizes are optimum, SNR of reconstructed signals are considerably improved by this scheme. For the luminance signals, which region is selected for the present pel is influenced on whether the pel is close to

(a) Scanned image

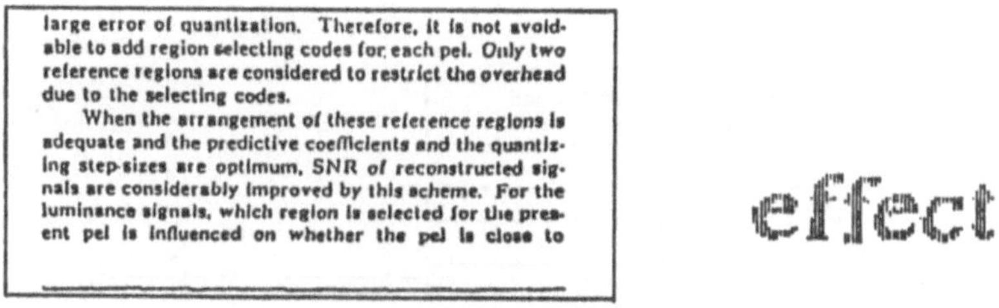
large error of quantization. Therefore, it is not avoidable to add region selecting codes for each pel. Only two reference regions are considered to restrict the overhead due to the selecting codes.

When the arrangement of these reference regions is adequate and the predictive coefficients and the quantizing step-sizes are optimum, SNR of reconstructed signals are considerably improved by this scheme. For the luminance signals, which region is selected for the present pel is influenced on whether the pel is close to

(b) Skew correction by our method

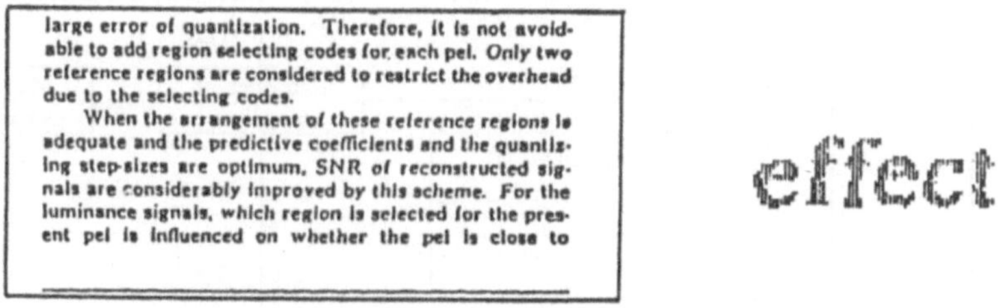
large error of quantization. Therefore, it is not avoidable to add region selecting codes for each pel. Only two reference regions are considered to restrict the overhead due to the selecting codes.

When the arrangement of these reference regions is adequate and the predictive coefficients and the quantizing step-sizes are optimum, SNR of reconstructed signals are considerably improved by this scheme. For the luminance signals, which region is selected for the present pel is influenced on whether the pel is close to

(c) Skew correction by pixel by pixel method

Fig. 2. Example of skew correction image.

spacing, and (2) to perform the segmentation procedure efficiently without special hardware. For purpose (2), our algorithm avoids the time consuming pixel by pixel processing like that in a projection profile, and uses only the rectangles which are generated by a simple operation on the blocks of SB code. Since the SB coding scheme is an information preserving coding, we can extract any information about a binarized document image from the blocks of SB code. Our algorithm is designed to accomplish the following objectives:

- Separate and classify a document into text, tables or enclosed articles, pictures (graphics), and field-separators.
- Determine the direction of text lines (vertical or horizontal).
- Separate text strings from a table or an enclosed article.

- Extract several kinds of field-separators.
- Have robustness for more complex document layout structures which cannot be handled by simple recursive projection profile methods.

The flow chart of the algorithm is shown in Figure 3 and the processing steps are described below in detail.

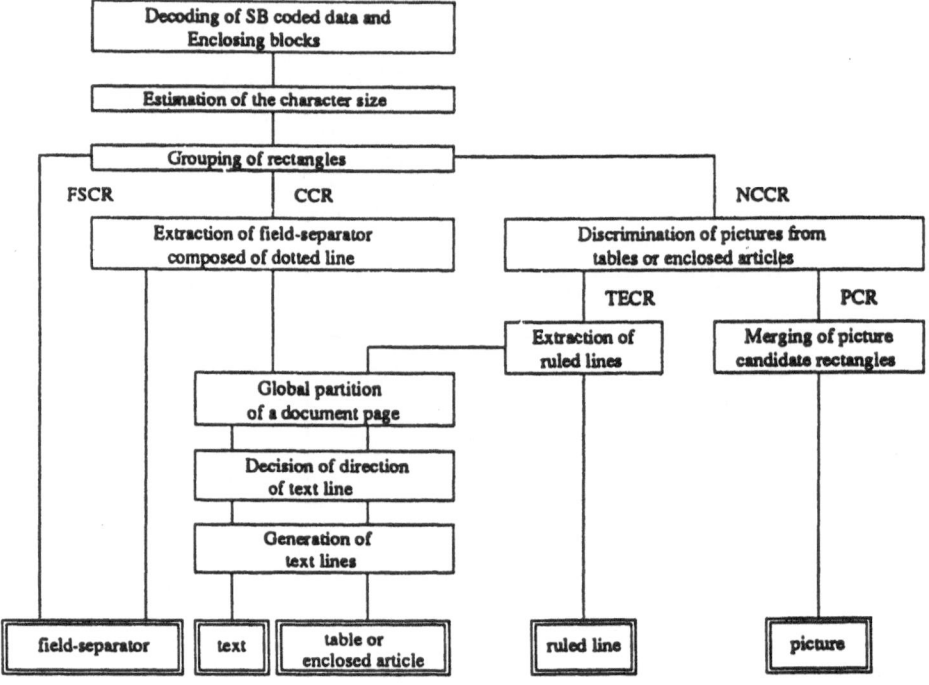

Fig. 3. Flow chart of region segmentation.

(1) Decoding of SB coded data and generation of SB code block enclosures. The blocks of SB code are enclosed by minimal size rectangles and then adjacent rectangles are merged into larger rectangles.

(2) Estimation of character size. From the histograms of horizontal and vertical sizes of rectangles, the most frequently occurring values of R_h^f and R_v^f are determined respectively. These sizes represent the approximate horizontal

and vertical dimensions of small characters which appear in the main text of a document.

(3) Grouping of rectangles. All rectangles are classified into one of three groups according to their sizes using the following conditions:

if $(R_x/R_y > 20)$ or $(R_y/R_x > 20)$
then   field-separator candidate rectangle ($FSCR$)
else if $(R_x > 5 \cdot R_h^f)$ and $(R_y > 5 \cdot R_v^f)$
then   non-character candidate rectangle ($NCCR$)
else   character candidate rectangle (CCR),

where R_x and R_y are the horizontal and vertical sizes of a rectangle. $NCCR$'s are considered to be the rectangles which are generated from tables, figures, or enclosed articles.

(4) Discrimination of pictures from tables or enclosed articles. All $NCCR$'s are classified as 1)pictures or 2)tables or enclosed articles by the following condition. Let Sr the area of an $NCCR$ and St the total area of CCR's which are contained in the $NCCR$.

if $(St > 0.2 \cdot Sr)$
then   a table or enclosed article candidate rectangle ($TECR$)
else   a picture candidate rectangle (PCR)

(5) Merging of picture candidate rectangles. Adjacent PCR's are merged into a single rectangle and from the picture region. In this step, all rectangles contained in picture regions are discarded.

(6) Extraction of ruled lines in tables or enclosed articles. For all $TECR$'s, horizontal or vertical lines are traced based on blocks of SB code contained in the $TECR$ and the ruled lines are extracted.

In the case of horizontal line tracing, the process is shown in Figure 4. For each leftmost block in a $TECR$, adjacency relation to other blocks is examined within the tracing region and adjacent blocks are merged into a single rectangle. If the rectangle has an aspect ratio of greater than 20, it will be extracted as a ruled line.

(7) Extraction of field-separators composed of dotted lines or other small size figures. Using the procedure similar to step (6) and the same trace region, CCR's whose horizontal or vertical sizes are less than $0.5 \cdot R_h^f$ or $0.5 \cdot R_v^f$, respectively, are traced.

(8) Global partitioning of a document page.
   (i) Text region extraction. A document page is divided into a grid and in each grid element, the existence of CCR's is checked. For the grid elements which contain CCR's, labeling is performed and elements with

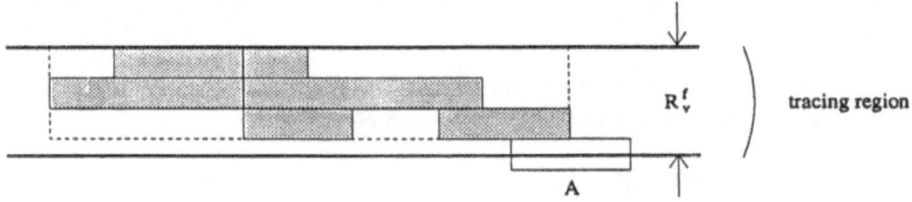

Since block A is out of region,
it is not merged.

Fig. 4. Ruled line tracing.

the same label are enclosed by rectangles. These rectangles form the text region of a document. Since the selection of mesh size has little dependence on the type of document processed, we arbitrarily selected a 16×16 pixel size grid for a document scanned with 200 dpi resolution.

(ii) Partitioning by field-separators. A text region extracted in the above step is partitioned by field-separators extracted in steps (3) or (7).

(9) Determination of text line orientation. For each text region, the direction of text lines is determined by the following method.

(i) We obtain D_x and D_y for each CCR in a text region by the distances D_r, D_l, D_a, D_b to the 4-neighboring (right, left, above, below) CCR's as follows:

$$D_x = min\{D_r, D_l\},$$
$$D_y = min\{D_a, D_b\}.$$

(ii) We compute the average values $\bar{D}_x, \bar{D}_y$ of D_x's and D_y's for all CCR's in the text area, and determine the direction of text line as follows.

If $\bar{D}_x < \bar{D}_y$ **then** horizontal direction
else vertical direction.

(10) Generation of text lines. For each text area, CCR's are merged into rectangles according to the orientation determined in step (9), and form the text line.

4.1 Experimental Results

Figure 5 shows an example of region segmentation and Table 2 shows the results of segmentation for some sample documents. The document in Figure 5 has several components and a rather complex layout structure and is reproduced artificially to illustrate the performance of our method. In this experiment, documents are scanned with 200 dpi resolution, and processed on a SUN-3/160.

Table 2. Results of region segmentation.

Doc. No.	Extracted Sentence Rect.	Figure Areas	Field Seps	Table or Enclosed Article			CPU secs
				Areas	Lines	Contents	
1	53/53	2/2	2/2	2/2	22/20	58/58	79.4
2	49/50	0/0	3/3	2/2	8/8	34/33	42.9
3	124/123	3/2	13/13	0/0	0/0	0/0	38.9
4	48/48	0/0	5/5	2/2	19/19	45/44	55.2
5	50/50	0/0	4/4	1/1	5/5	19/19	37.3
6	49/49	2/2	1/1	2/2	10/10	57/57	43.4

5 Text and Mathematical Expression Recognition

In scientific papers, a wide variety of font styles and mathematical symbols are used, and the different font representations (*italic*, *slanted*, **bold** etc) of the same character or symbol can carry important meaning. With the present character recognition level, the classification of font styles is still very difficult. Also, the main purpose of this research is purely experimental implementation of a document recognition system for scientific papers on a work station. For these reasons, slightly modified versions of simple template matching [1, 12] and vectorizer and feature extraction [10] methods have been implemented for character recognition and large size mathematical symbol recognition, respectively. Our principal implementations or modifications are as follows:

- Template pattern matching with our own weighting method;
- Application of some heuristics to the classification of the confusing groups (c-e-o, i-l, b-h, etc);
- Use of character layout context similar to [10],
- Separation of merged characters with a breakpoint criterion function; and
- Two-dimensional mathematical expression recognition.

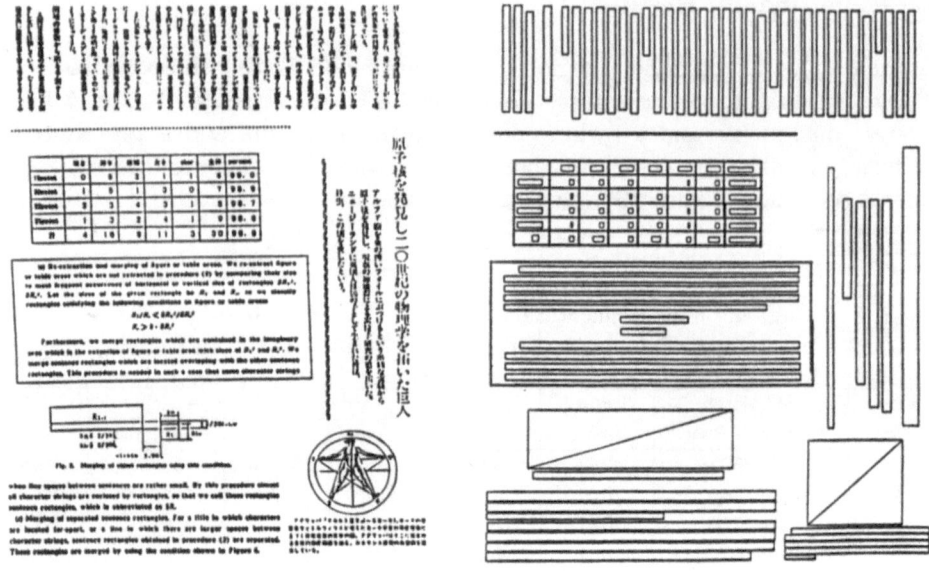

(a) Original document   (b) Result of segmentation

Fig. 5. An example of region segmentation.

5.1 Mathematical Expression Recognition

A wide variety of mathematical expressions can be recognized by using only the layout structures of symbols without parsing them. Parsing methods require a knowledge of syntax definitions of expressions which are described in a form of grammar [13]. This grammar includes the precise definition of various production rules which can become difficult for wide variety of expressions. Our method finds an expression structure from the two-dimensional relative positions of symbols within an expression. The basic procedure of this method is based on the partitioning of a given expression into components by recursive horizontal and vertical projection profiles cutting. Horizontal cutting extracts the relationship between components arranged vertically and vertical cutting does the same for horizontally arranged components. These relationship are represented by a tree structure. Some additional checking procedures are performed on the tree to correct any improper relationship between components caused by simple projection profile cuttings.

(1) Segmentation by recursive projection profile cutting

Because a mathematical expression consists of horizontally located subexpressions, vertical cutting (cutting by the vertical projection profile [14]) is applied first. Then, horizontal cuttings are attempted for each cut region. This procedure is repeated recursively until further vertical or horizontal cutting becomes impossible. After this procedure, the segmentation by labeling is carried out in order to divide a subexpression like $\sqrt{x+y}$ into separate elements which cannot be dealt with by the projection profile cut. The layout structure of an expression derived by this segmentation process is represented in the form of the tree with horizontal or vertical links representing corresponding cuttings. In this tree representation, the labeled segments are connected temporally by the horizontal links for further processing. Figure 6 illustrates the segmentation process and Figure 7 shows an example of a tree structure representation.

(2) During the segmentation process, symbols consisting of multiple parts, for example 'i', ':', '=', etc, are separated into individual components. In this case, merging of the separated components is carried out by examining the relative locations, the ratio of vertical sizes, and the ratio of areas whose rectan

(3) Structure analysis

In the above procedure, most syntax information of a expression is represented correctly by the tree structure. However some remains incorrect due to the simplicity of the recursive projection profile cut or labeling method. In this step, two types of corrections are performed. One type of correction is for the recognition of subscripts or superscripts, and their subexpressions. This can be done by examining the relative layout in the vertical direction among enclosed rectangles which are connected in the horizontal links. Another type of correction is performed for matrix structures and bounding relations between root signs and their enclosed subexpressions when large size parentheses and root symbols are recognized, respectively.

48   M. Okamoto and A. Miyazawa

$$\tan 2n\theta = \frac{\sum_{r=0}^{n-1}(-1)^r \binom{2n}{2r+1}\tan^{2r+1}\theta}{\sum_{r=0}^{n}(-1)^r \binom{2n}{2r}\tan^{2r}\theta}.$$

(a) Original image

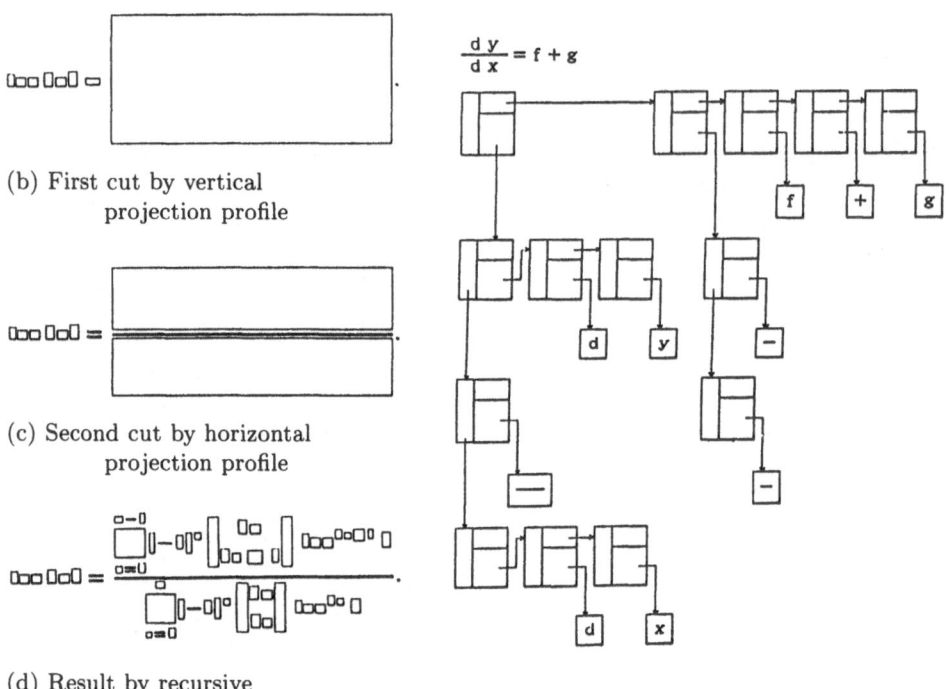

(b) First cut by vertical
     projection profile

(c) Second cut by horizontal
     projection profile

(d) Result by recursive
     projection profile

Fig. 6. Partitioning by recursive
projection profile.

Fig. 7. Tree structure of a mathematical
expression.

5.2 Reproduction of Recognized Documents

The recognition results for text areas with mathematical expressions can be reproduced on a bitmap display or a printer by the TEX [17] program. For this purpose, a simple program which converts encoded text to a format accepted by TEX has been developed. Two-byte codes are used to represent the many kinds of symbols and font styles recognized in our system. The conversion from recognized expressions to TEX format can be done directly according to the two-dimensional links in the tree structure.

$$\frac{\partial p_j}{\partial \alpha_l} = -\int \left\{ \prod_{\substack{l=1 \\ l \neq i, j}}^{k} \Phi(u + \alpha_j - \alpha_l) \right\} \qquad \frac{\partial p_j}{\partial \alpha_i} = -\int \left\{ \prod_{\substack{l=1 \\ l \neq i,j}}^{k} \Phi(n + \alpha_j - \alpha_i) \right\}$$

$$V = \begin{bmatrix} v_x \\ v_y \\ v_t \end{bmatrix} = \begin{bmatrix} \cos \psi_V \cos \phi_V \\ \sin \psi_V \cos \phi_V \\ \sin \phi_V \end{bmatrix}. \qquad \hat{V} = \begin{bmatrix} v_x \\ v_y \\ v_z \end{bmatrix} = \begin{bmatrix} \cos \psi_v & \cos \phi_v \\ \sin \psi_v & \cos \phi_v \\ \sin \phi_v \end{bmatrix}.$$

$$\mathrm{SNR} = \frac{\left| \int_{-W}^{+W} G(-x) f(x)\, dx \right|}{n_0 \sqrt{\int_{-W}^{+W} f^2(x)\, dx}} \qquad SNR = \frac{\left| \int_{-w}^{+w} G(-x) f(x) dx \right|}{n_o \sqrt{\int_{-w}^{+w} f^2(x) dx}}$$

$$P_{GLI} = \frac{\dfrac{R_{CI}}{2}}{\dfrac{R_L}{2} + \dfrac{R_{CI}}{2}}, \qquad P_{GL1} = \frac{\dfrac{R_{C1}}{2}}{\dfrac{R_L}{2} + \dfrac{R_{C1}}{2}},$$

(a) Original expressions   (b) Recognition results

Fig. 8. Examples of expression recognition.

Figure 8 shows some results of mathematical expression recognition. In this example, the rejected characters are indicated by '?', and recognition errors in the subscript expressions seem to be caused by the low resolution of the scanner.

6 Implementation and Experiments

All the algorithms used in our system were written in C and run on a SUN-3/160. Figure 10 shows the flow chart of the document recognition process. As an input device, a 200 dpi resolution commercial scanner was used. The scanned data was encoded by SB coding scheme and stored in files for the further processing. Pre-recognition was performed for one or two pages of papers to construct a template pattern library, prior to the actual tests. In these tests, table and picture areas were excluded and the distinction between text lines and mathematical expressions was specified manually. Figure 9 shows an example of a text area recognition result reproduced by the TEX . In this example, because the reproduction by TEX used the same layout structure which was obtained in the region segmentation step, the ends of lines were not aligned. Although only a small-scale trial was carried out, the overall speed was about 5 characters per second with a recognition rate of 91 to 97%.

7 Conclusion

The rapid increase of hardware performance of work stations seems to make an implementation of a document recognition system possible. The main purpose of our experimental implementation was to examine and realize the possibility of such a system on a work station and to evaluate methods needed in the various stages from the scanning step to the recognition phase. The important areas in which our current system can be improved or further studied are as follows:

- Implementation of an improved classifier which can deal with characters of various fonts and sizes. But in this case, we will need a secondary classifier which can identify the type of fonts (*italic, slanted,* **bold** etc).
- An improved region(block) classifier which can discriminate between sentences and mathematical expression areas automatically. This classification can be implemented partially by using some knowledge about how mathematical expressions are arranged in a paper.
- A partial syntax checker which will improve mathematical expression recognition. After we classify some principal symbols, we can apply simple syntax related to those symbols in order to correct recognition results.
- Development of a screen editor for text containing mathematical expression for post-editing.

References

[1]   K. Y. Wong, R. G. Casey, and F. M. Wahl, "Document Analysis System," *IBM J. Res. Develop.*, vol. 26, no. 6, pp. 647–656, 1982.

[2]   S. N. Srihari, "Document Image Understanding," *Proc. IEEE Computer Society Fall Joint Computer Conf.*, pp. 87–96, Nov. 1986.

[3]   M. Okamoto, K. Kawata, and M. Tamai, "Segmented Block Coding Scheme of Document Images and Its Data Compression," *Trans IECE Japan*, vol.E68, no. 2, pp. 113–114, 1985.

[4]   F. M. Wahl, M. K. Y. Wong, and R. G. Casey, "Block Segmentation and Text Extraction in Mixed Text/image Documents," *Computer Vision, Graphics, Image Processing*, vol. 20, pp. 375–390, 1982.

[5]   O. Nakamura, M. Ujiie, N. Okamoto, and T. Minami, "A Character Segmentation Algorithm for Mixed-Mode Communication," *Trans. IECE Japan*, vol.J66-D, no. 4, pp. 437–444, 1983.

[6] T. Akiyama and I. Masuda, "A Method of Document-Image Segmentation Based on Projection Profiles, Stroke Densities, and Circumscribed Rectangles," *Trans. IECE Japan*, vol,J69-D, no. 8, pp. 1187–1196, 1986.

[7] L. A. Fletcher and R. Kasturi, "A Robust Algorithm for Text String Separation from Mixed Text/Graphics Images," *IEEE Trans. Pattern Anal. Mach. Intelligence*, vol. 10, no. 6, pp. 910–918, 1988.

[8] M. Okamoto, H. Nishizawa, and H. M. Twaakyondo, "Skew Normalization and Segmentation of Document Images Using Segmented Block Coding," *IECEJ Technical Report*, OS87-9, pp. 13–18, 1987.

[9] D. Wang and S. N. Srihari, "Classification of Newspaper Image Blocks Using Texture Analysis," *Computer Vision, Graphics, Image Processing*, vol. 47, 1989, pp327–352.

[10] S. Kahan, T. Pavlidis, and H. S. Baird, "On The Recognition of Printed Characters of Any Font and Size," *IEEE Trans. Pattern Anal. Mach. Intelligence*, vol. PAMI-9, no. 2, pp. 274–288, 1987.

[11] T. Pavlidis, "A Vectorizer and Feature Extractor for Document Recognition," *Computer Vision, Graphics, Image Processing*, vol. 35, pp. 111–127, 1986.

[12] R. G. Casey and C. R. Jih, "A Processor-Based OCR System," *IBM J. Res. Develop.*, vol. 27, no. 4, July 1983.

[13] K. S. Fu, *Syntactic Methods in Pattern Recognition*, Academic Press, pp. 245–252, 1974.

[14] Y. Nakano, H. Fujisawa, and J. Higashino, "A Fast Algorithm for the Skew Normalization of Document Images," *Trans. IECE Japan*, vol.J69-D, no. 11, pp. 1833–1834, 1986.

[15] M. Okamoto and H. Nishizawa, "A Experimental Implementation of Document Recognition System for English Papers Containing Mathematical Formulas," *IECEJ Technical Report*, PRU88-158, pp. 89–96, 1989.

[16] H. S. Baird, "The Skew Angle of Printed Documents," in *Proc. SPSE 40th Conf. and Symp. on Hybrid Imaging System*, pp. 21–24, 1987.

[17] D. E. Knuth, *The TEXbook*, Addison–Wesley, Reading, MA, 1987.

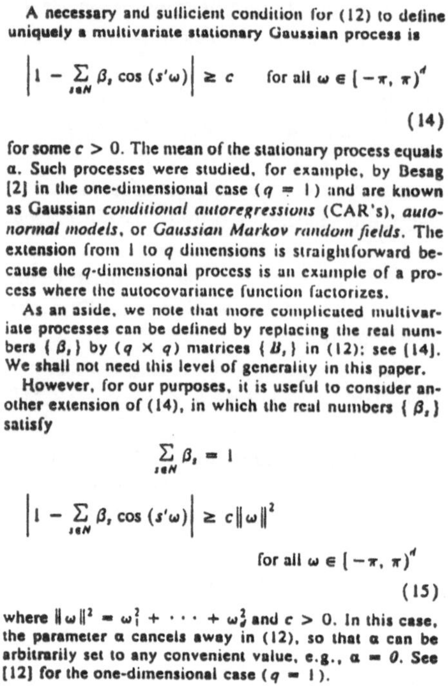

A necessary and sufficient condition for (12) to define uniquely a multivariate stationary Gaussian process is

$$\left|1 - \sum_{s \in N} \beta_s \cos(s'\omega)\right| \geq c \qquad \text{for all } \omega \in [-\pi, \pi)^d \tag{14}$$

for some $c > 0$. The mean of the stationary process equals α. Such processes were studied, for example, by Besag [2] in the one-dimensional case ($q = 1$) and are known as Gaussian *conditional autoregressions* (CAR's), *autonormal models*, or *Gaussian Markov random fields*. The extension from 1 to q dimensions is straightforward because the q-dimensional process is an example of a process where the autocovariance function factorizes.

As an aside, we note that more complicated multivariate processes can be defined by replacing the real numbers $\{\beta_s\}$ by $(q \times q)$ matrices $\{B_s\}$ in (12): see [14]. We shall not need this level of generality in this paper.

However, for our purposes, it is useful to consider another extension of (14), in which the real numbers $\{\beta_s\}$ satisfy

$$\sum_{s \in N} \beta_s = 1$$

$$\left|1 - \sum_{s \in N} \beta_s \cos(s'\omega)\right| \geq c\|\omega\|^2 \qquad \text{for all } \omega \in [-\pi, \pi)^d \tag{15}$$

where $\|\omega\|^2 = \omega_1^2 + \cdots + \omega_d^2$ and $c > 0$. In this case, the parameter α cancels away in (12), so that α can be arbitrarily set to any convenient value, e.g., $\alpha = 0$. See [12] for the one-dimensional case ($q = 1$).

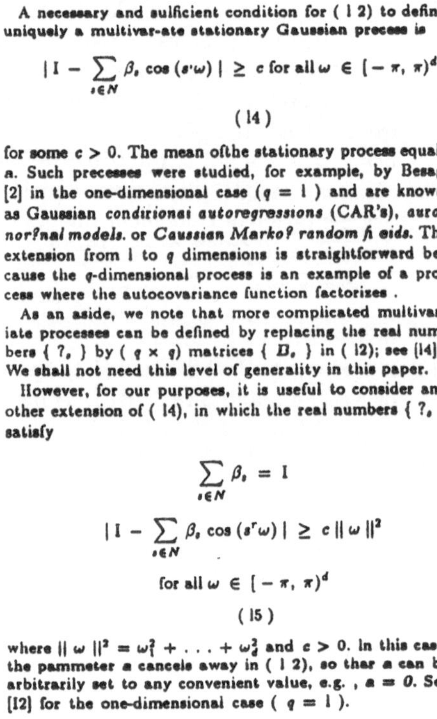

A necessary and sulficient condition for (1 2) to define uniquely a multivar-ate stationary Gaussian precess is

$$| I - \sum_{s \in N} \beta_s \cos(s'\omega) | \geq c \text{ for all } \omega \in [-\pi, \pi)^d$$

(14)

for some $c > 0$. The mean ofthe stationary process equals a. Such precesses were studied, for example, by Besag [2] in the one-dimensional case ($q = 1$) and are known as Gaussian *condirionai autoregressions* (CAR's), *auronor?nal models.* or *Caussian Marko? random fi eids.* The extension from 1 to q dimensions is straightforward be· cause the q-dimensional process is an example of a process where the autocovariance function factorizes .

As an aside, we note that more complicated multivariate processes can be defined by replacing the real numbers { ?, } by ($q \times q$) matrices { B_s } in (12); see [14] . We shall not need this level of generality in this paper.

IIowever, for our purposes, it is useful to consider an? other extension of (14), in which the real numbers { ?, } satisfy

$$\sum_{s \in N} \beta_s = I$$

$$| I - \sum_{s \in N} \beta_s \cos(s^r\omega) | \geq c \| \omega \|^2$$

for all $\omega \in [-\pi, \pi)^d$

(15)

where $\| \omega \|^2 = \omega_1^2 + \ldots + \omega_d^2$ and $c > 0$. In this case, the pammeter a cancels away in (1 2), so thar a can be arbitrarily set to any convenient value, e.g. , a = *0*. See [12] for the one-dimensional case ($q = 1$).

(a) Original image (b) Recognition result reproduced by TEX

Fig. 9. An example of document recognition.

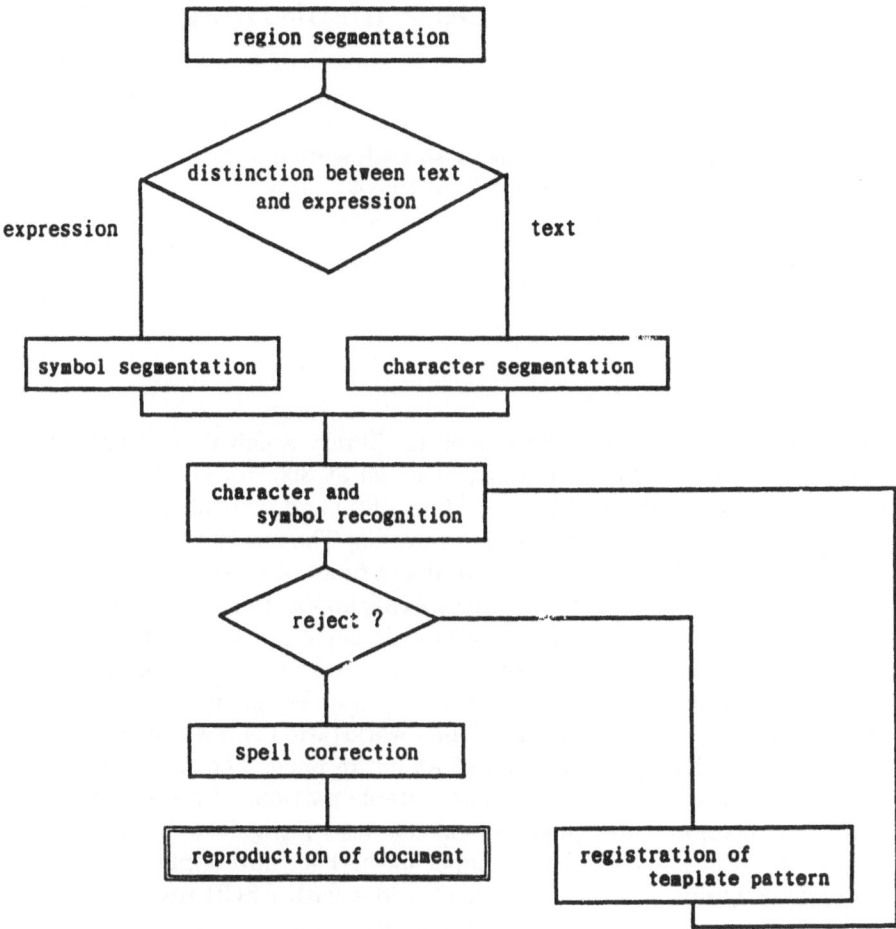

Fig. 10. Flow chart of document recognition process.

Towards a Structured-Document-Image Utility

George Nagy

Department of Electrical, Computer, and Systems Engineering,
Rensselaer Polytechnic Institute, Troy, NY 12180-3590, USA

Digitized documents are preprocessed for library archival and distribution. Pages from technical journals scanned at 300 dpi are recursively segmented with multiple alternating horizontal and vertical cuts according to publication-specific layout information. The resulting rectangular blocks are labeled concurrently in terms of functional components such as *author block, title, abstract*. Three specific applications for integrating paper-based information into an electronic environment are described. The first will allow library users to interactively select and view portions of a page-image, such as illustrations, subtitles, or text paragraphs, when either the screen resolution of their workstation or low transmission rates prevent viewing the bitmap of an entire page. The second application will automate the selection of suitable portions of the document (*e.g.*, abstracts) for subsequent optical character recognition for full-text search of journals and reports in paper form. The third application will automatically link pixel maps of illustrations with ASCII text files. All three applications are based on syntactic processing of binary document images.

1 Introduction

Librarians face an extraordinary problem in attempting to bring vast numbers of printed documents into the electronic Information Age. While progress is being made in creating full-text on-line files, information stored as print-on-paper persists. We are developing a methodology for integrating paper-based information into an electronic environment to improve information services through networked resource sharing. We use generic and publication-specific layout information to automatically divide scanned pages of technical articles into nested blocks corresponding to meaningful logical entities. Examples of the entity blocks that are located and labeled on the page are *titles* and *subtitles, authors, abstracts, illustrations*, and *references*. Three specific library applications of document images processed in this way are discussed. The first will allow library users to interactively select and view portions of a page-image when either the screen resolution of their workstation or low transmission rates (below c. 10 Mbs) prevent viewing the multimillion-byte bitmap of an entire page. This project will be demonstrated in conjunction with the RPI Library's existing on-line file of 1988 IEEE titles, authors and abstracts. The second application will allow automating the selection of suitable portions of the document (for instance, abstracts and reference lists) for subsequent optical character recognition for full-text search of large archival files of technical journals and reports in paper form. Additional information intended to facilitate OCR, such as column formats, line spacing and character size, will also be provided. The third application will automatically link pixel maps of illustrations with ASCII text files.

We first discuss alternative approaches to the computerization of the storage and retrieval of the large body of existing paper-based holdings in libraries. We then present the status of our current research on document segmentation and labeling techniques, followed by an explanation of how we propose to apply the techniques we have developed to both searching and interactively accessing scanned documents.

1.1 Alternative Storage and Information Sharing Technologies

Currently, documents in paper form are kept on shelves and in microfilm form in specialized cabinets. Other than hauling documents off the shelf or cabinet, copying, wrapping, addressing, and consigning them to the United States mail or a commercial messenger service, the only alternative for sending them to a remote destination is facsimile. Facsimile is used increasingly by libraries of all types, but still requires bringing the document to the facsimile transmitter and sending it over the low-speed telephone network. Perhaps because all this is far from an on-line, "real-time" operation, facsimile, though improving as a technology, is still not a major means for library access.

Some types of information, primarily that which is highly structured and has a wide audience, such as patents, statutes, and library indexes, have been converted to computer-readable alphanumeric form for direct access from end-user terminals. Capture can be accomplished by key entry (a very costly operation, even in third-world countries which have geared up to this cottage industry), as a by-product of the printing process, or by Optical Character Recognition (OCR). Current OCR technology does not, however, produce acceptable results without manual post-editing even on simple texts. The major reasons for this are the extraordinary diversity of typefaces (several *thousand* in common use), the large number of touching characters, and the complexity of the format of much printed material that precludes maintenance of the appropriate reading order in the coded text without semantic analysis [Nagy 82].

The current cost of bulk conversion (OCR + post-editing) varies from $2 to $5 per page of printed text depending on the complexity of the layout, the quality of the printing and paper, the desired accuracy, and the amount of formatting to be preserved. Although conversion to ASCII form provides immense flexibility in terms of automated search and access to the material, much of the layout information is inevitably lost. This renders the result irritating to read on either a screen display or printout. Another major drawback of OCR is that illustrations and mathematical formulas cannot be processed. While improvements in scanning resolution (most current OCR devices scan at only 240 or 300 dots per inch) will decrease the amount of post-processing necessary, many of the problems will not yield to increased scanning resolution. Hence OCR is not likely to provide the complete solution for the conversion of the paper backlog.

Scanning entire pages and storing them on mass storage devices such as digital compact disk or optical disk is considerably less expensive than conversion to ASCII, and the format of the document is preserved. Document images on CD can be disseminated either by physical means (*i.e.*, mailed) or through communication networks. However, this technology suffers from the inherent disadvantage that the smallest accessible unit is the page image. Even if a user wanted to read only the title of a page or a single figure caption, the entire page image — at 300 dpi, about 1 Megabyte in uncompressed form — must be accessed. While with hardware compression/decompression a page can be transmitted over a telephone line in a *fraction of a minute* (hardly flipping through the pages!), a second problem is even more serious. Very few display screens attached to general purpose workstations can accommodate the image at full resolution. Once the resolution is reduced to allow an entire page to be displayed at once, legibility is lost. To scroll the full-resolution image horizontally and vertically while reading it is both too slow and too irritating.

The *structured document image file* technology described below offers a potential solution to these problems. It is relatively scale-invariant with respect to the size of the collection. It can be adapted to *international exchange* of databases since the method is not language sensitive. Widely used publications could be scanned in *national centers*, using high-speed optical scanners and dedicated computers for processing. Smaller specialized collections could be scanned and processed at *regional libraries* with medium-speed scanners and general-purpose computers. The technology is within reach of even *small libraries* which could use desk-top scanners attached to personal workstations. Furthermore, the scanning could be performed wherever the documents are housed physically, and the processing completed at *library service centers*. The information processed at any center can be accessed elsewhere through communications networks.

Our intention is to combine the following emerging technologies and press them into the service of libraries.

- Optical page scanning and image compression as a means of storing on digital media documents that are now on paper or microform. Scanning is comparable in cost to microfilming, and the per-byte cost of optical jukeboxes is dropping rapidly.
- Development of data structures compatible with current standards for international document architectures for representing layout information in scanned documents.
- Digital image processing using syntactic and statistical pattern recognition and artificial intelligence search methods to extract layout structure and determine significant entities on printed pages.

- Optical character recognition with preprocessing by page analysis to preserve reading order and provide selective access.
- Structured document file transmission over digital networks.

We propose to demonstrate the method in three library-oriented applications:

- Provide a selective browse mechanism via personal computers or other workstations with network access to *interactively selected portions of page images* of IEEE technical publications. The viability of this demonstration is based on the Rensselaer Libraries' experimental INFOTRAX system which already provides faculty and student access to index information and full-text abstracts of 1989 IEEE publications.
- Use current OCR technology in conjunction with page analysis to provide ASCII input of selected portions of paper documents for *full-text searches*. We do not propose to carry out research on automated searching, just to provide a cost-effective means of applying available techniques to existing hard-copy collections.
- Show that automated page analysis can provide links from references to illustrations in ASCII text files to the *illustrations* themselves stored digitally in non-ASCII form. Access to compressed grey-scale images and line drawings is an order of magnitude more difficult on workstations than access to ASCII text because of the diversity of storage, compression, and display formats. Nevertheless, users who have the appropriate software and hardware must be able to access illustrations. Color is, of course, even more difficult, but the proposed methodology can eventually also be extended to color.

2 Method

The equipment used for experimentation consists of a 300 dpi Microtek scanner and several SUN 3/60 workstations. Software was collected and developed for the display of digitized pages and of segmentation trees and boundaries in various formats, as illustrated below.

The knowledge-base required for the segmentation and labeling of documents is organized into *logical* and *layout* categories in a hierarchy ranging from generic to publication-specific knowledge. Relevant entity-class and layout geometry was collected from ten samples each of three different journals. This data was used in the development of a knowledge base that takes full advantage of the *X-Y tree* structure of nested blocks devised specifically for images of printed pages [Nagy 84, Nagy 86]. A separate set of 95 samples was collected for experiments on block classification by statistical pattern recognition techniques. Horizontal and vertical block profiles were extracted for each sample. A set of 16 *profile primitives* was defined and coded for classification purposes.

In our original approach, samples of pages of technical journal articles were scanned and segmented into X-Y trees using a naive black/white *transition segmentation* of thresholded block profiles. We found that at 300 dpi the typical journal page yields upwards of 15,000 tree nodes (blocks), but the number of nodes is not a sensitive function of the scanning resolution. The smallest indivisible blocks are character fragments, such as the dot on an *i*. About a dozen logical entities were identified on transition-segmented pages in a single-column journal *(Artificial Intelligence)* using a thirty-rule knowledge base and a KEE expert-system shell [Thomas 88]. For validation purposes, faithful synthetic versions of pages from two different journals were generated with *troff* using macros that correspond to the desired logical entities. We were able to verify that the KEE-generated labels correspond to the right macro calls and to the correct position information from the user registers. This method could not, however, be extended to complex multi-column pages because transition segmentation does not respect logical boundaries.

In our current approach, we use a collection of *block-grammars* for simultaneous segmentation and identification of logical entities using the Unix tools *lex* and *yacc*. The essence of this method is to transform a *two-dimensional* segmentation and labeling problem into a tree-structured set of *one-dimensional* segmentation and labeling problems. Each segmentation of a block in a given direction generates a new set of *labeled* sub-blocks. Each of these sub-blocks then engenders a string that allows segmenting the sub-block in the direction orthogonal to the direction in which the parent block was segmented. The parameters (*i.e.*, the *grammar*) of the parse depend on the label of the block to which it was applied. The process terminates at leaf-nodes, which are characterized by having labels for which no grammars are available. Large leaf blocks (such as illustrations), that cannot be subdivided into X-Y trees, are further classified by statistical pattern recognition techniques. Earlier experiments on parsing *synthesized* pages of technical journals are reported in [Nagy 88, Viswanathan 88], while current experiments on *scanned* pages are described in detail in a companion paper [Viswanathan 91]. Examples of the classification of a full-text page and of a page containing some figures are shown in Figures 1 and 2. The labels reflect the hierarchical organization of the page. For example, COM stands for composite entry (two columns). COM COL for one column of a composite, and COM COL REF for a reference paragraph in a composite column.

Some segmentation and labeling errors committed when parsing a block may not be discovered until an unsuccessful attempt is made to parse immediate or distant offsprings of the block where the error was made. When this happens, the algorithm backtracks and tries to parse (with alternative grammars) the ancestors of the block where it failed. Since the algorithm cannot determine at what level an uncorrectable error occurred, it returns the X-Y tree whose labeled leaf-blocks cover the largest area. This can be accomplished efficiently with a branch-and-bound technique [Viswanathan 90].

One possible application of structure analysis is remote browsing. We have implemented a prototype system for this purpose. The system configuration is shown in Figure 3. An example of an iconic display of the page structure, and of the system's response to clicking the mouse on the part of the icon to be selected, are shown in Figure 4. We have demonstrated this remote browsing system, loaded with two-dozen documents, both over a local area network between Rensselaer workstations, and over the Internet with the host at Rensselaer

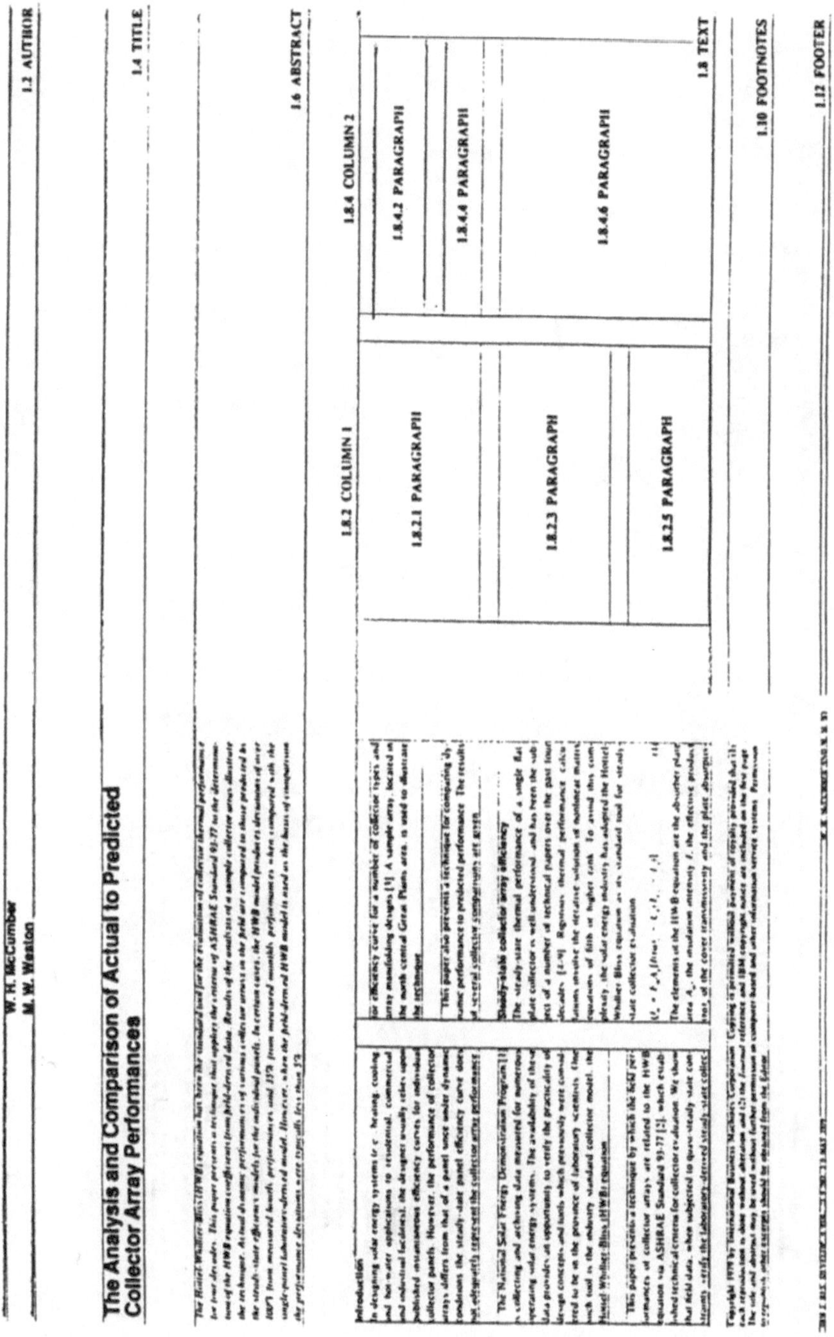

Fig. 1. Top-down segmentation and labeling using a syntactical approach.

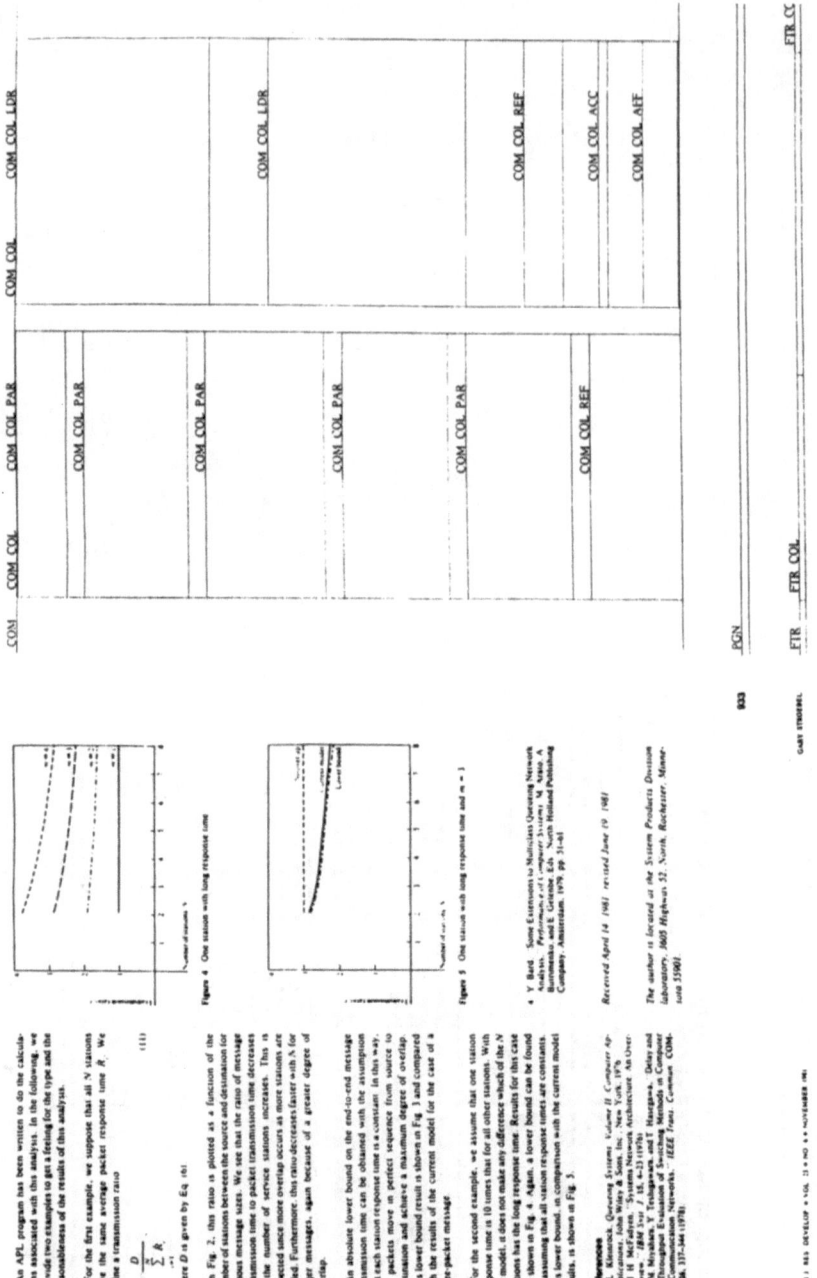

Fig. 2. Syntactic analysis and labeling of a page with text, references, and line-drawings.

and the query station at the University of Nebraska-Lincoln, and vice-versa. Recently the remote browser has been ported to the X-11 window manager, for eventual use on PCs.

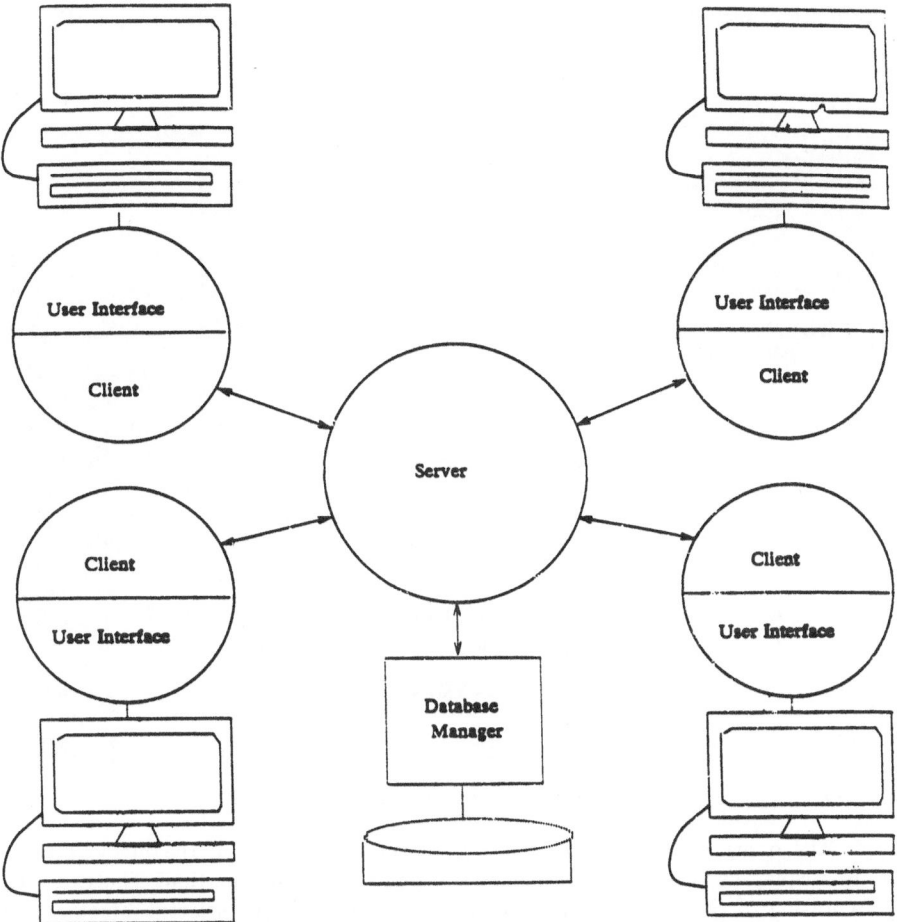

Fig. 3. The remote browsing system is implemented as a central server connected to query stations by the INTERNET. The user selects menu items to request information. The user interface converts these selections into requests which are sent to the server. The database manager extracts the requested data and sends it back to the query stations. The user interface displays the selected item.

For preprocessing documents for OCR, only the extraction of *layout*, rather than *logical*, information is necessary. This can be accomplished using bottom-up processing without any publication-specific knowledge. The method is based on the extraction of language-dependent *character prototypes* whose position relative to the baseline is fixed. Our intention is to pursue this method as far up as the labeling of various paragraph types, (*left-justified, right-justified, hanging,* etc.), and to merge the bottom-up *layout-tree* with the *top-down* logical tree, but so far we have concentrated on text-line extraction. The ability of the system to cope with tightly spaced or overlapping lines of text, that would stretch most conventional OCR systems, is illustrated in Figure 5. The system has been extended to several exotic alphabets. Details are in [Kanai 90a, Kanai 90b].

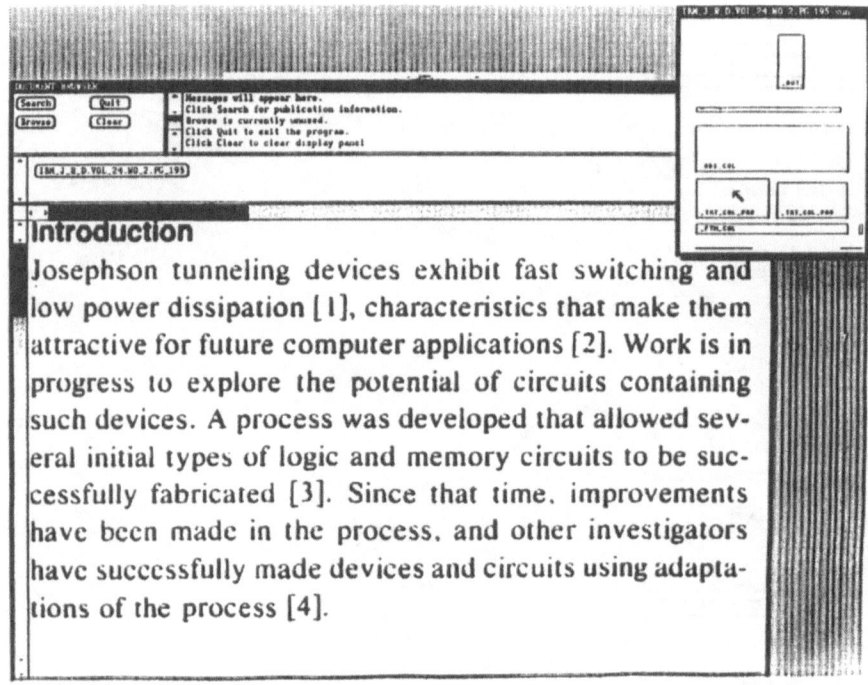

Fig. 4. The query station display consists of the control panel, the message panel, and the display canvas. The user enters the publication information. The geometric representation of the requested page appears as a menu. The selected block is then displayed.

It is clear that all processed documents have to be compressed before archival. Available compression techniques, including the three Unix utilities (*compact, compress,* and *pack*) and Level 3 and 4 CCITT codes, were investigated. The facsimile CCITT codes provide about twice the compression of the Unix routines on pages of text. Our original intent was global compression followed by retrieval of blocks from the coded page images. However, *block-by-block compression* is much simpler and does not introduce a large overhead at the segmentation level required for remote browsing.

Potentially much higher compression rates can be achieved on the textual portions by storing only the first instance of each character pattern and storing

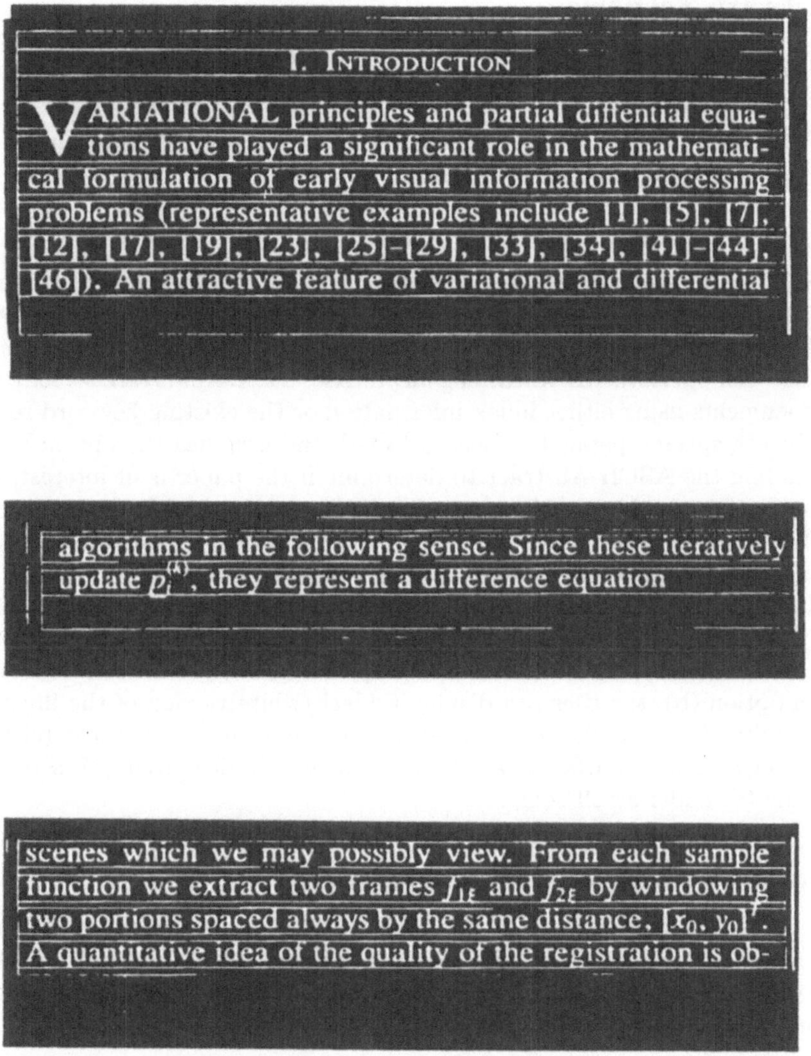

I. INTRODUCTION

VARIATIONAL principles and partial diffential equations have played a significant role in the mathematical formulation of early visual information processing problems (representative examples include [1], [5], [7], [12], [17], [19], [23], [25]–[29], [33], [34], [41]–[44], [46]). An attractive feature of variational and differential

algorithms in the following sense. Since these iteratively update $p_i^{(k)}$, they represent a difference equation

scenes which we may possibly view. From each sample function we extract two frames $f_{1\varepsilon}$ and $f_{2\varepsilon}$ by windowing two portions spaced always by the same distance, $[x_0, y_0]$. A quantitative idea of the quality of the registration is ob-

Fig. 5. Examples of tightly spaced or overlapping lines of text that are correctly segmented using character prototypes.

pointers to this pattern for all subsequent instances. While this can be achieved by clustering the patterns [Ascher 74], current commercial OCR systems provide a more convenient and effective solution. Using OCR to identify a representative pattern of each class is particularly appropriate if we wish to both encode the text in ASCII for information retrieval and compress the document for faithful page-image reconstruction.

3 Library Scenarios

To demonstrate the application of our methods in a library context, we propose the following scenarios.

3.1 IEEE Article Image Retrieval

This demonstration will build on our prototype remote browsing system:

- The user logs on to the mainframe using a PC or SUN workstation connected through either a 19,200 bits/sec or a 1 Mbits/sec link (we want to study the difference).
- The user opens the IEEE catalog file in INFOTRAX and searches for relevant documents using either index information or the existing keyword search.
- Once a specific paper has been selected, the user has the option of either reading the ASCII Abstract to determine if the paper is of interest, or immediately opening the document image file for that document.
- The user selects one of the following categories: (a) subheadings, (b) figure captions, (c) references, or (d) author's sketch.
- If option (a) or (b) was selected, the blocks corresponding to the lines of print constituting the subheadings or figure captions are displayed. In option (a), the user can display successive paragraphs of text under the selected heading. In option (b), the user can display a black/white version of the illustration or table. If (c) or (d) was selected, the image of the specific text (either list of references or author's sketch) is immediately displayed one screen at a time (or under scroll control).

3.2 Selective OCR for Full-Text Search

The scenario for selective OCR is simpler, although interfacing the document processing with commercial OCR systems has not proved easy. Currently we are experimenting with a trainable system (IBM's *TextReader*), and with a non-trainable system intended for set type (Caere's *OmniPage*).

- Library support staff, at a workstation, opens the document image file and views images of the titles and authors of *IEEE* documents.
- The staff will then select one of the following fields: (a) title, (b) author (c) abstract (d) references.
- The nested blocks of text corresponding to the selected field are extracted from the entire document image and transferred to a separate file. This file is then reformatted for OCR, with as much useful ancillary information as possible about baselines, column boundaries, and type size.
- The file is transferred to the OCR device (this step may be "off line"). The OCR system accepts the segmented image data and produces ASCII text.
- The ASCII text is reformatted into a form suitable for full-text search, and title and author information is extracted and converted into standard form by library personnel.

3.3 Links from Text File to Illustrations

The purpose of this demonstration is to show that one can conveniently access line art and half-tone illustrations, stored in a separate file in a different format from the figure captions. This project is only in the design phase.

- The user opens the IEEE article image file, selects an article as above, and enters the keyword "CAPTIONS."
- The entire set of figure captions from that article, in image form, are displayed, and one of the captions is selected.
- The corresponding image is decompressed and displayed in black-and-white if it is line art, and in dithered (digital halftone) form if it is a photograph.
- We also intend to convert the figure captions to ASCII using OCR, and invoke the illustrations by means of "hot button" type links from ASCII versions of the text.

The three library applications share the following processing steps:

- *Raster scan* of a document page using a 300 dpi Microtek black/white flatbed scanner (but 400 dpi is needed for fine detail). Grey-level scanning would provide increased fidelity for halftones.
- *Construct a labeled X-Y tree* by means of the following techniques applied separately or together:
  1. *Simple transition segmentation* based on block profiles followed by block labeling using an inference engine and a knowledge base of rules or frames. We intend to use the Standard Generalized Markup Language (SGML) or the Office Document Architecture (ODA) scheme for labeling the X-Y tree for compatibility with documents created by publishers using text-formatting and typesetting systems.
  2. *Concurrent segmentation and labeling* using a syntactic features and a page grammar that embodies publication-specific layout information.
  3. *Block classification* using profile features and statistical pattern recognition.
  4. *Bottom-up reconstruction* from blocks of connected components and a low-level generic typesetting model for printed lines and paragraphs.
- *Compress* the binary document image, *block by block*, using standard CCITT (fax) compression. This can be accomplished either in hardware or software, but for a production operation the compression chip (commercially available) is mandatory.
- Depending on the block identity, apply specific treatments to each block. For instance, halftones can be block-coded or, if the original scan was binary, they could be scanned with a *dithered* threshold (a technique used by binary scanners to preserve grey tones). Line drawings can be vectorized for more efficient storage, though the CCITT 2-D code (Level 4) is almost as efficient. Finally, either all or specific segments of text can be sent to the OCR subsystem, together with column layout, baseline, and type-size information. At this point, the links from the text to the illustrations can be automatically inserted.

– Simple *parameter learning* techniques can be applied to increase the yield
of correctly processed documents by adjusting the various segmentation and
labeling parameters according to the statistics of the documents that have
already been successfully processed [Spencer 89].

4 Evaluation

Since our proposed system is not intended for selecting relevant documents from
a database, conventional information retrieval metrics such as *precision* and *recall*
do not apply. Nor do *legibility* and *readability* of the displaced information, since
they depend more on the type of display used than on our contribution. We will,
however, provide quantitative data on the following aspects:

– *Segmentation error:* the fraction of blocks that are sufficiently mutilated to
interfere with understanding of their contents. We will report the error rate
for material of various degrees of complexity.
– *Labeling error:* the fraction of blocks that are mislabeled (for instance "figure
caption" instead of "subheading") as a function of layout complexity.
– *Preprocessing time:* the approximate number of CPU seconds necessary for
segmenting and labeling a typical printed page, as a function of the level of
desired detail. (Remote browsing and illustration-to-text links require much
less detail than preprocessing a page for OCR.)
– *Compression/decompression time:* The amount of time required to encode
and decode a document, as a function of the compression factor achieved,
and of whether the task is performed by software or hardware.
– *Post-editing:* the manual correction of missegmented and mislabeled blocks
is an optional operation. Its desirability in a given application is based on a
trade-off between operator time and user convenience.
– *Retrieval time:* unlike preprocessing and compression, decompression and
retrieval will be performed in an interactive setting each time the document
is accessed. Hence we must determine how long it takes to retrieve and
display a block as a function of block size and level in the X-Y tree. (This
measure applies only to remote browsing and links to illustrations, and not
to OCR.)
– *Storage requirements:* since the compression efficiency of the algorithms we
propose to use has already been widely studied, we need only assess the
storage overhead introduced by the X-Y tree.
– *Usability of missegmented/mislabeled pages:* we do not expect to be able to
process 100% of the material automatically without error. We will therefore
determine how much user effort is required to assimilate poorly segmented
or labeled pages in comparison to assimilating correctly processed pages.
Missegmented pages will cause additional horizontal and vertical scrolling,
while mislabeled pages will result in additional, unnecessary blocks being
retrieved and displayed.
– *OCR accuracy:* because character misidentifications typically occur in strings
and may also alter the correct reading order, OCR performance is notoriously

difficult to define and measure. Instead, we will report the amount of post-editing necessary for (1) segments of a page entered into the OCR system as a raw bitmap and, (2) the same segments after preprocessing based on the X-Y tree.

We have collected preliminary observations on segmentation error, labeling error, and processing time on a training sample of 31 pages and a test sample of 24 pages drawn from the *IBM Journal of Research and Development* and the *IEEE Transactions on Pattern Analysis and Machine Intelligence*. Some of the samples were scanned in our laboratory, while others were taken from the CD-ROMs distributed by the IEEE to selected research libraries in a pilot project. Some of the results are reported in this volume [Viswanathan 91], with additional details in [Viswanathan 90].

5 Conclusion

Image segmentation and labeling with syntactic methods has been the subject of intensive research for several decades, but progress in practical applications has been slow. We are therefore directing our efforts to a more restricted but important class of problems, the analysis of printed pages of technical journals, where success can be achieved.

We believe that structured document image files represent the most viable approach for applying computer and communications technology to the enormous body of existing documents on paper and microfiche. No competing technology currently exists for remote interactive access to documents containing complex mathematical expressions, foreign alphabets, line drawings, and other illustrations. The benefits offered can only increase with further technological developments resulting in higher speed digital networks, faster and higher resolution optical scanners, larger and less expensive bit-mapped displays, widespread use of color, and more sophisticated methods for segmenting and labeling documents and for optical character recognition.

A major strength of the approach is the preservation of the original layout of the documents, which not only augments reading comprehension but also often conveys indispensable information on its own. The method also offers a natural basis for increasing the scope and cost-effectiveness of existing automated indexing and cross-referencing tools which require access to selective portions of a document in computer-readable alphanumeric form.

Acknowledgments

The author fully acknowledges the essential contributions to the project of Professors Sharad Seth (UNL) and Spotswood Stoddard (now with Tandem Computers), Mukkai Krishnamoorthy, Thomas Spencer, and Massimo Ancona (U. Genova), and former and current students Alan Bonebrake (UNL), Alan Burkle, Melvin Choi (UNL), Kevin Damour, Neil Ferraiuolo, Junichi Kanai, J.

Li (UNL), Marina Maculotti (U. Genova), Nagesh Shirali, Mathews Thomas, Mahesh Viswanathan, and Jim Yu. The library-oriented aspects are the direct results of collaboration with Pat Molholt, Associate Director of Rensselaer Libraries. We are grateful for valuable suggestions and software to Dr. Henry Baird of AT&T Bell Laboratories. The project was funded in part by US West Advanced Technologies Sponsored Research Program and by the US Department of Education College Library Technology and Cooperation Grants Program.

References

[Ascher 74]   R. N. Ascher and G. Nagy, "A Means for Achieving a High Degree of Compaction on Scan-digitized Printed Text," *IEEE Trans. Computers C-23*, 11, pp. 1174–1179, October 1974.

[Kanai 86]   J. Kanai, M. S. Krishnamoorthy, and T. Spencer, "Algorithms for Manipulating Nested Block Represented Images," *Advance Printing of Paper Summaries, SPSE's 26th Fall Symp.*, Crystal City, Arlington, VA, 1986.

[Kanai 90a]   J. Kanai, "Text Line Extraction Using Character Prototypes," *Pre-proceedings, IAPR Workshop on Structural and Syntactic Pattern Recognition*, pp. 182–191, Murray Hill, NJ, 1990.

[Kanai 90b]   J. Kanai, "Knowledge-based Document Image Analysis System," *PhD Thesis*, Dept of Electrical, Computer, and Systems Engineering, Rensselaer Polytechnic Institute, Troy, NY, December 1990.

[Maculotti 88]   M. Maculotti, "Strutture Dati ed Algoritmi per il Riconoscimento di Testi con Formule Matematiche," *Laurea Thesis*, Univ. Genova, July 1988.

[Nagy 68]   G. Nagy, "Preliminary Investigation of Techniques for Automated Reading of Unformatted Text," *Comm. ACM*, Vol. 11, No. 7, pp. 480–487, 1968.

[Nagy 82]   G. Nagy, "Optical Character Recognition — Theory and Practice," In L.N. Kanal and P.R. Krisnaiah (eds.), *Handbook of Statistics II*, North–Holland, Amsterdam, pp. 621–649, 1982.

[Nagy 84]   G. Nagy and S. Seth, "Hierarchical Representation of Optically Scanned Documents," *Proc. IEEE 7th ICPR*, Montreal, Canada, pp. 347–349, 1984.

[Nagy 86]   G. Nagy, S. Seth, and S. D. Stoddard, "Document Analysis with an Expert System," In E.S. Gelsema and L.N. Kanal (eds.), *Pattern Recognition in Practice II*, pp. 149–159, 1986.

[Nagy 88]   G. Nagy, J. Kanai, M. S. Krishnamoorthy, M. Thomas, and M. Viswanathan, "Two Complementary Techniques for Digitized Document Analysis," *Proc. ACM Conf. on Document Processing Systems*, Sante Fe, NM, pp. 169–176, December 5–9, 1988.

[Nagy 90]   G. Nagy, "Document Analysis and Optical Character Recognition," In V. Cantoni, L. P. Cordella, S. Levialdi, G. Sanniti di Baja (eds.), *Progress in Image Analysis and Processing*, World Scientific, Singapore, pp. 511–529, 1990.

[Spencer 89]   T. Spencer, "Automating the Transition from Paper to Hypertext," *Proc. Fourth Annual Rocky Mountain Conf. on Artificial Intelligence*, Denver, pp. 33–36, June 1989.

[Thomas 88]   M. Thomas, "Knowledge Representation Schemes for Document Analysis System," *Master's Thesis*, Dept of Electrical, Computer, and Systems Engineering, Rensselaer Polytechnic Institute, Troy, NY, March 1988.

[Viswanathan 89]   M. Viswanathan and M. S. Krishnamoorthy, "A Syntactic Approach to Document Segmentation," *I.A.P.R. Workshop on Structural and Syntactic Pattern Recognition*, Pont-à-Mousson, France, September 1988, In R. Mohr, T. Pavlidis, and A. Sanfeliu (eds.), *Structured Pattern Analysis*, World Scientific, Singapore, pp. 197–215, 1989.

[Viswanathan 90]   M. Viswanathan, "A Syntactic Approach to Document Segmentation and Labeling," *PhD Thesis*, Dept of Electrical, Computer, and Systems Engineering, Rensselaer Polytechnic Institute, Troy, NY, December 1990.

[Viswanathan 91]   M. Viswanathan, "Analysis of Scanned Documents — A Syntactic Approach," In this volume.

[Yu 86]   J. Yu, "Document Analysis Using X-Y Tree and Rule-Based System," *Master's Thesis*, Dept of Electrical, Computer, and Systems Engineering, Rensselaer Polytechnic Institute, Troy, NY, December 1986.

ANASTASIL: A System for Low–Level and High–Level Geometric Analysis of Printed Documents

Andreas Dengel

German Research Center for Artificial Intelligence (DFKI),
Kaiserslautern Site, P.O. Box 20 80, D–6750 Kaiserslautern, Germany

This paper focuses on the knowledge-based document analysis system ANASTASIL (Analysis System to Interpret Areas in Single–sided Letters). The system identifies important conceptual parts (logical objects) within business letters, like recipient, sender or company-specific printings. Thereby, the system works completely independent of text recognition. Instead, it only utilizes geometric knowledge sources. These are: global geometric knowledge about logical object arrangements, and local geometric knowledge about formal features of logical objects (*e.g.* extensions, typical font sizes, etc). As a result, a document image is classified by labeling area items by corresponding logical object designators after hypothesizing and testing geometric properties of the captured physical units (layout objects). Due to this strategy, ANASTASIL can be envisioned as a key for expectation-driven further analysis of logical objects by text or graphic recognition. The system has been completely implemented and has achieved some remarkable results. It is composed of a low-level geometric analysis module for image processing tasks and a high-level geometric analysis module that performs logical labeling of layout objects. The implementation was done on a SUN 3/60 workstation in C and Common-Lisp and will be soon available in the MacIntosh environment.

1 Introduction

Paper documents are a natural medium to satisfy our needs for information and communication. Today's paper documents are so closely adapted to human reading procedures that the process of understanding is often neglected.

Considering automatic analysis of paper documents, the intention is to convert printed information into an equivalent symbolic representation. This process can be seen as the inverse of desktop publishing, where the abstract internal representation of a document should be transformed in all aspects on a paper sheet. Despite the growing dissemination of scanners and the advances in available character recognition systems, the automatic conversion of printed information that can be used for practical applications is restricted to few recognition tasks. The structuring and interpretation of printed information is still a human privilege.

Considering the needs of modern offices, many companies desire to convert existing as well as incoming paper documents into an electronic representation that allows information management including content-based retrieval and distribution. Thus, there is a pressing need for document analysis systems that should be used as intelligent interfaces between paper and electronic media. Due to the large amount of information and the multitude of diversity of printed material (e.g., meeting announcements, purchase orders, articles), reading by machine with partial understanding of information is still a fairly much unsolved problem. Nevertheless, the state of the art in this research field seems to allow the realization of systems analyzing specific document classes, for which it is possible to describe their topology, their layout and their contents. Thereby, an automatic analysis should comprise reading as well as a narrow understanding. In this sense, an interesting field that will dominate the 90's unfolds itself with great challenges, in particular because of the integration of reading and comprehension.

The tasks of reading machines are described in numerous special applications in which they have already been successfully employed today. However, an understanding of textual information is rarely included . Several papers address such systems, some of which are based on text recognition [1, 2] while others primarily make use of structural information [3, 4, 5].

Documents considered here are mixed-mode paper sheets that may contain text, graphics and images. The contents of a document is structured in two ways. A layout structure divides a document in nested rectangular areas, like text or graphic blocks, images, lines, words and characters. A logical structure describes the relationships between conceptual parts, e.g, title, company logo, recipient or footnote of a letter. In this sense, we use the standardized designations and notations of ODA (Office Document Architecture)[6]. Thereby, the layout structure is characterized by layout objects and the logical structure by logical objects. Normally, office documents can have different degrees of layout structuring, ranging from highly standardized formats, like order forms, to totally unstructured memos, while the logical structure depends on the relations and references captured within the information (e.g., a reference in a text to a previous chapter or to a figure).

According to the recommendations of ODA, two aspects of a document are of interest. The first is to consider a document as its image, to allow for printing and displaying. The second is to consider its textual representation for document editing or layout revision. Such a representation of a document could be expressed by formalisms that obey the ideas of ODA. The contents of a document, like mentioned above, are physically and semantically structured according to layout and logical aspects. They both are hierarchical structures, but provide a different view of the same content. In Figure 1, an example of a business letter is shown. It illustrates the layout as well as the logical view and their relationships to the contents of the letter.

The layout structure divides the content into hierarchically nested layout

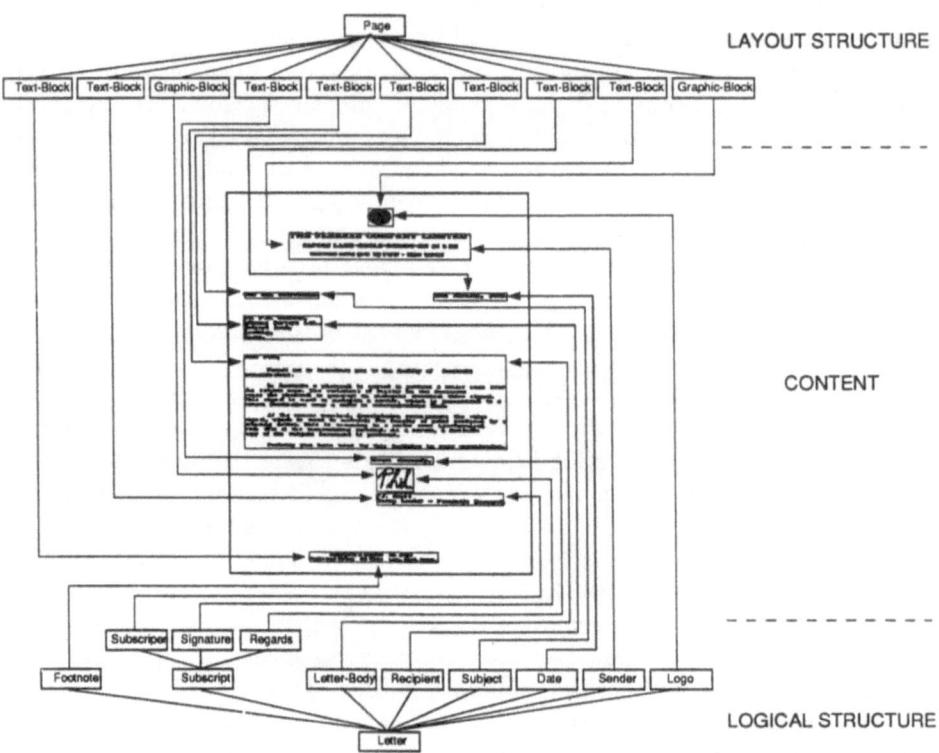

Fig. 1. Layout structure and logical structure of a business letter up to the block level.

objects. In the example, only the top-level layout objects are shown. In practice, all text-blocks are divided into text-lines. The lines in turn are divided into words and so on, while graphic-blocks could be compressed, stored in raster form, or could be divided into graphical primitives (*e.g.*, lines, rectangles, etc).

The logical structure divides the contents of the letter into a hierarchy of logical objects. Again in the example, only top-level logical objects are shown, except the *subscript* that is divided into *subscriber*, *signature* and *regards*. In addition, the *recipient* also could further be divided into *name*, etc, similarly the the *name* could further be divided into *first-name* and *last-name*.

This paper discusses a research effort that is intended to develop an experimental system for an automatic pre-analysis of business letters. The key idea is to have a tool that is able to convert printed documents into a representation which provides a basis for a further processing of the captured textual information (recognition, understanding) and to permit the integration of paper documents in document transition systems and the use of context-sensitive editors [7]. To reach this goal, document image preprocessing (normalization, classification of different information modi, segmentation), as well as logical labeling are applied. In addition, our system produces symbolic representations of a document that comprise its layout structure as well as classified top-level logical objects which provide a basis for the establishment of the logical structure of the document (see also Figure 1). While layout and logical structure of a document are important for document manipulation and rendering [6], it is especially valuable to know about top-level logical objects (*e.g.*, recipient, sender, or footnote of a letter) to perform document creation, filtering, or retrieval [8]. As a result, it will become possible to manage paper documents as well as electronic ones in a uniform representation by a centralized electronic archive. In this work, the result of the analysis is a data structure that conforms to the document architecture standard ODA defined by the International Standardization Organization (ISO) [9]. Section 2 first describes the system architecture and than gives an overview of the contents of the rest of the paper.

2 System Architecture

For a correct reading and interpretation of text parts within a document, the knowledge about the arrangement on the page is an essential knowledge source as well as an excellent orientation point. Documents which are created with today's text systems fulfill, for most cases, a minimum amount of formal criteria, that is at most not reflected, but directly used by a human reader for detecting and recognizing information. While the structuring of information in electronic documents often plays a minor role (*e.g.* e-mail), the layout of paper documents within a particular document class, e.g. publications, business letters, or application forms, is almost characteristic. The additional use and specific arrangement of graphical information parts have a supplementary effect. For example, the identification of a specific company logo, considered in a certain context, potentially allows conclusions about the contents of a document.

Considering these assumptions, the basic idea of our system is to support text recognition having a restricted view to document portions with respect to the context designated by their logical label. To this end, the logical labeling of layout objects is only based on geometric knowledge, like position, extensions (height and width), and formal shape features (number of lines or words, typical font height, etc.). A consideration of textual information as a knowledge source for a logical labeling is completely avoided. That means a text recognition is initiated just after the logical labeling. The whole geometric document analysis can be split into a low-level and a high-level geometric analysis (see also Figure 2).

This article describes the basic concepts, processing modules and techniques of the system ANASTASIL. Thereby, it focuses on the internal representation of the analysis results that conforms with the definitions of ODA. In principle, the application of ANASTASIL is not restricted to a certain document class, but due to the complexity of the general case, our system is implemented only for business letters. The system is based on different knowledge sources that have a hybrid representation. The different components of the system and their composition are shown in Figure 2.

Normally, incoming business letters are scanned in our environment at a resolution of about 200 dpi. To automatically process the resulting raster image, our system is composed of different processing modules.

For a low-level geometric analysis, a document *preprocessing module* first searches the dominant linear structure which results in determining the skew with which the document has been scanned and enables to correct it. In the next step, a top-down segmentation procedure is initiated to stepwise refine the physical structure of the captured information and to map the different physical components into a hierarchically nested data structure. The resulting description represents the layout structure of a given document page and is used as the input for a high-level control structure, that attempts to classify the different layout objects as logical objects.

A *document architecture* model captures the geometric knowledge that is necessary for a logical labeling. It is composed of a so called geometric tree and a statistical database (SDB). The tree can be interpreted as the global (conceptual) geometric view to documents. It is modeled as a specialization hierarchy, describing different arrangements of logical objects of business letters at different abstraction levels. In addition, a statistical database (SDB) provides a local and isolated view to the geometric properties of individual logical objects. It captures different rule sets that are based on the examination results of a few hundred business letters and that describe individual geometric features of, *e.g.*, sender, subject or date.

The document architecture model is the basis for a *control structure* (inference machine) that attempts to perform a logical labeling of layout objects. The task comprises a traversing of the geometric tree whereby hypotheses about the logical meaning of layout objects are generated only by considering their arrangements on the page. For the verification of the hypotheses, the appropriate set of geometric rules in the SDB is applied. This hypothesize and test strategy is supported by different tools. The most important are: a relevance check, several validation functions and an agenda.

If the logical labeling of a given document (layout structure) fails, a *knowledge acquisition component* is activated to allow the addition of new geometric knowledge. This knowledge can be local (new description for a logical object) or global (new arrangement of logical objects). The component is coupled with a structure editor that allows the definition of structural knowledge. Subsequently, the new knowledge is automatically added to the document architecture model by a model generator.

The *user interface* of ANASTASIL is realized as a development tool. It comprises the above mentioned structure editor and a simple explication component. The explication component provides a basis to validate the system behavior. That means: visualizing the analysis steps and decisions of the control, the developer gets feedback about the quality of the used validation functions and relevance checker.

The rest of the paper is structured as follows. Section 3 concentrates on

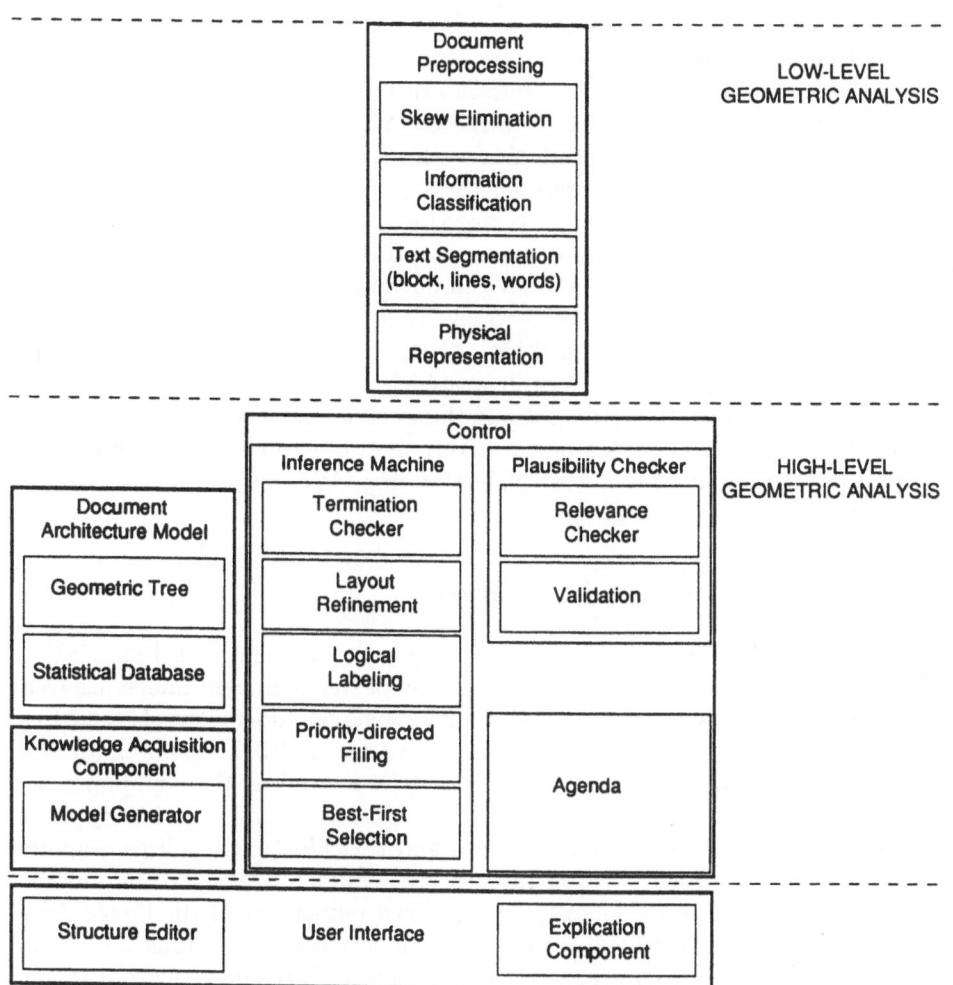

Fig. 2. System architecture of ANASTASIL.

the low-level geometric analysis. It proposes a method to detect the virtual skew within a scanned document image and subsequently illustrates our results and experiences in top-down segmentation techniques. Finally, an internal data structure is presented. It conforms to the ODA requirements for layout objects and moreover fits the representation needs for a logical labeling.

Section 4 of the paper focuses on the high-level geometric analysis. First, the document architecture model is described, mainly concentrating on techniques of how to utilize and to represent structural geometric knowledge for logical labeling. Consequently, the section outlines the principle concepts of the entire labeling procedure and the necessary tools and then illustrates techniques for a geometric knowledge acquisition. At the end of the section, the internal representation of logical objects is illustrated.

Section 5 discusses the strengths and the weaknesses of the system. It further explains how the results could be effectively used to support further processing steps, like text recognition or text understanding. At the end of the section, an overview of future work is given.

3 Low-Level Geometric Analysis

As a starting point, we examine a scanned paper document (pixel matrix). To obtain layout objects, automatic segmentation of the document image has to be initiated. This is an essential early step for later stages (document classification, graphics coding, etc.). It comprises the separation of multilevel (photographical) and bilevel (textual and graphical) information as well as their mapping into nested layout objects of different levels. The goal is to split the binary image into component-like characters, text-lines and text-blocks, as well as graphics- and image-parts. In practice, two strategies are possible: starting bottom-up from the pixel data or stepwise following a top-down refinement of the image. Most bottom-up clustering methods are working in a very time consuming way1. Top-down segmentation, by contrast, is fast but almost all techniques are degraded by small skew within the image. Consequently, the captured skew angle has to be detected and canceled by inverse rotation of the document image.

In the ANASTASIL system, we prefer top-down segmentation techniques. For the necessary skew detection, we have developed a method which works especially well for document images and is extremely fast.

3.1 Skew Angle Detection

The procedure we use to handle the problem of skew angle detection is called *left margin search* (LMS) [10]. After having scanned an A4-sized document, we obtain an image of about 1400×1750 pixels. Following the approach of Trincklin [11], we create a vector V of size n, with $n \leq 1750$, denoting the number of raster image lines. Consequently, we choose a column j of the image which is on the right of the boundary of the scanned document. V contains at position i the distance between column j and the first black pixel at line i. Taking the example of Figure 3, the vector V contains at positions 1 to 10 the following values:

i	1	2	3	4	5	6	7	8	9	10	...
V[i]	0	43	43	45	39	37	32	28	24	21	...

In the next step we try to determine straight line segments which describe the left margin of layout objects (words, text lines or blocks). This is different from Trincklin's approach, where all possible straight line orientations (at top, left and bottom of a layout object) are taken into account. Trincklin's strategy causes problems in the case of documents with a complex structure containing many small text blocks. Considering the LMS approach, it is not relevant how much text blocks a document may contain, because the horizontal space between them is not considered. The gradient of the straight line defines its angle with respect to the vertical orientation. By weighting it with the length of the line we obtain a distribution function over all possible angles. The dominant angle (maximum) defines the skew $\mathcal{L}$ of the image data (see Figure 3).

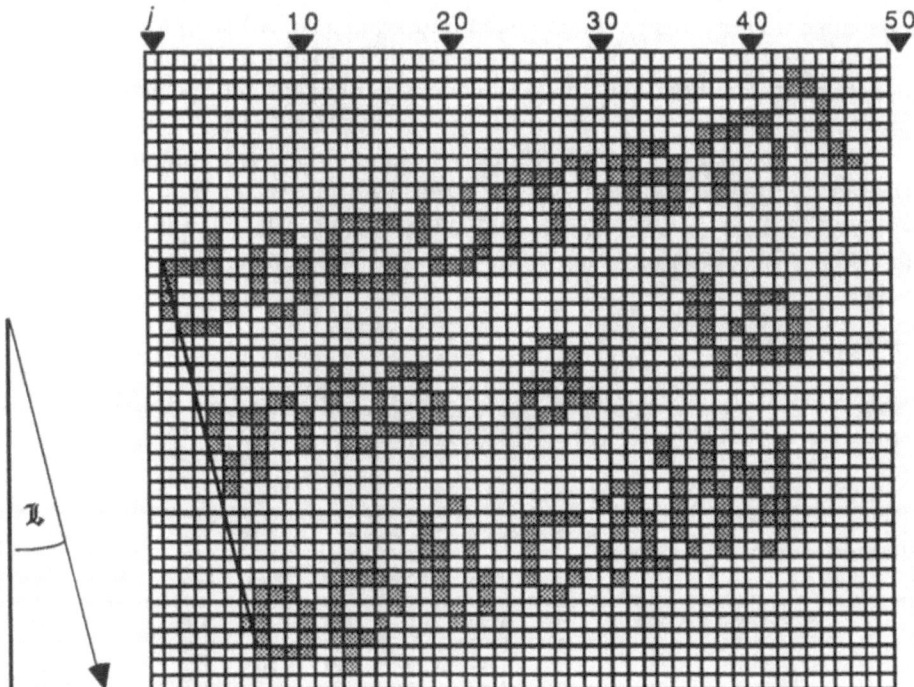

Fig. 3. Example of document image scanned at 75 dpi.

To realize this goal, we have established a filter to eliminate all points $P(i, V[i])$ that are not relevant for skew angle detection.

The algorithm starts with an empty set T_0, to which point $(1, V[1])$ is added. Continuing with $i = 2$, the procedure tests for every two points $(i - 1, V[i - 1])$ and $(i, V[i])$ if they are adjacent, whereby the adjacency is defined along the eight main directions.

If these two points are adjacent, point $(i, V[i])$ is added to T_0. Otherwise the procedure tries to find a point, which has an Euclidean distance to point $(i - 1, V[i - 1])$ that is less than one-and-a-half times a factor ϑ, which describes the minimal line height for T_0. ϑ J is taking into account line spacing and basically is initialized by a six pixel font height. If no point is found that satisfies the criteria, a new set T_1 is opened and the algorithm iterates.

This filtering procedure creates different sets of points, which describe the left margins of text lines or blocks. Using the method of minimal distances, the procedure determines straight line segments of maximal length which define the dominant skew within the document image.

We have compared the LMS approach to the methods of Trincklin and Postl [12], with respect to results, accuracy of results and run-time [10]. Thereby, the resulting skew is defined by the angle with the highest measure of belief. Accuracy of a result means the dominance, in which the resulting angle can be determined. All three approaches have been implemented on a SUN 3/60 in C. The comparison is illustrated giving three examples: a business letter, a newspaper which is relatively smudged and an article. All these examples have been considered with two different skew angles. In Figure 4, the black horizontal lines starting from the right side of the document images, represent the elements of vector V.

Table 1 contains appropriate results. Assuming there is a dominant text-line orientation, the LMS may be expected to run 3 times faster than the approach of Trincklin and 10 times faster than Postl's approach. On the average, our approach needs about 0.8 seconds to detect the skew angle in a 2.5 million pixel object.

Table 1. Document image (in dots), exact skew and recognized skew by the tree approaches (in Grad [°]), as well as CPU time (msec).

Document	Image Size	Exact Scew	Smallest Squares [Trincklin]		Sm. Squares [Trincklin] (mod.)		Left Margin Search		Simulated Skew Scan [Postl]	
			Scew	Time	Scew	Time	Scew	Time	Scew	Time
1	3507x2480	btw. -10 a. -9	-10	6199	-10	4866	-9	2816	-10	13282
1	3507x2480	0	0	5899	0	4383	0	2500	0	13332
2	1727x1423	19	19	1749	20	1299	20	533	19	8066
2	1755x1445	-19	-19	2149	-19	1633	-15	683	-19	8149
3	2333x1650	9	9	3033	9	2299	9	799	9	13332
3	2333x1650	btw. -4 a. -3	-4	3233	-4	2416	-4	900	-4	13349

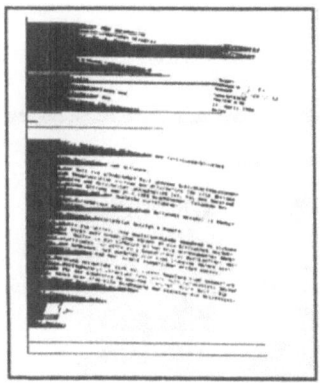  

Fig. 4. Skew angle detection in document images. V-values of zero are not considered.

3.2 Segmentation

After having normalized the skewed image, it is possible to use different segmentation methods. In our system, we use two of the most known techniques. They both are top-down approaches. The Run-Length-Smearing Algorithm (RLSA) [13] and projection profile cuts, proposed by Nagy *et al.* [14, 15].

Smearing. The RLSA can be applied to identify text-blocks as well as to find lines and words. In particular, two matrices A and B are calculated by exploring the given document image. Consequently, the matrices are combined by an logical "OR." Matrix A represents the smeared raster image in horizontal direction while matrix B corresponds to the smeared vertical image. Smeared means that all pixels between any two black pixels are also set to be black, if they do not exceed a certain threshold Δx (in vertical direction) or Δy (in horizontal direction). Applying a subsequent logical "OR"-operation, a matrix C is calculated which captures smeared image regions corresponding to segments that represent (text-)blocks, lines, or words with respect to the values of Δx and Δy. In Figure 5, an example of an input document and the corresponding smeared document image is shown. The image has a resolution of about 200 dpi, Δx and Δy have size 25.

The RLSA is a straight forward segmentation method that avoids time consuming backtracking. Another strength is the fact that only by altering Δx and Δy, the algorithm can be used for block segmentation as well as for line and word segmentation. Thus a classification in text, graphic or image parts is easy. For example, when a block which has a relative large size can not be segmented into line segments, it can be assumed that the block captures graphic or image information.

In contrast, if font size is a criterion to map sequenced lines in different text-blocks, smearing faies. In addition, the parameters Δx and Δy can not be

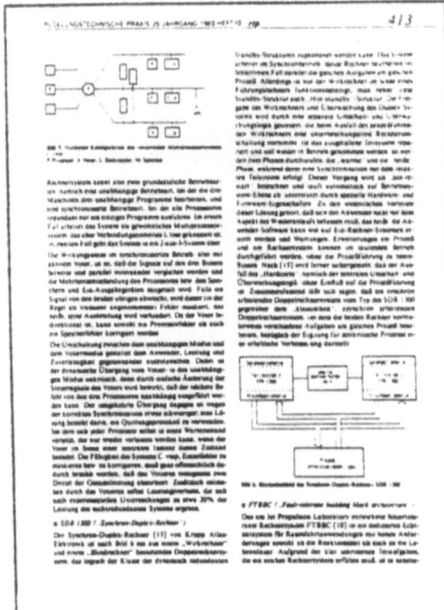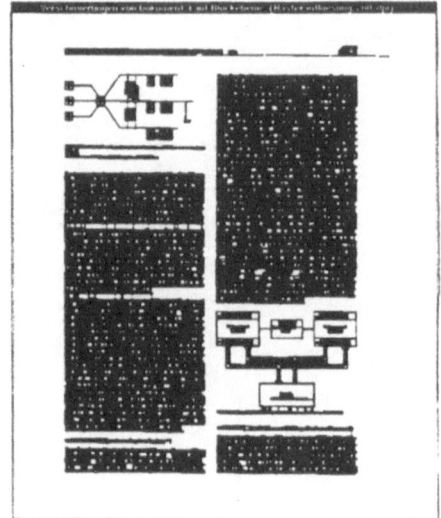

Fig. 5. Example of document image and smeared image regions (200 dpi, Dx = 25, Dy = 25).

dynamically adapted. They have to be set a specific value for each segmentation level (block, line, word). As a consequence, the method only is capable to work independent up to a specific font size.

Profiling. Profiling is a top-down approach. Profiling utilizes the nested structure of document information and also is based on the assumption that all text lines have no skew. It decomposes a rectangle into subrectangles. The decomposition is performed on different levels, first blocks, then lines and finally words are segmented. At each level, the subdivisions are executed in the same direction, either horizontally or vertically. To determine the location where the division has to take place, the local peaks of the profiles are considered (ref. Figure 6). They correspond to white gaps between paragraphs, lines or words and differ with respect to these segmentation levels. For the classification of the different information modi on the block level, the characteristics of the profile can be utilized. Text blocks are characterized by having ranges of thick black peaks, separated by white gaps of non-pixel areas. Graphics, by contrast have a relatively uniform profile. Figure 6 shows typical differences in horizontal projection profiles of text and graphical information.

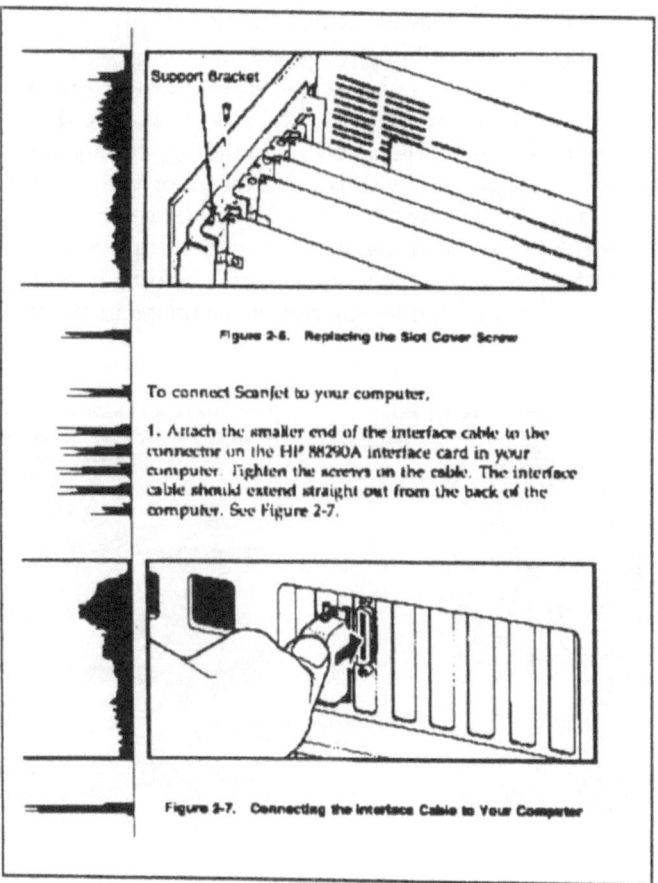

Fig. 6. Typical horizontal projection profile of text and graphics.

Nagy proposes the x-y-tree [14] as a special technique of projection profile cuts. He describes an attributed grammar to generate a x-y-tree without giving details to define cuts. Moreover, the proposed procedure does not work without backtracking, whereby the efficiency decreases. Therefore, we have improved the described algorithm to avoid backtracking [16].

Thus profile cuts also can be applied without backtracking. In contrast to smearing, the values for distances, for example, between blocks are not fix, but rather depend on the individual image features (profile). Thus, the procedure is largely independent from different font sizes. Moreover, the method works extremely time-efficient.

Comparison. Both techniques need nearly the same time. The time ranges from 50 to 120 CPU seconds using profiling and from 90 to 170 CPU seconds using the smearing algorithm. Both methods have failed in segmenting news paper articles. Smearing is more tolerant in the case the scanned image has a small skew, but needs more memory while run-time [16].

In practice, we prefer the profiling approach, because it supports our analysis strategy. As a result of both techniques, we obtain layout objects of the block level, as well as of the line and word level. Each object is described by geometric data, like position (left-upper corner) and surrounding rectangle. Respecting the example of Figure 5, Figure 7 illustrates the result of the block segmentation by applying smearing (a) and profiling (b). As can be seen, smearing results in determining 4 blocks in the headline of the document and 8 blocks including 2 graphic-blocks in the rest of the document image. Profiling in contrast considers the headline as one block and divides the rest of the image in 19 blocks, including 2 graphic-blocks.

 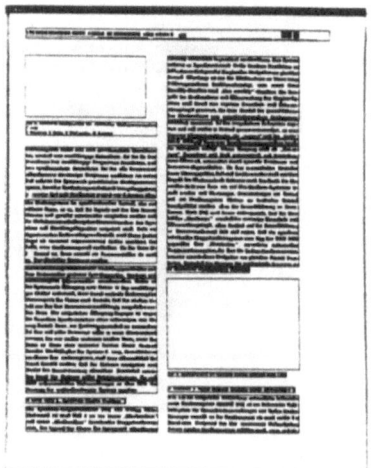

Fig. 7. Results of smearing (a) and profiling (b) on the block segmentation level applied to the example (200 dpi) of Figure 5.

3.3 Document Layout Representation

So far, we have described how the layout structure of a document can be established while analyzing its image. The following paragraphs describe how the results of the low-level geometric analysis are represented in ANASTASIL.

For the internal representation of layout objects of different abstraction levels, we prefer an object-centered representation of the real world that fits well the purposes of the ODA-standard [17]. That is, every entity existing in the application domain is expressed as an object of this model, the so-called *schema*, in

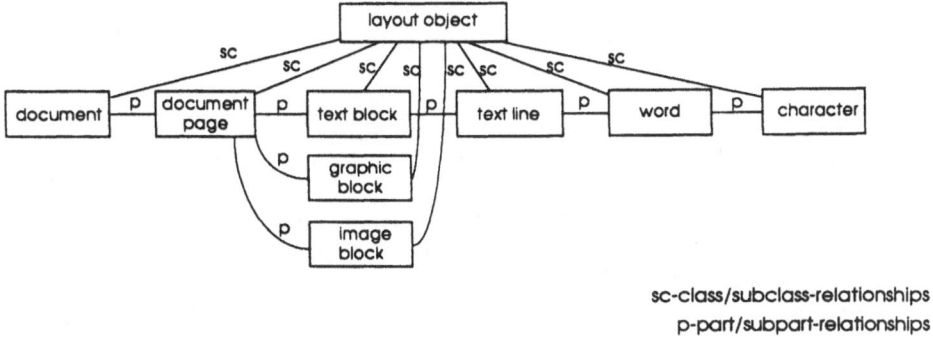

Fig. 8. Hierarchy of layout objects.

which descriptive, operational, and organizational aspects of the real world are integrated. In other words, a schema (not to be confused with a DB-schema!) is the symbolic representation of a real world entity (roughly analogous to *frame* or *unit* in other representation systems). It is always identifiable by a unique schema name and is composed of a set of attributes. The attributes may again be further described by aspects in order to characterize an object in more detail. Attributes are of different kinds. A schema may possess declarative attributes (slots) describing descriptive aspects of an object, procedural attributes (methods) that describe operational aspects, and structural attributes (abstraction relationships) used for expressing organizational relationships of the application domain.

Layout objects are complex structures composed by other layout objects. Thus, a document page is composed by several text blocks, which, in turn, contain several text lines. The latter ones are built of words that are composed of characters (see Figure 8).

Therefore, all layout objects hold the same information, however, with partially different semantics, *i.e.*, all of them are complex objects built of distinct components (ref. Figure 9).

The class *layout object* describes the aspects which every character, word, text-line, etc. has in common. That is:

x-origin, y-Origin   position of left-upper corner of circumscribing
                          rectangle
width, height   size of circumscribing rectangle

The different semantics of their components are then specified in the corresponding subclass by means of particular attributes and the aspects *possible-*

values and *cardinality*. It is important to point out the different types of attributes supported by the underlying representation model (see also [18]):

layout object
has-subclasses (document, document page, ... , character) terminal own-slot
x-origin   terminal instance-slot
     possible-values (integer)
     cardinality [1 1]
y-origin   terminal instance-slot
     possible-values (integer)
     cardinality [1 1]
width   terminal instance-slot
     possible-values (integer)
     cardinality [1 1]
height   terminal instance-slot
     possible-values (integer)
     cardinality [1 1]

document page
subclass-of (layout-object)   terminal own-slot
in-document   nonterminal instance-slot
     possible-values (instance-of (document))
     cardinality [1 1]
has-text-block   nonterminal instance-slot
     possible-values (instance-of (text block))
     cardinality [1 ∞]
has-graphic-block   nonterminal instance-slot
     possible-values (instance-of (graphic block))
     cardinality [0 4]

Fig. 9. Representation of layout objects as schemas.

- Ownattributes (*i.e.*, own-slots and own-methods), as subclass-of in Figure 9, are used to describe properties of the object itself, and as such may have values.
- Instance-slots and instance-methods, on the other hand, describe properties of the object's instances, and have, therefore, no values (*e.g.*, x-origin, y-origin, width, and height).
- Own-slots and instance-slots are further classified in nonterminals or terminals. Nonterminal slots indicate part-of properties (*i.e.*, the components) of objects since their values correspond to other objects of the knowledge base

(*e.g.*, in-document, has-text-block, and has-graphic-block). Terminal slots, on the other hand, describe either characteristics of the objects themselves (terminal own-slots) or of their instances (terminal instance-slots).

Therefore, the abstraction concept of aggregation can be represented by means of user-defined attributes [17], allowing for the specification of several kinds of relationships, each of with very fine semantics (observe, for example, the distinct integrity constraint associated to has-text-block, has-graphic-block, which can not be expressed by systems supporting aggregation by means of one single part-of relationship).

This internal data structure representing the layout of a document at hand is the input for a high-level classification tool that attempts to perform a logical labeling which is based on geometric knowledge.

4 High-Level Geometric Analysis

The task of automatic comprehension of a document is one of the necessary and most important goals of the document analysis. If it will become possible to automatically extract the logical structure of a document, it would be easier to initiate a further analysis of a specific document part. If, for example, the layout blocks referring to the addressee can be recognized, an OCR-procedure enables further expectation-driven recognition of captured text by matching it with prestored sets of zipcodes or destination cities [19].

Shapes of documents differ greatly. Documents represent medical records, reports, protocols, letters and other texts, but also plans and drafts. Any document is characterized by its contents and its internal organization. There are documents with a prescribed structure and documents having a more complex and flexible structure. If it would become possible to describe such structures in a homogeneous way, it would also be possible to determine the logical structure of a document by using AI techniques.

4.1 Document Architecture Model

Geometric Tree. Documents which are created with today's text systems normally fulfill a minimum amount of formal criteria. This trend towards uniformity makes identifying individual logical objects a lot easier. The typical image of a printed document has several contiguous regions or blocks, that correspond to logical objects that are significant for a document class. Considering business letters, we can state the following points:

- Some of the letter parts are mandatory, some are optional. Business letters range from simple letters, containing few logical objects (sender, recipient, date, subject and letter-body) to complex letters with several additional parts, like logos, graphics, company specific printings, etc.
- Logical objects have certain geometric and semantic features.
- Spatial relationships hold among the different logical objects.

To describe structural knowledge, we have developed a formalism for document page representation that provides a global view to logical object arrangements on a paper sheet. The structural elements of a document page, like columns, paragraphs, titles, lines and words of text are generally laid out as rectangular blocks. Orientation of textual information is along horizontal and vertical directions, determined by the rectangular shape of a typical sheet of paper. Thus, a document page is considered as a rectangle, having a characteristic width and height. To describe its spatial structure, the page is divided into smaller rectangles by vertical and horizontal cuts. Model cuts are placed in such a way that they do not intersect with textual or graphical areas. The subrectangles can be recursively divided in the same way, until the layout of the page is described in sufficient detail. To refine annotate the logical structure, different rectangles are assigned a label which describes their logical meaning (ref. the nodes in Figure 10). To model knowledge about more than one document layout and to obtain a very compact knowledge representation, we use a specialization hierarchy, called geometric tree. It describes a global hierarchy for possible logical object arrangements permitting to describe them in different specification levels (arrangement classes). Figure 10 illustrates the principle of the tree.

In a geometric tree, a node is a specialization of its parent node, while at the same time it is a generalization of its child nodes. Thus, the root of the tree represents the most general document layout description. Every document belongs to this class. The internal representation is organized in a way that parental characteristics, for example, their layout features, are inherited by children. Moreover, only the layout features which distinguish a child from its siblings are stored at child nodes. Common aspects are stored in the parent node [18]. The main advantages of such a tree are due to its straightforward representation of position, extension, size, and spatial relationships of objects within the domain of document page representation and subsets of it. Consequently, most document pages can be partitioned into nested rectangular areas by order, position, and orientation of cuts as well as by assignment of logical labels. The number of terminal nodes within the tree used in our experiments is about 40.

Statistical Data Base. Several arrangement classes of the geometric tree described above, only represent global geometric descriptions of possible basic structures within the document class business letter. Additionally, it is necessary to have a local view to possible logical objects within business letters to represent corresponding geometric knowledge about them.

Therefore, we have established a statistical database (SDB). It contains results of a statistical evaluation of a few hundred business letters. As a result thereof, we describe the usual logical parts of a business letter by their general intrinsic characteristics. For example, the recipient in a business letter can usually be characterized by the following features:

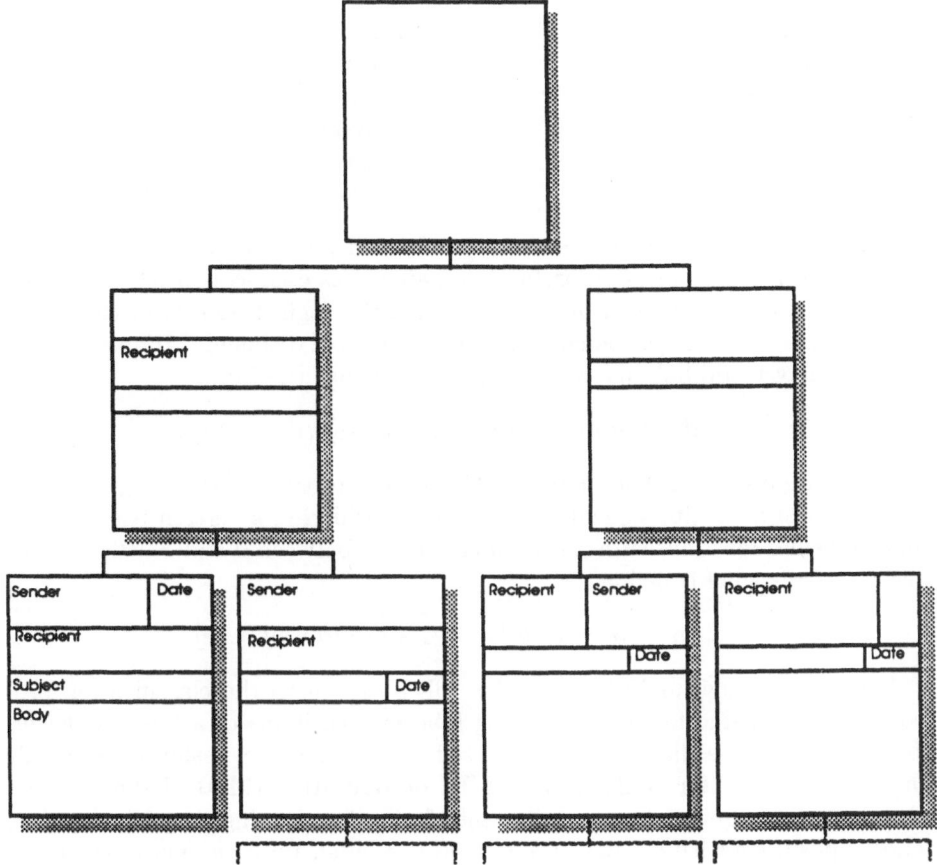

Fig. 10. Principle of a geometric tree.

- the position of the recipient is in the first upper third of the page;
- the left margin of the recipient is within the left quarter of the page;
- the horizontal extension is not longer than a third of the page width;
- the recipient is not written in an extremely large or small font;
- the recipient consists of four to six text lines, which are left justified.

Note again that there are no features with respect to content information. Up to this processing step, we do not employ any recognition procedure for the analysis of textual information. To limit the search time and to avoid all problems in connection with textual recognition, we concentrate only on geometric features of logical objects. To this end, we describe the following logical parts:

– sender   – letter-body,
– date   – preprintings,
– signature   – footnote,
– recipient,   – company-logo,
– theme (subject, title, ...),   – senter-short-form,
– initials,   – company-specific-printings.

The different features we use are transformed into subsets of *if-then* rules, one for each feature. These subsets are organized as **case**-constructs and again form a global set of description rules for an entire logical object. In the action part of a rule, measures of belief (MB) or measures of disbelief (MD) are stored, corresponding to probability values. Thus, a rule has the form:

if *<feature>* **then** *<measure-of-(dis-)belief>*

The measure-of-(dis-)belief thereby reflects the probability resulting from the verification of a specific logical object while considering a certain feature. The possible values for a measure-of-(dis-)belief range between 0 and 1, whereby the measure-of-disbelief is defined as:

measure-of-disbelief = 1 - measure-of-belief.

Later on, during analysis, the rules will be given to the classification procedure as knowledge for understanding labeled-area items of a business letter. To know how a specific value is then used, we furthermore assign to each rule whether it is used for confirmation (MB) or refutation (MD) of the assigned label. Figure 11 shows an appropriate set of rules for locating the recipient. The denoted positions within a page are related to the left upper corner of the page.

The whole SDB consists of about 71 such rule packages [20]. This organization of the SDB allows a straightforward testing of intrinsic features of given layout blocks as well as its easy extension by new rules. When new rules are added to the database, measures-of-belief as well as measure-of-disbelief for existing rules may have not to be altered, because every subset is independent from each other

4.2 Logical Labeling

For a logical labeling of layout objects resulting from the low-level geometric analysis, the geometric tree plays a central role. It is used as a decision tree. Starting at the root of the tree, a search is initiated that results in finding a path from the root to one of its leaves, thereby successively refining the layout of a given document. With each step on this path, the document has to be matched to document arrangement classes, represented by corresponding nodes. Figure 12 shows the explication component during the tree search.

As a result, a measure of belief is calculated that expresses the degree of similarity of an arrangement class in the geometric tree and the layout structure of the document at hand. In an earlier paper, we have described this process in sufficient detail [21]. While matching a given business letter with the arrangement

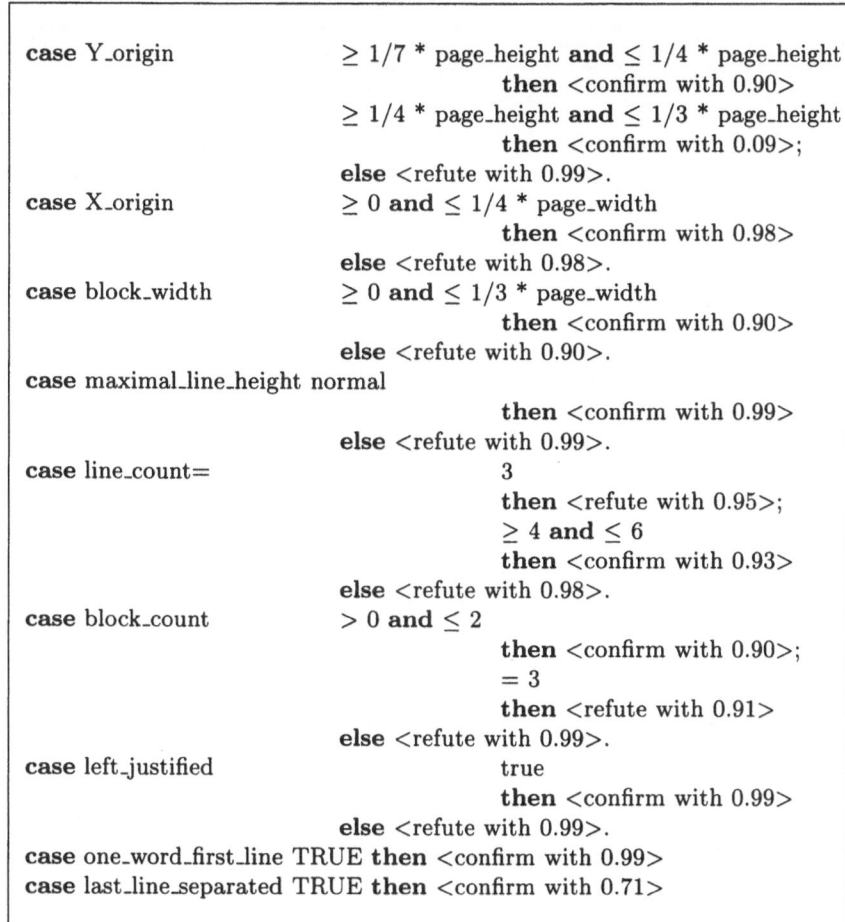

Fig. 11. Rules describing the logical object recipient.

classes of the geometric tree, several resulting rectangular areas are assigned a logical label. Thereby, a label indicates a hypothesis for the possible constituent within the appropriate area. To verify a hypothesis, the appropriate set of rules in the SDB is considered and matched with the geometric properties of the layout objects within the labeled area. The labeling of a specific area amounts to match the containing layout blocks against the appropriate set of description rules in the SDB.

Whereas probabilistic approaches, like the Bayesian formulas, refer to conditional probabilities, the SDB is based upon the combination of completely independent events with their respective probabilities, To this end, we use Dempster-Shafer's rules of combining probabilities [22]. Every two pieces of single MB's and MD's for specific features f_i are iteratively combined by the following formulas:

$$MB(H, f_1 \text{ and } f_2) := MB(H, f_1) + MB(H, f_2) - MB(H, f_1) * MB(H, f_2)$$

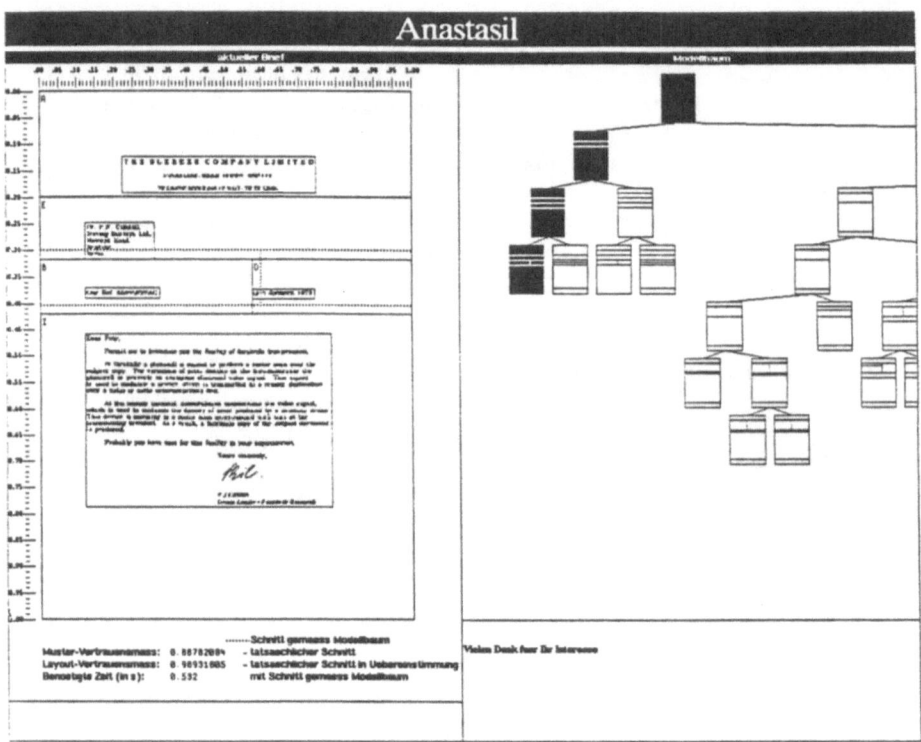

Fig. 12. Explication component while the geometric tree search (left window screens the intermediate or final results, right window visualizes the tree search).

$$MD(H, f_1 \text{ and } f_2) := MD(H, f_1) + MD(H, f_2) - MD(H, f_1) * MD(H, f_2)$$

As a result, we obtain two global values for the **confirmation or refutation** of a certain hypothesis H, respectively. To combine both values, another formula is used. It expresses for every hypothesis H the confidence value $MB_{Logik}(H)$ for its **confirmation and refutation**.

$$MB_{Logik}(H) := MB(H) * (1 - MD(H))/(1 - MB(H) * MD(H))$$

Combining resulting measures of belief while hypothesizing and testing [23], we are able to quantify the degree of similarity between the current document layout and the nodes in the model tree. While handling different intermediate results for document arrangement class matching, the use of the decision tree allows for easy reduction of the search space. Moreover, the user gets the comfortable feeling that he is controlling the situation such that some classification errors in the last analysis step can be immediately corrected by backtracking.

All intermediate decisions are collected in an agenda [3]. In every stage of the analysis, it provides the best intermediate solution for further examination. That means, to perform one step on the path in the geometric tree, the intermediate solution with the highest measure of belief is chosen to generate a more specific layout. Thus we perform a best-first search, which represents a variant of the uniform-cost search [24]. Figure 13 shows different examples of classification results obtained by ANASTASIL.

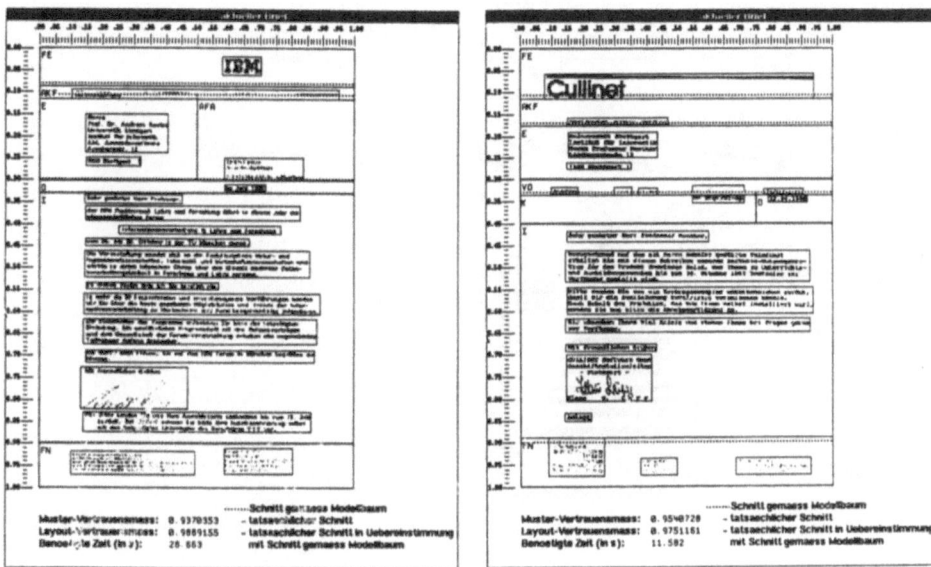

Fig. 13. Results of document classification.

4.3 Representation of Logical Objects

While logical labeling, all labeled area items that can be successfully verified, are represented as instances of corresponding logical objects. In ANASTASIL, logical objects are compared to the areas resulting from the matches against the arrangement classes in the geometric tree. Thus, they also describe the aspect *x-origin*, *y-origin*, *width* and *height* that are common with layout object aspects, but moreover they have additional aspects like:

parts   layout objects (subtree of the layout structure)

	captured within this area
label	label designating the respective logical object
measure-of-belief	measure of similarity resulting of the hypothesis verification

After logical labeling, the document at hand is represented as an instance of one terminal node of the layout hierarchy in the geometric tree. It is composed of instances of the class area that represent in common a fully classified business letter (see Figure 14).

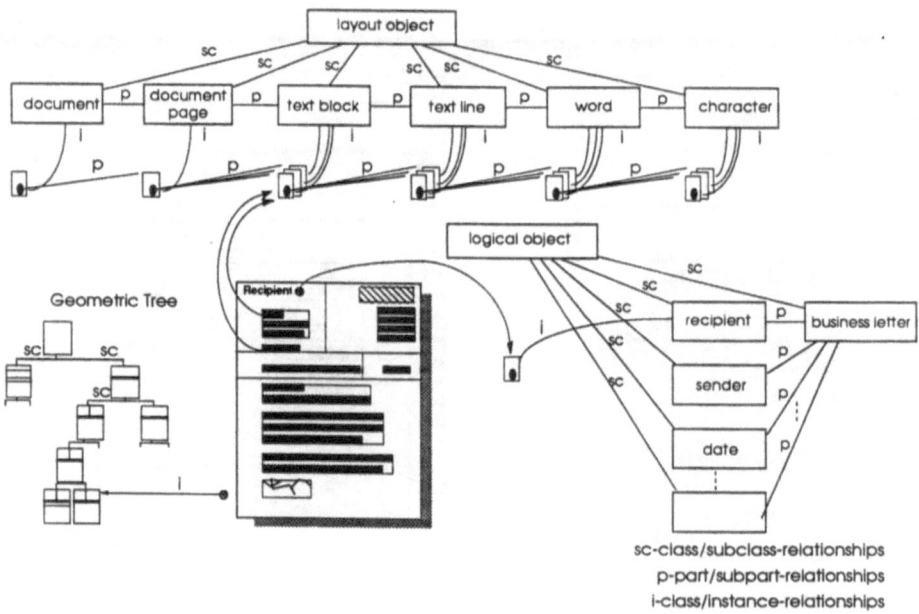

Fig. 14. Representation of logical objects.

4.4 Geometric Knowledge Acquisition

In the last sections, I have described how geometric knowledge about documents can be represented and how it can be applied for an automatic logical labeling. An important aspect while developing knowledge-based systems is the question about the correctness and completeness of the underlying knowledge sources. For that reason, it is necessary to also consider knowledge acquisition tools, providing mechanisms for knowledge base modification and extension.

In ANASTASIL, a such component concentrates on geometric knowledge acquisition. That is a special model generator coupled with a graphic structure editor which allows for an easy manipulation of geometric knowledge.

In the case of arrangement knowledge, defined by the arrangement classes of the geometric tree, a top-down strategy is applied. For every input document, the system searches for an intermediate solution that is "as good as possible." In other words, the system attempts to classify a given document as far as much by matching it with the predefined arrangement classes. However, if the measure of similarity decreases rapidly during one analysis step, the system uses the model generator. The model generator itself activates the structure editor and presents the match in a specific window on the screen. The user himself is now able to employ different graphical facilities and thus complete the layout description of the pattern by setting or deleting cuts and labels. The result is a new arrangement class. Subsequently, the new graphical pattern is converted into the internal representation. This is done by the model generator which automatically extends the knowledge sources by the new knowledge. In particular, the geometric tree is extended by modifying the appropriate subtree. Therefore, a common super-layout-class of the old subtree and the new layout-class forms the root of the new subtree [25].

This procedure can be illustrated by an example. In Figure 15(a), a subtree of the geometric tree is shown. The root of this subtree represents the best intermediate solution (*actual node*) that can be derived by the system's control. Assume that in all other subtrees of the model, no match that make sense can be performed. In the subtree of Figure 15(a), the subclasses of the *actual node* also do not make sense while matching. Consequently, the structure editor allows the completion of the layout pattern of *actual node*. The model generator then takes the new pattern, matches it against the two subclasses of *actual node* to decide which subtree of *actual node* may be extended by the new pattern. Subsequently, the corresponding subtree have to be modified by generating a pattern (*) as being the superclass of the root of this subtree and the new pattern (**) defined by the user (ref. Figure 15(b)). In all subsequent runs of the system the new pattern is available as geometric knowledge.

The acquisition of new logical object knowledge is hard to realize because the existent SDB is based on statistical examinations. This condition is not fulfilled in the case a new logical object does exist for the first time and therefore must be included in the SDB. Nevertheless, we have realized a procedure that allows the definition of geometric properties of new logical objects and, with respect to the internal syntax, their transformation into a subset of rules.

For the definition of local geometric knowledge, the system also provides graphic support to facilitate the input of formal features of logical objects. When a new logical object has to be defined, a dialog is started that performs a user interview of about geometric features of the new object. After defining the designator of the new object, its geometric properties have to be find out. Their

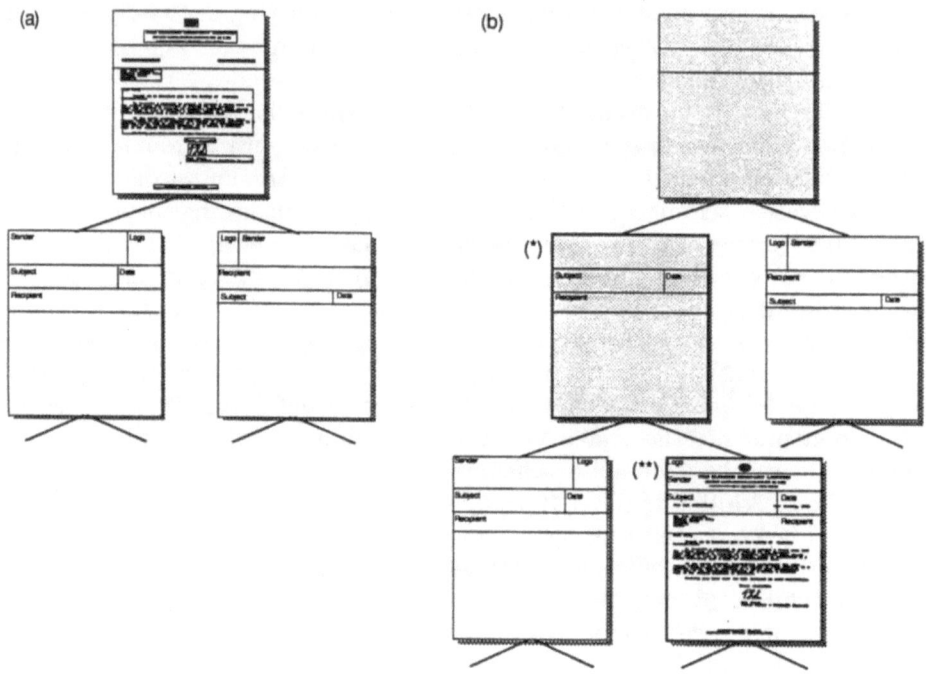

Fig. 15. Principles of geometric knowledge acquisition.

definitions are considered as guide lines. That means, they are not stored as fixed values, but rather are transformed by the model generator in intervals which are of a similar manner like these ones illustrated in the example of Figure 11. The example shown in Figure 16, illustrates this interview technique provided by the structure editor.

In the example, the editor asks for the averaged distance of the new logical object up from the top margin of the paper sheet. Thereby, the illustrated rectangles are visual aids that help to explain the actual question.The scale on the right-hand-side of the rectangles represents the set of possible values of the actual feature. After moving the scale marker by the mouse and setting a value for the actual feature, the model generator generates an appropriate rule. This is done with respect to the interval in the environment of the defined value (represented by the grey region within the scale). A corresponding confidence value is set to be 0.99 for all values within the interval. Outside of this interval, the

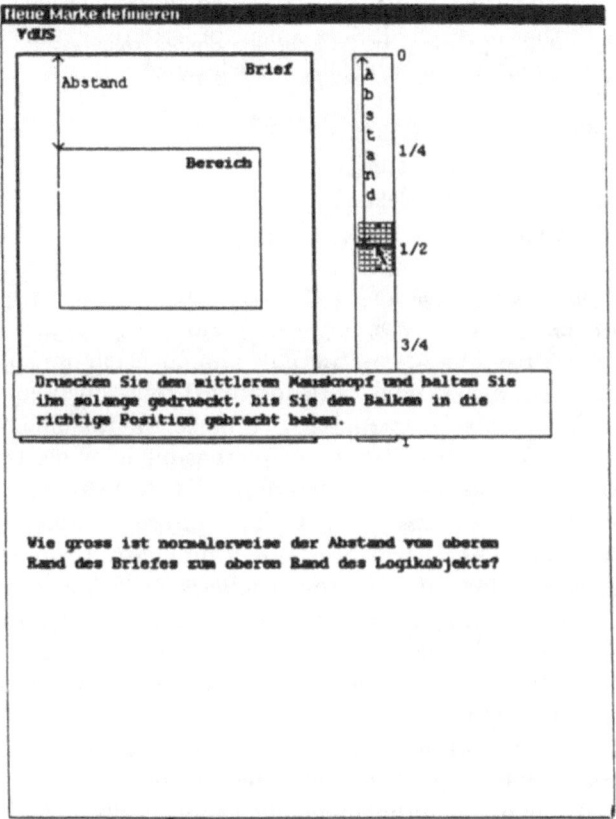

Fig. 16. Interview-mechanism provided by the structure editor of ANASTASIL.

value for refutation is set to be 0.01.

Using this technique, all geometric properties that are relevant for the new object are defined and transformed into the rule syntax.

5 Discussion and Future Work

This paper presents the topics of the document analysis system ANASTASIL and concepts for document representation that conform to the ODA standard. The main goal of this research effort has been the attempt to develop a system that is capable to classify important logical objects within business letters without any text recognition. Rather, the system is based on different knowledge sources that consider geometric aspects of information arrangements and geometric features of information parts. The system utilizes these knowledge sources to perform a logical labeling and moreover provides facilities for geometric knowledge acquisition.

As a result, the identified logical objects can be directly used as an orientation instrument for further processing. Subsequent procedures could start at a point where the global comprehension begins. For example:

- What is the date of the letter?
- Who is the sender of the letter?
- What is the subject of the letter?
- Who is the recipient of the letter?

Thus, a further goal-oriented partial processing of a document with specialized procedures, like reading algorithms or methods for graphical recognition is possible. Moreover techniques for a partial comprehension of captured information can be applied. Then, editors with improved functions allow the symbolic addressing of components of documents, or make the document accessible as a raster image, to edit parts of the text, to transmit it by electronic means or re-produce it on paper. In this sense, the ANASTASIL system is a starting point for a successor project launched at DFKI. The project is titled "Automatisches Lesen und Verstehen" (ALV) which means "Automatic Reading and Comprehension." The ALV project aims to provide a basis for bridging the gap between reading (from binary image to correct ASCII code) and comprehension (from correct ASCII code to the contents of a document) of textual information. For that purpose, we intend to integrate methods used in pattern recognition as well as image and language processing.

Taking measurements from a binary image as a starting point, the task of the ALV project is to provide relationships between document parts, to interpret them and thus, to comprehend the intended meaning of the document. The entire project is divided into the three phases: structure analysis, text recognition and partial text analysis. The structure analysis phase is performed by ANASTASIL.

Text recognition should attempt to recognize textual information within image screens using visual features. Therefore, characters should not be considered in an isolated manner but rather, redundant structural information of words is to be utilized [26]. The use of appropriate logical dictionaries should assist word-based text recognition within logical objects.

Words serve as a basis for the extraction of the meaning from a text. They allow for initiation of an expectation-driven partial analysis within logical objects. Thereby, the complexity of a logical object itself determines the technique to be applied. So, comprehension of a document is restricted to an extraction of important contextual statements within several text parts. Caused by relations between these statements and the identified logical objects, contextual dependencies of a document can be recognized. Thus, they could be represented by a logical structure.

The ALV project aims to develop a system that integrates partial results of different analysis phases, to relate and to test them against each other and, if appropriate, to correct them. Analysis of the contents of a document does not only depend on correct text recognition; it is also coupled with the task of identifying logical objects that are concealed within a document's layout. Thus, it is possible to assume an expectation-driven attitude. The ALV-project has a planned period of about three years starting in October 1990. The staff is about five researchers.

Acknowledgements

The author gratefully acknowledges the work of Eberhard Schweizer, Günther Reichert, Jochen Butz, Ernst Melchinger, who have been involved in this document analysis project. The author also acknowledges the support and assistance given by Gerhard Barth, Rainer Bleisinger Frank Hönes and Walter Olthoff.

References

[1] S. N. Srihari and G. W. Zack, "Document Image Analysis," *Proc. 8th ICPR*, Paris, pp. 434–440, 1986.

[2] H. Eirund and K. Kreplin, "Knowledge Based Document Classification Supporting Integrated Document Handling," *Proc. COIS 1988*, Palo Alto, CA, pp. 189–196, 1988.

[3] A. Dengel and G. Barth, "High Level Document Analysis Guided by Geometric Aspects," *Int'l J. on Pattern Recognition and AI*, Vol. 2, No. 4, pp. 641–656, 1988.

[4] G. Nagy, "Document Analysis and Optical Character Recognition," *Proc. 5th Int'l Conf. on Image Analysis and Processing*, Positano, Italy, 1989.

[5] F. Esposito *et al.*, "Experimental Page Layout Recognition System for Office Document Automatic Classification: An Integrated Approach For Inductive Generalization," *Proc. 10th ICPR*, Atlantic City, NJ, pp. 557–562, 1990.

[6] W. Horak, "Office Document Architecture and Office Document Interchange Formats: Current Status of International Standardization," *Computer*, pp. 50–60, 1985.

[7] W. Luhn and A. Dengel, "Modellgestützte Segmentierung und Hypothesengenerierung für die Analyse von Papierdokumenten," In H. Bunke, O. Kübler, and P. Stucki (eds.), *Proc. 10th DAGM–Symposium Mustererkennung*, Zürich, Informatik-Fachbericht 180, Springer–Verlag, Berlin, pp. 226–232, 1988.

[8] N. M. Mattos, B. Mitschang, A. Dengel, and R. Bleisinger, "An Approach to Integrated Document Processing & Management," *Proc. COIS-90*, Boston, MA, pp. 118–123, 1990.

[9] ISO, International Standards Organization: Information Processing — Text and Office System Document Structures, Part 2, Office Document Architecture Draft Proposal.

[10] A. Dengel and E. Schweizer, "Rotationswinkelbestimmung in binären Dokumentbildern," In H. Burkardt, H. Höhne, and B. Neumann (eds.), *Proc. 11th DAGM–Symposium Mustererkennung*, Hamburg, Informatik-Fachberichte 219, Springer–Verlag, Berlin, pp. 274–278, 1989.

[11] J.-P. Trincklin, Conception d'un Système d'Analyse de Documents: Etude et Réalisation d'un Module d'Extraction de la Structure Physique de Documents à Support visuel, Ph.D. Dissertation, Université de France-comte, Besançon, 1984.

[12] W. Postl, "Detection of Linear Oblique Structures and Skew Scan in Digitized Documents," *Proc. 8th ICPR*, Paris 1986, p. 240.

[13] K. Y. Wong, R. G. Casey, and F. M. Wahl, "Document Analysis System," *IBM J. Res. Dev.*, 26 (6) 1982.

[14] G. Nagy and S. Seth, "Hierarchical Representation of Optically Scanned Documents," *Proc. 7th ICPR*, Montreal, p. 347, 1984.

[15] G. Nagy, S. Seth, and S. Stoddard, "Document Analysis with an Expert System," *Pattern Recognition in Practice II*, Elsevier Science Publ. B. V, pp. 149–155, 1986.

[16] E. Schweizer, Erfassung, "Justierung und Segmentierung von Dokumentstrukturen," *Diploma Thesis*, CS Dept, Univ. Stuttgart, 1989.

[17] N. M. Mattos, "Abstraction Concepts — The Basis for Data and Knowledge Modeling," *Proc. 7th Int'l Conf. on the Entity-Relationship Approach*, Roma, Italy, pp. 331–350, 1988.

[18] A. Dengel, N. M. Mattos, and B. Mitschang, "An Integrated Document Management System," *Proc. SPIE / IEEE — Applications of Artificial Intelligence VIII*, Orlando, FL, pp. 368–369, 1990.

[19] S. N. Srihari, C.-H. Wang, P. W. Palumbo, and J. J. Hull, "Recognizing Address Blocks on Mail Pieces: Specialized Tools and Problem-Solving Architecture," *AI Magazine*, Vol. 8 No. 4, Winter 1987, p. 25.

[20] J. Butz, "Untersuchung und Definition von Struktureigenschaften in Bürodokumenten, sowie deren Bewertung mit Hilfe von kontinuierlichen Bewertungsmassen," *Bachelor Thesis*, CS Dept, Univ. Stuttgart, 1988.

[21] A. Dengel and G. Barth, "ANASTASIL: A Hybrid Knowledge-based System for Document Layout Analysis," *Proc. 11th IJCAI*, Detroit, MI, pp. 1249–1254, 1989.

[22] G. Shafer, *A Mathematical Theory of Evidence*, Princeton Univ. Press, 1976.

[23] A. Dengel, "Automatische Visuelle Klassifikation von Dokumenten" (in German), *Ph.D. Thesis*, CS Dept, Univ. Stuttgart, February 1989.

[24] A. Barr and E. A. Feigenbaum, *The Handbook of Artificial Intelligence, Vol. 1*, William Kaufmann Inc., Los Angeles, CA, 1981.

[25] E. Melchinger, "Geometrische Wissenserwerbskomponente," *Bachelor Thesis*, CS Dept, Univ. Stuttgart, 1988.

[26] F. Hönes, R. Bleisinger, and A. Dengel, "Intelligent Word-based Text Recognition," *Proc. OE-90, Symposium on Advances in Intelligent Systems* (Machine Vision and System Integration), Boston, MA, November 1990.

A Top-Down Approach to
the Analysis of Document Images

Hiromichi Fujisawa[1] and Yasuaki Nakano[2]

[1] Central Research Laboratory, Hitachi, Ltd, 1–280 Kokubunji, Tokyo 185, Japan
[2] Shinshu University, 500 Wakasato, Nagano 380, Japan

Top-down methods for document image understanding to extract information from documents are presented. A language FDL, Form Definition Language, is first introduced which can represent generic layout structures as a set of rectangular regions, each of which are recursively defined in terms of inclusive rectangular regions. To identify concrete layout structures, the generic descriptions are matched against input document images, and specific items on a page are extracted. Although this approach is powerful, it is rather complex and a simplification is possible. A language SFDL, a simplified version of FDL, can be used for rather regular document forms to describe characteristic patterns of the document form in terms of templates. Templates are rectangular regions among which spatial constraints are defined without recursions. By matching such templates, input document images can be classified, and bibliographic items such as a title and author's name can be extracted. Experiments have shown promising results and it can be applied to an automatic document filing system.

1 Introduction

Many attempts in document image understanding have been made from early 80s. Early research on document image understanding can be classified into several classes. The first one is to analyze complex page layouts such as newspapers, to extract articles consisting of a title, text and photographs for instance [1, 2]. The second one is to read printed documents with unknown layouts by enhancing character segmentation methods [3, 4]. Another domain of document understanding is for analyzing complex tabular forms to recognize hand-printed Kanji's to enter information to computer systems [5]. Some recent attempts also include address analysis of mail pieces [6].

One of the important applications of such technology is automatic information extraction for *automated document filing* [7, 8]. Document image filing systems using optical disks, which are being used in many offices, can store tens of thousands of document pages in terms of digital images [9]. In such a system, ease of information retrieval is very important. Currently, to file documents, users have to digest the contents of the documents, and then enter index information such as a title, author's name, keywords, etc. through a key-board. Therefore, automatic extraction of such index information from input documents is significant to liberate users from key-typing. To realize automatic information extraction, the system needs to identify locations of index information on a document page and to recognize characters in the identified areas. Automatic document page classification is also necessary to identify front pages and their type.

Higashino *et al.* proposed a top-down document analysis method aiming at such applications [10, 11]. The feature of the approach is document layout knowledge used to parse two-dimensional physical document structures. They devised a knowledge representation language FDL, Form Definition Language, to describe generic layout structures of documents. The structures are represented in terms of rectangular regions, each of which are recursively defined in terms of smaller rectangular regions. These generic descriptions are then matched against input document images to determine specific layouts. As a result, index information such as titles, author's names, etc. can be extracted from front pages effectively. Although this top-down method is powerful, it is rather complex because of recursions.

In this paper, we propose a simplified method for document classification and information extraction. We have developed a software prototype system to evaluate the method. Experiments on about 190 document pages have shown promising results.

2 The Form Definition Language with Recursion

We will briefly describe an image analysis method using FDL which utilizes generic knowledge about document layout rules. A document page can be considered as consisting of rectangular regions, each of which again consists of another set of rectangular regions. A similar representation scheme is adopted in the ODA/ODIF, Office Document Architecture and Interchange Format [12], which is going to be an international standard of document representation. This recursive definition of rectangular regions is illustrated in Figure 1. Each block is a rectangle and, if it is a text block for instance, it consists of "line blocks" each of which again consists of "word blocks." The word blocks then consist of character cells which enclose connected character patterns of black picture elements (pixels).

In general, form blocks in a document are given characteristic labels such as "title," "author," "affiliation," etc. By using these labels, the document structure can be represented as

        (DOC (title X1)
              (author X2)
              (affiliation X3)
              (classification X4)
              (abstract X5)

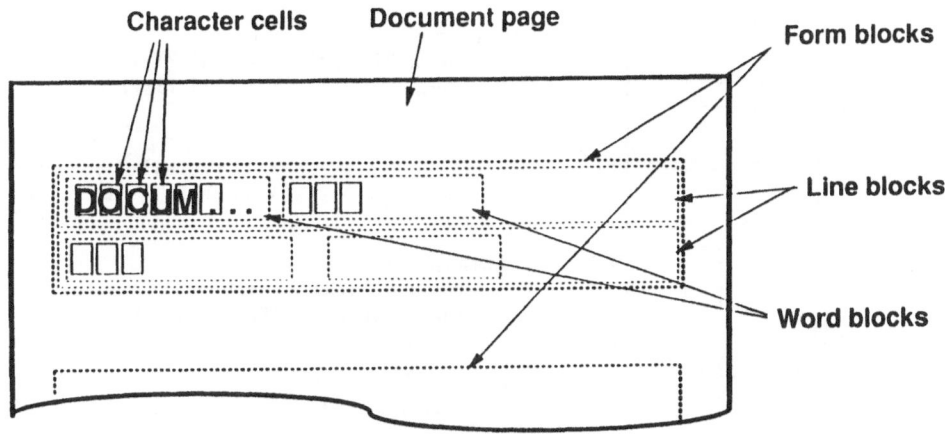

Fig. 1. Hierarchical structure of a document image.

(body X6))

where "DOC" is the label of the whole document, and "title," "author," etc. are labels of form blocks. Variables X1 through X6 represent subdivided regions each of which includes corresponding image patterns. In this way, the structure can be represented in a frame type expression. In order to determine the physical layout structure, however, more specific information about the layout knowledge is required. Language FDL is the one to codify this kind of knowledge.

The grammar of FDL makes the representation of recursive rectangular structures very easy. An illustrative example of such document description is shown in Figure 2. An exemplar geometrical (physical) structure of a page is shown in Figure 2 (a). In this example, the whole page is given a name of form F, and is consisted of forms F1 and F2. Here in FDL, blocks at any level are called "forms" to treat them uniformly. The form F1 then consists of two vertically separated forms F11 and F12. This arrangement of the form blocks can be defined as in Figure 2 (b).

In these expressions, the first "defform" statement defines the generic layout of form F, by specifying the locations of two forms F1 and F2 using the "form" statements, and by specifying spatial relationships between F1 and F2. In Figure 2 (b), the following defform statements define the layout structures of forms F1, F2, F11, etc.

The location of a rectangle is represented by a quadruple consisting of the minima and maxima of X- and Y-coordinates as in (?Xs1 ?Xe1 ?Ys1 ?Ye1), where the origin is set on the left upper corner of the form. In general, it is not possible to specify the values in the quadruples in advance. Therefore, these quadruples can be represented in terms of variables whose mnemonics start with ?. In the example of Figure 2, the location of form F1 is defined to be at (?Xs1 ?Xe1 ?Ys1 ?Ye1) in its parent form F. The locations of forms F11 and F12 in the form F1 can be specified similarly. In this manner, hierarchical description becomes possible.

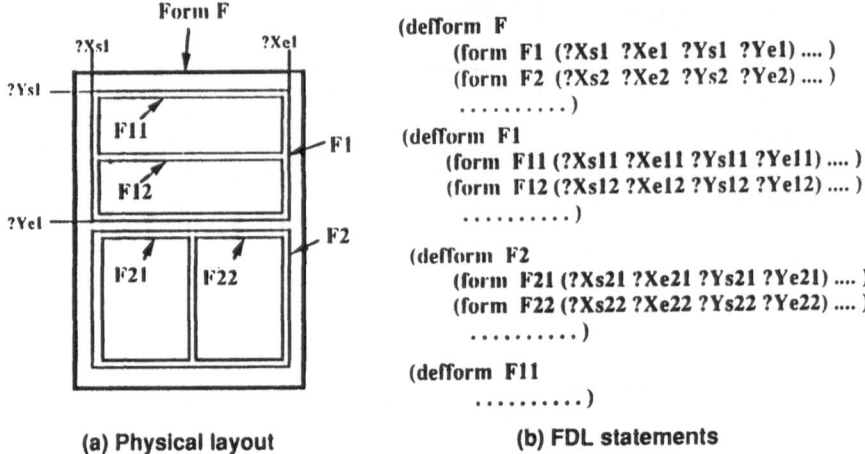

(a) Physical layout   (b) FDL statements

Fig. 2. An illustrative example of generic document layout description in FDL.

Here, spatial relationships among these forms are more important. Otherwise, such regions cannot be identified. Although it is not shown in Figure 2, FDL facilitates the capability to represent such relationships by describing conditions on those variables.

Spaces in-between rectangular regions are very important in describing such relationships. For example, to identify two form F1 and F2, the horizontal space bar between these two forms plays the role of boundary. Normally, between two different blocks, there is a wider gap between adjacent character lines. Therefore, FDL has "space" statement which declares the existence of such a space bar, and which expresses the conditions on those variables. In the case of Figure 2, for instance, a condition "$?Ys2 - ?Ye1 > S$" is declared in the defform statement of F, where S is a threshold representing a minimum gap between these two forms F1 and F2. Normally, the threshold S can be defined in terms of a font height multiplied by a coefficient which is greater than one.

In the image analysis stage, these layout descriptions are matched against connected pattern components which are extracted from the input image. One-to-one correspondence between a form definition and a set of aligned patterns is then tried to find. When the matching process succeeds, the values of the variables in these quadruples are instantiated. These derived values can be in either absolute coordinates or relative ones in a parent form. In conjunction with FDL, FDE or Form Dividing Engine has been developed which interprets the form definition statements and guides the image analysis process [10, 11].

It should be noted that the layout description is generic in the sense that variables can be used and they are determined according to input images. Because of this feature of the method, the description and analysis of the layout become possible, even though the sizes or physical, absolute locations of the regions are variable. The matching process is top-down in nature. It resembles the parsing process in the grammatical analysis of sentences, but is two-dimensional.

An experimental system implemented on a general purpose computer using a LISP language has shown the effectiveness of this approach. A further extension of this method includes extraction of logical document structures. A more detailed description of this method will be found elsewhere [10, 11, 13].

3 A Simplified Top-Down Method

The document image analysis method using FDL is powerful, but is complex to be implemented on small machines. The main reason of the complexity is in the recursive description of document layouts. The recursion is indispensable to analyze the entire structure of documents, but is unnecessary for some restricted purposes. An example of such purposes is to extract bibliographic items from rather restricted types of documents.

In this section, we present a language SFDL, Simplified Form Description Language, to describe characteristic patterns of document forms. Such patterns are defined in terms of templates among which spatial constraints can be defined. By not supporting recursive description, the range of analysis is limited, but it remains sufficiently wide to cover practically important applications.

The proposed method consists of three steps: preprocessing of document images, extraction of connected pattern components, and matching with layout descriptions written in SFDL. In the matching step, connected pattern components are matched to a plurality of SFDL descriptions, each of which is defined for a class of document pages. As a result, one description that matches to the input is identified. Therefore, the process can be considered as document class recognition. In this process, important form blocks are extracted as by-products. By supplying these block images to a well-established character recognition process, automatic extraction of bibliographic items is completed. The details of each step will be explained in the following sections.

3.1 Run-Length Filtering as Preprocessing

In most document analysis systems, a slowest step is often that of merging character cells into a line block. The expense of the merging process is excessive sometimes, because only a few character cells are actually used in following steps. For this reason, we attempt to extract text line patterns from the original image by applying image preprocessing. It will reduce the number of connected pattern components, reducing the amount of computation in the template matching.

The preprocessing method we use is a run-length filtering whose principle is shown in Figure 3. For each scanned line of pixels, the run length of each white pixel run, say W, is compared to a predetermined threshold T. If W is less than (or shorter than) T, this white run is changed to a black run, and the adjacent black runs are merged. By doing so, character patterns can be merged into a line pattern as shown in Figure 3 (b). The threshold value T is determined in advance according to the statistics of font sizes being used. After the run-length filtering, connected pattern components are extracted by a labeling method [14]. It is hoped that most of the connected components form character line patterns.

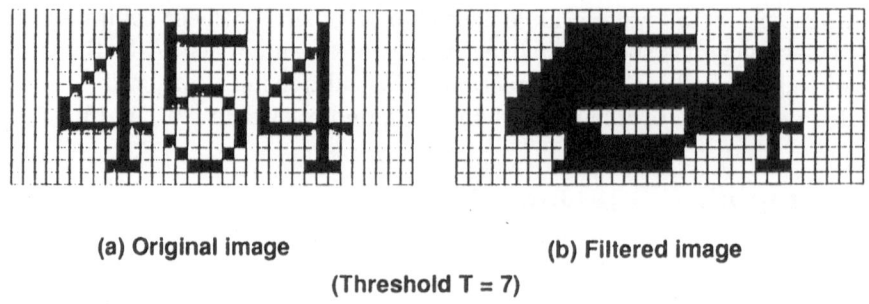

(a) Original image   (b) Filtered image

(Threshold T = 7)

Fig. 3. Run-length filtering.

As the run-length filtering is vulnerable to the skew of documents and to small noises between blocks, a skew normalization and noise removing operations are applied to realize robust filtering. The details of the preprocessing can be found elsewhere [15].

In the case of Wong *et al.*, the run-length filtering is applied in both horizontal and vertical directions [3]. In our method, on the other hand, the filtering is operated only in the horizontal direction because its role is restricted to the preprocessing for obtaining candidates of line patterns. The main task of the image analysis is in the steps following the preprocessing, which will be described in Section 3.3.

An example of a preprocessed image is shown in Figure 4 with the corresponding original image. The sample is a front page of a patent application document which will be explained in Section 4.1.

3.2 The Grammar of SFDL

An important function of an automated filing system is a classification of pages of documents, since many different documents will be stacked for automatic entry. Classes include those of a front page (header page), title page, text page, figure page, etc. In the case of such documents that require automated filing, pages have typical features in their layout styles. Especially, front pages have characteristic features, in other words, some regularities. For instance, pages have fixed areas and variable areas. Such regular forms include patent application forms.

Therefore, the idea proposed here to make classification is that of matching input features to the registered features. Matching is based on the existence of typical areas and their consistent geometrical (spatial) interrelationships. This feature matching enables the document classification and, at the same time, it enables the identification of important areas of titles, author's names, etc. Language SFDL has been devised to describe such layout features. In this language, templates can be defined that specify pattern areas which are selected as characteristic patterns on a page. Normally, such a pattern is a string of characters. Then, spatial relations can be defined to constrain some geometrical interrelationships among these pattern areas. There should be as many templates defined

 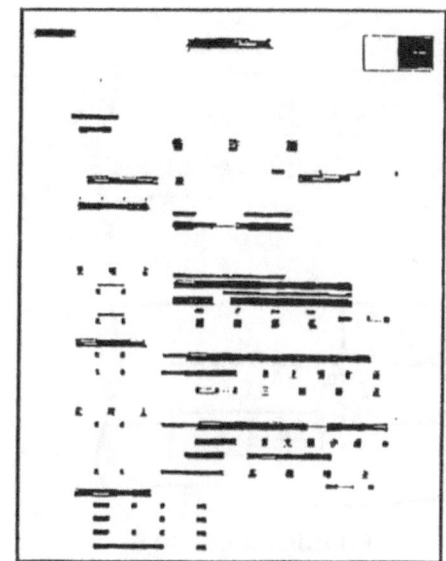

(a) Original document image   **(b) Preprocessed image**

Fig. 4. Preprocessing applied to a front page of a Japanese patent application form.

as to correctly identify a document class. A template for a characteristic pattern can be defined by a following TEMPLATE statement:

label TEMPLATE [*n*]

where *label* represents an arbitrary name attached to the template, and *n* is an optional identification number. In SFDL, upper case and lower case letters represent reserved words and parameters, respectively.

Spatial constraints on characteristic patterns are defined in terms of absolute and relative constraints. There are four kinds of constraints that can be specified by language SFDL, as shown in Figure 5. Absolute constraints can be specified by three kinds of modifier statements, or AREA, SIZE and EDGE statements. The styles of the statements are as follows:

    AREA   *l r t b*
    SIZE   *w*1 *w*2 *h*1 *h*2
    EDGE *π a*1 *a*2

Here, parameters *l*, *r*, *t*, and *b* of an AREA statement define the left, right, top and bottom limits on template locations, respectively, as shown in Figure 5 (a). Size parameters *w*1, *w*2, *h*1, and *h*2 are lower and upper bounds on the width and height of the template.

In an EDGE statement, *π* specifies one of the four edges of a template, *i.e.* one of the letters L, R, U and B which represent the left, right, upper and bottom

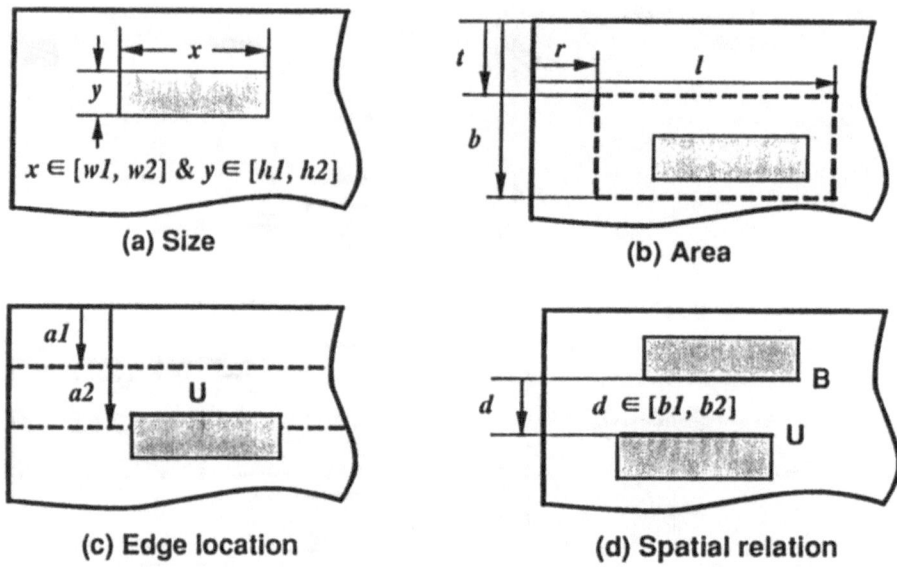

Fig. 5. Spatial constraints on templates.

edge, respectively. The parameters $a1$ and $a2$ are lower and upper bounds on the edge position.

Relative constraints restrict the alignment of any two patterns that are to be included in the corresponding template. For instance, the following REL statement specifies a spatial relation between two patterns to be included in the templates labeled as *label1* and *label2*.

REL $\alpha\$label1 = \beta\$label2$ $a1$ $a2$

Here, α and β specify one of the four edges of a temple as in the EDGE statement, and $a1$ and $a2$ are bounds of the difference between the two specified edges. For instance, the following example statement:

REL   U\$ABC1 = B\$ABC2   150   230

specifies that two patterns included in templates ABC1 and ABC2 align themselves such that the vertical distance between the upper edge of ABC1 and the lower edge of ABC2 should be between 150 mm and 230 mm (Figure 5 (d)).

An example of a form description is shown in Figure 6, where the name of the form is given by the DEFINE statement as FRONTPAGE-1. Statements below the header statement are definitions of templates and their interrelationships. What is meant by the form description is depicted in Figure 9, where the purpose is to identify a class of patent application documents shown in Figure 4. In an application, there are as many number of form descriptions as the number of document page classes to be identified.

```
              DEFINE      FRONTPAGE-1
      A11     TEMPLATE
              AREA        600 850 400 800
              SIZE        30 60 30 60
      A12     TEMPLATE
              AREA        800 1050 400 800
              SIZE        30 60 30 60
      A13     TEMPLATE
              AREA        1000 1250 400 800
              SIZE        30 60 30 60
      A2      TEMPLATE
              AREA        320 770 560 860
              SIZE        200 300 20 40
      A3      TEMPLETE
              AREA        300 750 660 980
              SIZE        200 300 20 40
      A4      TEMPLATE
              AREA        680 1650 660 980
              SIZE        200 1000 20 60
              REL         L$A12 = L$A11 150 230
              REL         U$A12 = U$A11 -20 20
              REL         L$A13 = L$12 150 230
              REL         U$A13 = U$A12 -20 20
              REL         L$A2 = L$A11 -350 -260
              REL         U$A2 = U$A11 80 160
              REL         L$A3 = L$A2 -50 -10
              REL         U$A3 = U$A2 80 120
              REL         L$A4 = R$A3 50 300
              REL         U$A4 = U$A4 -50 100
              END
```

Fig. 6. SFDL statements for the layout features of type-1 front page.

3.3 Matching with SFDL Statements

Connected pattern components extracted from a preprocessed image as in Figure 4 (b) are matched against form descriptions which are represented in terms of templates explained in the previous section. If each template in a form description finds a text line pattern(s) (connected pattern component) enclosed in the specified area, and all templates in the same form description suffice the geometrical constraints, then, the image is considered to match the form description, and is assigned the corresponding page class. When such a match does not occur, the next form description is tried to match. If the input image matches none of the descriptions, it is rejected as having unknown page class.

The SFDL matching algorithm is explained following a PAD (Program Analysis Diagram) shown in Figure 7. At the start of the matching process, connected pattern components extracted from the preprocessed image are listed in a set P of candidate line patterns p_i. And a set of templates, $T_k = \{t_{kj}\}$, is read out from form description file F. File F has as many sets, Ts, as the number of forms defined. By using the SIZE, AREA and EDGE statements as constraints, candidate line patterns that are not located in any of template areas are excluded from the candidate list P. In this step, each line pattern is identified a template t_{kj} that includes it. In the next step, every line pattern p_i is tested if there exists other line pattern q that meets the geometrical constraints defined in the REL statement for template t_{kj}. If there exists one, it is remained as it is. Otherwise, the line pattern is excluded from the candidate list. And this elimination process is repeated until no change in the candidate list occurs.

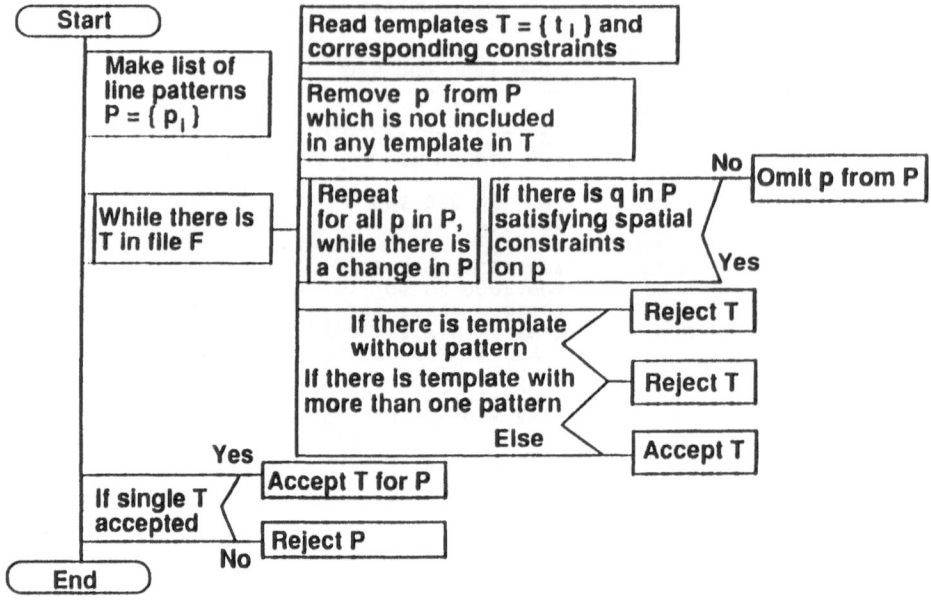

Fig. 7. SFDL matching algorithm.

After the elimination process, it is tested if there remains at least one candidate line pattern for each template. If it is true, the matching succeeds and the form T_k is recorded as a candidate of the page class. On the contrary, if there is any template that includes no candidate line pattern, the matching is a failure. Sometimes, there remain templates that have more than one pattern. This case is also a failure as a definition.

If the matched description T_k is unique after matching all the form descriptions in file F, the corresponding page class is accepted. If the uniquely matched description is not the right one, then it means a misclassification. If there are no descriptions or more than one descriptions matched to the input, on the other hand, it is rejected.

3.4 Form Description for Identifying Page Class

Describing page forms in terms of templates and constraints is a task for setting up the system for use. To automate document filing, documents to be stored automatically should be studied in advance so that classes and their features are identified by the system designer. Then, form descriptions are written manually from detailed observations on typical sample images. By carrying out several

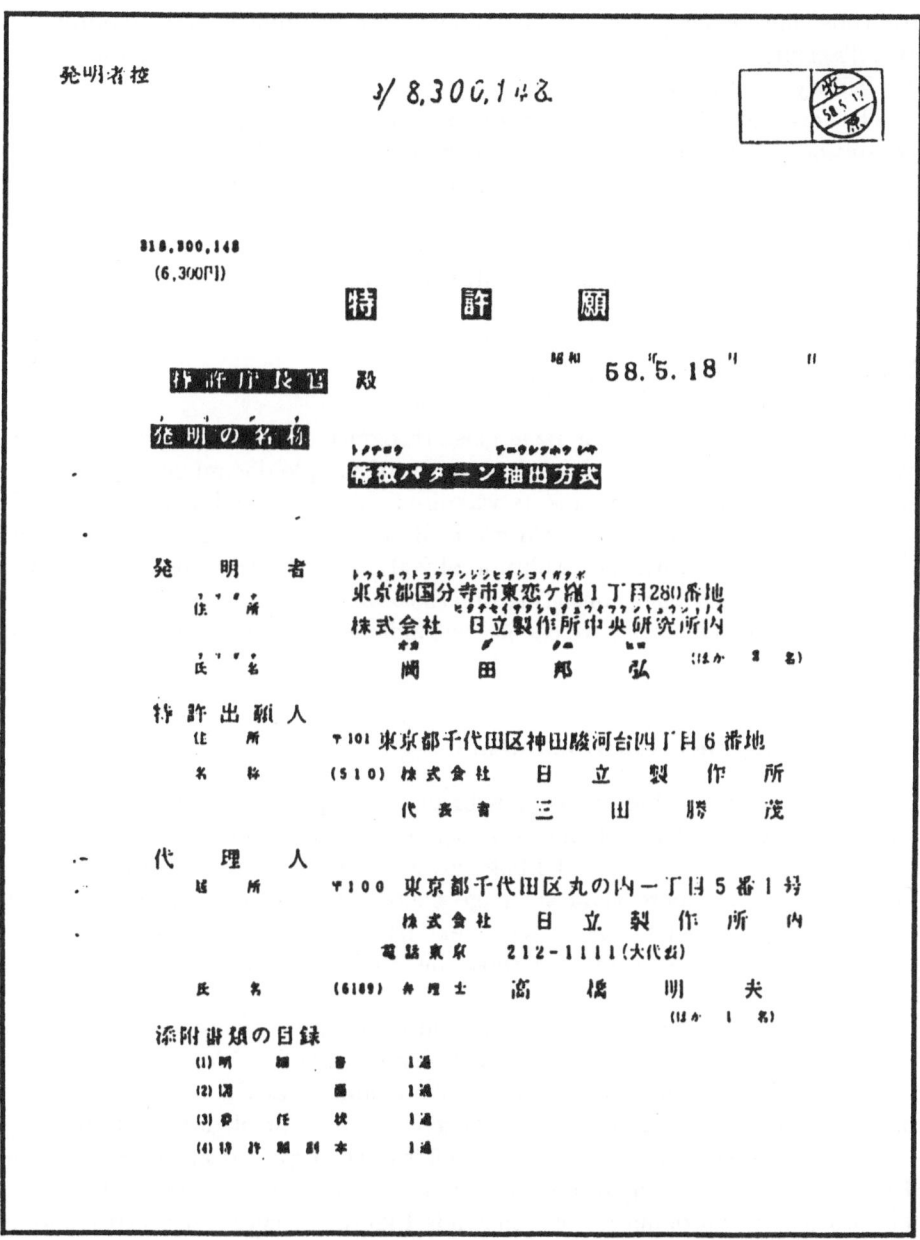

Fig. 8. Identified template regions.

test runs, misclassified and rejected images are examined, and inappropriate form descriptions are corrected. This elaboration process must be repeated until satisfactory results are expected.

The form description process corresponds to a training process for pattern recognition. What is different from pattern recognition is that structural features are to be extracted from samples and codified in a language like SFDL. After identifying structural features, parameters should be trained. Automatic learning of the form descriptions is an interesting issue as a next target to develop. It will be learning from samples with some abstraction process.

4 Experiments

Two series of experiments for page class recognition have been carried out to evaluate the method. In the first series, a set of sample documents of 106 pages from patent application documents was used. In the second series, a set of 81 pages from Japanese Patent Disclosure Bulletin (JPDB) was used. These documents were scanned with the resolution of 200 dot/inch and converted to binary digital images, each page consisting of 1728 × 2287 pixels. The recognition experiments for the two sets were carried out independently with two separate sets of form descriptions.

4.1 Patent Application Documents

Sample documents include two types of patent applications depending on the kind of inventions. It is assumed that these documents are stacked randomly and scanned into the document filing system automatically. By examining the samples, there are more than six page classes, which are front page type-1, front page type-2, patent claim page, text page, figure page, separator sheets, and others. Separator sheets are those inserted in-between successive patent applications.

Other page classes are those such as a supplementary front page, corrections, and so on. We classify these pages as miscellaneous, and we do not prepare form descriptions for this miscellaneous class. We assume that the recognition of this class succeed if a page of this class is rejected as a result of classification.

The form description shown in Figure 6 is of the type-1 front page written in SFDL. The corresponding graphical explanation of the constraints is illustrated in Figure 9. A result of matching is shown in Figure 8, where areas corresponding to the matched templates are shown as inverted regions.

The score of the page class recognition experiment for the patent application documents is shown in Table 1. Eight pages are rejected among which only two are actually misclassification. The rejections for the two were due to noises which caused improper preprocessing. As described before, the miscellaneous pages are considered correctly recognized because they are properly rejected.

Training of form descriptions has been repeated four times in trial and error. The repetition was required to cope with unknown situations and parameter

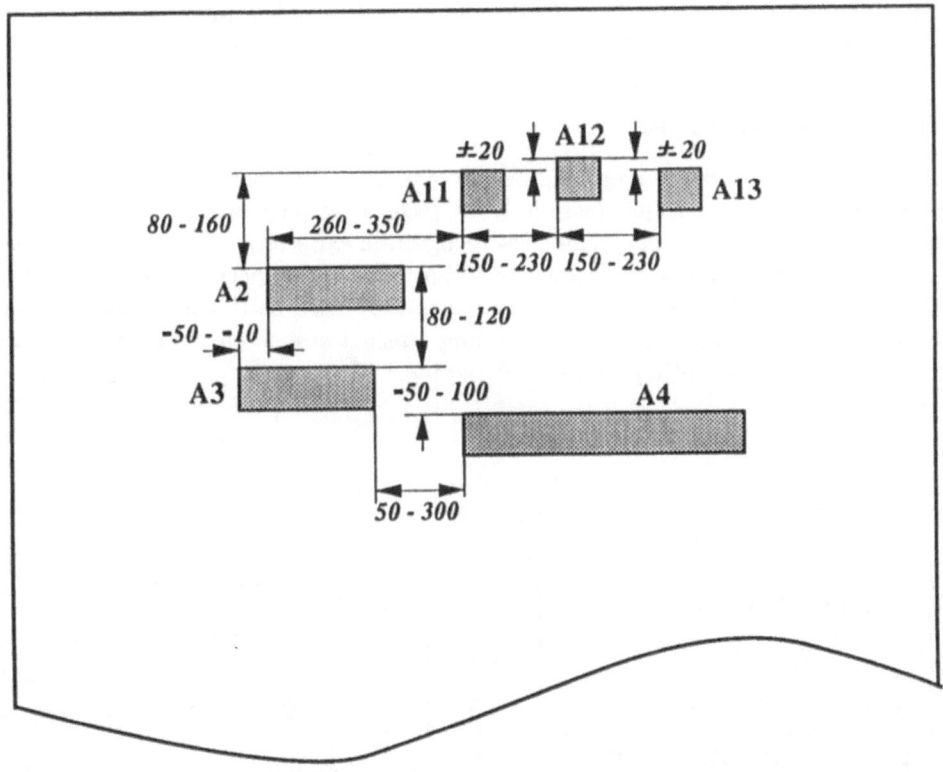

Fig. 9. Geometrical constraints on template defined for type-1 front page.

Table 1. Results of page class recognition for Japanese patent application forms.

Input Page Class	Recognized Class							
	A	B	C	D	E	F	Reject	Total
A.Separator Sheet	3	0	0	0	0	0	0	3
B. Front Page Type-1	0	7	0	0	0	0	1	8
C. Front Page Type-2	0	0	3	0	0	0	0	3
D. Claim Page	0	0	0	11	0	0	0	11
E. Text Page	0	0	0	0	45	0	1	46
F. Figure Page	0	0	0	0	0	29	0	29
X. Miscellanea	0	0	0	0	0	0	6	6
Total	3	7	3	11	45	29	8	106

adjustments. All 106 pages are used as training samples; in other words, the training set and the test set are identical in this experiment.

4.2 JPDB Documents

We have defined three page classes for Japanese Patent Disclosure Bulletin (JPDB) documents, which include front page, text page without figures, and text page with figures. The page class recognition experiment for this set of documents has given the score shown in Table 2. In the experiment, all 81 pages have been correctly recognized. Forty pages were used as training samples and remaining pages were tested. The training finished in a single cycle because the form structure was rather simple and the most of the variation could be anticipated.

Table 2. Results of page class recognition for Japanese disclosure bulletins.

Input Page Class	Recognized Class				
	A	B	C	Reject	Total
A. Fron Page	16	0	0	0	16
B. Text Page without Figure	0	40	0	0	40
C. Text Page with Figure	0	0	25	0	25
Total	16	40	25	0	81

5 Conclusion

A simple but effective method for document analysis has been proposed. A language SFDL, a simplified version of FDL, has been developed. By using SFDL, the form of a document can be described in a simple form without recursive expressions.

In order to treat text lines directly in the form matching, the run-length filtering is applied to input images as preprocessing. In the image analysis, form descriptions are matched against the preprocessed patterns, and the page classes of input are identified. Bibliographic items such as a title and author's names can be extracted as a result of this matching process. Images in the extracted regions are sent to a character recognition process and then converted into code information.

The experiments of the proposed method have been carried out for two sets of patent related printed documents. For the patent application documents, 104 pages out of 106 pages were correctly recognized and two were misrecognized because of noise. For the second set of patent disclosure documents, all 81 pages were correctly recognized. If we average the results of two series of experiments, the recognition accuracy becomes 99%. The effectiveness of this approach has been proved in spite of the simplified capability in form description.

Future research should be directed to a development of automatic form description generation, which is machine learning of structures from samples. It will include automatic structural feature extraction and abstraction process. By incorporating the learning capability, this approach will realize a full automatic filing function for the optical document filing system.

Acknowledgements

The authors would like to express their gratitude to M. Fujinawa, E. Hadano, and J. Higashino of Central Research Laboratory for their software tools. They also would like to extend their thankfulness to T. Hananoi and K. Kurino of Hitachi Odawara Works for their collaboration and valuable discussions.

References

[1]   J. Toyoda and Y. Noguchi, "Study of Extracting Japanese Newspaper Article," *Proc. 6th ICPR*, pp. 1113–1115, 1982.

[2]   K. Inagaki, T. Kato, T. Hiroshima, and T. Sakai, "MACSYM: A Hierarchical Image Processing System for Event-driven Pattern Understanding of Documents," *Pattern Recognition*, Vol. 17, No. 1, pp. 85–108, 1984.

[3]   K. W. Wong, R. G. Casey, and F. H. Wahl, "Document Analysis System," *IBM J. of Research and Development*, Vol. 26, No. 6, pp. 647–656, 1982.

[4]   T. Akiyama and I. Masuda, "A Segmentation Method for Document Images without the Knowledge of document Formats," *Trans. Japanese Institute of Electronics and Communication Engineers*, Vol. J66-D, No. 2, pp. 111–118, 1982 (in Japanese).

[5]   Y. Nakano, H. Fujisawa, O. Kunisaki, K. Okada, and T. Hananoi, "A Document Understanding System incorporating with Character Recognition," *Proc. 8th ICPR*, Paris, pp. 801–803, 1986.

[6]   C. H. Wang, P. W. Palumbo, and N. Srihari, "Object Recognition in Visually Complex Documents: An Architecture for Locating Address Blocks on Mail Pieces," *Proc. 9th ICPR*, pp. 365–367, 1988.

[7]   H. Fujisawa, "Artificial Intelligence as applied to Optical Image Filing," *Proc. Int'l Symp. on Optical Memory*, Tokyo, 1987, also in Japanese J. of Applied Physics, Vol. 26, Supplement 26-4, 1987.

[8]   Y. Nakano and H. Fujisawa, "A Method of Document Understanding for Automatic Filing," *Trans. Japanese Inst. of Electron. and Comm. Eng.*, Vol. J71-D, No. 10, pp. 2050–2058, 1988 (in Japanese).

[9]   H. Masuzaki, N. Takahashi, and Y. Kurosu, "HITFILE 650E Optical Disk Filing System," *Hitachi Review*, Vol. 38, No. 5, pp. 257–264, 1989.

[10] J. Higashino, H. Fujisawa, Y. Nakano, and M. Ejiri, "A Knowledge-based Segmentation Method for Document Understanding," *Proc. 8th ICPR*, Paris, pp. 745–748, 1986.

[11] H. Yashiro, T. Murakami, Y. Shima, Y. Nakano, and H. Fujisawa, "A New Method of Document Structure Extraction using Generic Layout Knowledge," *Proc. Int'l Workshop Industrial Applications of Machine Intelligence and Vision*, MIV-89, Tokyo, pp. 282–287, April 1989.

[12] ISO/TC97/SC18, "Office Document Architecture (ODA) and Interchange Format," *DIS8613*, Mar. 1988.

[13] H. Fujisawa, H. Yashiro, J. Higashino, Y. Shima, Y. Nakano, and T. Murakami, "Document Analysis and Decomposition Method for Multimedia Contents Retrieval," *Proc. 2nd Int'l Symp. Interoperable Information Systems*, ISIIS-88, Tokyo, pp. 231–238, Nov. 1988.

[14] Y. Shima, T. Murakami, M. Koga, H. Yashiro, and H. Fujisawa, "A High Speed Algorithm for Propagation-type Labeling based on Block Sorting of Runs in Binary Images," *Proc. 10th ICPR*, Atlantic City, pp. 655–658, June 1990.

[15] Y. Nakano, Y. Shima, H. Fujisawa, J. Higashino, and M. Fujinawa, "An Algorithm for the Skew Normalization of Document Image," *Proc. 10th ICPR*, Atlantic City, pp. 8–13, June 1990.

[16] Y. Tsuji, "Document Image Analysis for generating Syntactic Structure Description," *Proc. 9th ICPR*, pp. 744–747, 1988.

Analysis of Scanned Documents
– a Syntactic Approach

Mahesh Viswanathan

Department of Electrical, Computer, and Systems Engineering,[1]
Rensselaer Polytechnic Institute, Troy, NY 12180–3590, USA

Pages from technical journals are analyzed with a syntactic approach to hierarchically identify the spatial structure of a scanned document image and to assign logical labels to its component blocks. These blocks may be fields of text, tables and figures. Publication-specific knowledge is used in the segmentation and labeling of the blocks. The information is meticulously coded in the form of block-grammars used to describe the relationships between the various entity classes or blocks. Lexical and syntax analysis tools, Lex and Yacc, are used to segment and label the blocks. These block-grammars can be generated manually or from a parameter table. Further extensions involving multiple grammars and backtracking algorithms are also discussed.

1 Introduction

Our objective is to identify the spatial structure of scanned pages of technical journals and to assign logical labels like 'title', 'authors', to its various components without using optical character recognition. This system identifies the most significant components first and then further processes these to obtain smaller, but still significant blocks. All of the experiments have been conducted on photocopied pages of the *IBM Journal of Research and Development* (*IBM*) scanned at 300 dpi.

Intended applications of such a system include data compression for document transmission and archival, document entry for information processing and retrieval systems, and remote browsing selected portions of page images. Another application is for preprocessing complex documents for optical character recognition [Kahan 87].

The document is represented hierarchically using the X-Y tree data structure [Nagy 84, Nagy 88]. In this representation, each node corresponds to a rectangular block. The root is the largest rectangular block, usually the initial binary image. The root is segmented into major regions such as 'text', 'footer', 'composite' blocks, and these form the children of the root node. Further subdivisions result in columns, paragraphs, figures, and so on.

---

[1] Presently at IBM Storage Systems Product Division, San Jose, CA 95193, USA

The X-Y tree data structure permits the transformation of a two-dimensional image analysis problem into a sequence of quasi-independent one-dimensional (string) problems. (The results of analyzing a string can be expressed as apriori knowledge for the analysis of its successor strings.) All legal decompositions of a block in a specified direction are prescribed by means of a context-free grammar applied to the string extracted from the block. A parsed string has both the partitions and the label of each partition specified. Since lower-level profile-strings are a result of higher-level segmentations, we have to construct grammars for every segmentable node, and these cannot be merged into a single grammar. These block-grammars are constructed based on a training set of 21 *IBM* pages.

The earlier results presented in [Viswanathan 88] were obtained on journal pages synthesized at 67 dpi using the *troff* typesetting program. The intent of the experiments was to show that it is feasible to simultaneously segment and label the various logical objects using block-grammars. This was also extended to lower levels in the hierarchy to separate the columns in the main text portion of the document, and label the components of each column as section-titles and paragraphs of text. The processing was carried out by a single shell program which includes a routine to generate the node to be processed next.

Similar shell programs are now used for processing *scanned* images. There are two sources of difficulties introduced by scanned images not found in synthetic documents: noise and skew. Typically, a photocopied journal page has noise specks of 1–5 pixels height and width peppered across the document. For the present, small noise specks are eliminated by deleting leaf nodes smaller than 5×5 pixels in a separate preprocessing step. Allowances are also made for noise in the grammars. Skew is avoided by careful scanning. (We also used a de-skewing program obtained from Olivetti Corporation, Italy, on test pages from *IEEE Transactions on Pattern Analysis and Machine Intelligence* (*PAMI*), another publication that we analyzed, but, in this article, we will focus only on *IBM* pages.)

The advances reported in this paper, apart from extending the technique to scanned images, include the analysis of *IBM* non-title pages which include formulas and graphic objects like photographs, line-drawings and tables. Certain blocks can be precisely labeled only after processing beyond the third level (generally, the last level processing in our experiments). Such blocks are assigned temporary labels in the first pass and then relabeled after post-processing. This approach is used in labeling *reference* sections.

An automatic grammar generation method from parameter tables is also described. This is followed by a discussion of two backtracking algorithms, *Exact Parse* and *Maximum Area*, that are used to analyze all the training and test pages are discussed. Both these algorithms use multiple grammars to segment and label documents. These parameter table (PT) generated grammars are used in both algorithms. Results of processing IBM pages and a discussion of the results are next presented, followed by a conclusion.

2 Syntactic Approach Definitions

A few definitions are required to provide a formal definition of page layout in terms of profiles. A comprehensive list is given in [Viswanathan 89]. A smaller list of more frequently used definitions are provided here.

- The horizontal/vertical **1-D profile** is a 1-dimensional integer-valued function, $f(i)$, whose value is the number of black pixels in the row/column (scan-line) 'i'.
- A thresholded profile, **Tprofile(i)**, is defined such that Tprofile(i) = 1 when $f(i) > \theta$, and is zero otherwise.
- A **segmentable block** is a block corresponding to a leaf-node (of the X-Y tree of the page obtained so far) that contains some black pixels.
- A **black atom** is an **all-1** substring of the segmentable block-profile. It is the smallest indivisible partition of a segmentable block-profile (*e.g.*, *lines of print, character blocks*).
- A **white atom** is an **all-0** substring between two black atoms (*e.g.*, *inter-line* or *inter-paragraph spaces*).
- **Atom length** is the number of symbols in an atomic substring. (The word "length" avoids the directional bias associated with "height" and "width.")
- A **black entity** is a contiguous sequence of black and white atom pairs followed by a black atom (*e.g.*, *author blocks, lines of print* and *word blocks*).
- A **white entity** is a white atom separating two black entities or the beginning/end of entire profile-string from first/last black entity (*e.g.*, *word spaces, spaces between author-title blocks*).
- **Entity class** is a logical label assigned to an entity (*e.g.*, *title/author* (white entity), *title, paragraph*).
- A **publication-specific block-grammar** is a set of rules that specify allowable segmentations of the block-profile into labeled entities ("interpretations") according to attributes based on the lengths of the atoms. A single profile may have zero, one, or several valid interpretations.
- **Entity valence** is the number of black atoms in an entity (*e.g.*, *three black atoms in title entity*).
- **Cardinality** is the number of entities in a block (profile-string) with a given entity class label (*e.g.*, *[0–1] for header*, indicating an optional entity and at most one per page).
- **Class precedence** determines the partial order induced by the linear order of the classes of entities in a segmentable block. The block-grammar may impose restrictions on the permissible pairwise precedences (*e.g.*, *authors before title*).

All of these attributes can be expressed as string properties for manipulation in Lex [Lesk 75] and Yacc [Johnson 75]. A context-free grammar describes the logical layout of entities in a document block; the nonterminals correspond to logical entities like `title block`, or `bottom margin`, while the terminals correspond to the black and white atoms. From our experience, it appears that each entity is dependent only upon the entities that immediately precede and succeed it. Therefore, the grammar derived is a *regular grammar*.

3 Knowledge Acquisition and Grammar Generation

It is important that the document pages selected for processing are all from a period wherein the publisher's layout format remained uniform. A set of grammars can be generated based on such a uniformity. For our experiments, we selected sample *IBM* pages from the years 1979–84.

Entities are processed in a top-down order, starting with the root of the X-Y tree (the whole page), down to sub-blocks that result in paragraphs as children. All entities of interest in any publication are known beforehand. Blocks that produce text lines as child nodes are leaf nodes and never processed. Therefore, *IBM* pages are processed only up to three levels.

All document primitives (precedence, cardinality, black entities, white entities, valence and atom lengths) are extracted from every segmentable sub-block of a publication, and block-grammars are constructed for each. The sub-blocks to be analyzed are decided by visual inspection of the sample documents. To create grammars over a whole set of training samples is not a simple task, since the grammars are constructed one level at a time. A block-grammar for level 1 is constructed (from information acquired at the top level) from all the training samples and it incorporates all of the nuances of the varied layouts. Failed parses are used to improve the block-grammar. Grammar construction can be simplified by using partial X-Y trees — collecting all the nodes with the same label, profiling them, calculating their atom run lengths, and then by visual inspection, applying labels to the runs. The corresponding document sub-blocks are identified and the measurements are recorded. These may then used in parameter tables for automatic grammar generation or directly in manually constructed grammars. The final tweaking is performed when the whole hierarchy of grammars is used to process each training sample.

4 Grammar Generation for a Document Block

The generation of a block-grammar for a sample document block is presented in this section. Consider a segmentable block with only *title* and *author* entities from a sample *IBM* page (Figure 1). There are three entities to be labeled: title, author, and the separating white entity. The measurements (in pixels) for the author entity are: $(35–39)(26–27)\{1,1\}$ (*i.e.*, (black_atom_range) (white_atom_range) {valence}), for title entity: $(66–67)(8)\{2,2\}$ and (246) for author/title white entity. The cardinality of both entities is 1 and the author block always precedes the title block.

Three Lex stages and one Yacc stage are involved in the simultaneous segmentation and labeling process. The *Tprofile* of the segmentable block is the input to the first Lex stage. All the black and white atom ranges are sorted to give two mutually exclusive black ranges (35–39 and 66–67), and three white ranges (8–8, 26–27, and 246–246). Identifiers are generated corresponding to each atom and a token (symbol) string is produced. Here, the Lex statement,

1{35,39}   {putchar ('a');}

places an "*a*" in the output corresponding to every black atom of length $>= 34$ and $<= 50$ in the `Tprofiles` and similarly,

0{8,8}   {putchar ('A');}

places an "*A*" in the output for white atoms. The second Lex stage accepts the atom identifiers of the first stage and produces tentative entity labels. For example, *(aB){3,3}a* would be the author entity definition. (The valence range, *{3–3}*, applies to the black and white atoms, *a* and *B*, collectively.) Tentative entity labels are generated for each matching entity definition. (If the intersection of the definition of different entities is not null, the ambiguity is resolved only in the Yacc stage.) Since the title and author definitions are unambiguous, unique labels are generated for the Yacc stage. After Stage 2, the document block may be considered segmented, but not fully labeled. As each tentative entity label is released to the Yacc stage, the entity locations are calculated by accumulating the atom runs that combine to form the previous entities.

The following is an example of a sample Yacc program, the third stage. (The lower-case symbols are nonterminals, the upper-case symbols are terminals received from the second Lex stage, "*s*" is the start symbol and "*ε*" is the end symbol.)

```
s : AUTHOR s1
s1 : WHITE_AUTHOR/TITLE s2
s2 : TITLE s3
s3 : ε
```

The order in which the productions are presented depends on the order in which the entities appear in the document block. The number of productions for each entity depends on the number of entity descriptions that may be matched (including ambiguous entity descriptions).

Entities that are unnecessarily split in Stage 2 are merged in Stage 4. The entities that can be split and are to be merged must be known beforehand. In our application, text blocks, figure captions, formulas, and composite blocks are merged (if split). This stage is implemented in Lex. Unlike the other three stages which are constructed for each document sub-block, this stage grammar is common to all sub-blocks.

5 Analysis of IBM Pages

The analysis of *IBM* pages based on photocopies of a diverse set of title pages of articles is described in this section. Based on the 9 *IBM* title pages in the training set, the final definitions for author, title and white_author/title were:

(34–50)(11–29){1,12}, (55–78)(1–18){1,3} and (210–270). Grammars were developed for segmenting and labeling two levels completely, and the third level only for the columns, with each grammar consisting of three stages. The Yacc-stage grammar for the top level (horizontal pass and ignoring interspersed white entities for brevity) is of the form:

s : *HEADER* s0 | *AUTHOR* s1
s0 : *AUTHOR* s1
s1 : *TITLE* s2
s2 : *ABSTRACT* s3
s3 : *TEXT* s4
s4 : *TEXT* s5 | *FOOTNOTES* s6
s5 : *FOOTNOTES* s6
s6 : *FOOTER* s7
s7 : ϵ

Only one terminal symbol is shown for each entity above, but overlapping entity definitions cause multiple terminal symbols. Multiple **text** entities (*cardinality* forces repetition of terminal symbol/s for that entity) resulting from the parse above are merged in a concatenation stage after the Yacc stage.

At the second level, each single column entity (*i.e.*, **title**, **author**, **abstract**) obtained from the first level is processed to eliminate the margins. Double-column entities (*i.e.*, **text**, **footnotes**, **footer**) are split into columns. At the third level, these columns are split into *paragraphs* and *section-titles* (Figure 1, right).

A diverse set of logical objects may appear in non-title pages (see Figure 2). (A total of 12 pages form the training set.) These include text-paragraphs, line-drawings, photographs, tables, schematics, references, acceptance notice, author-affiliation, section-titles, page-number and footer. Even though *IBM* has a two-column format, objects such as tables, line-drawings and photographs may occur in either single-column or double-column formats.

In non-title pages, at the first level, there are only two entities, *composite* and *footer*. In the last page of an article, however, the page number may also be separated. The Yacc-stage grammar is:

s : *COMPOSITE* s1
s1 : *COMPOSITE* s2 | *PAGE_NUMBER* s3 | *FOOTER* s4
s2 : *COMPOSITE* s1
s3 : *FOOTER* s4
s4 : ϵ

Multiple **composite** blocks are due to double-column **tables** or **figures**. **Figures** (line-drawings and photographs) and **tables** that extend across two columns can be segmented and labeled during the first horizontal pass. They could be more precisely labeled (*i.e.*, as line-drawings, photographs, or tables) using a block-profile classification algorithm described in [Nagy 89].

At the second level, the two-column **composite** block is vertically divided into columns. There are two major columns of **text** and a column corresponding to the **page-number**. The **footer** is also separated into single-line columns at this level.

Each column is separately processed at the third level. Line-drawings are boxed, and therefore, photographs and line-drawings can be easily distinguished from other objects. These are located closer to the top of the page than all other objects though more than one of each may be present in a single column. A **figure** is characterized by a graphic portion followed by the caption (text). For example, the high-level layout description for **figure** entity is: [large_black_atom][white_space]([black_atom][white_atom])valence.

The *large_black_atom* and *white_space* correspond to the boxed graphic portion and the following white space (between the figure and its caption), while the rest of the definition is for the figure caption. (The valence above is applicable only to the figure caption.)

Other labels are assigned as dictated by the entity descriptions developed for each block, and labeled using these grammars. Without adequate 2-D or lower level information, it is nearly impossible to distinguish between text-paragraphs and references. Hence, the references section is also labeled as *paragraph*. The complete set of possible labels is presented in Figure 3.

6 Segmentation to Five Levels

Certain blocks can be labeled accurately with lower-level information. Most significant is the references section. In order to relabel certain paragraphs as "*references*," more information is required about that document sub-block. The reference section is typeset as follows:

(reference block − > [reference_number][white_space][reference_body]).

"Resegmentation" block-grammars are constructed to analyze all nodes with the label *paragraph*. The other new label applied is *paragraph_under_section-titles*, by analyzing the first lines of paragraphs (section-titles usually do not extend all the way across a column).

The resegmentation process was applied to both title and non-title pages in the training set. Two errors were made in 9 title pages. In one instance, a two-line section-title was labeled "*paragraph*," and in another, an introductory statement to an equation was labeled "*paragraph_under_section-title*." Figures 1 and 2 show results from five levels of processing. Labels *_TXT_COL_PAR* and *_COM_COL_PAR* (from three processing levels) are replaced by *_TXT_COL_PTL*, *_COM_COL_PTL* and *_COM_COL_REF*.

7 Automatic Grammar Generation and Multiple Block-Grammars

The approach that has been taken so far consists of writing down block-grammars *by hand* for a specific class of documents, and then segmenting and labeling any

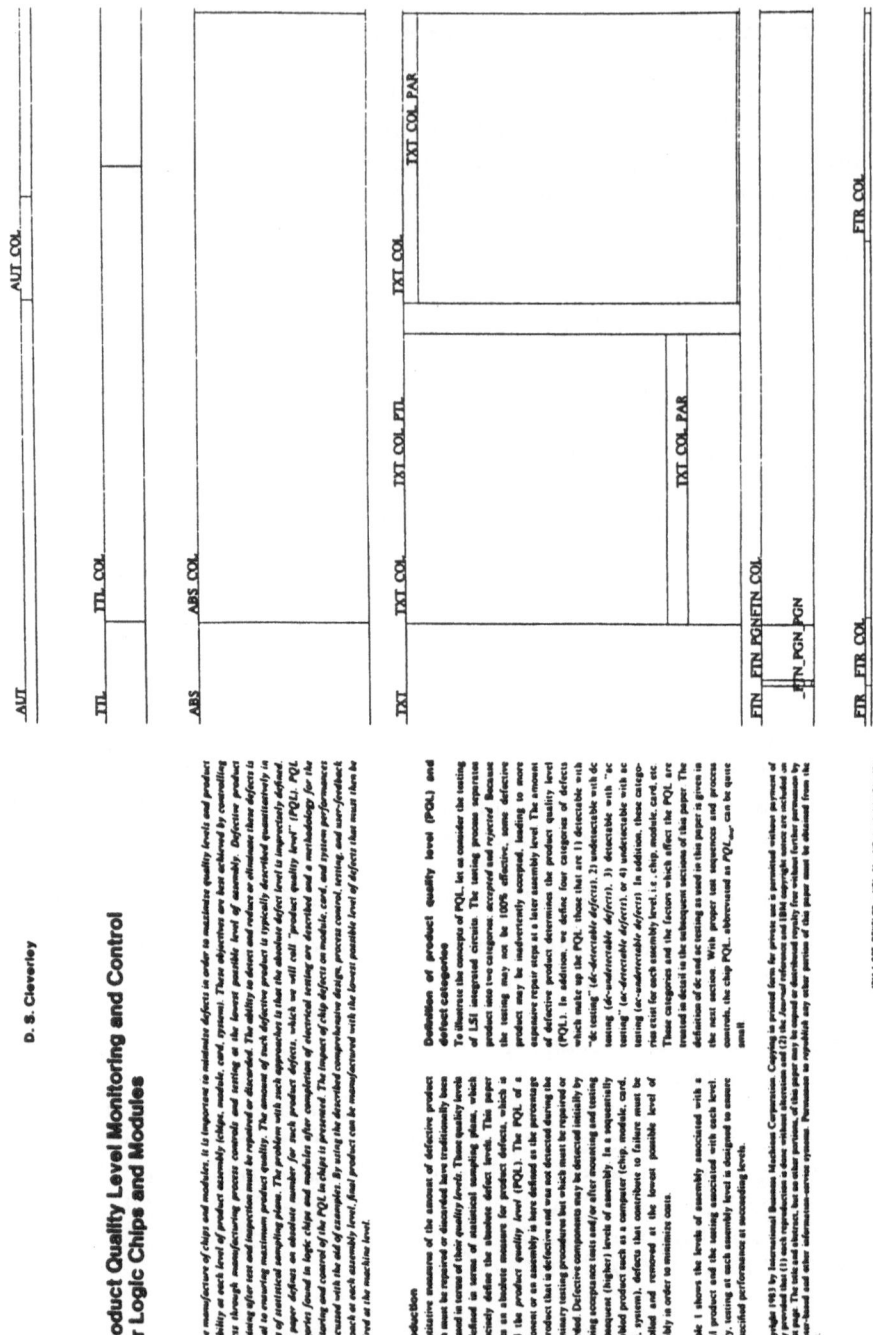

Fig. 1. IBM title page from the training data (reduced photocopy) and X-Y tree. The page is processed up to three levels using grammars, and then resegmented to five levels to identify section-titles and references. One paragraph under a section-title is assigned a new label (_TXT_COL_PTL). The other remains unrecognized.

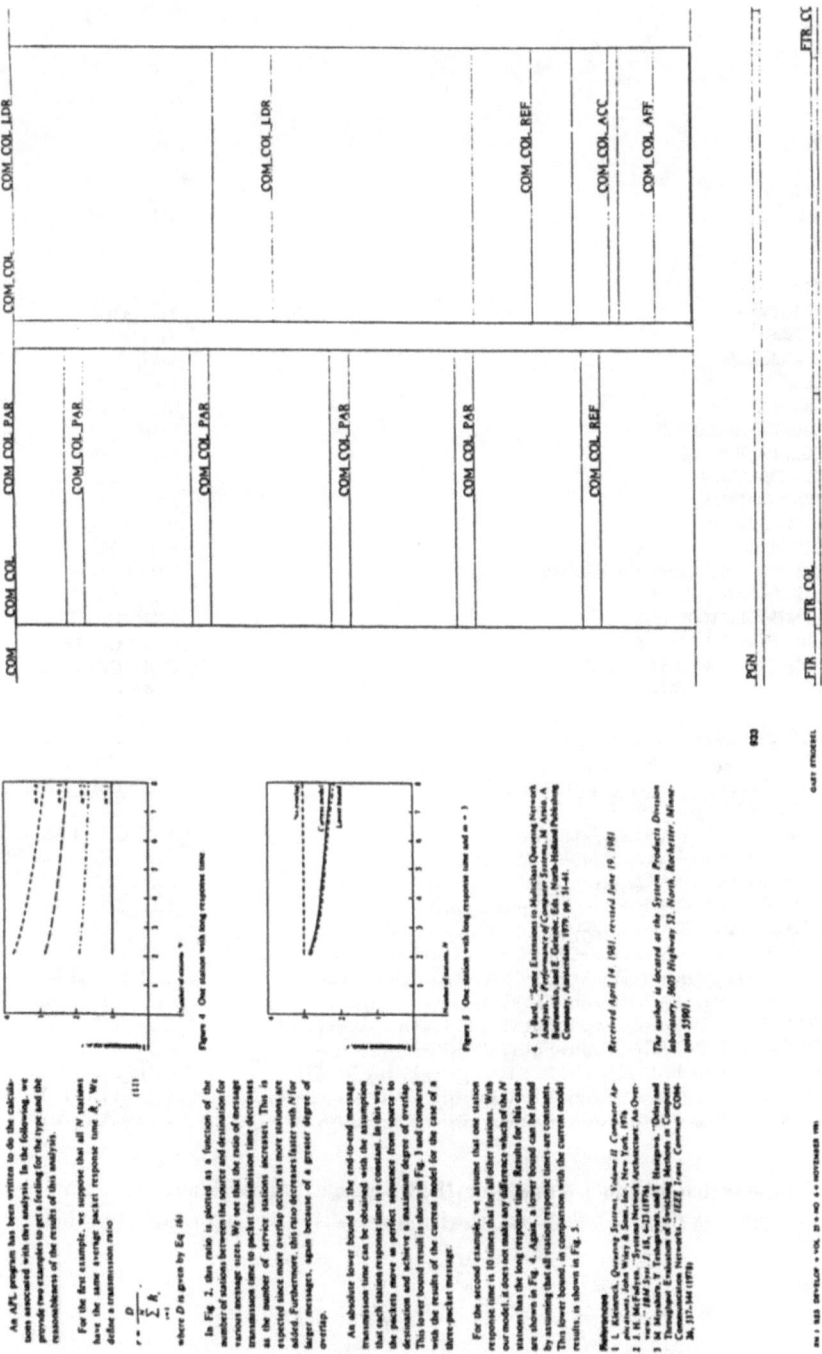

Fig. 2. IBM non-title page from the training data (reduced photocopy) and X-Y tree (three levels). "Figures" are labeled as "line-drawings" after analyzing the distribution of black pixels in the figure profiles (an example of profile classification). Other labels assigned may be "photograph" or two-column "table." Both reference blocks are assigned correct (new) labels (_COM_COL_REF).

TITLE_PAGE	–
NON-TITLE_PAGE	–
HEADER	_HDR
AUTHOR	_AUT
TITLE	_TTL
ABSTRACT	_ABS
TEXT	_TXT
COMPOSITES	_COM
FOOTNOTES	_FTN
PAGENUM	_PGN
FOOTER	_FTR
HEADER-COLUMN	_HDR_COL
AUTHOR-COLUMN	_AUT_COL
TITLE-COLUMN	_TTL_COL
ABSTRACT-COLUMN	_ABS_COL
TEXT-COLUMN	_TXT_COL
COMPOSITES-COLUMN	_COM_COL
COMPOSITES-COMPOSITES	_COM_COM
COMPOSITES-PAGENUM	_COM_PGN
FOOTNOTES-COLUMN	_FTN_COL
FOOTNOTES-PAGENUM	_FTN_PGN
PAGENUM-PAGENUM	_PGN_PGN
FOOTER-COLUMN	_FTR_COL
FOOTNOTES-PAGENUMBER-PAGENUMBER	_FTN_PGN_PGN
TEXT-COLUMN-PARAGRAPH	_TXT_COL_PAR
TEXT-COLUMN-SECTIONTITLE	_TXT_COL_STL
COMPOSITES-COLUMN-PARAGRAPH	_COM_COL_PAR
COMPOSITES-COLUMN-TABLES	_COM_COL_TBL
COMPOSITES-COLUMN-FIGURE	_COM_COL_FIG
COMPOSITES-COLUMN-SECTIONTITLE	_COM_COL_STL
COMPOSITES-COLUMN-ACCEPTANCE	_COM_COL_ACC
COMPOSITES-COLUMN-AFFILIATION	_COM_COL_AFF
COMPOSITES-PAGENUMBER-PAGENUMBER	_COM_PGN_PGN
TEXT-COLUMN-PARAGRAPH-FIRSTLINE	_TXT_COL_PAR_FLN*
TEXT-COLUMN-PARAGRAPH-RESTOFLINES	_TXT_COL_PAR_RPR*
COMPOSITES-COLUMN-PARAGRAPH-FIRSTLINE	_COM_COL_PAR_FLN*
COMPOSITES-COLUMN-PARAGRAPH-RESTOFLINES	_COM_COL_PAR_RPR*
TEXT-COLUMN-PARAGRAPH-FIRSTLINE-PARAGRAPH	_TXT_COL_PAR
TEXT-COLUMN-PARAGRAPH-FIRSTLINE-PARAUNDERTITLE	_TXT_COL_PTL
TEXT-COLUMN-PARAGRAPH-RESTOFLINES-PARAGRAPH	_TXT_COL_PAR
TEXT-COLUMN-PARAGRAPH-RESTOFLINES-PARAUNDERTITLE	_TXT_COL_PTL
COMPOSITES-COLUMN-PARAGRAPH-FIRSTLINE-PARAGRAPH	_COM_COL_PAR
COMPOSITES-COLUMN-PARAGRAPH-FIRSTLINE-PARAUNDERTITLE	_COM_COL_PTL
COMPOSITES-COLUMN-PARAGRAPH-FIRSTLINE-REFERENCES	_COM_COL_REF
COMPOSITES-COLUMN-PARAGRAPH-RESTOFLINES-PARAGRAPH	_COM_COL_PAR
COMPOSITES-COLUMN-PARAGRAPH-RESTOFLINES-PARAUNDERTITLE	_COM_COL_PTL
COMPOSITES-COLUMN-PARAGRAPH-RESTOFLINES-REFERENCES	_COM_COL_REF

Fig. 3. Complete list of block labels for IBM Journal pages. The labels used in the X-Y tree are also shown. Labels marked with an asterisk are intermediate labels.

given document in that class. The main disadvantages are: a) that the page-grammar has to be derived by hand, and b) there is no backtracking if there is a problem in segmentation or labeling at any lower level. The former can be overcome by automatic generation of block-grammars from a set of parameters (entity, valence, cardinality, etc), and the latter by associating more than one block-grammar with each of the segments.

The automatic grammar generation process begins with a table of parameters like the one shown in Figure 4. The format of the table is fixed and it is filled by hand. The necessary information is extracted by examining a set of training samples. Strict adherence to the entity definitions (viz., [black_atom-white_atom-valence]) is imperative. A set of programs were written that attempt to mimic the manual grammar writing procedure to the maximum extent possible while obtaining **all** the necessary information entirely from a table. Atom lengths in the parameter tables are specified in printer's points, and are translated into scan-lines (using a program) for the purpose of generating the grammars. (Figure 4, however, shows a table filled with atom lengths specified in pixels.)

A	B	C	D	E	F	G	H	I	J	K	L	M	N	O	P
1	1	0	0	50	100	1	1	0	1	0	1	W_H	TOP	1	HEADER
1	2	1	5	101	300	1	1	0	1	0	1	W_A	TOP	1	AUTHOR
1	3	25	29	0	0	1	1	0	1	1	1	HEADER	W_H	1	W_HA
1	4	0	0	101	150	1	1	0	1	0	1	W_HA	HEADER	1	AUTHOR
1	5	34	50	11	29	1	12	1	1	1	1	AUTHOR	W_A	1	W_AT
1	6	0	0	210	270	1	1	1	1	0	1	W_AT	AUTHOR	1	TITLE
1	7	55	150	1	18	1	3	1	1	1	1	TITLE	W_AT	1	W_TB
1	8	0	0	151	209	1	1	1	1	0	1	W_TB	TITLE	1	ABSTRACT
1	9	23	48	3	19	2	15	1	1	1	1	ABSTRACT	W_TB	1	W_BX
1	10	0	0	40	350	1	1	1	1	0	1	W_BX	ABSTRACT	1	TEXT
1	11	25	500	1	39	9	34	1	2	1	1	TEXT	W_BX	2	W_XN W_XX
1	12	0	0	60	100	1	1	0	1	0	1	W_XX	TEXT	1	TEXT
1	13	0	0	50	80	1	1	1	1	0	1	W_XN	TEXT	1	FOOTNOTES
1	14	29	72	1	8	3	5	1	1	1	1	FOOTNOTES	W_XN	1	W_NF
1	15	0	0	151	209	1	1	1	1	0	1	W_NF	FOOTNOTES	1	FOOTER
1	16	3	25	1	2	1	2	1	1	1	1	FOOTER	W_NF	1	W_F
1	17	0	0	50	209	1	1	1	1	0	1	W_F	FOOTER	1	BOTTOM

```
A - Level (Topmost level = 1)          I - Minimum Cardinality
B - Unique ID                          J - Maximum Cardinality
C - Minimum Black Atom Length          K - Color (Black = 1, White = 0)
D - Maximum Black Atom Length          L - Direction of Cut (H = 1, V = 0)
E - Minimum White Atom Length          M - Logical Label
F - Maximum White Atom Length          N - Logical Label of Preceding Node
G - Minimum Valence                    O - Number of Succeeding Nodes
H - Maximum Valence                    P - Labels of Succeeding Label/s
TOP and BOTTOM - Dummy Nodes
```

Fig. 4. Parameter table for IBM Title Page — Top Level. Atom lengths may be specified in printer's points, but are converted to pixels (as shown here) before grammar generation. (At 300 dpi, 1 point = 4.2 pixels.)

All the sample title and non-title pages were processed using table-generated grammars. Except for the case of a *table* being labeled as *paragraph* in one page in the training set (tables have definitions that are very close to those of paragraphs), the results matched those of the manually generated programs.

The motivation for multiple grammars comes from different styles of layout for different instances of the same entity. The different instances may occur in different volumes or within the same issue by sections, *e.g.*, Research Contribution versus a Computing Practice article. Even within the same article, the cover page differs significantly in style from the other pages. Layout formats of the *IBM* Journal have changed since 1984, but it must be possible to add new grammars to accommodate these changes. Also, complicated grammar constructions (complex in terms of the number of entities) can be simplified by increasing the number of grammars. However, the most compelling reason for multiple grammars is recovery from erroneous labelings.

In processing a page using multiple grammars, the set of grammars (for any block) are placed in a queue and accessed sequentially.

Only when a grammar fails is the next applied. Erroneous segmentations and labelings can be detected and recovered through backtracking. If a certain block cannot be segmented or labeled at any level, it can be due to any one of three reasons. One, the block does not conform to its grammatical description; the solution is to apply the next grammar. (If none exists, backtrack.) Two, the labeling was erroneous at a higher level; backtrack to the previous level and apply the next grammar. This step is recursive. Finally, such a block layout may be unexpected and all the grammars fail, in which case we must be satisfied with a partially labeled page.

8 Two Algorithms for Analyzing Document Pages

In technical documents, it is quite possible that there may be more than one legal parse for some profile-strings. Multiple grammars are constructed for this purpose. A publication-specific entity-grammar is defined for each label that can be assigned to a block in the segmentation of a page. To accommodate multiple interpretations of a block with the same label, the entity-grammar G_L for block label L is defined as a list of block-grammars, g_L, where each list element, g_L, represents a distinct interpretation [Viswanathan 90]. The failure of the process means that some sub-block in the segmentation could not be assigned a label according to our syntactic model.

Segmentation and labeling errors committed when parsing a block may not be discovered until an unsuccessful attempt is made to parse immediate or distant descendants of the current block where the error was made. The two backtracking algorithms implemented try to parse the block with alternate grammars. Since it is not possible to know beforehand at what level the uncorrectable error occurred, separate alternate grammars have to be designed for sub-blocks of the image where multiple legal interpretations are possible. In the *Exact Parse* algorithm, this would result in a failure of the parse at this block and all of its parent blocks. On the other hand, we may be content with an inexact parse which succeeds in labeling all but a small fraction of a page. Then, a *Maximum Area* (branch-and-bound) algorithm is used. Both algorithms use the same set of block-grammars.

The basic difference between using a single set of block-grammars and multiple grammars has to do with the action taken when a failure occurs; instead of reporting a failure to higher levels, the algorithm must try another interpretation for the block, if available. The search is performed in *breadth-first* order in the *Exact Parse* algorithm. This algorithm is very similar in spirit to the AND_OR method of searching. An OR-node corresponds to the alternate profile-grammars that can be tried for the label being sought for the node block. An AND-node corresponds to the branching due to segmentation of a block (child blocks generated as a result of processing the block) by profile parsing.

In the exact parse approach for multiple interpretation, either all the blocks are segmented and labeled, or no blocks are labeled. However, we may want to obtain the best labeling possible with the available block-grammars, even if the labeling is not complete. The best labeling is defined here as that with the maximum cumulative area of the labeled blocks. This algorithm avoids trying an alternative grammar unless it can increase the total labeled area. It is a recursive algorithm that tries to label blocks by executing a *depth-first* traversal of the tree underlying a document as it is segmented. The AND-nodes of the exact parse algorithm are replaced by SUM, and the OR-nodes are replaced by the MAX operation. The trick is to avoid labeling and segmenting sub-blocks by *pruning* subtrees, if even with correct labelings, the maximum labeled area cannot be increased over the current bound.

9 Results

The experiments and results of the analysis of *IBM* pages (test set) are presented. The two algorithms incorporating multiple grammars are applied. Parameter table generated grammars are designed strictly on the basis of the layout and format of the training samples. The test set (6 title and 6 non-title pages) was processed **once** using methods that worked best on the training data. All experiments were run on a SUN-3/60 computer.

About 30 pages were photocopied from 1979–84 *IBM* journal issues. The test set was randomly picked from these. Each page was carefully aligned on the scanner bed to minimize skew and all (noise) specks smaller than 5×5 were removed. The segmentations and labelings are illustrated by photocopies of document pages and their X-Y trees. No post-processing was performed, but we expect the same results obtained for the training data.

The segmentation and labeling produced by the two algorithm are identical when the *Exact Parse* algorithm succeeds. Therefore, a single set of figures are used to illustrate results for both algorithms. In each category, title and non-title, one fully successful example and one partially successful example is presented. Title pages and their X-Y trees are presented in Figures 5 and 6, while non-title pages (with results) are presented in Figures 7 and 8. The number of grammars constructed for each document block in these *IBM* pages is presented in Table 1. Table 2 presents statistics which include the number of grammars applied, blocks labeled, mislabelings, unprocessed blocks, maximum area labeled and processing time for each page.

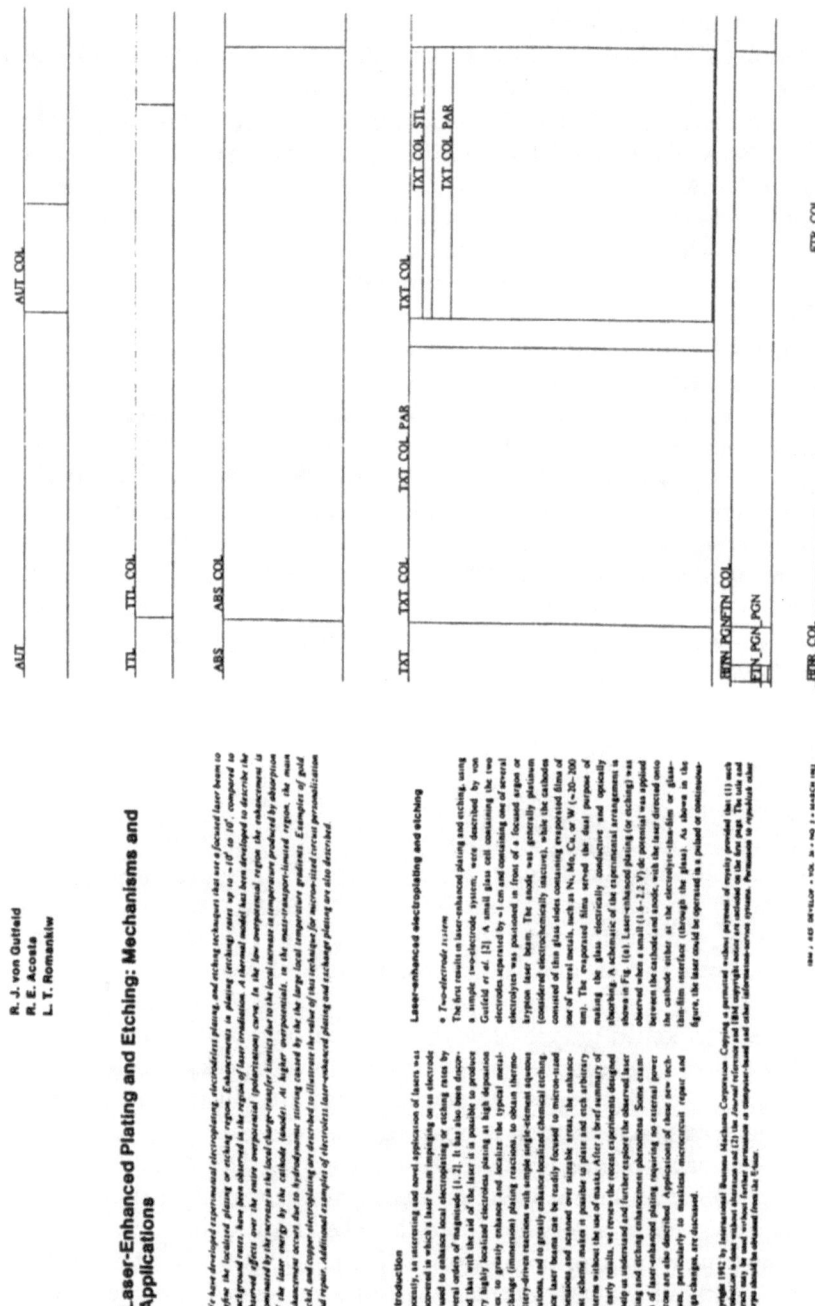

Fig. 5. IBM title page 1 from the test data (reduced photocopy) and X-Y tree (three levels). The page is fully labeled using the *exact parse* algorithm. A section-title and a subtitle are not identified.

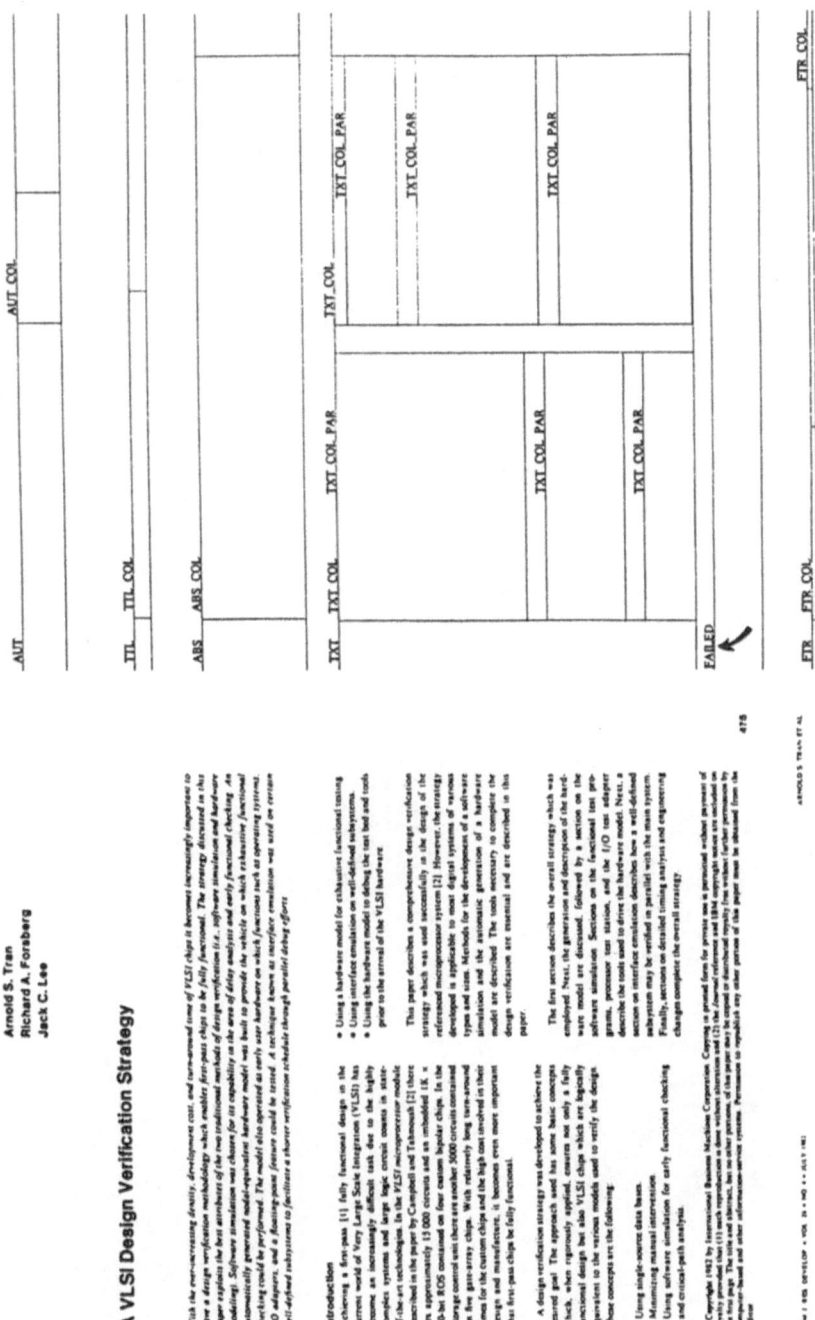

Fig. 6. IBM title page 2 from the test data (reduced photocopy) and X-Y tree (three levels). The *exact parse* algorithm failed because the footnote block could not be processed. The area labeled by the *maximum area* (94%) algorithm is shown.

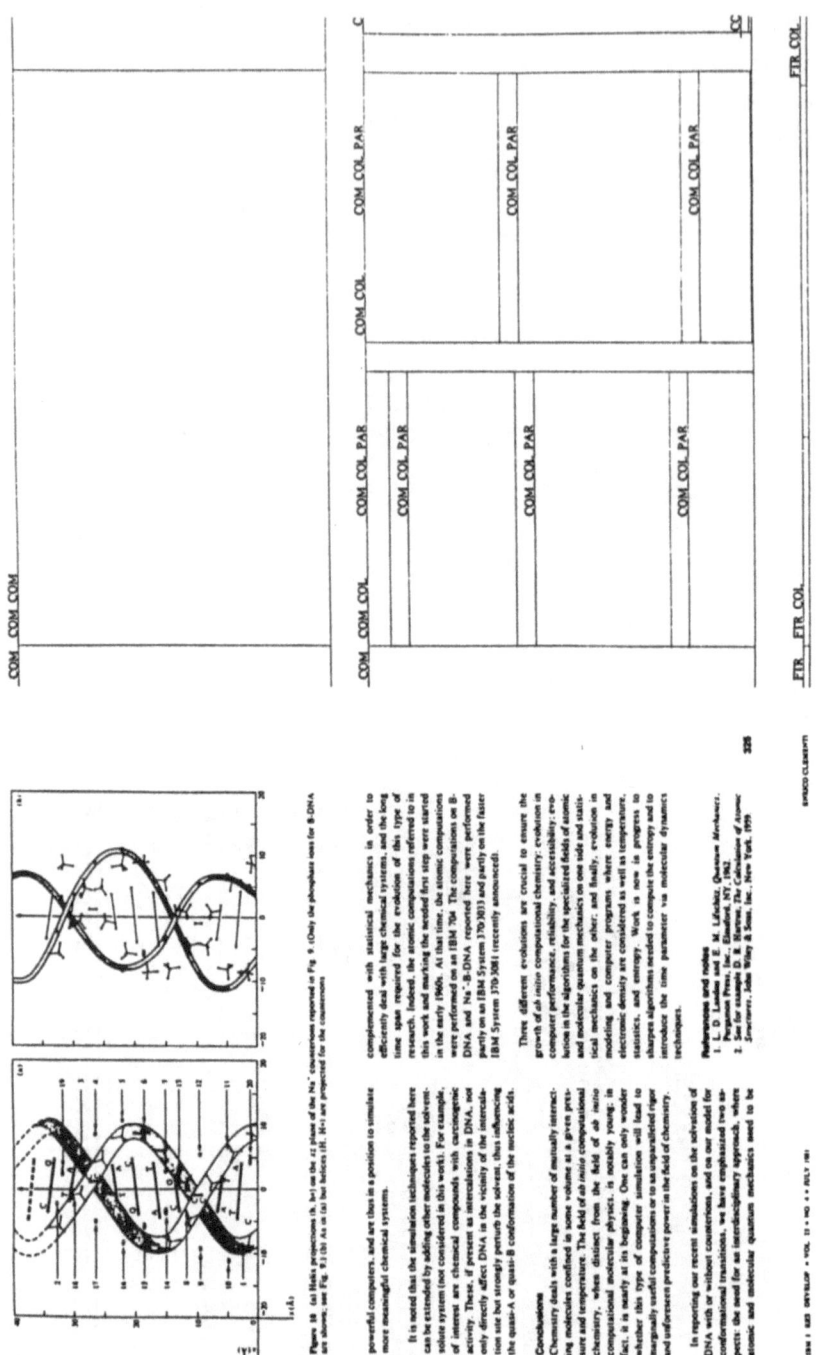

Fig. 7. IBM non-title page 1 from the test data (reduced photocopy) and X-Y tree (three levels). The page is fully labeled using the *exact parse* algorithm. Two section-titles remain unidentified.

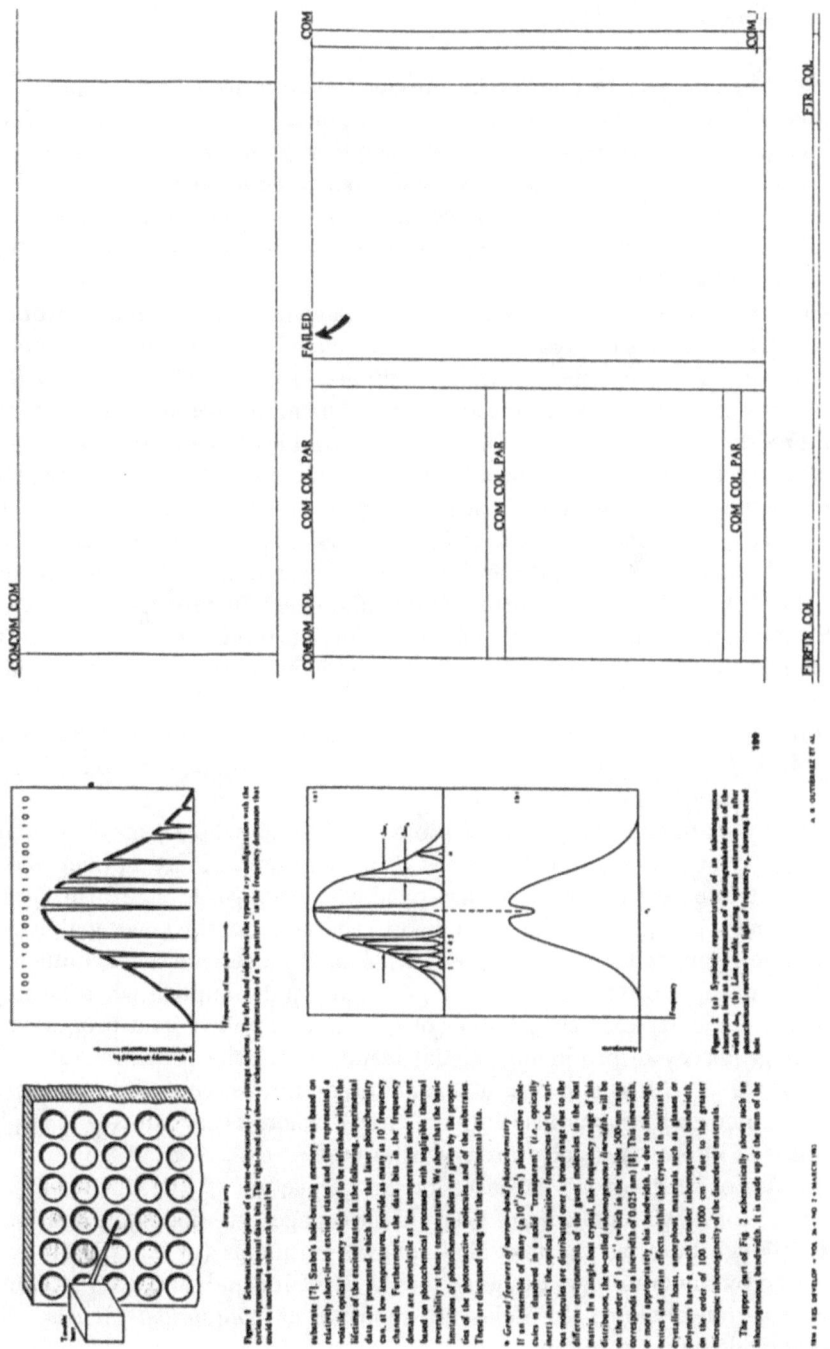

Fig. 8. IBM non-title page 2 from the test data (reduced photocopy) and X-Y tree (three levels). The *exact parse* algorithm failed because the right text column could not be processed. The area labeled by the *maximum area* (80%) algorithm is shown.

10 Discussion of Results

The experiments and results of the previous section are discussed here. A distinction between title and non-title pages is made in the design and construction of block-grammars. In algorithms using multiple grammars, the grammars for title and non-title pages are ordered (such that all title-page grammars precede all non-title-page grammars), and the grammar that successfully labels a document completely has to be the appropriate one. If a grammar fails, alternate grammars are applied.

The time required to process a document page increases with algorithm complexity and the number of blocks to be processed. The *Maximum Area* algorithm, which incorporates pruning to eliminate unnecessary search subtrees, executes more slowly than the *Exact Parse* algorithm. The number of blocks visited translates directly to the number of blocks whose profiles have to be calculated. As the first step in obtaining the profile of a each document block, the whole document image (approximately 1 Megabyte) is read from the hard disk. The average time spent by the system on this is 5.7 seconds. This means that in processing a page, about 1 minute is spent in just repeatedly reading the image repeatedly from the disk. At least two-thirds of the time spent in processing a document page is spent in obtaining the threshold projection profiles of blocks — 67% for *Maximum Area* and 77% for *Exact Parse*. (This is in spite of the fact that the C program for obtaining the threshold profile is optimized.)

Multiple grammars are used when more than one format exists for a document block, but it is most relevant in recovery from erroneous parses. The order in which block-grammars are arranged does not significantly alter the processing time for a document. The profile of a block (*e.g.*, the whole page) is calculated only once at any level even if a series of page-grammars are applied. So, if a title-page grammar fails (because the page was a non-title page), the profile is retained and the next grammar is applied to the same profile (saving almost 90% of the time required to process the block). Failed parses, however, induce more searches causing more node visits and grammars to be applied when backtracking occurs. This explains the number of grammars applied (and proportionally, the time required) in producing partial results using the *Maximum Area* algorithm (Table 2). But this is still a considerable improvement over an unpruned search method (which was also implemented), where every subtree is explored regardless of improved labeled area or otherwise.

The list of mislabelings is based on an inspection of the documents. The missed section-titles of the *IBM* Journal title pages are the same font size (9 point), though bold, as the text that follows. Formulas (or equations) are *not* recognized by the grammars designed for the *IBM* Journal, and are therefore not reported as mislabelings (formulas are reported as "*paragraphs*"). Also, figure blocks include figure captions.

Out of the 12 title and non-title pages that form the test data, 7 are fully labeled, *i.e.*, the *Exact Parse* algorithm labeled 100% of the area of each page. The missed blocks in the other 5 pages are two footnotes blocks, a page-number block and two text columns. The grammars for these blocks were not robust

Table 1. IBM title and non-title pages: grammars for the *exact parse* and *maximum area* algorithms. Table shows document entities and the number of grammars available to process each entity. Grammars used in resegmentation are also included. ("Composite" and "Paragraph" are abbreviated "Comp" and "Para" respectively.)

IBM Pages - Number of Block Grammars Exact Parse and Maximum Area Algorithms	
Document Blocks	**# Grammars**
Title: Page	3
Non-Title: Page	3
Title: Header	2
Title: Author	2
Title: Title	2
Title: Abstract	2
Title: Text	2
Non-Title: Composite (Comp)	4
Title: Footnotes	4
Title: Footer	2
Non-Title: Footer	2
Non-Title: Page-number	2
Title: Text_Column	2
Non-Title: Comp_Column	4
Title: Footnotes_Page-number	2
Non-Title: Comp_Page-number	2
Title: Text_Column_Para	1
Non-Title: Comp_Column_Para	1
Title: Text_Column_Para_First-line	1
Title: Text_Column_Para_Rest-of-Para	1
Non-Title: Comp_Column_Para_First-line	1
Non-Title: Comp_Column_Para_Rest-of-Para	1

Table 2. IBM title and non-title pages: statistics for the *exact parse* (EP) and *maximum area* (B&B) algorithms. The tables show the number of grammars applied (generated automatically from parameter tables), total number of labeled blocks (B&B), maximum area labeled (B&B), and processing time for each analyzed document. Documents that could not be parsed using a particular algorithm are indicated with an "F" (failure) in the Time column. ("Section-title," "Reference," "Column," and "Page-number" are abbreviated "SecT," "Ref," "Col," and "Pgn" respectively.)

No.	# Grammars Applied	Total # of Nodes	Mislabelings	Unprocessed Blocks	Area Labeled	Time (m:s) EP	Time (m:s) B&B
\multicolumn{8}{|c|}{IBM Title Pages - Parameter Table Grammars TEST Set: Exact Parse and Maximum Area Algorithms}							
1	12	20	*None*	*None*	100%	3:07	4:05
2	26	21	SecT	Footnotes_Pgn	99%	F	9:44
3	25	20	SecT (2)	Footnotes	94%	F	9:00
4	14	20	SecT (2)	*None*	100%	3:14	4:20
5	11	21	SecT	*None*	100%	2:57	3:53
6	35	20	SecT (2)	Footnotes	94%	F	12:24

No.	# Grammars Applied	Total # of Nodes	Mislabelings	Unprocessed Blocks	Area Labeled	Time (m:s) EP	Time (m:s) B&B
\multicolumn{8}{|c|}{IBM Non-title Pages - Parameter Table Grammars TEST Set: Exact Parse and Maximum Area Algorithms}							
1	12	18	SecT, Ref	*None*	100%	2:42	3:36
2	10	18	*None*	*None*	100%	2:40	3:28
3	23	14	SecT	Text Col-2	80%	F	7:24
4	15	18	SecT (2), Ref	*None*	100%	3:09	4:17
5	33	13	SecT	Text Col-1	66%	F	12:28
6	9	17	SecT (3)	*None*	100%	2:33	3:19

enough to parse them. The *Maximum Area* algorithm repeatedly analyzes almost the entire page in an effort to label the blocks left unlabeled in the first pass, thereby doubling the number of grammars applied using the *Exact Parse* algorithm (Table 2). Every test sample that is partially labeled had some portion of the search tree pruned.

From the three partially labeled title pages, we find that non-title-page grammars can parse title pages. In each case, the failure of any of the title-page grammars to improve upon the labeled area prompts the application of non-title-page grammars. The page is parsed at the top level but further parsing fails, leaving the labels assigned by the title-page grammars as the final labelings.

11 Conclusion and Further Work

A syntactic approach to document segmentation and labeling was presented. Publication-specific knowledge was represented in the form of block-grammars. A document page was hierarchically processed and only the most significant blocks were extracted at each level in the hierarchy. The extraction of document blocks for which no grammars have been constructed terminated the analysis of the document. Generation of grammars from parameter tables and multiple grammar analysis of document blocks were investigated.

Grammars were designed and constructed for only two publications. Analysis of the *IBM* Journal was first conducted. The process of extracting all the parameters for the various stages and writing down the grammars took about 3–4 months. On the other hand, the *PAMI* Journal, which came later, took a few weeks. Part of the reason was the design of a system to automatically generate grammars. This obviated the time-consuming process of manual grammar generation. But, another level of automation is called for in order to make dramatic improvements in the time taken to extract these parameters. A minimum number of observations must be made, but beyond that a supervised or unsupervised learning algorithm can aid the adaptation of the primitives in the parameter table.

Processing a document using one of the algorithms described in this thesis takes about 3 minutes. To warrant use in the real world, a significant speed-up is imperative. Solutions include implementing the profiler on a parallel machine. However, partitioning the data for allocation to the different processors is an overhead. Another solution could be the use of special purpose or custom-built chips. These should provide improvement in execution speed. Immediate and significant speed-up can be achieved by eliminating the repeated disk access required in loading a document image onto the computer main memory every time a block-profile is computed.

Block-grammars are predictable and extensible. Also, from a practical point of view, such an approach provides access to text, illustrations and formulas in a document page. By using the X-Y data structure in conjunction with this approach, the original layout of documents is preserved. This system can be used in combination with optical character recognition and remote browsing.

References

[Johnson 75]   S. C. Johnson, "Yacc : Yet Another Compiler-Compiler," Computing
                    Science Technical Report No. 32, AT&T Bell Laboratories, Murray
                    Hill, NJ, 1975.

[Kahan 87]   S. Kahan, T. Pavlidis, and H. S. Baird, "On the Recognition of
                    Printed Characters of any Font and Size," *IEEE Trans. on Pattern
                    Analysis and Machine Intelligence*, Vol. 9, No. 2, pp. 274–288, March
                    1987.

[Lesk 75]   M. E. Lesk, "Lex — A Lexical Analyzer Generator," Computing
                    Science Technical Report No. 39, AT&T Bell Laboratories, Murray
                    Hill, NJ, 1975.

[Nagy 89]   G. Nagy, "Document Analysis and Optical Character Recognition,"
                    In V. Cantoni, L. P. Cordella, S. Levialdi, and G. Sanniti di Baja
                    (eds.), *Proc. 5th Int'l Conf. on Image Analysis and Processing*, Posi-
                    tano, Italy, Sept. 1989, World Scientific, Singapore, pp. 511–529,
                    1990.

[Nagy 88]   G. Nagy, J. Kanai, M. S. Krishnamoorthy, M. Thomas, and M.
                    Viswanathan, "Two Complementary Techniques for Digitized Doc-
                    ument Analysis," *Proc. First ACM Conf. on Document Processing
                    Systems*, Santa Fe, NM, pp. 169–176, Dec. 1988.

[Nagy 84]   G. Nagy and S. Seth, "Hierarchical Representation Of Optically
                    Scanned Documents," *Proc. 7th ICPR*, Montreal, Canada, 1, pp.
                    347–349, 1984.

[Viswanathan 88]   M. Viswanathan, and M. S. Krishnamoorthy, "A Syntactic Ap-
                    proach to Document Segmentation," *Proc. IAPR Workshop on
                    Structural and Syntactic Pattern Recognition*, Pont-a-Mousson,
                    France, pp. 148–165, Sept. 1988.

[Viswanathan 89]   M. Viswanathan, and M. S. Krishnamoorthy, "A Syntactic Ap-
                    proach to Document Segmentation," In R. Mohr, T. Pavlidis, and A.
                    Sanfeliu (eds.), *Structural Pattern Analysis*, World Scientific, Singa-
                    pore, pp. 197–215, 1989 (revision of [Viswanathan 88]).

[Viswanathan 90]   M. Viswanathan, *A Syntactic Approach to Document Segmentation
                    and Labeling*, Doctoral Thesis, Dept Electrical, Computer, and Sys-
                    tems Engineering, Rensselaer Polytechnic Institute, Troy, NY, Oc-
                    tober 1990.

Character and Symbol Recognition

Structural Analysis and Description of Curves by Quasi-Topological Features and Singular Points

Hirobumi Nishida and Shunji Mori

RICOH Research and Development Center, 16–1 Shin-ei-cho, Kohoku-ku, Yokohama, Kanagawa 223, Japan

We propose a compact and concise description method of curves in terms of the quasi-topological features and the structure of each singular point. By quasi-topological features, we mean the convexity, loop, and connectivity. The quasi-topological structure is analyzed in a hierarchical way, and algebraic structure is presented explicitly on each representation level. The lower-level representations are integrated into the higher-level one in the systematic way. When a curve has singular points (branch points), the curve is decomposed into components each of which is a simple arc or a simple closed curve by decomposing each singular point. The description scheme is applied to character recognition.

1 Introduction

Structural pattern recognition comes from the idea to describe a complex pattern in terms of a hierarchical composition of simpler subpatterns [1]. The key to realize this attractive idea of structural pattern recognition consists in selection of the pattern primitives and the rules (grammars [2]) of composition of primitives into the higher-level representation.

A number of authors have considered the class of *thin line pictures* and have proposed various methods for describing such patterns in terms of structural models [3]. The grammar for describing the chromosome [4] is a representative work in the early days. A pioneer of the high-order pattern grammars is Shaw [5], who introduced the concepts of *head* and *tail*, and the binary operators +, ×, −, and * explicitly. However, selection of primitives is not addressed explicitly, and we find a problem of how the primitives and the relations of primitives are composed into the higher-level representation of the shape in the hierarchical and structural information tree.

Mori [6] proposes the *primitive sequence* to give an answer to this problem. This approach tries to integrate local features (primitives) into global features (primitive sequences) and ignore local deformation by capturing global features of the shape. However, since the primitive is defined in terms of quasi-convex functions [7], which are complex compared to monotone functions, it is complicated to construct primitive sequences. Furthermore, the description is ambiguous, because no structural relationship is defined on primitive sequences. Thus, we find the following criteria for structural description of curves:

Criterion 1 *Primitives are simple enough to be computed easily. (See the criteria for primitive selection of Pavlidis [3].)*

Criterion 2 *Algebraic structure is introduced to higher-level representation (global feature) as well as to lower-level.*

Mori [8, 9] also propose an algebraic system in terms of primitives of monotone functions (L-type primitives) and binary operations on primitives. The primitives can be computed easily, but they are defined for contours on a discrete image plane. For instance, the curve shown in Figure 5(d) cannot be represented by Mori's scheme. Furthermore, since the shape is represented by a string of primitives and local operations on primitives, it is not clear what kind of global feature is described by Mori's scheme. Thus, the following criteria should be considered:

Criterion 3 *Systematic rules are presented to integrate local features into global description, and it should be clear what kind of global feature is described by the description scheme.*

Criterion 4 *Any continuous curves can be represented by the description scheme.*

For Criteria 1 and 4, Jakubowski [10, 11] proposes a quantitative and explicit composition of primitives for simple curves. The primitives are defined in terms of axial and sloped straight line segments, and convex and concave segments. An xy-monotone curve is defined as a composition of the primitives, and a transducer is given to extract concatenations of monotone curves. Moreover, a chain of monotone curves is characterized by the components (*key*) and the length (*order*). However, the global structure of the curve is not analyzed in terms of the algebraic structure of the set of keys and orders. Therefore, no solution for Criteria 2 and 3 is given by Jakubowski. Few methods satisfy these four criteria (see [12, 13]), although a key to compact and concise description of shape lies in Criteria 2 and 3.

On the other hand, shape description methods should be applicable to practical problems. Character recognition is a good application of shape description. Mori [6, 14] classifies shape description techniques in OCR into two groups:

(1) Geometrical feature representation,
(2) Quasi-topological feature representation.

Geometrical feature representation techniques describe the shape in terms of line segments and singular points such as branching and crossing [15]. Such features as singular points are intuitively appealing, but high-quality thinning methods need be developed in practice. Furthermore, since curves are poorly represented by a series of vectors in prototypes (models), it is necessary to apply dynamic programming techniques [16] or graph distance measures for attributed relational graphs [17] in matching of prototypes and objects. However, they have heavy computational complexities, and the matching does not always give reasonable results because it is sensitive to definition of heuristic cost functions.

On the other hand, Mori's description scheme [8] is an instance of quasi-topological ones. The character shape is described by background or contours features, and curves are represented flexibly by loops or convexity (concavity). Analysis of such features is easier than development of high-quality thinning methods, but background or contour features are sometimes counterintuitive. Therefore, the two techniques are complementary, so another criterion is given here from the viewpoint of practical application.

Criterion 5 *Geometrical and quasi-topological feature representation are integrated.*

It has been thought that shape description should be invariant to coordinate transformations, namely rotation, size, and translation. However, when we address shape description for pattern analysis and recognition, objects in the real world are so complex that we need to put some constraints on invariance. Otherwise, shape analysis and description would be too complicated to be applied to practical problems. Furthermore, strict invariance causes side effects in some applications. For instance, rotation invariance will cause confusion of '6' and '9', 'M' and 'W', and so on. Therefore, we address only size and translation invariance in this paper, because our main application is document image analysis.

Criterion 6 *The shape description is size and translation invariant.*

This paper presents a method for structural and hierarchical description of curves satisfying Criteria 1 through 6. In Section 2, we introduce analysis and description of quasi-topological structure of simple arcs or simple closed curves. By quasi-topological features, we mean the convexity, loop, and connectivity. In Section 3 we analyze and describe structure of general curves with singular points (branch points). The reader will find that a new description method given here satisfies Criteria 1 through 6. In Section 4, we show that closed curves have the specific structure in terms of our description scheme. Furthermore, in Section 5, we mention an application of the description scheme to character recognition, showing the experimental results on hand-printed numerals. All the proofs for theorems are given in the appendices.

2 Quasi-Topological Structure of Curves

In this section, we consider description of the quasi-topological structure of curves. We assume that the curve is a simple arc or a simple closed curve. From Criterion 6, the description depends on only directions of the coordinate axes.

In this paper, we take the coordinate system as shown in Figure 2: the x-axis goes from the left to the right horizontally, and the y-axis from the bottom to the top vertically.

Figure 1 and Figure 14 are a flow chart and a hierarchical diagram of analysis and description of quasi-topological structure of curves. In Figure 1, the items in boxes are the objects on each representation level, and the ones in ellipses are the operations on the objects. The arrows in Figure 1 mean that the higher-level representation is given by applying the operations to objects on the lower-level. First, the four classes of curve primitives are defined explicitly (Section 2.1). Each primitive has the two end points called *head* and *tail*, and a primitive can be concatenated to others only at its head or tail. The four types of binary operations on the primitives are defined by classifying the concatenations of primitives according to the direction of convexity (2.2). We show that the operators have algebraic properties explicitly (2.3). Next, the primitive sequences are generated by linking the binary operations of primitives. A label is given to each primitive sequence according to the properties of the primitives and their concatenations forming the sequence (2.4). A primitive sequence can be connected with others by sharing its first or last primitive. In other words, two binary operations are introduced to primitive sequences. Moreover, we show that the operations can be applied only if the labels of the two primitive sequences satisfy the specific relations (2.5). Finally, the quasi-topological structure of a curve is described by a string of primitive sequences (2.6).

2.1 Primitives of Curves

The xy-monotone curve is a curve whose x and y values are either non-increasing or non-decreasing as one traverses the curve. Let the two end points of an xy-monotone curve be $H (x_0, y_0)$ and $T (x_1, y_1)$, where H and T are determined in such a way that $x_0 < x_1$ if $x_0 \neq x_1$, and $y_0 < y_1$ if $x_0 = x_1$. The point H is called the *head* of the curve, and T is the *tail*. The xy-monotone curve is classified according to the order relation of the x and y coordinates of the head and the tail.

(1) $x_0 < x_1$ and $y_0 = y_1$ (denoted by ' $-$ ' below and illustrated in Figure 2(a))
(2) $x_0 < x_1$ and $y_0 < y_1$ (' $/$ ', in Figure 2(b))
(3) $x_0 = x_1$ and $y_0 < y_1$ (' $|$ ', in Figure 2(c))
(4) $x_0 < x_1$ and $y_0 > y_1$ (' $\backslash$ ', in Figure 2(d))

The primitives of curves are defined as these four classes of xy-monotone curves.

Example 2.1 Figure 3 illustrates decomposition of curves into primitives. *A2, A4, B0, B2, C0, C2, C4,* and *C6* are primitives of the type ' $/$ ', and the others ' $\backslash$ '.   □

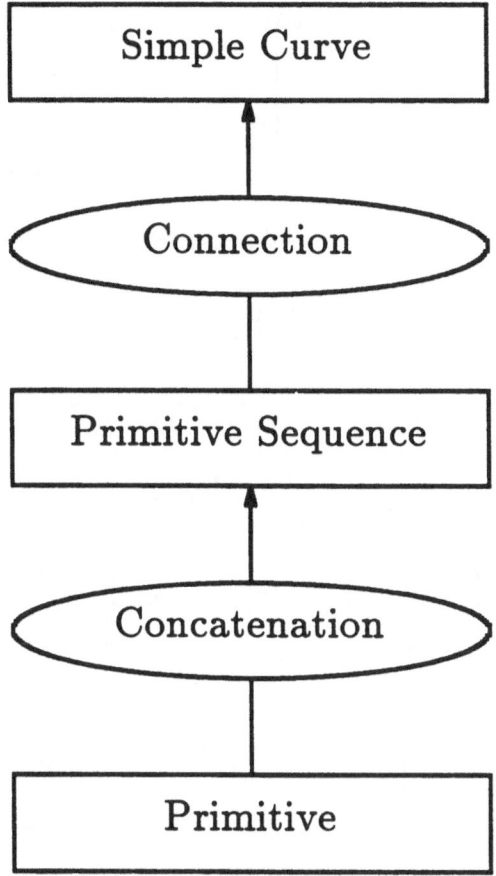

Fig. 1. Analysis of quasi-topological structure of curves. The items in boxes are the objects on each representation level, and the ones in ellipses are the operations on the objects.

2.2 Concatenation Operators of Primitives

We define the binary operators of the primitives. Following Shaw's scheme [5], we assume that a primitive can be concatenated to others only at its head or tail. Furthermore, we assume that a curve formed by a concatenation of two primitives is not a primitive (an xy-monotone curve) any more. Before introducing the binary operators, we define some notations and functions.

Definition 1 $\Delta(a, b)$, where a and b are primitives. Suppose that two primitives a and b are concatenated. Let P be a point in the intersection of a and b, and let P_a and P_b be points sufficiently close to P such that P_a and P_b are contained in only a and only b respectively. $\Delta(a, b)$ is defined as

$$\Delta(a, b) = sign \begin{vmatrix} x_a - x_p & x_b - x_p \\ y_a - y_p & y_b - y_p \end{vmatrix}, \tag{1}$$

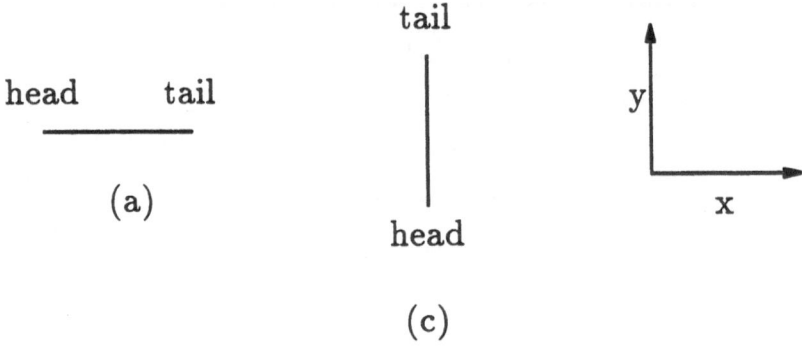

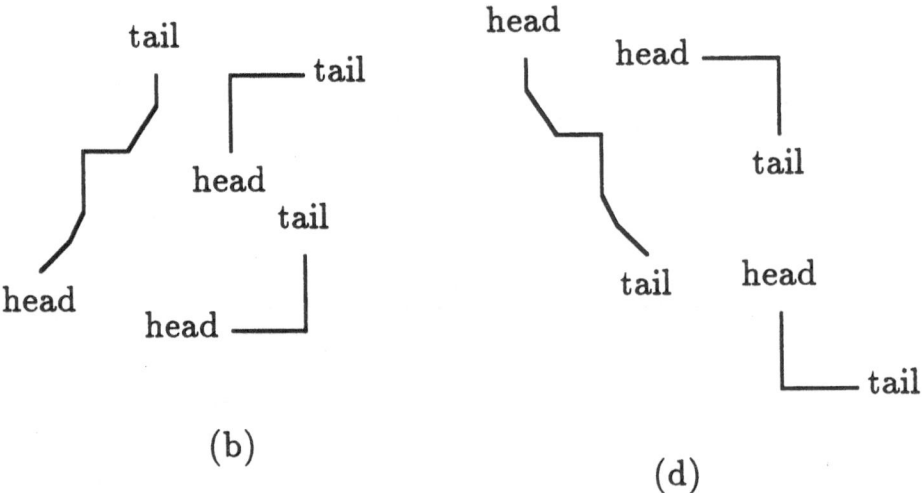

Fig. 2. Four types of curve primitives. (a) : ' — ', (b) : ' / ', (c) : ' | ', (d) : ' \ '.

$$\text{sign } x = \begin{cases} -1 & \text{if } x < 0 \\ 0 & \text{if } x = 0 \\ 1 & \text{if } x > 0 \end{cases}$$

where (x_p, y_p), (x_a, y_a), and (x_b, y_b) are the coordinates of P, P_a, and P_b respectively.   □

Definition 2 $prm(a)$, where a is a primitive. $prm(a)$ denotes the primitive type of a. $prm(a) \in \{ | , / , - , \backslash \}$.   □

Definition 3 $[\, a, A, \alpha \; ; \; b, B, \beta \,]$, where a and b are two primitives, $A = prm(a)$, $B = prm(b)$, and $\alpha, \beta \in \{head, tail\}$. $[\, a, A, \alpha \; ; \; b, B, \beta \,]$ means that primitives a ($prm(a) = A$) and b ($prm(b) = B$) are concatenated at α of a and β of b in such a way that $\Delta(a, b) = 1$ (see Figure 4).   □

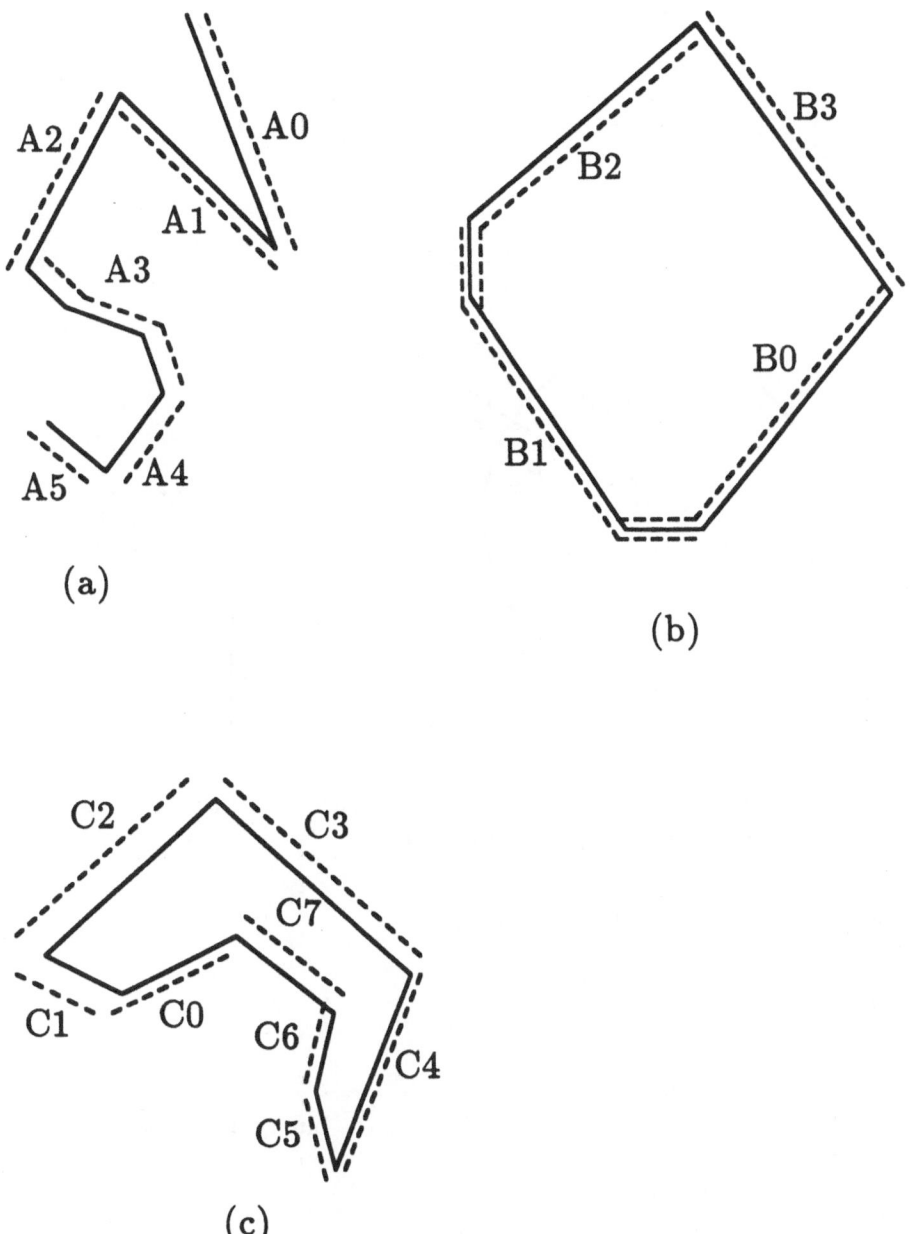

Fig. 3. Decomposition of curves into primitives. , A4, B0, B2, C0, C2, C4, and C6 are primitives of the type ' / ', and the others ' \ '.

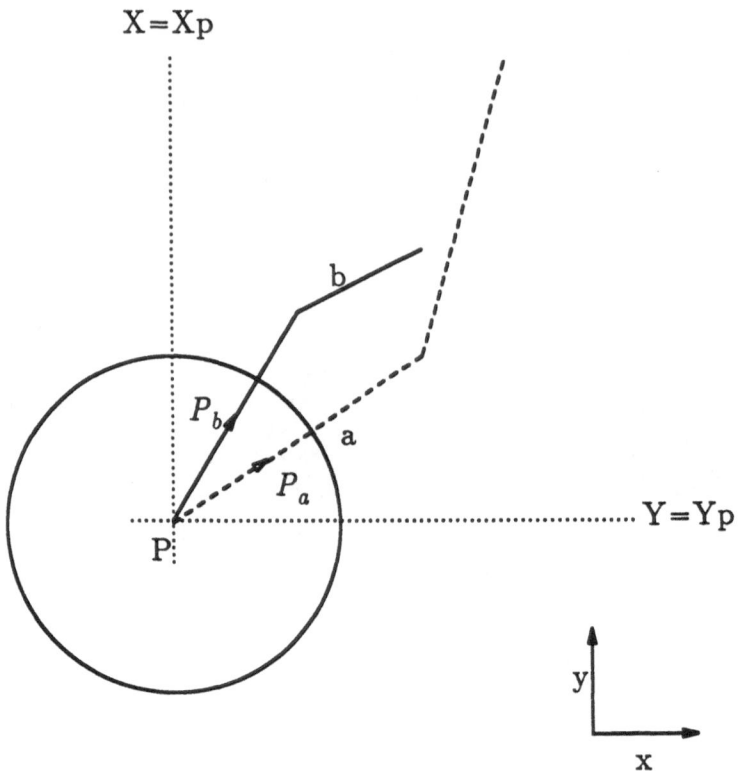

Fig. 4. Two primitives a and b are concatenated in such a way that the pair of vectors (PP_a, PP_b) constitutes the right-hand system.

Definition 4 $\overline{\alpha}$, where $\alpha \in \{head, tail\}$.

$$\overline{\alpha} = \begin{cases} tail & if\ \alpha = head \\ head & if\ \alpha = tail \end{cases} \tag{2}$$

$\square$

Now, for two primitives a and b, we define the binary operations

$$a \xrightarrow{j} b, \quad j = 0, 1, 2, 3, \tag{3}$$

where j is the characteristic number of the operator and denotes the direction of convexity formed by the concatenation of primitives. Note that the operation (3) is not compatible with

$$b \xrightarrow{j} a,$$

and that two primitives a and b satisfy $\Delta(a, b) = 1$ as shown in Figure 4. The operation (3) is defined for each type of concatenation of primitives by the following rules:

Rule 1 (Downward convex)

$$a \xrightarrow{\ 0\ } b$$

for

(a) [a, /, *head* ; b, \, *tail*],
(b) [a, |, *head* ; b, \, *tail*],
(c) [a, /, *head* ; b, |, *head*],
(d) [a, /, *head* ; b, /, *head*].

They are illustrated in Figure 5.

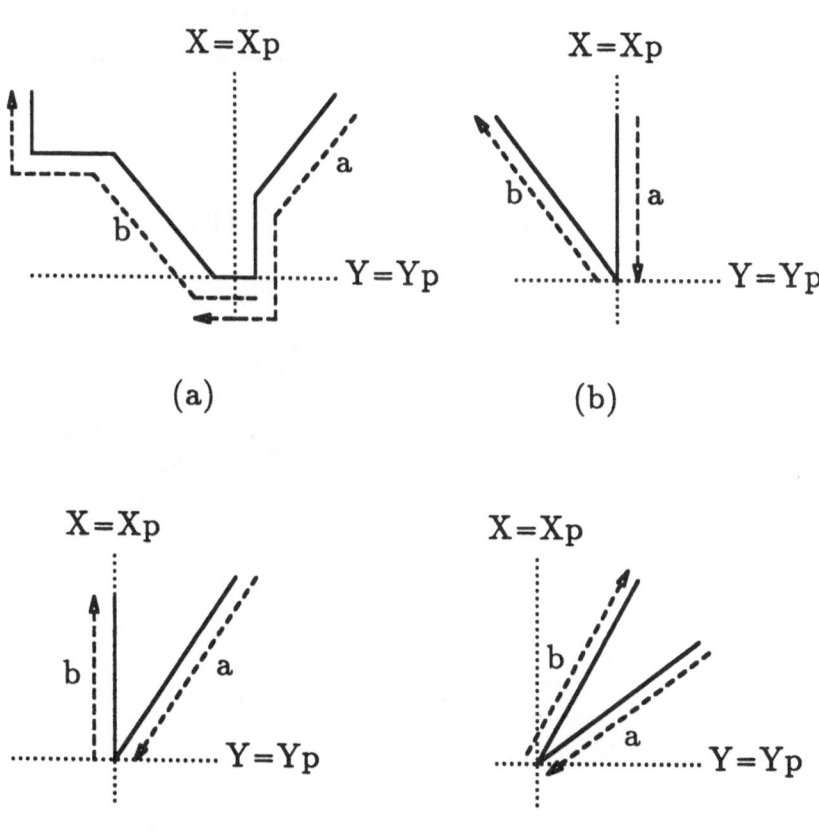

Fig. 5. Illustrations of the concatenation '0'.

Rule 2 (Leftward convex)

$$a \xrightarrow{\ 1\ } b$$

for

(a) $[\, a, \; \backslash, \; head \; ; \; b, \; /, \; head \,]$,
(b) $[\, a, \; -, \; head \; ; \; b, \; /, \; head \,]$,
(c) $[\, a, \; \backslash, \; head \; ; \; b, \; -, \; head \,]$,
(d) $[\, a, \; \backslash, \; head \; ; \; b, \; \backslash, \; head \,]$

They are illustrated in Figure 6.

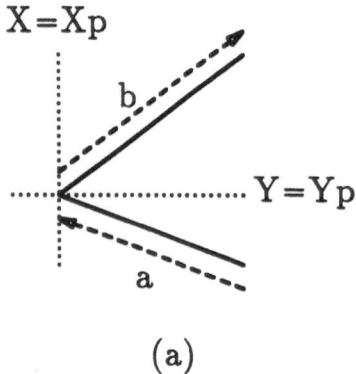

(a)

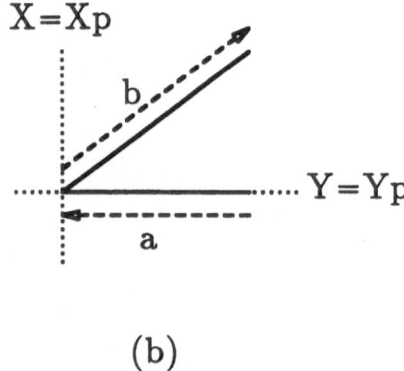

(b)

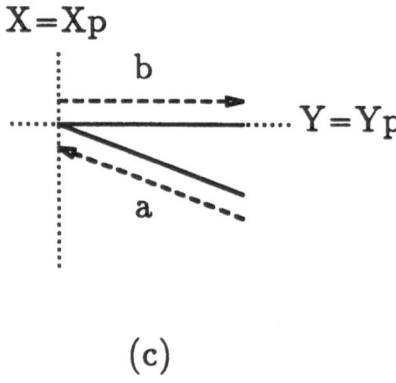

(c)

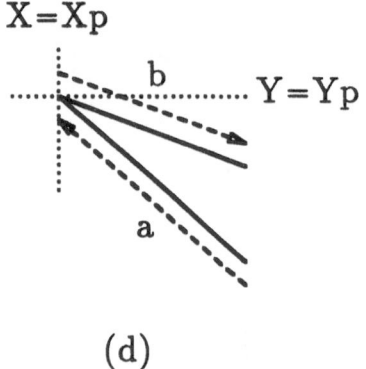

(d)

Fig. 6. Illustrations of the concatenation '1'.

Rule 3 (Upward convex)

$$a \xrightarrow{\;2\;} b$$

for

(a) $[\, a, \; /, \; tail \; ; \; b, \; \backslash, \; head \,]$,
(b) $[\, a, \; |, \; tail \; ; \; b, \; \backslash, \; head \,]$,
(c) $[\, a, \; /, \; tail \; ; \; b, \; |, \; tail \,]$,
(d) $[\, a, \; /, \; tail \; ; \; b, \; /, \; tail \,]$.

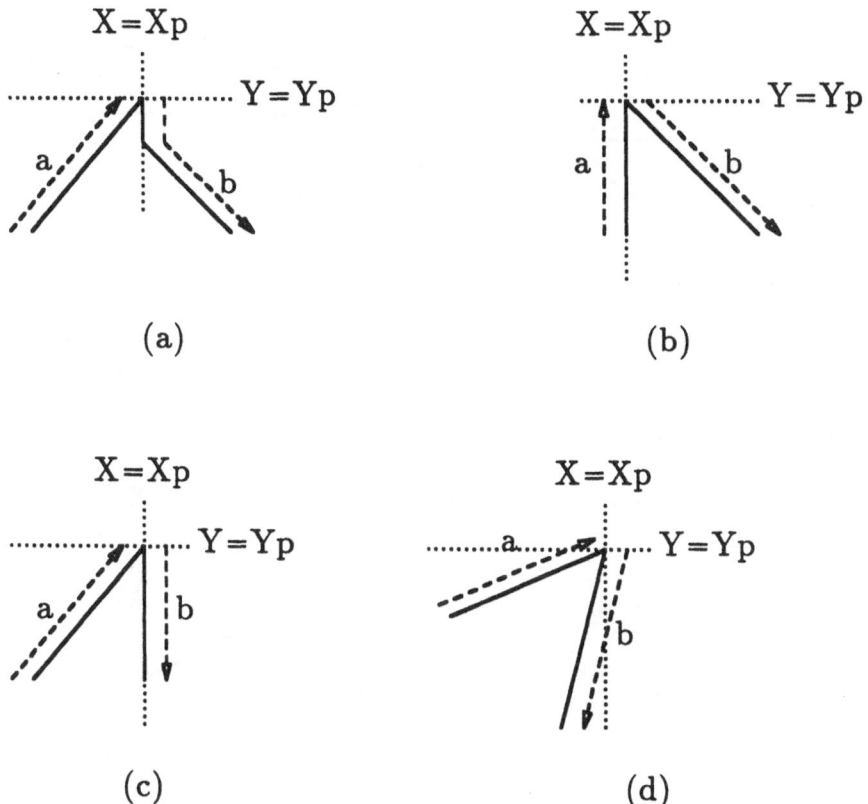

Fig. 7. Illustrations of the concatenation '2'.

They are illustrated in Figure 7.

Rule 4 (Rightward convex)

$$a \xrightarrow{3} b$$

for

(a) [a, \, *tail* ; b, /, *tail*],
(b) [a, −, *tail* ; b, /, *tail*],
(c) [a, \, *tail* ; b, −, *tail*],
(d) [a, \, *tail* ; b, \, *tail*]

They are illustrated in Figure 8.

Rule 1, 2, 3, and 4 correspond to downward, leftward, upward, and rightward convexity, respectively. In other words, the directions of convexity have correspondence to elements of the set $\{0, 1, 2, 3\}$. In the following, we will show that

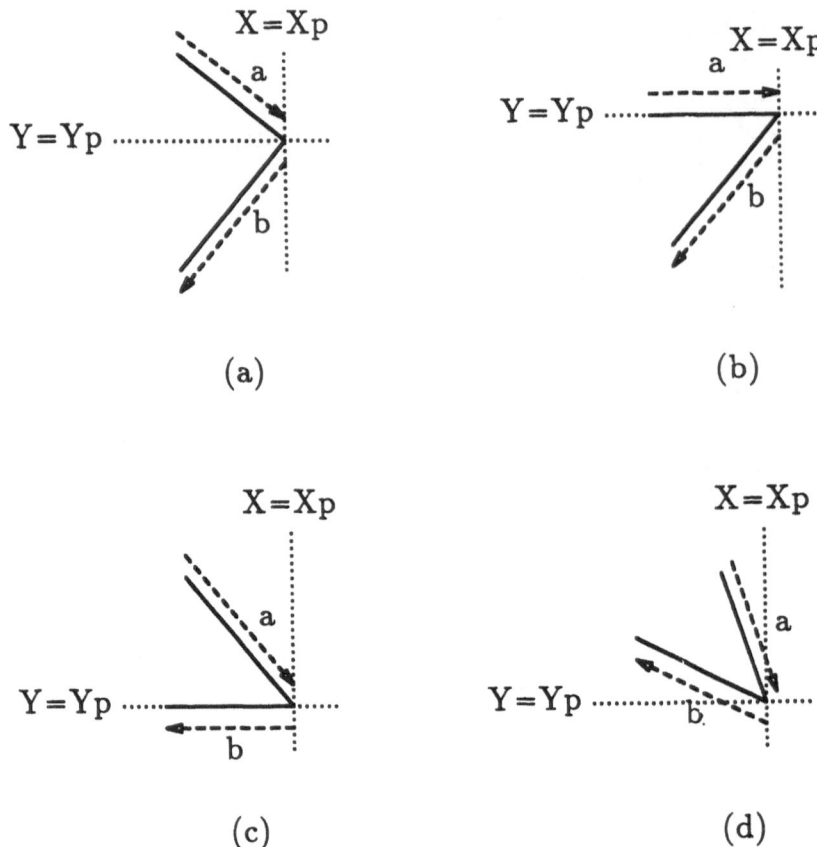

(a)   (b)

(c)   (d)

Fig. 8. Illustrations of the concatenation '3'.

structure of curves with complex shape is represented in terms of simple arithmetic operations on the set $Z/(4)$, which is the residue-class system of integer with respect to 4. In addition, Table 1 summarizes these four rules.

Remark 1 When two primitives of the types ' / ' and ' \ ' are concatenated ([a, /, $head$; b, \, $tail$], [a, \, $head$; b, /, $head$], [a, /, $tail$; b, \, $head$], and [a, \, $tail$; b, /, $tail$]), the intersection of the primitives can be a horizontal or vertical line segment instead of a single point, as shown in Figure 3(b) and Figure 5(a). In the other cases, the intersection of the two primitives is always a single point.   □

Example 2.2 We apply the binary operations to the primitives in Figure 3 as follows:

$$A0 \xrightarrow{3} A1, \ A2 \xrightarrow{2} A1, \ A3 \xrightarrow{1} A2, \ A3 \xrightarrow{3} A4, \ A4 \xrightarrow{0} A5;$$
$$B0 \xrightarrow{0} B1, \ B1 \xrightarrow{1} B2, \ B2 \xrightarrow{2} B3, \ B3 \xrightarrow{3} B0;$$

$$C0 \xrightarrow{0} C1, \ C1 \xrightarrow{1} C2, \ C2 \xrightarrow{2} C3, \ C3 \xrightarrow{3} C4,$$

$$C4 \xrightarrow{0} C5, \ C5 \xrightarrow{1} C6, \ C7 \xrightarrow{3} C6, \ C0 \xrightarrow{2} C7.$$

□

Table 1. Concatenation rules of two primitives.

j	a	b	a	b	a	b	a	b
0	/h	\t	h	\t	/h	h	/h	/h
1	\h	/h	−h	/h	\h	−h	\h	\h
2	/t	\h	t	\h	/t	t	/t	/t
3	\t	/t	−t	/t	\t	−t	\t	\t

2.3 Algebraic Properties of Concatenation Operators

We have defined the binary operations

$$a \xrightarrow{j} b, \quad j = 0, 1, 2, 3$$

for primitives a and b. Now, we show the properties of the concatenation operators, from which we will derive algebraic properties of the higher-level representation of the curve structure.

Definition 5 $corner(a \xrightarrow{i} b)$, where a and b are two primitives, and $i \in \{0, 1, 2, 3\}$.

$$corner(a \xrightarrow{i} b) = \begin{cases} 1 & if \ prm(a) = prm(b), \\ 0 & otherwise. \end{cases} \tag{4}$$

□

Let a, b, and c be primitives, and let i and $j \in \{0, 1, 2, 3\}$ be the characteristic numbers of the operators. The concatenation operator has algebraic properties as follows:

Property 1 If

$$a \xrightarrow{i} b, \ a \xrightarrow{j} c,$$

then

$$i - j \equiv 2 \ (mod \ 4).$$

Property 2 If

$$a \xrightarrow{i} b, \ c \xrightarrow{j} b,$$

then

$$i + corner(a \xrightarrow{i} b) \equiv j + corner(c \xrightarrow{j} b) + 2 \ (mod \ 4).$$

Property 3 If

$$a \xrightarrow{i} b, \ b \xrightarrow{j} c \ (prm(b) \in \{ \ / \ , \ \backslash \ \}),$$

then

$$j \equiv i + corner(a \xrightarrow{i} b) + 1 \ (mod \ 4).$$

Property 4 If

$$a \xrightarrow{i} b, \ b \xrightarrow{j} c \ (prm(b) \in \{ \ | \ , \ - \ \}),$$

then

$$j - i \equiv 2 \ (mod \ 4).$$

Figure 9 illustrates these properties:

(a) $a \xrightarrow{2} b, \ a \xrightarrow{0} c$;
(b) $a \xrightarrow{2} b, \ c \xrightarrow{0} b$;
(c) $a \xrightarrow{1} b, \ b \xrightarrow{2} c \ (prm(b) = \ / \ )$;
(d) $a \xrightarrow{0} b, \ b \xrightarrow{2} c \ (prm(b) = \ | \ )$.

2.4 Primitive Sequence of Curves

For a simple arc or a simple closed curve, we can cover the curve with the minimum number of primitives, and apply the concatenation operators to each pair of the primitives. By linking the binary operations on primitives, the following sequence is generated:

$$a_0 \xrightarrow{j_1} a_1 \xrightarrow{j_2} \cdots \xrightarrow{j_{n-1}} a_{n-1} \xrightarrow{j_n} a_n. \tag{5}$$

The sequence (5) is called the *primitive sequence*. In the following, we give a label to the primitive sequence according to the properties of the primitives and their concatenations.

When a curve consists of two primitives or more and the primitive sequence on the curve is not infinitely cyclic, it is decomposed into primitive sequences (5), where there exists neither b nor c such that

$$b \xrightarrow{j_0} a_0 \ (j_0 = 0, 1, 2, or \ 3),$$

$$a_n \xrightarrow{j_{n+1}} c \ (j_{n+1} = 0, 1, 2, or \ 3).$$

In addition, the end points of the primitive sequence on the primitives a_0 and a_n are called the *h-point* and the *t-point* respectively. Since any operation of two primitives

$$a \xrightarrow{*} b$$

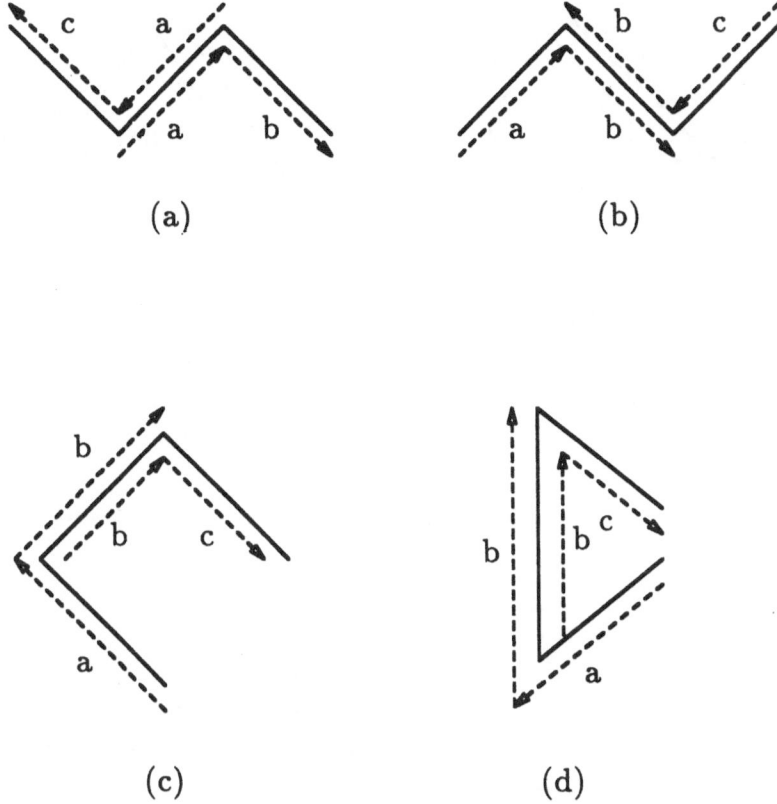

Fig. 9. Illustrations of properties of concatenations of primitives.

satisfies $\Delta(a, b) = 1$, we always turn to the right at any joints of primitives when we traverse a curve composed of one primitive sequence from the h-point to the t-point (see Figure 9(c), 9(d), and Figure 10).

The label of the primitive sequence, *PS-label* for short, $\langle ps, idr \rangle$ is given to the sequence (5) composed of $n + 1$ primitives by the following formulae:

$$ps = (n + 1) + L + M, \tag{6}$$

$$idr = j_1, \tag{7}$$

where L is the number of concatenations

$$a_i \xrightarrow{j_{i+1}} a_{i+1} \ (i = 0, 1, \ldots, n - 1)$$

such that $prm(a_i) = prm(a_{i+1})$, and M is the number of a_i $(i = 1, 2, \ldots, n-1)$ such that $prm(a_i) \in \{\ |\ ,\ -\ \}$.

Figure 10 shows instances of curves with the PS-label $\langle 5, 0 \rangle$. In the figure, h and t denote the h-point and the t-point of the primitive sequence, respectively. The curves shown in Figure 10(a), 10(b), 10(c) and 10(d) are examples of $L = M = 0$, $L = 1$, $L = 2$, and $M = 1$, respectively.

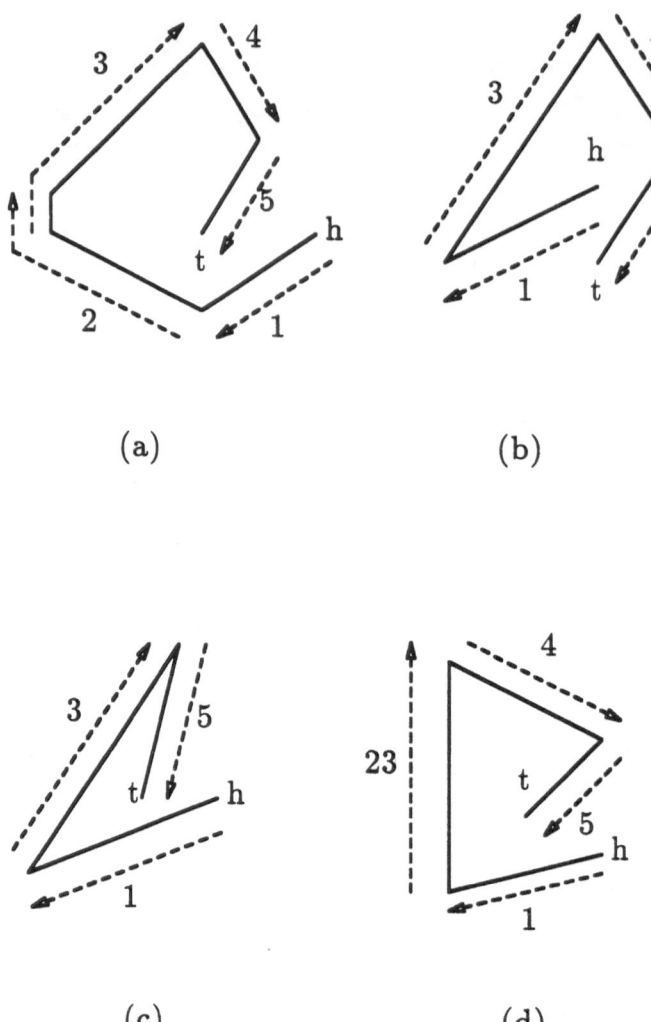

(a)   (b)

(c)   (d)

Fig. 10. Instances of curves with the PS-label $\langle 5,0 \rangle$, where 'h' and 't' denote h-point and t-point respectively: (a) $L = M = 0$; (b) $L = 1$, $M = 0$; (c) $L = 2$, $M = 0$; (d) $L = 0$, $M = 1$.

idr denotes the initial direction of the rotation. The meaning of *ps* can be interpreted in the following way: If $L = M = 0$ (Figure 10(a)), then ' / ' and ' \ ' appear alternately in the primitive sequence:

$$1 \xrightarrow{0} 2 \xrightarrow{1} 3 \xrightarrow{2} 4 \xrightarrow{3} 5.$$

When $prm(a_i) = prm(a_{i+1})$ (Figure 10(b) and 10(c)), one ' \ ' (' / ') is thought to be skipped between a_i and a_{i+1} because of an excessive change of the direction of the curve. For instance, if the primitive '2' on the curve in Figure 10(a) gets smaller and smaller, then it is finally removed and we get the curve in Figure 10(b):

$$1 \xrightarrow{0} 3 \xrightarrow{2} 4 \xrightarrow{3} 5.$$

Moreover, we get the curve in Figure 10(c) by removing the primitive '4' from the curve in Figure 10(b):

$$1 \xrightarrow{0} 3 \xrightarrow{2} 5.$$

Similarly, when $prm(a_i) \in \{ \, | \, , \, - \, \}$ (Figure 10(d)), ' / ' and ' \ ' are thought to be merged into ' | ' or ' − '. For example, if we collapse the primitives '2' and '3' in Figure 10(a), then they are finally merged into '23' in Figure 10(d):

$$1 \xrightarrow{0} 23 \xrightarrow{2} 4 \xrightarrow{3} 5.$$

Thus, it is reasonable to add L and M to the number of the primitives a_i so that ps is invariant in such variations. This argument is formalized by the following theorem:

Theorem 1 *For $n \geq 2$,*

$$ps - 2 = \sum_{i=1}^{n-1}\left\{(j_{i+1} - j_i) \ (mod \ 4)\right\} + corner(a_{n-1} \xrightarrow{j_n} a_n). \tag{8}$$

When the primitive sequence is infinitely cyclic on a simple closed curve as

$$\cdots \xrightarrow{j_{n-1}} a_{n-1} \xrightarrow{j_n} a_n \xrightarrow{j_0} a_0 \xrightarrow{j_1} a_1 \xrightarrow{j_2} \cdots \xrightarrow{j_n} a_n \xrightarrow{j_0} a_0 \xrightarrow{j_1} \cdots, \tag{9}$$

the PS-label $\langle 0, 0 \rangle$ is given to the curve.

When a curve is composed of one primitive, the PS-label is given to the curve in the following way: $\langle 1, 0 \rangle$ for ' − ', $\langle 1, 1 \rangle$ for ' / ', $\langle 1, 2 \rangle$ for ' | ', and $\langle 1, 3 \rangle$ for ' \ '.

Example 2.3 By linking the binary operations in Example 2.2, the following primitive sequences are generated:

$$E_1 : A0 \xrightarrow{3} A1 \quad \langle 3, 3 \rangle \ (prm(A0) = prm(A1) = \ \backslash \ ),$$

$$E_2 : A3 \xrightarrow{1} A2 \xrightarrow{2} A1 \quad \langle 3, 1 \rangle,$$

$$E_3 : A3 \xrightarrow{3} A4 \xrightarrow{0} A5 \quad \langle 3, 3 \rangle,$$

$$E_4 : \cdots \xrightarrow{2} B3 \xrightarrow{3} B0 \xrightarrow{0} B1 \xrightarrow{1} B2 \xrightarrow{2} B3 \xrightarrow{3} B0 \xrightarrow{0} \cdots \quad \langle 0, 0 \rangle,$$

$$E_5 : C0 \xrightarrow{0} C1 \xrightarrow{1} C2 \xrightarrow{2} C3 \xrightarrow{3} C4 \xrightarrow{0} C5 \xrightarrow{1} C6 \quad \langle 7, 0 \rangle,$$

$$E_6 : C0 \xrightarrow{2} C7 \xrightarrow{3} C6 \quad \langle 3, 2 \rangle.$$

E_1, E_2, and E_3 are illustrated in Figure 11, where $p1$, $p4$, and $p5$ are the h-points, and $p2$, $p3$, and $p6$ are the t-points of E_1, E_2, and E_3, respectively. E_4 is an infinitely cyclic sequence as illustrated in Figure 12. Similarly, any convex closed curve has the label $\langle 0, 0 \rangle$. E_5 and E_6 are illustrated in Figure 13, where $p7$ and $p9$ are the h-points, and $p8$ and $p10$ are the t-points of E_5 and E_6 respectively. $\square$

2.5 Connection of Primitive Sequences

We have obtained primitive sequences on a simple arc or a simple closed curve. Next, we consider connection of primitive sequences. Let two primitive sequences e_0 and e_1 be

$$e_0 : a_0 \xrightarrow{i_1} a_1 \xrightarrow{i_2} \cdots \xrightarrow{i_m} a_m,$$
$$e_1 : b_0 \xrightarrow{j_1} b_1 \xrightarrow{j_2} \cdots \xrightarrow{j_n} b_n.$$

Let the PS-labels of e_0 and e_1 be $\langle ps_0, idr_0 \rangle$ and $\langle ps_1, idr_1 \rangle$ respectively. For any pair of primitives a and b which are concatenated to one another, either

$$a \xrightarrow{*} b$$

or

$$b \xrightarrow{*} a$$

is satisfied. Moreover, there do not exist c_0, d_0, c_1, or d_1 such that

$$c_0 \xrightarrow{*} a_0, \quad a_m \xrightarrow{*} d_0, \quad c_1 \xrightarrow{*} b_0, \quad b_n \xrightarrow{*} d_1.$$

Therefore, e_0 and e_1 are connected by sharing a_0 (b_0) or a_m (b_n). The connection is classified as follows:

h-connection: The primitive a_0 is identical to the primitive b_0. Two primitive sequences are connected to one another by sharing the first primitive of each one (see Figure 9(a)).

t-connection: The primitive a_m is identical to the primitive b_n. Two primitive sequences are connected to one another by sharing the last primitive of each one (see Figure 9(b)).

These are denoted by

$$e_0 \xrightarrow{h} e_1 \ (or \ e_1 \xrightarrow{h} e_0), \tag{10}$$

$$e_0 \xrightarrow{t} e_1 \ (or \ e_1 \xrightarrow{t} e_0), \tag{11}$$

respectively. Recall that we always turn to the right at the joint of primitives when we traverse a curve composed of one primitive sequence from the h-point to the t-point. Thus, when we traverse a curve composed of two primitive sequences e_0 and e_1, we turn to the right (left) at the joints of primitives on e_0, while we turn to the left (right) at the joints on e_1.

Example 2.4 We examine connection of the primitive sequences in Example 2.3. Since the primitive sequences E_1 and E_2 share the primitive $A1$,

$$E_1 \xrightarrow{t} E_2.$$

Notice that the direction of the primitive $A1$ is reversed. Similarly, we have

$$E_2 \xrightarrow{h} E_3, \ E_5 \xrightarrow{h} E_6, \ E_5 \xrightarrow{t} E_6.$$

$\square$

Next, we show that h-connection and t-connection can be applied to two primitive sequences only if the two PS-labels satisfy the following specific relations:

Theorem 2 *If*

$$e_0 \overset{h}{\text{---}} e_1,$$

then

$$idr_0 - idr_1 \equiv 2 \ (mod \ 4), \tag{12}$$

and if

$$e_0 \overset{t}{\text{---}} e_1,$$

then

$$ps_0 + idr_0 \equiv ps_1 + idr_1 + 2 \ (mod \ 4). \tag{13}$$

Corollary 1

$$e_0 \overset{h}{\text{---}} e_1, \ e_0 \overset{t}{\text{---}} e_1 \ (ps_0 \geq ps_1 \geq 2),$$

then

$$ps_0 \geq 3, \ ps_0 \equiv ps_1 \ (mod \ 4), \ idr_0 - idr_1 \equiv 2 \ (mod \ 4). \tag{14}$$

2.6 Description of Quasi-Topological Structure of Curves

We have constructed the primitive sequences and their connections for a simple arc or a simple closed curve. Now, we can describe the quasi-topological structure of the curve by the labels and the connections of the primitive sequences.

(1) The curve is a simple arc.

Suppose that the curve consists of n primitive sequences e_i $(i = 1, 2, \ldots, n)$, and e_i is connected to e_{i+1} $(i = 1, 2, \ldots, n-1)$ in such a way that

$$e_i \overset{c_{i+1}}{\text{---}} e_{i+1} \ (c_i \in \{h, t\}),$$

where $c_{i+1} = t$ if $c_i = h$, and $c_{i+1} = h$ if $c_i = t$, $i = 2, 3, \ldots, n-1$. By linking the connections of the primitive sequences, the following string is generated:

$$e_1 \overset{c_2}{\text{---}} e_2 \overset{c_3}{\text{---}} e_3 \overset{c_4}{\text{---}} \cdots \overset{c_{n-1}}{\text{---}} e_{n-1} \overset{c_n}{\text{---}} e_n. \tag{15}$$

Let the PS-label of e_i be $\langle ps_i, idr_i \rangle$. By substituting e_i by $\langle ps_i, idr_i \rangle$, the quasi-topological structure of the curve is described as

$$\langle ps_1, idr_1 \rangle \overset{c_2}{\text{---}} \langle ps_2, idr_2 \rangle \overset{c_3}{\text{---}} \cdots \overset{c_n}{\text{---}} \langle ps_n, idr_n \rangle. \tag{16}$$

(2) The curve is a simple closed curve.

Similarly, a string of the primitive sequences is generated.

$$e_1 \xrightarrow{c_2} e_2 \xrightarrow{c_3} \cdots \xrightarrow{c_{n-1}} e_{n-1} \xrightarrow{c_n} e_n \xrightarrow{c_1} e_1^*.$$

The mark '$*$' means that the string is cyclic, and that the last element is identical to the first one. Since the string above is cyclic, and h and t appear alternately in the sequence ($c_1, c_2, \ldots, c_n$), n must be an even number for a closed curve. Then, the quasi-topological structure of the curve is described as

$$\langle ps_1, idr_1 \rangle \xrightarrow{c_2} \langle ps_2, idr_2 \rangle \xrightarrow{c_3} \cdots \xrightarrow{c_n} \langle ps_n, idr_n \rangle \xrightarrow{c_1} \langle ps_1, idr_1 \rangle^*. \qquad (17)$$

Example 2.5 For the curves shown in Figure 3, the primitive sequences and their connections have been obtained in Example 2.4. Lists of the primitive sequences are generated as follows:

$$Figure\ 3(a) : E_1 \xrightarrow{t} E_2 \xrightarrow{h} E_3,$$

$$Figure\ 3(b) : E_4,$$

$$Figure\ 3(c) : E_5 \xrightarrow{h} E_6 \xrightarrow{t} E_5^*.$$

Therefore, the quasi-topological structure of each curve

$$(a) : \langle 3,3 \rangle \xrightarrow{t} \langle 3,1 \rangle \xrightarrow{h} \langle 3,3 \rangle,$$

$$(b) : \langle 0,0 \rangle,$$

$$(c) : \langle 7,0 \rangle \xrightarrow{h} \langle 3,2 \rangle \xrightarrow{t} \langle 7,0 \rangle^*.$$

□

In summary of this section, Figure 14 gives the hierarchical representation of the quasi-topological structure of the curve shown in Figure 3(a). In the figure, the same symbols are used as Examples 2.1 through 2.4.

3 Structural Description of General Curves

In the previous section, we assumed that curves are simple arcs or simple closed curves. However, curves in the real world have branch points. In this section, we consider structural description of general curves with branch points.

High-quality thinning is a key technology for analysis of line drawings. We mention new thinning methods which are non-pixelwise and based on decomposition techniques (Section 3.1). Next, by decomposition of each singular point, the curve is decomposed into components (*strokes*) each of which is either a simple arc or a simple closed curve (3.2). We describe the structure of the curve by the quasi-topological structure of each stroke (3.3) and the adjacent structures of the primitive sequences on the singular point (3.4). Consequently, a compact and concise description of the curve structure is obtained (3.5).

3.1 Thinning of Line Drawings

Curves in the real world are not ideal in the mathematical sense in that they have thickness. The first step of structural analysis of curves is to extract lines in the mathematical sense from line drawings. Many algorithms for pixelwise thinning have been proposed, but they have intrinsic limitation due to local processing. Therefore, their output is hard to be used for structural analysis of curves directly, because the figures of branch points and corners are distorted and counterintuitive. On the other hand, some non-pixelwise thinning methods have been developed, such as [18, 19]. They give a rough description and features of lines, but a more adequate and fine representation is necessary for structural description of curves.

To resolve this problem, new non-pixelwise thinning methods have been developed on the basis of decomposition techniques. The principle is the following: First, the image is decomposed into simple/regular parts (lines) and complex/singular parts (branching and crossing). (It is similar to the idea of regularity and singularity of line drawings by Simon and Baret [20].) Next, the simple/regular parts are analyzed and described as thin lines. Finally, the residual parts (complex/singular parts) are analyzed in conjunction with neighboring simple/regular parts, and they are described as junctions of lines or endpoints.

Based on the principle, two methods have been developed so far:

(1) a thinning method based on the cell structure [21],
(2) a description method of line drawings by cross section sequence graph and its application to thinning [22].

Details of the thinning methods are described in the referenced papers.

The output from the thinning is a piecewise linear curve expressed in terms of the undirected graph $G = (V, E)$, where V is the set of vertices and E is the set of edges. Moreover, we assume that the graph $G = (V, E)$ is a simple graph (a graph which contains neither a self loop nor a multiple edge). The coordinate function

$$coord : V \longrightarrow R^2$$

is defined for each element v in V, where $coord(v)$ corresponds to the coordinates of v. Figure 15 and Figure 16 show examples of images and results of thinning, respectively.

3.2 Decomposition of Singular Points

The vertex in V whose order (the number of edges incident to the vertex) is equal to or more than 3 is called a singular point of G. For instance, the vertices p, q, and r in Figure 16 are singular points, the orders of which are 4 for p and q, and 3 for r.

For each singular point v, introduce n new vertices v_i such that $coord(v_i) = coord(v)$, $i = 1, 2, \ldots, n$ (n is the order of v). Next, for n vertices w_i ($i = 1, 2, \ldots, n$) which are adjacent to v, add virtual edges (v_i, w_i) ($i = 1, 2, \ldots, n$), and remove the vertex v. Though the vertices v_i $(i = 1, 2, \ldots, n)$ have the same coordinates as v, they are regarded as different from each other. After applying this operation, the graph G is decomposed into connected components each of which is a simple arc. Figure 17(a) depicts a singular point of the order 5, and Figure 17(b) illustrates the result of the operation mentioned above.

Let $coord(v)$ be (x_0, y_0) and $coord(w_i)$ be (x_i, y_i). Now, compute $S(i, j)$ $(i < j, i, j = 1, 2, \ldots, n)$:

$$S(i, j) = \frac{\mathbf{q_i} \cdot \mathbf{q_j}}{\left| \mathbf{q_i} \right| \cdot \left| \mathbf{q_j} \right|}, \tag{18}$$

where

$$\mathbf{q_k} = (x_k - x_0, y_k - y_0), \quad k = 1, 2, \ldots, n.$$

Next, find the sequence

$$S(i_1, j_1) \leq S(i_2, j_2) \leq \cdots \leq S(i_m, j_m) \tag{19}$$

such that

$$S(i_1, j_1) = \min \Big\{ S(i, j) \,\Big|\, i, j \in I, i < j \Big\},$$

$$S(i_k, j_k) = \min \Big\{ S(i, j) \,\Big|\, i, j \in I - \bigcup_{\lambda=1}^{k-1} \{i_\lambda, j_\lambda\}, i < j \Big\}$$

for $k = 2, 3, \ldots, m$, where $I = \{1, 2, \ldots, n\}$ and $m = \lfloor n/2 \rfloor$ ($\lfloor r \rfloor$ is the greatest integer that is equal to or smaller than r). Then, connect a pair of edges (v_{i_k}, w_{i_k}) and (v_{j_k}, w_{j_k}) by regarding the two vertices v_{i_k} and v_{j_k} $(k = 1, 2, \ldots, m)$ as identical.

A series of the above operations is called the *singular point decomposition*. It decomposes the vertex v into $\lceil n/2 \rceil$ ($\lceil r \rceil$ is the smallest integer that is equal to or greater than r) vertices, and generates $\lceil n/2 \rceil$ pairs of edges incident to v. Moreover, the graph obtained by applying the singular point decomposition to the graph G is called the *stroke graph* of G. Each connected component of the stroke graph is called a *stroke*, and it is either a simple arc or a simple closed curve. Therefore, the curve is decomposed into *unicursal* components by taking account of the smoothness of directional changes at the singular points.

Figure 17(c) illustrates the decomposition of the singular point shown in Figure 17(a). Since $n = 5$ in this case, three pairs of edges $\{1, 3\}$, $\{2, 4\}$, and $\{5, \phi\}$ are connected by the procedure mentioned above.

Remark 2 Definition of $S(\cdot, \cdot)$ depends on the application and on the complexity of the shapes. We gave above the simplest one [23] suitable for simple shapes such as numerals and Roman alphabets. When local feature around the singular point is complex, *i.e.*, for some l

$$S(i_l, j_l) \approx S(i_l, k), \quad j_l \neq k$$

or

$$S(i_l, j_l) \approx S(k, j_l), \quad i_l \neq k,$$

decision should be made in terms of global features of adjacent curves (sequences of edges) rather than the local rules for adjacent edges. The above definition of $S(\cdot, \cdot)$ can be replaced by the absolute value of the curvature at the singular point estimated from curve fitting [24]. Medioni and Yasumoto [25] used cubic B-splines for curve representation, and Liao and Huang [26] applied Bernstein-Bezier curve fitting to stroke segmentation for handwritten Chinese characters. □

Example 3.1 The graphs shown in Figure 18 are obtained by applying the singular point decomposition to the graphs in Figure 16. The singular point p is decomposed into $a1$ and $a3$, q is into $b1$ and $b4$, and r is into $c1$ and $c3$. The graph in Figure 16(a) is transformed into the stroke graph which consists of a simple arc $(a0, a1, a2, a3, a4)$, the one in Figure 16(b) into the stroke graph of two simple arcs $(b0, b1, b2)$ and $(b3, b4, b5)$, and the one in Figure 16(c) into the stroke graph of two simple arcs $(c0, c1, c2)$ and $(c3, c4)$. □

3.3 Analysis of Quasi-Topological Structure of Strokes

Since each stroke obtained by the singular point decomposition is either a simple arc or a simple closed curve, we can describe the quasi-topological structure of each stroke.

Example 3.2 For curves in Figure 18, each stroke is decomposed into primitives as shown in Figure 19. $U0, U2, U4, V0, V2, W0, W2$, and $W4$ are primitives of type ' / ', and the others ' \ '. Next, by constructing concatenations of primitives and linking them, the following primitive sequences are generated:

$$F_1 : U0 \xrightarrow{2} U1 \xrightarrow{3} U2 \xrightarrow{0} U3 \xrightarrow{1} U4 \xrightarrow{2} U5 \quad \langle 6, 2 \rangle,$$

$$F_2 : V1 \xrightarrow{1} V0 \quad \langle 2, 1 \rangle,$$

$$F_3 : V2 \quad \langle 1, 1 \rangle,$$

$$F_4 : W1 \xrightarrow{1} W0 \quad \langle 2, 1 \rangle,$$

$$F_5 : W1 \xrightarrow{3} W2 \xrightarrow{0} W3 \quad \langle 3, 3 \rangle,$$

$$F_6 : W4 \quad \langle 1, 1 \rangle.$$

Moreover, since F_4 and F_5 share the primitive $W1$,

$$F_4 \overset{h}{\text{---}} F_5.$$

Figure 20 depicts the two primitive sequences F_4 and F_5. $p1$ and $p2$ are the h-points, and $p0$ and $p3$ are the t-points of F_4 and F_5 respectively. □

3.4 Structure of Singular Points

We give description of singular points. As shown in Figure 21, there are three types of adjacent structures of two primitive sequences on the singular point: X-type (crossing), K-type (touch), and T-type. Let two primitive sequences e_i and e_j be

$$e_i : a_0 \xrightarrow{i_1} a_1 \xrightarrow{i_2} \cdots \xrightarrow{i_m} a_m,$$

$$e_j : b_0 \xrightarrow{j_1} b_1 \xrightarrow{j_2} \cdots \xrightarrow{j_n} b_n.$$

The structure of the singular point v is described by the binary relation of two primitive sequences e_i and e_j containing v:

$$[e_i, \sigma] \xrightarrow{\chi} [e_j, \tau], \tag{20}$$

where $\chi \in \{X, K, T\}$, and $\sigma, \tau \in \{hp, tp, h, t, \phi\}$. χ denotes the adjacent structure of e_i and e_j on v, and σ (τ) denotes the position of v on the primitive sequence e_i (e_j):

$$\sigma = \begin{cases} hp & \text{if } v \text{ is the h-point of } e_i, \\ tp & \text{if } v \text{ is the t-point of } e_i, \\ h & \text{if } v \text{ lies on } a_0, \text{ but it is not the h-point of } e_i, \\ t & \text{if } v \text{ lies on } a_m, \text{ but it is not the t-point of } e_i, \\ \phi & \text{otherwise.} \end{cases}$$

When e_i is composed of one primitive $(m = 0)$,

$$\sigma = \begin{cases} hp & \text{if } v \text{ is the head of the primitive } a_0, \\ tp & \text{if } v \text{ is the tail of the primitive } a_0, \\ \phi & \text{otherwise.} \end{cases}$$

If the PS-label of e_i is $\langle 0, 0 \rangle$, σ is set to be ϕ. τ is determined in the same way as σ. Since $\lceil N/2 \rceil$ pairs of edges are generated on the singular point v of the order N, the structure of v is described by at least $\lceil N/2 \rceil \times (\lceil N/2 \rceil - 1)/2$ of the forms of (20).

Example 3.3 For the primitive sequences obtained in Example 3.2, we describe the structure of each of the singular points in Figure 16 as follows (see also Figure 18, Figure 19, and Figure 20). The singular point p in Figure 16(a) lies on the primitives $U2$ and $U4$ in the primitive sequence F_1 (see Figure 19(a)). The singular point q in Figure 16(b) lies on the primitive $V1$ in the primitive sequence F_2 and $V2$ in F_3 (see Figure 19(b)). The singular point r in Figure 16(c) lies on the primitive $W0$ in the primitive sequence F_4 and the head $c3$ (Figure 18(c)) of the primitive F_6 (see Figure 19(c) and Figure 20). Therefore, we have

$$p : [F_1, \phi] \xrightarrow{X} [F_1, \phi],$$

$$q : [F_2, h] \xrightarrow{X} [F_3, \phi],$$

$$r : [F_4, t] \xrightarrow{T} [F_6, hp].$$

□

3.5 Structural Description of Curves

We have obtained the primitive sequences, their connections, and the adjacent structures of primitive sequences on the singular points. Now, we can describe the structure of a curve by the quasi-topological structure of each stroke and the structure of each singular point. Since each stroke is either a simple arc or a simple closed curve, it is described in the form of (15) or (17). On the other hand, the structure of each singular point is described in the form of (20).

Example 3.4 For the curves represented as stroke graphs in Figure 18, the structure of each curve is described as follows. For the curve shown in Figure 18(a),

$$stroke(a0, a1, a2, a3, a4) : \langle 6, 2 \rangle (F_1),$$

$$singular\ point(a1, a3) : [F_1, \phi] \xrightarrow{\ X\ } [F_1, \phi].$$

For the curve shown in Figure 18(b),

$$stroke(b0, b1, b2) : \langle 2, 1 \rangle (F_2),$$

$$stroke(b3, b4, b5) : \langle 1, 1 \rangle (F_3),$$

$$singular\ point(b1, b4) : [F_2, h] \xrightarrow{\ X\ } [F_3, \phi].$$

For the curve shown in Figure 18(c),

$$stroke(c0, c1, c2) : \langle 2, 1 \rangle (F_4) \xrightarrow{\ h\ } \langle 3, 3 \rangle (F_5),$$

$$stroke(c3, c4) : \langle 1, 1 \rangle (F_6),$$

$$singular\ point(c1, c3) : [F_4, t] \xrightarrow{\ T\ } [F_6, hp].$$

□

4 Structure of Closed Curves

In this section, we analyze the structure of closed curves in terms of the properties of the PS-labels. The properties show the geometrical meanings of the PS-label. We assume that the closed curve C is composed of n primitive sequences $e_1, e_2, \ldots, e_n$ (n is an even number) such that

$$e_1 \xrightarrow{\ h\ } e_2 \xrightarrow{\ t\ } e_3 \xrightarrow{\ h\ } \cdots \xrightarrow{\ h\ } e_n \xrightarrow{\ t\ } e_1^* . \tag{21}$$

Let the PS-label of e_i be $\langle ps_i, idr_i \rangle$. Now, we give the total amount T of the directional change along the curve C in terms of the PS-labels.

Theorem 3 *The total amount T of the directional change along the curve C is given by*

$$\left|T\right| = \frac{\pi}{2}\left|\sum_{i=1}^{n}(-1)^i ps_i\right|. \tag{22}$$

Theorem 3 suggests that ps_i represents the rotation number along the primitive sequence e_i. Furthermore, $T = \pm 2m\pi$ (m is an integer) for closed curves, and $T = \pm 2\pi$ for simple closed curves in particular. Thus, we obtain the following corollary:

Corollary 2 *If the curve C is a closed curve, then*

$$\sum_{i=1}^{n}(-1)^i ps_i \equiv 0 \ (mod \ 4). \tag{23}$$

In particular, the curve C is a simple closed curve, then

$$\sum_{i=1}^{n}(-1)^i ps_i = \pm 4. \tag{24}$$

Example 4.1 Figure 22 illustrates the argument of Theorem 3 and Corollary 2. As shown in Examples 2.1 through 2.4, the simple closed curve shown in Figure 3(c) consists of the primitives $C0, C1, \ldots, C7$ each of which is a straight line segment (see Figure 3(c)), and is composed of two primitive sequences E_5 and E_6 (see Figure 13). The PS-labels of E_5 and E_6 are $\langle 7,0\rangle$ and $\langle 3,2\rangle$ respectively. Figure 22(a) depicts the directional change along the primitive sequence E_5 when we traverse it from $p7$ (h-point) to $p8$ (t-point) in Figure 13(a), and Figure 22(b) depicts the directional change along the primitive sequence E_6 when we traverse it from $p9$ (h-point) to $p10$ (t-point) in Figure 13(b). Then, the directional changes along the primitive sequences E_5 and E_6 are given by

$$(7-2) \cdot \pi/2 + \Psi + \Omega,$$

$$(3-2) \cdot \pi/2 + \Psi + \Omega,$$

respectively. Notice that the directions of the primitives $C0$ and $C6$ are reversed in Figure 13(a) and Figure 13(b), and that Ψ and Ω in Figure 22(a) are the same values as Ψ and Ω in Figure 22(b) respectively. Therefore, the total amount T of the directional change along the curve is given by

$$\left|T\right| = \left|\left\{(7-2) \cdot \pi/2 + \Psi + \Omega\right\} - \left\{(3-2) \cdot \pi/2 + \Psi + \Omega\right\}\right|$$
$$= 2\pi.$$

□

Finally, we mention the relationship between the PS-label set and singular points on a closed curve. The following corollary is derived from Theorem 3 and Corollary 2:

Corollary 3 *If*

$$\sum_{i=1}^{n} (-1)^i ps_i \neq \pm 4,$$

then there is an X-type singular point on the closed curve C.

5 Application to Character Recognition

We mention an application of our curve analysis and description technique to hand-printed character recognition. We do not describe the recognition system in detail, but give an outline of the system we have been developing and show experimental results on numerals. A flow chart of the system is shown in Figure 23. We assume that each character is extracted from the image. We have described new structural analysis/description of curves in Section 3. In the following, each part of the character recognition system is described briefly.

5.1 Parameterization of Shapes

Since the description method ignores metric information such as length, curvature, angle, or position, sometimes objects representing different symbols have the identical structure. For instance, as shown in Figures 24 and 25, some instance of '6' has the same structure as some of '0'. Therefore, parameterization of shapes is necessary to give more information to shape description.

We have four types of shapes:

(1) primitive sequence — representing global features of the curve, characterized by PS-label.
(2) primitive — representing local features of the curve, characterized by the type.
(3) singular point — characterized by adjacent structures of primitive sequences,

We use the normalization method similar to Baird's method [27]: We normalize with respect to the bounding box (the upright rectangle just enclosing the shape) of the character by scaling the longest side of the box to unity and preserving aspect ratio. The center of the bounding box is set to be the origin (0, 0).

In selecting parameterization, it is required that a small change of the shape should cause a small displacement in the parameter space. By taking account of this requirement, the parameterization is defined in the following way:

(1) primitive sequence with PS-label $\langle ps(> 0), idr \rangle$ — (gx, gy, dx, dy, x_{hp}, y_{hp}, x_{tp}, y_{tp})
   (gx, gy) is the center coordinates of the bounding box of the primitive sequence, and dx and dy are width and height of the bounding box. (x_{hp}, y_{hp}) is the location of h-point, and (x_{tp}, y_{tp}) is that of t-point.

(2) primitive sequence with PS-label $\langle 0, 0 \rangle$ — (cx, cy, T, dx, dy)
(cx, cy) is the center coordinates of the loop, and dx and dy have the same meaning as (1). T is the *thinness-ratio* defined by

$$T = 4\pi A / P^2,$$

where A is the area and P is the perimeter of the loop. A famous theorem in geometry is that thinness-ratio has a maximum value of 1, which is achieved if the shape is a circle.

(3) primitive — (cx, cy, cvx, dx, dy)
(cx, cy) is the center coordinates of the chord (line segment connecting the end points of the primitive). dx and dy are the lengths of projections of the arc to x and y axes, respectively. Since the primitive type (' / ', ' \ ', ' | ', ' — ') is known for the arc, the direction is uniquely determined from dx and dy. cvx represents *convexity* defined in a special way: Suppose that the primitive is composed of the point sequence $(P_1, P_2, \ldots, P_n)$, where P_1 is the head of the primitive and P_n is the tail. Now, let S be the signed area of the polygon $(P_1, P_2, \ldots, P_n, P_1)$. Then, cvx is defined by

$$cvx = \frac{2 \cdot S}{\overline{P_1 P_n}}.$$

(4) singular point and endpoint — (x, y)
(x, y) is the coordinates of the point.

5.2 Dictionary

Dictionaries have been manually created in structural approaches of character recognition [28, 29]. Even if it is semi-automatically created, heuristic methods have been employed [30]. A strong advantage of our description scheme is that since the shape structure is represented in the well-organized form, character shapes can be classified automatically in the systematic way [31]. Thus, clustering the thin line curves by the structural similarity in terms of our description scheme, we can construct the dictionary automatically from the training data. From the practical viewpoint, it is more important to reject too distorted or ambiguous data than force to read them. Since hand-printed characters have various patterns of deformation, we have multiple models for one character. Each model has the quasi-topological structure of each stroke and the list of singular points, with each primitive sequence and singular point having the sets of eligible labels and structures, respectively. For instance, a model for the numeral '6' is described as follows:

- symbol : 6
- Quasi-Topological Structure of Strokes

Stroke $1 : E$

– Eligible Labels for Primitive Sequences

$$E : \{\langle 3, 0\rangle, \langle 3, 3\rangle, \langle 4, 2\rangle, \langle 4, 3\rangle, \langle 5, 2\rangle, \langle 5, 3\rangle, \langle 6, 2\rangle\}$$

– Eligible Structures of Singular Point

$$S(optional) : \Big\{[E, t] \xrightarrow{T} [E, hp], [E, hp] \xrightarrow{T} [E, \phi],$$

$$[E, t] \xrightarrow{X} [E, h], [E, h] \xrightarrow{X} [E, \phi]\Big\}.$$

This model can cover all the shapes illustrated in Figure 24, while techniques such as contour or background analysis require several models for those shapes. This example shows that our description method can cope with various deformation patterns with the smaller dictionary. Moreover, statistics (mean and standard deviation) are computed for shape parameters during dictionary creation process.

5.3 Structural Matching and Distance Calculation

Structural matching of the object and models is based on the string matching of PS-labels on each stroke and the structural matching of singular points. Since the character shape is described in terms of global features, the description is not sensitive to local deformation. Therefore, we employed neither cost functions nor editing operations [32] for finding optimal correspondence between two strings, but we applied the *exact* string matching method, in which two string are matched against one another only if they are identical. A formal description on matching is given in Appendix of D.

If the object is matched with a model, Mahalanobis distance (Euclidean distance from the mean, scaled component-wise by standard deviation) is computed for parameters on structural components (primitive sequences, primitives, singular points), and the final decision is made on the basis of the distance. For instance, the curves shown in Figures 24 and 25 are matched with models for both '0' and '6', but detailed classification is made based on the parametric information.

5.4 Experiment on Loosely Constrained Data

It should be noted that correct recognition ratio depends heavily on the quality of data given. In our case, a set of hand-printed data was obtained from 251 people. Shown the standard shapes of the hand-printed numerals, they were asked to write numerals normally and neatly under no specification for a writing device. Naturally, many characters deviate from the standard shapes as usual as shown in Figure 26 for example, and many people ignored the standard shape. In this sense, we may call the data *loosely constrained data* with a variety of writing styles and instruments. The data were digitized at 200 dpi with binary levels. Thus, we acquired 13,400 characters in total for 10 numerals.

Training and test sets were disjoint, selected in the ratio 1:1 in a randomized manner from the data set. We used the thinning method by cross section sequence graph [22] as a thinning algorithm. In postprocessing of thinning, small fluctuations nearly vertical or horizontal are smoothed, because the structural description is sensitive to them. The result on the test set is shown in Table 2, with the number of models created from the training set.

Table 2. Experimental results of hand-printed numeral recognition using the new curve description technique. The thinning method based on cross section sequence graph was used for thinning. The experiment was made on the loosely constrained data set of 13,400 samples. A part of the data set is shown in Figure 26.

	Recognition(%)	Rejection(%)	Substitution(%)	Model
0	99.3	0.4	0.3	3
1	99.7	0.2	0.1	3
2	98.9	0.5	0.6	5
3	99.3	0.1	0.6	4
4	97.7	2.0	0.3	5
5	99.4	0.6	0.0	5
6	99.1	0.9	0.0	2
7	98.7	0.8	0.5	5
8	95.7	3.8	0.5	10
9	98.9	0.9	0.2	4
	98.7	1.0	0.3	46

5.5 Experiment on Totally Unconstrained Data

Another experiment was performed on totally unconstrained handwritten numerals. The data set consists of about 127,000 samples collected from 319 people (different from the writers of the loosely constrained data set) without any specification of writing styles or devices. The loosely constrained data set was used as the training set, and the test was made on the whole of the totally unconstrained data set in the same way as Section 5.4. Therefore, the nature of the test set is quite different from the training set. Note that we neither added nor modified functionalities in the program or models/parameters in the dictionary to accommodate unconstrained data. The result is that

- Recognition : 95.4%
- Rejection : 2.9%
- Substitution Error : 1.7%

It is remarkable, because we used only one algorithm (see [33, 34]) and the dictionary created from the loosely constrained data set without any tuning or adjustment for unconstrained data.

5.6 Comparison with Contour Analysis Techniques

To show flexibility of the curve description technique introduced in Section 3, we give experimental results on hand-printed numerals recognition using contour analysis technique, as well as our technique. Since a contour is a simple closed curve, the description technique in Section 2 can be applied to contours. A contour is smoothed by Gaussian filter and small fluctuations nearly vertical or horizontal are removed. Then, the contour is described by quasi-topological structure with geometrical parameters in the same way as Section 5.1. The thinning method based on cell structure was used for thinning [21]. For both techniques, structural matching and distance calculation were also done in the same way.

Since the result is influenced by image quality and preprocessing, we removed poor image quality samples from the loosely constrained data set mentioned above to give unbiased comparison of two methods. Thus, in the experiments, we used 11,500 characters in total written by 220 subjects. Training and test sets were disjoint, selected in the ratio 1:1 in a randomized manner from the samples.

We compare two methods from the viewpoint of recognition ratio and the number of models. The results on the test set are shown in Tables 3 and 4. From the tables, it is found that our method gave a better result than contour analysis, because both rejection and substitution error ratios are less than contour analysis technique, and the number of models in our method is only two thirds of that of contour analysis. Therefore, our technique can cope with various patterns of deformation and agrees with human intuition. The flexibility and reliability of our method has been verified by experiment.

Table 3. Experimental result of hand-printed numeral recognition using the new curve description technique. The thinning method based on cell structure was used for thinning. The experiment was made on 11,500 samples, which is a subset of the loosely constrained data set.

	Recognition(%)	Rejection(%)	Substitution(%)	Model
0	99.2	0.8	0.0	3
1	99.6	0.0	0.4	2
2	99.5	0.5	0.0	5
3	98.0	2.0	0.0	4
4	98.9	1.1	0.0	2
5	98.5	1.5	0.0	4
6	99.8	0.0	0.2	2
7	99.2	0.6	0.2	2
8	98.5	1.5	0.0	9
9	99.4	0.4	0.2	4
	99.1	0.8	0.1	37

Table 4. Experimental result of hand-printed numeral recognition using contour analysis technique. The experiment was made on the same data as Table 3.

	Recognition(%)	Rejection(%)	Substitution(%)	Model
0	98.6	1.0	0.4	6
1	98.9	1.1	0.0	3
2	98.6	1.4	0.0	4
3	98.0	1.9	0.1	4
4	94.4	4.6	1.0	9
5	97.9	2.1	0.0	5
6	97.9	2.1	0.0	5
7	98.5	1.1	0.4	4
8	96.6	3.2	0.3	12
9	94.0	4.8	1.2	6
	97.6	2.0	0.4	58

5.7 Discussion

Hand-printed character recognition has been a main research theme in pattern recognition. The prime difficulty in research and development of the technology lies in the variety of deformation of the shape. Various methods such as contour analysis and background analysis [28, 29] have been proposed. Since most of the practical methods utilize some kinds of distance measures or matching methods on the feature space in which the features are position dependent, the normalization on the image is indispensable for coordinate transformation. In other words, image normalization has been a main method to cope with shape deformation. However, it is difficult to know the extent of displacement of the image with respect to the standard coordinate system before recognizing it. It implies that malfunction of normalization distorts the shape and results in rejection or substitution error. Furthermore, most of curve representation techniques have been *ad hoc*, and dictionary creation relies on hand-tuning in structural methods.

We describe the shape of characters by two types of features, *i.e.*, symbolic, qualitative, and discrete features (quasi-topological features and singular points), and statistical, quantitative and continuous features (geometrical parameters). The former is regarded as dominant information, while the latter is secondary information attached to structural components. The structural description is size and translation invariant, so normalization of image is not necessary for global feature extraction. Parameters of each shape are computed in the normalized scale, but the normalization has no side-effect, because it is applied to abstract geometrical parts such as curves and points. Moreover, statistical constraints for deformation can be put on the structural description in terms of the parameterization of shapes, and the categories with the same structure can be discriminated by statistical analysis of geometrical parameters. The structural description and parameterization are simple and agree with human intuition. Therefore, we can construct hybrid recognition systems in cooperation with statistical methods [35], and key features to distinguish confusing characters [36] can be analyzed quantitatively on the basis of the structural description and the parameterization of shapes.

Since different strokes were written independently, they should have independent information and their transformations should be independent from each other. We have shown that singular point decomposition is a clue to the compact and flexible description of curves, and deformed characters can be recognized easily and effectively. Our recognition method is close to on-line character recognition techniques, while primitive sequences have nothing to do with time sequences of handwriting. The experimental result shows stability and effectiveness of our method.

Furthermore, a systematic and rigorous description scheme of shapes is a basis for systematic clustering of character shapes. We have also developed a new method for clustering character shapes in terms of quasi-topological features and singular points, and applied it to dictionary creation [31].

6 Conclusion

We have presented an algebraic description of the curve structure. The primitive of curves are defined simply and explicitly (Criterion 1), and systematic rules are given to integrate local operations to global description system (Criterion 3). We have shown that the description is compact, has rigorous mathematical properties in that algebraic structure is introduced to higher-level representation (Criterion 2). The description is size and translation invariant (Criterion 6), and can be applied to any continuous curves (Criterion 4). The analysis is simple and fast, and the description is composed of few components with rich features. Furthermore, a unified approach of shape description of characters has been presented by integrating geometrical and quasi-topological feature representation techniques (Criterion 5). As an application of our description scheme, we have given an outline of hand-printed numeral recognition system. The experimental results shows that the scheme is very powerful to represent the shape of hand-printed characters.

A Proof of Theorem 1

Consider a subsequence

$$a_{i-1} \xrightarrow{j_i} a_i \xrightarrow{j_{i+1}} a_{i+1}, \quad i = 1, 2, \ldots, n-1.$$

If $prm(a_{i-1}) = prm(a_i)$ $(i = 1, 2, \ldots, n-1)$, then

$$j_{i+1} \equiv j_i + corner(a_{i-1} \xrightarrow{j_i} a_i) + 1$$
$$\equiv j_i + 2 \ (mod \ 4).$$

from Property 3. Next, if $prm(a_i) \in \{ \mid, - \}$ $(i = 1, 2, \ldots, n-1)$, $j_{i+1} - j_i \equiv 2$ (mod 4) from Property 4. In other cases, $j_{i+1} - j_i \equiv 1$ (mod 4) from Property 3, because $corner(a_{i-1} \xrightarrow{j_i} a_i) = 0$. Thus,

$$\sum_{i=1}^{n-1} \left\{ (j_{i+1} - j_i)(mod\ 4) \right\} + corner(a_{n-1} \xrightarrow{j_n} a_n)$$
$$= (n-1) + L + M$$
$$= ps - 2.$$

B Proof of Theorem 2

The condition for h-connection is directly derived from Property 1 and the definition of PS-label. On the other hand, from Theorem 2.4,

$$i_m \equiv idr_0 + ps_0 - 2 - corner(a_{m-1} \xrightarrow{i_m} a_m),$$

$$j_n \equiv idr_1 + ps_1 - 2 - corner(b_{n-1} \xrightarrow{j_n} b_n).$$

Therefore, applying Property 2, we have for t-connection

$$ps_0 + idr_0 - 2 \equiv (ps_1 + idr_1 - 2) + 2 \ (mod\ 4).$$

C Proof of Theorem 3

For simplicity, we assume that the curve C consists of primitives each of which is a straight line segment (see Figure 3(c)). Let a primitive sequence e_i on the curve C be

$$a_0 \xrightarrow{j_1} a_1 \xrightarrow{j_2} \cdots \xrightarrow{j_{n-1}} a_{n-1} \xrightarrow{j_n} a_n.$$

Now, we compute the directional change when we traverse a curve composed of the primitive sequence e_i from the h-point to the t-point (see Figure 13). Let θ_k be the counterclockwise angle between the positive x-axis and a_k, $k = 0, 1, \ldots, n$. The direction of a_k is the same way as the traversal of e_i from the h-point to the t-point (see Figure 13 and Figure 22). Define Ψ_i and $\Omega_i \in (0, \pi/2]$ as

$$\Psi_i = \theta_0 - \kappa \frac{\pi}{2} \quad \left(\kappa \frac{\pi}{2} < \theta_0 \leq (\kappa+1)\frac{\pi}{2}, \ \kappa \in \{0, 1, 2, 3\} \right), \tag{25}$$

$$\Omega_i = (\lambda+1)\frac{\pi}{2} - \theta_n \quad \left(\lambda \frac{\pi}{2} \leq \theta_n < (\lambda+1)\frac{\pi}{2}, \ \lambda \in \{0, 1, 2, 3\} \right). \tag{26}$$

(see Figure 22 and Figure 27). Then, we can compute the directional change K_i along e_i in the following way:

Lemma 1 *The directional change K_i along the primitive sequence e_i is given by*

$$K_i = (ps_i - 2) \cdot \pi/2 + \Psi_i + \Omega_i, \tag{27}$$

when we traverse a curve composed of e_i from the h-point to the t-point (see Figure 13 and Figure 22).

Lemma 1 can be proved by induction on ps_i. Now, we give the proof of Theorem 3 in the following:

$$\Psi_{2i} = \Psi_{2i-1}, \ \Omega_{2i} = \Omega_{2i+1} \ (i = 1, 2, \ldots, n/2, \ \Omega_{n+1} = \Omega_1),$$

because

$$e_{2i-1} \overset{h}{\text{---}} e_{2i}, \ e_{2i} \overset{t}{\text{---}} e_{2i+1} \ (e_{n+1} = e_1).$$

Recall that when we traverse a curve composed of e_i and e_{i+1}, we turn to the right (left) at the joints of primitives on e_i, while we turn to the left (right) at the joints on e_{i+1}. Thus, the total amount T of the directional change along the curve C is given by

$$|T| = \left| \sum_{i=1}^{n} (-1)^i K_i \right|$$

$$= \left| \sum_{i=1}^{n} (-1)^i \left\{ (ps_i - 2) \cdot \pi/2 + \Psi_i + \Omega_i \right\} \right|$$

$$= \left| \frac{\pi}{2} \sum_{i=1}^{n} (-1)^i ps_i + \sum_{i=1}^{n/2} (\Psi_{2i} - \Psi_{2i-1}) + \sum_{i=1}^{n/2} (\Omega_{2i} - \Omega_{2i+1}) \right|$$

$$= \frac{\pi}{2} \left| \sum_{i=1}^{n} (-1)^i ps_i \right|,$$

because n is an even number.

In general, we can obtain the same result as Theorem 3 in the following way: Let a sequence $(a_1, a_2, \ldots, a_N)$ be the minimum number of primitives that cover the curve C, where a_i is joined to a_{i+1}, $i = 1, 2, \ldots, N$ $(a_{N+1} = a_1)$. Now, we choose one point P_i in the intersection of a_i and a_{i+1}, and approximate the curve C by connecting P_i and P_{i+1}, $i = 1, 2, \ldots, N$ $(P_{N+1} = P_1)$, by straight line segments. By the same argument as above, we obtain the equation (22).

D Structural Matching

Structural matching of an object and a model is described. First of all, the description scheme of the model I of curves is given formally in the following:

$$Q(I) = (M^{(I)}, N_P^{(I)}, N_S^{(I)}, C^{(I)}, \pi^{(I)}, st^{(I)}, \sigma^{(I)}, mp^{(I)}, ms^{(I)}).$$

$M^{(I)}$ is the number of strokes in the curve, $N_P^{(I)}$ is the number of primitive sequences, and $N_S^{(I)}$ is the number of singular points. $C^{(I)}$ is the set of connections of primitive sequences:

$$C^{(I)} \subseteq \left\{ i \overset{c}{\text{---}} j \ \middle| \ 1 \leq i, j \leq N_P^{(I)}, c \in \{h, t\} \right\}.$$

$\pi^{(I)}(i)$ denotes the eligible labels of the i-th primitive sequence:

$$\pi^{(I)} : \{1, 2, \ldots, N_P\} \longrightarrow 2^{\Pi},$$

where

$$\Pi = \Big\{ \langle 0, 0 \rangle \Big\} \bigcup \Big\{ \langle ps, idr \rangle \ \Big| \ ps = 1, 2, \ldots, \ idr \in \{0, 1, 2, 3\} \Big\}.$$

$st^{(I)}(i)$ denotes the stroke index to which the i-th primitive sequence belongs:

$$st^{(I)} : \{1, 2, \ldots, N_P^{(I)}\} \longrightarrow \{1, 2, \ldots, M^{(I)}\}.$$

$\sigma^{(I)}(k)$ denotes the eligible structure of the singular point k:

$$\sigma^{(I)} : \{1, 2, \ldots, N_S^{(I)}\} \longrightarrow 2^{\Sigma(I)},$$

where

$$\Sigma(I) = \Big\{ [i, p_i] \xrightarrow{\chi} [j, p_j] \ \Big| \ 1 \le i, j \le N_P^{(I)},$$

$$\chi \in \{X, K, T\}, p_i, p_j \in \{hp, h, o, t, tp\} \Big\}.$$

$mp^{(I)}$ and $ms^{(I)}$ are mappings:

$$mp^{(I)} : P \longrightarrow \{0, 1\},$$

$$ms^{(I)} : S \longrightarrow \{0, 1\}.$$

If $mp^{(I)}(i) = 0$ ($ms^{(I)}(j) = 0$), then the i-th primitive sequence (j-th singular point) is optional. If $mp^{(I)}(i) = 1$, then the i-th primitive sequence is mandatory. If $ms^{(I)}(i) = 1$, then the i-th singular point must exist if the primitive sequences forming the point exist.

Example D.1 In the model given in Section 5.2,

$$M^{(I)} = N_P^{(I)} = N_S^{(I)} = 1,$$

$$C^{(I)} = \phi,$$

$$\pi^{(I)} : 1 \mapsto \{\langle 3, 0 \rangle, \langle 3, 3 \rangle, \langle 4, 2 \rangle, \langle 4, 3 \rangle, \langle 5, 2 \rangle, \langle 5, 3 \rangle, \langle 6, 2 \rangle\},$$

$$st^{(I)} : 1 \mapsto 1,$$

$$\sigma^{(I)} : 1 \mapsto \Big\{ [E, t] \xrightarrow{T} [E, hp], [E, hp] \xrightarrow{T} [E, \phi],$$

$$[E, t] \xrightarrow{X} [E, h], [E, h] \xrightarrow{X} [E, \phi] \Big\},$$

$$mp^{(I)} : 1 \mapsto 1, \quad ms^{(I)} : 1 \mapsto 0.$$

□

The description of an object (curve) O is given formally in the similar way:

$$Q'(O) = (M^{(O)}, N_P^{(O)}, N_S^{(O)}, C^{(O)}, \pi^{(O)}, st^{(O)}, \sigma^{(O)}),$$

where the same notations are used as $Q(I)$.

Structural matching of an object and a model is formalized in the following: An object O is matched with a model I if surjections f and g:

$$f : \{1, 2, \ldots, N_P^{(I)}\} \longrightarrow \{1, 2, \ldots, N_P^{(O)}\} \bigcup \{\phi\}$$

$$g : \{1, 2, \ldots, N_S^{(I)}\} \longrightarrow \{1, 2, \ldots, N_S^{(O)}\} \bigcup \{\phi\}$$

are found that satisfy the following:

(1) If $f(i) = f(j) \neq \phi$ for $i, j \in \{1, 2, \ldots, N_P^{(I)}\}$, then $i = j$.

(2) If the primitive sequence i in the model is mandatory, then a corresponding element must exist in the object: If $mp^{(I)}(i) = 1$ for $i \in \{1, 2, \ldots, N_P^{(I)}\}$ then there exists $j \in \{1, 2, \ldots, N_P^{(O)}\}$ such that $f(i) = j$.

(3) If a corresponding element is found in the object for the primitive sequence i in the model, then PS-label of $f(i)$ must be a member of $\pi^{(I)}(i)$: If $f(i) \neq \phi$ for $i \in \{1, 2, \ldots, N_P^{(I)}\}$, then $\pi^{(O)}(f(i)) \in \pi^{(I)}(i)$.

(4) Connection of primitive sequences defined in the model are also preserved in the object under the correspondence f:

$$C^{(O)} = \left\{ f(m) \overset{c}{-} f(n) \,\middle|\, m \overset{c}{-} n \in C^{(I)}, f(m) \neq \phi, f(n) \neq \phi \right\}.$$

(5) Strokes in the model I have a one-to-one correspondence to strokes in the object O: If $f(m) \neq \phi$ and $f(n) \neq \phi$, then $st^{(I)}(m) = st^{(I)}(n)$ if and only if $st^{(O)}(f(m)) = st^{(O)}(f(n))$.

(6) If $g(i) = g(j) \neq \phi$ for $i, j \in \{1, 2, \ldots, N_S^{(I)}\}$, then $i = j$.

(7) If the singular point i in the model is mandatory, and, for some primitive sequences forming the singular point i, corresponding elements are found in the object, then a corresponding singular point must exist in the object: If $ms^{(I)}(i) = 1$ for $i \in \{1, 2, \ldots, N_S^{(I)}\}$, and $f(m) \neq \phi$ and $f(n) \neq \phi$ for some

$$[m, p_m] \overset{\chi}{-} [n, p_n] \in \sigma^{(I)}(i),$$

then there exists $j \in \{1, 2, \ldots, N_S^{(O)}\}$ such that $g(i) = j$.

(8) If a corresponding element is found in the object for the singular point i in the model, then a structure of $g(i)$ must be a member of $\sigma^{(I)}(i)$: If $g(i) \neq \phi$ for $i \in \{1, 2, \ldots, N_S^{(I)}\}$, then there exists some

$$[m, p_m] \overset{\chi}{-} [n, p_n] \in \sigma^{(I)}(i)$$

such that

$$[f(m), p_m] \xrightarrow{\chi} [f(n), p_n] \in \sigma^{(O)}(g(i)).$$

The mapping f is found by the consistent labeling algorithm [37, 38] with constraints (1) through (5). If f is found out successfully, then g is found with constraints (6) through (8) under the mapping f. When several correspondences f and g are found, the best one is taken on the basis of Mahalanobis distance in the parameter space mentioned in Section 5.1. Computational complexity is a serious problem in syntactic or structural pattern recognition techniques. However, the shape is described in terms of global features, so the number of elements is not large in our description technique. For instance, in case of numerals, the number of primitive sequences or singular points is at most 4. Therefore, computational complexity is not serious in our approach.

Acknowledgements

We would like to express our gratitude to Prof. Theo Pavlidis for his valuable comments on this study. We also thank Dr. Noboru Murayama, the managing director of engineering in RICOH R & D center, for valuable advice and encouragement. Mr. Toshihiro Suzuki carefully read earlier drafts of this paper and made many useful comments.

References

1. K. S. Fu, *Syntactic Pattern Recognition and Applications*, Prentice–Hall, Englewood Cliffs, NJ, 1982.
2. K. S. Fu and T. L. Booth, "Grammatical inference: introduction and survey — part 1,2," *IEEE Trans. on Pattern Analysis and Machine Intelligence*, vol. PAMI-8, no. 3, pp. 343–375, May 1986.
3. T. Pavlidis, "Structural pattern recognition: primitives and juxtaposition," In S. Watanabe (ed.), *Frontiers of Pattern Recognition*, Academic Press, New York, 1972.
4. R. Ledley, L. Rotolo, T. Golab, J. Jacobsen, M. Ginsberg, and J. Wilson, "FIDAC: film input to digital automatic computer and associated syntax-directed pattern recognition programming system," In J. Tippet, D. Beckowitz, D. Clapp, L. Koester, & A. Vanderburgh, Jr, (eds.), *Optical and Electro-Optical Information Processing*, MIT Press, Cambridge, MA, 1965.
5. A. C. Shaw, "The formal picture description scheme as a basis for picture processing system," *Information and Control*, vol. 14, pp. 9–52, 1969.
6. S. Mori, "A non-metric model of hand-printed characters," *Researches of Electrotechnical Laboratory*, vol. 798, August 1979. (in Japanese)
7. O. L. Mangasarian, *Nonlinear Programming*, McGraw–Hill, New York, 1969.
8. S. Mori, "An algebraic structural representation of shape," *Trans. of IECE Japan*, vol. J64-D, no. 8, pp. 705–712, August 1981. (in Japanese)

9. S. Mori and M. Doh, "A sequential tracking extraction of shape features and its constructive description," *Computer Vision and Image Processing*, vol. 19, pp. 349–366, August 1982.

10. R. Jakubowski, "Extraction of shape features for syntactic recognition of mechanical parts," *IEEE Trans. on Systems, Man, and Cybernetics*, vol. SMC-15, no. 5, pp. 642–651, September/October 1985.

11. R. Jakubowski, "A structural representation of shape and its features," *Information Sciences*, vol. 39, pp. 129–151, 1986.

12. T. Pavlidis, *Structural Pattern Recognition*, Springer Series Electrophysics 1, Springer–Verlag, Berlin, 1977.

13. T. Pavlidis, "Algorithms for shape analysis of contours and waveforms," *IEEE Trans. on Pattern Analysis and Machine Intelligence*, vol. PAMI-2, no. 4, July 1980.

14. S. Mori and T. Sakakura, *The fundamentals of Image Recognition[1] — Preprocessing, and Feature extraction of Shape –*, Ohm, Tokyo, August 1986. (in Japanese)

15. C. H. Cox, P Coueignoux, B. Blesser, and M. Eden, "Skeletons: a between theoretical and physical letter descriptions," *Pattern Recognition*, vol. 15, no. 1, pp. 11–22, 1982.

16. V. A. Kovalevsky, "Sequential optimization in pattern recognition and pattern description," *Proc. IFIP Congr. 68*, pp. 1603–1607, 1969.

17. A. Sanfeliu and K. S. Fu, "A distance measure between attributed relational graphs for pattern recognition," *IEEE Trans. on Systems, Man, and Cybernetics*, vol. SMC-13, no. 3, pp. 353–362, May/June 1983.

18. M. Sakauchi and Y. Osawa, "The AI-MIDAMS: Drawing data processor based on multi-dimensional pattern data structure," *Annual Report of CFE, Institute of Industrial Science, Univ. of Tokyo*, pp. 146–153, 1985.

19. T. Pavlidis, "A vectorizer and feature extractor for document recognition," *Computer Vision, Graphics, and Image Processing*, vol. 35, pp. 111–127, 1986.

20. J. C. Simon and O. Baret, "Regularities and singularities in line pictures," In this volume.

21. T. Suzuki and S. Mori, "A thinning method based on cell structure," In C. Y. Suen (ed.), *Frontiers in Handwriting Recognition*, CENPARMI, Concordia Univ., Montreal, pp. 39–52, April 1990.

22. T. Suzuki and S. Mori, "A description method of line drawings by cross section sequence graph and its application to thinning," *Technical Report of IEICE Japan*, no. PRU 90–22, June 1990.

23. K. Kobayashi, F. Yada, K. Banno, K. Yamamoto, and H. Nambu, "Recognition of hand-printed characters by stroke matching method," *Trans. IECE Japan*, PRL 81–33, 1981.

24. T. Pavlidis, *Algorithms for Graphics and Image Processing*, Computer Science, Rockville, MD, 1982.

25. G. Medioni and Y. Yasumoto, "Corner detection and curve representation using cubic B-Splines," *Computer Vision, Graphics, and Image Processing*, vol. 39, pp. 267–278, 1987.

26. C. W. Liao and J. S .Huang, "Stroke segmentation by Bernstein-Bezier curve fitting," *Pattern Recognition*, vol. 23, no. 5, pp. 475–484, 1990.

27. H. S. Baird, "Feature extraction for hybrid structural/statistical pattern classification," *Computer Vision, Graphics, and Image Processing*, vol. 42, pp. 318–333, 1988.

28. C. Y. Suen, M. Berthod, and S. Mori, "Automatic recognition of hand-printed characters — the state of the art," *Proc. of the IEEE*, vol. 68, no. 4, pp. 469–487, April 1980.

29. S. Mori, K. Yamamoto, and M. Yasuda, "Research on machine recognition of hand-printed characters," *IEEE Trans. on Pattern Analysis and Machine Intelligence*, vol. PAMI-6, no. 4, pp. 386–405, July 1984.

30. K. Yamamoto and S. Mori, "Recognition of hand-printed characters by outermost point method," *Pattern Recognition*, vol. 12, pp. 229–236, 1980.

31. H. Nishida and S. Mori, *An approach to automatic construction of structural models for character recognition*, in preparation.

32. W. H. Tsai and S. S. Yu, "Attributed string matching with merging for shape recognition," *IEEE Trans. on Pattern analysis and Machine Intelligence*, vol. PAMI-7, no. 4, pp. 453–462, July 1985.

33. J. J. Hull, A. Commike, and T.-K. Ho, "Multiple algorithms for handwritten character recognition," In C. Y. Suen (ed.), *Frontiers in Handwriting Recognition*, CENPARMI, Concordia Univ., Montreal, pp. 117–131, April 1990.

34. C. Y. Suen, C. Nadal, T. A. Mai, R. Legault, and L. Lam, "Recognition of totally unconstrained handwritten numerals based on the concept of multiple experts," In C. Y. Suen (ed.), *Frontiers in Handwriting Recognition*, CENPARMI, Concordia Univ., Montreal, pp. 131–144, April 1990.

35. K. S. Fu, "A step towards unification of syntactic and statistical pattern recognition," *IEEE Trans. on Pattern Analysis and Machine Intelligence*, vol. PAMI-5, no. 2, pp. 200–205, March 1983.

36. R. Legault, C. Y. Suen, and C. Nadal, "Classification of confusing handwritten numerals by human subjects," In C. Y. Suen (ed.), *Frontiers in Handwriting Recognition*, CENPARMI, Concordia Univ., Montreal, pp. 181–194, April 1990.

37. R. M. Haralick and L. G. Shapiro, "The consistent labeling problem: part 1," *IEEE Trans. on Pattern Analysis and Machine Intelligence*, vol. PAMI-1, pp. 173–184, April 1979.

38. R. M. Haralick and G. L. Elliott, "Increasing tree search efficiency for constraint satisfaction problems," *Artificial Intelligence*, vol. 14, pp. 263–313, 1980.

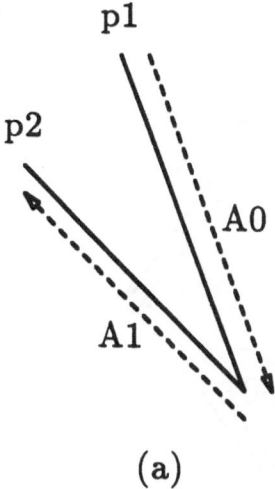

(a)

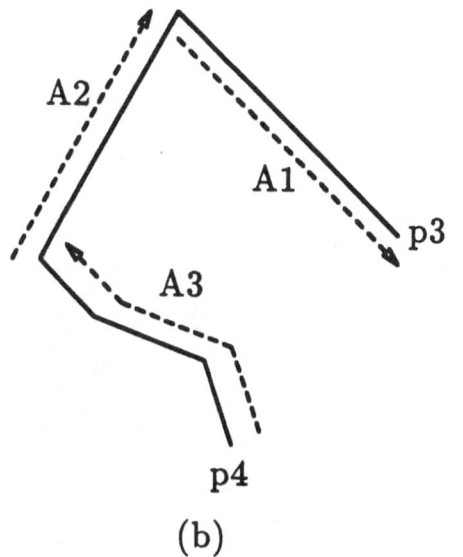

(b)

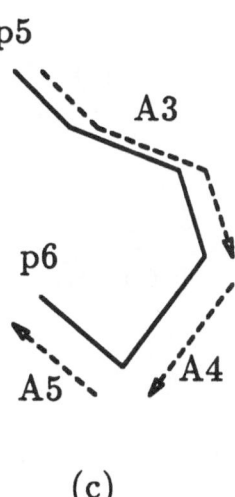

(c)

Fig. 11. Decomposition of the curve in Figure 3(a) into primitive sequences: (a) E_1 $\langle 3, 3 \rangle$, (b) E_2 $\langle 3, 1 \rangle$, (c) E_3 $\langle 3, 3 \rangle$.

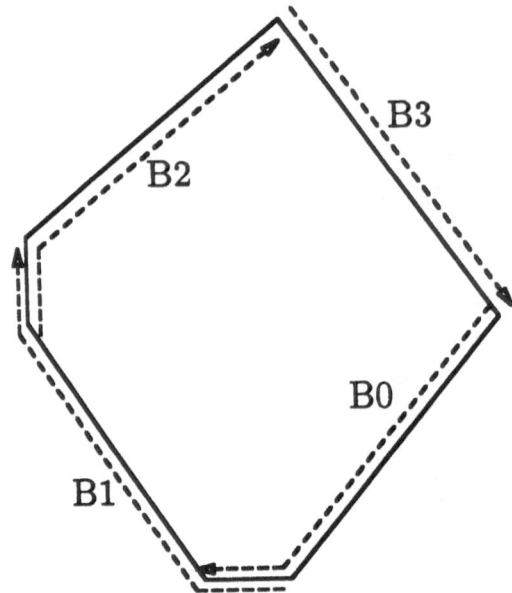

Fig. 12. The primitive sequence E_4 of the PS-label $\langle 0, 0 \rangle$.

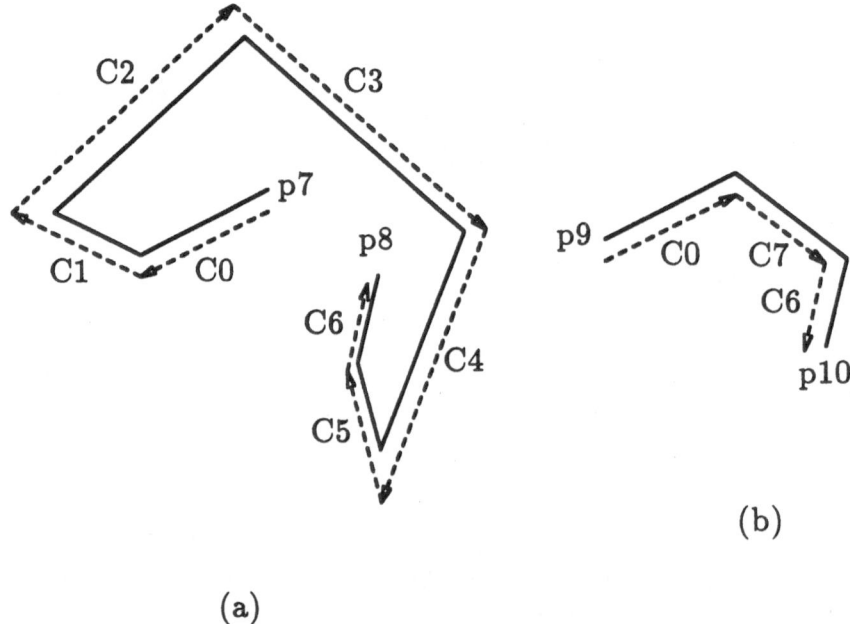

(b)

(a)

Fig. 13. Decomposition of the curve in Figure 3(c) into primitive sequences: (a) E_5 $\langle 7, 0 \rangle$, (b) E_6 $\langle 3, 2 \rangle$.

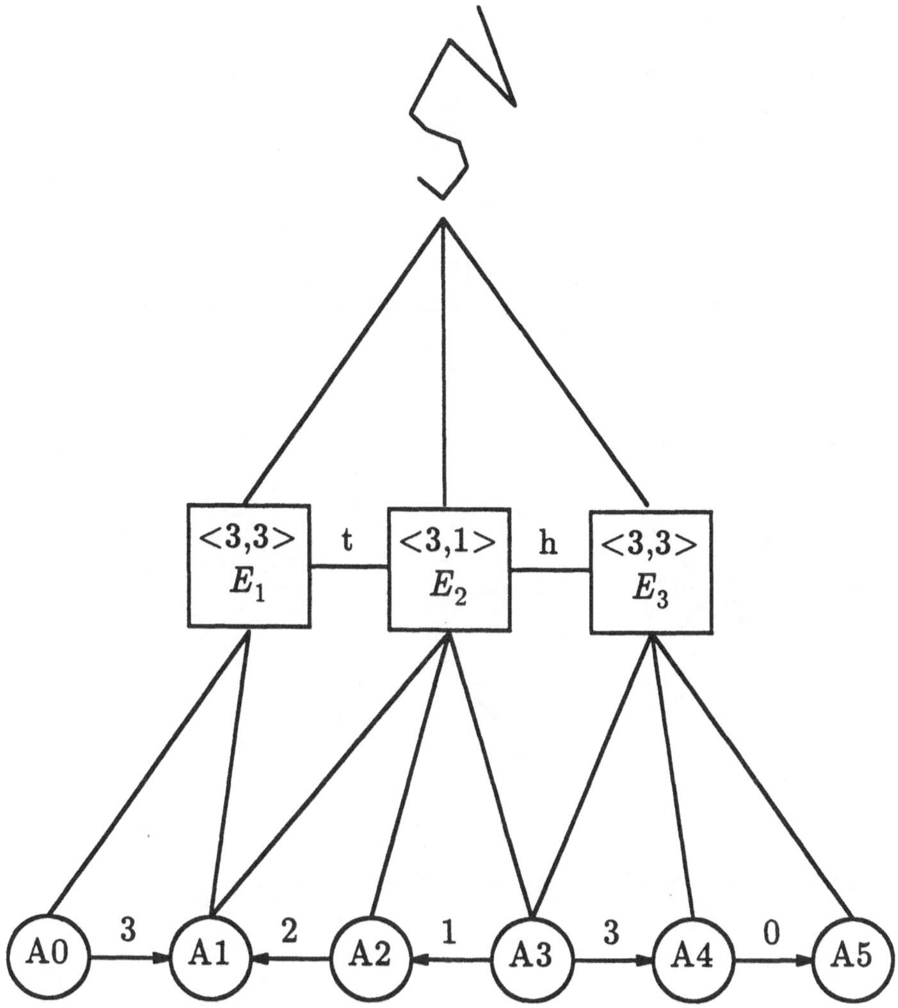

Fig. 14. The quasi-topological structure of the curve shown in Figure 3(a).

Fig. 15. Examples of line pictures.

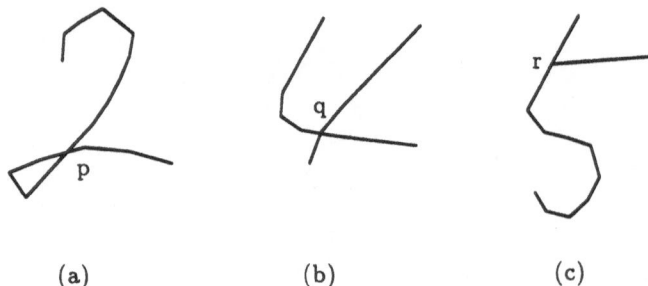

(a)   (b)   (c)

Fig. 16. Thinned line pictures. p, q, and r are singular points of the orders 4, 4, and 3, respectively.

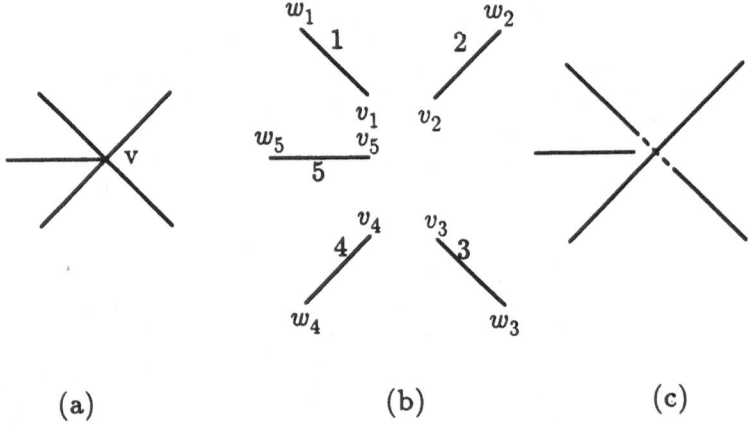

(a)   (b)   (c)

Fig. 17. Decomposition of a singular point whose order is 5.

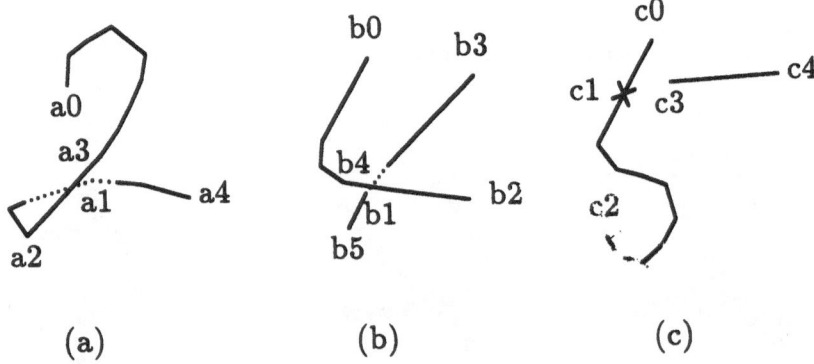

(a)   (b)   (c)

Fig. 18. Singular point decomposition. The point p in Figure 16(a) is decomposed into $a1$ and $a3$, q in Figure 16(b) into $b1$ and $b4$, and r in Figure 16(c) into $c1$ and $c3$.

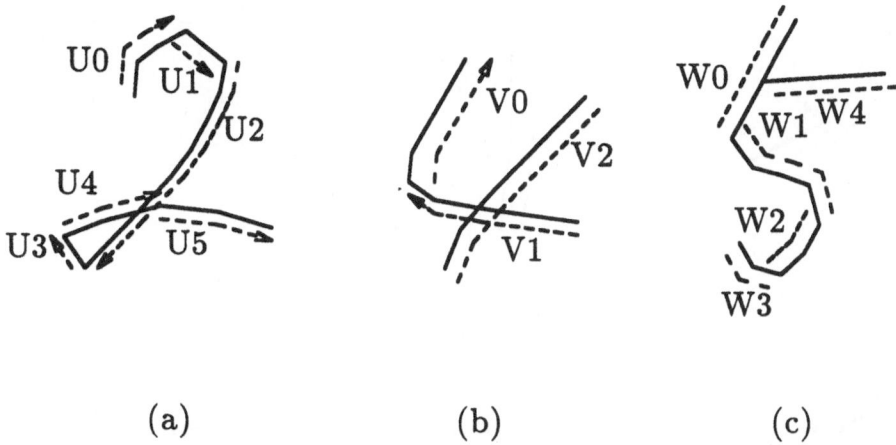

(a)   (b)   (c)

Fig. 19. Decomposition of strokes into primitives for the curves shown in Figure 18. (a), (b), and (c) correspond to Figure 18(a), 18(b), and 18(c) respectively.

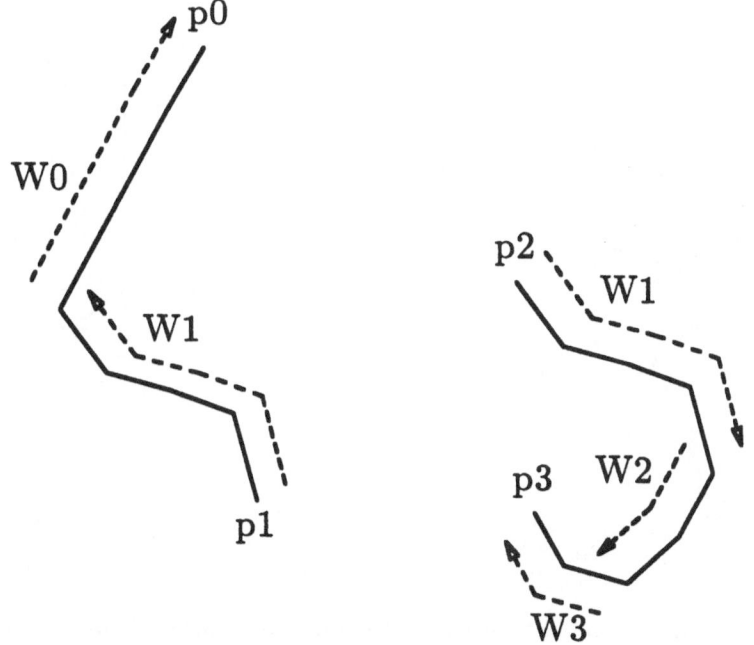

Fig. 20. Decomposition of a stroke into primitive sequences. The primitive sequence on the left has the PS-label $\langle 2, 1 \rangle$, where $p1$ is h-point, and $p0$ is t-point. The right one has the PS-label $\langle 3, 3 \rangle$, where $p2$ is h-point, and $p3$ is t-point.

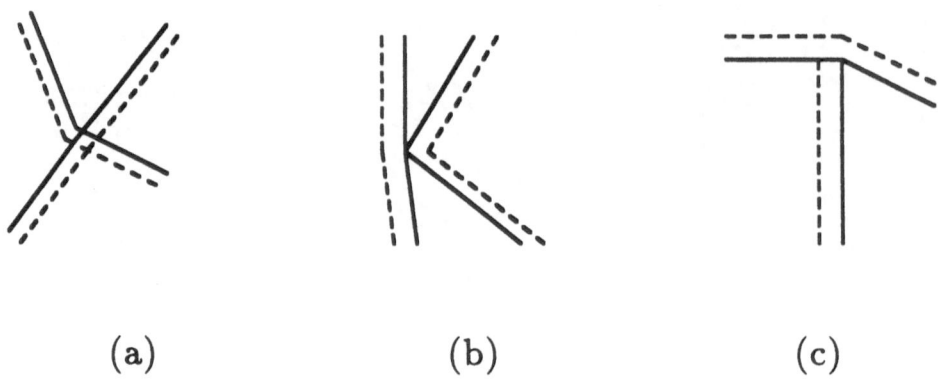

Fig. 21. Illustrations of the adjacent structures of two primitive sequences on singular points. (a), (b), and (c) are X, K, and T-type respectively.

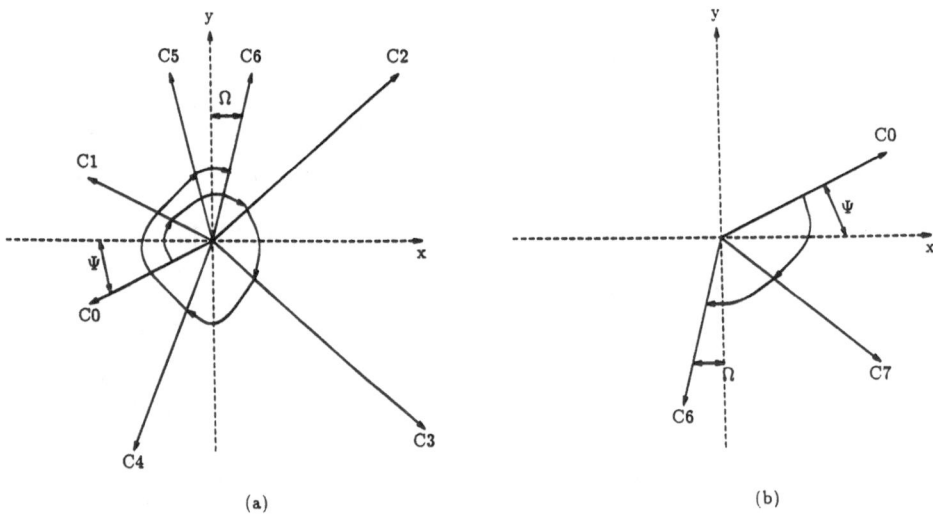

Fig. 22. The directional change along the primitive sequences: (a) E_5 (see Figure 13(a)), (b) E_6 (see Figure 13(b)).

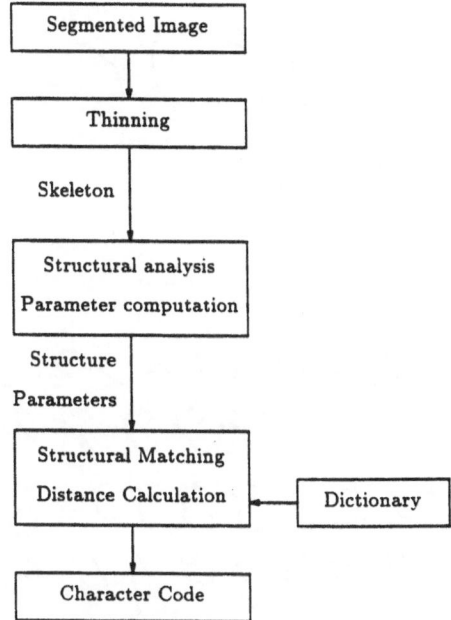

Fig. 23. Components of hand-printed character recognition system.

Fig. 24. Examples of '6'.

Fig. 25. Examples of '0'.

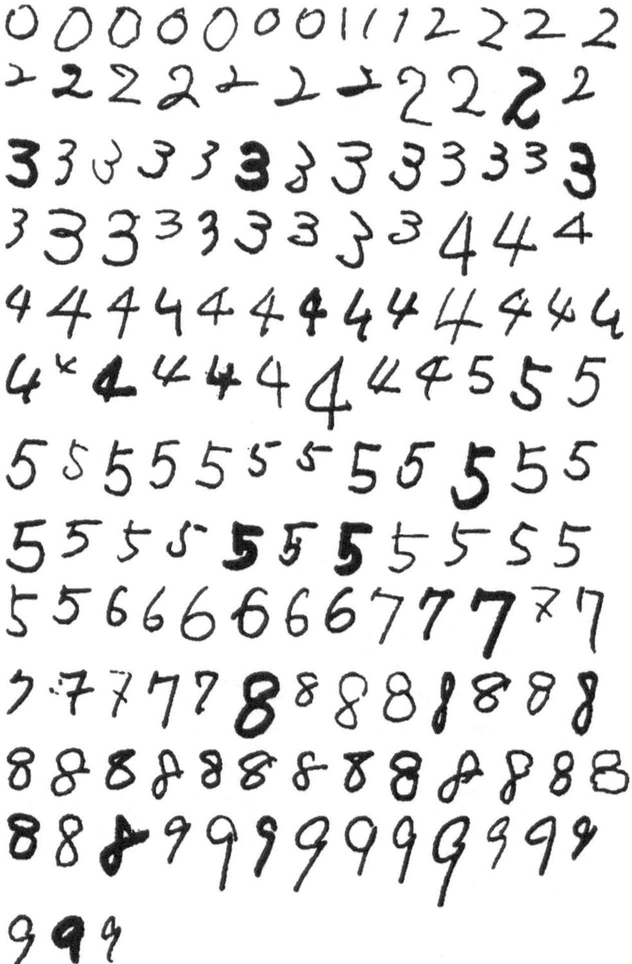

$$0\ 0\ 0\ 0\ 0\ 0\ 0\ 1\ 1\ 1\ 2\ 2\ 2\ 2$$
$$2\ 2\ 2\ 2\ 2\ 2\ 2\ 2\ 2\ 2\ 2\ 2$$
$$3\ 3\ 3\ 3\ 3\ 3\ 3\ 3\ 3\ 3\ 3\ 3$$
$$3\ 3\ 3\ 3\ 3\ 3\ 3\ 3\ 3\ 4\ 4\ 4$$
$$4\ 4\ 4\ 4\ 4\ 4\ 4\ 4\ 4\ 4\ 4\ 4$$
$$4\ 4\ 4\ 4\ 4\ 4\ 4\ 5\ 5\ 5$$
$$5\ 5\ 5\ 5\ 5\ 5\ 5\ 5\ 5\ 5\ 5\ 5$$
$$5\ 5\ 5\ 5\ 5\ 5\ 5\ 5\ 5\ 5\ 5$$
$$5\ 5\ 6\ 6\ 6\ 6\ 6\ 6\ 7\ 7\ 7\ 7$$
$$7\ 7\ 7\ 7\ 7\ 8\ 8\ 8\ 8\ 8\ 8\ 8$$
$$8\ 8\ 8\ 8\ 8\ 8\ 8\ 8\ 8\ 8\ 8\ 8$$
$$8\ 8\ 8\ 9\ 9\ 9\ 9\ 9\ 9\ 9\ 9\ 9$$
$$9\ 9\ 9$$

Fig. 26. Examples of the data used in the experiment of hand-printed character recognition.

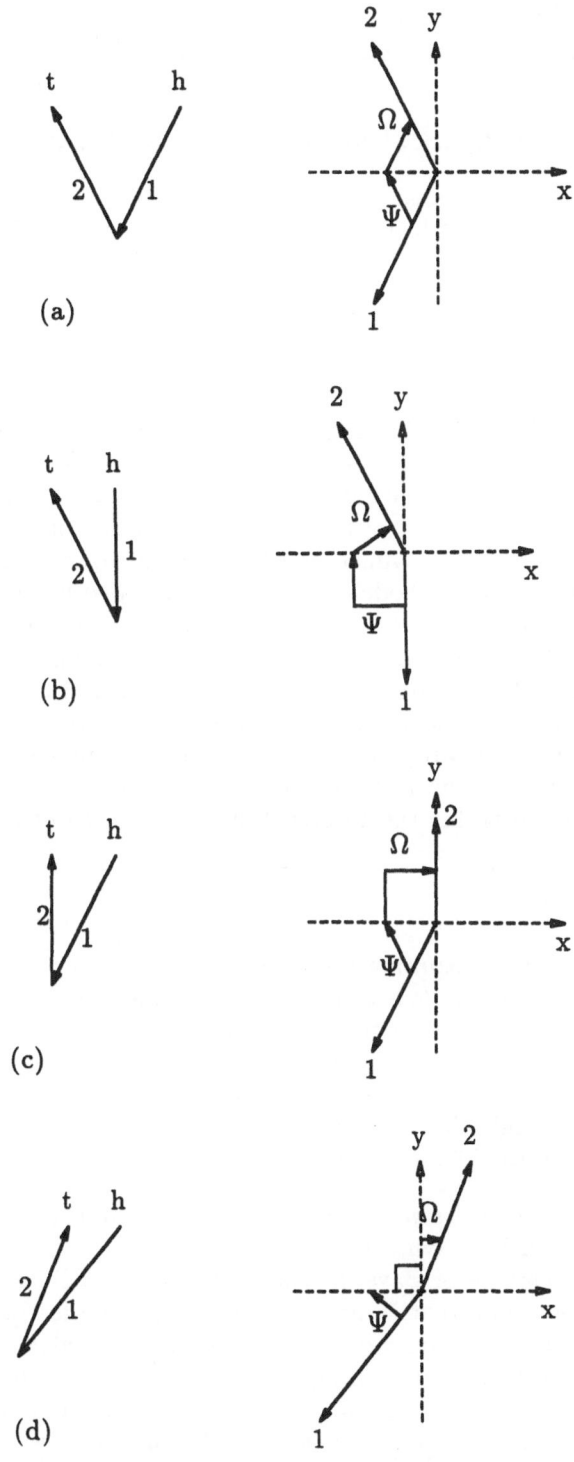

Fig. 27. Directional change along curves composed of two primitives.

Combination of Decisions by Multiple Classifiers

Tin Kam Ho, Jonathan J. Hull, and Sargur N. Srihari

Department of Computer Science,
State University of New York at Buffalo,
Buffalo, NY 14260, USA

A technique for combining the results of classifier decisions in a multi-classifier recognition system is presented. Each classifier produces a ranking of a set of classes. The combination technique uses these rankings to determine a small subset of the set of classes that contains the correct class. A group consensus function is then applied to re-rank the elements in the subset. This methodology is especially suited for recognition systems with large numbers of classes where it is valuable to reduce the decision problem to a manageable size before making a final determination about the identity of the image. Experimentation is discussed in which the proposed method is used with a word recognition problem where 40 classifiers are applied to degraded machine-printed word images and where a typical lexicon contains 235 words. A 96.6% correct rate is achieved within the 10 best decisions for 817 test images.

1 Introduction

In practical pattern recognition problems, a large number of features can often contribute to recognition. It is common to represent all such measurements in a single descriptor, such as a feature vector. A classifier decides the class identity by evaluating a discriminant function or distance function defined for such a descriptor [7].

An effective single classifier over a large set of features may be difficult to design because of the following reasons:

1. Different *classifier designs* are appropriate for different feature subsets. The alternatives include syntactic or various statistical classifier designs such as nearest-neighbor or Bayesian classifiers. Each classifier can itself contain valuable knowledge that is difficult to represent in a feature descriptor.
2. Different *types of feature measurements*. Parameter values that describe features may be measured on a nominal, ordinal, interval or ratio scale. The physical meaning of the parameters can be so different that they cannot be easily normalized to one single scale. For instance, we can be interested in higher level features such as the location of a perceptual entity (*e.g.* an

edge, an end point etc.), and also a lower level feature like a count of all the black pixels in the image. Though a descriptor can always be developed to represent such a collection of features, it is nontrivial to define a meaningful distance function for such a descriptor. Arbitrary combination of such a mixture of scales may result in meaningless operations [22].

3. Different *recognition approaches* may be appropriate for the same recognition problem, and there may be no meaningful distance function defined on the feature values computed by all the approaches. Each method may contribute information not given by another one. For instance, one approach may recognize the object as a whole, whereas another approach may recognize the components of the object and then derive consistent decisions.

Moreover, variables of different types can be sensitive to different input conditions, such as various patterns of image degradation, and the characteristics of the classes if a variable input class set is given. It is not easy to optimize the performance of a single classifier using a large collection of feature variables under all circumstances.

Recently, it has been observed that a multiple classifier system can be advantageous in pattern recognition problems involving diverse features ([11, 13, 14, 19, 23]). A multiple classifier system applies a number of independent classifiers in parallel to each image and combines their results to generate a single decision. A multiple classifier system overcomes some of the disadvantages of a single classifier approach listed earlier in the following ways:

1. Different similarity measures and classification procedures can be defined for various feature subsets such that the information contained in each subset is best utilized.
2. Feature measurements on different scales can be matched separately in their corresponding scales, such that the evaluation operations will be appropriate for all the feature types.
3. Different approaches for recognition can be applied by using different classifier designs that are appropriate for the individual methods.
4. Features sensitive to different input conditions can be separated and *dynamically selected* when knowledge of the input conditions is available. Post classification selection is also possible if a confidence measure can be associated with the classification decisions.

A critical question for a multiple classifier approach is whether one can combine the decisions of the individual classifiers and obtain one classifier with performance better than any one working in isolation. In this paper, we demonstrate that this is possible, and propose a method that can be used to combine the decisions of individual classifiers to obtain a classification procedure which performs better than the individual classifiers.

We assume that the decisions of each classifier are given as rank orders of a given set of classes. The proposed combination methods are primarily based on these rank orders. In levels of strength in measurement, rank orders are weaker than the distance measures used by the individual classifiers but stronger than categorical decisions (either accepted to be a certain class or rejected, such as the decisions produced by many syntactic classifiers) [15, 24]. By using rank orders, we avoid the problem of combining a mixture of scales used by different classifiers. Nevertheless, more information can be utilized than the methods that rely on only categorical decisions. In fact, it has been well known in the theory of multidimensional scaling, that rank orders provide sufficient information to recover most of the distance relationship of a set of objects [6, 21]. Categorical decisions can be regarded as degenerate rank orders.

The decision combination is performed in two stages. A candidate set of classes is first derived. A group consensus function is then applied to re-rank the classes in the candidate set by combining the rankings assigned by the classifiers.

2 The Intersection Approach and the Union Approach

Assume that in a multiple classifier system, each classifier produces a ranking of a set of allowable classes by evaluating a measure of distance between the feature descriptors obtained from the image and those stored as prototypes. We will call the classes ranked near the top as the *neighborhood* of the true class. The objective of recognition is to produce a neighborhood that contains the true class. Perfect recognition will be achieved when the true class is the only member of the neighborhood.

To produce a candidate set from a set of rankings, two opposite approaches are possible. In the first approach, a large neighborhood is obtained from each classifier, and their intersection is then output as a set of candidates. Hence a class will be an output candidate if and only if it is in *all* the neighborhoods. In other words, a decision is made if it is confirmed by all classifiers. In the second approach, a small neighborhood is obtained from each classifier. The *union* of these neighborhoods is output as a set of candidates. A class is output as a candidate if and only if it is in *at least* one of the neighborhoods.

Obviously the intersection approach is appropriate only when all the classifiers have moderate worst case performance, such that thresholds on neighborhood sizes can be selected in a way that the candidate set can be small, while the true class is not missed. However, for a set of specialized classifiers working on small subsets of features, this is usually not achievable, since each classifier may perform poorly for certain types of inputs. We propose that the union approach is preferred for combining a set of highly specialized classifiers, because the strength of any individual classifier can be preserved, while its weakness can be compensated for by other classifiers.

Besides these two approaches, an intermediate approach is also possible that relies on a voting scheme to determine which class should be included in the candidate set, though the design of the voting scheme is more difficult than either the intersection or the union approach. Practical requirements such as the maximum error rate allowed need to be considered.

The following discussions in this paper are mostly based on the union approach. We will first show how the worst case performance can be improved by using our method to determine the sizes of the neighborhoods, and then describe how the set of output candidates can be re-ranked by combining the rankings from the individual classifiers.

3 Related Studies

One way to organize a set of feature-based classifiers is as a decision tree. Decision trees have a sequential and hierarchical organization. They are well-studied; a survey of decision tree methods is given in [18]. The topology of the tree is determined according to an optimization criterion, like minimizing the probability of misclassification and expected test cost.

Haralick [10] gives the error bounds when the intersection approach is applied to combine results from multiple Bayesian classifiers. An example problem is given where the use of multiple classifiers is motivated by the need to use multiple resolutions in various feature dimensions. Selection of different feature subsets to discriminate certain classes from others is also discussed.

Mandler and Schuermann [16] describe a method for combining independent classifier decisions based on the Dempster-Shafer theory of evidence. This method involves a series of transformations of computed pattern distances into confidence values, which are then combined by the rules of evidence theory.

The application of committee methods to two-class problems and an algorithm for the construction of a minimal committee is discussed in [17], where the final decision is made by majority vote. This method cannot be easily generalized to a many-class problem.

Hull *et al.* in [13, 14] demonstrate the usefulness of multiple algorithms for character recognition, with the decisions combined by a decision tree method and an earlier version of the approach described in this paper. Suen *et al.* in [23] propose the use of several experts for handwritten character recognition, with the decisions combined by majority vote. The voting makes use of of a single decision from each classifier. In case that a classifier does not discriminate among a set of decisions, its vote is split evenly among this decision set. Nadal *et al.* in [19] describe several heuristic rules for combining decisions by a similar set of classifiers.

In a problem with hundreds of classes and many classifiers, a rule is needed which will determine a consensus ranking from the rankings given by a group of individual decision makers. Such a rule is referred to as a *group consensus function* or a *social welfare function* [20]. Conditions on such functions and possibility theorems on various assumptions have been discussed in [1, 2, 9]. The logic of committee decisions and of elections, as well as a history of mathematical theory of committees and elections are presented in [4]. A formal analysis of social choice functions, with much emphasis on the study of majority functions is presented in [8]. A theory of distances between partial orders is given in [5].

4 The Recognition System

The proposed algorithm for classifier combination anticipates a recognition system like the one shown in Figure 1.

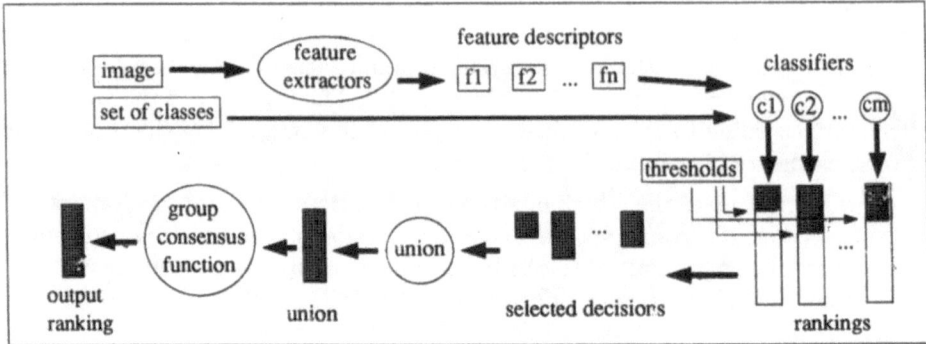

Fig. 1. A multiple-classifier recognition system.

A set of classifiers are applied to an input image. Each classifier produces a ranking of a set of allowable classes. A small number of classes are chosen from the top of each ranking by a set of thresholds. The union of these subsets of the set of classes is ranked by a group consensus function, and then output by the recognition system.

The proposed algorithm chooses the set of thresholds to minimize the size of the union and maximize the probability that it contains the class of the input image. We are concerned with cases where there are a large number of classes (500 or more) [12].

To choose the thresholds, the classifiers are first applied to a set of training data. A performance table for the training set like the one shown in Table 1 can then be obtained. The left half of the table shows the rankings of the *true class* in each image by each of the classifiers. We perform a transformation that takes the minimum ranking in each row and produces the right half of the table. The rankings can be partial orders, but, for convenience, we convert all of them into total orders by resolving ties using an arbitrary order in the set of classes. This data structure is the basis of the proposed technique for threshold selection.

5 Proposed Algorithm for Threshold Selection

This section presents a formal description of the algorithm for threshold selection in a multi-classifier recognition system.

Table 1. Example performance table for a training set.

$I_i \backslash C_j$	$rank^i_j$				$rowmin^i_j$			
	C_1	C_2	C_3	C_4	C_1	C_2	C_3	C_4
I_1	3	12	1	24	0	0	1	0
I_2	1	5	29	12	1	0	0	0
I_3	34	3	4	6	0	3	0	0
I_4	9	7	6	7	0	0	6	0
I_5	4	36	5	5	4	0	0	0
I_6	16	2	3	4	0	2	0	0
$colmax_j$					4	3	6	0

Let $rank^i_j$ be the ranking of the *true class* in image i by classifier j, where $i = 1, 2, ..., n$ and $j = 1, 2, ..., m$.

Define
$$rowmin^i_j = \begin{cases} rank^i_j & \text{if } \forall l, 1 \leq l \leq m, rank^i_j \leq rank^i_l \\ 0 & \text{otherwise} \end{cases}$$
$$colmax_j = Max_i (rowmin^i_j)$$

we can then claim that $\forall i, \exists j$ such that $rank^i_j \leq colmax_j$.

Proof: (by contradiction) otherwise, $\exists k$, we have $\forall j \; rank^k_j > colmax_j$.
Then $\exists l$, $rowmin^k_l = Min_j (rank^k_j) > colmax_j$ \qquad (1),
and $colmax_j \overset{(def)}{\geq} rowmin^k_l \overset{(1)}{>} colmax_j$ which is a contradiction.

This claim says that for any image I_i in the training set, if we take top $colmax_j$ decisions from classifier C_j for each j, and take the *union* of all these decisions, then the true class for image I_i *must be* contained in this union. The $colmax_j$ values are the thresholds determined by this method. The thresholds can then be used to obtain unions for other test sets.

Intuitively, $colmax_j$ for classifier j is the worst case decision by classifier j, when no other classifiers can do better than it. Consider an ideal system such that we know, by observing the performance on a training set, that for any input image, there exists a classifier which will rank its true class at the top. In this case all the $colmax_j$'s equal to one, that is, we only need to consider the top decisions from all the classifiers. Consider another system that there is only one classifier. In this case $colmax_1$ is the worst case rank given by that classifier.

6 Observations

For any j, if $colmax_j = 0$, then classifier j is redundant, in the sense that its decision is always inferior to some other classifiers. Classifier C_4 in Table 1 is redundant in this sense.

Let $\{C_{j_1}, C_{j_2}, ..., C_{j_k}\}$ be any subset of the original classifier set, and let the *maximum union size* be defined as

$$MUS = \sum_{j=j_1}^{j_k} colmax_j$$

For the example given in Table 1, $MUS = 4 + 3 + 6 = 13$. That means all the true classes for the images in this training set will be included in a union of size *at most* 13, which is smaller than the number of decisions needed from any individual classifier for the same correct rate.

Yet one may notice that for the example in Table 1, if we use only the classifier subset $\{C_1, C_2\}$, or $\{C_2, C_3\}$, and obtain the thresholds $colmax_j$ following the aforementioned procedure, we will need a union of even smaller size (11 in both cases). In fact, the smallest union size (10) can be obtained if we use the subset $\{C_1, C_3\}$. This observation leads to a method for classifier subset selection.

7 Classifier Subset Selection

A method for classifier subset selection can be derived based on the previous observations.

If MUS is minimized over all possible subsets, then $\{C_{j_1}, C_{j_2}, ..., C_{j_k}\}$ is the theoretical minimum-union-size (optimal worst case performance) classifier subset for the training set.

A direct implementation of this selection technique would require evaluation of MUS over the power set of the classifiers and thus is not a polynomial algorithm. The complexity may preclude its application to larger classifier sets. One simplification is to omit the subset selection procedure, and use all the classifiers except the redundant ones. Another simplification is to approximate the theoretical optimum by a greedy algorithm, which aims at stepwise reduction of MUS by adding new classifiers.

Whereas MUS is the theoretical maximum size of the union, the true maximum or average union size can be determined experimentally by actually obtaining all the decisions and forming the unions. Hence the minimum MUS does not necessarily give an optimal experimental union size. But this is a useful measure in the absence of more knowledge of the mutual dependence among the classifiers.

The performance of this method on test sets will depend on how well the training set represents the population. This includes both the quality of the images and the distribution of the classes in the training images.

8 Dynamic Feature Selection

Consider an *oracle* that will always select the best classifier C_j for each image I_i. If such an oracle is available, we can take the top $colmax_j$ decisions from classifier C_j only, and ignore the decisions by other classifiers. In this case MUS

is the maximum $colmax_j$, which could be much smaller than the MUS given by the union.

Such an oracle will perform what we may call *dynamic feature selection*. It selects the best feature set for recognition for each image. The selection can be based on confidence of feature detection, or possible association of the classifier performance with other characteristics of the image like some global features, or some estimation of the degradation pattern in the image. Dynamic feature/classifier selection can be done on a set of features/classifiers that are *statically* determined to be useful when all possible cases are taken into consideration.

One way to approximate such an oracle is to compute some mutually exclusive conditions from the images. A training set can be partitioned according to the computed conditions. Classifier performance can be measured separately on each partition. The best classifier for each partition can hence be determined. For the test set, similar conditions can be computed and the best classifier will be selected.

Note that this kind of selection is an intermediate method between two extremes, one being a static single classifier method and the other is with one classifier for each class that responds well for patterns of only that class. In the latter case selection of the best classifier is equivalent to the original classification problem in difficulty.

9 Combination of Rankings

The candidate classes contained in the set derived by either the union or the intersection approach can be further ranked by combining the rankings they received from the individual classifiers. One useful combination scheme is referred to as the *Borda Count* [20]. In the original definition, the rankings given by all the classifiers are considered. For any particular class c, the Borda count is the sum of the number of classes ranked below c by each classifier. If a candidate subset is selected from the set of allowable classes, in computing this count, we will consider the classes included in this subset only. Our definition is given as follows:

For any class c in the candidate subset S, let $B_j(c)$ be the number of classes in S which are ranked below the class c by classifier C_j. $B_j(c)$ is zero if $c \notin S$. The Borda count for class c is $B(c) = \sum_{j=1}^{m} B_j(c)$. The final ranking is given by arranging the classes in the union so that their Borda counts are in descending order.

This count is dependent on the agreement among the classifiers. Intuitively, if the class c is ranked near the top by more classifiers, its Borda count tends to be larger.

10 Example Application

The approach is illustrated with examples from a word recognition system. The input to the system includes an image of a machine-printed word, and a given lexicon which contains the word. We are developing a holistic word shape based recognition system *without* applying character segmentation. It is desired that a ranking of the lexicon be produced such that the target word should be as close to the top as possible. The rankings can then be combined with the decisions from an isolated-character-based recognizer.

A set of global and local features are identified and computed for each input image. Global features describe some overall characteristics of a word, and local features describe certain locally detectable characteristics.

The global features used include the case of the word, which says whether the word is in purely upper, purely lower or mixed case, and a word length estimate, which is a range of possible numbers of characters in the word. In our application, purely lower case words are not considered. The shape of the same word is different when printed in upper or mixed case, and hence separate feature prototypes are needed for the different cases. Exact estimate of the case reduces the number of word prototypes to be compared by half. Estimates of word length further reduce the size of the lexicon. However, the amount of the reduction depends on the accuracy of the estimate.

The local features that are used include geometrical characteristics such as endpoints, edges, vertical and horizontal strokes, diagonal strokes, curves, distribution of strokes, some topological features like dots, holes, and bridges between strokes [11], as well as a set of template defined features described in [3]. Table 2 summarizes the detection methods for the features used in our design.

Table 2. Summary of structural features used in word recognition.

Global Features	Extraction Method
Case	Analysis of separation between reference lines, horizontal projection profile, and connected components
Word length	Analysis of vertical projection profile and connected components
Local Features	Extraction Method
Template defined features	Convolution
Stroke distribution	All direction run length analysis
Stroke edges	Run length analysis
End points of skeleton	Convolution
Holes and dots	Connected component analysis
Vertical and horizontal strokes	Run length analysis
Curves and diagonal strokes	Chain code analysis
Bridges between strokes	Connected component analysis

The recognition algorithm first filters the lexicon according to the computed global features (case and word length estimate). Local features are then extracted. A fixed area partition grid of 4 × 10 is used to describe the location of the local features. A set of 36 different descriptors are used to represent the local features and their locations. They are in different forms including two feature vectors, 5 symbol strings for 5 different subsets of the features, as well as 29 digit strings, one for each feature. Each descriptor is compared to the counterpart in the prototypes by a distance function, which is either a city-block distance [7] or a string edit distance [25]. Four composite distance functions are also used. A nearest-neighbor classifier is implemented using each of these distances. This results in 40 classifiers in total, each produces a ranking of the filtered lexicon. The level of resolution of the rankings varies among the different classifiers. Classifiers 1 and 2 use a refined distance measure so that the rankings are mostly total orders. The other classifiers that use string edit distances produce partial orders most of the time. The partial orders are converted into total orders by the alphabetical order of the words. The rankings are then combined using our proposed union approach and re-ranking method. Table 3 gives a summary of these descriptors and the corresponding distance functions. Table 4 gives a summary of the features used by the 40 classifiers.

Table 3. Summary of feature descriptors and corresponding distance functions.

Features	Descriptor	Example	Distance Function
template features	1280 dimensional vector	[5 0 4 2 ....]	city-block distance
stroke distribution	160 dimensional vector	[10 26 0 0 ....]	city-block distance
relative location of edges end points, ascenders, descenders, holes, dots, curves etc.	symbol strings, one for each feature subset. each symbol represents a specific feature	$AOOAD$	minimum edit distance
horizontal position of edges, end points, ascenders, descenders, holes, dots, curves etc.	digit strings, one for each feature. digits are positions w.r.t. the 10 width partitions	2334567	minimum edit distance, where edit costs are differences of digit values

11 Experimental Results

The recognition system has been developed using a collection of images of *machine-printed* postal words obtained from live mail. They were scanned at roughly 200 ppi and binarized. The font and quality of the images vary. We used a measure of density (number of black pixels divided by image area) to assess the image quality. Figure 2 shows some example images with low, medium and high density levels. In the database we have roughly the same number of images in each of these three categories.

The available images were divided into separate training sets and testing sets. The feature extractors were developed and modified by observing performance in

Table 4. Summary of features used by the classifiers.

Classifier	Features	Distances
1	convolution generated feature vector	city-block distance
2	stroke distribution vector	city-block distance
3	symbol string for edge features	string edit distance
4-11	location strings for edge features	string edit distance
12		sum of distances for 4-11
13	symbol string for endpoint features	string edit distance
14-18	location strings for edge features	string edit distance
19		sum of distances for 14-18
20-22	symbol strings for letter shape features	string edit distance
23		sum of distances for 20-22
24-39	location strings for letter shape features	string edit distance
40		sum of distances for 24-39

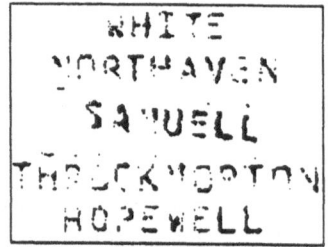 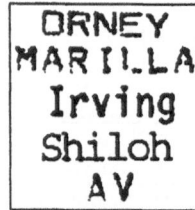 

Fig. 2. Example images with low, medium and high density levels.

a small initial training set of about 200 images. Feature prototypes for characters were 179 font samples. Feature prototypes for the words in the lexicon were obtained by synthesizing feature descriptors computed for the characters.

A set of 1675 images, different from those we used in developing the feature extractors, were used to test the classifier combination algorithm. Input lexicons contained postal words including city names and street names. A different lexicon was associated with each input image, depending on other information in the address block from which the input image was extracted. The average size of the input lexicon was 235 words.

We allowed a rejection option in case assignment (which duplicated the size of the lexicon for the reject cases), and flexible ranges for word length estimate so that for 1634 images (97.55% of total), the true word remained in the filtered lexicon, *i.e.* the computed global features were correct. The average size of the *filtered* lexicon was 68 (words). This set was divided into two halves randomly as a training set and a testing set, each containing 817 images. The 40 classifiers were applied to both sets.

To derive the neighborhood thresholds, we constructed the ranking table for the training set. Table 5 gives the performance of the 40 classifiers on these 817 images, the maximum rank needed to get all the true words if each classifier was used in isolation, as well as the computed neighborhood thresholds. As observed from the computed thresholds, only classifiers 1, 2, 3, 4, 6, 8, 9, 10, 11, 12, 13, 16, 18, 19, 21, 22, 26, 37, and 40 were contributing, and the others were redundant. The maximum union size was determined to be 53, much smaller than the maximum rank required for each classifier. The average union size was determined to be 28 after the unions were actually computed, which was 53% of the average size of the filtered lexicons. That is, on the average, 47% of the candidate classes could be eliminated from further consideration after the union was computed. If an oracle selecting the best classifier for each image was available, the top choice correct rate would be 96.0%, and the correct rates at top 2,3,4,5,10 choices would be 98.2%, 99.1%, 99.4%, 99.8%, and 100% respectively.

Table 5. Summary of performance on training set and neighborhood thresholds.

Classifier	1	2	3	4	5	6	7	8	9	10	11	12	13	14	15	16	17	18	19	20
% corr. top 1	89	90	67	9	5	21	12	14	21	18	19	42	39	13	5	6	21	24	35	30
% corr. top 2	92	93	77	14	7	30	17	21	27	35	27	54	51	22	8	12	29	34	45	38
% corr. top 3	92	95	82	17	9	36	22	25	34	41	34	58	57	27	11	16	36	42	51	44
% corr. top 4	93	96	84	20	11	40	24	28	37	45	39	63	62	30	12	23	42	46	55	47
% corr. top 5	94	97	85	23	13	43	27	31	42	47	45	67	66	33	14	35	44	49	58	50
% corr. top 10	96	98	90	44	41	55	39	47	51	57	60	77	78	55	42	47	56	59	69	60
thresholds	3	8	10	1	0	5	0	2	1	2	3	1	2	0	0	1	0	2	1	0

Classifier	21	22	23	24	25	26	27	28	29	30	31	32	33	34	35	36	37	38	39	40
% corr. top 1	12	11	28	22	4	26	6	5	6	3	5	6	5	7	8	6	8	5	8	27
% corr. top 2	18	19	38	29	7	33	14	7	9	6	8	12	8	10	13	9	12	15	12	36
% corr. top 3	22	26	45	33	10	37	17	9	11	9	12	15	10	12	17	12	16	18	17	43
% corr. top 4	26	32	50	37	12	40	22	11	16	11	14	18	13	14	18	14	26	22	19	46
% corr. top 5	30	36	52	40	14	43	25	13	34	13	18	20	15	17	21	17	29	27	22	51
% corr. top 10	46	53	65	56	41	52	47	41	48	40	33	28	38	35	33	34	45	44	41	64
thresholds	1	3	0	0	0	3	0	0	0	0	0	0	0	0	0	0	5	0	0	5

The same feature extractors and *contributing* classifiers were then applied to the set of 817 test images, which were different from all the images used in various training stages. Similar input lexicons were used. After the classifiers produced the rankings, the neighborhood thresholds were applied to select a number of top decisions from each classifier. The union of these selected decisions was formed. The classes in the union were re-ranked using the Borda count which was computed on the rankings of classifier 1 and 2. Table 6 gives the performance of the 40 classifiers on these 817 images. As can be seen from the performance table, some of the 40 classifiers, when working in isolation, are very poor in (macroscopic) performance over the whole test set. However, the union combination was better than any of the individual classifiers. After the union computation and reranking, the correct rate at top choice was 94%. The correct rates at the top 2,3,4,5 and 10 choices were 96%, 97%, 97%, 98%, and 99% respectively. Degraded by the errors in the global feature computation stage, this was equivalent to 96.6% correct rate at top 10 choices for the input test set. The average union size was determined to be 28. The union included the true class in 99.3% of all the test images.

Table 6. Summary of performance on testing set.

classifier	1	2	3	4	6	8	9	10	11	12	13	16	18	19	21	22	26	37	40	union
% corr. top 1	92	92	67	9	23	16	21	17	22	43	39	7	26	34	12	10	32	7	29	94
% corr. top 2	94	96	76	14	32	23	28	33	31	55	53	12	33	45	19	18	36	10	38	96
% corr. top 3	95	96	80	17	38	28	35	40	36	61	60	15	39	51	23	24	43	14	44	97
% corr. top 4	96	97	83	19	42	31	38	44	40	66	64	22	42	55	27	28	46	24	51	97
% corr. top 5	96	97	84	21	45	33	43	47	44	69	68	37	45	58	31	31	47	28	54	98
% corr. top 10	97	98	90	46	57	48	53	57	58	78	81	47	56	73	48	47	57	42	68	99

This experiment showed that the combination performance was better than those of the individual classifiers. However, we did not perform a combinatorial subset selection procedure due to the complexity involved. Therefore it is possible that the combination of certain subsets of these 40 classifiers performs better than what has been achieved.

12 Conclusions and Future Work

A technique was presented for combining the rankings of a large set of classes by the classifiers in a multi-classifier pattern recognition system. The combination algorithm first determines a candidate set of classes and then derives a consensus ranking on the candidate set. A method was shown that utilizes the results of applying the classifiers to training data to determine a set of thresholds on the rankings. The ranked subsets obtained by applying the thresholds are then combined with a union operation and re-ranked by a group consensus function. This technique discovers those classifiers that are redundant and removes them from the recognition system. A further methodology was discussed for selecting a subset of the non-redundant classifiers that minimizes the union size.

The proposed technique was applied to a word recognition problem that used 40 classifiers and involved an average of 235 classes. The data were binary images of machine printed words that were scanned on a postal OCR at 200 pixels per inch. In many cases the image quality was very poor. Applying the strategy to a testing set resulted in a 96.6% correct rate within the top 10 choices.

The use of Borda count to combine rankings is one among many other possible methods. It is believed that some descriptive statistics, such as measurement of correlation among the classifiers, should be taken into account in ranking combination. Follow up work will include studies of the possible applications of other group consensus functions to classifier ranking combination, consideration of correlation measures for the classifiers, as well as the functional dependence of the combined performance on the individual classifier performances. Our goal will be to identify some necessary conditions on the individual classifier performance such that the combined performance will be *always* better.

The multiple classifiers can be organized at multiple stages such that some subsets of the classifiers can be combined first, and the results are then combined at the next stage. Use of both the intersection approach and the union approach in the same system is also possible.

Future work will also include investigation of an oracle that selects the best feature sets dynamically. This is possible if some of the feature subsets are selectively ignored, based on top-down constraints such as the discriminative power of a particular feature with respect to the input class set, or bottom-up information such as a measurement of the degradation in the image and the confidence of feature detection.

Acknowledgements

The support of the Office of Advanced Technology of the United States Postal Service is gratefully acknowledged. The authors appreciate the valuable suggestions by the reviewers of an earlier version of this paper. The discussions with Dr. David Sher of SUNY at Buffalo were especially helpful. Peter Cullen, Michal Prussak and Piotr Prussak assisted in the development of the database for the experiments.

References

1. K. J. Arrow, *Social Choice and Individual Values*, Cowles Commission Monograph 12, John Wiley, New York, 1951, 2nd ed., 1963.
2. K. J. Arrow and H. Raynaud, *Social Choice and Multicriterion decision-making*, MIT Press, Cambridge, Mass., 1986.
3. H. S. Baird, H. P. Graf, L. D. Jackel, and W. E. Hubbard, "A VLSI Architecture For Binary Image Classification," In J.-C. Simon (ed.), *From Pixels to Features*, pp. 275–286, North–Holland, Amsterdam, 1989.
4. D. Black, *The Theory of Committees and Elections*, Cambridge Univ. Press, Cambridge, U.K., 1958, reprinted 1963.
5. K. P. Bogart, "Preference Structures I: Distances between Transitive Preference Relations," *J. of Mathematical Sociology*, 3, pp. 49–67, 1973.
6. C. H. Coombs, *A Theory of Data*, John Wiley, New York, 1964.
7. R. O. Duda and P. E. Hart, *Pattern Classification and Scene Analysis*, Addison-Wesley, Reading, MA, 1973.
8. P. C. Fishburn, *The Theory of Social Choice*, Princeton Univ. Press, Princeton, 1972.
9. L. A. Goodman and H. Markowitz, "Social Welfare Functions Based on Individual Rankings," *The American J. of Sociology*, 58, pp. 257–262, 1952.
10. R. M. Haralick, "The Table Look-Up Rule," *Comm. in Statistics — Theory and Methods*, A5, 12, pp. 1163–1191, 1976.

11. T. K. Ho, J. J. Hull, and S. N. Srihari, "A Word Shape Analysis Approach to Recognition of Degraded Word Images," *Proc. USPS Advanced Technology Conf.*, Washington, D. C., pp. 217–231, November 1990.

12. J. J. Hull, "Feature Selection and Language Syntax in Text Recognition," In J.-C. Simon (ed.), *From Pixels to Features*, pp. 249–260, North–Holland, Amsterdam, 1989.

13. J. J. Hull, A. Commike, and T. K. Ho, "Multiple Algorithms for Handwritten Character Recognition," *Proc. the International Workshop on Frontiers in Handwriting Recognition*, Montreal, pp. 117–124, 1990.

14. J. J. Hull, S. N. Srihari, E. Cohen, C. L. Kuan, P. Cullen, and P. Palumbo, "A blackboard-based approach to handwritten ZIP Code recognition," *Proc. Third United States Postal Service Advanced Technology Conf.*, Washington, D. C., pp. 1018–1032, May 1988.

15. D. H. Krantz, R. D. Luce, P. Suppes, and A. Tversky, *Foundations of Measurement, Volume I, Additive and Polynomial Representations*, Academic Press, 1971.

16. E. Mandler and J. Schürmann, "Combining the Classification Results of Independent Classifiers Based on the Dempster/Shafer Theory of Evidence," In E. S. Gelsema and L. N. Kanal (eds.), *Pattern Recognition and Artificial Intelligence*, pp. 381–393, North–Holland, Amsterdam, 1988.

17. V. D. Mazurov, A. I. Krivonogov, and V. L. Kazantsev, "Solving of Optimization and Identification Problems by the Committee Methods," *Pattern Recognition*, 20, 4, pp. 371–378, 1987.

18. B. M. E. Moret, "Decision Trees and Diagrams," *Computing Surveys*, 14, pp. 593–623, December 1982.

19. C. Nadal, R. Legault, and C. Y. Suen, "Complementary Algorithms for the Recognition of Totally Unconstrained Handwritten Numerals," *Proc. 10th ICPR*, Atlantic City, NJ, Vol.I, pp. 443–449, 1990.

20. F. S. Roberts, *Discrete Mathematical Models, with Applications to Social, Biological, and Environmental Problems*, Prentice–Hall, Englewood Cliffs, NJ, 1976.

21. A. K. Romney, R. H. Shepard, and S. B. Nerlove, *Multidimensional Scaling, Theory and Applications in the Behavioral Sciences*, Vol. I and II, Seminar Press, 1972.

22. S. S. Stevens, "Measurement, Statistics, and the Schemapiric View," *Science*, 161, 3844, pp. 849–856, 1968.

23. C. Y. Suen, C. Nadal, T. A. Mai, R. Legault, and L. Lam, "Recognition of Totally Unconstrained Handwritten Numerals Based on the Concept of Multiple Experts," *Proc. the International Workshop on Frontiers in Handwriting Recognition*, Montreal, pp. 131–140, April 1990.

24. P. Suppes, D. M. Krantz, R. D. Luce, and A. Tversky, *Foundations of Measurement, Volume II, Geometrical, Threshold, and Probabilistic Representations*, Academic Press, 1989.

25. R. A. Wagner and M. J. Fischer, "The String-to-String Correction Problem," *J. of the ACM*, 21, 1, pp. 168–173, January 1974.

Resolving Ambiguity in Segmenting Touching Characters

Shuichi Tsujimoto and Haruo Asada

Toshiba Research and Development Center,
1, Komukai Toshiba-cho, Saiwai-ku, Kawasaki 210, Japan

This paper presents an efficient and powerful character segmentation method which enables touching characters in a document to be read accurately at high speed. The character segmentation phase extracts characters from a text line. Connected components in a text line image may have to be segmented or combined to form recognizable characters. For example, the character 'i' is formed by combining two components. Touching characters are segmented to identify each character. Segmenting touching characters is an open problem, whose solution would advance the field. Touching characters have several candidates for their break position, which are then confirmed by recursive segmentation and recognition, and finally by the determination of the linguistic context. There are several possible candidates at each stage. For example, several candidates for the break position of touching characters are nominated. Any segmented area might possibly fit several alternative characters. Therefore, an efficient resolution of ambiguity at each stage is significantly critical and indispensable for practical text reading. The authors' approach is based on knowledge about character composition (*e.g.* an 'm' is like a combination of an 'r' and an 'n'), as well as knowledge about omni-fonts. Knowledge about character composition compresses the number of recursive segmentation and recognition. Knowledge about omni-fonts reduces the number of linguistic context adaptations. The proposed method resolves ambiguity at each stage, and hence achieves a 120 character per second text reading speed.

1 Introduction

A multitude of printed documents, such as newspapers, magazines, technical manuals, and other publications, have been published. Also, various kinds of machine/computer-aided text processing, such as desktop publishing, text database management, and machine translation, *e.g.*, English-to-Japanese translation, have been activated. Automation is widely demanded in the area of conventional manually operated keyboard computer input. A text reader meets this requirement. The text reader automatically analyzes each page in a document and recognizes each character in a page for input to a computer.

The text reader generally consists of two phases: a document analysis phase and a character segmentation phase. The document analysis phase extracts text lines from a page for recognition. This procedure consists of finding and extracting document items, like graphics, photographs, and text lines. This document analysis phase should be designed to achieve robustness even for multi-columned and multi-articled documents with graphics and photographs.

The character segmentation phase extracts characters from given text lines, which have been obtained in the document analysis phase. This procedure consists of finding and extracting characters to be recognized. This character segmentation phase should be designed to have robustness even for touching characters.

A text line is composed of words, each of which consists of characters. Thus, a text line has a hierarchical structure. Figure 1 shows a character segmentation overview. First, the connected area of a text line image is defined as a component. A component may have to be segmented or combined to form recognizable characters.

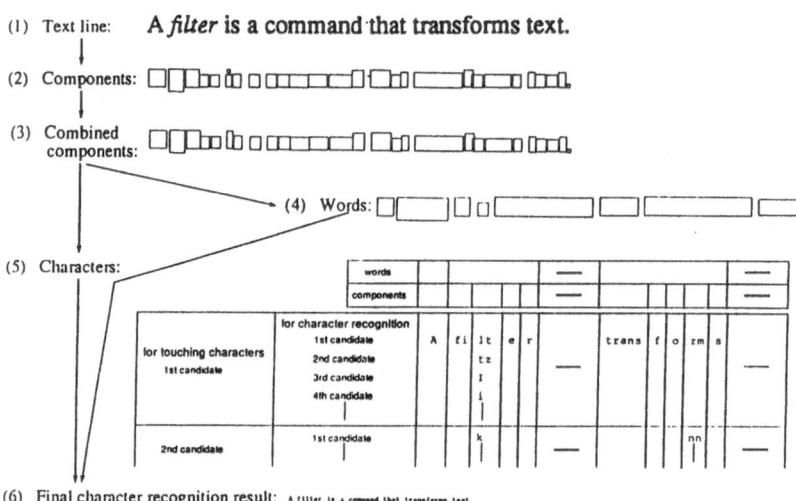

Fig. 1. Character segmentation overview.

Next, components above and below one another are combined. In Figure 1, the 'i' is formed by combining two components. Components too small to have the potential for forming characters may be regarded as noise to be removed. Words are detected by examining spaces between components.

Practical applications require a text reader to be able to read a document accurately at high speed. Segmenting touching characters is of major importance to meet this requirement. However, it is impossible to determine the number of individual characters contained in touching characters prior to the segmentation of touching characters, since an 'm' may have the same size as the combination of an 'r' and an 'n'. Character pitch information is not available for a document whose character pitch is proportional. Therefore, it is required to efficiently determine whether an input image consists of an 'r' and an 'n', or represents an 'm'. Up to now, Babaguchi, *et al.* [1] and Maeda, *et al.* [2] extracted characters from Japanese handwritten documents. Spitz [3] extracted characters from multi-lingual documents. Baird, *et al.* [4, 5] discussed the segmentation of touching characters. Casey and Nagy [6, 7] built a recursive segmentation and classification method for touching characters. Kooi, *et al.* [8] analyzed the contour of an image of touching characters.

This paper presents an efficient and powerful character segmentation method for touching characters. The segmentation procedure nominates candidates for the break position for touching characters. Then, recursive segmentation and recognition [6, 7] and the determination of the linguistic context confirm the candidates. There are several ambiguities at each stage. For example, touching characters have several candidates for their break position. A segmented area fits several alternative characters. The presented approach employs knowledge about character composition and knowledge about omni-fonts to resolve the ambiguity in an efficient manner.

Knowledge about character composition, *e.g.* a 'd' is like a 'c' and an 'l', avoids the necessity for implementing extra recursive segmentation and recognition. Knowledge about omni-fonts reduces the number of linguistic context adaptations. This approach achieves a speed of 120 characters per second with a correct character recognition rate of 99.7%.

Section 2 presents the authors' approach for segmenting touching characters. Section 3 describes the character segmentation method in detail. Section 4 shows experimental results achieved for a variety of documents.

2 Proposed Approach

It is often appropriate that problem parts should be sequentially solved in multiple phases, where several candidates stand. Ambiguity remains unresolved at a phase where a candidate identifying the solution for a problem cannot be successfully sought. There are generally two different approaches to this problem. One is the approach where ambiguities at each phase are deferred till the final phase. The other is the approach where ambiguity at each phase can be positively resolved in the said phase. The former is applied to problems where the final phase should be more emphasized than the other phases. The latter is applied to problems where phases should be individually and sequentially managed. The authors' approach for touching character segmentation belongs to the former rather than the latter.

The procedure for segmenting touching characters consists of four phases: (1) Break position candidates for touching characters are nominated and combined to construct a decision tree. (2) Possible candidates are searched for in the decision tree. (3) The area segmented by possible candidates is recognized to fit several alternative characters. (4) Determining the appropriate linguistic context confirms the characters. Resolving ambiguities at each phase is very important in order to segment touching characters due to two reasons. One is efficiency which enables the problem parts to be solved at high speed. The other is powerfulness which prevents ambiguities at a phase which will lead to mistaken confirmation. Without this powerfulness, a Roman numeral "III" might be mistakenly changed to an English word "ill" when determining a candidate 'i' for recognizing the first letter of the input word, may have been deferred to its linguistic context. As another example, numerals "50" and "200" might be mistakenly changed to English words "SO" and "ZOO", respectively.

Each component, defined as a connected area in a text line image, identifies a single character or touching characters. Some prior works employed the concept of aspect ratio to discriminate a component representing touching characters from a component representing a single character. However, aspect ratio alone is insufficient information, especially for a document whose character pitch is proportional. For example, in Figure 1, the single character 'A' has a greater aspect ratio than "lt", which is comprised of two characters. In the authors' approach, the component representing touching characters is determined on the basis of the character recognition result. First, a component is recognized as a single character. Then, the component whose similarity in recognition is less than an *a priori* similarity (described in Section 3.4 in detail), is determined to represent touching characters.

The procedure for segmenting touching characters involves several ambiguities. For example, (1) each component image has several candidates nominated for break position. (2) An individual component may fit several possible touching characters. In Figure 1, the "lt" portion of the word "filter" fits the combination of an 'l' and a 't', a 'k', and so on. (3) Each segmented area may fit several alternative characters. In Figure 1, the 'l' segment of the word "filter" fits an 'l', a 't', an 'I', an 'i', and so on. To resolve ambiguities, the authors define a new metric to evaluate the degree of touching in an image, as well as employing knowledge about character composition, and knowledge about omni-fonts. Knowledge about character composition avoids the necessity for carrying out a complete search in a decision tree. Knowledge about omni-fonts reduces the number of candidates adapted to a linguistic context. A new metric can be employed to exhibit the degree of touching and hence can nominate a sufficient number of candidates.

3 Character Segmentation Method for Touching Characters

This section describes a way to segment touching characters, based on break cost as a metric to evaluate the degree of touching , knowledge about character composition, and knowledge about omni-fonts. First, break cost nominates candidates for the break position for touching characters. Next, a decision tree, describing the search order for the candidates, is constructed. Candidates which allow a segmented area to be recognized with acceptance is searched utilizing a recursive segmentation and recognition approach [6, 7]. Knowledge about character composition avoids the necessity for implementing a complete search. Knowledge about the linguistic context confirms the candidates, whose numbers are reduced by the knowledge about omni-fonts.

3.1 New Metric for Segmenting Touching Characters

Prior works employed the vertical projection of the touching character image at each column to find positions to separate touching characters. The authors introduce a new metric for break cost. This break cost is defined at each position between neighboring columns. It is calculated by accumulating the black pixel amount of the image obtained by the AND operation between neighboring columns. Figure 2(b) shows the vertical projection of Figure 2(a), while Figure 2(c) shows a new metric capable of exhibiting a prominent connection between the left-hand and right-hand areas in Figure 2(a).

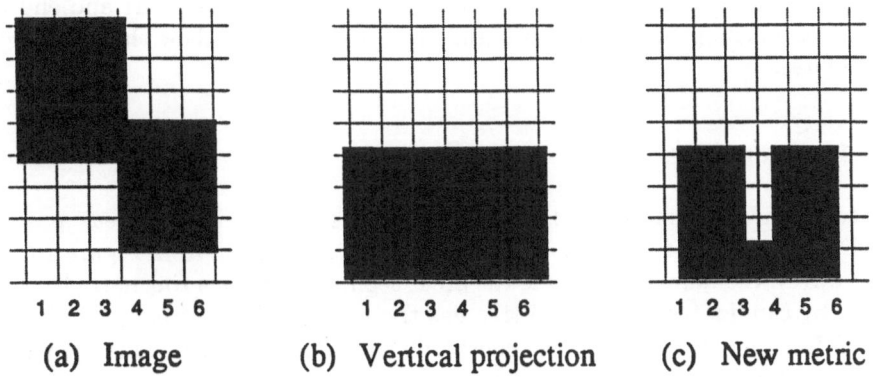

(a) Image   (b) Vertical projection   (c) New metric

Fig. 2. Break cost for segmenting touching characters.

The break cost is calculated for an image being raised up for touching characters whose font is regarded as italic as shown in Figure 3.

3.2 Candidates for Break Position

The authors assume that some changes in break cost can be found when two characters touch with each other. The candidates for a break position are obtained by finding local minimums of a smoothed break cost function. Multiple candidates are set at smooth local minima. Candidates are also set at both the start and end positions for touching characters. Figure 4(a) shows an example

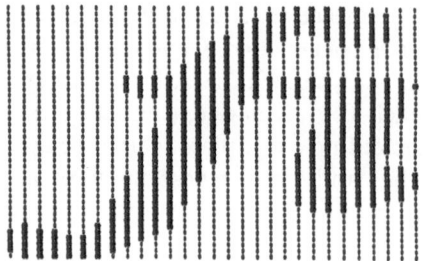 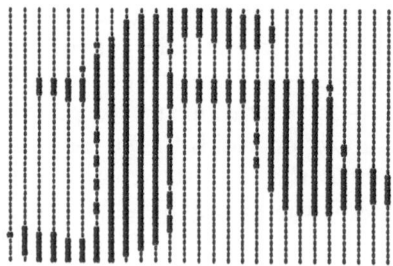

(a) Italics font image   (b) Italics font image being raised up

Fig. 3. Italic font characters.

of touching characters. The break cost for Figure 4(a) is shown in Figure 4(b), whose smoothed break cost function is shown in Figure 4(c). The arrows indicate the candidates for the break position.

There are two kinds of candidates. One has a higher possibility to be selected as the final break position than the other. If the break cost distribution around a candidate shows a dominant sharp peak, then advantage is given to that specific candidate. Advantage is also given to candidates at both the start and end positions of touching characters. In Figure 4(c), thick arrows show the advantaged candidates.

3.3 Decision Tree

A decision tree is constructed to represent the search order for break position candidates,. Figure 4(d) shows the decision tree constructed from Figure 4(c). In Figure 4(c), the numbers indicate the areas segmented from a touching character image by candidates. A decision tree has the following properties:

(1) Each node, except for the root node which has a NULL value, represents a subset of the segmented area, which may identify a single character. For example, in Figure 4(d), the subset {**2, 3**} corresponds to a node, which identifies an 'h'. (2) Each node has a list of the segmented area, whose first element is geometrically connected to the last element of the preceding node in a depth-first order. In other words, the daughters of a node represent succeeding characters. For example, the subset {**1**} has five daughters {**2**}, {**2, 3**}, {**2, 3, 4, 5, 6**}, {**2, 3, 4, 5**}, and {**2, 3, 4**}. The depth of the tree represents the order in which the characters segmented from touching characters are being managed. (3) The daughters of each node are sequentially ordered in the following ways.

(a) Among segmented areas ended by advantaged candidates, a smaller segmented area precedes the others. For example, the subset {**1**} precedes the subset {**1, 2**} among the daughters of the root node.

(b) Among adjacent segmented areas ended by candidates which are not advantaged, a larger segmented area precedes the others. For example, the subset

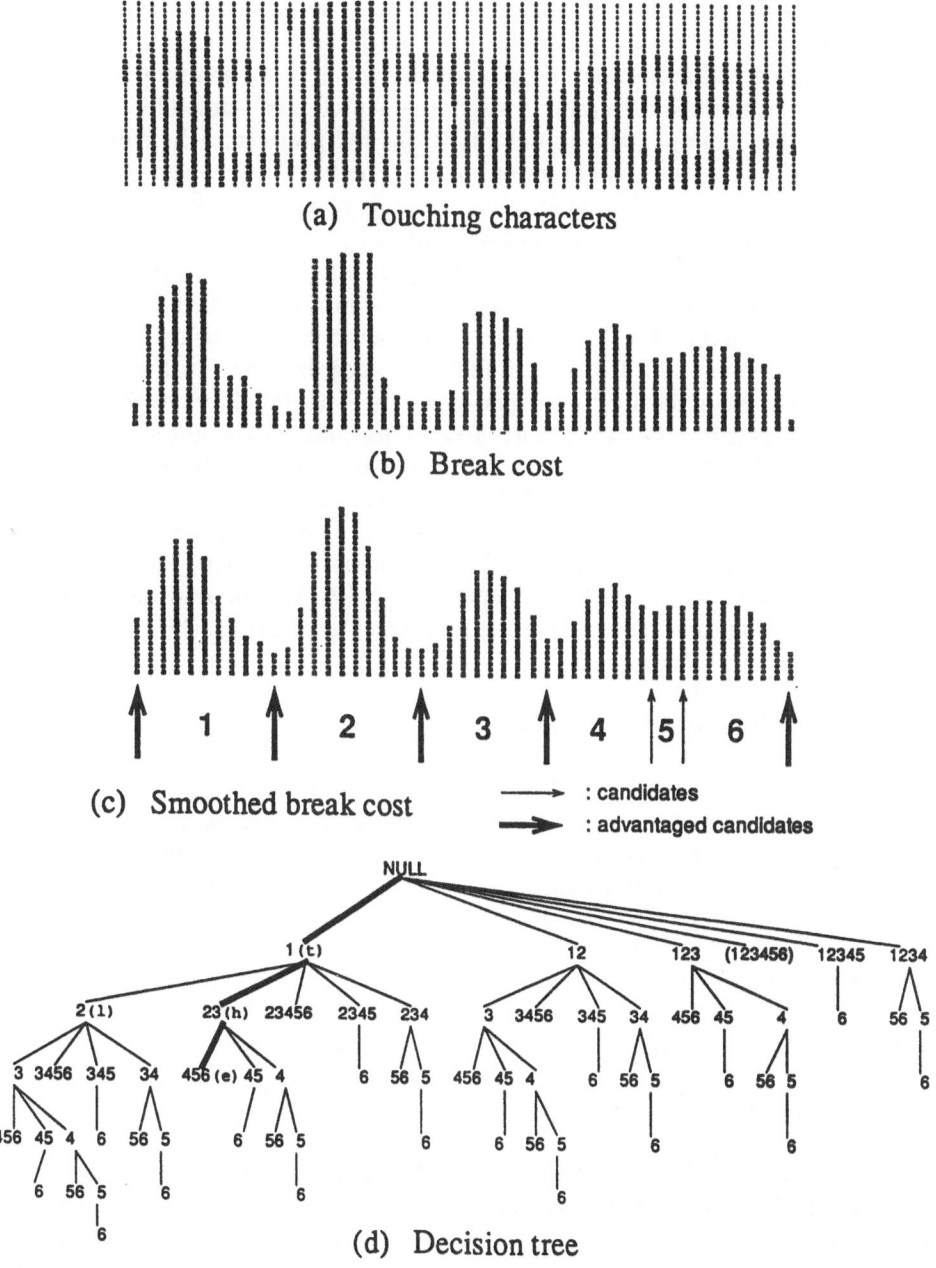

(a) Touching characters

(b) Break cost

(c) Smoothed break cost

⟶ : candidates

⟹ : advantaged candidates

(d) Decision tree

Fig. 4. Segmentation of touching characters.

{**1, 2, 3, 4, 5**} precedes the subset {**1, 2, 3, 4**} among the daughters of the root node.

(c) A segmented area ended by a candidate which is not advantaged succeeds the smallest segmented area among larger segmented areas ended by advantaged candidates. For example, the subset {**1, 2, 3, 4, 5**} succeeds the subset {**1, 2, 3, 4, 5, 6**} among the daughters of the root node. This sequence determination method reflects the fact that advantaged candidates can be searched for in advance of candidates which are not advantaged.

Each node is searched for in a depth-first order in the decision tree. If a node is recognized with acceptance, then its daughter is searched for. Otherwise, its sisters are searched for. The criterion for character recognition acceptance is described in Section 3.4. The subset {**1**} was recognized first in Figure 4. Since the subset was recognized as a 't' with acceptance, its daughters were examined. Subset2 was recognized as an 'l' with acceptance, but the daughter subsets {**3**}, {**3, 4, 5, 6**}, {**3, 4, 5**}, and {**3, 4**}, were not recognized with acceptance. So, the path for subset {**2**} was ignored. In the next step, the sister of subset {**2**} was examined. A similar procedure is applied to the decision tree until the path arriving at a leaf node is found. Search will finish once that path is found, to save time. In Figure 4, subsets {**1**} representing a 't', {**2, 3**} representing an 'h', and {**4, 5, 6**} representing an 'e', were finally segmented from touching characters.

3.4 Knowledge about Omni-fonts

Each node in a decision tree is recognized by the multiple similarity method [9], which is designed to be insensitive to the varieties of omni-fonts. Several recognition candidates are obtained. When similarities for the first and second candidates are denoted as $s1$ and $s2$, respectively, the condition for accepting the recognition result is as follows.

> **if** $(s1 < th1)$
>   rejected
> **else if** $(s1 - s2 > th2)$
>   accepted
> **else** conflict

Thresholds $th1$ and $th2$, are statistically examined for each character category.

"Conflict" suggests that both the first and second candidates for character recognition are ambiguous. For example, an 'l', an 'I', a '1', and an 'i' belong to this "conflict" category. However, when the first candidate is an 'l' but the second candidate is an 'm', then this recognition result should be rejected. For "conflict" characters, their images are also examined in detail. For example, for an 'l', an 'I', a '1', and an 'i', whether or not a dot exists should be examined. The existence of a dot is facilitated by measures such as the number of combined components described in Section 1. For a 'c', and an 'e', whether or not a hole exists in the character should be examined.

"Accepted" and "conflict" characters are regarded as being recognized with acceptance. The difference is that, in employing a linguistic context, an "accepted" character fits the first candidate in recognition, while a "conflict" character fits several alternative candidates. This classification ("accepted"/ "conflict"/ "rejected") enables the system to save time. Also, this classification can prevent the recognition results from being mistakenly changed by implementing a linguistic context, as described in Section 2.

3.5 Knowledge about Character Composition

Figure 5 shows another example of touching characters where the character segmentation procedure fails. Two subsets, {**1, 2**} representing an 'n' and {**3, 4, 5, 6**} representing an 'n', are selected. If all possible paths arriving at leaf nodes were to be searched, subset {**1**} representing an 'r', and {**2, 3, 4, 5, 6**} representing an 'm', would also be selected. Since searching entire paths requires additional processing time, the authors employ knowledge about character composition to solve this problem. As an example of such knowledge,

- 'm' is regarded as an 'r' and an 'n',
- 'q' is regarded as a 'c' and a 'j',
- 'k' is regarded as an 'l' and a 'c',
- 'B' is regarded as a '1' and a '3',
- 'H' is regarded as an 'I', a '-', and an 'I',
- "mm" is regarded as an 'n', a 'u', and 'n',
- "ck" is regarded as a 'd' and a 'c',

With these kinds of knowledge, another path can be generated automatically. The authors have prepared more than thirty examples of knowledge. In Figure 5, knowledge about an "nn" builds the hypothesis of another possible path representing an 'r' and an 'm'. After searching a decision tree, subsets {**1**} representing an 'r' and {**2, 3, 4, 5, 6**} representing an 'm', are also confirmed. The final path for touching characters is not determined by this procedure, but the result is deferred for a linguistic context procedure. In Figure 1, a "transforms" confirms a combination of an 'r' and 'm' rather than 'n' and 'n'.

4 Experimental Results

The proposed algorithms were implemented on a hand-made recognition board consisting of a RISC processor (10 MIPS) and a VRAM (4 MByte). A scanner whose resolution was 300 dpi, was directly connected to the recognition board. No special hardware was used.

Experiments were carried out on 32 documents taken from magazines, journals, newspapers, manuals, letters, scientific papers, and so on. These documents were printed with various kinds of fonts, and contained many touching characters.

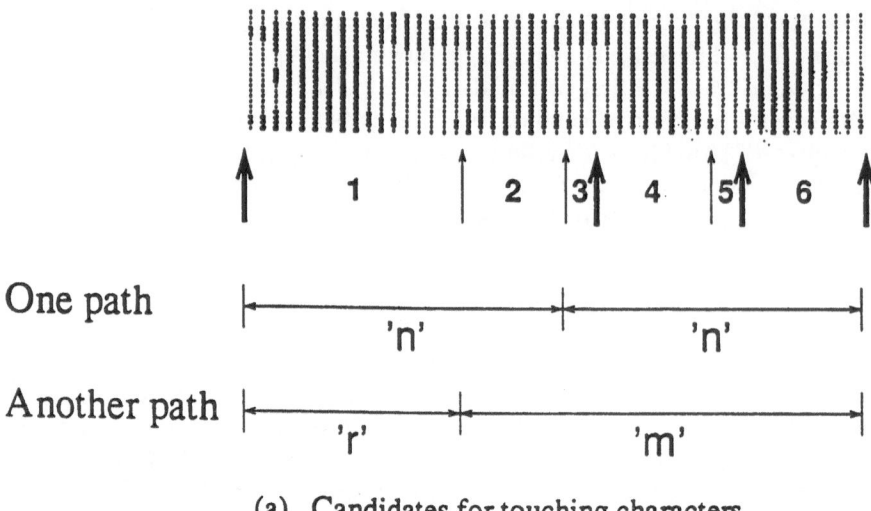

(a) Candidates for touching characters

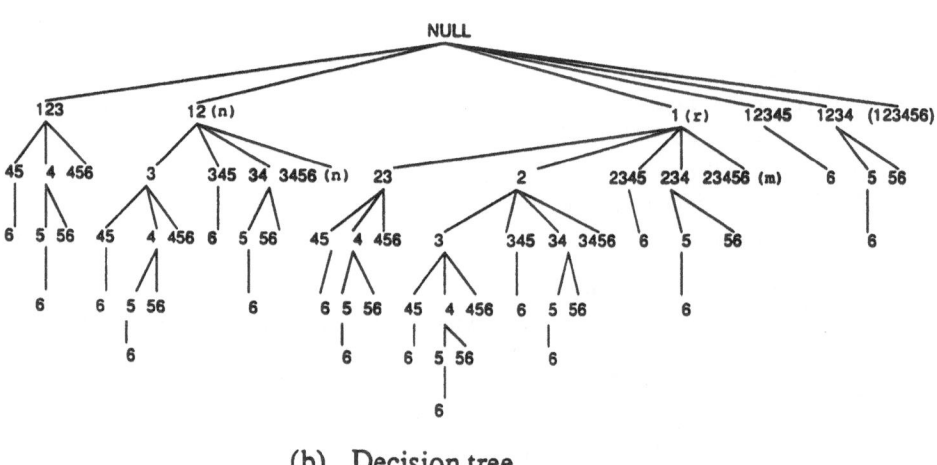

(b) Decision tree

Fig. 5. Touching 'r' and 'm'.

The correct recognition rate was 99.7% on the average for xerox copies of original good quality documents. The overall processing speed, from document analysis to character recognition, was 60 to 120 characters per second, depending on the quality of the input documents.

In 17% out of an error of 0.3%, character segmentation failed to separate an individual character from touching characters for three reasons. One reason was because the candidates for a touching character break position were not correctly nominated, due to complicated touching. Figure 6(a) shows an example of tangled touching, where two-dimensional distribution analysis of an image is required. Another was because another path fit before the path representing a break position for touching characters was found. Figure 6(b) shows an example where one path, representing a 'T', a '1', a 'J', and an 'R',was accepted in spite of another path representing a 'T', a 'U', and an 'R'. Knowledge about character composition could not effectively work. The last reason was because a character was rejected due to errors in character recognition on the path arriving at a leaf node of the decision tree. Figure 6(c) shows an example where the character identifying an 'a' was not recognized with acceptance.

5 Conclusion

This paper has presented an efficient and powerful method for segmentation of touching characters. This approach employs knowledge about character composition as well as knowledge about omni-fonts to resolve ambiguity in segmenting touching characters.

Experiments were carried out for documents commonly encountered in daily use, in order to evaluate the presented approach. Software realization achieved a speed of 120 characters per second with 99.7% accuracy.

However, a few problems still remain unsolved as described in Section 4. Further research should be directed to solving these problems. One problem was due to insufficiency of candidates nominated for the break position. A two-dimensional analysis of an image is required to solve this problem. Another problem was due to the avoidance of a complete search in a decision tree. The condition indicating a complete search in a decision tree should be designed. The last problem was due to failure in searching a decision tree. A measure to counteract the case where no paths were sought out in a decision tree can be considered. A feedback approach may be introduced to solve this problem. Knowledge about grammatical rules or semantics will also be required in the near future. Without them, it is difficult to distinguish "modem" from "modern", because an 'm' looks like a combination of an 'r' and an 'n'.

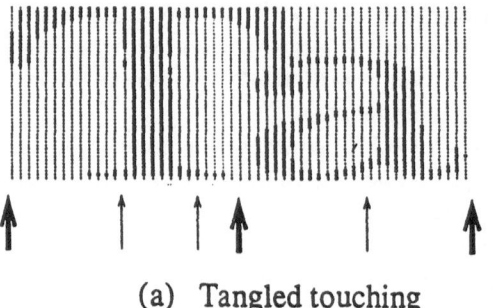

(a) Tangled touching

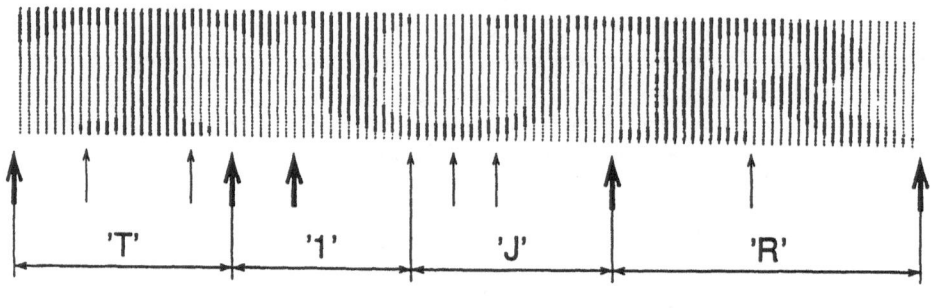

(b) Some available paths

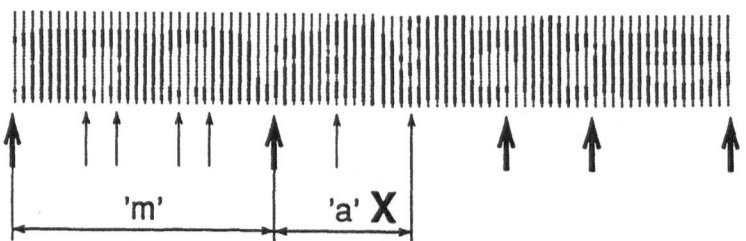

(c) Character not recognized with acceptance

Fig. 6. Problems in segmenting touching characters.

References

[1] N. Babaguchi, M. Tsukamoto, and T. Aibara, "Knowledge Aided Character Segmentation from Handwritten Document Images," *Proc. 8th ICPR*, Paris, pp. 573–575, 1986.

[2] Y. Maeda, F. Yoda, K. Matsuura, and H. Nambu, "Character Segmentation in Japanese Hand-written Document Images," *Proc. 8th ICPR*, Paris, pp. 769–772, 1986.

[3] A. L. Spitz, "Layout Structure Recognition in Multilingual Documents," *Pre-Proc. 1990 IAPR Workshop on Syntactic & Structural Pattern Recognition*, Murray Hill, NJ, pp. 497–497, 1990.

[4] H. S. Baird, S. Kahan, and T. Pavlidis, "Components of an Omnifont Page Reader," *Proc. 8th ICPR*, Paris, France, pp. 344–348, 1986.

[5] S. Kahan, T. Pavlidis, and H. S. Baird, "On the Recognition of Printed Characters of Any Font and Size," *IEEE Trans. Pattern Anal. Machine Intell.*, Vol. PAMI-9, No. 2, pp. 274–288, 1987.

[6] R. G. Casey and G. Nagy, "Recursive Segmentation and Classification of Composite Character Patterns," *Proc. 6th ICPR*, Munich, pp. 1023–1026, 1982.

[7] G. Nagy, "Document Analysis and Optical Character Recognition," *Proc. 5th Int'l Conf. Image Anal. and Processing*, Pasitano, Italy, pp. 1–19, 1989.

[8] R. Kooi and W. C. Lin, "An On-Line Minicomputer-Based Systems for Reading Printed Text Aloud," *IEEE Trans. Systems, Man, & Cybernetics*, Vol. SMC-8, No. 1, pp. 57–62, 1978.

[9] T. Iijima, H. Genchi, and K. Mori, "A Theory of Character Recognition by Pattern Matching Method," *Proc. 1st Int'l Joint Conf. Pattern Recognition*, Washington D.C., pp. 50–57, 1973.

Handwriting

Off–line Identification With Handwritten Signature Images: Survey and Perspectives

Robert Sabourin[1], Réjean Plamondon[2], and Guy Lorette[3]

[1] Laboratoire Scribens, Ecole de Technologie Supérieure, Département de Génie de la Production Automatisée, 4750 Henri-Julien, Montréal QC, Canada H2T 2C8
[2] Laboratoire Scribens, Ecole Polytechnique de Montréal, Département de Génie Electrique, C.P. 6079, Succ. "A," Montréal QC, Canada H3C 3A7
[3] IRISA, Université de Rennes 1, Campus de Beaulieu, 35042 Rennes Cedex, France

The first part of this paper presents a survey of the literature on automatic handwritten signature verification systems using binary or gray-level images, and focuses primarily on preprocessing techniques, feature or primitive extraction methods, comparison processes, and performance evaluation. With these previous studies in mind, we propose, in the second part of this paper, an image-understanding system based on the extraction of a novel representation of handwritten signature images. This approach is text insensitive. A structural match between a reference primitive set Pr and a test primitive set Pt takes into account the geometric shape and spatial relations between primitives. Finally, the local comparison of gray levels between pairs of primitives next to each node of the static solution path N results in a pseudodynamic similarity measure $\vartheta_d(Pr, Pt)$. This scheme allows the elimination, with a certain degree of success, of skilled forgeries such as tracings and photocopies, showing marked gray-level dissimilarity along the signature line.

1 Introduction

Off-line signature verification problems are generally considered to be more difficult than on-line ones [7]. A signature image can easily be copied optically or mechanically. Moreover, timing and dynamic information are highly degraded in a static specimen. Although part of this information can be recovered by expert document analysts using specific skills and techniques [23, 24, 25], most of their methods cannot be implemented easily in a computer environment. A few papers proposing ways of dealing with this problem have been reported in the literature. Sakai *et al.* have proposed an interactive hybrid system to collect and display the static and dynamic features of a test and a reference signature on a CRT screen, using a color code [3]. This system was used to help a clerk examine specific features of a signature, and the final decision about the specimen's authenticity was left to him. Ammar *et al.* have tried recently to extract indirectly and use pressure information from a signature image [1, 2]. Apart from this recent paper, most of the work done in this area thus far has been concerned with static feature analysis only.

The design of off-line signature verification systems requires the solution of five types of problems: data acquisition, preprocessing, feature or primitive extraction, the comparison process, and performance evaluation.

2 Data Acquisition

Different types of acquisition devices are used for off-line signature verification systems, including TV vidicon cameras, CCD matrix cameras, and electro-optical scanners. The size of the image may be up to 512×512 pixels in area and with up to 256 gray levels of quantization. Off-line data entry systems may also be simulated by ordering (X,Y) coordinate pairs issued from a digitizing tablet as with a raster scanning.

3 Preprocessing

This step deals with the preparation of the relevant information: nonuniformity correction for sensor elements, localization of the signature in the picture, extraction of the signature from the background, slicing, solving thresholding and filtering problems, segmentation, and data reduction.

Since most of the applications covered by these studies are related to the automatic validation and processing of specific paper forms (such as checks), the finding of a signature in this context is not a difficult problem and may be solved with the help of a window operator [4]. However, as suggested by Nagel [4, 5, 6], this problem might become more serious if the form standard permits a large number of variations. If no artifice is used (e.g. signing with special ink), the problem of extracting a signature image from its background is not a trivial one. Thresholding and slicing techniques have been proposed [1, 6, 8] but are generally insufficient in practice in a noisy background for which restoration techniques are also necessary [1].

Indeed, the efficiency of slicing and thresholding techniques is directly related to the selection of the cut point from a gray-level histogram of the picture. The problem is then reduced to finding a point on the frequency distribution that separates the peaks of a bimodal curve, where the peak representing the signature is almost lost in noise. The use of the Laplacian or the Sobel operator has been proposed as a border or stroke detector. In the first case, the threshold is fixed to select pixels above the 85% valve in the cumulative Laplacian distribution [5, 6]. In the second, the modulus gradient vector of the gray-level signature is used, with the threshold fixed at the point where the modulus variations in the pixel distribution function become less than 1% [8]. This latter approach offers the advantage of being independent of the thickness of the strokes and of the overall length of the signature.

However, for practical cases where specimens are noisy, these techniques have to be improved. A four-step preprocessing operation has recently been proposed by Ammar et al. [1] (background equalization and reduction, noise reduction by averaging, automatic thresholding and image extraction). This approach has been found to be successful in removing the overlapping in a signature as well as in the signing line, at the cost, however, of eliminating some parts of the signature in about 2% of samples.

Depending on the features needed at the next stage, the preprocessing algorithms can perform more specific operations on the extracted image. Pre-screening operators are used to eliminate points that are judged to contain little information on writer identity [14, 15, 16]. Window operators have been used by Brocklehurst to improve the image [17]. A tracking algorithm has been applied by Nagel and Rosenfeld to identify and label all connected components in the picture [6]. Based on the hypothesis that high-pressure regions are indicated by higher gray levels in an image, a high pressure threshold selection algorithm has been proposed by Ammar *et al.* [1] to extract the high-pressure regions of a signature. This mechanism is based on the evaluation of a pressure factor, i.e. the ratio of the high-pressure area to the binary signature area. Recently, Sabourin and Plamondon [10, 11] have proposed a new version of a centroidal linkage region-growing-with-merging algorithm to perform signature segmentation. Using the statistics of directional data, atomic regions characterized by local uniformity in the orientation of the gradient are extracted. This scheme allows the extraction of signature areas characterized by gray levels with a very low signal/noise ratio.

4 Feature or Primitive Extraction

The division of feature or primitive extraction methods into those involving text-sensitive and those involving text-insensitive features, as has been proposed for document expertise [18], cannot be strictly applied to signatures since the number of characters or symbols in a specimen is limited and often irrelevant (in an alphabetical context). Similarly, since the time information is not available from the image data, the function approach to feature or primitive extraction is not a really an appropriate distinction for static techniques [7]. Attempts at feature or primitive selection are better categorized by their global or local approaches to the problem, although an efficient system will probably incorporate both global and local feature or primitive extraction [13]. Moreover, none of the feature or primitive sets selected thus far preserves enough information to allow a reconstruction of the handwritten specimens.

In the global approach, the signature image is taken and processed as a whole; features or primitives are deduced from the global aspect of a signature. In other cases, features are evaluated from local parameter values which are averaged over the signature. In both cases, structural aspects encountered in signatures are taken into account in the local and global descriptions. Nemcek and Lin [16] have used the Hadamard transform on binary images as a means for data reduction and feature selection, the resulting spectrum constituting the feature set. A Sobel operator has been applied by Sabourin and Plamondon [8] to gray-level handwritten signature images, and the angular behavior of the resulting intensity gradient (assumed to reflect the stroke orientation) has been used as a feature set. A close-fitting polygon has also been computed to evaluate the overall shape of a signature and to serve, once normalized, as basic features [15]. Sabourin and Plamondon have proposed a feasibility study on the use of some graphometric techniques, and, in particular, the rhythmic line of the signature has been used [9].

Chuang [21] has divided the signature into upper, middle, and lower zones, initial and end strokes (a process familiar to graphoanalysts), and performed a sequential analysis of each sub-image to extract features related to each resulting zone and its proportionalities. A single study has been reported to date describing the extraction of some global dynamic features from a static image. Indeed, Ammar *et al.* [1, 2] have worked with a set of features mainly related to pressure measurements, as extracted from gray-level images: the vertical position of the baseline of the high-pressure and of the binary image, a pressure factor and threshold, the highest gray level in the extracted signature image, the dynamic range on the gray scale for a signature, and its area measured as the number of pixels.

In the second approach, a set of local attributes is computed. Many of these features are known to be stable, according to document examiner expertise [23, 24, 25]. However, most of the studies dealing with local features also incorporate some global ones. For example, Brocklehurst [17] has proposed the use of the overall length of the signature (global) with a set of local features likes slope measurements, the distance from the left-hand end of the designated space provided for a signature to the point at which the signature begins, concavity measures, etc. Nagel and Rosenfeld [4, 5, 6] have also worked with characteristics extracted from signatures segmented into vertical and horizontal zones. Assuming that a signature spelling was known, these authors detected tall letters in a specimen. Two global features (the ratio of signature width to short-stroke height and to long-stroke height) and two types of local features (the ratio of the height of a long stroke to the height of the short strokes immediately preceding it and the slope features of appropriate long letters) were retained for their studies, the number of these local features being dependent on the number of tall letters in a signature.

Most of the work done so far in the area of off-line signature verification has been concerned mainly with the statistical approach. Few studies deal with structural approaches using primitives. In his work, Requier [30] has used the linear strokes of signatures as primitives in a simulated off-line verification system. Nouboud *et al.* [19, 20] used as primitives the segments of the polygonal envelope of a signature. In a recent paper, Ammar *et al.* [22] described signature features and relations among them using a character string (the Global Description of a Signature (GDS)) and a hierarchical tree structure as a local description.

5 Comparison Processes and Performance Evaluation

As for the on-line system [7], the comparison process is based on the assumption that feature sets or structural descriptions extracted from genuine signatures are more stable than those of forgeries: that is, that intrapersonal variations are smaller than interpersonal variations. So, an unknown signature may be recognized or rejected according to its similarity to the reference signature representation first specified by an indirect identifier.

To evaluate this similarity, three approaches have been tried, two involving statistical or data analysis and one involving structural analysis. Considering signature verification as a non-standard two-class problem (since the class of forgeries cannot be specified), a first group of researchers [1, 6, 21] has used weighted distances. These methods compute a distance measured between the reference set and the test set. The decision is taken according to the value of this distance criterion with respect to a decision threshold, this threshold being pre-established with the help of a training set of genuine signatures. Assuming some a priori probability [16], or by limiting their studies to random forgeries [8], some authors have used maximum likelihood classifiers and linear discriminant functions. This second approach also assumes statistical interdependence of gaussian distributed features. The third approach is typically a structural one. Requier [30] has proposed a method using graph and subgraph isomorphism for signature verification. Nouboud et al. [19, 20] have used dynamic programming to compare segments related to the polygonal envelope of a signature.

Table 1 summarizes the results obtained thus far by the research groups involved in off-line signature verification. Since the performance evaluation method differs greatly from one approach to another, these experimental results are again difficult to compare. The table shows the type of input data used in each author's study, a description of the data base used for the training or test experiments or both, the number and type of features with the comparison method, the error rates as reported according to type I (ε_1) and type II (ε_2) definitions. The last column reports a few comments that might be helpful in analyzing the results.

Generally speaking, it has been observed that type I and type II errors of the order of a few percent can be obtained at the present time for systems working with simple and random forgeries. Only one system has been tested with skilled forgeries, and these specimens were not reliably detected [17]. According to expert document analysts, skilled forgery detection will not be efficient with these systems as long as dynamic and static features are not exhaustively extracted from a written specimen [23, 24, 25]. This is corroborated by observations from human perception experiments that knowledge of the drawing methods can greatly influence the recognizability of distorted characters [26].

Some authors have commented on their system failures [16, 17], two major causes of which are reported: first, scanning problems or signal quantization errors, resulting in incomplete specimen acquisition, due to the thinness of the trace or the color of the ink used [16]; second, excessive natural variations in the signatures of a few users [17].

6 A New Approach

Incorporating some knowledge from expert document analysts [23, 24, 25] seems to us the best way of obtaining a significant improvement in the performance of

Table 1. Performance of static signature verification systems.

AUTHORS	INPUT IMAGE RESOLUTION / FEATURE DESCRIPTION	TRAINING AND/OR TEST DATA BASE (Specimens x Writers)	COMPARISON METHOD	ERROR RATES	COMMENTS
AMMAR, YOSHIDA, FUKUMURA (1986) [1]	256 x 1024 grid 256 gray levels 7 global pressure features	200 genuines (20 S x 10 W) 200 forgeries (20 S x 10 imitators)	weighted distance	$\epsilon_1 = 6\%$ $\epsilon_2 = 4\%$	freehand forgeries leave-one-out method with threshold for maximizing performances
BROCKLE-HURST (1985) [17]	60 pixels/cm binary 7 local characteristics	2820 genuines (60 S x 47 W) (equal number of unseen forgeries)		$\epsilon_1 = 5\%$ $\epsilon_2 = 5\%$	6 S/W as reference acceptation training threshold at 95% true acceptation
CHUANG (1977) [21]	100 x 300 grid binary global features	2400 genuines (6 S x 400 W) 1600 forgeries (4 S/user)	weighted distance	$\epsilon_1 = 20\%$ $\epsilon_2 = 20\%$	3 S/W as reference freehand forgeries acceptation training threshold fixed at 95% genuine acceptation
NAGEL, ROSENFELD (1977) [6]	500 pixels/inch 64 gray levels 2 types of local global features	11 genuines (6 S x 1 W + 5S x 1W) 14 forgeries (9 S x 1 W + 5S x 1W)	weighted distance	$\epsilon_1 = 8\%$ $\epsilon_2 = 0\%$ $\epsilon_1^1 = 12\%$ $\epsilon_2^2 = 0\%$	freehand forgeries average result of single and double jacknife method
NEMCECK, LIN (1974) [16]	128 x 256 grid binary 14 features from Hadamar spectra	600 genuines (40 S x 15 W) 120 forgeries (10 users imitated 3 S/user, 4 imitators)	maximum likelihood classifier	$\epsilon_1 = 11\%$ $\epsilon_2 = 41\%$	30 S/W training 10 S/W test freehand forgeries training threshold at 96% genuine acceptation
NOUBOUD (1989) [20]	384 x 510 64 gray levels sig. envelope	1000 genuines (10 S x 100 W) 6 S/W for reference	dynamic programming	$\epsilon_1 = 2\%$ $\epsilon_2 = 8\%$	with personal threshold
PHELPS (1982) [15]	resolution not specified close-fitting polygon	3 genuines (3 S x 1 W) 6 forgeries (3 S x 2 W)	similarity of overlapping area		incomplete results
SABOURIN PLAMONDON (1986) [8]	128 x 512 grid 256 gray levels angular histogram image gradient	760 genuines (40 S x 19 W)	maximum likelihood and linear discrim.	$\epsilon_1 = 1.5\%$ $\epsilon_2 = 7\%$	random forgeries only 15 S/W for training 25 S/W for test
SABOURIN PLAMONDON (1987) [9]		800 genuines (40 S x 20 W)	nearest neighbour classifier	$\epsilon_1 = 0.57\%$ $\epsilon_2 = 0.03\%$	5 ref./signer
	rhythmic line	63 genuines from 1 W 117 simulated forgeries from 6 amateur forgers	nearest neighbour classifier	$\epsilon_1 = 3.5\%$ $\epsilon_2^1 = 0\%$	features extracted interactively at a graphic terminal 6 ref./signer
		17 skilled forgeries from 1 professional forger		$\epsilon_1 = 1.8\%$ $\epsilon_2 = 47.1\%$	6 ref./signer
SABOURIN PLAMONDON (1990) [14]	128 x 512 grid 256 gray-levels set of primitives	224 genuines, pen #1 (28 S x 8 W) 160 tracing forgeries (10 S/user, pen #1) (10 S/user, pen #2) 224 photocopies (28 S/user)	structural matching (static)	$\epsilon_1 = 0.0\%$ $\epsilon_2 = 1.34\%$ $\epsilon_2 = 100\%$ $\epsilon_2 = 98.9\%$ $\epsilon_2 = 96\%$	3 S/W as reference random forgeries $\beta = 0.0$ comparison threshold selected from the random forgeries experiment, tracing forgeries from 1 writer
		224 genuines, pen #1 (28 S x 8 W) 160 tracing forgeries (10 S/user, pen #1) (10 S/user, pen #2) 224 photocopies (28 S/user)	structural matching (static + pseudo-dynamic)	$\epsilon_1 = 8.93\%$ $\epsilon_2^1 = 1.79\%$ $\epsilon_2 = 6.25\%$ $\epsilon_2 = 78.8\%$ $\epsilon_2 = 61.2\%$	3 S/W as reference random forgeries $\beta = 5.0$ comparison threshold selected from the random forgeries experiment, tracing forgeries from 1 writer

Automatic Handwritten Signature Verification Systems (AHSVS) [13]. As stated in [12, 13], Locard [25] has proposed many characteristics belonging to genuine handwritten signatures which are imperceptible to the average forger and very difficult to imitate. These characteristics are related to local variation in aspect ratio, orientation, relative position, shading, etc., between pairs of characters. This scheme seems to be more powerful than the individual letter's shape or general design which is very easily perceived by the average forger and therefore easier to imitate [23, 24, 25].

In the light of these previous studies [1, 6, 8, 9, 15, 16, 17, 20, 21], we propose an image-understanding system [10, 11, 12, 13, 14, 32] based on the extraction of a novel signature representation from gray-level images [10, 11] for automatic signature verification. By an image-understanding system we mean the separation of the local and global evaluation functions [28] for the analysis of the handwritten signature and the detection of skilled forgeries. The approach considered in the present work [10, 11, 12, 13, 14] is text insensitive because no attempt is made to segment specific letters from the semantic part of the signature. Two classes of features, static and pseudo-dynamic, are taken into account for the representation of the scene. The former includes the geometric shape and spatial relations (N,S,E,O,N_E,N_O,S_E,S_O, and ADJ_TO) between some primitives extracted from the signature line [12]. The latter is associated with the gray-level variation inside the primitive [14]. By considering simultaneously these two classes of features, and the separation from the local interpretation of the primitives followed by the global interpretation of the scene, we have designed a general-purpose image-understanding system for the interpretation of handwritten signature images. This system is view-point dependent [27] and tailor-made for this purpose.

The spatial sampling of handwritten signatures produces an image format of 128×512 pixels. The preprocessing stage of the AHSVS (see Figure 1) is responsible for producing the signature image where each pixel from the gray-level image has a label $L_s(m, n)$ signifying that the pixel at location (m, n) is either a background or a signal picture element. The preprocessing phase is subdivided into two stages: the gradient computation and the background elimination processes [10, 11]. The gradient at location (m, n) is evaluated over the entire gray-level image with the Sobel operator. The resulting filtered image is then analyzed by the background elimination process. Because the handwritten signature is characterized by a high gradient activity, the density function $F(|\nabla|)$ is computed and a threshold T is automatically settled. Finally, those pixels at location (m, n) where the gradient activity is high, that is to say $|\nabla|(m, n) \geq T$, are associated with a label $L_s(m, n) = 1$, and $L_s(m, n) = 0$ otherwise.

The signature image is thereafter analyzed by the primitive extraction process that is responsible for the production of the primitive sets necessary for the structural analysis of the handwritten signature by the comparison process. The strategy adopted here takes into account the collinearity of neighboring signal-pixels (labeled as $L_s(m, n) = 1$) in the directional plane $\Theta(m, n)$ of the gradient space. This task is performed in two steps [10].

First, the signal-pixels are merged into atomic regions characterized by the

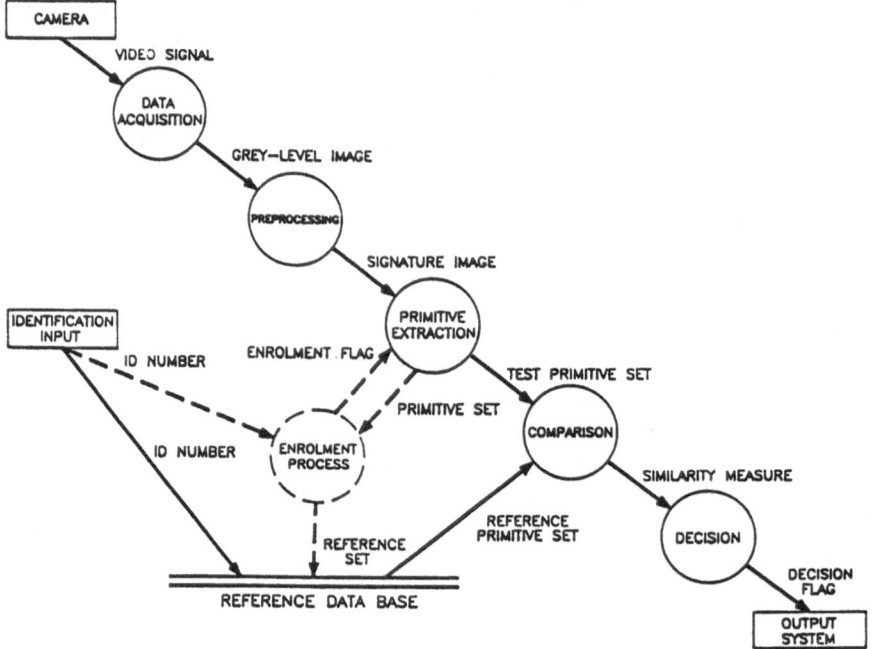

Fig. 1. The data-flow diagram of the proposed AHSVS using gray-level images.

uniformity of a local property, i.e. the orientation $\Theta(m, n)$ of their gradient vectors. The resulting atomic regions belong to the signature line or represent spurious noise elsewhere in the scene. The initials, "ar", depicted in Figures 2(a) and 2(b) (reference and test images), will serve as a case study to illustrate the various stages of the proposed AHSVS. The enlargement of the letter "r" (Figure 2(a)) depicted in Figure 2(c) shows the atomic region partitions in the gradient space.

The second step of the primitive extraction process is responsible for generating the primitive set [11]. The High-Level-Merging process (HLM) starts with the elimination of sparse atomic regions. The HLM process continues with a hierarchical merging strategy in growing collinear atomic regions. The growth is therefore limited by the resulting circular variance $\bar{R}$. The latter sub-process is used repeatedly in varying a growing constraint $\bar{R}_m$, considering a fixed directional constraint $\bar{\Theta}_m$ related to the local organization in the directional data located at the common border of neighboring atomic regions. This scheme acts as a zoom procedure focusing the attention of the HLM process on the biggest homogeneous regions from the atomic region set. The resulting primitive set is therefore characterized by a collection of arbitrarily shaped primitives. The degree of merging in the HLM process depends on the enrollment flag status (Figure 1). When this status has a TRUE value, the resulting set is a reference primitive set Pr where the growth is limited only by the presence of directional discontinuities along the handwritten signature line. In the case of a test primitive set Pt,

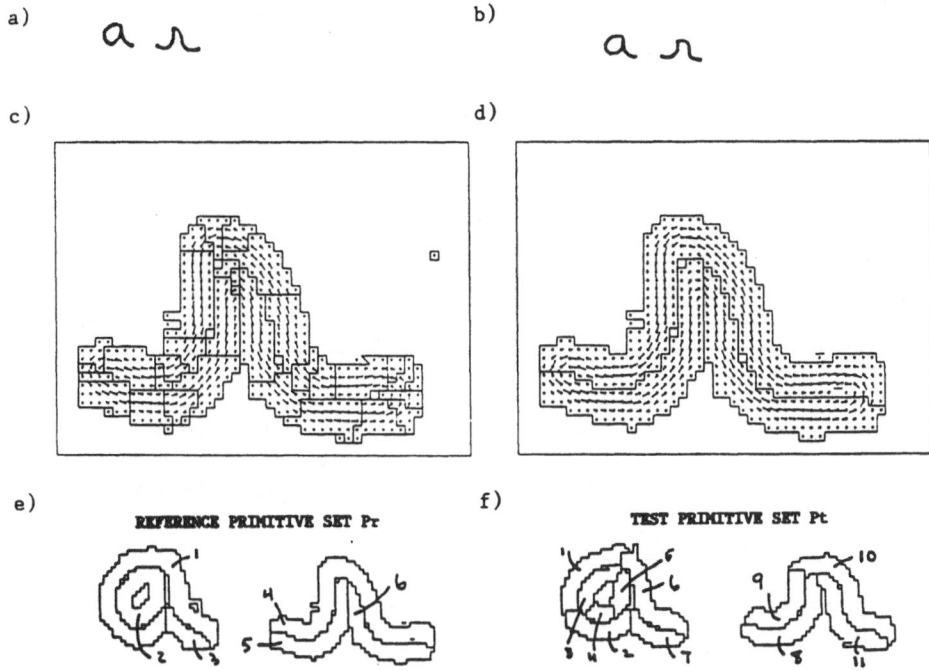

Fig. 2. Reference (a) and test (b) images. The atomic region set is shown in the gradient space (c) with the enlargement of the letter "r" from (a), followed by the corresponding reference primitives (d). Finally, the representation of the reference (e) and the test (f) primitive sets Pr and Pt.

the HLM process limits the growth depending on a circular constraint $\bar{R}_m$ (for example, the reference primitives $Pr_i \in Pr$ depicted in Figure 2(d), resulting from the application of the HLM process to the atomic regions of Figure 2(c)). The final results obtained from the extraction of the reference primitive set Pr from the reference image (Figure 2(a)) and the test primitive set Pt from the test image (Figure 2(b)), are shown in Figures 2(e) and 2(f) with cardinalities of $N_r = 6$ and $N_t = 11$ primitives. Examples of reference primitive sets Pr taken from handwritten signature images are also depicted in Figure 3.

The comparison process is therefore responsible for the structural match between a reference primitive set Pr and a test primitive set Pt, resulting in a global similarity measure $\vartheta(Pr, Pt)$.

The first stage of the comparison process, the Local Interpretation of Primitives (LIP), is related to the final merging of test primitives $Pt_v \in Pt$. The LIP process is responsible for the labeling of all test primitives $Pt_v \in Pt$, given a reference primitive set Pr. The A^* algorithm previously proposed [29] is replaced by a partially informed best-first BF^* strategy governed by a new evaluation function $f(n) = f(g(n), h(n))$, where heuristics are embedded in $f(n)$ [12]. The

a)

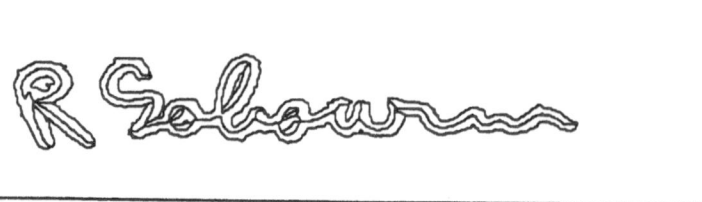

b)

Fig. 3. Examples of reference primitive sets Pr for two writers enrolled in the proposed AHSVS data base [13].

evaluation function $f(n)$ is now defined by the relation

$$f(n) = [w_1 * (1 - SHAPE(Pt_{v:n}, Pr_i))] + [w_2 * AREA(Pt_{v:n}, Pr_i)]$$
$$+ [w_3 * DIST(Pt_{v:n}, Pr_i)] + [w_4 * A\_R(Pt_{v:n}, Pr_i)], \qquad (1)$$

where $\sum_{k=1}^{4} w_k = 1$, and $0 \leq f(n) \leq 1$.

Each term used in the definition of the evaluation function $f(n)$ is related in some way to graphometric features used by the expert document analysts [13]. The first term $SHAPE(Pt_{v:n}, Pr_i)$ gives the similarity of shape between the collection of test primitives $Pt_{v:n} \in Pt$ and the reference primitive $Pr_i \in Pr$. The shape factor is related to the measure of planar shapes using binary shape matrices obtained from the polar sampling of the silhouette of primitives $Pt_{v:n}$ and Pr_i. The next term $AREA(Pt_{v:n}, Pr_i)$ is related to the difference in area between the test primitive subset $Pt_{v:n}$ centered around the test primitive Pt_v and tentatively interpreted as reference primitive Pr_i. The relative difference in area is justified by the fact that all test and reference images for each writer are taken under similar experimental conditions. The $AREA(Pt_{v:n}, Pr_i)$ feature should permit the rapid elimination of primitives with the same shape but with great dissimilarity in proportion. In the same way, $DIST(Pt_{v:n}, Pr_i)$ enables discrimination between two primitives on the basis of their local position. Two primitives similar in shape and equally prominent must be discriminated finally by their local positions. For example, if two lines with the same orientation have to be matched, $DIST(Pt_{v:n}, Pr_i)$ acts as a local constraint in the intelligent local template matching, limiting the merge of test primitives on the basis of their respective X positions from the start of the handwritten signature. This is also carried out by the term $A\_R(Pt_{v:n}, Pr_i)$ related to the relative difference-in-aspect ratio between $Pt_{v:n}$ and Pr_i.

The local confidence rating between a test primitive subset $Pt_{v:\gamma} \in Pt$, tentatively labeled as primitive $Pr_i \in Pr$, is given by

$$F_i(v) = 1 - f(\gamma), \tag{2}$$

where $0 \leq F_i(v) \leq 1$.

The local confidence rating $F_i(v)$ takes a value near unity for a perfect match between the subset of test primitives $Pt_{v:\gamma} \in Pt$ in the neighborhood of test primitive Pt_v, and the reference primitive $Pr_i \in Pr$. The local interpretation of Pt_v as Pr_i terminates with the set of primitives

$$Pt_{v:\gamma} = Pt_v, \ldots, Pt_\gamma \in Pt \tag{3}$$

The second stage of the comparison process, the Global Interpretation of the Scene (GIS), completes the analysis with the evaluation of a solution path N, produced by the structural matching of the primitive sets Pr and Pt, and followed by the validation of the resulting solution with the comparison of corresponding pseudo-dynamic features taken along the solution path N.

The first stage of the GIS process involves the evaluation of a static similarity $\vartheta_s(Pr, Pt)$ between the test primitive set Pt and a reference primitive set Pr. The state space graph $G' = (V', E')$ is defined as an oriented graph where nodes (states) are grouped in $k \geq 2$ disjoint subsets $V_i, 1 \leq i \leq k$ (phases). So, the set of nodes V' may be defined as the union of all subsets, as $V' = V_1 \cup V_2 \cup \cdots \cup V_i \cup \cdots V_k$. As previously stated [12, 14], a greedy algorithm seems a sufficient search mechanism for the global interpretation of handwritten signature images. This scheme is computationally less costly than the dynamic programming used in [29]. The static cost (similarity) at node $v \in V_i$ may be defined as

$$S_{i-1,i}(u, v) = (R_{i-1,i}(u, v) + F_i(v))/2 \tag{4}$$

The factor $R_{i-1,i}(u, v)$ represents the similarity in spatial relations between pairs of reference primitives Pr_{i-1} and Pr_i taken from the reference handwritten signature image represented by the primitive set Pr, and the spatial relations between pairs of corresponding test primitives Pt_u and Pt_v from the test primitive set Pt. Finally, node $v \in V_i$, where the accumulated cost $COST_i(v)$ is maximum, is pushed on list $N_i = v$. Assuming the use of a greedy algorithm at the GIS stage, the cost $COST_i(v)$ is therefore defined by the expression [12, 14]:

$$COST_i(v) = COST_{i-1}(u) + (\Omega_i * S_{i-1,i}(u, v)), \tag{5}$$

where $u = N_{i-1}$, $v \in V_i$, $< u, v > \in E'$, $3 \le i \le k - 1$, and

$$N_i = \arg \max_{v \in V_i} COST_i(v) \qquad (6)$$

Note also that

$$0 \le R_{i-1,i}(u,v) \le 1 \quad \text{(the similarity in spatial relations)} \qquad (7)$$
$$0 \le \quad F_i(v) \quad \le 1 \quad \text{(the local confidence rating)} \qquad (8)$$
$$0 \le \quad \Omega_i \quad \le 1 \quad \text{(the normalization factor)} \qquad (9)$$

Moreover, the initial conditions are as follows:

$$COST_1(1) = 0 \qquad (10)$$
$$N_1 = s \qquad (11)$$
$$COST_2(v) = \Omega_2 * F_2(v), \forall v \in V_2 \qquad (12)$$
$$N_2 = \arg \max_{v \in V_2} COST_2(v) \qquad (13)$$

The final step is therefore:

$$N_k = t \qquad (14)$$
$$COST_k(t) = COST_{k-1}(N_{k-1}) \qquad (15)$$

The normalization factor defined by $\Omega_i = AREA(Pr_i)/AREA(Pr)$ takes into account the ratio, in area, of the reference primitives related to each phase $(Pr_i \equiv V_i) \in V'$ to the entire area of the reference primitive set Pr. This permits an additional penalty for primitives not yet included in the definition of V'. Finally, Ω_i emphasizes prominent reference primitives in set V' in the evaluation of a global static similarity measure $\vartheta_s(Pr, Pt)$, defined as follows:

$$\vartheta_s(Pr, Pt) = COST_k(t) \qquad (16)$$

where of course $0 \le \vartheta_s(Pr, Pt) \le 1$.

A pseudo-dynamic similarity measure $\vartheta_d(Pr, Pt)$ is therefore computed at the end of the GIS process with the use of the resulting solution path $N = s, \nu_1, \nu_2, \cdots, \nu_{k-1}, t$. A pseudo-dynamic feature is evaluated from the local analysis of the gray levels inside pairs of primitives $\nu_i = Pr_i, Pt_{v:\gamma}$ located on the solution path N (Figure 4). The pseudo-dynamic feature adopted here is the proportion of "black-labeled pixels" obtained from a discriminant analysis of gray-level histograms computed for each of the primitives $Pr_i \in Pr$ and $Pt_{v:\gamma} \in Pt$, where $Pr_i, Pt_{v:\gamma} \in N$ [14]. This feature is called pseudodynamic because it reflects the effect of the writing process dynamics, which produces gray-level variations along the signature line. The pseudo-dynamic similarity measure $\vartheta_d(Pr, Pt)$ is defined as:

$$\vartheta_d(Pr, Pt) = (\Omega_2 * F_2(v) * D_2^\beta(v)) + \sum_{i=3}^{k-1}(\Omega_i * S_{i-1,i}(u,v) * D_i^\beta(v)) \qquad (17)$$

REFERENCE   TEST

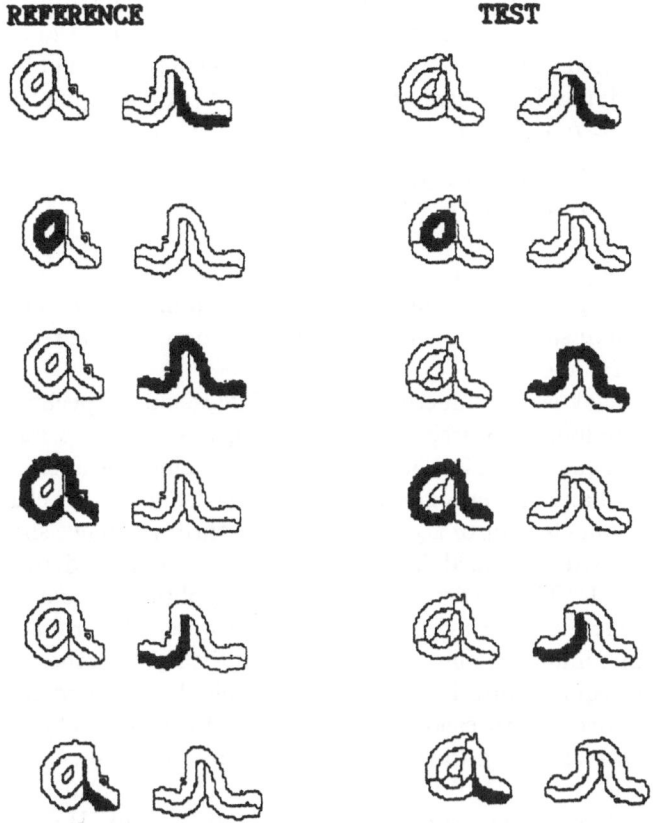

Fig. 4. Primitives pairs located on static solution path N and considered in the evaluation of the pseudo-dynamic similarity measure $\vartheta_d(Pr, Pt)$.

where $u = N_{i-1} \in V_{i-1}$, $v = N_i \in V_i$, $|N| = k$, $N_1 = s$, $N_k = t$, and

$$0 \leq \quad F_i(v) \quad \leq 1 \quad (the\ local\ confidence\ rating) \tag{18}$$

$$0 \leq S_{i-1,i}(u, v) \leq 1 \quad (the\ static\ similarity\ measure) \tag{19}$$

$$0 \leq \quad D_i(v) \quad \leq 1 \quad (the\ pseudo-dynamic\ similarity\ measure) \tag{20}$$

$$0 \leq \quad \beta \quad \leq 5 \quad (the\ scaling\ factor) \tag{21}$$

$$0 \leq \quad \Omega_i \quad \leq 1 \quad (the\ normalization\ factor) \tag{22}$$

The pseudo-dynamic factor $D_i(v)$ acts as an additional penalty when the cost of the static solution path N is revalued. Define the pseudo-dynamic features

$$DYN(i) = \omega_i(k_i^*) \tag{23}$$

$$DYN(v) = \omega_v(k_v^*) \tag{24}$$

where $\omega_i(k_i^*)$ $(\omega_v(k_v^*))$ represents the proportion of black pixels defined at gray-level threshold k_i^* (k_v^*), which is evaluated automatically with a discriminant analysis of the gray level density functions proposed by Otsu in [31], and computed from pixels belonging to the reference primitive Pr_i ($Pt_{v:\gamma}$).

$D_i(v)$ is defined as the relative similarity in the proportion of black pixels between pseudo-dynamic features $DYN(i)$ and $DYN(v)$ belonging to the primitive pair $Pr_i, Pt_{v:\gamma} = \nu_i \in N$, i.e.

$$D_i(v) = 1 - \frac{|DYN(i) - DYN(v)|}{MAX(DYN(i), DYN(v))} \tag{25}$$

with of course $0 \leq D_i(v) \leq 1$.

The resulting pseudo-dynamic cost $D_i(v)$ is used in equation (17) for the evaluation of the final similarity measure $\vartheta_d(Pr, Pt)$ between the test and reference primitive sets Pt and Pr.

An experiment was conducted [14] with 224 genuine specimens from eight writers, 224 random forgeries, 160 tracing forgeries from one forger using two kind of tracing pens and 224 photocopies of the genuine specimens. Let ω_1 be the class of genuine handwritten signatures and ω_2 be defined as the class of forgeries. A test image from class ω_1 or ω_2 is compared to three reference signature images for a specific writer enrolled in the AHSVS, and identified by a specific ID number (Figure 1). The best similarity $\vartheta_d(Pr, Pt)$ obtained from the comparison process is therefore dispatched to the decision process. The probability functions of resulting maximum similarity measures $\vartheta_d(Pr, Pt)$ are therefore computed considering an equal a priori probability for each class ω_1 and ω_2, say $P[\omega_1] = P[\omega_2] = 0.5$. A decision threshold τ_{ra} is settled with the help of random forgeries at the value corresponding to the total minimum error rate ε_{tmin} [14].

In the static case ($\beta = 0$ in equation (17)), experimental results with random forgeries show a type I error rate of $\varepsilon_1 = 0.0\%$, a type II error rate of $\varepsilon_2 = 1.34\%$, resulting in a total minimum error rate of $\varepsilon_{tmin} = 0.67\%$ for the proposed AHSVS. Considering the same decision threshold τ_{ra}, tracing forgeries and photocopies were not eliminated (see Table 1). Using the proposed pseudodynamic scheme with $\beta = 5$ in equation (17), a new decision threshold τ_{ra} is computed with the random forgeries. Using this threshold (Table 1), tracing forgeries (pen number 1) showing a thicker signature line than the genuines can be eliminated with a type II error rate of $\varepsilon_2 = 6.25\%$, at the expense of a higher type I error rate of $\varepsilon_1 = 8.93\%$. The corresponding type II error rate for the random forgeries experiment is now equal to $\varepsilon_2 = 1.79\%$.

7 Conclusion

A new scheme is advocated for the design and analysis of automatic handwritten signature verification systems using gray-level images [32]. The use of a novel handwritten signature representation allows local analysis of gray levels along the signature line, enabling the elimination of skilled forgeries such as tracings and the photocopies showing great gray level dissimilarity along the signature line. The concept of combining the structural matching of gray-level images with the separately considered local interpretation of primitives and the global interpretation of the scene is not new in the field of computer vision [27, 29], but major improvements to the method have been presented [10, 11, 12, 13, 14, 32].

Acknowledgements

This work was supported by grant A0915 to Réjean Plamondon from NSERC CANADA, and by FIR grant to Robert Sabourin from Ecole de Technologie Supérieure. The preparation of this paper was completed when Réjean Plamondon was a Fellow of the Netherlands Institute for Advanced Studies.

References

[1] M. Ammar, Y. Yoshida, and T. Fukumura, "A New Effective Approach For Off-Line Verification of Signatures by Using Pressure Features," *Proc. 8th ICPR*, Paris, France, pp. 566–569, October 1986.

[2] M. Ammar, Y. Yoshida, and I. Fukumura, "Feature Extraction and Selection for Simulated Signature Verification," *Proc. 3rd Int'l Symp. on Handwriting and Computer Applications*, Montréal, pp. 167–169, 1987.

[3] T. Sakai, T. Kanade, and Y. Ariki, "Multi-Feature Display of On-line Signatures by Color TV Display," *Proc. 2nd Int'l Joint Conf. on Pattern Recognition*, pp. 303–304, Copenhagen, 1974.

[4] R. N. Nagel and A. Rosenfeld, "Steps Toward Handwritten Signature Verification," *Proc. 1st Int'l Joint Conf. Pattern Recognition*, pp. 59–66, 1973.

[5] R. N. Nagel, "Computer Detection of Freehand Forgeries," Ph.D. thesis, Univ. Maryland, 1976.

[6] R. N. Nagel and A. Rosenfeld, "Computer Detection of Freehand Forgeries," *IEEE Trans. on Computers*, vol. C-26, no. 9, pp. 895–905, September 1977.

[7] R. Plamondon and G. Lorette, "Automatic Signature Verification and Writer Identification, The State of The Art," *Pattern Recognition*, Vol. 22, No. 2, pp. 107–131, 1989.

[8] R. Sabourin and R. Plamondon, "Preprocessing of Handwritten Signatures From Image Gradient Analysis," *Proc. 8th ICPR*, Paris, France, pp. 576–579, October 1986.

[9] R. Sabourin and R. Plamondon, "On the Implementation of Some Graphometric Techniques for Interactive Signature Verification: A Feasibility Study," *Proc. The Third Int'l Symp. on Handwriting and Computer Applications*, Montréal, Canada, pp. 160–162, 1987.

[10] R. Sabourin and R. Plamondon, "Segmentation of Handwritten Signature Images Using The Statistics of Directional Data," *Proc. 9th ICPR*, Rome, Italy, pp. 282–285, November 1988.

[11] R. Sabourin and R. Plamondon, "Segmentation of Handwritten Signature Images: A Structural Approach," Tech. Report TR89a, Ecole de Technologie Supérieure, Montréal QC, Canada, 1989.

[12] R. Sabourin and R. Plamondon, "Structural Interpretation of Handwritten Signature Images," Tech. Report TR90a, Ecole de Technologie Supérieure, Montréal QC, Canada, 1990.

[13] R. Sabourin and R. Plamondon, "Progress in the Field of Automatic Handwritten Signature Verification Systems Using Gray-level Images," *Proc. International Workshop on Frontiers in Handwriting Recognition*, Montréal, April 1990.

[14] R. Sabourin and R. Plamondon, "Steps Toward Efficient Processing of Handwritten Signature Images," *Vision Interface 90*, Halifax, Nova Scotia, May 1990.

[15] R. I. Phelps, "A Holistic Approach to Signature Verification," *Proc. ICPR*, vol. 2, p. 1187, 1982.

[16] W. F. Nemcek and W. C. Lin, "Experimental Investigation of Automatic Signature Verification," *IEEE Trans. on SMC*, pp. 121–126, January 1974.

[17] E. R. Brocklehurst, "Computer Methods of Signature Verification," NPL Report DITC 41/84, pp. 1–12, May 1984. Also in: *J. of the Forensic Science Society*, Vol. 25, pp. 445–457, 1985.

[18] V. Klement, R. D. Naske, and K. Steinke, "The Application of Image Processing and Pattern Recognition Techniques to the Forensic Analysis of Handwriting," *Int'l Conf. on Security Through Science and Engineering*, Berlin, pp. 5–11, September 1980.

[19] F. Nouboud, "Contribution à l'étude et à la Mise Au Point d'un Système d'Authentification de signatures Manuscrites," Thèse de Doctorat, Université de Caen, France, 1988.

[20] F. Nouboud, F. Cuozzo, R. Collot, and M. Achemlal, "Authentification de Signatures Manuscrites par Programation Dynamique," *Proc. Congrès PIXIM*, Paris, pp. 345–960, 1988.

[21] P. C. Chuang, "Machine Verification of Handwritten Signature Images," Proc. *Int'l Conf. on Crime Countermeasures, Sciences and Eng.*, pp. 105–109, 1977.

[22] M. Ammar, Y. Yoshida, and I. Fukumura, "Description of Signature Images and Its Application to their Classification," *Proc. 9th ICPR*, Rome, Italy, pp. 23–26, 1988.

[23] W. R. Harrison, *Suspect Documents, Their Scientific Examination*, Chicago, Nelson-Hall, 1981.

[24] O. Hilton, *Scientific Examination of Questioned Documents*, Elsevier, NY, revised edition, 424 Pages, 1982.

[25] E. Locard, *Les Faux en Ecriture et leur Expertise*, Payot, Paris, 1959.

[26] J. J. Freyd, "Representing The Dynamics of a Static Form," *Memory Cognition* 11, pp342–346, 1983.

[27] T. O. Binford, "Survey of Model-Based Image Analysis Systems," *Int'l J. of Robotics Research*, Vol. 1, No. 1, Spring 1982.

[28] M. A. Fischler and R. A. Elschlasser, "The Representation and Matching of Pictorial Structures," *IEEE Trans on Computers*, C-22, No.1., pp. 67–92, 1973.

[29] M. D. Levine, "A Knowledge-Based Computer Vision System," In E. M. Riseman and A. R. Hanson (eds.), *Computer Vision Systems*, Academic Press, New York, 1978.

[30] J. P. Requier and G. Lorette, "Reconnaissance de Signatures Manuscrites," *Actes du 2e Congrès AFCET-IRIA*, Reconnaissance des Formes et Intelligence Artificielle, Tome III, pp. 298–307, 1979.

[31] N. Otsu, "A Threshold Selection Method from Gray-Level Histograms," *IEEE Trans. on SMC*, Vol. SMC-9, No. 1, pp. 62–66, 1979.

[32] R. Sabourin, "Une Approche de Type Compréhension de Scène Appliquée au Problème de la Vérification Automatique de l'Identité par l'Image de la Signature Manuscrite," Ph.D. Thesis, Ecole Polytechnique de Montréal, 1990.

Difficult Cases
in Handwritten Numeral Recognition

Raymond Legault, Ching Y. Suen, and Christine Nadal

Centre for Pattern Recognition and Machine Intelligence,
Concordia University,
1455 de Maisonneuve Boulevard West, Montreal, Canada H3G 1M8

One avenue to improve the performance of computer systems for the recognition of handwritten data is to develop a better grasp of human expertise in this area. Through an experiment, we investigate the clues and cues used by humans to recognize the most confusing samples of our database. Four algorithms are also applied, individually and in a combined manner, to the same difficult data set. Machine and human performances are compared. Such knowledge should be used to refine the existing algorithms which are proved to be clearly inferior to the human experts in recognition of unconstrained handwritten numerals.

1 Introduction

To match human performance in computer recognition of handwritten characters is not an easy task. Every literate human has an expertise in this area which has been acquired and refined over many years, from early school training to adult life.

After more than 20 years of sustained research in the area of off-line computer recognition of totally unconstrained handwritten numerals, the best efforts have resulted in 90-95% recognition rates, with 1-3% substitution rates. See, for example, references [Beu73, HSC+88, KDS90, KS88, LS88, LBD+90, MS90].

These numeral recognition systems obviously have no difficulty with samples which are well-formed and resemble the standards for each class. Their challenge is to maintain the same high performance levels with numerals which have been distorted or written in more 'personal' styles. The systems must then incorporate much more knowledge and their development can become a painstaking task. A situation of diminishing returns often arises, where efforts to repeatedly refine classification schemes produce smaller and smaller gains in overall reliability. In this respect, the combination of complementary algorithms into multi-expert systems [SNM+90] appears to be a much more promising alternative which can but eliminate errors, without losing much in the recognition rate.

In order to gain new insights and further bridge the gap between human and machine recognition, we have decided to develop experiments focusing on the most difficult cases in numeral handwriting recognition. To this end, we selected 360 of the most confusing samples from our database of 17 000 segmented digits from handwritten zip codes.

First, an experiment was conducted to investigate human recognition of these confusing samples. Here the goal was to explore and grasp better what makes up human expertise in this area. What are the key cues and clues which are used to recognize digits, despite the diversity of shapes which can be encountered in each class? When the more obvious distinctive features are absent or altered, what other indicators are relied on by human subjects and with what confidence levels? A better understanding of these questions could lead to some improvements in feature selection and classification strategy [NW60].

Second, we applied 4 distinct recognition algorithms, as well as their combination [SNM+90], to the same difficult data set. We then carefully compared the classification results obtained by this combination of expert algorithms to those drawn from groups of human subjects.

In the following section, we describe the experiment with human subjects and present some general results. Then Section 3 offers a detailed comparison between machine and human performance in classifying the 360 difficult samples. Finally, Section 4 explores further some of the aspects for which humans are clearly superior to our multi-expert system.

2 An Experiment with Human Subjects

2.1 Description

The digits were presented to human subjects in their original size, framed in 25 mm x 25 mm boxes. Three framed numerals were placed on each page, alternatively on the left- and the right-hand side of successive pages. For each sample, a table of 11 empty class boxes (labeled 'zero', 'one', 'two',..., 'nine' and 'nil') was provided as well as 6 lines for writing comments. For each sample, the subjects were asked to first enter scores in 1 or more of the 11 empty boxes, giving the identity of the digit. The sum of the scores had to be 100, but this total could be distributed in any way to indicate relative confidence levels concerning the class to which the sample belonged. The 11th box, marked 'nil', was to indicate that the sample "did not really look like a digit". After identifying the digit, the subjects were required to write down the key factors which motivated their score distribution, trying to rank their arguments in decreasing order of importance.

The experiment was administered[1] to 9 human subjects: 5 researchers specialized in handwriting recognition (including the authors) and 4 volunteer (paid) students. In the rest of this paper, we will refer to the 2 groups as 'the experts' and 'the volunteers' respectively.

---

[1] On average, 15-20 hours were required to complete the experiment.

2.2 General Results

Consider each of the 2 groups in turn and let n be the number of subjects in that group. For a given experimental sample x, let $c_i(k)$ be the score entered by subject i in class box k, for $i = 1 \ldots n$, $k = 0 \ldots 10$ ($k = 10$ refers to class box marked 'nil'). We then define the group result $C(k)$, for class box k, as the average of individual scores in that box:

$$C(k) = \frac{1}{n} \sum_{i=1}^{n} c_i(k) \qquad \text{for } k = 0 \ldots 10 \qquad (1)$$

Figure 1 presents plotted curves of the percentage of samples which are classified as a function of t, a confidence level threshold. Each dotted line represents the results from a specific subject and the solid line gives the group result. For different values of t, the graph gives the percentage of samples classified by the individuals (equation 2) and by the group (equation 3) for which we have:

$$Max_k \ c_i(k) \geq t \qquad \text{for } k = 0 \ldots 9 \qquad (2)$$
$$Max_k \ C(k) \geq t \qquad \text{for } k = 0 \ldots 9 \qquad (3)$$

Within each group, we see important differences in the classification rate of individual subjects. Thus, at the 80% (or more) confidence level, the rates vary from 17% to 68% among experts, and from 13% to 74% among volunteers.

Figure 2 presents the *group* recognition, rejection and substitution rates as a function of t. The solid lines represent the recognition rates. The dotted lines represent the rejection rates, which were obtained from the 'nil' scores. The dashed lines represent the substitution rates; substitutions[2] refer to a classification which is different from that of the original database. Note that these graphs leave out a number of confusing samples for which no single $C(k)$ received the minimum of 60%.

As a rule, we see that the volunteers tend to make many more rejections than the experts and more substitutions as well. At higher confidence levels (80-100%), volunteers recognize more, substitute more and reject many more samples than experts. We can say that they are more categorical in their judgment. But at lower confidence levels (60-80%), experts are able to recognize more, substitute fewer and reject much fewer samples than volunteers. Thus, as expected, it appears that the experts' judgment is more cautious and nuanced (*i.e.* based on a broader range of considerations) which enables them to achieve a better performance overall.

Figure 3 shows samples which serve to illustrate this tendency. The volunteers uniquely classified numerals (a), (b) and (c), with confidence levels above 90%. Together as a group, they scored (a) as '6'(93%); (b) as '6'(95%); and

---

[2] Some of these 'substitutions' were expected. We selected a few of the 360 samples because we thought they had originally been misclassified when the database was first built.

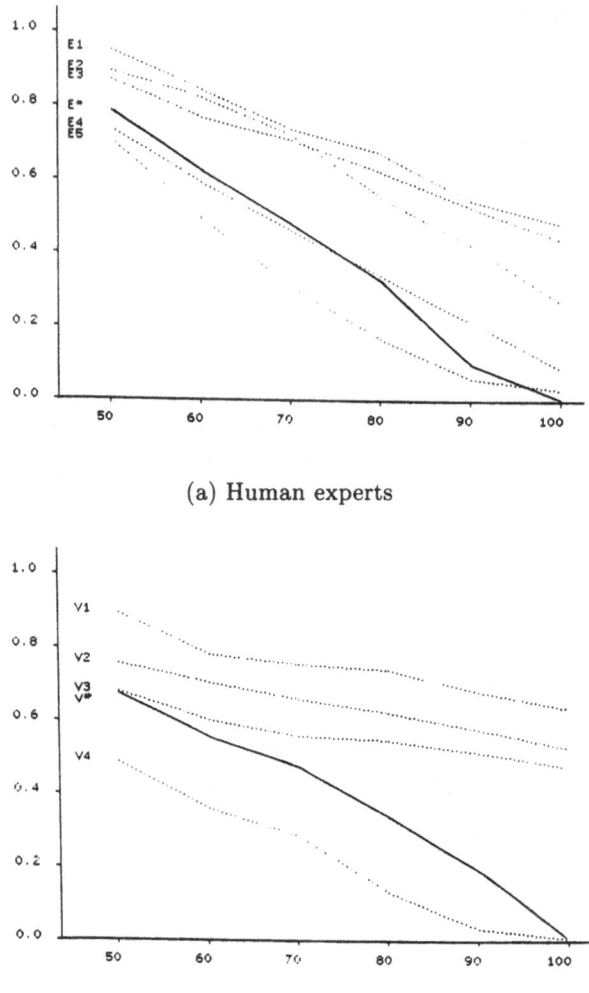

(a) Human experts

(b) Human volunteers

Fig. 1. Classification rates *versus* confidence levels.

(c) as '8'(93%). The experts, on the other hand, saw the possibility that these samples could have other identities. Their combined scores were as follows: for (a), '6'(62%), **and '4'**(32%); for (b), '6'(64%) **and '5'**(36%); for (c), '8'(64%) **and '6'**(30%). For numeral (d), experts and volunteers actually disagreed concerning its most probable identity. The scores for the experts were **'7'**(67%) and '4'(23%), whereas the scores for the volunteers were '7'(7%), and **'4'**(88%).

Table 1 presents the individual scores for the sample shown in Figure 3(d). It can be seen that all experts, except one, saw this sample as being more likely a '7' than a '4'. All student volunteers saw it the other way around. We also see that one expert (E3) had absolutely no hesitation in identifying a '7' and two

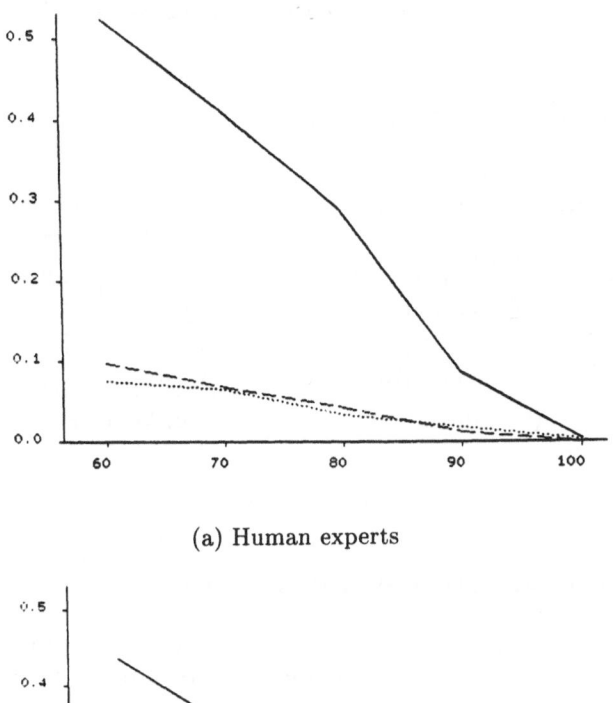

(a) Human experts

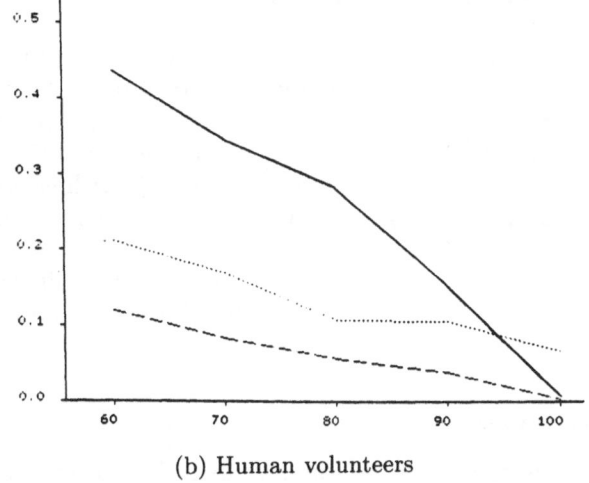

(b) Human volunteers

Fig. 2. Recognition (solid), rejection (dotted) and substitution (dashed) rates *versus* confidence levels.

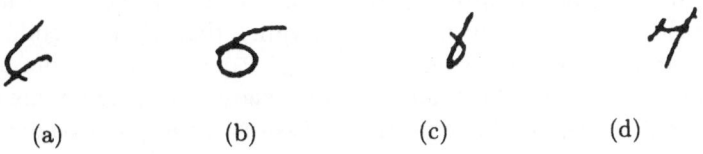

(a)   (b)   (c)   (d)

Fig. 3. A few samples from the experiment.

volunteers were equally convinced that the sample was a '4'!

Table 1. Individual scores (%) for a sample.

	4	7	Nil
E1	10	90	
E2	25	75	
E3		100	
E4	20	50	30
E5	60	20	20
E(Aver.)	23.0	67.0	10.0

(a) Experts

	4	7	Nil
V1	90	10	
V2	100		
V3	100		
V4	60	20	20
V (Aver.)	87.5	7.5	5.0

(b) Volunteers

3 Machine *versus* Human Performance

Very promising results are presented in [SNM+90] which considers the combination of multiple experts as a new direction to improve performance in the recognition of unconstrained handwritten characters. In that paper, the 4 algorithms used were developed independently and rely on different features and classification strategies. When results from these 4 algorithms are combined, the substitution rate drops dramatically, without affecting the recognition rate much at all.

These 4 algorithms are used here with the same difficult data presented to human subjects. The result of their combination is then compared to the decision of the human experts.

3.1 Overall Comparison

For a given human group, the information available for each sample is in the form of the scores $C(k)$. In order to compare human and machine performance, we want first to establish a criterion from which *unambiguous classification* by groups of humans will be defined.

Let S_1 be the highest score $C(k)$ and S_2 be the second highest score $C(k)$, for $k = 0 \ldots 9$. Let the score $C(10)$ be expressed as S_{nil}. For unambiguous classification, it seems only natural to require that S_1 be significantly larger than S_2 and also significantly larger than S_{nil}. Equation 4 gives our *unambiguous classification criterion*. The 2 constants were chosen after examining many values with the goal of keeping the number of substitutions at a reasonable level. Using larger values did not really reduce the number of substitutions while smaller values increased it fairly rapidly.

$$(S_1 \geq 2.5\ S_2)\ and\ (S_1 \geq 1.75\ S_{nil}) \tag{4}$$

For a given sample, assume that equation 4 is satisfied and let $S_1 = C(k_1)$. If k_1 coincides with the original identity of the sample, then we have a case of correct recognition; on the other hand, if k_1 does not coincide with the sample's original identity, we have a substitution.

Initially, when the unambiguous classification rule was applied to the experts' scores, a recognition rate of 51.9% and a substitution rate of 7.3% were obtained. However we must keep in mind that the initial classification of samples in the database was performed manually for over 17 000 samples by one individual. In this situation, the chances of misclassification were much greater than in the present experiment, where 5 experts focus their attention on only 360 samples. For this reason, it seems only natural to use the experts' decision as the reference. Hence any classification by this group which was different from the original classification resulted in a change of the sample's identity.

Table 2. Comparing the results of the four algorithms and their combination (%).

	Recognition	Substitution	Rejection
Algorithm # 1	44.2	19.2	36.6
Algorithm # 2	56.1	31.4	12.5
Algorithm # 3	55.0	19.4	25.6
Algorithm # 4	54.2	17.2	28.6
Combined Algo.	47.8	6.4	45.8

Once these changes were made, we submitted the data set to the 4 algorithms mentioned in [SNM+90]. Table 2 shows the results obtained. As we expected, the combination of algorithms eliminates a significant portion of the errors introduced by the individual algorithms. For the combination system, the criterion for unique classification is an agreement among more than 2 of the 4 algorithms. In the following sections of this paper, the results obtained using this rule will be referred to as *the machine performance*.

Table 3. Machine *versus* human results (%).

	Recognition	Substitution	Rejection
Experts	59.2	0.0	40.8
Volunteers	46.4	6.1	47.5
Machine	47.8	6.4	45.8

Table 3 presents the performance of the human experts and volunteers obtained using the unambiguous classification criterion (equation 4). All samples for which the rule was not satisfied, were considered as rejected. For the purpose of comparison, the combined machine performance is also given. We notice that overall the machine rates are similar to those given by the group of volunteers. This is quite an accomplishment and further validates the concept of multi-expert recognition systems for unconstrained handwritten data. However we should not conclude from this that human performance has now been matched.

3.2 A More Detailed Examination of Machine Results

In this section, we use the human experts' classification as a reference. First, we consider the set of 213 samples which they unambiguously recognized and we examine how the multi-algorithm recognizer and the human volunteers performed on these samples. Secondly, we carry out a similar analysis for the set of 147 samples which human experts rejected.

3.2.1 The subset of samples recognized by human experts. Here we are dealing with the "easiest" of our set of 360 difficult samples, those for which human experts provided clear-out identifications. Consequently, we would expect a relatively better machine performance on this subset, as compared to the overall results of Table 3.

Table 4 (a) gives the percentage of those samples which are recognized, substituted and rejected by the volunteers and the machine. It is clear that the expected improvement in performance is present for the volunteers but not for the 4-algorithm combination, despite the relative sophistication of the member algorithms.

Table 4. Performance results for subsets of original 360 pattern database.

	Rec.	Sub.	Rej.
Volunteers	70.0	0.5	29.5
Machine	49.3	6.6	44.1

(a) 213 easier samples

	Rec.	Sub.	Rej.
Volunteers	12.2	14.3	73.5
Machine	45.6	6.1	48.3

(b) 147 more difficult samples

3.2.2 The subset of samples rejected by human experts. Here we consider the 147 samples for which the experts' group scores did not satisfy equation 4. Table 4 (b) compares the results for the machine and the human volunteers. It is clear that the multi-algorithm combination does not identify the inherent difficulty of the subset and "recognizes" more than 45% of them; the volunteers do the same thing but only for approximately 12% of them. Furthermore, for these 12% (18 samples) the classification by the volunteers generally coincides with the class given the largest score by the experts.

For the samples rejected by human experts, if we study the confidence level given in each class box, we can distinguish between 2 categories which we label "confused" and "unrecognized". We call confused a sample for which 2 (rarely 3) of the 10 classes obtain a relatively high score. On the other hand, an unrecognized pattern is one for which the *'nil'* box gets significant votes.

More precisely, the rule introduced in section 3.1 is now expanded as follows to incorporate these new classification types.

$$
\begin{aligned}
&if\ (S_{nil} \geq 50) && then\ ``Unrecognized" \\
&else\ if\ (S_1 < 2.5\ S_2) && then\ ``Confused" \\
&else\ if\ (S_1 \geq 1.75\ S_{nil}) && then\ ``Recognized" \\
&else\ if\ (S_2 \geq 10) && \\
&\quad and\ (S_1 + S_2 > S_{nil})\ then\ ``Confused" \\
&\quad\quad\quad\quad\quad\quad else\ ``Unrecognized"
\end{aligned}
\tag{5}
$$

For a given pattern, let $S_1 = C(k_1)$ and $S_2 = C(k_2)$. Clearly if the difference between S_1 and S_2 is not large enough, this pattern can be considered as a confusion between the classes k_1 and k_2. Similarly, if the group score S_{nil} is large enough, the pattern should be classified as unrecognized.

When the above rule is applied to the human experts' group scores, 48 of the 147 samples are considered unrecognized and 99 are confused. These 99 confused samples can be regrouped into 20 confusing pairs. Figure 4 shows an example of each. These are samples for which S_1 and S_2 are almost the same. Each numeral is labeled in the form C-D(x-y), where C and D are the 2 most likely classes for the sample and x and y are the respective percentages of total score for these samples.

Ideally we would like a machine recognition scheme that is able to differentiate the unrecognized and confused categories and to give for each roughly the same counts as those given by human experts. Furthermore, in the case of confused samples, the machine should produce the same confusing pairs as human experts do. Unfortunately, our 4-algorithm combination does not fulfill these expectations.

For the 48 samples unrecognized by experts, only 1/3 have 2 or more algorithms classifying them as rejects. Rejection from the machine means *not recognized as one of the possible 10 classes* and is in fact unrecognized. For another 1/3 of these samples, the 4 algorithms disagree on the identification and classify them as confusing. For the last 1/3 of the 48 samples, the machine classifies them uniquely. Furthermore, in 75% of the cases this class agrees with the original identity of the pattern, and in 25% of the cases the outcome is a substitution. On the other hand, the group of volunteers agrees much more with the experts. Their scores assign 42 of the 48 samples to the unrecognized category.

The same type of study was made on the samples classified as confusing by the group of human experts. It was found that for more than 1/2 of the 99 samples, the machine combination has uniquely classified the pattern. For 1/4 of the patterns the machine gave an unrecognized verdict. In the remaining 1/4 of the cases, the algorithms show a confusion which does not necessarily

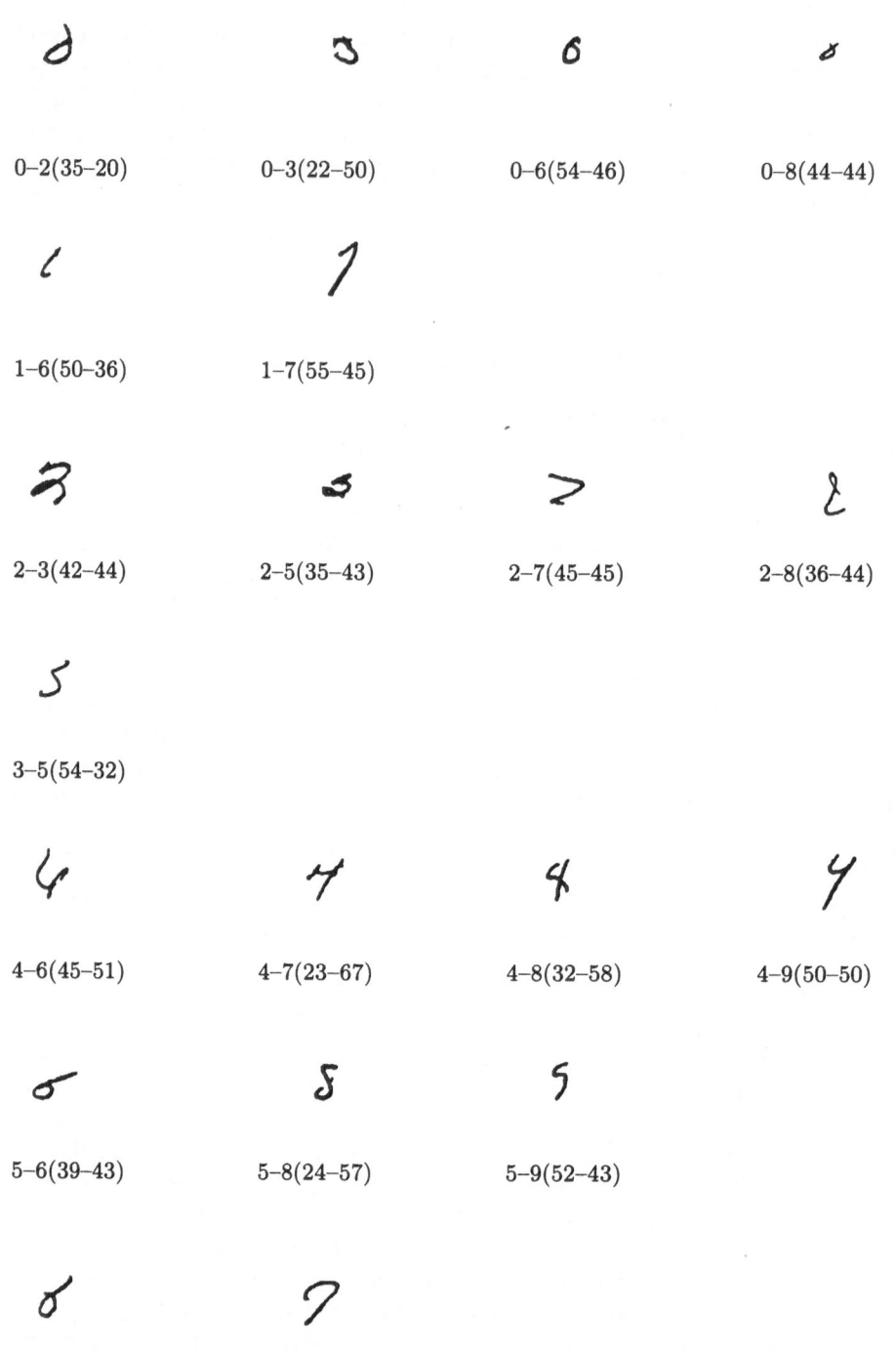

Fig. 4. Examples of confusing samples.

correspond to the pair of digits found in the human confusion: for 35% of this last portion, the machine and the humans were hesitating on the same pair; for 55% of the samples, at least one digit member of the human pair appears in the machine pair; finally 10% of the time, the machine pair is totally different from the human confusing pair.

4 Possible Improvement to Machine Performance

In the past section we have seen how a multi-expert numeral recognition system can greatly improve performance, compared to individual algorithms. A more careful examination of the results also revealed some weaknesses, when compared to a group of human experts: (1) the machine can produce substitutions for samples whose identity is unambiguous to humans; (2) the machine cannot differentiate between the samples which humans identify unambiguously and the samples which they find confusing; (3) for this last category of confusing samples, the machine does not generally provide the correct list of 2 (rarely 3) most likely classes for the numeral.

The above weaknesses of our multi-expert system are also weaknesses of the individual algorithms which compose it. Consequently, they can only be overcome by bringing more refinement into each algorithm. One avenue to accomplish this is to draw more deeply upon human expertise and incorporate more knowledge into the algorithms. A careful study of the confusing pairs of our human experiment (see Figure 4) should be useful in this regard. Many samples of the same pair — with varying degrees of confusion — should be examined, scrutinizing in parallel the motivations noted down by human experts.

We now proceed to do so for one particular case: the 4–9 confusing pair. The choice of this pair is motivated by the fact that 4–9 substitutions appear to be the most common type of substitution reported in the literature.

4.1 Case Study: the 4–9 Confusing Pair

Figure 5 shows many samples which can be used to investigate the 4–9 confusing pair. The samples on line (a) are clearly recognized as '4' by the group of human experts. The samples on line (e) are clearly recognized as '9'. Lines (b), (c) and (d) contain confusing samples: line (b) has numerals which are seen as closer to '4' than to '9' (the respective percentages for the last digit on that line are 60–40); line (c) has numerals just as likely to belong to either class (50–50); line (d) has numerals which are seen as closer to '9' than '4' (the label for the last sample on that line being 4–9(31–59)).

We now summarize the clues and cues which have been repeatedly invoked by our 5 human experts to justify their classification. Since most of the samples represented in Figure 5 have an opening at the top, we will discuss here only features related to what will be referenced as the open-4 and open-9 types of patterns.

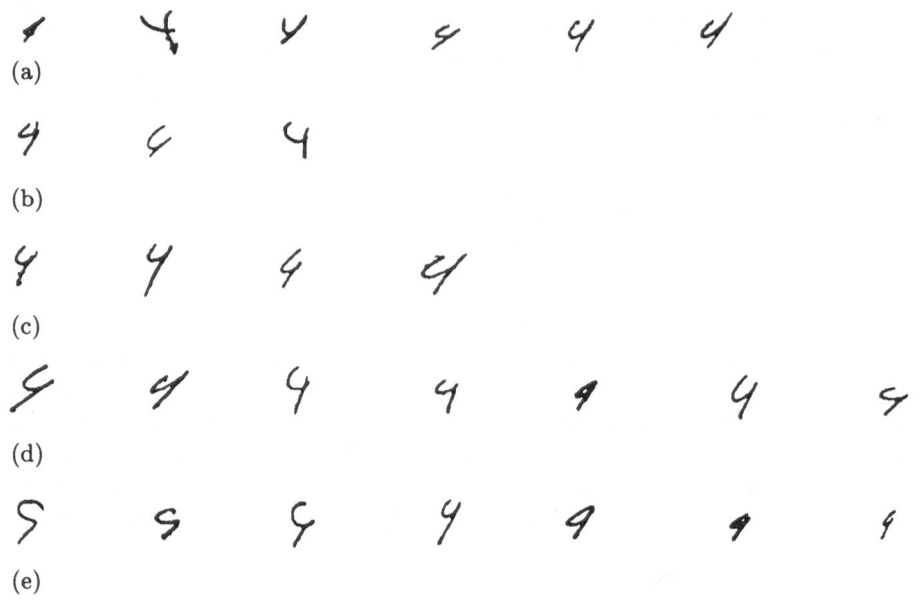

Fig. 5. Samples for study of the 4–9 confusing pair.

4.1.1 The open-4. Most human experts are regarding the open-4 digit as made of 2 strokes: one L-shape segment to the left and one vertical bar to the right of the pattern. A lift of the pen is assumed between the drawing of these 2 components. The point where the 2 strokes meet is referenced to as the crossing or junction point. It determines the middle part (middle height) of the character. The inner part of the L-shape stroke together with the top of the vertical bar enclose a region called the top cavity. Similarly, to the left of the vertical stroke, below the junction point, we find an area referred to as the bottom cavity. Using this terminology we can present the clues and cues detected by the human experts on the open-4 experimental samples.

1. Regarding top endpoints
   (i)   large horizontal gap between 2 endpoints
   (ii) top right endpoint as high or higher than top left endpoint
   (iii) top left endpoint may be pointing north or even to the west.
2. Regarding top cavity
   (i) a sharp direction change at the bottom right of the top cavity indicates 2 distinct strokes
   (ii) 2 sides of the cavity (1 segment extending downwards from each top endpoint) tend to be parallel
3. Regarding top left profile: L-shape
   (i) top of L: segment extending from the top left endpoint is very straight

(ii) angle of L: at middle height the stroke corner can be quite sharp

(iii) bottom of L: after the sharp corner, the segment is straight and horizontal

(iv) right end of L: the last portion of that stroke extends slightly beyond (to the right of) the vertical stroke

4. Regarding bottom part

(i) short bottom leg (low junction point)

4.1.2 The open-9. For the majority of human experts, the open-9 digit is described as being written as a single stroke, the writing instrument always touching the paper surface. Nevertheless, to ease the comparison, we decided to divide the pattern into 2 components resembling the ones found in the description of the numeral '4': the vertical bar and what we preferred to call the loop (or the looping component).

1. Regarding top endpoints

(i) top left endpoint pointing north-east or even east

(ii) large vertical gap between 2 top endpoints

2. Regarding top cavity

(i) no sudden direction change along the inner contour

(ii) tends to be much rounder — loop

3. Regarding top left profile: loop

(i) top of loop: segment from the top left endpoint to 'corner' tends to be curved, not straight

(ii) angle of loop: middle left 'corner' is rounder

4. Regarding bottom part

(i) bottom leg tends to be longer

(ii) cavity at top of the bottom leg reaches higher than the loop angle (see 3(ii))

(iii) pronounced leg inclination more likely in 9 than 4

4.1.3 Discussion. We see that human experts rely on various factors to guide their classification. Some of these are used by one or more of our algorithms; but others are not. For examples, clues 2(i) and 2(ii) for open-4 appear important to some human experts and have not really been used in machine recognition to our knowledge.

It remains difficult to determine exactly how to use all the listed clues to improve machine recognition. For humans, some of these are key, while others simply act as confirmation. For example, a criterion which can establish that the pattern was drawn in 2 distinct strokes is a very important key. The sharp angle change near the crossing point inside the top cavity strongly suggests that the L-shape (left part) is a separate stroke and is not extending into the vertical bar in a natural way without lifting the pen. These keys are decisive and lead to an open-4 classification.

On the other hand, features regarding the top endpoints and their relative height and distance are not decisive. We can see in Figure 5 that it is only a tendency, not a necessary condition. Some samples classified as the numeral '9' have the vertical bar (right endpoint) extending higher than the left side and some pattern recognized as '4' show the opposite. Such features can only be used to increase or reduce the confidence level of a decision which should be based on stronger features.

The other problem we want to mention here is that seeing a feature is very different from having the computer successfully measure and analyze it. Most recognition schemes have a tendency to begin with a preprocessing stage to either thin the pattern or smooth its contour. By doing so we overpass some of the small imperfections on the contour due to digitization or binarization; consequently, the information on subtle or sharp direction changes (ex: inside top cavity near the junction) is often lost. To have the preprocessing reduced to a minimum so that all information is kept would mean to keep also the unwanted imperfections.

The above analysis can be used to improve the algorithms to better recognize members of the numeral classes '4' and '9'. Similarly, we can study the comments given by the human experts for all confusing pairs in the experimental database to further improve the recognition algorithms on their individual weaknesses.

5 Conclusions

We have presented some results of an experiment dealing with human and machine recognition of the most difficult cases of handwritten numerals. Based on the combined classification of human experts, we were able to differentiate among 3 levels of difficulty for these patterns: unambiguous, confusing, and unrecognizable. On the other hand, it was also shown that combined algorithms, although having a performance comparable to humans, presently have an arbitrary classification scheme: they substitute samples which are unambiguous to humans; they cannot differentiate between unambiguous and confusing patterns; they do not hesitate on the same class pairs as the humans when the sample is confusing.

In order to improve machine performance, we feel we need a better understanding of what makes up the human expertise in the recognition of the different handwritten numerals. A detailed study of the clues and cues used by humans for the classification of 4's and 9's gave us a set of features which can be divided in two categories: decisive keys and confirmation elements.

Using these features should help us refine the algorithms in their decision making process for the numerals 4 and 9. Similarly we can study the comments given by the human experts for all the confusing pairs in the experimental database to further improve the recognition algorithms on their individual weaknesses. By gradually grasping more of the human expertise, the machine could eventually match their performance.

Acknowledgements

We would like to thank L. Lam and T. A. Mai for their cooperation as expert human subjects in this experiment, as well as for providing us with the results of their own computer algorithms when applied to the set of 360 most confusing samples. We also greatly appreciated the suggestions of Dr. M. Komoda of the department of Psychology in the preparation of the experiment with human subjects. Finally we thank Ari Wiener who prepared and administered preliminary experiments and also supervised the final experiment with the 4 student volunteers.

This work was supported by a strategic research grant awarded by the Natural Sciences and Engineering Research Council of Canada and an FCAR team research grant awarded by the Ministry of Education of Quebec.

References

[Beu73]   M. Beun. A flexible method for automatic reading of handwritten numerals. *Philips Tech. Rev.*, 33:89–101,130–137, 1973.

[HSC+88] J. J. Hull, S. N. Srihari, E. Cohen, C. L. Kuan, P. Cullen, and P. Palumbo. A blackboard-based approach to handwritten zip code recognition. In *Proc. U.S. Postal Service Advanced Technology Conf.*, pages 1018–1032, 1988.

[KDS90]   A. Krzyzak, W. Dai, and C. Y. Suen. Unconstrained handwritten character classification using modified backpropagation model. In *Proc. Int. Workshop on Frontiers in Handwriting Recognition*, pages 155–166, Concordia University, Montreal, April 1990.

[KS88]   C. L. Kuan and S. N. Srihari. A stroke-based approach to handwritten numeral recognition. In *Proc. U.S. Postal Service Advanced Technology Conf.*, pages 1033–1041, 1988.

[LBD+90] Yan Le Cun, B. Boser, J. S. Denker, D. Henderson, R. E. Howard, W. Hubbard, L. D. Jackel, and H. S. Baird. Constrained neural network for unconstrained handwritten digit recognition. In *Proc. Int. Workshop on Frontiers in Handwriting Recognition*, pages 145–154, Concordia University, Montreal, April 1990.

[LS88]   L. Lam and C. Y. Suen. Structural classification and relaxation matching of totally unconstrained handwritten zip-code numbers. *Pattern Recognition*, 21(1):19–31, 1988.

[MS90]   T. Mai and C. Y. Suen. A generalized knowledge-based system for the recognition of unconstrained handwritten numerals. *IEEE Trans. Syst. Cybern.*, 20(4):835–848, 1990.

[NW60]   U. Neisser and P. Weene. A note on human recognition of handprinted characters. *Information and Control*, 3:191–196, 1960.

[SNM+90] C. Y. Suen, C. Nadal, T. A. Mai, R. Legault, and L. Lam. Recognition of handwritten numerals based on the concept of multiple experts. In *Proc. Int. Workshop on Frontiers in Handwriting Recognition*, pages 131–144, Concordia University, Montreal, April 1990.

Recognition of Hand-Printed Chinese Characters and the Japanese Cursive Syllabary

Kazuhiko Yamamoto and Hiromitsu Yamada

Image Understanding Section, Electrotechnical Laboratory,
Tsukuba Science City, Ibaraki 305, Japan

We describe a method for the recognition of hand-printed Chinese characters (Kanji) and Japanese cursive syllabary characters (Hiragana). The system preclassifies using cellular features and then classifies by a combination of feature extraction of line segments, an extreme-point method, and a relaxation matching method. Relaxation is a technique using contextual information to reduce local ambiguities: initial probabilities are assigned to matches between pairs of the line segments in the dictionary and the input, and then iteration finds acceptable combinations of the matches. The system was trained and tested on the ETL8 database; recognition results were 99% correct on the "good quality" data set, and 94.6% on the "poor quality" data set.

1 Introduction

The main difficulties in the recognition of Kanji characters result from:

1. The number of character categories used daily in Japan is large.
2. The structure of Chinese character patterns is more complex than that of alphanumeric characters. Chinese characters are not only characters but are also pictures that are complex structures of line segments.
3. There are many sets of characters that are similar by shape.

We propose a method combining relaxation with feature extraction, for the recognition of Kanji (Chinese characters used in Japan) and Hiragana (the Japanese cursive syllabic alphabet). Automatic extraction of line segments is more difficult for Hiragana, since they are more cursive than Kanji. We also describe a new method for the extraction of line segments, which improves on a previously published method using a relaxation matching method [1].

Due to the large size of the symbol set, fast preclassifiers are run first. There are many matching methods [3] which can be used for preclassification. We use a cellular feature matching [2] method, chosen for its simplicity and high speed.

2 Extraction of Line Segments

We propose a new method, called the "extreme point" method, which is an improvement upon the "outermost point" method [4]. By fixing a specific allowance for the calculation of inner products, deciding the comparison of directional vectors for each of the plurality of directions on the basis of this allowance, and providing the system with a switching function capable of setting specific directions in a non-responding status, the system is allowed to exclude unnecessary components due to noise and, at the same time, effect polygonal approximation [5] which faithfully reflects the characteristic of the given pattern.

The extraction of feature line segments in the extreme point method will be described in detail below. For simplicity of description, the operation of this system is assumed here as involving the eight directions $(D_1, D_3, D_5, ...D_{15})$, namely the 16 directions of Figure 2 minus the even-numbered directions as shown Figure 1.

When the pattern shown in Figure 2 is given to be recognized, for example, the point P_1 at the uppermost corner of the pattern is regarded as the point for starting the tracing of the contour of this pattern and, at the same time, the point P_1 itself constitutes a candidates for the outermost point in the direction D_{13}. Since the contour is traced clockwise, there is a possibility that the origin P_1 will be decided simultaneously as a common extreme point in the directions D_{13}, D_{15}, D_1, and D_3. To preclude this possibility, therefore, in the output switches for the extreme points illustrated in Figure 3(A), those for the directions $D_5, ...D_9$, and D_{11} are turned ON (non-responding status; shown enclosed with a circle "o" in the picture) and those for the directions D_{13}, D_{15}, D_1, and D_3 are turned OFF. When the difference, δ_i, between the projection of a candidates extreme point and that of a point of the contour being traced, on the same given direction exceeds the allowance ε, the candidates extreme point is fed out as a true extreme point. This allowance ε is fixed, depending on the degree of minute irregularities in the contour of the pattern which are to be ignored in the approximation. Here, the value indicated by the two-headed arrow in Figure 2 is used as the allowance. The calculation of the projection is expressed by the formula (1) shown below,

$$\Delta_i = |a_j| \times cos\theta_{ij} = |a_j| \times \frac{(a_j, e_i)}{|a_j| \times |e_i|} = \frac{(a_j, e_i)}{|e_i|}$$

Where θ_{ij} denotes the angle formed by the vector a of the point of contour e_i. The point at which the projection Δ_i reached its maximum constitutes the outer most point in the direction i. There is a total of 16 specific directions as illustrated in Figure 1. The value, e_i, of the directional vector in the right side of the formula is not necessarily "1." By assuming $e_i \times \epsilon$ for all the directions, the calculation of the projection can be carried out only by the calculation of inner products (a_j, e_i). The tracing of the contour from the point P_1 is started. At various points of the contour, inner products (a_j, e_i) are calculated with respect to all the directions, and decisions are made as to whether the difference between the two projections mentioned above exceeds the allowance ϵ in each of the directions for which the output switches for extreme points have been turned OFF. When the difference is not greater than the allowance ϵ, the current point of contour or the candidates extreme point, whichever has a greater projection, is taken as the candidates extreme point. When the difference exceeds the allowance ϵ, the candidate extreme point is fed out as a true extreme point and the output switch for the extreme point for the direction in which this output is obtained is turned ON and the output switch for the extreme point for the direction diametrically opposite the direction of the output is turned OFF, and the current point of the contour is taken as a candidate extreme point.

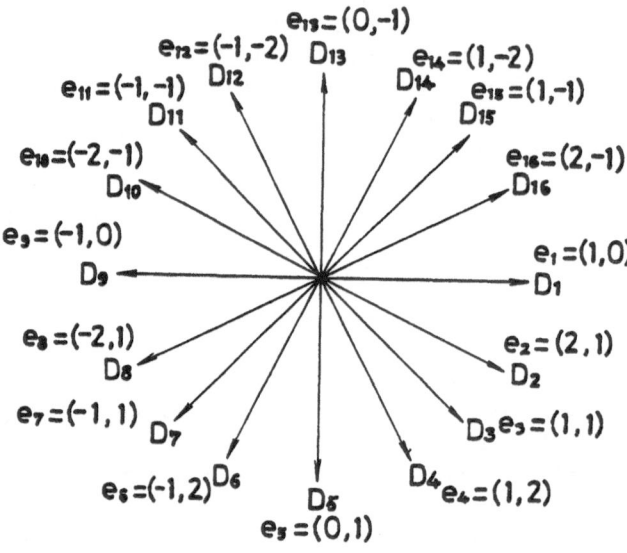

Fig. 1. The individual direction involved in seeking the extreme points and the directional vectors in such directions.

With respect to the direction for which the output switch for the extreme point is kept ON, the tracing of the contour is advancing away from that direction and the extreme point has already been fed out. Consequently, the current point of the contour is forcibly taken as a candidates extreme point. In Figure 2, at the point P_2, the difference δ_2^1 of the two projections of the points P_1 and P_2 in relation to the direction D_{13} exceeds the allowance ϵ so that the point P_1 is fed out as the true extreme point in the direction D_{13}. In Figure 3(A), the output switch for the extreme point for the direction D_{13} is turned ON and the output switch for the extreme point for the direction P_5 is turned OFF. At the point P_3 , since the difference δ_3^1 between the two projections of the points P_1 and P_3 with respect to the direction D_{15} exceeds the allowance ϵ, the point P_1 is fed out as the true extreme point in the direction D_{15}, the output switch for the extreme point for the direction D_{15} is turned ON, and the output switch for the extreme point for the direction D_7 is turned OFF. At the time that the tracing of the contour has passed the point P_4, the output switch for the extreme point for the directions D_1, D_3, D_5, and D_7 are kept OFF and those for the directions D_9, D_{11}, D_{13}, and D_{15}, are kept ON as illustrated in Figure 3(B). At the point P_5, since the difference δ_5^4 between the two projections with respect to the direction D_7 with the point P_4 exceeds the allowance ϵ, the point P_4 is fed out as the true extreme point in the direction D_7.

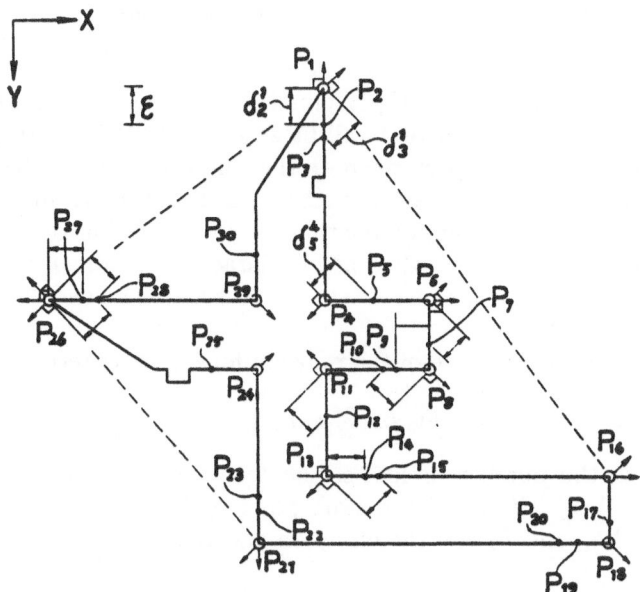

Fig. 2. An explanatory pattern illustrating the process of extraction of extreme points.

By tracing the contour and feeding out the extreme points wherever the difference between two projections exceed the allowance ϵ as described above, a polygonal approximation of the pattern is obtained, it is a pattern which disregards minute concavities and convexities not exceeding the allowance ϵ as occurring between the points P_1 and P_4 and between the point P_{25} and P_{26}. In Figure 2, the points $P_1, P_4, P_6, P_8, P_{11}, P_{13}, P_{16}, P_{18}, P_{21}, P_{24}, P_{26}$, and P_{29}, are fed out as extreme points to afford a polygonal approximation which faithfully preserves the feature of the pattern given to be recognized. In accordance with the conventional "outermost point listing method" [4], only the five points $P_1, P_{16}, P_{18,21}$ and P_{26}, are obtained as outermost points. Thus, the approximated pattern consequently obtained assumes a convex hull as shown by the dotted line in Figure 2 which no longer preserves the shape of the pattern.

At the time that the tracing of the contour of the pattern is the started, the output switches for the extreme point for some of the direction involved are turned ON.

When a pattern such as that illustrated in Figure 4(A), for example, is polygonally approximated on the condition of $\epsilon = 0$, the result of this approximation

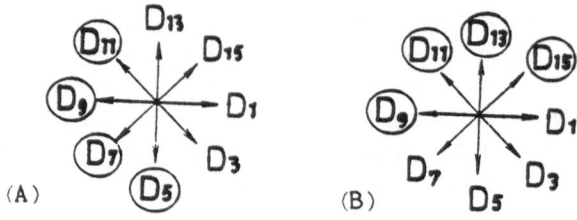

Fig. 3. The operation of the output switch for extreme points.

will be as shown in Figure 4(B). If polygonal approximation is performed on the condition of $\epsilon \geq$ 2 × 64, the result will be as shown in Figure 4(C). When this polygonal approximation is performed on the condition of $\epsilon = 2$ (corresponding to two meshes in 64 × 63 meshes), the result will be as shown in Figure 4(D).

We used the polygonal approximation on the condition of $\epsilon = 2$. As can be seen in Figure 4(D), this method has a characteristic threat relatively many points are extracted in the area where the contour makes a bend. So, some points are excluded by stages.

A line segment O_k is a side of the polygon for input pattern.

$$O = (O_k)_{k=1}^{\varphi} = (X_{sk}, Y_{sk}, \theta_k, L_k, X_{ek}, Y_{ek})_{k=1}^{\varphi} \tag{1}$$

Where φ is the number of line segments of the polygon; (X_{sk}, Y_{sk}) and (X_{ek}, Y_{ek}) are the positions of the start point and the end point for the line segment k; and θ_k and L_k are the direction and the length of the line segment k.

2.1 Neighboring Segments' List

There are two kinds of neighboring segments lists for segment k. The neighboring segments for the start point of k are defined as the segments which have end points within a radius of ρ of the start point of k. The neighboring segments for the end point of k are similarly defined as the segments which have start point of k. The neighboring segments lists are denoted by $(E_1, ..., E_{nsk})$, $(E_1, ..., E_{nek})$

where $nsk \leq 4$ and $nek \leq 4$ are the numbers of neighboring segments for the start point and the end point of segment k.

3 Preclassification

3.1 Cellular Features

Reduced cellular feature $Z(X, Y, \Theta)$ is defined on cellular space with meshes of 7 × 7 and each cell has 8 intracells for 8 directions. Each intracell stores the strength of the edge whose direction is just normal to the direction Θ of the intracell. These intracell features are representing geometrical features of the input pattern around cell. One example is shown in Figure 5.

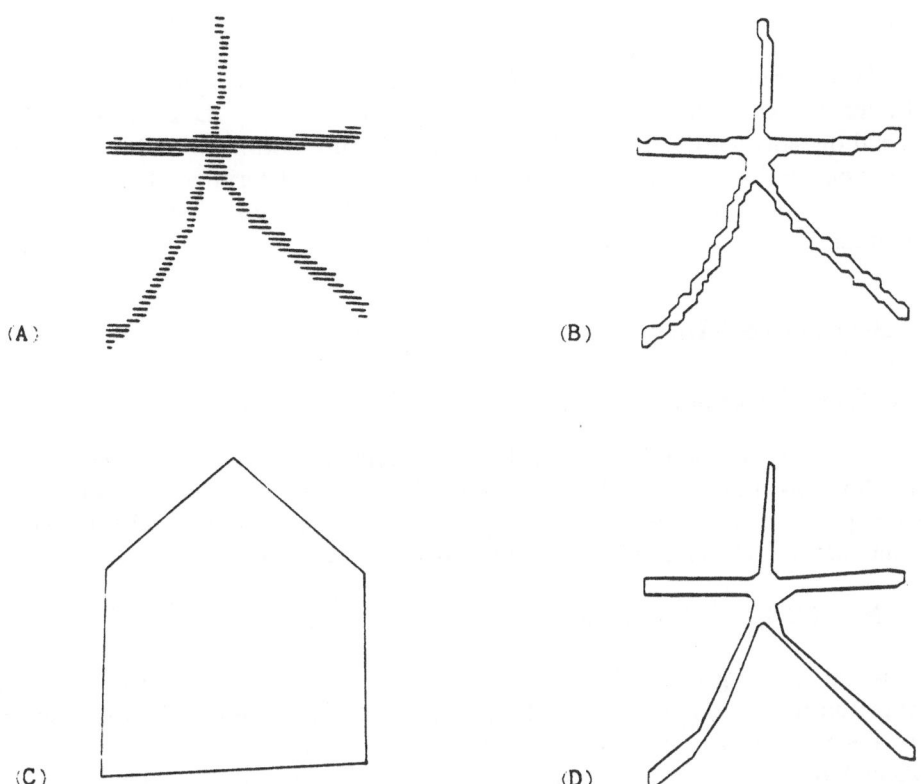

(A)

(B)

(C)

(D)

Fig. 4. Input pattern and its polygonal approximation for different value ϵ: (A) the original image; (B) polygon for $\varepsilon = 0$; (C) polygon for $\varepsilon > \sqrt{2}.64$; and (D) polygon for $\varepsilon = 2.0$.

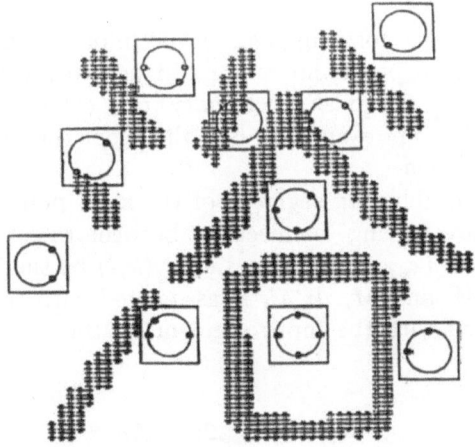

Fig. 5. Sampled cellular features. The filled points on the circle in the box show the intracells whose values are larger than a given threshold.

3.2 Distance Calculation

Preclassification dictionary $H_J = (x, y, \Theta)$ of a category J is an average value of reduced cellular features $Z_J(x, y, \Theta)$ for training data of the category J. The Euclid distance between the reduced cellular feature pattern Z and the preclassification dictionary pattern H_J of preclassification determines the candidate category set of the input character. Ten candidate categories which have tenth minimal distance are selected.

4 Structure Matching

4.1 The Dictionary

Each category has only one mask; thus the dictionary of characters is composed of 956 masks. Each mask M is composed of φ_M segments and each segment M is composed of the six features $(x_{sk}, y_{sk}, \theta_k, L_k, x_{ek}, y_{ek})$ together with the start points list and the end points list of the neighboring segments:

$$M = (M_i)_{i=1}^{\phi_M} = (x_{si}, y_{si}, \theta_i, L_i, x_{ei}, y_{ei}, [E_1, ..., E_{nsi}], [E_1, ...E_{nei}])_{i=1}^{\phi_M} \qquad (2)$$

In the learning stage of the dictionary, each feature of mask segment M_i is evaluated from a set of associated segments of training data by the relaxation process to be described later. The features $(x_{si}, y_{si}, \theta_i, L_i, x_{ei}, y_{ei})$ of M_i are calculated from the average values of features $(x_{sl}, y_{sl}, theta_l, L_l, x_{el}, y_{el})$ of input segment k for the training set of the same category. The neigh-bori ng segments list of the mask is assigned from the neighboring segments list of the first data of the training set.

4.2 Relaxation Matching

Relaxation is a technique for using contextual information to reduce local ambiguities. At first initial probabilities are assigned to the match between pairs of the line segment i in the mask (dictionary) of a category and k in the input. Initially, all $i - k$ pairs are examined, but all except the most probable one are damped at each iteration.

Let M_j be the neighboring segment of the start point of segment M_i. We assume that there are "spring" connections between the start point (x_{si}, y_{si}) of M_i and the end point (x_{ej}, y_{ej}) of M_j. Let $r_{ij}^s(k, l)$ be the initial tension in the spring connecting M_i and M_j. If M_i is associated with the input segment o_k, and M_j is associated with the input segment o_l, then $r_{ij}^s(k, l)$ is evaluated as follows:

$$r_{ij}^s(k, l) = \Delta x + \Delta y$$

$$\Delta x = max(min(1 - \frac{1}{16} \times (D_s^x(i, j) - D_s^x(k, l) + \alpha_{25}), 1), 0)$$

$$\Delta y = max(min(1 - \frac{1}{16} \times (D_s^y(i,j) - D_s^y(k,l) + \alpha_{25}), 1), 0)$$

$$D_s^x(i,j) = x_{si} - x_{ej}$$

$$D_s^y(i,j) = y_{si} - y_{ej}$$

Where $alpha_{25}(=2)$ is a threshold of invariance for small differences.
The end point tension $r_{ij}^e(k,l)$ is defined analogously.

The probability $p_{i(k)}^{(t)}$ is evaluated by the tension in the spring connecting the segments as follows:

$$P_{i(k)}^{(t+1)} = \frac{Q_{i(k)} \times P_{i(k)}^{(t)}}{\sum_{k'} Q_{i(k')} P_{i(k')}^{(t)}}$$

$$Q_{i(k)} = \frac{Q_{i(k)}^s + Q_{i(k)}^e}{nsi + nei}$$

$$Q_{i(k)}^s = \sum_j^{nsi} (Max \ r_{ij}^s(k,l) \times P_{j(l)}^{(t)})$$

$$Q_{i(k)}^e = \sum_{j'}^{nsi} (Max \ r_{ij'}^e(k,l') \times P_{j'(l')}^{(t)})$$

Where t is the number of iterations.

The relaxation operation dynamically changes the probability according to the compatibility between the configurations of mask segments and the input segments. The distance D_J between mask J and the input is defined as follows: The $\bar{k}$ of association function is chosen out of all pairs (i,k) for i, because $p_{i(\bar{k})}$ is at its highest probability after iteration time T.

$$D_j = \frac{\sum_{i \in \phi'} (1 - R_{i(\bar{k})}) + \sum_{i\phi'} 1 + \sum_{k \in \phi''} 1}{\phi_M}$$

$$R_{i(\bar{k})} = \frac{\sum_j^{nsi} r_{ij}^s(\bar{k}, \bar{l}) P_{j(\bar{l})} + \sum_{j'}^{nei} r_{ij'}^e(\bar{k}, \bar{l'}) P_{j'(\bar{l'})}}{nsi + nei} P'_{(\bar{k})}$$

Where ϕ' is the set of matched mask segments, ϕ'' is the set of unmatched mask segments, and ϕ''' is the set of unmatched input segments. The resulting category J is that for which the distance D_J is the shortest within candidate categories.

An illustrative example of the relaxation matching is shown in Figure 6. Upper left picture is input character and upper right is a polygonal approximation of the input. Down left categorize are candidates of the input and the top of them is a result category because its distance between the mask and the input is the shortest. Down right pattern is the mask of the resulting category and dotted lines shown the match between the line segment of the mask segment and the input.

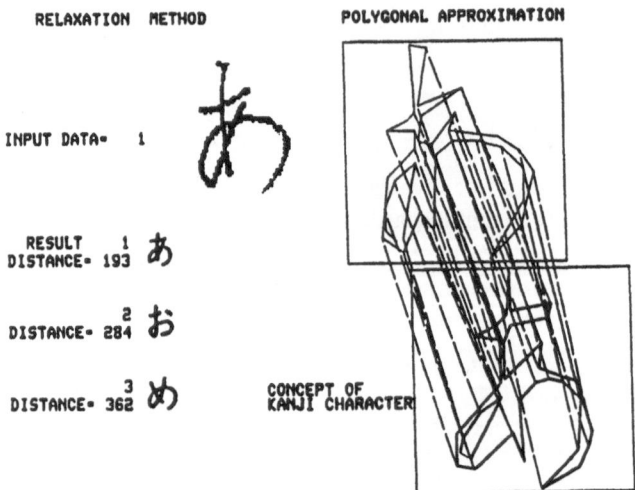

Fig. 6. An illustration of relaxation matching.

5 Experiments

The hand-printed character data base ETL-8 was used which is binarized and normalized to 64×63 in size. The ETL-8 consists of 160 data sets and each data set consists of 952 categories (881 Kanji characters and 71 Hiragana characters). The preclassification dictionary and the main dictionary was created with 80 training data sets which are odd data sets. Recognition tests were done using the second data set which is good quality, and the 34th data set which is poor quality. The preclassification rates which included the correct category in the first ten candidates are shown in Table 1. Table 2 gives total recognition rates, and Table 3 shows some examples.

Table 1. Preclassification rates (the correct category is included in the ten categories).

Data set	Tenth preclassification rate
2nd	99.8 %
34th	98.4 %

6 Conclusion

Some concluding remarks are listed as follows:

1. The cellular feature is a very useful feature for preclassification of Kanji characters and Hiragana characters.

Table 2. Experimental results (A).

Recognition method	Recognition rate (%)	
	2nd data set	34th data set
simple matching(7)	76.2	44.2
Directional feature matching(7)	95.9	73.6
Cellular feature matching(2)	97.4	82.9
Extreme poiny and relaxation matching	99.0	93.0

(#) shown the reference paper.

Table 3. Recognition examples (B).

Good quality data set(2nd) | Poor quality data set (34th)

Input	Result		Input	Result
	Code			Code
	Distance			Distance

2. The extreme point listing method for extraction of line segments work well even for cursive syllabary characters.
3. The effectiveness of the combining relaxation matching method and the extreme point method has been proved even for poor quality data.

Acknowledgements

The authors wishes to thank Dr. Mori and Dr. Yasuda for their comments.

References

[1] K. Yamamoto, and A. Rosenfeld, "Recognition of hand-printed Kanji characters by a relaxation," *Proc. 6th ICPR*, Munich, pp. 395–398, 1982.

[2] Ryu-ichi Oka, "Hand-printed Chinese-Japanese characters recognition by using cellular feature," *Proc. 6th ICPR*, Munich, pp. 783–785, 1982.

[3] S. Mori, "Research on machine recognition of hand-printed Chinese characters," *Proc. Int'l Conf. Chinese-Language Computer Society*, pp. 373–387, Sep. 1982.

[4] K. Yamamoto *et al.*, "Recognition of hand-printed characters by outer most point method," *Pattern Recognition*, Vol. 12, pp. 229–236, 1980.

[5] H. Yamada *et al.*, "A polygonal approximation based on the extreme point method," *Annual Conf. of IECE of Japan*, 1377, 1983 (in Japanese).

[6] S. Mori *et al.*, "Data bank of Kanji characters," *Bulletin of ETL*, Vol. 43, No. 11, pp. 752, 1980, (in Japanese).

[7] T. Saito *et al.*, "An analysis of hand-printed Chinese characters," *J. of IECE of Japan*, Vol. J65-D, pp. 550–557, 1982.

Regularities and Singularities in Line Pictures

Jean–Claude Simon and Olivier Baret

Laforia / CNRS and ENPC, Paris, France

The main difficulty of Pattern Recognition is the interpretation of the
iconic picture, the pixels, into primitive features. The interest of a feature
classification as "regular" and "singular" is recalled and justified. These
ideas are applied to line images, and particularly to handwritten words.
On the graph representation of a word, a regular feature, the "axis,"
is found; it allows to segment the word representation and to obtain
a descriptive chain. Examples of such symbolic descriptions are given,
with their interpretation as a word among a list of 25 words. The results
are of the order of 87% success, 3% substitution on one handwriting.
Preliminary results show that it may be extended to large categories of
handwriting.

1 Introduction

1.1 Definitions

An "item of information," or more simply an "information" is a couple consisting
of a concrete representation and it(s) interpretation(s) [1].

A "concrete representation," more simply a "representation" is any real
means representing an object. For instance, the waves of light radiated by an
object are a representation of the object; pressure waves are a representation
of a speech sound; a "picture"[1] on a piece of paper is the representation of a
scene. Inside a computer representations are strings of symbols taken from a
finite alphabet, *i.e.* a coding. A "set of pixels," numerical samples, allow the
representation of a picture, in a computer memory.

An "interpretation" is the result of an operation (a program) using as input
a representation. As examples, a human being interprets the pressure waves
falling on his ears as a speech, the light waves falling on his eyes as the image of

---

[1] From dictionary definitions, an image is "a visible representation of something,"
a picture is "a surface representation of an object or a scene, as by a painting,
drawing, engraving, or photograph; also a mental image." Thus "picture" is preferred
to "image" to speak of the representation of an image in a computer.

a scene. It is difficult to grasp what are precisely these human interpretations, but for computing machines it is clear that the result of an interpretation is a new representation.

A "quantity of information" is the amount of memory in "bytes," usually octets, necessary to store a representation. Along the interpretation sequence, which is typical of Pattern Recognition (P.R.), the quantity of information decreases. The identification of an object, a word, which is the final interpretation, request usually the minimal quantity of information. It is the ultimate "compression" of the initial quantity of information (the set of pixels). As comprehension increases, the quantity of information decreases.

1.2 Computing Complexity

Every mathematical object does not find its representation in the computable world. For example mathematical "real numbers" may request an infinite quantity of information. The computing type "float" or "real" is not exactly a real number in the sense of mathematics. A mapping in mathematics may be defined only by its properties. How to implement a mapping does not concern usually a mathematician. The inverse is true in computing. Any operation (program) on a representation should be exactly defined from elementary operations. The result of an operator (program) is also exactly defined by a new representation. But the properties of the mapping is not always clear.

The price to pay for constructivity (*i.e.*, for well defined operations, which allow to obtain a well defined output from a well defined input) is computing complexity, *i.e.* the number of elementary operations and/or quantity of information necessary to obtain the output from the input representation [2].

P.R. is typically a problem implying computing complexity. The goal of P.R. is to map constructively the set of initial representations into the set of names. To build up this mapping "in extension," *i.e.* template matching is quite hopeless as it is an exponential-time algorithm, and thus intractable. The only circumventions are (see [1], Chapter 1) :

- to lower the dimension of a P.R. problem, *i.e.* to solve several problems of smaller dimensions;
- to decompose the identification mapping in several hierarchized subidentifications;
- to allow errors, exchanging in a way exactness for computing speed, for example use polynomial operators

1.3 From Pixels to Features

The first level of recognition from pixels to features is specially difficult to implement, and its success conditions the final identification [3].

As we pointed out, the initial representation of a picture in a computer is a set of N pixels (the "iconic" representation). Thus a picture can be viewed as a "point" into a N dimension euclidian space $\mathcal{R}^N$.

By definition, a "feature" is the result of the interpretation of p pixels, usually on a compact support, a "window" of the picture (a subspace $\mathcal{R}^p$ of $\mathcal{R}^N$). The problem is to determine operators (programs) which decide of the existence of the corresponding feature inside a given window. On which properties can we rely to find such operators ?

- *On properties of $\mathcal{R}^p$* , such as neighborhood, distance measures. If samples of a feature occupy a region of such a metric space, we may suppose that by continuity the points of this region and of a neighborhood probably represent the same feature. However, it is clear that most of the points of $\mathcal{R}^p$ are just "noise."
- *On properties of the interpretation and of the corresponding operator.* Interpretation (the feature) and the corresponding operator (the identification program) may have some interesting properties such as *invariance to transformations* of the object [5].

First step towards the identification of objects, feature identification is the birth of linguistic concepts. $\mathcal{R}^N$ is a undifferentiated space in the sense that the type of any "point" is equivalent. A feature space is quite different. It is finite, and it has differentiated types. The following steps of recognition operate on representations which are already words or phrases of a language. The step from pixels to features allow to progress in comprehension from a world without meaning, the "chaos" of the Greeks.

2 Regular and Singular Features

2.1 Errors and Complexity of Operators

Edge or contour detection from an iconic picture (a picture representation stored in memory as a set of pixels) is a good example of the difficulties of P.R. . Several edge detector have been proposed, but on real pictures they perform badly, in the sense that they miss edges where we see one or find edges where there is not any. A lot of efforts has been devoted to improve edge operators, increasing badly the computing complexity, but without a complete success. The same may be said for consonant detection in speech signals.

Of course, exponential matching algorithms will remain intractable, whatever the computing power. Today all the identification operators in use are of polynomial types; but they should not overpass errors of a few percent, which is not true for consonants or edges.

On the other hand, vowel identification is simple and errors are of a few percent. For pictures, texture identification, line identification (in a line picture) is also of low complexity and the errors are small. The common character of these features is the *periodicity of their iconic representation* and thus the *invariance to translation* of the identification operators.

2.2 Regular and Singular Classes of Features

From the above remarks, it seems likely to classify features in two classes:

- *The regular class* is made of features, of which the iconic representation is periodic or quasiperiodic, such as vowels, features, lines. Their identification is invariant versus the translation of the pixel representation.
- *The singular class* is made of features which are the *complements* of the the features of the regular class. In fact they are the "*accidents*" or "*catastrophes*" of the regular features: consonants for vowels; edges for textures; extremities, crossings, cusps, forks for line pictures.

In the literature, two approaches to "picture segmentation" may be found: an edge-based approach, a "region growing" approach.

In the first, edges are found and, if possible, are joined so as to form close contours of objects. In the second, the pixels are clustered into compact supports, with the help of a similarity measure to find quasi uniform regions.

Recently, Pavlidis has proposed the use of residual analysis for feature extraction. Quoting [4] : "pictures are considered as consisting of three parts: smooth, features and noise. After a smoothing operation, the difference between the result and the original has the characteristic of noise in areas away from features. Systematic trends in the difference indicate features such as "edges or corners." In our terminology, smooth regions are those of regular features. What Pavlidis call features is our singular features. He points out that smoothed (regular) regions are the predictable part (any periodic signal is predictable), and that the feature (singular) regions are obtained by residual analysis.

Quite similarly, we have proposed in [5, 6] a *complemental* approach to feature detection. The principle is: *First find the regions of regular features, and then subtract these regions from the iconic representation. What remains are regions of singular features.* Examples are given in the following.

3 Line Pictures

3.1 What is a Line?

From now, we deal with "line pictures," *i.e.* the image representations obtained from lines on sheets of paper. The iconic representation is either a set of numerical samples (grey level picture) or of binary samples (binary picture).

Let us discuss first the grey picture of a line. Without any line, "background" pixels are obtained, images of the empty sheet of paper. Their amplitude may vary, according to the sensor sensitivity and the light on the sheet. Usually it is a regular region in our sense. But it may be also a picture in itself as on bank checks. Let us assume that it is uniform and white. To black lines on the sheet correspond new values of pixels, sampling a 2dimension signal. The shortest pulse, in a direction orthogonal to the line, should have a minimum width w. If the sampling criterion is respected, at least three pixels along the orthogonal direction have values different of the local background pixels. For a detailed discussion see [3] or [1], Chapter 6. This requires usually at least 300 d.p.i. (dots per inch) or 12 pixels/mm.

In practice, it is convenient to obtain a binary picture, in which the 0 pixels belong to the background, the 1 pixels belong to the line. It is a delicate operation, as the thresholding value may vary according to the position in the image. From a "correct" sampling, *at least 3 black pixels* should be obtained in all directions. Unfortunately 300 d.p.i. slows down the scanning of the sheet, and takes a fair amount of memory. Engineers work currently with 150 or even less d.p.i. The results are binary pictures which do not respect the above criterion of at least 3 black pixels. These uncorrect" pictures may create difficulties in the following operations. Though some preprocessing techniques may restore a correct picture, it is always better to obtain a correct picture at the start.

The shortest possible line is the point, which in a correct picture is represented by at least a 3 × 3 black pixel support.

Definitions: A "quantum" is a 3 × 3 black pixel support, named so in the memory of Gabor. We may now answer to the question "What is a line": In a binary picture a "line" is a sequence of quantums (quanta), which more or less overlap. It may be noticed that the localization of the "feature point" is anywhere inside a quantum, and the localization of the feature "line" is anywhere inside a band of at least three pixel thick.

The above ideas have been applied to find "lines" in printed character binary representations, as it will be shown in the following Section 3.3.

3.2 Representation of A Line

In the former paragraph 3.1, we have discussed the binary representation of a line, as it should be obtained at the input of the first level, *i.e.* at the input of the feature finding operators. Once a line has been found, any convenient representation may be used, such as a *chain of black pixels*. But may we underline that such a representation is in fact impossible to obtain from a system "optical linear sensor plus a thresholding operation." Such a representation of a line image by chains of pixels does generate a graph, as it will be seen later.

Remarks on skeletonization. A lot of efforts has been put to obtain "skeletons," representations by chains of pixels, either of grey or binary pictures. On grey pictures, morphological techniques are favored [8], on binary pictures "thinning" techniques. The last one, of linear complexity, give birth to parasitic chains, the "dendrites," which may be quite a problem. The underlying idea is still to get a representation of a line as a *chain of pixels* (see 4.1).

Several other representations can be used to represent a line at the iconic level: the Freeman code, discrete vectors, even polynomials such as splines

3.3 A First Complemental Approach to Feature Detection

Let us assume that the picture representation is binary. Lines defined, as above at Section 3.1, are the regular features of a line image. The principle on which

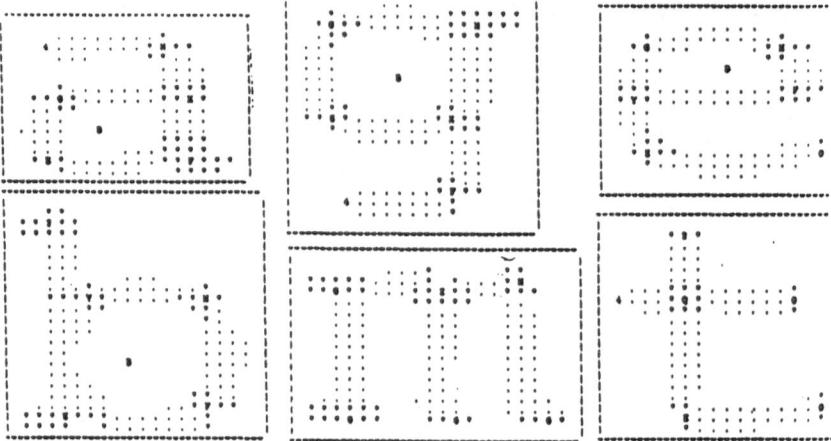

Fig. 1. Singular features of printed characters.

works the identification of a line is to grow a region of black pixels, such that it may be considered as a line, and to stop when it is no more possible. In more details, let us consider horizontal scans of rank $i = 0, 1, 2, \ldots$. Any sequence of at least 2 black pixels is a "line precursor," $a_i, b_i, c_i, \ldots$. A sequence of $a_i, b_i, \ldots$ may cover an area, which may be considered as a "quantum." As it was said, covering quanta may be a line segment, according to some rules. The orientation of such a line element may vary between 45 degrees around the vertical direction. In the same way, vertical scans would find line elements 45 degrees around the horizontal direction [5]. Figure 1 gives several examples of lower case printed characters, treated with the above techniques. The dot pixels '.' belong to line elements, the star pixels '*' are the black pixels which remain when the former dot pixels have been removed. They are the support of the singular features: forks, like Z in 'm', X in 'a' and 'g', Y in 'b' and 'e'; crossings like Q in 't'; changes of direction G, H, E, F; extremities 0,1,...,7. The nature of these singular features is found by the direction of the line elements adjacent to them. This technique of finding the singular features is quite robust, and much less prone to errors than a direct approach. The rate of error is well under 1%.

Figure 2 & 3 show the same technique applied to handwriting, from iconic binary pictures [9]. Again, the results are quite robust. On Figure 2, the black pixels belonging to a line are the small dots, the remaining black pixels are the thick dots. They belong to supports of singular features. Figure 3 gives interpretations of these singular features, according to the directions of the lines which join them; for example, Q, crossing; G, E, H, F, changes of direction; 0,1,...,7, extremities.

However this technique favors horizontal and vertical line elements. This is why the changes of direction G, H, E, F appear preferentially. It is justified for most printed characters, except such as 'x', 'y', 'z', for which conflicts may appear at 45 degrees; but it may be less valuable as handwriting singularities.

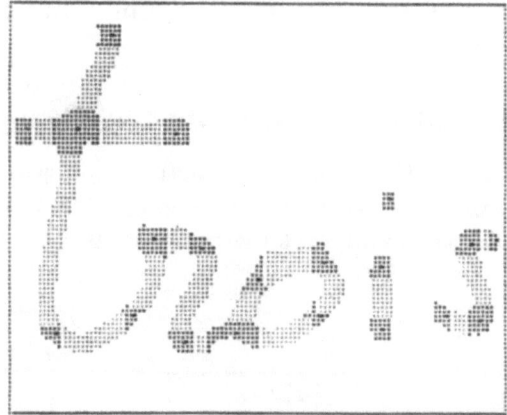

Fig. 2. The complemental approach applied to handwriting: case 1.

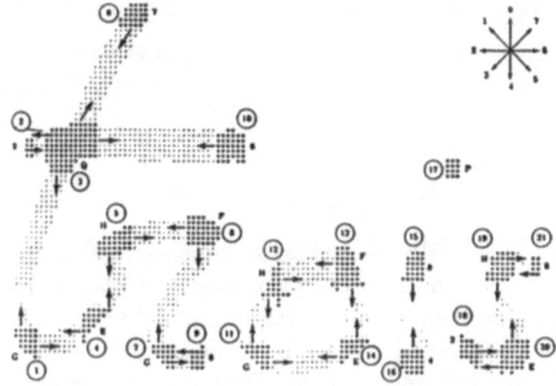

Fig. 3. The complemental approach applied to handwriting: case 2.

On the other hand, the line finding algorithm assumes that a line is at least three pixels thick, and in practice sometimes, as the reader may notice on Figure 1, two pixels thick in a direction orthogonal to the line element. On Figure 2 and 3 the rule of at least three pixels thick is always respected. But as we underlined, in practice binary files do not respect this condition. The optical sensor scans at speeds such that only one or two black pixels are sampled (100 dpi instead of 300 dpi). Then the initial binary representation of a line is very noisy and could even be interrupted. Some preprocessing techniques allow to restore a correct representation. But it may be more interesting in practice to try to find directly the representations of lines as chains of pixels. This is what is done in the following Section 4.

4 The Axis, a Regular Feature of the Chaingraph Representation

4.1 The Chaingraph Representation of a Line Picture

The thinning algorithm of A. Leturcqs thesis [10] is used from now on. Figure 4 shows the result on the handwritten word "million." The iconic input representation is in black. The chaingraph is superposed on it in white.

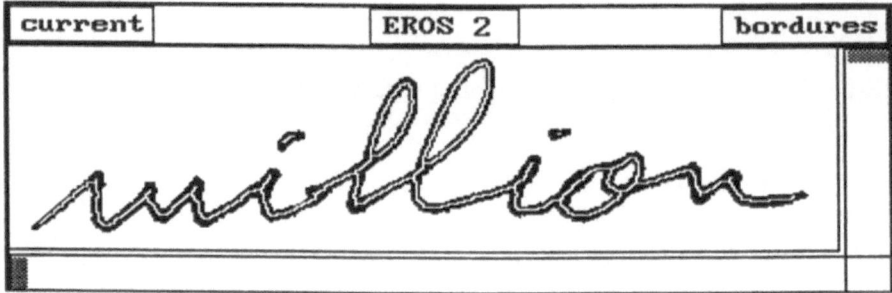

Fig. 4. The chaingraph of the handwritten word "million".

Such a "chaingraph" [2] is made of arcs (chains of pixels), connecting vertices (singularities such as extremities, forks, crossings). The "circuits" of this graph being found are reduced to labeled vertices. A final graph G is obtained.

Figure 5 shows the graph G on which the "axis" is to be determined. The "loops" (inside of circuits) are in black. The lines are represented by chains of black pixels. The two 'l' of million are found as elongated loops, later named S. The white lines inside the black loops, being the result of a thinning, denote the elongated character of the loop.

4.2 Definition of the Axis

Remarks on handwriting. Occidental handwriting consists in displacing a pen from left to right in an oscillating movement, with loops, legs (descenders), poles (ascenders). As an example, in the handwritten word of Figure 4, "million," the 'l' is a pole and a loop, the 'o' is a loop. Legs and poles are respectively under and above the main body of the word. If the word is loosely written, as words which are written fast and often (some signatures for instance), the loops, legs

---

[2] Since "skeleton" has a precise mathematical definition, "chaingraph" is preferred. The only properties required are i) to be made of 4-connected chains of pixels, ii) to be included in the black iconic representation.

palette		SING 2		bordures

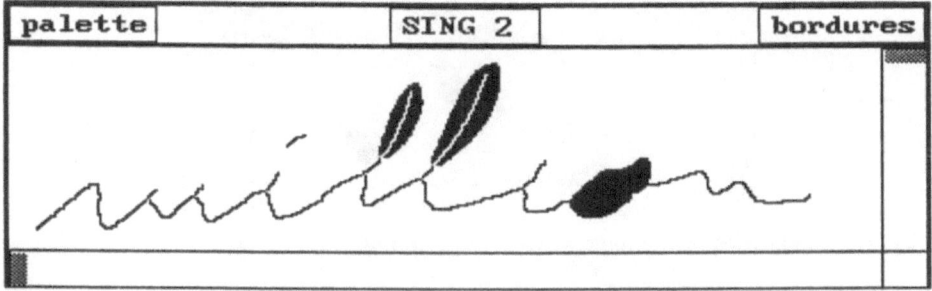

Fig. 5. The graph G of the handwritten word "million".

and poles, diminish and sometimes disappear. Only a sort of oscillating wiggle remains; let it be called an "**axis**." The normally written word may be restored from this axis. In fact, any written word may be restored from an arbitrary "axis," as the reader may convince himself. The graph G may be not connected, if for instance the writer lifts the pen.

palette	Primitives	CHAINES 2			bordures
Aff_cadres	AffBase	ChnNo		ChnCompl	ChnRestr

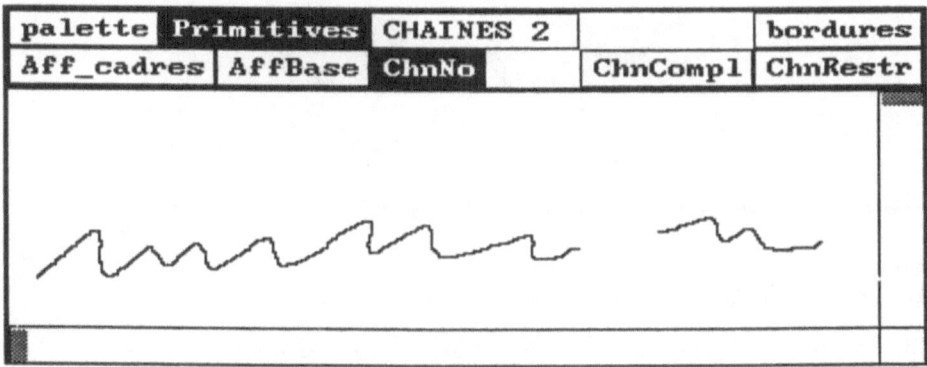

Fig. 6. The "axis" of the handwritten word "million".

Being more formal, the axis is a shortest path in graph G, which respects some further conditions, such as remaining into the main body part of the word (it should not enter into ascenders or descenders).

Figure 6 shows in black the chains, which are the axis of the graph G of Figure 5, and thus of the handwritten word "million."

Applying now the *complemental approach*, the axis is subtracted from G, the singularities appear; as it is shown by Figure 7. The addition of Figure 6 and Figure 7 restores Figure 5. The sequence for the word "trente" is given by Figure 8.

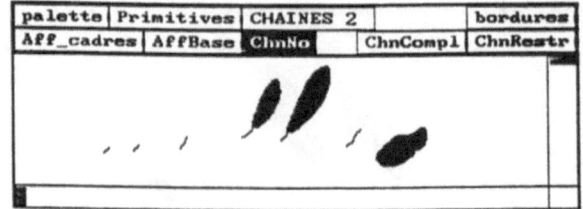

Fig. 7. Singularities of the handwritten word "million".

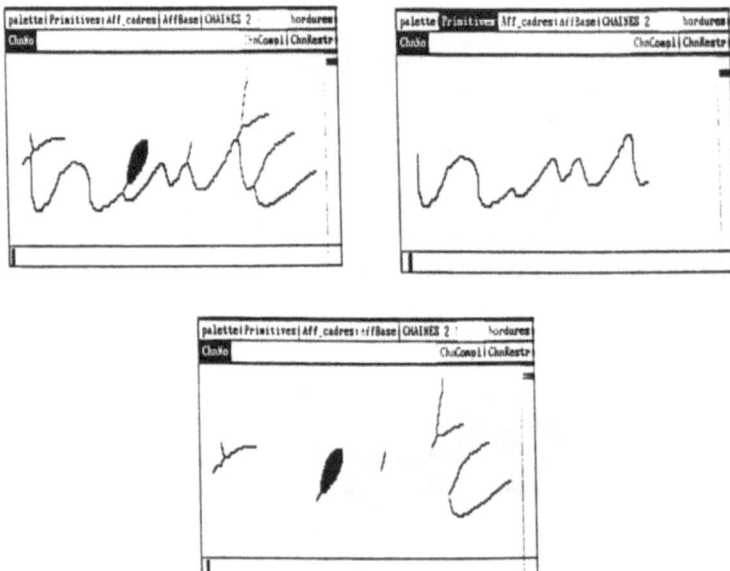

Fig. 8. The chaingraph G, the axis, the singularities for the word "trente".

4.3 Symbolic Description of a Handwritten Word

The interest of the sequence of processes, described above is *to segment the word*, and thus to find the *singularities*. Some are parasitic such as the small vertical segments of "million," but some may represent an 'i'. The loops, round or elongated, the 't' appear clearly on Figure 7 and Figure 8; thanks to the axis extraction.

A "symbolic description" is obtained by a scan of the graph G from left to right, registering the elements. The following chains represent the word "million" of Figures 4 and 5, the word "trente" of Figure 8.

"million"   ⇒   C3:C1:T1:C1:T1:C1:T1:C1:**T1(S)**:C1:**T1(S)**:C1:T1:C1:
                B:C3:C1:C3:C1:

"trente"   ⇒   **T012**:C1:C3:C1:**S**:C1:C3:C1:T1:C1:**T1(T01)**:C1 :**T00**:

The singularities are in **bold** characters. The chains are made of fields, of which the delimiters are ':'. Inside a field is a string of symbols, such as:

- T_i, with $i \in \{0, 1, 2, 3\}$, for East, North, West, South quadrants; T_{ij}, or T_{ijk}, with $i, j, k \in \{0, 1, 2, 3\}$;

- Ci, with $i = 0, 1, 2, 3$, for a curve; for example C1 is a concavity, C3 a convexity.;

- B is a round loop, S is an elongated loop (like in 'l'), F is a loop which has been closed;

- ii (not in the above chains) is an interruption; '(' and ')' are further down replaced by 'd' and 'f', for practical syntactic reasons.

- Finally, ascenders and descenders are denoted by hk, bl, with $k, l \in \{0, 1, ..., 9\}$, with k, l smallest for largest distance from the axis.

4.4 Finding Ascenders and Descenders

A controlled "smearing" allows to find the "body" of the hand-written word. Figure 9 gives in black the area of the body of the word "million." Every feature which is outside above is an ascender, outside under a descender. This technique is much safer than those based on histograms, which suppose that the word is written on an horizontal line (true for printed material).

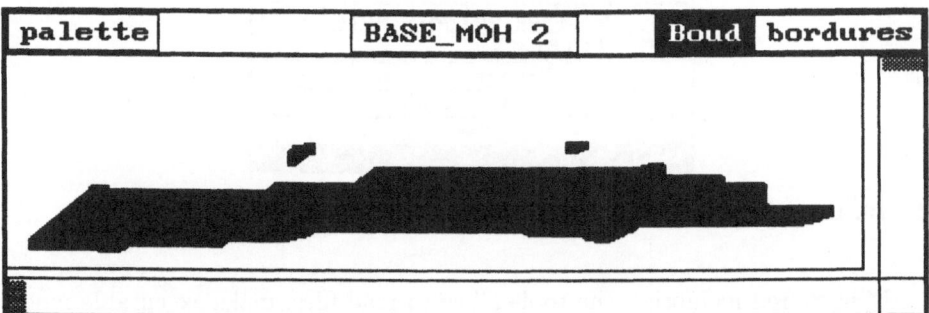

Fig. 9. The "body" of the handwritten word "million".

With *hk* and *bl* in *italics*, the chains for "million" and "trente" are now:

"million" $\Rightarrow$ C3:C1:T1:C1:T1:C1:T1:C1:**T1**d*h0*Sf:C1:**T1**d*h0*Sf:C1:T1:C1:
            B:C3:C1:C3:C1:

"trente" $\Rightarrow$ *h7***T0***h41h32*:C1:C3:C1:**S**:C1:C3:C1:T1:C1:**T1**d**T01***h0*f:C1:**T00**:

5 Description of the Equipment and Main Results

5.1 The Experimental Hardware and Software

Pictures of handwritten words are digitized by a MICROTEK scanner, which delivers binary iconic files. The machines on which the processes are performed are IBM 6151130. The operating system is AIX, a version of UNIX System V. Tools have been developed under X Windows. Figure 10 gives an example of the command panel.

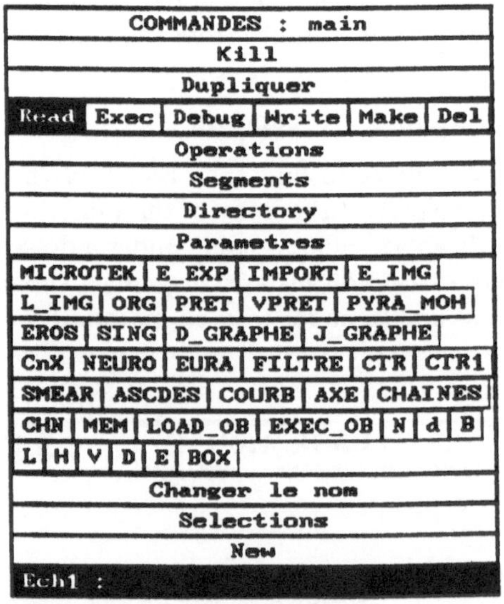

Fig. 10. Example of a command panel.

Using shared memories, the tools allow to read files, make executable modules, execute modules or macros, transmit parameters, display screens, etc. The one letter modules are preprocessing modules which allow to restore degraded files of pictures.

5.2 Some Examples of Descriptive Chains

Let us give some examples of descriptive chains of words by the same writer. The first field is the label of the word; the second the name of the file; the third

a measure of the length of the word versus a 10mean of all the chains; the others are the descriptive chain itself. "un" gives the example of a word which does not have any singularity, but apart some parasitic T1, displays only an axis.
Word "**un**":

1:k100:37:	C1:C3:C1:C3:C1:T1:C1:
1:k101:43:	C1:T1:C1:C3:T3:T1:C1:
1:k102:44:	C1:T1:C1:C3:T3:T1:C1:
1:k103:44:	C1:T1:C1:C3:C1:C3:C1:
1:k104:47:	C1:C3:C1:C3:C1:T1:C1:
1:k105:36:	C1:T1:C1:C3:C1:C3:C1:
1:k106:49:	C1:T1:C1:C3:C1:T1:C1:
1:k107:45:	C1:C3:C1:C3:C1:C3:C1:
1:k108:46:	C1:T1:C1:C3:C1:T1:C1:
1:k109:46:	C1:T1:C1:C3:C1:T1:C1:

Word "**trente**":

18:k100:96:	T01:C1:ii:C3:C1:T1dSf:C1:T1:C1:T1:C1:T1dT01h0f:C1:B:C1:
18:k101:94:	T01:C1:ii:C3:C1:S:C1:C3:C1:T1:C1:T0dh2T0h01h0f:C1:T1dh1Sf:C1:
18:k102:96:	T01h0:C1:C3:C1:B:C1:T1:C1:T1:C1:T1dT01h0f:C1:T0dSf:
18:k103:100:	T01:C1:ii:C3:C1:T1dSf:C1:C3:C1:T1:C1:B1h0:C1:
18:k104:90:	b2F1:ii:C3:C1:B:T1:C1:T1:C1:T1dh0S0h2f:C1:T1:C1:
18:k105:104:	T001:ii:C3:C1:B:C3:C1:T1:C1:T1dT0h21h0f:C1:T1dSf:C1:
18:k106:101:	T01h0:C1:ii:C3:C1:S:C1:T1:C1:T1:C1:T1dT01h0f:C1:T00:
18:k107:86:	T01h0:C1:C3:C1:S:C1:C3:C1:T1:C1:T1dT01h0f:C1:T00:
18:k108:91:	C1:C3:C1:S:C1:C3:C1:T1:C1:T1dT01h0f:C1:T00:
18:k109:89:	T01h2:C1:C3:C1:B:T1:C1:T1:C1:T1dT01h0f:C1:T1dSf:C1:

Word "**mille**":

23:k100:91:	C1:C3:C1:T1:C1:C3:C1:T1dh0Sf:C1:T1dh0Sf:C1:T1dh2Sf:C1:
23:k101:81:	C1:C3:C1:T1:C1:T1:C1:h0F:C1:T1dh0Sf:C1:
23:k102:97:	C3:C1:C3:C1:C3:C1:T1:C1:h0F2h0:C1:T1:C1:
23:k103:86:	C1:T1:C1:T1:C1:T1:C1:T1dh0Sf:C1:T1dh0Sf:C1:T1dSf:C1:
23:k104:99:	C3:C1:C3:C1:T1:C1:T1:C1:T1dh0Sf:C1:T1dh0Sf:C1:T1dh0Sf:C1:
23:k105:100:	T1:C1:C3:C1:T1:C1:T1:C1:ii:h0S:C1:T1dh0Sf:C1:T0dh1Sf:C1:
23:k106:94:	C3:C1:C3:C1:T1:C1:T1:C1:h0F:C1:T1dh2Sf:C1:
23:k107:96:	C3:C1:T1:C1:T1:C1:T1:C1:T1dh0Sf:C1:T1dh0Sf:C1:T00:
23:k108:86:	C3:C1:C3:C1:C3:C1:T1:C1:T1dh0Sf:C1:T1dh0Sf:C3:C1:T1:C1:
23:k109:97:	C3:C1:C3:C1:T1:C1:T1:C1:T1dh0Sf:C1:T1dh0Sf:C1:T1h1:C1:

Word "**million**":

24:k100:129:	T13:C3:C1:T1:C1:T1:C1:T1dh0Sf:C1:T1dh0Sf:C1:T1:C1:B:C3:C1 :C3:C1:

24:k101:143:   C1:C3:C1:C3:C1:T1:C1:ii:h0S:C1:T1dh0Sf:C1:T1:C1:B:C3:C1:
                T1:C1:
24:k102:134:   C1:T1:C1:T1:C1:T1:C1:h0F2h2:C1:T1:C1:B:C3:C1:T1:C1:
24:k103:150:   C1:C3:C1:T1:C1:T1:C1:T1dh0Sf:C1:T1dh0Sf:C1:T1:C1:B:C3:C1:
                T1:C1:
24:k104:140:   C3:C1:T1:C1:T1:C1:T1:C1:T1dh0Sf:C1:T1dh0Sf:C1:T1:C1:B:C3:
                C1:C3:C1:
24:k105:149:   C3:C1:C3:C1:T1:C1:T1:C1:T1dh0Sf:C1:T1dh0Sf:C1:T1:C1:B:C3:
                C1:C3:C1:
24:k106:154:   C3:C1:T1:C1:T1:C1:T1:C1:T1dh0Sf:C1:T1dh0Sf:C1:T1:C1:B:C3:
                C1:C3:C1:
24:k107:157:   C3:C1:T1:C1:C3:C1:T1:C1:T1dh0Sf:C1:T1dh0Sf:C1:T1:C1:T0:C1:
                B:C3:C1:C3:C1:
24:k108:155:   C3:C1:T1:C1:T1:C1:T1:C1:T1dh0Sf:C1:T1dh0Sf:C1:T1:C1:B1:C1:
                C3:C1:T1:C1:
24:k109:144:   C3:C1:T1:C1:C3:C1:C3:C1:ii:h0S:C1:T1dh0Sf:C1:T1:C1:B:C3:
                C1:C3:C1:

Word "**milliard**":

25:k100:167:   C1:C3:C1:T1:C1:T1:C1:T1dh0Sf:C1:T1dh0Sf:C1:T1:C1:B:C1:T1:
                C3:C1:T0:C1:T1h0:C1:
25:k101:170:   C3:C1:T1:C1:T1:C1:T1:C1:T1dh0Sf:C1:T1dh0Sf:C1:T1:C1:ii:B0:
                C1:C3:C1:S1dh0Sf:C1:
25:k102:183:   C1:C3:C1:T1:C1:T1:C1:T1dh0Sf:C1:T1dh0Sf:C1:T1:C1:B1:C1:T1:
                C3:C1:F1h0:C1:
25:k103:178:   C1:T1:C1:T1:C1:T1:C1:T1dh0Sf:C1:T1dh0Sf:C1:T1:C1:B1:C1:C3:
                C1:T0dSf:C1:T1dh0Sf:C1:
25:k104:187:   C3:C1:T1:C1:C3:C1:T1:C1:T1dh0Sf:C1:T1dh0Sf:C1:T1:C1:B:C1:C3:
                C1:S:T1h0:C1:
25:k105:188:   C3:C1:T1:C1:T1:C1:T1:C1:T1dh0Sf:C1:T1dh0Sf:C1:T1:C1:B:C1:C3:
                C1:B:T1h0:C1:
25:k106:194:   C3:C1:C3:C1:T1:C1:T1:C1:T1dh0Sf:C1:T1dh0Sf:C1:T1:C1:B:C1:T1:
                C1:C3:C1:T0:C1:T1h0:C1:
25:k107:177:   T1:C1:C3:C1:C3:C1:T1:C1:T1dh0Sf:C1:T1dh0Sf:C1:T1:C1:B1:C1:
                C3:C1:T0:C1:T1dh0Sf:C1:
25:k108:189:   C3:C1:C3:C1:C3:C1:T1:C1:T1dh0Sf:C1:T1dh0Sf:C1:T1:C1:B1:C1:T1:
                C1:T0:C1:B:T1h0:C1:
25:k109:186:   C3:C1:C3:C1:C3:C1:T1:C1:T1dh0Sf:C1:T1dh0Sf:C1:T1:C1:F:C1:C3:
                C1:S1h0:C1:

It is interesting to compare "mille," "million," "milliard." From these chains,
it is easy to restitute "by hand" a picture of the graph G. It could of course be
done automatically, though the coding is rather primitive (no indication of the
length of the segments for instance). Compression of the quantity of information
is of the order of 100.

5.3 Recognition Techniques

These chains may be analyzed by some simple programs in awk, a tool of UNIX. But a more refined technique has been developed by O. BARET, in two steps: find "anchor singularities" in the unknown chain; match dynamically a candidate word and the unknown chain.

5.3.1 Finding anchor singularities. A chain is scanned to find "anchors," *i.e.* singularities, which very probably represent a letter or a group of letters. For example the field :T1dT01h0f: likely represents a 't'. When one or more anchors are found, some candidate words are selected in the list of possible words (25 in our specific problem). A special treatment is initiated if no anchor is found (as in "un").

The library of anchors has about *sixty rules*, the first part being a regular expression (as in lex, awk, grep). The alphabet of symbols is given at paragraph 4.3. A singularity is a well formed subchain of these symbols, representing a "tree"; thus to be analyzed by automatas, as Unix regular expressions. Either the subchain is accepted or rejected by a rule. No distance measurement is implemented at this step.

5.4.1 Dynamic matching of a candidate word to the chain. When one or more "anchors" are found, candidate words are selected among the list of 25 words. The program finds out if the remaining fields (often axis parts) may match the remaining letters. Another library allows to implement these matchings. If the number of letters to be explained is greater than the number of available fields, the word is rejected (a rather severe rule).

Otherwise, a dynamic matching is performed, trying to match the maximum number of letters of the candidate word for each subchains. If no match is possible, rejection of the word.

A figure of merit M is obtained for each candidate word which is not rejected, as the percentage of explained primitives versus the total number of primitives. For example, M=100% if every fields of the chain correspond to a letter of the candidate word, except some fields which may be a "liaison field," such as C1, or ii. The following list gives such results for the k104 file of words.

                k104 1   un(57) REC
                k104 2   deux(70) douze(70) dix(20) onze(10) REC
                k104 3   trois(100) REC
                k104 4   quatre(100) REC
                k104 5   REJ
                k104 6   six(100) dix(100) sept(42) onze(28) REC
                k104 7   sept(81) deux(9) neuf(9) seize(9) REC
                k104 8   huit(100) sept(18) vingt(18) REC
                k104 9   neuf(66) REC
                k104 10   dix(100) six(62) onze(37) REC
                k104 11   onze(100) seize(77) douze(44) REC

k104 12   quinze(69) douze(61) treize(53) seize(53) REC
k104 13   treize(100) REC
k104 14   quatorze(100) quinze(50) treize(43) douze(25) REC
k104 15   quatorze(50) seize(50) quinze(33) REC
k104 16   seize(100) REC
k104 17   vingt(23) REC
k104 18   trente(100) treize(61) trois(46) dix(23) onze(23) douze(23)
           quatre(15) quinze(15) seize(15) mille(15) deux(7) REC
k104 19   quarante(100) quatre(40) quatorze(40) quinze(35) REC
k104 20   cinquante(100) REC
k104 21   soixante(88) trente(55) quarante(55) REC
k104 22   cent(100) REC
k104 23   mille(100) REC
k104 24   million(100) milliard(84) REC
k104 25   milliard(100) million(71) REC

For the time being, the libraries of rules of each step have been implemented
by hand. Use is made of the tools of UNIX, such as grep, awk, lex, yacc.

5.4 Statistical Results

Up to now the recognition package is designed for a maximum facility to test new
algorithms, and is not optimized in speed. On an IBM workstation 6151/130,
the rate of recognition is approximately **one word / second**. At the end of
1989, the results are the following:

On one writer:

Percentage of correctly recognized words	**87%**
Percentage of rejected words	**10%**
Misrecognition rate	**3,55%**

The "misrecognition rate" is the percentage of words recognized in error
versus the total number of words accepted.

On several writers (integers from 0 to 9):

A	k20?	k30?	k70?	k80?	k90?	k120?	k140?
Pc	66	53	48	75	70	66	62
Pr	21	28	24	15	20	22	24
T	17	26	37	12	13	16	18

A	name of the file,
Pc	percentage of success,
Pr	percentage of rejects,
T	misrecognition rate.

These results were achieved without changing the libraries of primitives and of chain matching.

Each file has 25 words, the current french words to write numbers. Each writer has written 10 times the 25 words, They are entered under the name kij, i being a number recording the writer (for example 10, 20, 120), j a number from 0 to 9 (the ten files of a writer). Samples of the written words are given in the Appendix.

5.5 The Quality of the Binary Files

The nature of the binary file is somewhat critical. We underlined that a "line" should be represented by at least three pixels along the orthogonal direction of the line (see paragraph 3.1). Lifting of pen causes damaging interruptions. Some restoration techniques may be applied to improve the quality. Scanning the original iconic picture in 4 directions: 0,+45, 90,-45 degrees, give 4 *one-dimensional* signals. *One-dimensional filters* check for each directions if the gaps of 3 or less 0-pixels, between "10" and "01" configurations, may be filled up by 1-pixels; and this accordingly to several context sensitive rules, implemented by an error-correcting code. For instance, the following results have been obtained on "k10X" files (X = 0-4):

file	correct	rejected	substitution
k100	from 80% to 88%	from 12% to 8%	from 9% to 4%
k101	from 76% to 80%	from 20% to 16%	from 5% to 4%
k102	from 76% to 88%	from 20% to 12%	from 5% to 0%
k103	from 76% to 92%	from 20% to 8%	from 5% to 0%
k104	from 88% to 100%	from 12% to 0%	from 0% to 0%

Though interesting, these results show that the quality of the files is quite essential to obtain good results. Undoubtedly, this is a weakness of the algorithm as a whole. In addition, some similar files give different results, which up to know do not seem predictable by an *a priori* examination. In other words, as an example k100 and k104 look very much alike; but if the second allows a 100% recognition, the second is limited to 88%.

6 Conclusion

These results seem encouraging, according to the fact that *the learning phase has been performed on one writer only*. Now we are testing the largest possible group of writers; and undoubtedly we will have numerous surprises. We have to admit that the technique is sensitive to the quality of the iconic file, which may be highly degraded by the use of blue ink or ball pen. Restoration techniques of 5.5 are then quite valuable, but *a priori* criteria of application should be devised.

Up to now the number of rules is modest, and we may increase this number, without slowing notably the recognition rate. Now that the recognition system is complete, we may look for the following improvements:

1. A more precise determination of the primitive; for example, 8 quadrants instead of 4 for the segment directions, some metric indication on segments.
2. A feedback at the graph level, in case of a low security of the last decision phase.
3. An automatic restoration algorithm for degraded files.
4. A semiautomatic learning algorithm to cover the maximum types of writers.

It is worth to underline that the progress comes from the application of new ideas: *in a word find a regular feature, the "axis"; then by complementation of the axis, find the singularities* [11]. Such ideas, which proved useful also for printed character recognition, may be applied in several other domains of P.R.

Acknowledgment

This basic study is supported by the Direction Générale des Postes Françaises.

References

[1]   J. C. Simon, *Pattern and Operators*. MacGraw-Hill in North America, North Oxford Acad. in Europe, (1986).
[2]   M. R. Garey and D. S. Johnson, *Computers and Intractability*. W. H. Freeman, San Francisco (1979).
[3]   J. C. Simon (ed.), *From Pixels to Features*, North–Holland, Amsterdam (1989).
[4]   T. Pavlidis, "Residual Analysis for feature extraction," pp. 219–227, in [3] (1989).
[5]   J. C. Simon, "Invariance in P. R., Application to line images," *Image and Vision Comp. Jr.* 4, 1, pp. 11–23 (1986).
[6]   J. C. Simon, "A complemental approach to feature detection," pp. 229–236 In [3] (1989).
[7]   J. Serra, *Image Analysis and Mathematical Morphology*, Vol. II, Academic Press, Chaps. 11–13 (1988).
[8]   K. L. Heng, "Analyse d'une image de ligne: des pixels aux primitives." Thèse Univ P. et M. Curie, May 1986.
[9]   J. M. Lery, "Reconnaissance de lécriture manuscrite monoscripteur: description symbolique des mots par un graphe de primitives." Thèse Univ. P. et M. Curie, June 1989.
[10] A. Leturcq, "La reconnaissance des caractères manuscrits sans apprentissage." Thèse Univ. P. et M. Curie, March 1990.
[11] J. C. Simon and O. Baret, "Formes régulières, formes singulières, application à la reconnaissance de l' éricriture manuscrite." *C. R. Acad. Sc. Paris*, T.309, série II, 19, pp. 1901–1906, December 1989.

Appendix

Samples of the original handwritten words; each paragraph is from a different writer, except the first three, on this page.

un deux trois quatre cinq six sept huit neuf dix
onze douze treize quatorze quinze seize
vingt trente quarante cinquante soixante cent
mille million milliard   k 100

un deux trois quatre cinq six sept huit neuf
dix onze douze treize quatorze quinze seize
vingt trente quarante cinquante soixante
cent mille million milliard   k 101

un deux · trois quatre cinq six sept huit neuf
dix onze douze treize quatorze quinze seize
vingt trente quarante cinquante soixante
cent mille million milliard   k 104

un deux trois quatre cinq six sept huit neuf
dix onze douze treize quatorze quinze seize
vingt trente quarante cinquante soixante
cent mille million milliard.   k204

un deux trois quatre cinq six sept huit neuf dix
onze douze treize quatorze quinze seize
vingt trente quarante cinquante soixante cent mille
million milliard   k301

Un deux trois quatre cinq six sept huit neuf
dix onze douze treize quatorze quinze seize
vingt trente quarante cinquante soixante
cent mille million milliard   k705

un deux trois quatre cinq six sept huit neuf
dix onze douze treize quatorze quinze seize
vingt trente quarante cinquante soixante
cent mille million milliard.   k806

un deux trois quatre cinq six sept huit neuf
dix onze douze treize quatorze quinze seize
vingt trente quarante cinquante soixante
cent mille million milliard.   h 902

un deux trois quatre cinq six sept
huit neuf dix onze douze treize
quatorze quinze seize vingt trente
quarante cinquante soixante cent
mille million milliard   h 1207

un deux trois quatre cinq six sept huit
neuf dix onze douze treize quatorze quinze
seize vingt trente quarante cinquante soixante
cent mille million milliard .   k 1402

Graphics, Maps, and Technical Drawings

An Overview of Techniques for Graphics Recognition

Rangachar Kasturi[1], Rajesh Raman[1], Chakravarthy Chennubhotla[1], and Lawrence O'Gorman[2]

[1] Department of Electrical and Computer Engineering,
   The Pennsylvania State University, University Park, PA 16802, USA
[2] AT&T Bell Laboratories, 600 Mountain Avenue, Murray Hill, NJ 07974, USA

An overview is presented of algorithms and techniques for document image analysis with an emphasis on those for graphics recognition and interpretation. Topics covered are data capture, segmentation into text and graphics regions, vectorization, identification of graphical primitives, and generation of succinct image interpretations. This paper is primarily survey in nature, but an effort is made to provide information to evaluate and compare techniques, both through reference to more focused articles, as well as through our own experience.

1 Introduction

Document image analysis addresses the problem of creating a higher level description of the contents of paper-based documents. In particular, efficient algorithms for intelligent interpretation and succinct description of mixed text and graphics documents have many immediate applications. For example, they permit conversion of paper-based engineering drawings into a CAD compatible form; provide a mechanism for archiving documents such as journals and news magazines; and facilitate integration of vector-oriented graphics databases and raster-oriented images in applications such as geographic information systems.

In a typical document image analysis system, the input is a raster image obtained from optically scanning a document page. Such documents as technical manuals, for example, may contain text, half-tone images, as well as graphical components such as block diagrams, circuit diagrams, illustration of mechanical parts, and flow charts. The objective is then to segment such an image into its meaningful text, image, and graphics regions, and further analyze each of these to generate a succinct description. Ideally, such a description should include the page structure and format information such as the size and location of various blocks and columns of text, and the size and font style of characters. It should contain adequate information to obtain a fairly accurate reconstruction of the original document. In addition, it must be at a level of description that facilitates document modification and information interchange between various systems. It is in this respect that document analysis systems differ from conventional data compression systems. An intelligent interpretation system may also combine data in the document with the knowledge about the domain to create an even higher level description. For example, line data from orthographic views in a mechanical part drawing can be combined with the rules and conventions followed in engineering drafting to generate three-dimensional object description. The problems that are to be solved to accomplish the document analysis goals are essentially the same as the ones that have been addressed by the image processing and computer vision communities for many years. Many of the algorithms and techniques such as noise filtering, line detection, segmentation, feature recognition and classification, pattern matching, semantic interpretation, consistent labeling, and object hypothesis and verification are useful in analyzing document images. The primary difference between document image analysis and traditional 3-D computer vision is in the nature of input data; while computer vision systems operate on two dimensional perspective projections of three dimensional scenes, objects in document images are inherently two dimensional; one practical difference is that a document image is often much larger than a typical scene image. These differences, among others, lead to the development and use of algorithms for document image analysis that are similar in goal but often different in method than computer vision techniques.

The objective of this paper is to present an overview of the algorithms and techniques for document image processing for graphics recognition and interpretation. It should be noted that, although optical character recognition (OCR) falls within the context of document image analysis, we do not cover this area, since OCR techniques have been covered extensively in the literature. We also limit the focus to images containing binary information.

A common sequence of steps taken for document image analysis for graphics interpretation is listed here:

1. Data capture and preprocessing;
2. Region segmentation;
3. Vectorization;
4. Feature extraction; and
5. Graphics recognition and interpretation.

Data capture and preprocessing includes operations such as scanning, noise filtering, and thresholding for converting a paper-based document to a reasonably noise-free binary image. These are discussed in Section 2. A typical image of a document contains regions of text, graphics, and half-tone images. It is then necessary to segment a mixed image into separate regions to facilitate application of appropriate algorithms to each class. For example, text regions can be used as input to an OCR system; graphics regions to a graphics interpretation system, and image regions to a data compression system or an image interpretation system as appropriate. These region segmentation algorithms are described in Section 3. Binary raster graphics images contain solid objects (completely filled regions) and objects made up of thin lines. While thin lines are adequately represented by their core-lines, solid objects are best represented by their boundaries. For dashed lines, it is necessary to track syntactically continuous segments to generate a compact line description. These vectorization and line following operations are performed to facilitate recognition and these are discussed in Section 4. Since straight lines and curves are basic components in a graphics diagram, detection of feature points such as corners and points of transitions from straight lines to curves is an important step in graphics recognition. Locating such points is made difficult by the artifacts introduced during digitization and preprocessing. Algorithms for feature extraction are discussed in Section 5. The extracted features and the associated line and curve description files are then processed by a semantic interpretation system that includes task-dependent graphics recognition and interpretation algorithms. For example, to process a hierarchical organization chart, simple polygon recognition algorithm is adequate; for an electrical schematic recognition system, matching is performed to identify various electrical components and their interconnections; and for interpretation of 3-D objects represented by their 2-D projections, knowledge-based algorithms are required to combine information in multiple views and generate a three dimensional object description. Some of these techniques are discussed in Section 6. Finally, a brief summary is presented in Section 7.

2 Data Capture and Preprocessing

2.1 Scanning

A bit-mapped binary image array is typically obtained by scanning a paper-based document at an appropriate sampling resolution. Many of the scanners include the thresholding operation, and output a binary image. Thresholding is applied separately if the images are captured using video digitization or other data capture techniques which output gray level images.

Scanners may be broadly classified as belonging to one of the three types: drum type, flat- bed type, or continuous roll feed type. Drum scanners contain a rotating drum on which the document is mounted and a sensor that captures the changes in the light intensity along a line of the document. Flatbed type scanners use a linear array of light sensors mounted on a carrier. The carrier moves in the plane of the flat table containing the document. In the continuous roll feed type scanners, the document is fed into the scanner at a controlled speed and a linear sensor array captures the intensity changes along the entire width of the document [Ejiri et al. 90].

An important parameter to be determined in selecting a scanner is the resolution. Although higher resolution scanning yields data with greater fidelity, it also implies larger memory and storage requirements. For example, changing the resolution from 200 dpi (dots per inch) (8 dots per mm) to 300 dpi (12 dots per mm) more than doubles the image size. The image array for a typical A0 size (1,189 mm × 841 mm) mechanical part drawing scanned at a resolution of 250 dpi contains nearly 100 million pixels. For such large documents, image partitioning with overlap is the method of choice for data processing. The choice of the resolution is determined by the minimum feature size in the document. The rule of thumb for character recognition [Casey and Wong 90] recommends scanning at a resolution that is at least two pixels across the minimum width strokes. For example, for recognition of characters in a typed document with a minimum stroke width of 0.2 mm it is adequate to scan the document at 300 dpi. Note that, if the objective is to recognize the font style as well as the ASCII code of the character, much higher resolution is needed. Also, when document quality is low, higher resolution facilitates recognition in later stages. For applications where features are larger and less complex, such as for recognizing lines in a circuit diagram, it may be adequate to use much lower resolution. For example, [Okazaki et al. 85] use 80 dpi for line following and 240 dpi for character recognition in a circuit diagram.

In certain applications such as for geographic maps or large scale integrated (LSI) circuit cell diagrams, different features are distinguishable only by their colors. Recently, color scanners have become more widely available. [Ejiri et al. 90] describes a system in which color codes are assigned to various pixels in an image during scanning. Boundary pixels and pixels in which several lines with different colors overlap are assigned an uncertainty code. A combination of dichromic mirrors and trimming filters having peak transmittances at 455 nm, 515 nm, 675 nm, and 765 nm is used in their scanning system. This is capable of discriminating up to 12 commonly used colors in documents.

2.2 Thresholding

For documents with a good contrast against a uniform background, data capture is straightforward. Binary scanners are available that combine scanning with thresholding at a fixed threshold. However, many documents have a wide range of background and object gray levels. For these, a fixed threshold applied to a gray level image often does not generate images with clear separation between the object and background. For these cases, it is best to first obtain gray-scale images from the scanning stage, enabling separate digital image processing methods to be used to extract the binary information.

[Holdermann and Kazmierczak 72, Peleg and Rosenfeld 79, Ting and Prasada 80, Wang et al. 81, Weszka 78, Nagin et al. 82] describe general pre-processing techniques, entailing filtering and thresholding. The objective is to separate objects regions from the background and noise. Because of variations in average intensities, spatially adaptive thresholding is performed by analyzing gray-level values within local windows across the image to determine local thresholds [Rosenfeld and Kak 82, Casey and Wong 90]. These local neighborhoods should be large enough to guarantee that both foreground and background pixels are included, but not so large as to average over nonuniform background intensities. Ideally, the threshold should be insensitive to noise but sensitive to edges of characters and lines [Wong 78]. [Morrin 74] sets the threshold to the average of high-gradient pixels. This reduces bias imposed by setting the threshold at the valley between high and low peaks in the intensity histogram — where one peak, usually the background, has much greater area than the other. [White and Rohrer 83] describe a dynamic thresholding algorithm for separating characters from background. The threshold is continuously changed using a two-dimensional running average of gray level values. A low-cost implementation of this algorithm in digital hardware is also described. A more sophisticated algorithm, called Integrated Function Algorithm, in which the width of the text strokes, sharpness of the text edges, and contrast ratio are used in making the threshold decision is also described in their paper. [Watson *et al.* 84] describe a local double adaptive thresholding algorithm to extract lines and regions from gray level images of line drawings. An upper cut-off is computed by multiplying the average gray level within a square window by a cutoff factor. Only those pixels having values greater than a lower threshold are used in computing the average to avoid biasing the average value. Only the ridge-line pixels of convex ridges have values greater than the upper cut-off. These are marked. Regions are identified by marking those pixels which are greater than a region threshold but less than the upper cut-off. Region pixels are then represented by following and encoding their contours. [Mitchell and Gillies 89] describe a thresholding method for preprocessing mail pieces. First, background white level normalization is done by estimating the white level and subtracting this level from the raw image. Then, segmentation of characters is accomplished by applying various thresholds and selecting the image with the least noise content. Noise content is measured as the sum of areas occupied by components that are shorter and thinner than empirically determined parameters. An image thresholded at four different thresholds is shown in Figure 1. Frame 3 in this figure is selected since this measure of noise content is minimum there. For a more extensive treatment of thresholding techniques, the paper [Sahoo, *et al.* 88] contains a recent survey.

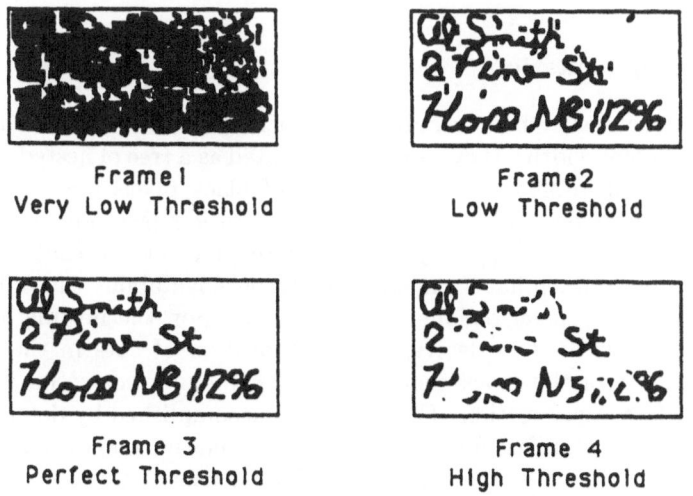

Frame 1
Very Low Threshold

Frame 2
Low Threshold

Frame 3
Perfect Threshold

Frame 4
High Threshold

Fig. 1. Illustration of adaptive global threshold [Mitchell and Gillies 89].

2.3 Preprocessing

Simple noise reduction filters are generally applied to the binary image data obtained from scanning and thresholding. In its simplest form, single pixel voids are filled and protrusions are deleted by iteratively passing a 3 × 3 pixel filter window over the image [Shih and Kasturi 88]. Morphological operations [Jain 89] such as erosion, dilation, open, close, and prune may also be applied to filter some of the digitization artifacts and noise. For most man-made graphics, such as characters, it is desirable to remove noise, but retain corners. This necessitates a tradeoff between noise reduction and retention of the symbol corners. The choice of the preprocessing filters and their parameters is clearly application dependent since what is considered to be noise in one application is possibly a feature for another.

3 Region Segmentation

After binarization, the document image typically consists of regions of text, graphics, and halftone images. Since different techniques are applied to process each of these, they are usually first segmented into these different regions. [Srihari and Zack 86, Casey and Wong 90] classify block segmentation algorithms into two categories: Top-down, or knowledge based methods, that work with a knowledge of the nature of the document; and bottom-up, or data driven methods, that continuously refine data by layered grouping operations. However, since many of the algorithms use a combination of these two methods, we refrain from categorizing the methods described below.

3.1 Block Segmentation

Since most documents have rectangular block structures separated by white regions of different widths, they can be represented as a tree of nested rectangular blocks. Projection profile plots of the sums of black pixels upon horizontal or vertical axes have been used for block segmentation [Masuda *et al.* 85, Zen and Ozawa 85]. [Baird 90] analyzes the white pixel blocks that enclose text regions to achieve a similar segmentation. Knowledge about the differences in the widths of white pixel regions, which depend upon the nesting level of the block structure, is used in determining the location of cuts in the projection profiles. In most of the block segmentation techniques, correction for skew is necessary before segmentation. This is usually accomplished by determining the projection profiles at different angles. Note that when the orientation is very close to the true orientation of the page, large fluctuations in the projection profile are observed. This phenomenon is used to estimate the skew angle of the image in [Srihari and Govindaraju 89]. [Baird 90] describes an efficient algorithm in which the skew angle is determined accurately by first computing the projection profile at coarse intervals, then recalculating them at closer intervals near the correct orientation.

The run-length smearing method [Wong *et al.* 82] broadly segments an image into regions of text, graphics, and images using a statistical feature classification technique. The algorithm changes white pixels to black if the number of white pixels separating black pixels is less than a threshold. This smearing is applied in both horizontal and vertical direction, and these are combined using a logical AND operation. Features are calculated for each block of smeared black pixels [Casey and Wong 90, Wahl 83], including height, eccentricity, black pixel density, and mean length of pixel runs. These features are then used to segment the image into text, black solid lines, graphics, and halftone images. The smearing method fails when there is too much skew of the document, or when the pattern of characters or graphics in the image has not been anticipated in the segmentation rules. For instance, a dense field of random straight lines may be classified as text.

3.2 Text-string Segmentation

Although the two methods described above are capable of broadly segmenting an image into text and non-text regions, they are unable to segment text strings that are enclosed in graphics (*e.g.*, tables, maps, engineering drawings). [Fletcher and Kasturi 88] describe a Hough transform-based algorithm for segmenting text-strings in a mixed text/graphics image. (For a review of Hough transform techniques, their implementation, and performance see [Illingworth and Kittler 88].) Since the Hough transform method is invariant to document skew, text strings in any orientation are detected. The algorithm determines the thresholds adaptively, thus making it invariant to changes in size and font style of text strings. This algorithm has been enhanced to handle text strings that are connected to graphics [Gattiker 88]. A brief summary of the algorithm is given below.

There are five steps in the algorithm: connected component generation; preprocessing the components to eliminate those that are most likely graphics; grouping the remaining components using the Hough transform; logically grouping these strings into textual word and phrase groups; and post processing of these strings to further refine the strings. The first four steps are described in detail in [Fletcher and Kasturi 88]. The final step, post-processing, is described in [Gattiker 87, Kasturi *et al.* 90] and consists of two parts: separation of repeated symbols and dashed line segments grouped as text, and the removal of characters connected to graphics. As an illustration, the images before and after applying the algorithm are shown in Figures 2 and 3. Note that the original image contains text strings of various fonts, sizes, and orientations. Further, there are characters connected to graphics and text completely enclosed within graphics. Also, there are graphics strings such as asterisk's and dashed lines which satisfy most of the heuristics for text strings. Despite these complications, the algorithm correctly segments the image as can be verified in Figure 3.

The Hough transform has also been used by [Srihari and Govindaraju 89] for analyzing textual images. Their system detects text skew angle, determines the

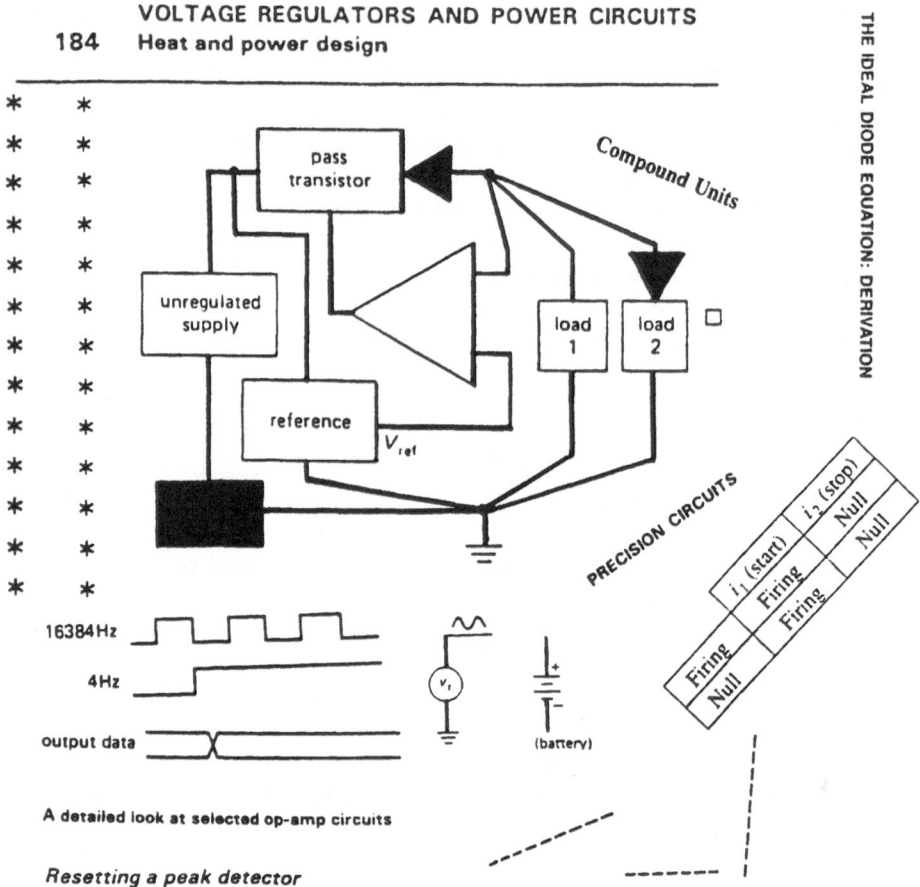

Fig. 2. Test image input to text string separation algorithm.

signature of a text line, segments text into lines, and determines whether the text is right-side-up.

3.3 Other Segmentation Methods

A measure, called the neighborhood line density, obtained by computing the "complexity" of an image at every black pixel has been used by [Kida *et al.* 86] to separate characters from graphics. [Doster 84, Meynieux 86] describe clustering methods for text block segmentation of long text strings, using a method based on grouping nearby connected components. A technique that merges connected components to characters, then to words, strings, paragraphs and columns, is described in [Nagy *et al.* 85]. In their rule-based approach, these entities are described by their widths, aspect ratios, number of cuts, etc. When combined with knowledge about the standard format used by a particular publication, these features are used to determine the page layout of a document. [Dori 89]

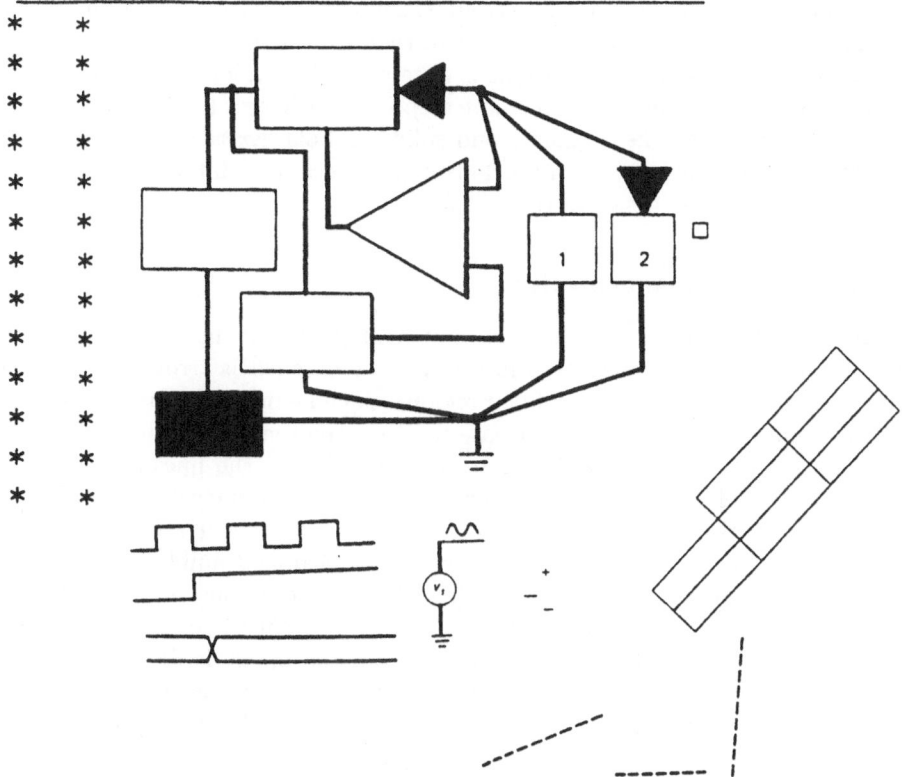

Fig. 3. Graphics image after text string separation.

describes a syntactic/geometric approach for recognition of interpretation lines (*e.g.* dimensioning lines describing measurements of the object) and associated components in engineering drawings.

After region segmentation, a document can be separated into different images, each containing only one class of objects such as text, graphics, or halftone images. Each of these images require different techniques for further analysis. In the remainder of this paper we consider techniques for processing graphics images such as line drawings, circuit diagrams, flow charts, maps, and engineering drawings.

4 Extraction and Description of Lines and Solid Regions

The amount and type of processing applied to graphics data in a raster image is usually application dependent. If the graphics image is a part of a predominantly textual document and the objective is simply data archiving for later reconstruction, then use of any one of the well known data compression techniques [Jain 89] is adequate. On the other hand, if information is to be extracted from data for such applications as indexing image components from a pictorial database, modification of graphics in a CAD system [Karima *et al.* 85], or determining locations in a geographical information system, then extensive processing to extract objects and their spatial relationships is necessary. Such a level of description is attained through a series of intermediate steps. At the lowest level, graphics data is processed to locate line segments and solid symbols. Extracting the location and attributes of these is an important step for graphics interpretation. This process is discussed in detail in this section.

4.1 Solid Region Segmentation

A typical graphics image contains lines and symbols. While most of the graphics symbols are formed by thin lines, some of the symbols such as arrow-heads, diode symbols, and company logos are filled regions. Such symbols can be represented by their boundaries, while thin lines are used for the remaining entities.

To represent an image by thin lines and boundaries, the lines and solid regions must first be differentiated. One approach to determine solid regions is by erosion and dilation operations [Harada *et al.* 85, Shah 88, Kasturi *et al.* 90]. In this approach, the image is eroded by a predetermined number of pixels to completely remove all thin entities such as lines. The eroded image is dilated and a logical AND operation is performed to recover solid symbols. Note that, since dilation is not an exact inverse of erosion, the image is dilated by more pixels than it is eroded to completely recover the solid symbols. The boundaries of these solid symbols are then found, and used in the symbol recognition phase. The difference image, obtained by subtracting solid symbols from original image, contains only thin entities, and is processed by vectorization methods described below. There are also methods that simultaneously extract boundaries and core lines. In [Shih and Kasturi 89] several picture decomposition algorithms for locating solid symbols are evaluated. Wakayama's Maximal Square Moving (MSM) algorithm [Wakayama 82], in which black pixel regions are represented as a union of largest possible overlapping squares, was adapted by [Shih and Kasturi 89] for simultaneously locating the core-lines of thin entities and boundaries of solid regions. However, the algorithm is quite complex and requires numerous data structures and pointers to obtain the desired description. Another method in which core lines are found simultaneously with boundaries is the $k \times k$ thinning method [O'Gorman 90-1]. This method is described in the next section.

4.2 Thinning and Vectorization

For a line whose information can be represented by its path and perhaps width and color parameters, thinning and vectorization are often performed to facilitate subsequent processing. Thinning reduces digitized lines to one-pixel width. Vectorization represents this results in terms of connected chains and line segments.

A common thinning approach is to "peel" the region boundaries until the regions have been reduced to thin lines, *e.g.* [Hilditch 69]. This process is performed iteratively — on each iteration every image pixel is inspected within

3×3 windows, and single-pixel wide boundaries that are not required to maintain connectivity or end-lines are erased. In [O'Gorman 90-1], the $k \times k$ thinning method is proposed as a generalization of the 3×3 method to size $k \times k$ windows. Instead of erasing only one pixel on each iteration, k-2×k-2 pixels can be erased, and by doing this, fewer iterations are often required. This method can also be performed in parallel, and can be configured to obtain boundaries of filled regions, widths of lines, labels of lines (for instance for colored lines), as well as skeletons of thin lines.

Recent methods have been proposed to thin with a fixed number of steps not dependent on the maximum line thickness [Arcelli and di Baja 85, Sinha 87]. For these non-iterative methods, skeletal points are estimated from distance measurements with respect to opposite boundary points of the regions. Some of these methods require joining the line segments after thinning to restore connectivity, and also require a parameter estimating maximum thickness of the original image lines to limit the search for pairs of opposite boundary points. In general, these non-iterative methods are less regularly repetitive, not limited to local operations, and less able to be pipelined compared to the iterative methods; and this makes their implementation in special-purpose hardware less appropriate. All these algorithms can be performed in sequential, raster-scan order. Some of the iterative methods can be done in parallel, where operation at any pixel does not depend on results at any other pixel on a single iteration. Previous papers are well reviewed in recent literature. For a good background on thinning techniques, see [Pavlidis 82]. For comparisons of the iterative methods, see [Tamura 78, Naccache and Shinghal 84], and for the parallel techniques, see [Guo and Hall 89].

After thinning, the image can be processed to extract connected chains of pixels. In [Freeman 61], a code was introduced for representation of image lines as chains of pixels. This Freeman chain code represents a chain as a sequence of direction codes from one pixel to the adjacent one. This code is highly effective for compression of line images. However the code was designed for contours, without any provision for maintaining branching line structures. This is fine for compression, but for image analysis it is important to retain the complete line structure with all its branches and to know the topology at each junction. In [Harris *et al.* 82], the skeleton is coded with pixel values of 0, 1, 2, and 3 for background pixels, terminal (end of line) pixels, intermediate pixels, and junction pixels respectively. This, combined with chaining allows line segments and their interconnections to be easily determined. Another method that operates on the thinned image to preserve line features is described in [O'Gorman 90-2]. This Primitives Chain Code (PCC) is an extension of Freeman chain code, first designed for coding thinned fingerprint images. In addition to retaining connectivity information, PCC also preserves branching and junction topology information. With these additional features, subsequent pattern recognition steps are facilitated, and this code usually results in higher compression than the Freeman technique.

Unwanted in the thinned image are isolated lines and spurs off longer lines that are artifacts due to the thinning process or noise in the image. Many thinning methods, *e.g.* [Arcelli and di Baja 85], require that the binary image is noise filtered before thinning because noise severely degrades the effectiveness and efficiency of this processing. However noise can never be totally removed, and it is often difficult to distinguish noise from the signal in earlier stages. In [Jagadish and O'Gorman 89], image lines (between endpoints and junctions) are found, and descriptive parameters (length, type, location) are associated with them. This descriptive and contextual information is then used to remove the line artifacts.

Alternative approaches for vectorization have also been investigated. For example, [Ramachandran 80] describes a vector extraction and coding scheme intended to code vector representations of engineering drawings. This fits piecewise linear segments to outlines of black pixel regions. For each run of black pixels in a scan line, adjacent runs in subsequent scan lines are grouped to form outlines, and new vectors are generated whenever the change in vector orientation exceed a preset threshold. Compression ratios of up to 35:1 have been reported for this. [Shih and Kasturi 89] have applied this algorithm to obtain a trapezoidal approximation to black pixel regions. An image and its corresponding trapezoidal approximation with an angle variation threshold of 10 degrees are shown in Figure 4. The lines forming the trapezoids can then be processed to obtain line segment description. [Bley 84] describes a picture decomposition algorithm for segmenting electrical schematics. In this algorithm black pixel regions are approximated by rectangular blocks that are then analyzed to segment lines and symbols. The maximal square moving algorithm [Wakayama 82] has also been evaluated by [Shih and Kasturi 89] for its suitability in generating vector descriptions of lines.

Another approach implements vectorization using specialized hardware. Fastrak [Fulford 81] is an interactive line following digitizer that depends upon human interaction for tracking noisy data. [Ejiri *et al.* 90] describes two automatic digitizers, one for monochrome and the other for color documents, which can handle drawings up to A0 size (1,189 mm × 841 mm). The block diagram of the color digitizer is shown in Figure 5. Color codes are generated by the color detection circuit in real time and are processed by microprogram-controlled image processors designed to detect lines and contours. Longest possible straight lines are fit to pixels of the same color without applying any line thinning operations. The procedure is illustrated in Figure 6. This line fitting method eliminates the problems of twigs and other artifacts that are generated by thinning algorithms. This method of line tracking is efficient if the drawing contains mostly long straight lines. Post-processing is done on these detected lines to maintain "grid locking" (where lines are locked to a grid spaced at uniform intervals) This system is intended for digitizing LSI cell layout diagrams. Facilities for interactively editing digitized data are also provided.

[Watson *et al.* 84] describe a method for extracting lines from gray-level images of line drawings. The algorithm tracks the ridges of the gray-scale intensity surfaces, which are candidates for boundary regions between objects (lines) and background. The usual raster scan is made to pick up a starting pixel with a grey value not belonging to the background, and which is strong compared to

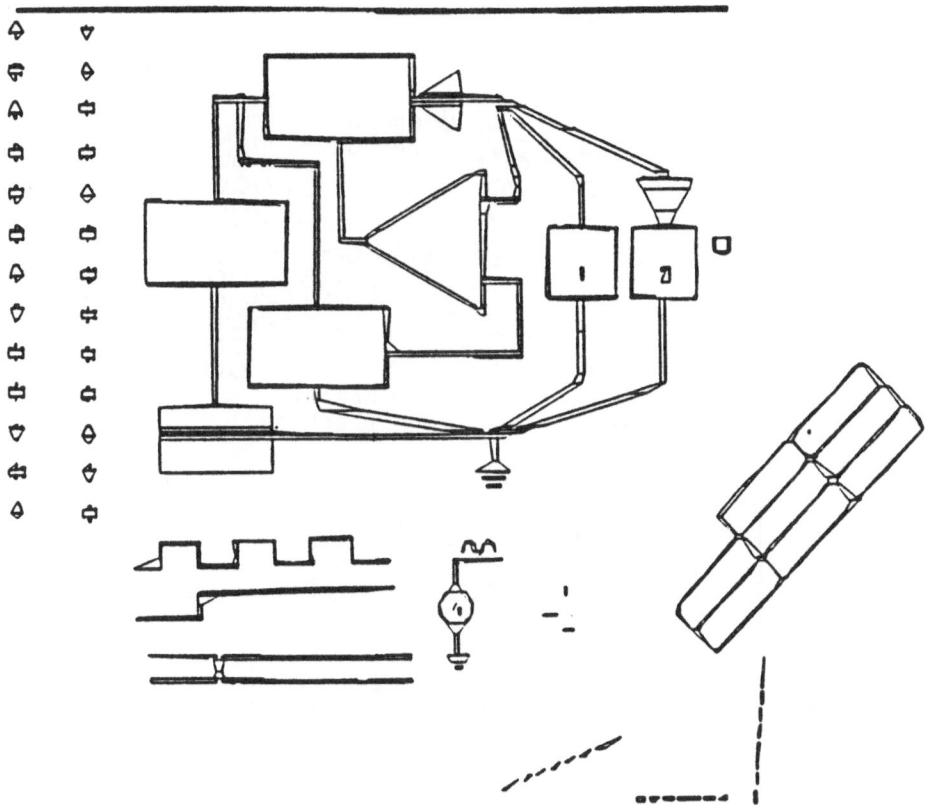

Fig. 4. Trapezoids enclosing black pixels in Figure 3 [Shih and Kasturi 89].

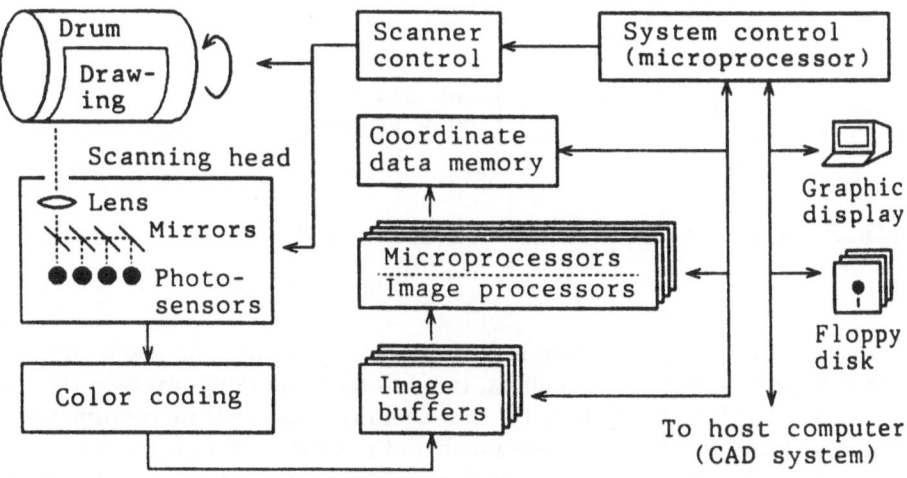

Fig. 5. Block diagram of color digitizer [Ejiri *et al.* 90].

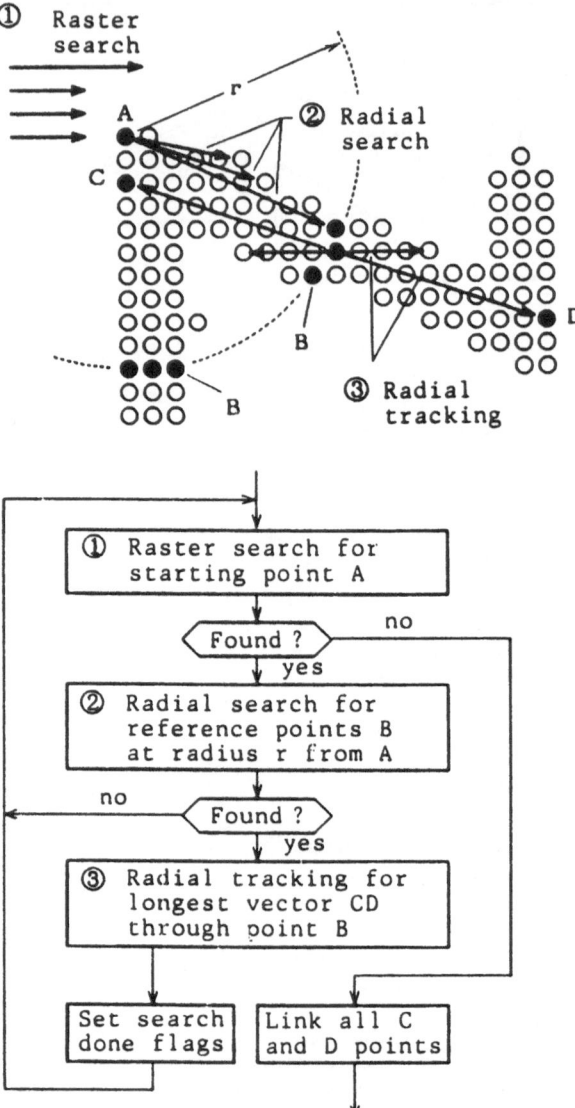

Fig. 6. Fitting longest vector to bit pattern [Ejiri *et al.* 90].

nearby tracked vectors. The line is then tracked such that the pixels have no
marked eight (3 × 3 mask) neighbors. In addition to marking pixels in the image, the line tracker also outputs the new chain code or absolute coordinates of
the pixels. The algorithm requires a number of parameters for proper operation.
It also generates a large number of short segments that require special handling.
[Haralick *et al.* 83] describe a method for topographical labeling of gray scale
image characteristics, such as peaks, ridges, valleys, etc., which can be applied

to line drawings to extract straight lines and curves.

Variations of these vectorization techniques as well as other approaches have been described in [Parker 88, Woetzel 78, Peuquet 81, Pavlidis and Cherry 82, Landy and Cohen 85, Pavlidis 84, Merelli *et al.* 85, Mori and Sakakura 84, Jimenez and Navalon 82].

4.3 Dashed Line Detection

After line segments are found, it is necessary to detect broken lines such as dashed lines by linking nearby segments that satisfy certain constraints. An algorithm for detecting such lines is described in [Kasturi *et al.* 90]. A dashed line may be made up of segments of equal lengths or may consist of alternating long and short segments. The algorithm identifies four segments having lengths l_1, l_2, l_3, and l_4 and inter-segment gaps $g_{1,2}$, $g_{2,3}$, and $g_{3,4}$ as a dashed line, if the following conditions are satisfied:

$$
\begin{aligned}
l_i < T_l & \quad i \in \{1,2,3,4\} \\
T_{g1} < g_{i,i+1} < T_{g2} & \quad i \in \{1,2,3\} \\
l_i = l_{i+2} & \quad i \in \{1,2\} \\
g_{i,i+1} = g_{i+1,i+2} & \quad i \in \{1,2\}
\end{aligned}
$$

Here T's are the length threshold parameters. Figure 7 illustrates the dashed lines detected in a portion of a map image using this algorithm.

Fig. 7. A portion of a map image and the dashed lines after detection and tracking.

[Ejiri *et al.* 90] describe a two-stage algorithm for detecting dashed lines. Line segments are grouped together using local constraints in the first stage. Context dependent global syntax rules are then applied in the second stage to resolve conflicts. The Hough transform is also useful to group together broken straight line segments. The segments grouped together should then be examined for consistency in inter-segment gaps.

Once the lines and object boundaries are located, feature points such as corners, inflection points, and junctions can be located. Techniques for obtaining these are discussed in the next section.

5 Feature Extraction

An important step in the recognition of objects for computer vision tasks involves localization of feature points. On edge, contour, or thinned images, these features include high curvature points as well as inflection points. From the methods in the previous section, chains of pixels are found for curves and boundaries. In this section, methods are given to find features on these chains, from which line segmentation can be performed. In graphics recognition applications, these features are used as critical points along a curve for performing piece-wise linear approximation and curve fitting. This results in a more concise description of the chain, and this description is also "higher level," that is it is closer to our goal of recognized graphics.

5.1 Polygonalization

Polygonal approximation is one common approach to analyzing curves. In the iterative endpoint fit algorithm [Ramer 72, Duda and Hart 73], a straight line segment is first connected between endpoints of the data. The perpendicular distances from the segment to each point on the curve are measured. If any distance is greater than a chosen threshold, the segment is replaced by two segments each from a segment endpoint to the curve point where distance to the segment is greatest. This process is iterated until all segments are within the threshold of the curve. In another class of methods [Tomek 74, Williams 78, Sklansky and Gonzalez 80, Williams 81, Pavlidis 82], a straight line fit is constrained to pass within a radius around each data point. The line segment is grown from the first point, and when further extension of the line segment causes it to fall outside the radius of a point, a new line is started. In another method [Kurozumi and Davis 82], a minimax approach is employed. The line segment approximations are chosen to minimize the maximum distance between the data points and the approximating line segment. For this method and for some of the other methods, segment endpoints must be adjusted to be within a gap tolerance of connecting segment endpoints. In another class of techniques, area versus distance is used as a measure of goodness of fit. [Wall and Danielsson 84] use a scan-along technique where, if the area deviation for each line segment exceeds a preset value, then a new segment is generated. [Wall 86] uses this polygonal approximation for generating a smooth cubic curve as an approximation to the original data. Images of the coastline of Great Britain and its polygonal approximations are shown in Figure 8.

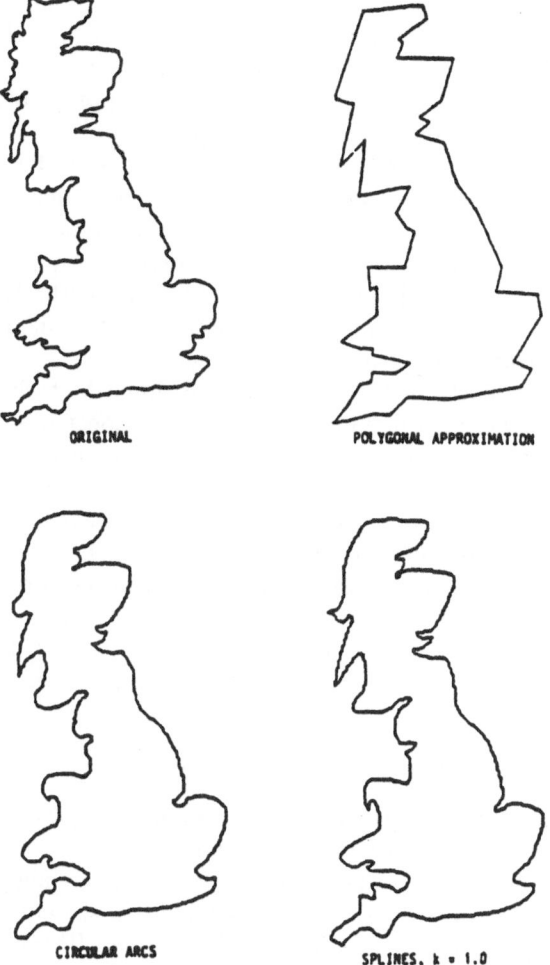

ORIGINAL   POLYGONAL APPROXIMATION

CIRCULAR ARCS   SPLINES, k = 1.0

Fig. 8. Illustration of polygonal, circular arc, and spline approximations [Wall 86].

[Leu and Chen 88] focus on uniqueness and accuracy of representation, two important issues of polygonal approximation. Uniqueness is achieved by starting the approximation simultaneously at places along the shape boundary where the arcs are closer to straight lines than their neighboring arcs. This is done by first calculating the maximum arc-to-chord deviation for each arc, and then finding the local minimum deviation arc (LMDA) by comparing each deviation with those of the neighboring arcs. Polygonal approximation is done by fitting lines to those LMDAs whose maximum arc-to-chord distance is less than a given tolerance. In [Imai and Iri 86], algorithms are discussed to perform piece-wise linear approximation to a curve with minimum cardinality, so as to cover a sequence of points by a minimum number of rectangles.

[Sirjani and Cross 88] have developed a two-pass algorithm for polygonal approximation. On chain-coded curves, they first mark all points that are potential candidates for the vertices of a polygon. In the second pass they do a sweep to remove all segments that have distance less than a threshold. Noisy curves can cause problems in the first pass, and selection of an appropriate threshold in the second pass is critical to obtaining good results.

Besides polygonal approximation methods, higher order curve and spline fitting methods are used where more precise approximations are required. These are more computationally expensive that most polygonalization methods, and can be more difficult to apply. Some of these are described in [Pavlidis 77, Pavlidis 78, Pavlidis 82, Davis 86]. Higher-order curve fitting methods are also used for beautification of hand-drawn and machine-approximated diagrams such as flow-charts, block diagrams, electrical schematics, etc.

One of the drawbacks of most of these polygonal fit techniques is that the operations are not performed symmetrically with respect to curve features such as corners and the centers of curves. The result is that the computed breakpoints between segments may be at different locations depending on starting and ending locations, or direction of operation of the line fit. Extensions can be made to some of the methods to produce fewer and more consistent breakpoint locations, but these procedures are usually iterative and can be computationally expensive. In the next section, curve fitting methods are performed from a different approach, that of detecting features first, then performing fits. It will be seen that these methods often produce better approximations than polygonalization.

5.2 Detection of Critical Points

Most of the algorithms for detecting critical points to segment lines into shorter segments follow the idea of [Attneave 54] and mark the local curvature maxima points as dominant. Five popular feature detection algorithms using this approach are the: angle detection procedures of [Rosenfeld and Johnston 73, Rosenfeld and Weszka 75], corner finding algorithm of [Freeman and Davis 77], dominant point detection method of [Sankar and Sharma 78], and vertex detection algorithm of [Anderson and Bezdek 84]. These have been compared and evaluated in [Teh and Chin 89], who also propose a method. The first three algorithms estimate the curvature at each point by fitting straight lines of varying lengths to pixels on either side of the point; points with local maxima of curvature are then labeled as dominant points. The [Shankar and Sharma 78] method locates dominant points using an iterative procedure. Local curvatures are first determined, and these values are then used for determination of more global maxima. The [Anderson and Bezdek 84] algorithm is significantly different from these local curvature estimation methods. It locates vertices based on cumulative tangential deflections that are calculated using statistical analysis. [Teh and Chin 89] describe a parallel algorithm for detecting dominant points in a closed curve in which the region of support for each point is determined based on local properties. [Fischler and Bolles 86] detect dominant points along a curve by analyzing the deviations of the curve from a chord. The points are marked as a critical point, or belonging to a smooth or noisy interval. These markings depend on whether the curve makes a single excursion away from the chord, stays close to the chord, or makes two or more excursions away from the chord, respectively. A drawback of many of these methods based on critical points of high curvature, is that inflection points due to smooth changes between segments (such as transitions from a circular arc to a tangential line) are not found.

Another reference in which curvature methods are compared is [O'Gorman 88-1]. In this paper, chosen methods are grouped into two families, the difference of slopes (DOS) family, and the Gaussian smoothing method. For the DOS methods, curvature is measured as the angular difference between the slopes of two line segments fit to the data around each curve point. The difference between the methods within the DOS family is in the arc-length of the gap between the two segments. It can be negative (for overlapping line fits), zero for a "hinged" line fit, or positive. Many popular methods fall into this family. For the Gaussian smoothing family of methods, a local second derivative estimate of curvature is first taken for each point along the curve, then a Gaussian smoothing filter is applied to the resulting curvature plot. In both cases, features are determined from the curvature plot. In [O'Gorman 88-2], it is shown that, for the DOS methods, signal-to-noise ratio is maximized when the gap between segments is positive and equals the arc-length of the corner curvature. This method, designated DOS+, is compared with the Gaussian smoothing method, and shown to have slightly better results in distinguishing a corner signal in a noisy chain with low signal-to-noise ratio. Use of the DOS+ method, and relationships between feature parameters and method parameters, are described in [O'Gorman 88-2]. An advantage of both the DOS and Gaussian smoothing families of methods over many others is that their results are symmetric with respect to curve features — an important criterion for judgement of feature detection methods.

Most of the critical point detection algorithms discussed above require parameters related to the minimum resolvable feature separation. However, features of different size and separation are usually present in a given image. Parameter values determined by the minimum size feature may not be adequate to smooth large features, and as a result, too many points may be detected as dominant points. One approach for solving this problem is to adaptively determine the parameters using local feature data — with no required user parameters. [Teh and Chin 89] describe such an algorithm. First, the region of support is adaptively determined using local properties, and local curvature is measured within this. Then, dominant points are detected by non-maxima suppression of local curvature. This algorithm has been compared with several other algorithms (as mentioned above). The comparison indicates that the adaptive method generates approximations with lower maximum error compared to others. Results of approximations by several algorithms on one of the test images in this paper are shown in Figure 9. Quantitative comparisons for this image are shown in Table 1. It is clear that the approximations generated by their algorithm compares well against non-adaptive methods. One drawback is evident though. It can be seen in Figure 9 that the output generated by the algorithm is sensitive to the direction of travel along the curve, and this results in asymmetrical approximations to symmetrical data. In addition, the effect of noise along the curve can cause the region of support to be incorrectly estimated, leading to poor results. Of course, were it not for the tradeoff between noise reduction and signal resolution, the problem would be much easier.

Table 1. Quantitative comparison of dominant point detection algorithms [Teh and Chin 89].

Algorithm		Input Parameters			Number of Dominant Pts n_d	Compression Ratio n/n_d	Max Error E_∞	Integral Sq Error E_2	CPU Time in Secs t
(1) Rosenfeld–Johnston	(a)	m	=	9	12	8.5	2.04	92.37	10.81
	(b)	m	=	4	30	3.4	0.74	8.85	8.00
(2) Rosenfeld–Weszka	(a)	m	=	9	14	7.3	1.56	59.12	15.24
	(b)	m	=	4	34	3.0	1.00	15.40	10.13
(3) Freeman–Davis	(a)	s = 3, m = 1			17	6.0	2.54	79.53	7.65
	(b)	s = 2, m = 1			19	5.4	1.41	23.31	9.46
(4) Sankar–Sharma		None			10	10.2	8.00	769.53	35.04
(5) Anderson–Bezdek	(a)	$\Delta\theta_t$ = 15°, m = 7, ε_{b1} = 0.75, d = 3			18	5.7	1.64	36.14	12.85
	(b)	$\Delta\theta_t$ = 15°, m = 3, ε_{b1} = 0.75, d = 3			29	3.5	1.18	6.43	12.04
(6) Teh–Chin :									
(a) k–cosine		None			22	4.6	1.00	20.61	9.66
(b) k–curvature		None			22	4.6	1.00	20.61	11.81
(c) 1–curvature		None			22	4.6	1.00	20.61	9.40

[Phillips and Rosenfeld 87] also discuss determination of region of support. To get feature points they use the arc-chord distance property. If P is a point on the curve and k the chosen arc length, then for every chord C whose arc has length k, and P in its interior, let $d(P, C)$ be the perpendicular distance from P to C. Let $M(P, C)$ be the maximum of these distances for all such chords. A graph of $M(P, C)$ against P is plotted. P is a feature point if the value of its corresponding $M(P, C)$ is a local maximum and it exceeds a certain threshold, which is a function of k. The partition points obtained depend on the k value, which is chosen as follows. First, determine the straight-line segment that best fits each k-point arc of the curve (in the least square sense) and compute the RMS error, e, corresponding to this fit. Then the value of k at which the function, $f(k) = e/k$, reaches a local minimum is chosen for that part of the curve.

The problem of feature point detection in digital curves may also be approached as a scale-space filtering problem [Witkin 83, Asada and Brady 86, Deguchi 88]. In [Deguchi 88], k-curvatures (for different values of k) are calculated by finding the differences in slopes of chords connecting pixels that are k pixels from the current point on either side. A plot of k-curvatures and the corresponding curve are shown in Figure 10. For an isolated vertex on a contour line (*i.e.*, no other feature points in the vicinity), the value of the k-curvature

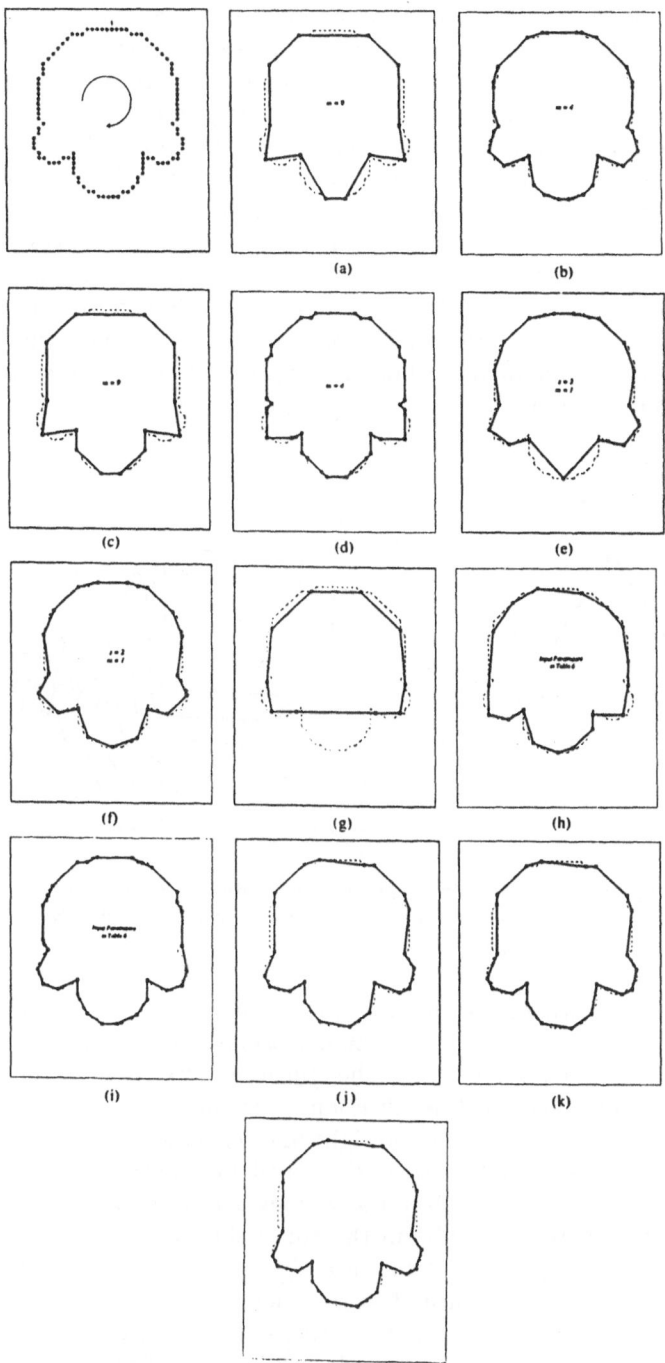

Fig. 9. Comparison of various dominant point detection algorithms on a curve with four semicircles [Teh and Chin 89]. Rosenfeld-Johnston algorithm with (a) m=9 and (b) m=4. Rosenfeld-Weszka algorithm with (c) m=9 and (d) m=4. Freeman-Davis algorithm with (e) s=3, m=1 and (f) s=2, m=1. (g) Sankar-Sharma algorithm. Anderson-Bezdek algorithm with (h) m=7 and (i) m=3. Teh-Chin algorithm (j) k-cosine, (k) k curvature, and (l) 1 curvature.

at the vertex is independent of the value of k. However, the width of the peak depends on the value of k; smaller values of k result in sharper peaks. To locate all vertices, the maximal and minimal points of curvature are found for some k. These are potential convex or concave feature points. The behavior of these maximum or minimum points is tracked as the value of k is decreased. At a curvature maximum point corresponding to a convex vertex, if the maximum value remains the same as k is decreased, then the vertex is a simple isolated vertex; if it decreases, then this indicates the possibility of another convex vertex in the neighborhood; and if the value increases, then a concave vertex in the neighborhood is possibly present. Similar conclusions are obtained for minimum points corresponding to concave vertices. The problem is that of converting these qualitative descriptions into an algorithm with appropriate parameters to be tolerant to the typically noisy data.

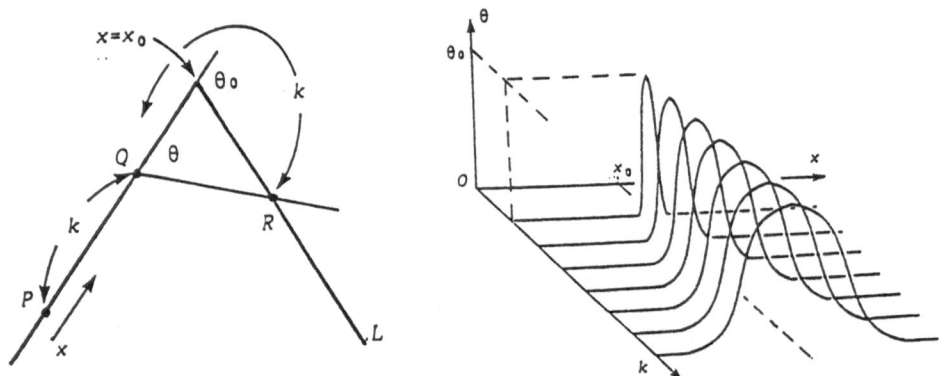

Fig. 10. K-curvature for a line segment containing a corner: (a) test data; (b) k-curvature plotted as a function of pixel position and k [Deguchi 88].

An adaptive filtering algorithm to smooth noisy curves has been described by [Saint-Marc et al.. 89]. To illustrate the performance of this algorithm, consider the closed curve shown in Figure 11. The objective is to locate all the vertices and other critical points such as the inflection point along the curved segment and points of transition from curve to straight line segments. This image is thinned, and the core-line (consisting of about 2500 pixels) is tracked to obtain an ordered list of pixels. The curvature at each point along the core-line is determined using a small region of support to obtain the curve shown in Figure 12. Because of artifacts introduced during digitization and thinning, this curve is not smooth. Smoothing is necessary to identify features such as vertices (peaks and valleys in the curvature plot), inflection points (zero-crossings in curvature), and smooth joins (points of transition from zero curvature to a significant value). A common filter used for smoothing noisy signals is the Gaussian filter. However, Gaussian filtering smooths both noise and data points. Alternatively, an adaptive filter

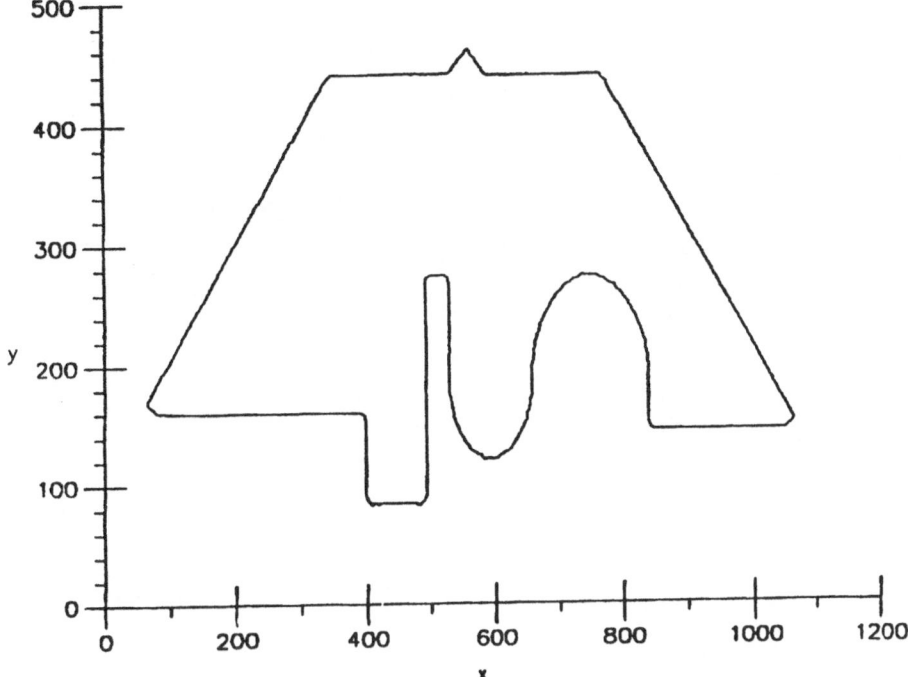

Fig. 11. A closed curve for evaluating adaptive smoothing algorithm.

that emphasizes intra-region smoothing over inter-region smoothing [Saint-Marc
et al. 89] is useful in this situation. This filtering approach is now described.

Let $I_0(s)$ be the signal before smoothing, and $I_t(s)$ the signal at the tth
iteration. The smoothed version of $I_t(s)$ is then defined at each point by:

$$I_{t+1}(s) = (1/R) \sum_{i=-1}^{+1} I_t(s+i) c_t(s+i)$$

where

$$R = \sum_{i=-1}^{+1} c_t(s+i)$$

and $c(s)$ is a coefficient array of same size as $I(s)$, having values close to zero at
region boundary points and one at region interior points. Thus, two points belonging to different regions are not averaged. Because the region boundary points
are not known *a priori*, an estimate of their location based on local curvature is
used in calculating $c(s)$ as follows:

$$c(s) = f(d(s)) = exp(-d^2(s)/2k^2)$$

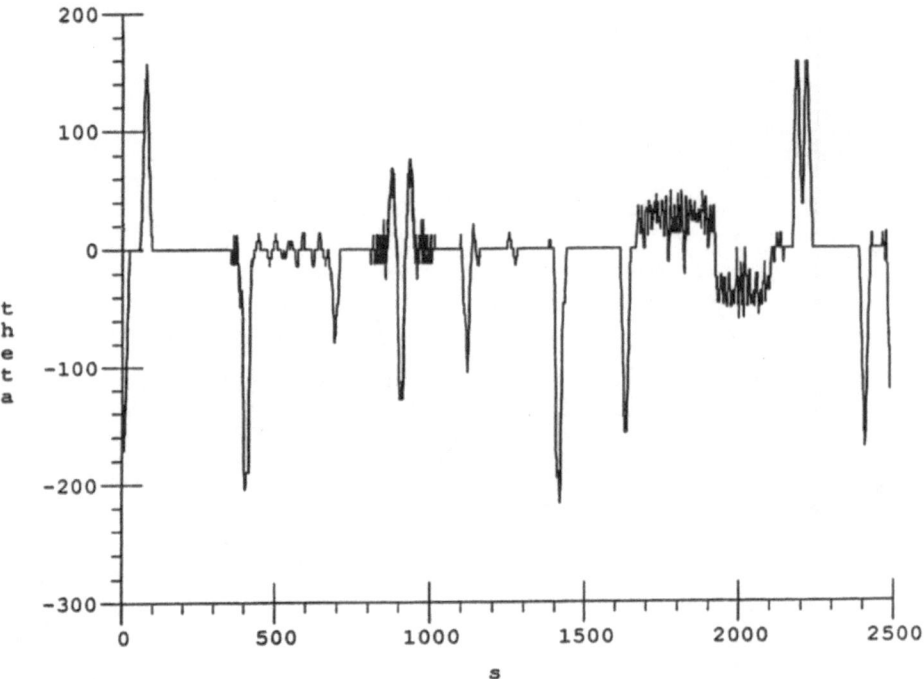

Fig. 12. Plot of curvature as a function of position.

where $d(s)$ is the magnitude of the gradient at s. Note that $f(0) = 1$ and $f(d(s)) \to 0$ as $d(s)$ increases; hence, $c(s)$ is small at discontinuities. If k is chosen to be small, then every feature will diffuse during iteration and the result will be the same as with Gaussian smoothing. If k is chosen to be large, then every discontinuity will stop diffusion and no smoothing will happen. The number of iterations determine the degree of smoothing obtained. Note that, in our example, the function to be smoothed is the curvature function and hence $d(s)$ represents the third derivative of the spatial function. The smoothed function after 75 iterations with $k = 40$ is shown in Figure 13. Note that there are still some fluctuations in the regions corresponding to circular arcs and the two diagonal lines. Two thresholds, one for peak detection and another for zero crossing detection are applied to this curve. Peaks (O's) and significant zero crossings (X's) detected are marked in Figure 13 and the corresponding points in the object are shown in Figure 14.

After detecting critical points, data is represented as a collection of line segments connecting feature points. Attributes of these segments are also computed. Curves are often approximated by piece-wise circular arcs. These line segment and feature point data along with their spatial relationships are retained in appropriate data structures. Information in these data structures is then used for graphics recognition. Techniques for graphics recognition and interpretation are discussed in the next section.

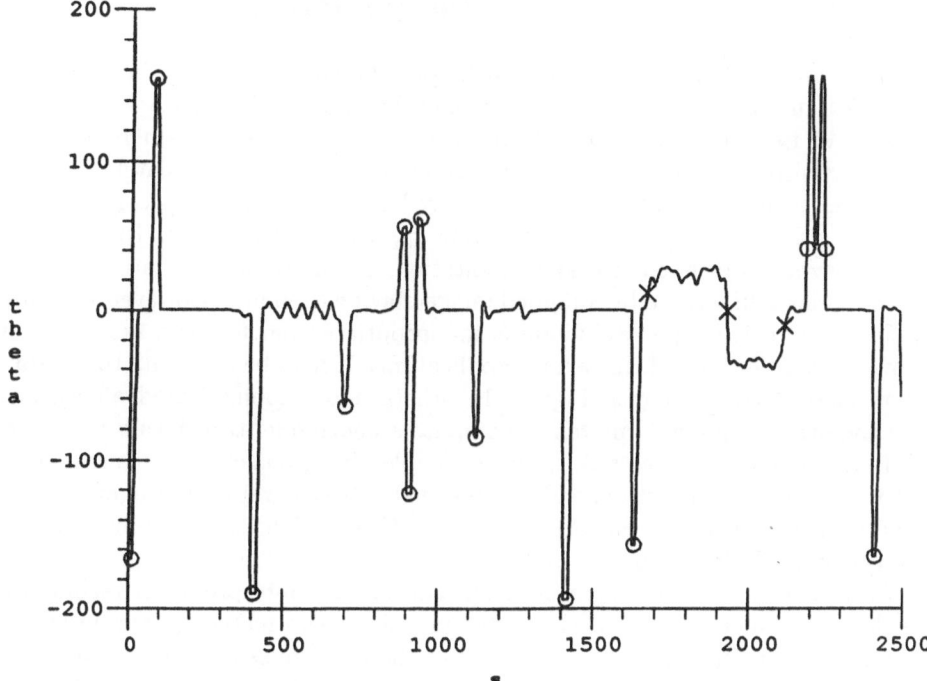

Fig. 13. Curvature after adaptive smoothing.

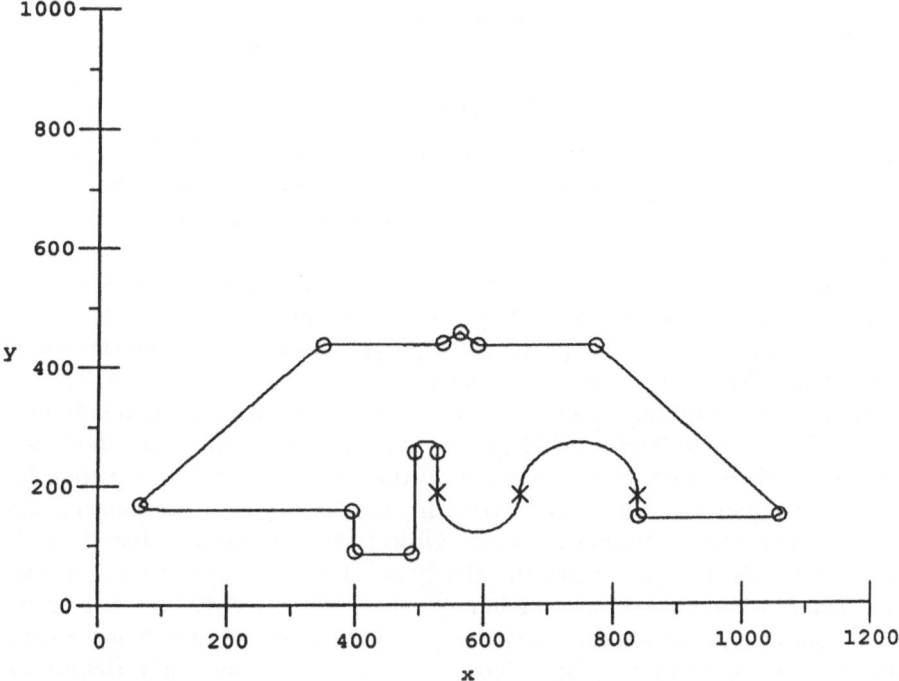

Fig. 14. Critical points.

6 Graphics Recognition and Interpretation

Recognition of graphical shapes and their spatial relationships is an important final task in most document analysis systems. The recognition process essentially
consists of two main steps: processing the input image to obtain representational primitives (as described in the previous sections), and matching these
primitives against similar primitives derived from known models. Techniques
used for graphics recognition are strongly application-dependent. To recognize
isolated symbols of fixed size and orientation, simple template matching techniques applied directly to bit-mapped image may be adequate. However for many
applications, this simple technique is inappropriate, and features as described
above must be extracted. In certain applications, it may be adequate to approximate closed contours by polygons. In others, more sophisticated algorithms
that hypothesize possible matches, compute scene/model transformations, and
verify the hypotheses are used. In more complex images such as maps and engineering drawings, context-dependent, knowledge-based graphics recognition and
interpretation techniques have been used. Different algorithms exhibit varying
degrees of flexibility, accuracy, and robustness.

In this section, various graphics recognition and interpretation techniques
are described, including hierarchical decomposition and matching, and interpretation based on structure-analysis. Most of the techniques described here make
use of the line and feature data obtained using techniques described in the previous sections. Recognition algorithms that operate directly on bit-mapped data
or those that are based on well known techniques such as signature analysis,
Fourier descriptors, etc. are not described here.

6.1 Hierarchical Decomposition and Matching

Techniques such as polygonal approximations are useful for shape recognition
only when the complete outline of the object is available. Although this is not a
serious restriction in most of the graphics recognition applications, occasionally
it would be necessary to recognize graphical shapes when some part of the symbol
is missing or hidden behind other shapes. Further, in some applications in which
the number of possible different shapes to be recognized is large, it may be
efficient to represent complex parts as a combination of already known simple
shapes along with their spatial relationships.

An object recognition system that creates a library of parts by hierarchical
decomposition is described in [Ettinger 88]. The library organization and indexing is designed to avoid linear search of all the model objects. The system has
hierarchical organization for both structure (whole object-to-component sub-
parts) and scale (gross-to-fine features). Object representation is based on the
Curvature Primal Sketch [Asada and Brady 86]. Features used are corner, end,
crank, smooth-join, inflection and bump, which are derived from discontinuities in contour orientation and curvature. Sub-parts consist of subsets of these
features, which partition the object into components. The model libraries are automatically built using the hierarchical nature of the model representations. The

recognition engine is structured as an interpretation tree [Grimson and Lozano-Perez 84]. A constrained search scheme is used for matching scene features to model features. Many configurations are pruned in the search space early in the search process using simple geometric constraints such as orientation difference, distance, and direction between pairs of features.

6.2 Structure Analysis Based Graphics Recognition and Interpretation

For recognition of drawings such as flow-charts, block diagrams, electrical schematics, mechanical part drawings, etc, structural analysis of lines and their interconnections is required to generate meaningful and succinct descriptions. For example, the flow chart shown in Figure 15 contains only 57 line segments (excluding hatching lines and filling patterns); but they form 74 different closed loops [Kasturi *et al.* 90]. A meaningful interpretation would be to identify the seven simple shapes, and describe other lines as interconnecting segments. Similarly, an unconstrained algorithm could interpret a table as a collection of many rectangles, whereas it would be more useful to describe it as a rectangle with horizontal and vertical bars. In case of electrical schematics it would be necessary to separate lines belonging to symbols from connecting lines.

An algorithm for generating loops of minimum redundancy is described in [El-Masri 88, Kasturi *et al.* 90]. In this algorithm, all terminal line segments are first separated since they cannot be a part of any closed loop. This removes the two short line segments at the top and bottom of Figure 15. All self loops are then separated (top rectangle and small shape fillings in Figure 15). This process is repeated, if necessary (to delete the short segment at the bottom of the top rectangle in Figure 15). A heuristic search algorithm is then applied to the remaining network to identify simple closed loops that are made up of no more than a predetermined number of line segments. This search algorithm is described with the help of Figure 16. In this figure, the current point C has been reached by following line segments AB and BC. The objective is to assign priorities to line segments at C for continuing the search for a closed loop. Line segment j is assigned the highest priority since it is collinear with BC. Next priority is assigned to k (angles a1 and a2 are equal) since it has the potential to form a regular polygon. Next priority goes to segment l that is parallel to AB (potential parallelogram, trapezoid). Final priority goes to segment m since it forms the sharpest convex corner at C. If none of these segments continue the path to form a closed loop, segment n is chosen during the final search for a closed loop. This loop finding algorithm employs a depth first search strategy. It correctly identifies the seven simple shapes that are present in the figure. In particular, the algorithm traces the outline of the hatched rectangle and thus separates hatching patterns from enclosing lines. The loops that are extracted are then compared with a library of *known shapes* shown in Table 2 for recognition and description. Those shapes that are not recognized are analyzed to verify if they can be described as partially overlapped *known shapes*. All other segments are described as interconnecting lines or hatching patterns. The sys-

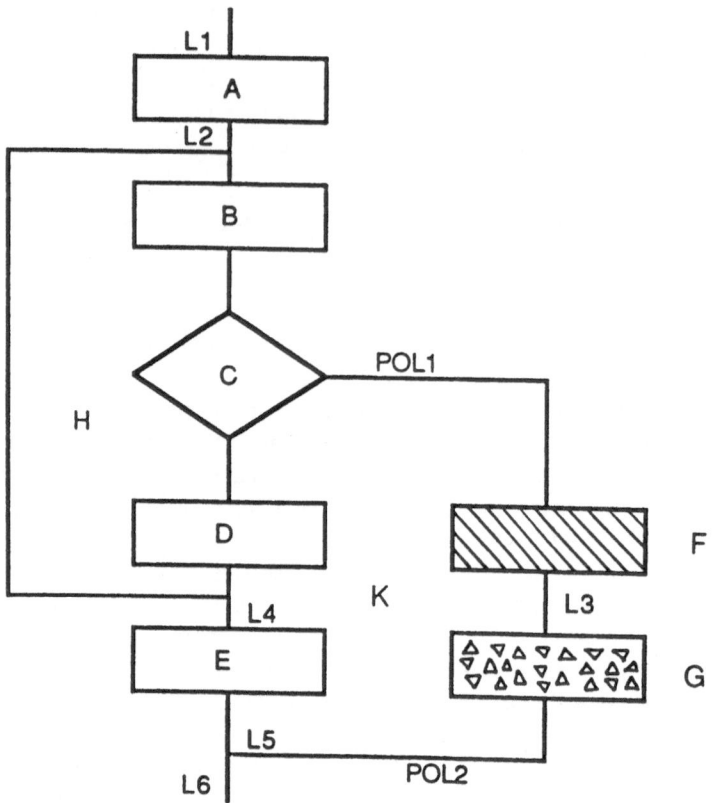

Fig. 15. A flow chart test image.

tem outputs all recognized shapes, their attributes and spatial relationships. The output generated by the system corresponding to the test image of Figure 17 are shown in Tables 3 and 4. The algorithm has been extended to describe graphics made up of circular arc segments [Bow and Kasturi 90]. Some of these techniques have also been used in a map-based geographic information system [Kasturi *et al.* 89].

[Ejiri *et al.* 90] apply structure analysis methods for recognition of engineering drawings and maps. To process LSI cell diagrams, solid lines and two types of broken lines in any one of six colors are recognized using the color digitizer described earlier. A loop-finding routine facilitates detection of overlapped lines denoted by a special mark. Structure analysis methods have also been used to recognize characters and symbols in logic circuit diagrams, chemical plant diagrams, and mechanical part drawings.

[Fahn *et al.* 88] describe a topology-based component extraction system to recognize symbols in electronic circuit diagrams. The objective is to extract

Table 2. Catalog of known shapes and their attributes [Kasturi *et al.* 90].

Known Shapes		Attributes
Triangle		P1, P2, P3
Rectangle		P, W, H, ∅
Rhombus		P, L, Θ, ∅
Parallelogram		P, L1, L2, Θ, ∅
Trapezoid		P, L1, L2, H, Θ, ∅
Regular Pentagon		P, L, ∅
Regular Hexagon		P, L, ∅
Quasi-Hexagon		P, L1, L2, Θ, ∅

∅:   Orientation of longer side (major axis in case of rhombus and quasi-hexagon) passing through P with respect to x axis

314   R. Kasturi et al.

Table 3. Recognized objects in Figure 17 and their attributes [Kasturi *et al.* 90].

	Object	Attributes
1	Regular Hexagon	P: (1258, 1081), L = 133, ϕ = 1.51
2	Parallelogram	P: (727, 1268), L1 = 292, L2 = 146, Θ = 46.1, ϕ = 0
3	Trapezoid	P: (73, 1081), L1 = 718, L2 = 390, H = 217, Θ = 90.68, ϕ = -0.16
4	Rhombus	P: (339, 1791), L = 220 Θ = 30.1, ϕ = -0.45
5	Trapezoid	P: (1220, 1194), L1 = 221, L2 = 150, H = 68.6, Θ = 65, ϕ = 0.77
6	Triangle	P1: (1295, 1153), P2: (1363, 1151), P3: (1325, 1122), Isoceles
7	Triangle	P1: (1396, 1826), P2: (1106, 1831), P3: (1256, 1971), Isoceles
8	Rectangle	P: (457, 1044), W = 835, H = 564, ϕ = -0.4, Table
9	Quasi-Hexagon	P: (692,1497), L1 = 440, L2 = 303, Θ = 89.1, ϕ = 3.0
10	Parallelogram	P: (765, 1790), L1 = 297.1, L2 = 148, Θ = 89.0, ϕ = -1.35, Single hatch: a1 = 135, d1 = 30
11	Traingle	P1: (1256, 1897), P2: (1399, 1755), P3: (1108, 1753), Isoceles
12	Polygon, irregular	Number of segments: 6, Center: (1556, 1706), Coordinates of vertices....

Table 4. Interconnecting lines and their attributes [Kasturi *et al.* 90].

	Objects	Spatial Relationships		
11	Triangle	Overlaps Object 7		
1	Regular Hexagon	Encloses Objects 5 and 6		
10	Parallelogram	Single Hatch		
3	Trapezoid	Small Shape Fillings		
Lines and Their Interconnections				
Line	Head	Tail	From	To
Single Segment Lines				
L1	(1404,1748)	(1399,1755)	--	11
L2	(910,1416)	(911,1271)	9	2
. . .	. . .	. . .	. . .	. . .
Lines With Multiple Segments				
PL1	S1: (330,1531) S2: (260,1537) S3: (265,1791) S4: (332,1790)	(260,1537) (265,1791) (332;1790) (339,1791)	--	4
PL2	S1: (1064,1715) S2: (1252,1719)	(1252,1719) (1252,1750)	10	11
. . .	. . .	. . .	. . .	. . .

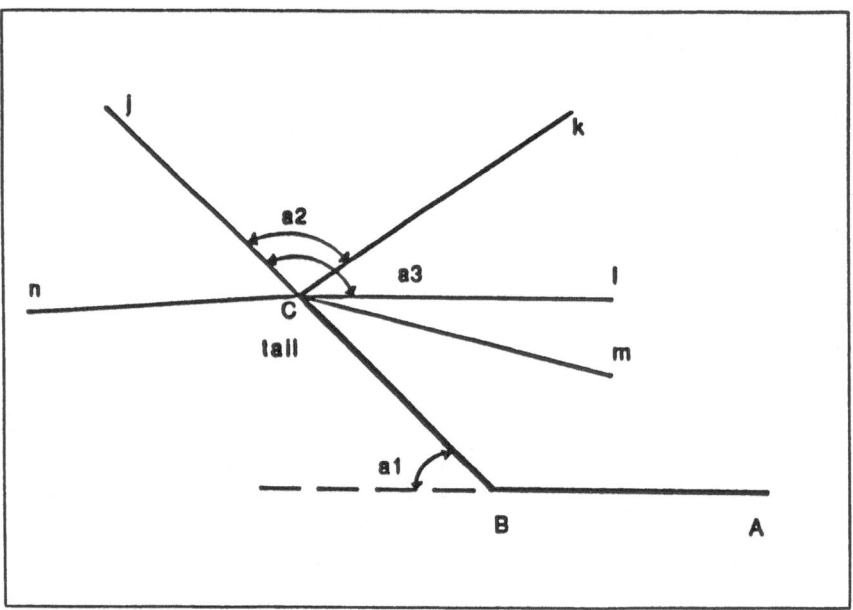

Fig. 16. Assignment of priorities.

circuit symbols, characters and connecting lines. Picture segments are detected using segment tracking algorithms. These are then approximated using a piecewise linear approximation algorithm. A topological search is done to form clusters of symbols or characters. A decision tree is used to assign picture segments to a class of primitives. Segments are clustered into component symbols using a context-based depth-first search method. The system is designed to recognize circuit symbols in four orientations, and connection lines that are horizontal, vertical or diagonal. The system has also been used to generate fair copies of hand-drawn circuit diagrams. In [Okazaki *et al.* 88], a loop-structure analysis system is described for recognition of circuit symbols.

A method for interpreting the 3-D shape of an object corresponding to multiple orthographic views in an engineering drawing has been described in [Lysak and Kasturi 90]. The technique is based on a bottom-up approach in which candidate vertices and edges are used to generate a set of possible faces, which are in turn assembled into enclosures representing the final object [Wesley and Markowsky 81]. A minimum of two views is required, and a maximum of six orthogonal views in a standard layout can be accommodated. All possible interpretations consistent with the input views are found, and inconsistent input views are recognized. The method can handle input views with small drafting errors and inaccuracies.

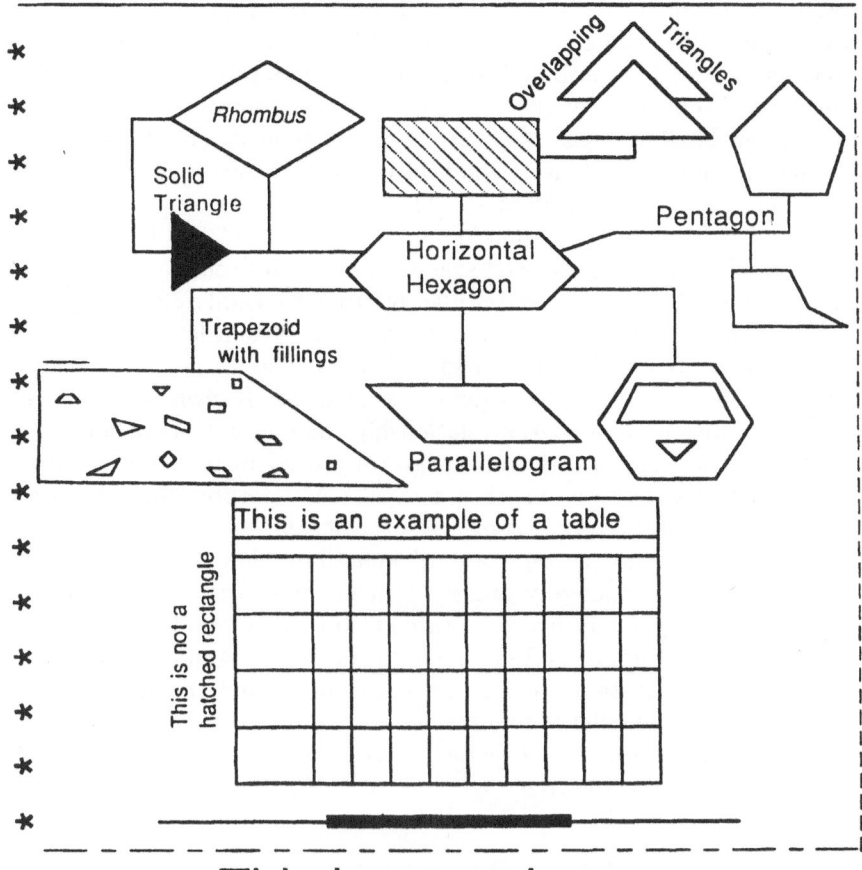

Fig. 17. A test image containing different shapes [Kasturi *et al.* 90].

6.3 Other Approaches for Recognition

The hypothesis-prediction-verification paradigm combines bottom-up and top-down techniques to take advantage of the system's knowledge of the objects. [Govindaraju *et al.* 89] uses this to locate human faces in newspaper photographs. A low-level Hough transform first detects the arcs and collinear edges in the image. A line-finder then uses back-projection from the Hough accumulator array to extract line segments in the original image. Then the curves and line segments are grouped together in this way to generate candidate regions for faces. Top-down methodology employs the spatial constraints (with respect to the photograph captions) and heuristics from photo-journalism, to eliminate inconsistent candidates returned by bottom-up Hough transform analysis, and verify these predictions.

Another approach to recognition is using relaxation. [Bunke and Allerman 81] use this method to analyze electrical schematics. A vector with probabilities of possible interpretations is first assigned to each vertex in the schematic. A vertex is a location where either several line segments touch each other or a line segment ends. The probabilities of the interpretations at various vertices are successively changed by the relaxation process in order to achieve unique and consistent labeling. This recognition engine depends on effective propagation along the matching vertices, good initial assignments, and convexity of the configuration space and the domain. The convexity requirement removes the danger of identifying local maxima/minima as global, but is difficult to satisfy.

Rule-based or knowledge-based systems have also been used as recognition engines [Nagy *et al.* 85, Niyogi and Srihari 86, Bley 84, Bunke 82, Huang and Tou 86]. [Niyogi and Srihari 86] describe a production system for document understanding. The control flow is described as follows. The image is first segmented and descriptions about various regions are obtained. Knowledge rules pertain to intrinsic properties and spatial relationships among various regions. Control rules are used to decide which knowledge rules need to be executed. Strategy rules are used to determine whether a consistent interpretation has been obtained. If the data from initial segmentation is insufficient, further processing is invoked. Such production systems are difficult to develop since the compilation of a knowledge-base is a lengthy process. Since segmentation is affected by noise and viewing conditions, any error generated at this stage could be propagated all the way to final interpretation. In [Bunke 82] symbol recognition is controlled by a decision tree that contains all *a priori* knowledge about the form of symbols. The decision tree has model configurations stored in terms of line segments. Image segmentation generates line segments that are then matched to the model configurations stored in the tree.

7 Summary

In this paper we have presented an overview of many algorithms and techniques that are useful in a graphics recognition system. In Section 2, data capture issues such as scanner resolution and thresholding for binarization were addressed. Since a typical graphics image contains regions of text as well as graphics, region segmentation techniques are used to separate the two. These were discussed in Section 3. Data conversion from bit-mapped form to line segment form is a necessary intermediate step in all but very simple graphics recognition systems. Vectorization by line-fitting, or thinning and line tracking methods, were discussed in Section 4. Algorithms for detection of feature points, and segmentation of concatenated lines into straight line segments and curves were given in Section 5. Techniques for recognition and description of graphics, such as hierarchical organization and matching, and structure analysis were described in Section 6.

Acknowledgements

We would like to thank S. T. Bow, R. T. Chin, K. Deguchi, M. Ejiri, B. T. Mitchell, and K. Wall for permitting us to reproduce several figures and tables from their papers.

8 References

I. M. Anderson and J. C. Bezdek, "Curvature and tangential deflection of discrete arcs: A theory based on the commutator of matrix pairs and its application to vertex detection in planar shape data," *IEEE Trans. PAMI*, 6(1):27-40, Jan. 1984.

C. Arcelli, L. P. Cordella, and S. Levialdi, "From local maxima to connected skeletons," *IEEE Trans. PAMI*, 3(2):134-143, Mar., 1981.

C. Arcelli and G. S. di Baja, "A width-independent fast thinning algorithm," *IEEE Trans. PAMI*, 7(4):463-474, Jul. 1985.

H. Asada and M. Brady, "The curvature primal sketch," *IEEE Trans. PAMI*, 8(1):26-33, Jan. 1986.

F. Attneave, "Some informational aspects of visual perception," *Psychol. Rev.* 61:183-193, 1954.

H. S. Baird, S. E. Jones, and S. J. Fortune, "Image segmentation using shape-directed covers," *Proc. 10th ICPR*, Atlantic City, New Jersey, 1990.

H. Bley, "Segmentation and preprocessing of electrical schematics using picture graphs," *Computer Graphics and Image Processing*, 28:271-288, 1984.

S. Bow and R. Kasturi, "A graphics recognition system for interpretation of line drawings," In R. Kasturi and M. M. Trivedi (eds.), *Image Analysis Applications*, Marcel Dekker, 1990.

H. Bunke and G. Allerman, "Probabilistic relaxation for the interpretation of electrical schematics," *Proc. ICPR*, pp. 438-440, 1981.

H. Bunke, "Automatic interpretation of lines and text in circuit diagrams," In J. Kittler, K. S. Fu, and L. F. Pau (eds.), *Pattern Recognition: Theory and Applications*, pp. 297-310, D. Reidel, 1982.

R. G. Casey and K. Y. Wong, "Document analysis systems and techniques," in *Image Analysis Applications*, R. Kasturi and M. M. Trivedi (eds), Marcel Dekker, 1990.

L. S. Davis, *Handbook of Pattern Recognition and Image Processing*, Academic Press, 1986.

K. Deguchi, "Multi-scale curvatures for contour feature extraction," *Proc. 9th ICPR*, pp. 1113-1115, 1988.

D. Dori, "A syntactic/geometric approach to recognition of dimensions in engineering machine drawings," *Computer Vision, Graphics, and Image Processing*, 47:1-21, 1989.

W. Doster, "Different states of a document's content on its way from the Gutenbergian world to the electronic world," *Proc. 7th ICPR*, Montreal, pp. 872-874, 1984.

R. O. Duda and P. E. Hart, *Pattern Classification and Scene Analysis*, Wiley-Interscience, New York, pp. 338-339, 1973.

M. Ejiri, S. Kakumoto, T. Miyatake, S. Shimada, and K. Iwamura, "Automatic recognition of engineering drawings and maps," in *Image Analysis Applications*, R. Kasturi and M. M. Trivedi (eds), Marcel Dekker, 1990.

W. El-Masri, *Recognition and Description of Graphical Primitives*, M. S. Thesis, Electrical Engineering, Penn State University, 1987.

G. J. Ettinger, "Large hierarchical object recognition using libraries of parameterized model sub-parts," *Proc. CVPR*, pp. 32-41, 1988.

C. S. Fahn, J. F. Wang, and J. Y. Lee, "A topology-based component extractor for understanding electronic circuit diagrams," *Computer Vision, Graphics and Image Processing*, 44:119-138, 1988.

M. A. Fischler and R. C. Bolles, "Perceptual organization and curve partitioning," *IEEE Trans. PAMI*, 8(1):100-105, Jan. 1986.

L. A. Fletcher and R. Kasturi, "A robust algorithm for text string separation from mixed text/graphics image," *IEEE Trans. PAMI*, 10:(6)910-918, Nov. 1988.

H. Freeman, "On the encoding of arbitrary geometric configurations," *IEEE Trans. Elec. Computers*, Vol. EC-10:260-268, 1961.

H. Freeman and L. S. Davis, "A corner-finding algorithm for chain-coded curves," *IEEE Trans. Computers* 26:297-303, March 1977.

N. C. Fulford, "The Fastrak automatic digitizing system," *Pattern Recognition*, 14:65-74, 1981.

J. R. Gattiker, *An improved algorithm for text-string separation from mixed text/graphics images*, M. S. Thesis, Electrical Engineering, Penn State University, 1988.

V. Govindaraju, D. B. Sher, R. K. Srihari, and S. N. Srihari, "Locating human faces in newspaper photographs," *Proc. CVPR*, pp. 549-554, San Diego, 1989.

W. E. L. Grimson and T. Lozano-Perez, "Model-based recognition and localization from sparse range or tactile data," *Intl. J. of Robotics Research*, 3(3):3-35, 1984.

Z. Guo and R. W. Hall, "Parallel thinning with two-subiteration algorithms," *Comm. ACM*, 32:359-373, 1989.

H. Harada, Y. Itoh, and M. Ishii, "Recognition of free-hand drawings in chemical plant engineering," *Proc. IEEE Workshop on Computer Architecture for Pattern Analysis and Image Database Management*, pp. 146-153, 1985.

R. M. Haralick, L. T. Watson, and T. J. Laffey, "The topographic primal sketch," *Int'l J. Robotics Res.*, 2:50-72, 1983.

J. F. Harris, J. Kittler, B. Llewellyn, and G. Preston, "A modular system for interpreting binary pixel representations of line-structured data," In J. Kittler, K. S. Fu, and L. F. Pau (eds.), *Pattern Recognition: Theory and Applications*, pp. 311-351, D. Reidel, 1982.

C. J. Hilditch, "Linear skeletons from square cupboards," *Machine Intelligence*, 4:403-420, 1969.

F. Holdermann and H. Kazmierczak, "Preprocessing of gray scale pictures," *Computer Graphics and Image Processing*, 1:66-80, 1972.

C. L. Huang and J. T. Tou, "Knowledge-based functional-symbol understanding in electronic circuit diagram interpretation," *Proc. SPIE Conf. Applications of Artificial Intelligence* 635, 1986.

J. Illingworth and J. Kittler, "A survey of the Hough transform," *Computer Graphics and Image Processing*, 44:87-116, 1988.

H. Imai and M. Iri, "Computational-geometric methods for polygonal approximations of a curve," *Computer Graphics and Image Processing*, 36:31-41, 1986.

H. V. Jagadish and L. O'Gorman, "An object model for image recognition," *IEEE Computer*, 22(12):33-41, Dec. 1989.

A. K. Jain, *Fundamentals of Digital Image Processing*, Prentice–Hall, Englewood Cliffs, NJ, 1989.

J. Jimenez and J. L. Navalon, "Some experiments in image vetorization," *IBM J. Res. Develop.*, 26(6):724-734, Nov. 1982.

M. Karima, K. S. Sadhal, and T. O. McNeil, "From paper drawings to computer aided design," *IEEE Computer Graphics and Applications*, pp. 24-39, Feb. 1985.

R. Kasturi, R. Fernandez, M. L. Amlani, and W. C. Feng, "Map data processing in geographical information systems," *Computer*, 22(12):10-21, 1989.

R. Kasturi, S. T. Bow, W. El-Masri, J. Shah, J. Gattiker, and U. Mokate, "A system for interpretation of line drawings," accepted for publication in *IEEE Trans. PAMI*, 1990.

H. Kida, O. Iwaki, and K. Kawada, "Document recognition system for office automation," *Proc. 8th ICPR*, pp. 446-448, Paris, 1986.

Y. Kurozumi and W. A. Davis, "Polygonal approximation by minimax method," *Computer Graphics and Image Processing*, 19, 248-264, 1982.

M. S. Landy and Y. Cohen, "Vectorgraph coding: efficient coding of line drawings," *Computer Vision, Graphics and Image Processing*, 30:331-344, 1985.

J. G. Leu and L. Chen, "Polygonal approximation of 2-D shapes through boundary merging," *Pattern Recognition Letters*, 7:231-238, 1988.

D. B. Lysak and R. Kasturi, "Interpretation of line drawings with multiple views," *Proc. 10th ICPR* (Pattern Recognition Systems and Applications Subconference), 1990.

I. Masuda, N. Hagita, T. Akayama, T. Takahashi, and S. Naito, "Approach to smart document reader system," *Proc. CVPR*, pp. 550-557, San Francisco, 1985.

D. Merelli, F. Mussio, and M. Padula, "An approach to the definition, description, and extraction of structures in binary digital images," *Computer Vision, Graphics, and Image Processing*, 30:19-49, 1985.

E. Meynieux, S. Seisen, and K. Tombre, "Bilevel information recognition and coding in office paper documents," *Proc. 8th ICPR*, pp. 442-445, Paris, 1986.

B. T. Mitchell and A. M. Gillies, "A model-based computer vision system for recognizing handwritten ZIP codes," *Machine Vision and Applications*, 2:231-243, 1989.

S. Mori and T. Sakakura, "Line filtering and its application to stroke segmentation of hand-printed Chinese characters," *Proc. 7th ICPR*, pp. 366-369, Montreal, 1984.

T. H. Morrin, "A black-white representation of a gray scale picture," *IEEE Trans. Computers*, 23(2):184-186, 1974.

N. J. Naccache and R. Shinghal, "SPTA: A proposed algorithm for thinning binary patterns," *IEEE Trans. Systems, Man, and Cybernetics*, SMC-14(3):409-418, 1984.

P. A. Nagin, A. R. Hanson, and E. M. Riseman, "Studies in global and local histogram guided relaxation algorithms," *IEEE Trans. PAMI*, 4:263-277, 1982.

S. Nagy, S. C. Seth, and S. D. Stoddard, "Document analysis with an expert system," In E. S. Gelsema and L. N. Kanal (eds.), *Proc. Int'l Workshop on Pattern Recognition in Practice 2*, pp. 149-159, Elsevier/North–Holland, Amsterdam, June 1985.

D. Niyogi and Srihari S. N., "A rule-based system for document understanding," *Proc. AAAI*, pp. 789-793, Philadelphia, 1986.

L. O'Gorman, "An analysis of feature detectability from curvature estimation," *Proc. CVPR*, pp. 235-240, Ann Arbor, Michigan, June 1988.

L. O'Gorman, "Curvilinear feature detection from curvature estimation," *Proc. 9th ICPR*, pp. 1116-1119, Rome, 1988.

L. O'Gorman, "kxk Thinning," *Computer Vision, Graphics, and Image Processing*, Vol. 51, 1990 (in press).

L. O'Gorman, "Primitives chain code," *Computer Vision, Graphics, and Image Processing*, 1990 (in press).

A. Okazaki, T. Kondo, K. Mori, and S. Tsunekawa, "Knowledge controlled pattern recognition technique for hand drawn logic symbols," *Proc. IEEE Workshop on Computer Architecture for Pattern Analysis and Image Database Management*, pp. 524-531, 1985.

A. Okazaki, T. Kondo, K. Mori, S. Tsunekawa, and E. Kawamoto, "An automatic circuit diagram reader with loop-structure-based symbol recognition" *IEEE Trans. PAMI*, 10(3):331-341, May 1988.

J. R. Parker, "Extracting vectors from raster images," *Computer and Graphics*, 12(1):75-79, 1988.

T. Pavlidis, *Structural Pattern Recognition*, Springer Series Electrophysics 1, Springer–Verlag, Berlin, 1977.

T. Pavlidis, "Survey: A review of algorithms for shape analysis," *Computer Graphics and Image Processing*, 7:243-258, 1978.

T. Pavlidis, *Algorithms for Graphics and Image Processing*, Computer Science Press, Rockville, Maryland, 1982.

T. Pavlidis and L. L. Cherry, "Vector and arc encoding of graphics and text," *Proc. 6th ICPR*, Munich, pp. 610-613, October 1982.

T. Pavlidis, "A hybrid vectorization algorithm," *Proc. 7th ICPR*, Montreal, pp. 490–492, 1984.

S. Peleg and A. Rosenfeld, "A min-max medial axis transformation," *IEEE Trans. PAMI*, 1:88-89, 1979.

D. J. Peuquet, "An examination of techniques for reforming digital cartographic data, Part 1: The raster-to-vector process," *Cartographica*, 18:34-48, 1981.

T. Y. Phillips and A. Rosenfeld, "A method of curve partitioning using arc-chord distance," *Pattern Recognition Letters*, 5:285-288, April 1987.

K. Ramachandran, "A coding method for vector representation of engineering drawings," *Proc. IEEE*, 68:813-817, 1980.

U. E. Ramer, "An iterative procedure for the polygonal approximation of plane curves," *Computer Graphics and Image Processing*, 1:244-256, 1972.

A. Rosenfeld and E. Johnston, "Angle detection on digital curves," *IEEE Trans. Computers*, 22:875-878, Sept. 1973.

A. Rosenfeld and J. S. Weszka, "An improved method of angle detection on digital curves," *IEEE Trans. Computers*, 24:940-941, Sept. 1975.

A. Rosenfeld and A. C. Kak, *Digital Picture Processing*, 2nd edition, Academic Press, 1982.

P. K. Sahoo, S. Soltani, A. K. C. Wong, and Y. C. Chen, "A survey of thresholding techniques," *Computer Vision, Graphics, and Image Processing*, 41(2):233-260, February 1988.

P. Saint-Marc, J. S. Chen, and G. Medioni, "Adaptive smoothing: a general tool for early vision," *Proc. CVPR*, San Diego, pp. 618-624, 1989.

P. V. Sankar and C. V. Sharma, "A parallel procedure for the detection of dominant points on a digital curve," *Computer Graphics and Image Processing*, 7:403-412, 1978.

J. D. Shah, *Vector Representation of Raster Scanned Images*, M. S. Thesis, Electrical Engineering, Penn State University, 1988.

C.-C. Shih and R. Kasturi, "Generation of a Line-Description File for Graphics Recognition," *Proc. SPIE Conf. on Applications of Artificial Intelligence*, 937:568-575, 1988.

C.-C. Shih and R. Kasturi, "Extraction of graphic primitives from images of paper-based drawings" *Machine Vision and Applications*, 2:103-113, 1989.

R. M. K. Sinha, "A width-independent algorithm for character skeleton estimation," *Computer Vision, Graphics, and Image Processing*, 40:388-397, 1987.

A. Sirjani and G. R. Cross, "An algorithm for polygonal approximation of a digital object," *Pattern Recognition Letters* 7:299-303, 1988.

J. Sklansky and V. Gonzalez, "Fast polygonal approximation of digitized curves," *Pattern Recognition*, 12:327-331, 1980.

S. N. Srihari and G. M. Zack, "Document image analysis," *Proc. 8th ICPR*, Paris, pp. 434-436, 1986.

S. N. Srihari and V. Govindaraju, "Analysis of textual images using the Hough transform," *Machine Vision and Applications*, 2:141-153, 1989.

H. Tamura, "A comparison of line thinning algorithms from digital geometry viewpoint," *ICPR*, Kyoto, Japan, pp. 715-719, Nov. 1978.

C. H. Teh and R. T. Chin, "On the detection of dominant points on digital curves," *IEEE Trans. PAMI*, 11(8):859-872, 1989.

D. Ting and B. Prasada, "Digital processing techniques for encoding of graphics," *Proc. IEEE*, 6:756-767, 1980.

I. Tomek, "Two algorithms for piecewise-linear continuous fit of functions of one variable," *IEEE Trans. Computers*, C-23(4):445-448, 1974.

F. M. Wahl, "A new distance mapping algorithm and its use for shape measurement on binary patterns," *Computer Graphics and Image Processing*, 23:218-226, 1983.

T. Wakayama, "A core line tracking algorithm based on maximal square moving," *IEEE Trans. PAMI*, 4(1):68-74, Jan. 1982.

K. Wall, "Curve fitting based on polygonal approximation," *Proc. 8th ICPR*, Paris, pp. 1273-1275, 1986.

K. Wall and P. E. Danielsson, "A fast sequential method for polygonal approximation of digitized curves," *Computer Graphics and Image Processing*,

28:220-227, 1984.

S. Wang, A. Y. Wu, and A. Rosenfeld, "Image approximation from gray scale medial axis," *IEEE Trans. PAMI*, 3:687-697, 1981.

L. T. Watson, K. Arvind, R. W. Ehrich, and R. M. Haralick, "Extraction of lines and drawings from grey tone line drawing images," *Pattern Recognition*, 17(5):493-507, 1984.

M. A. Wesley and S. Markowsky, "Fleshing out projections," *IBM J. Research and Development*, 25(6):934-954, Nov. 1981.

J. Weszka, "A survey of threshold selection techniques," *Computer Graphics and Image Processing*, 7:259-265, 1978.

J. White and G. Rohrer, "Image thresholding for optical recognition and other applications requiring character image extraction," *IBM J. Res. Dev.*, 27(4):400-411, 1983.

C. M. Williams, "Bounded straight-line approximation of digitized planar curves and lines," *Computer Graphics and Image Processing*, 16:370-381, 1981.

C. M. Williams, "An efficient algorithm for the piecewise linear approximation of planar curves," *Computer Graphics and Image Processing*, 8:286-293, 1978.

A. P. Witkin, "Scale-space filtering," *Proc. 8th IJCAI*, Karlsruhe, W. Germany, pp. 1019-1022, Aug. 1983.

G. Woetzel, "A fast and economic scan-to-line conversion algorithm," *Computer Graphics*, 12:125-129, 1978.

K. Y. Wong, "Multi-function auto-thresholding algorithm," *IBM Technical Disclosure Bulletin*, 21(7):3001-3003, 1978.

K. Y. Wong, R. G. Casey, and F. M. Wahl, "Document analysis system," *IBM J. Res. Dev.*, 26(6):647-656, 1982.

H. Zen and S. Ozawa, "Extraction of the fair document from mixed mode manuscript," *Proc. CVPR*, San Francisco, pp. 544-549, 1985.

High Quality Vectorization Based on a Generic Object Model

Osamu Hori and Akio Okazaki

Toshiba Research and Development Center,
1, Komukai Toshiba-Cho, Saiwai-Ku, Kawasaki 210, Japan

We propose a new method for high quality vectorization based on a generic object model. In conventional methods, the quality of vectorization has been regarded as the same thing as digitizing accuracy, which is evaluated in terms of the error between the original line-drawing and the resultant vector sequence. However, this accuracy does not always correspond to perceptual quality. Based on the discussion about possible distortions in a vectorization process which strongly affects perceptual quality, we introduce a generic model of an object. The generic properties are described in the object model, for example, "The object is a polygon whose corners all have a right angle" or "The object is composed of several pairs of almost parallel lines". The method consists of three processes: pre-vectorization, object recognition and shape modification based on an object model. The approximation line-figure which is first defined in the pre-vectorization process, is modified so as to meet the properties described in the object model. A cost function is derived from the model so that shape modification can be formalized as an optimization problem. A relaxation method is employed to save on computation time. Object recognition is needed for object model selection. The method was applied to geographic maps for urban planning to extract building polygons. Subjective evaluation on the extracted building shapes showed that 93.6% of the buildings were vectorized with high quality and that the number of buildings with insufficient quality was reduced to one twelfth.

1 Introduction

Raster-to-vector conversion is a key technique for automatic graphic information entry into CAD systems, data-base systems, data communication systems, etc. The purpose of this conversion is to obtain a vector representation for the original image without loss in the necessary pictorial information. There are two types in this technique. In engineering drawing recognition systems [1, 2, 3], raster-to-vector conversion is used as a pre-processing technique for symbol recognition and network analysis. It is important to preserve a topological features and geometric properties for this purpose. In automatic digitizing systems, on the other hand, both perceptual quality and digitizing accuracy are important because the vector data are not only used for various graphic data manipulations, such as the measurement of the area or perimeter, but also displayed for human interaction. In conventional systems [4, 5], perceptual quality has been regarded as the same thing as digitizing accuracy. Many reports [8, 9, 10, 11] have discussed digitizing accuracy in terms of the error between the original line drawing and the resultant vector sequence. However, this accuracy does not always correspond to perceptual quality, owing to the noises mixed in the image scanning process. For example, parallel lines are not always vectorized as parallel lines by the conventional methods. Two sides of a rectangle may not meet with a right angle. These facts lead to the degradation of vectorization quality, because human perception is very sensitive to even a slight distortion. A typical example, in which this problem arises, is discovered in the vectorization for buildings and roads in geographical map images. Certain complementary knowledge is needed in order to obtain an ideal shape for human perception by eliminating such distortions It is easy graphic information entry systems involving symbol recognition to obtain high quality vector representation by replacing detected symbols with a pre-determined template. The template is the most simple model for representing such knowledge. However, this approach cannot be applied to geographic map constituents like buildings and roads because they vary greatly in shape. Pavlidis has proposed an automatic method for beatifying drawings and illustrations from the same point of view [12]. He showed basic ideas for beatification and several examples to which beatification operations are effective. His method beatifies drawings and illustrations based on certain rules. However, it is not a trivial problem to decide automatically which rules should be applied to each sub-pattern in an line drawing. He did not mention the selection problem for beautification rules. Furthermore, it is considered that more efficient beautification algorithm is needed in the practical situation, in which the size of a line drawing is quite large. He did not show a practical beatification algorithm. In this paper, a generic object model for high quality vectorization is introduced instead of beautification rules. The pattern recognition techniques are used to extract target line patterns which should be beautified using the model. The model is efficiently utilized for transforming a shape with distortions into an ideal shape for human perception. The basic idea for high quality vectorization is described in Section 2. In Section 3, the method is applied to urban planning maps to vectorize building polygons. Finally, the effectiveness of the method is shown through subjective evaluations on the experimental results in Section 4.

2 The Basic Idea

This section discusses several kinds of distortions occurring in raster-to-vector conversion, which affects the quality of the obtained vector sequence. Then, an approach to obtaining a high quality vectorized shape is described.

2.1 What Affects Vectorization Quality?

It is often found that vectorized shape is "dirty" or "undesirable" for human perception, even if the accuracy is sufficient. The factors which lower the shape quality can be considered to be as follows.

(i) Local shape distortion, which has occurred in the processing stage of line structure extraction from an input image, by a thinning operation (or other skeleton extraction techniques) and line tracing. This kind of distortion often appears in the neighborhood of cross points. Typical distortion examples are shown in Figure 1.

(ii) Location error in the extraction of feature points, such as bending points, inflection points or maximum curvature, and inadequate selection of knots in line approximation. In most case, this causes lack of smoothness.

(iii) Delicate mismatch among the directions or the lengths of the vectors forming the total shape. For example, most building shapes, shown on an urban planning map, have several parallel vectors. This is a geometrical property expected by humans. However, the vectorized shapes do not always rigidly maintain the above property due to delicate error in knot location. This error cannot be overcome by local processing techniques alone. Human perception senses a kind of "dirtiness" in the entire vectorized shape.

Of the three types, (i) and (ii) are local distortions, while (iii) is a global distortion.

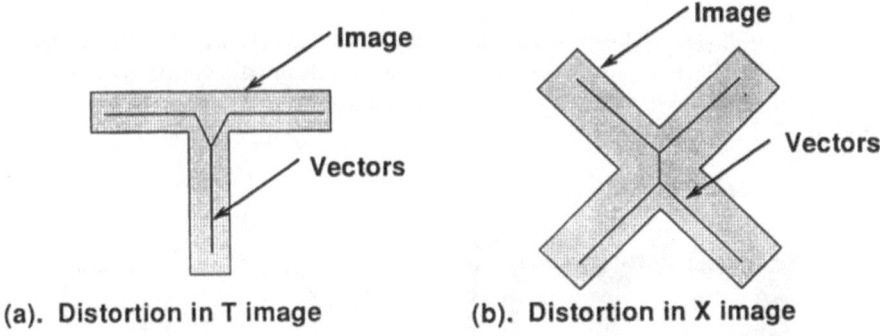

(a). Distortion in T image   (b). Distortion in X image

Fig. 1. Local distortion categories.

2.2 Approach

Considering the above-mentioned three distortion levels, a powerful recovering method for high quality vectorization has been designed. A functional block-diagram is shown in Figure 2. Pre-vectorization, which accomplishes line structure extraction, feature point detection and line approximation has been proposed [13] as an efficient and effective method for this processing. This method has been adopted to obtain the pre-vectorized shape without distortion caused by simple noise, such as short line segments.

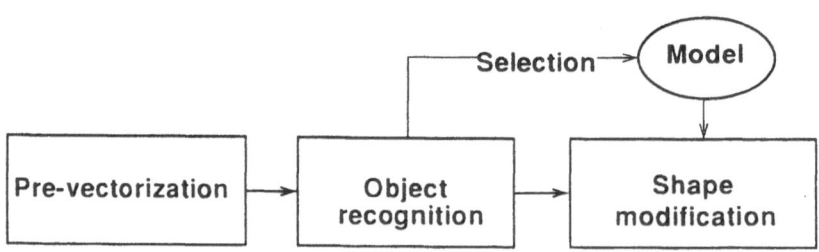

Fig. 2. Three sub-processes for high-quality vectorization.

Many techniques for recovering from local distortions (i) [8, 9, 10, 11] and (ii) [7] in the previous section have been proposed. However, they do not take distortion (iii), into consideration. It is observed that conventional methods are not applicable for line patterns such as buildings or roads in a map as shown in Figure 3(a). Mismatch in the sense of (iii) often occurs, because humans have a relatively severe shape model for these patterns in mind as shown in Figure 3(b). However, such patterns can not be strictly defined as templates because of variable shapes, although their shapes do obey certain rules. A generic model is introduced for the description of such rules. For example, generic properties such as: "The object is a polygon whose corners all have 90 degree angles," or "The object is composed of pairs of parallel lines" are described in the model. The pre-vectorized shape is improved in the form of a desirable shape which matches the generic model. Object recognition is accomplished in order to decide which object model is to be used for shape modification.

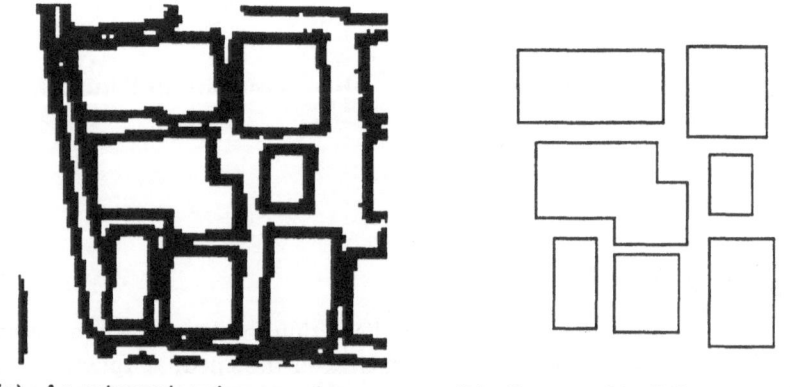

(a). An urban planning map image   **(b). Expected buildings vectors**

Fig. 3. Raster image and expected building vector.

Shape modification can be formalized as an optimization problem by introducing a generic object model, that is: (i) a cost function which outputs the similarity between the current vectorized shape and the generic model is defined; and (ii) each knot of the vectorized shape is shifted in a certain manner until the most optimal shape, which means minimum cost, is obtained. The optimization flow is shown in Figure 4. The initial input is a pre-vectorized shape. Knot shifting means a slight adjustment for shape quality improvement. The limit for the shifting distance is given *a priori* to preserve vectorization accuracy. The number of combinations for the knot shifting becomes larger as the shifting limit becomes larger. In that case, a strategy which reduces the number of combinations is needed to shorten processing time. An example of the strategy is shown in the next section.

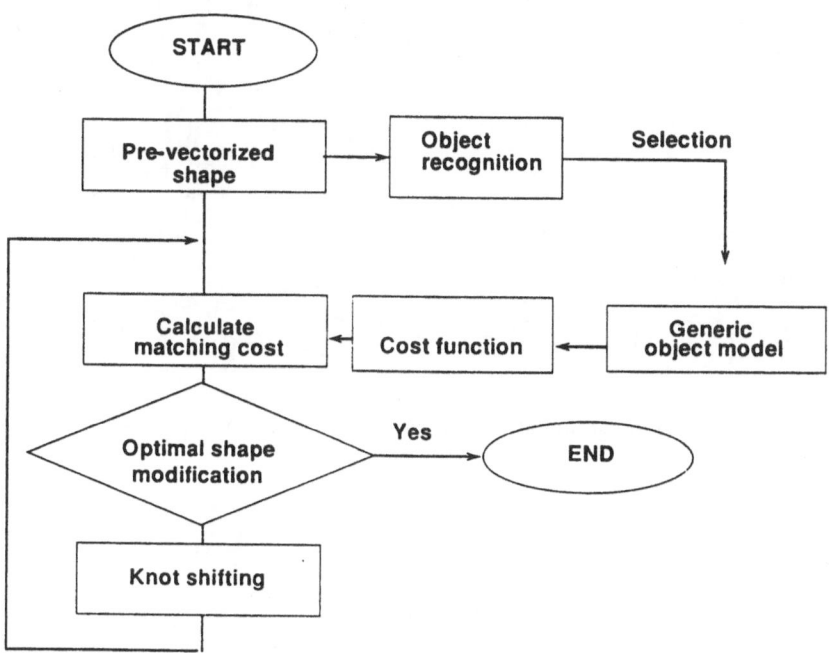

Fig. 4. Shape modification flowchart.

3 High Quality Vectorization for Buildings on Maps

In this section, the proposed method is applied to geographical maps used for urban planning. An example is shown in Figure 5. The vectorization process consists of three stages: pre-vectorization, object recognition and shape modification.

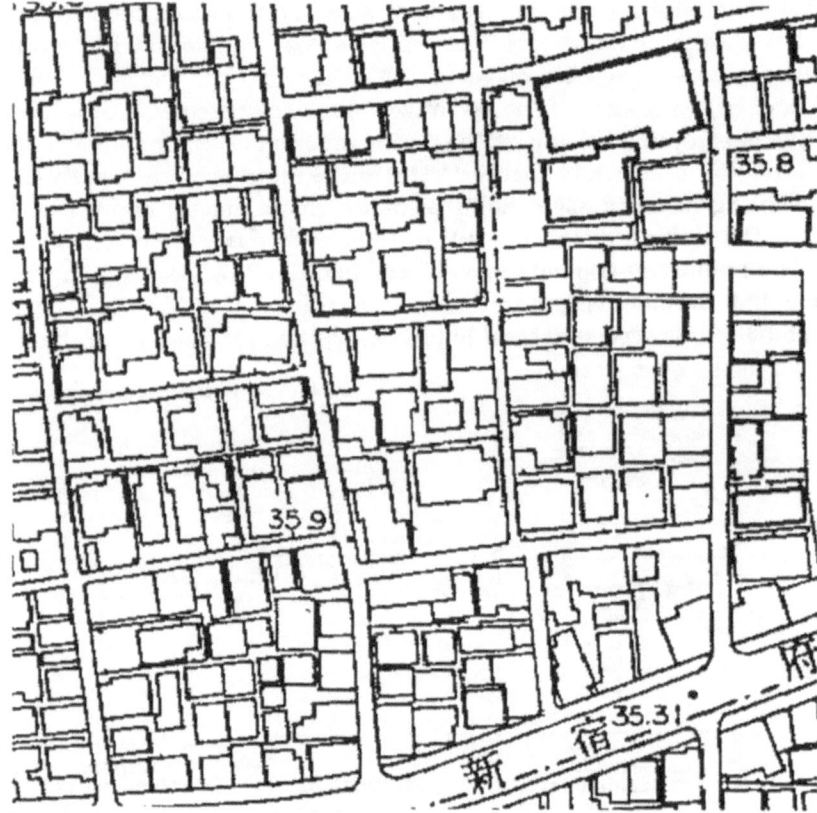

Fig. 5. Original map image for Shinjuku ward in Tokyo.

3.1 Pre-vectorization

In the pre-vectorization stage, candidate shapes for buildings are extracted and vectorized. Buildings are represented by their outline in maps. They are basically an isolated closed polygon. Candidate extraction can be accomplished by finding out closed loops. However, because building shapes touch neighboring ones and road boundaries in way places, it is not appropriate to use external contours for the closed loop extraction. Moreover, the thinning operation causes large distortions in shape when such touches occur. Therefore, internal contours are used to represent building candidates. Every internal contour is then eroded by a half of the line width, which is a predetermined value for a specific map. The resultant internal contour can be regarded as the skeleton of the original line. A vector sequence for the contour is finally generated using a line approximation algorithm.

3.2 Object Recognition

Candidate shapes for buildings include true buildings, loops surrounded by buildings, small loops in characters, and so on. In the object recognition stage, true building polygons are selected by a pattern recognition method described below. Two features, simpleness and size of a shape, are used for the recognition. The simpleness measure of a shape is defined as $area/(perimeter^2)$ [14]. The thresholds for the features are statistically determined. Figure 6 shows a two dimensional distribution of feature values for buildings and other loops. The number of samples was about 3,500, including 2,500 building polygons and 1,000 other loops. The symbol □ indicates buildings and × indicates other loops. Three lines as shown in Figure 6 which separate the distribution into two categories are found. Building polygons are effectively distinguished by the three lines. Line a and line b mean the size and simpleness threshold, respectively. Line c indicates that more complex buildings are allowed by the increasing size. This is because a large building is able to have a sufficiently large living space in spite of its complex shape.

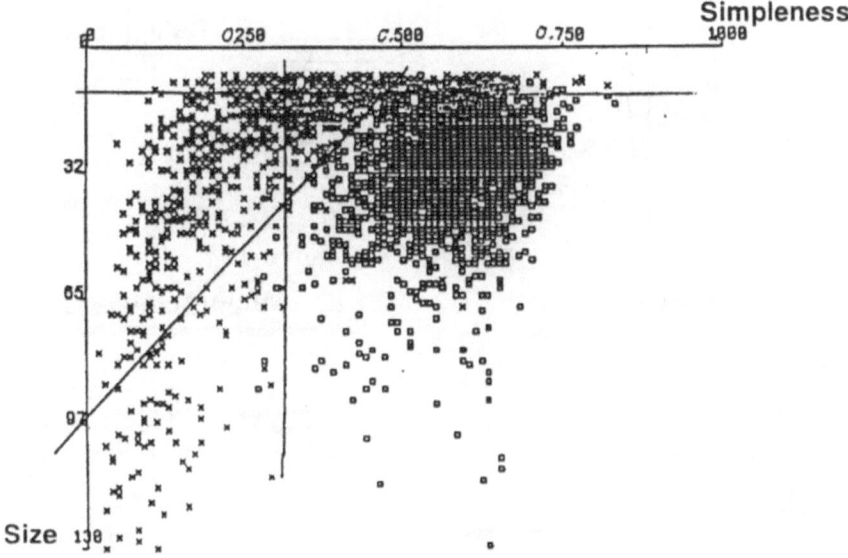

Fig. 6. Graph of relations between size and simpleness on closed polygons (□ are buildings, × are not buildings).

3.3 Shape-modification Based on a Generic Object Model

In this stage, the vector sequence obtained in the pre-vectorization stage is interactively modified so that the cost function derived from the generic model is minimized. The generic model of a building is described by the following two statements: (a) The building shape is a simple polygon. (b) The relation between the sides of a polygon is parallel or perpendicular, when and if possible. The cost function for this generic model is defined as follows. Figure 7(b) shows the histogram of the vector orientation weighted by the vector length. The horizontal axis indicates the frequency weighted by the vector length. The vertical axis indicates the vector orientation. If a building has a desirable shape, the histogram should have two sharp peaks whose distance along the vertical axis is 90 degrees. By taking the modulus of 90 for the orientation angle, Figure 7(b) is transformed into Figure 7(c) which has a single peak to simplify the evaluation. It is clear that all the vectors are either parallel or perpendicular to each other if the peak is single. Moreover, there are no redundant vectors, so the building is represented by the simplest possible polygon. Consequently, the variance for the histogram stands for the cost function.

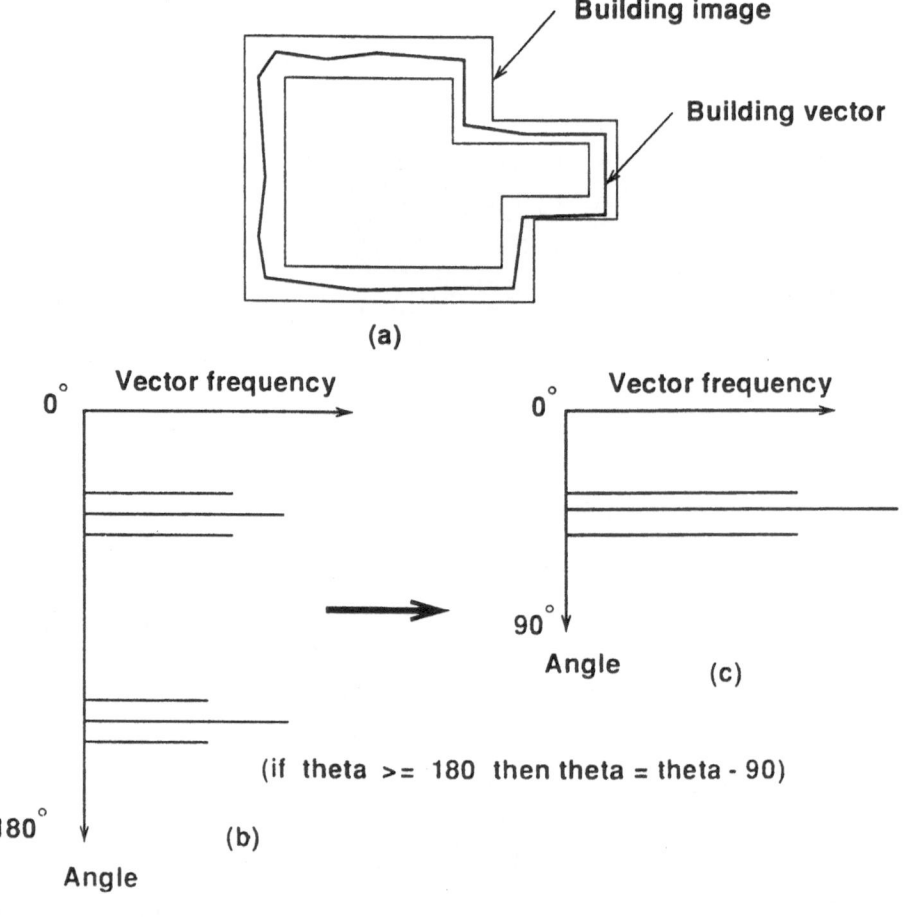

Fig. 7. Illustration of shape-modification for a building.

The next step is to select a combination of knot points for a vector sequence which minimizes the cost function. Knot points can be shifted within a certain range under the restriction that no vectors should stick out from the inside of an image of a building, as shown in Figure 8. If a building has m knot points and the shiftable range is $n \times n$ pixels, then the number of combinations would be enormous: $n^2 m$. Therefore, a relaxation method is employed to save on computation time. For a knot point, the histograms after shifting in $n \times n$ ways are evaluated and the best position for the knot point is determined. This operation is repeated for all the m knot points until a minimum variance is achieved for the histogram, as shown in the flow chart in Figure 9. The iterative k times operation reduce the calculation time to $n^2 m k$ and the histogram gradually forms a single sharp peak. The k times depends on drawings and determined empirically. Figure 10 shows an example of shape modification results. The shape of an extracted building, as shown in Figure 10(c), is modified into a good-shape, as shown in Figure 10(d). The round corner is sharpened and the relation between individual lines becomes vertical or parallel. A redundant knot point is also successfully eliminated. Histograms, as shown in Figure 10(b), indicate that the directions of lines are concentrated on a local peak after shape modification. Figure 11 shows several buildings before and after shape modification. Figure 12 shows the result of buildings extracted and modified from the image in Figure 5.

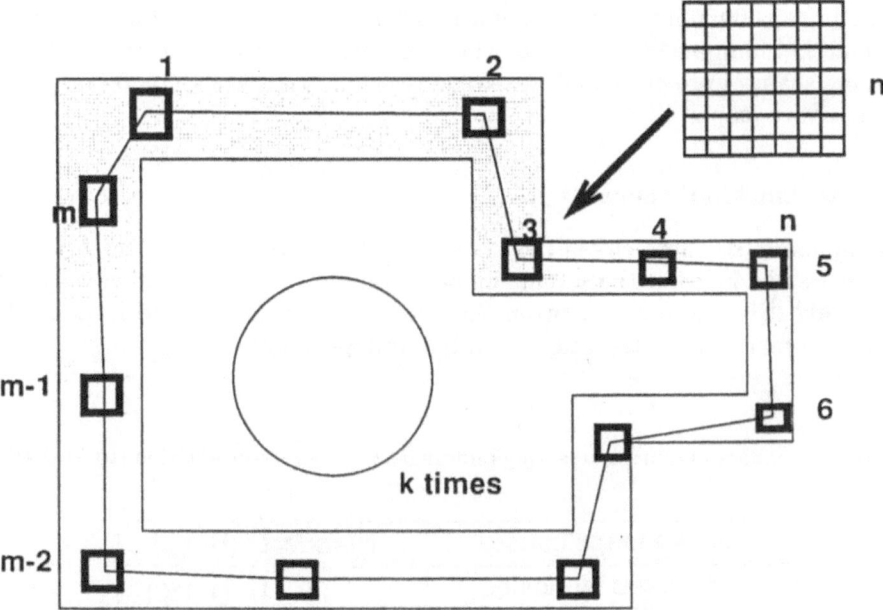

Fig. 8. Knot shifting ranges for vectors.

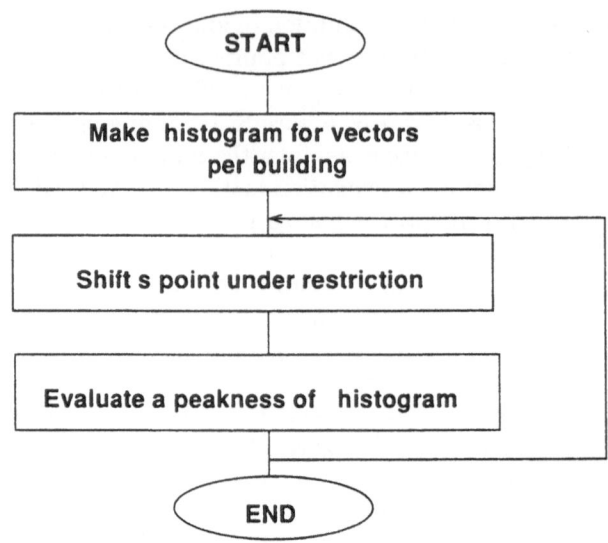

Fig. 9. Building shape modification process flowchart.

4 Experimental Results

About 65,000 buildings were extracted from twelve sheets of urban planning maps, 1000 × 600 mm in size, having a 1:2500 scale, with a resolution of 8 pixels per mm, in Shinjuku Ward, Tokyo. The recognition accuracy and the quality of building shapes were evaluated in sixteen selected local areas(64 × 64 mm size) on the above maps.

4.1 Recognition Accuracy

The number of isolated closed-polygons extracted in the first pre-vectorization process was 3,448, while the actual number of buildings was 2597. Some polygons were broken by noises and written characters on the map. Table 1 shows the number of failures in extracting actual building-polygons.

Table 1. Number of failures extracting buildings in first pre-vectorization (total: 2597).

Broken loops cause	Number	(Ratio)
Interrupted by noises	29	(1.1%)
Interrrupted by characters	53	(2.0%)
Total	82	(3.2%)

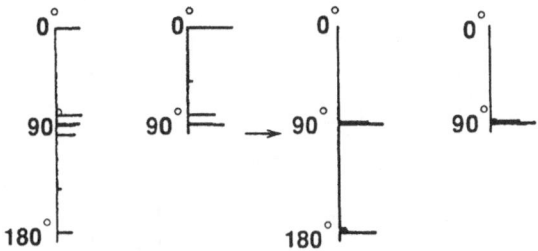

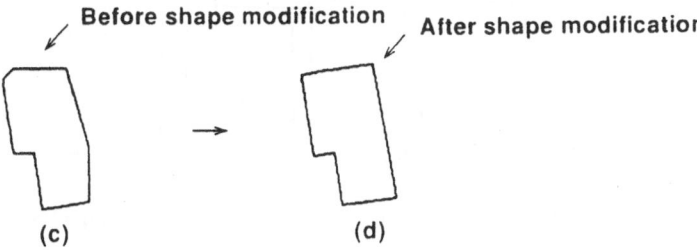

(a) Histograms before modification (b) Histograms after modification

Before shape modification   After shape modification

(c)   (d)

Fig. 10. Shape modification result.

After object recognition by the machine, a human checked the actual buildings. Table 2 shows the confusion matrix for object recognition. The correct building identification rate is the ratio of the number of extracted buildings to the number of actual buildings. The correct rate for other polygons is the ratio of the number of other polygons to that of incorrectly extracted other polygons. The experimental results indicate the correct ratio of buildings and other polygons were 98.2% and 93.9%, respectively. The system fails to recognize actual buildings as buildings in case that corners of buildings are not detected in pre-vectorization stage because they are not so sharp.

Table 2. Confusion matrix for building object recognition.

Human\machine	Buildings	Others	Total	Correct ratio
Buildings	2469	46	2515	98.2%
Others	58	875	933	93.9%
Total	2527	921	3448	97.0%

Pre-Vectorization should be improved in corner extraction robustness. On the other hand, most errors in elimination of other polygons are caused by misrecognition of holes in kanji characters and meaningless loops, as shown in Figure 5. In order to remove these errors, the system should deal with high level information, that is, contextual relations among elements in a map. That will be our

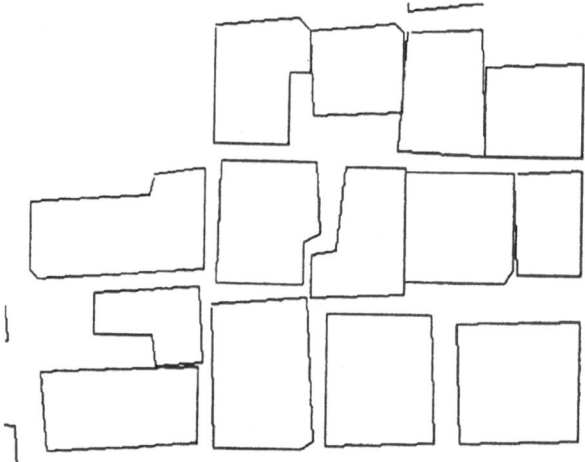

(a) Several buildings before shape modification

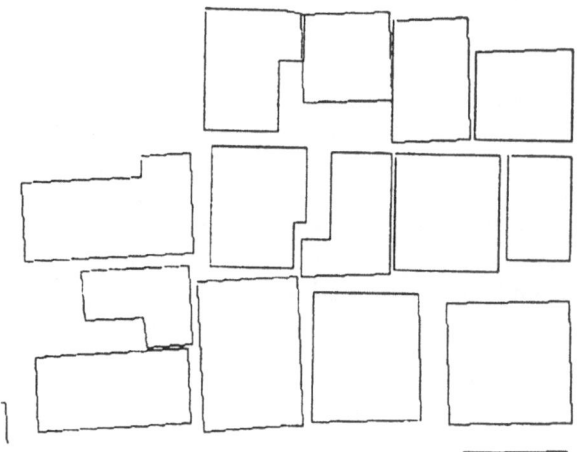

(b) Several buildings after shape modification

Fig. 11. Shape modification result.

future works. Consequently, 128 (82+46) building images failed to be extracted and 95.1% ((2597-128)/2597) of actual buildings images were extracted and recognized from these maps. 95.1% is a high rate. If all extracted buildings were acceptable, hand digitizing operation would have been reduced to one twentieth.

4.2 Shape Quality Evaluation

Shape quality evaluation was carried out by several human inspectors. A standard with four levels of quality, as shown in Table 3, was decided upon from

error

Fig. 12. Buildings extracted from a map of Shinjuku ward, Tokyo.

three points: the corner feature, shape quality and line location accuracy. A higher level indicated better shape quality. Building images in level 1 were not acceptable for the human perceptual criterion. Level 2 or 3 was equal to the quality for building shapes extracted with a hand digitizer. Buildings in Level 4 had perfect shapes. It is difficult to achieve Level 4 using a hand digitizer.

Tables 4 and 5 show the evaluation results for shapes before and after shape modification for the selected 885 buildings. Only 80% of the buildings were acceptable before shape modification. On the other hand, about 98% of the buildings were acceptable after shape modification while still retaining the location accuracy of the vectors. Moreover, the shapes of buildings in each level were improved in quality. The overall performance is shown in Table 6. Consequently, a high rate of 93.6% (95.1% x 98.4%) acceptable building shapes was successfully extracted by the proposed method. Hand digitizing operations were reduced to one twelfth.

Table 3. Building shape standards.

Worse   Not acceptable

Level\item	Corner feature	Shape	Location accuracy
1	With ambiguous corners	Poor	Outside line width (but not always)
2	With necessary corners	Normal	within line width
3	With sharp corners	Good	within line width
4	With minimum corners	Very good	within line width

Better   Acceptable

Table 4. Evaluation of shapes of buildings before shape modification.

Level	1	2	3	4	Total
Number	178	184	196	327	885
Ratio	20.1%	20.8%	22.1%	36.9%	100%

$\vdash$———— 79.9% ————$\dashv$

Table 5. Evaluation of shapes of buildings after shape modification.

Level	1	2	3	4	Total
Number	14	51	175	642	885
Ratio	1.6%	5.8%	19.8%	72.5%	100%

$\vdash$———— 98.4% ————$\dashv$

Table 6. Ratio of available buildings.

Process	Ratio
Object recognition	95.1%
Shape modification	98.4%
Total	93.6%

5 Conclusion

A new method for high quality vectorization has been proposed, which significantly improves the shape of buildings extracted from geographic maps. A generic model for building shapes was defined and effectively translated into a cost function which drove the extraction. The method is applicable to vectorization of other objects by changing the object model and defining a corresponding cost function.

Acknowledgment

The authors wish to thank Haruo Asada for his constructive discussions and useful suggestions.

References

[1] K. Ramchandran, "Coding Method for Vector Representation of Engineering Drawings," *Proc. IEEE* 68, pp. 813–817, 1980.

[2] M. Ejiri *et al.*, "Automatic Recognition of Design Drawings and Maps," *Proc. 7th ICPR*, Montreal, pp. 1296–1305, 1984.

[3] A. Okazaki *et al.*, "An Automatic Circuit Diagram Reader with Loop-structure-based Symbol Recognition," In *IEEE Trans. on PAMI*, Vol.10 No.3, pp. 331–340, 1988.

[4] A. Maeda and J. Shibayama, "Application of Automatic Drawing Reader for the Utility Management System," *IEEE Computer Society Workshop on CAPAIDM*, pp. 139–145, 1985.

[5] S. Suzuki and T. Yamada, "MARIS, Map recognizing input system," *Proc. Int'l Workshop on Industrial Applications of Machine Vision and Machine Intelligence*, Feb. 1987, p. 214.

[6] M. Sakauchi and Y. Ohsawa, "The AI-MUDAMS, The drawing processor based on the multidimensional pattern data structure," *Proc. IEEE Computer Society Workshop on CAPAIDM*, 1985, p. 146.

[7] S. Suzuki, "Graph-based Vectorization Method for Mine Patterns," *Proc. IEEE Computer Vision and Pattern Recognition*, pp. 616–621, 1988.

[8] C. Williams, "An Efficient Algorithm for the Piecewise Linear Approximation of Planar Curves," *Computer Graphics and Image Processing* 8, pp. 286–293, 1978.

[9] C. Williams, "Bounded straight-line approximation of digitized planar curves," *Computer Graphics and Image Processing* 16, pp. 370–381, 1981.

[10] J. Sklansky and V. Gonzales, "Fast polygonal approximation of digitized curves," *Pattern Recognition* 12, pp. 327–331, 1980.

[11] Y. Kurozumi and W. Davis, "Polygonal approximation by the minimax method," *Computer Graphics and Image Processing* 19, pp. 248–264, 1981.

[12] T. Pavlidis and C. J. Van Wyk, "An Automatic Beautifier for Drawings and Illustrations," *Proc. ACM SIGGRAPH '85*, pp. 225–234, 1985.

[13] S. Shimotsuji *et al.*, "A High Speed Raster-to-vector Conversion using Special Hardware for Contour Tracing," in *Proc. IAPR Workshop on COMPUTER VISION* (Special Hardware and Industrial applications), pp. 18–23, 1988.

[14] A. Rosenfeld and A. C. Kak, *Digital Picture Processing*, 2nd Edition, pp.265–266, Academic Press, NY (1982).

Recognizing Hand-Drawn Electrical Circuit Symbols with Attributed Graph Matching

Seong-Whan Lee

Department of Computer Science,[1] Chungbuk National University, Cheongju, Chungbuk 360–763, Republic of Korea

We propose a model-based approach to the recognition of hand-drawn electrical circuit symbols under arbitrary unknown similarity transformations (translation, rotation, and scale). A hybrid representation, called an attributed graph (AG), incorporating structural and statistical characteristics of image patterns, is used for matching an unknown symbol to models. We describe experimental results that suggest that AG matching is effective and efficient for this problem.

1 Introduction

CAD (Computer Aided Design) systems have been recognized as the most important tools for achieving advanced automation. The CAD performs a variety of functions: circuit analysis, logic simulation, test pattern generation, test type editing, layout design and generation, artwork data editing, and artwork checking, which are accomplished by various CAD software. The integrated CAD system automatically converts diagram into test tape and artwork tape [1, 2, 3, 4].

Although CAD is growing in importance, the initial design of circuit and logic diagrams is still often created manually by experienced engineers and manually drawn circuit diagrams are still often used in practice as important means for communication. Therefore, there is a need to extract the relevant data from a given diagram and to store it in a computer. The process of extracting relevant data is often performed manually or in an interactive manner, using a digitizing tablet, for example. Due to the imperfect performance of human operators, this process is rather time consuming and gives raise to several errors. As a consequence, there is an interest in industry in performing the recognition task leading from the diagram to its description automatically and automating the input process has been recognized as an important step in augmenting engineering design productivity and enhancing existing CAD capabilities [1, 2, 3, 4, 5, 6, 7, 8, 9, 10, 11, 12, 13, 14, 15, 16, 17, 18, 19, 20, 21]. Understanding diagrams by "seeing" is the ultimate goal of the input process automation.

---

[1] This work was supported in part by the System Engineering Research Institute, Korea Institute of Science and Technology under contract 90T032.

Schematic diagrams used in CAD systems include electrical circuit diagrams, flow charts, process diagrams, construction drawings, and piping and instrument diagrams. These diagrams consist of many components which can be classified into three groups: symbols, interconnection structures and denotations[1, 5, 6, 7, 8, 9, 10, 11, 12, 14, 20]. Figure 1 shows a typical example of an electrical circuit diagram.

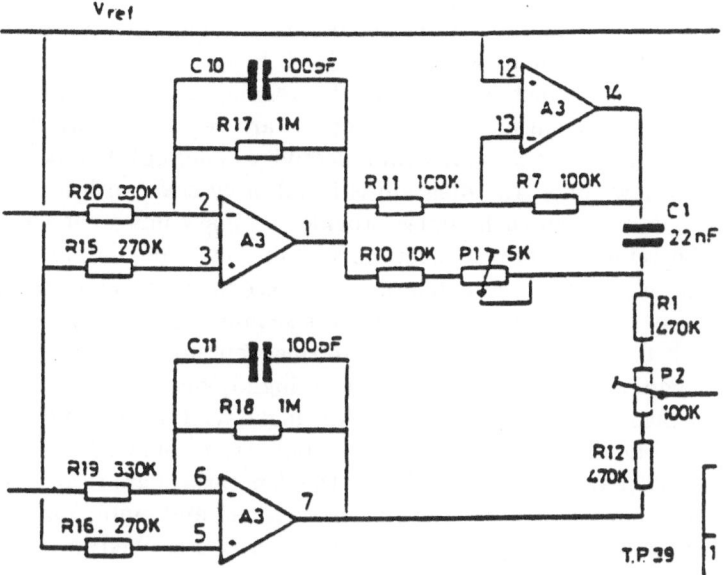

Fig. 1. An example of an electrical circuit diagram.

Symbols represent single elements in a schematic diagram. For each symbol there exist several terminals defining those points where symbols can be connected among each other. Interconnection structures are represented by straight horizontal or vertical lines emanating at the terminals of symbols. Denotations are character strings used for several purposes in schematic diagram. First, denotations can define physical properties of elements. The string "100pF" attached to a capacitor means, for example, the capacitance being 100pF. Second, denotations can be used for defining special elements. The denotation "A3" attached to an amplifier can define, for example, the special type of this amplifier among all other types. Third, denotations can be used for identifying certain components in a circuit diagram, *e.g.*, the terminals of a symbol. More than just one diagram is used normally for the representation of complex circuit. If one and the same element occurs in more than one diagram, it can be uniquely identified if identical denotations are used. The meaning of the individual components and the relation among them compose the information which a diagram presents. For understanding diagrams we have to discriminate each components, extract their meanings, and identify the relations among them; in short, recognize the diagrams given as image.

Study on the schematic diagram understanding has mainly concentrated on the understanding of electrical circuit diagrams [1, 2, 3, 6, 7, 8, 9, 10, 11, 13, 15, 16, 17, 20]. Several methods for recognizing electrical circuit diagrams have been studied such as syntactic methods based on decision trees [1, 3, 8, 9, 15, 20] and a programmed graph grammar [4], consistent labeling approaches [2, 19, 22], graph theoretic methods [11, 13, 14], a knowledge-based approach [16] and statistical methods using characteristic features [17, 18, 21].

Though most of existing approaches obtained their input images from the simple thresholding of the diagram image [1, 4, 5, 6, 8, 9, 10, 12, 13, 15, 16, 17, 18, 21], the diagrams which are available for reading are seldom just black and white. Due to their age, a number of diagrams are degraded; both line-drawing and background will have non-uniform reflectivity (shading). Furthermore, after being copied a few times, the diagram is in full grey scale with a great deal of noise. Thresholding from such copies provides a binary image which cannot be processed. Therefore, we are considering the full grey scale diagrams.

In general, electrical circuit diagrams are recognized through the following processing steps (Figure 2). The first step is scanning of a diagram image and thresholding it to obtain a binary image. In this step, noise removal and shading correction techniques may be used to obtain high quality input image. Second, the binary image is separated into line-drawings (symbols and interconnection structures) and denotations. Third, the symbols are recognized. Fourth, the interconnection structures are coded. Fifth, the denotations are recognized. Sixth, user interaction for the identification of unidentified and ambiguous symbols is performed. Finally, the electrical circuit diagram is described in the format of the CAD system database.

Since the denotations are expressed in terms of a character string, it appears that denotation recognition may be treated as separate research topic, *i.e.*, character recognition in a text. An important step in the recognition of electrical circuit diagrams is the separation of the binary image into symbols, interconnection structures and denotations [1, 5, 6, 7, 8, 9, 10, 11, 12, 14, 20]. We follow a top-down approach proposed by Groen and Munster [7], in which first the global topology of the electrical circuit diagram is investigated and different components in it are separated in advance from each other using cellular Logic (or morphologic) operations [26, 27] and component labeling and afterwards the different components found in the global analysis are recognized [32]. In this paper, we focus on the problem of recognizing symbols in electrical circuit diagrams in the absence of any information concerning the pose (translation, rotation and scale) of them. A new approach for separating different components in circuit diagrams will be described in [33].

In our scheme, a symbol is represented by an attributed graph (AG) which consists of a set of vertices and segments connecting them. AG is a hybrid representation incorporating structural and statistical characteristics of image patterns [11, 23, 24]. Both to the vertices and segments, various attributes may be attached. When observations as well as models are represented in AG, the problem of symbol recognition can be formulated as the problem of matching

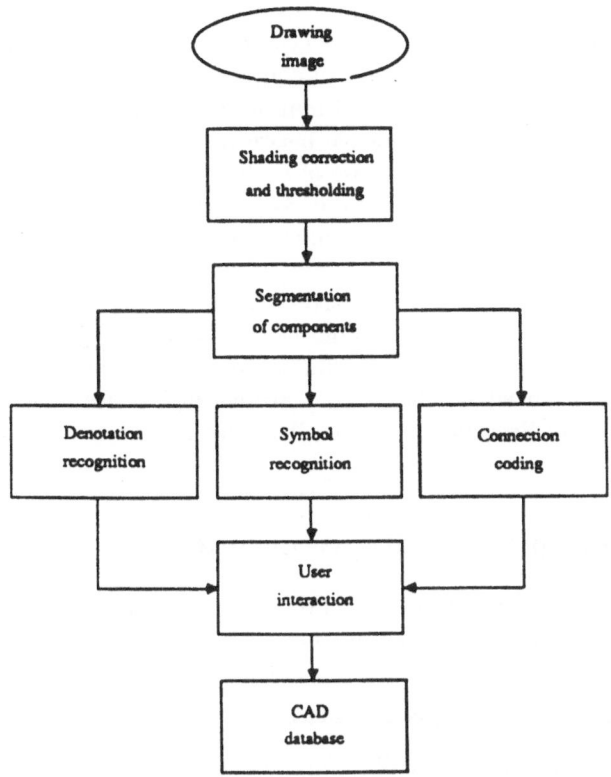

Fig. 2. An architecture for general electrical circuit diagram recognition system.

an observed AG (AG_O) against model AG's ($AG_M's$) to select one with the minimum distance.

Our scheme begins with an assumption that a particular set of vertices, called control vertices, are found reliably in observations. The use of control vertices yields two advantages. First, the amount of data to be processed is reduced by considering only control vertices. Therefore, the problem becomes tractable. Second, undesirable errors which may result from dealing with unstable vertices are minimized. In our current implementation, control vertices are selected manually from the AG_M during the model learning stage. In doing so, a few considerations should be made: First, control vertices must be stable. This means they must have a high probability of occurrence and, therefore, they are almost always present in $AG_O's$. Second, control vertices must contain reliable information about the pose of the AG_O. In other words, they should be in their general position in 2-D space, *i.e.*, they should not be in collinear position nor too close to each other.

The process of AG matching proceeds as follows. First, an AG_O is constructed from single-pixel-width line-representations of an observed symbol. Then, the pose of AG_O is estimated in terms of translation, rotation and scale with respect to each of $AG_M's$, based on the fast minimum square error transform we devised. By introducing the concept of control vertex and applying geometrical constraints in an early stage, a small number of candidate $AG_M's$ are selected. At the next step, the correspondence between components of observed AG after normalization ($AG_O{}^N$) and those of each AG_M is found for the given pose. Finally, distances between $AG_O{}^N$ and $AG_M's$ are calculated, based upon the correspondences, and $AG_O{}^N$ is classified as the AG_M with the minimum distance.

The rest of this paper is organized as follows. Section 2 describes an AG representation for observed and model electrical circuit symbol. A method for recognizing symbols using AG matching is presented in Section 3. In Section 4, the learning stage in which the $AG_M's$ are learned is described. Experimental results are given in Section 5, and, finally, concluding remarks are discussed in Section 6.

2 Construction of AG Representation

In this Section, we define attributes of our AG representation and describe construction steps for the AG representation.

2.1 Definition of AG Representation

Attributes of the AG are typically numerical measurements of the local structure formed by the primitives (segments or vertices) in single-pixel-width line-representation of a symbol. For the segment primitive, the length, the curvature and two vertices it connects are attributed. For the vertex primitive, the position, the type (end, corner or junction), the list of segments attached to this vertex and the list of angles of segments attached to this vertex are attributed. A typical example of an AG for the observed symbol is shown in Figure 3.

Quantitative informations are attached to these attributes and used to improve the efficiency of matching by constraining possible structural correspondences, as well as to improve the matching accuracy and reliability. These attributes also make it possible to calculate the degree of the match. So they give a probabilistic basis to how good a vertex or a segment matches. The AG_M is constructed during the learning stage and contains statistical attributes of the vertices and segments. For the segment, these are the number of occurrences, mean length, the variance in the length, mean curvature, and variance in curvature. For the vertex, these are the number of occurrences, the mean position, the variance in position, and the histogram of the number of segments.

2.2 Construction of an AG

2.2.1 Fast skeletonization. After shading correction and thresholding, the symbol patterns are processed to obtain their skeletons using the fast skeletonization algorithm of Vliet and Verwer [28]. Detailed description on shading

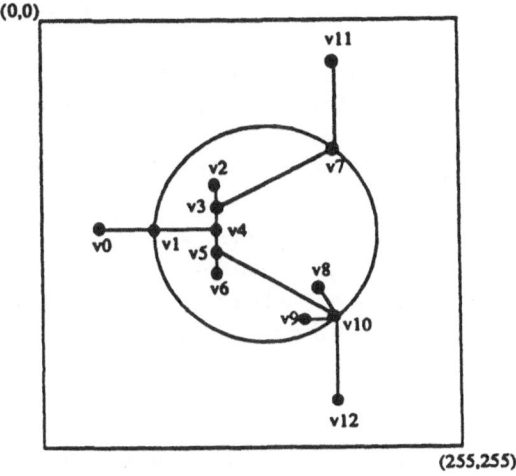

(0,0)

(255,255)

This AG consists of 13 vertices and 13 segments.

v_0: position: (15, 120), type: end, segment list: (s_0), angle list: (0)

v_1: position: (30, 120), type: junction, segment list: (s_0,s_1,s_2,s_3), angle list: (180,0,30,-30)

.
.

v_{12}: position: (150, 240), type: end, segment list: (s_{12}), angle list: (90)

s_0: length: 30, curvature: 0, adjacent vertex list: (v_0,v_1)

s_1: length: 50, curvature: 0, adjacent vertex list: (v_1,v_4)

.
.

s_{12}: length: 70, curvature: 0, adjacent vertex list: (v_7,v_{10})

Fig. 3. Graphical representation of a typical AG for an observed symbol.

correction and thresholding algorithms used is available on [25]. The key principle of the skeletonization algorithm is to process object contours. A queue is implemented to store the contours in each iteration for the next iteration. The contour can be passed from one operation to another as well. The time complexity of the algorithm is linear with the number of contour elements to be processed. The algorithm has been proven to be faster than any other known algorithm.

2.2.2 Line-tracking and piecewise segment approximation. AG's are constructed from these skeletons of symbol patterns. First, the different types of pixels in the skeleton image are marked: end, corner and junction pixels. A line-tracking technique is applied in which the different skeleton parts are found. An end of a skeleton part is found when an end, a junction or a starting pixel (closed contour) is encountered during the tracking. Next, the parts are approximated by piecewise straight or circular line-segments as follows:

1. The maximum distance is calculated between the part and the straight line-segment.
2. When this distance exceeds a threshold dc, a circular line-segment is calculated through the endpoints of the skeleton part and the pixel in the middle of the part.
3. The maximum distance between the circular line-segment and the skeleton part is calculated.
4. When this maximum distance is smaller than the one of the straight line approximation, the circular approximation is used.
5. When the maximum distance exceeds a threshold d_{max}, the skeleton part is split at the pixel of maximum distance to the straight line.
6. Above five steps are repeated on both resulting parts until the d_{max} condition is satisfied.

The AG representing the symbol pattern is built during the line tracking and piecewise approximation. The two initial end pixels of the skeleton part are of the type end; the pixels where the skeleton part is split are of the type corner. When the maximum distance between skeleton part and straight or circular line-segment is smaller than d_{min}, the segment is added to the list.

2.2.3 Error recovery. Because only the different line-segments, which might be split, are found during the contour-tracking, junctions have to be recovered afterwards. This gives in addition the possibility of incorporating the recovery of junctions which disappeared because of gaps in line-segments. The recovery consists of following steps:

1. Two close end points within a threshold d_{min} from each other are joined.
2. All segments with at least one end point and shorter than a threshold d_{min} are removed.
3. All other segments shorter than a threshold d_{min} are absorbed.
4. End points within a distance d_{min} from a straight or a circular line-segment are attached to it, resulting in a junction and the splitting of the straight or circular line-segment.
5. Two close segments within a threshold d_{min} from each other are joined.
6. Corners between straight line-segments with an angle close to 180° are deleted and the segments are joined.
7. Small loops are deleted.

3 Attributed Graph Matching

In the AG matching procedure, an unknown AG_O is matched to the different $AG'_M s$ and the AG_O is classified as the AG_M with the minimum distance. The normalized positions of the vertices in the AG_O are determined by the fast computational method for minimum square error transform [30]. This transform is described by a parameter vector, (r_0, s_0, Θ, c) where r_0, s_0 is the translation,

Θ is the rotation, c is the scale, such that the image (x_i, y_i) of an arbitrary point (r_i, s_i) of the AG_M is given by the following set of equations.

$$x_i = c \, cos\Theta(r_i - r_0) + c \, sin\Theta(s_i - s_0) \qquad (1a)$$

$$y_i = -c \, sin\Theta(r_i - r_0) + c \, cos\Theta(s_i - s_0) \qquad (1b)$$

Given an AG_O, a hypothesis (*i.e.*, a prediction of the position of the AG_O with respect to the AG_M) is generated by matching a set of control vertices in the AG_M to a set of compatible vertices in the AG_O.

3.1 Pose Estimation

In order to find the pose of the AG_O, the degree of the match between a vertex in the AG_O and a control vertex in the AG_M is calculated based upon pose-independent attribute of a vertex. The pose-independent attributes of each vertex can be the types of the vertex and angles between segments of the vertex. When the attributes are reliable and the AG_M is stable, there should exist only a few correspondences between a control vertex in the AG_M and a few vertices in the AG_O. When individual vertices do not carry sufficient information and, therefore, do not strongly constrain the number of possible correspondences, the geometry of combination of vertices can help.

We define an m-tuple control vertex vector by ordered m control vertices, and an m-tuple correspondence as a match between m-tuple control vertex vectors in the AG_M and the AG_O. An example of 4-tuple control vertex vector in the AG of Figure 3 can be (V_0, V_1, V_2, V_6).

In 2-D, we have to find 4 parameters (2 for translation, 1 for rotation, and 1 for scale). So the problem has four degrees of freedom. This means that two control vertices are the smallest number we can use to find the parameters. (Each control vertex gives 2 equations, 1 for x coordinate and 1 for y coordinate.) However, we are in that case very sensitive to noise present in the measurement of the position of the control vertices. That is the reason that we want to find a minimum square error transform. From a statistical point of view, we want to use as much control vertices as we can find. Unfortunately, the number of control vertices is a trade off between the computational burden and availability of control vertices on one side and the accuracy on the other. In our current implementation, quadruple correspondence (*i.e.*, the control vertex vector is 4-tuple) was used in order to make the problem much more tractable. Therefore, our pose estimation strategy involves generating 4-tuple correspondences between control vertices of the AG_M and vertices of the AG_O. The performance evaluation on the trade off is available on [32].

To incorporate geometric features in the matching of the control vertices, the set of control vertices is split into subsets of pairs. If there are n vertices in the AG_O, this results in $_nC_2 = n(n-1)/2$ candidate control vertex pairs to be evaluated. A control vertex pair has 4 degrees of freedom: position (2), orientation (1), and the distance between the vertices (1). Assuming that the scale is approximately known (eg. from the segment length distribution), the likelihood that a candidate control vertex pair in the AG_O corresponds to a control vertex pair in the AG_M can be calculated from this distance. Among them, only the 2n most likely candidate control vertex pairs are selected for further analysis. These 2n candidate control vertex pairs are combined to form candidate 4-tuple control vertex vectors. A candidate 4-tuple control vertex vector has 8 degrees of freedom: position and orientation (3), the distances of the two pairs (2), the angle between the candidate control vertex pairs (1), and the shift along the candidate control vertex pairs (2). The angle between the candidate control vertex pairs together with the pair-distances is used to calculate the degree of the match between the compatible 4-tuple control vertex vector in the AG_O and the 4-tuple control vertex vector in the AG_M.

If there are 2n candidate control vertex pairs in the AG_O, then there are as many as $_{2n}C_2 = n(2n - 1)$ candidate 4-tuple control vertex vectors to be evaluated. Among them, only the 4n most likely candidate 4-tuple control vertex vectors are selected for further analysis. Next, the fast minimum square error transform, which results in the transform parameters (translation, rotation and scale) and transform errors for the most likely 4n correspondences, is calculated. This transform has to be determined so as to minimize the transform error between the control vertex vector in the AG_M and the compatible control vertex vector in the AG_O. Then, a correspondence with minimum transform error is chosen for the best transform parameters. The transform errors obtained for candidate AG_M's are used to halt the matching if reasonable error, *i.e.*, error less than some threshold, has not been found.

3.2 Correspondence Finding and Conflict Resolution

After finding the pose of the AG_O, the positions of the vertices are known. Therefore a list of possible corresponding vertices in the AG_O is made for all the vertices in the AG_M. This primary matched list is based on the distance between the observed vertex and the model vertices in standardized coordinate system. All vertices within a distance d_{match} are considered as possible matches.

When there are multiple matches, structural information is used to resolve the ambiguity between the multiple matches. First the vertex type is considered and, when the vertex type is a corner, the angle of the corner is also taken into account. When there is still an ambiguity, the closest vertex is chosen in our current implementation.

The matched segments are found from the matched vertices. For the two vertices of each segment of the AG_O, the matched vertices of the AG_M are known, if any, and the matched model segment must be present between these two matched model vertices.

3.3 Distance Calculation

In this Section, we propose a distance measure between the AG_O and the AG_M cast in probabilistic terms. Suppose $S = (S_1, S_2, ..., S_{|S|})$ is a finite set of segments and $V = (V_1, V_2, ..., V_{|V|})$ is a finite set of vertices of the AG universe.

Then the probability that $AG_O{}^N$ is a true instance of AG_M, Prob (S, V), is defined to be

$$Prob(S, V)$$
$$= Prob(S_1, S_2, ..., S_{|S|}, V_1, V_2, ..., V_{|V|}) \tag{2}$$

By introducing independence assumption among each components (segments and vertices), Equation (2) can be expressed by

$$Prob(S, V)$$
$$= Prob(S_1)Prob(S_2)...Prob(S_{|S|})Prob(V_1)Prob(V_2)...Prob(V_{|V|})$$
$$= \prod_i Prob(S_i) \prod_j Prob(V_j) \tag{3}$$

If we adopt 3 features for each segment (chance of occurrence of the length of the segment, the chance of occurrence of the curvature of the segment, and the stability of the segment), and 3 features for each vertex (chance of occurrence of the distance between model and observed vertex, the chance of occurrence of the number of segments attached to this vertex, and the stability of the vertex), Equation (3) becomes

$$Prob(S, V)$$
$$= \prod_i Prob_{l,c,s}(S_i) \prod_j Prob_{d,n,s}(V_j) \tag{4}$$

If we assume independence among each feature in a component, Equation (4) can be expressed by

$$Prob(S, V)$$
$$= \prod_i Prob_l(S_i)Prob_c(S_i)Prob_s(S_i) \prod_j Prob_d(V_j)Prob_n(V_j)Prob_s(V_j) \tag{5}$$

As Prob (S, V) lies between 0 and 1, the distance between $AG_O{}^N$ and AG_M can be defined to be

$$DIST(AG_O^N, AG_M)$$
$$= log(1/Prob(S, V))$$
$$= -[\sum_i (logProb_l(S_i) + logProb_c(S_i) + logProb_s(S_i))$$
$$+ \sum_j (logProb_d(V_j) + logProb_n(V_j) + logProb_s(V_j))] \tag{6}$$

Therefore, the distance measure is computed by the contributions of each segment and vertex of the $AG_O{}^N$. The distance of a segment match consists of three parts based upon the chance of occurrence of the length of the segment ($Prob_l(S_i)$), the chance of occurrence of the curvature of the segment ($Prob_c(S_i)$), and the stability of the segment ($Prob_s(S_i)$). The distance of a

vertex match consists of three parts based upon the chance of occurrence of the
distance between model and observed vertex $(Prob_d(V_j))$, the chance of occurrence of the number of segments attached to this vertex $(Prob_n(V_j))$, and the
stability of the vertex $(Prob_s(V_j))$. When a segment or a vertex is not matched,
a minimum likelihood is assigned.

$Prob_s(S_i)$ and $Prob_s(V_j)$ are computed as the number of occurrences of each
s_i and v_j divided by the total number of learning samples, and $Prob_n(V_j)$ is
computed as the number of segments attached to v_j divided by histogram of
same number of segments in AG_M. $Prob_l(S_i)$, $Prob_c(S_i)$ and $Prob_d(V_j)$ are
computed in terms of a set of likelihoods indicating the conditional probability
that a component (vertex or segment) will have some particular value for some
feature in the $AG_O{}^N$, given that its corresponding feature in the AG_M has some
particular probability distribution.

Since each feature of a component (vertex or segment) except for the features
for the occurrence of a component and the number of segments attached to a
vertex occurs naturally, we have assumed that, given a sample set of observation (*i.e.*, learning set), there is a continuous distribution across some interval
of values. We model the probability density of each feature of a component by a
Gaussian (normal) distribution. A Gaussian distribution is characterized by the
clustering of values about a mean or average value. Given the standard deviation of this distribution (or given an estimated variance), well-known statistical
methods are used to compute a probability. Each model component contains the
expected values of features (*e.g.*, length and curvature for segments and distance
for vertices) as a distribution of expected value (*i.e.*, mean value and variance). A
reliable estimate of the variance can be derived from empirical evidence because
the number of observations is significant.

The final result of matching is a correspondence list and a numerical measure
of the distance of the model and the observation. The log distance values are
rarely exactly zero. Hence every component in the model increases the overall log
distance, even if it has a close match. The log distance for different models can not
be compared unless they are normalized to remove this effect. We normalize the
distance measure by dividing by the total number of correspondences included
in the distance measure.

4 Learning Model AG's

The $AG_M{}'s$ described in earlier Sections are constructed by a model learning
stage. From an ensemble of observations, which is called the "learning set,"
and, in our case, a collection of symbol images, the structural components and
their attributes are extracted to construct model. Learning is performed on the
learning set; that is, the images contain only an example of the pattern class to
be learned. This helps to assure that only the "significant" set of control vertices
are found in the AG_M.

4.1 Learning Algorithm

The learning algorithm begins with an empty AG_M. For the first symbol in the learning set, control vertices are selected by the human supervisor and following procedures are repeated for each sample symbol in the learning set:

1. A pose (translation, rotation, scale) is obtained which places the AG_M at the position, orientation, and the scale of the pattern in the sample image. This pose is hypothesized by the system and confirmed by the human supervisor.
2. For each control vertex in the AG_M, the correspondence to the most likely control vertex in the AG_O is determined and displayed.
3. As each correspondence is found, the mean and standard deviation of the probability distributions for the attributes are incrementally calculated, and the chance of occurrence for the control vertices is updated.
4. The most likely correspondences are then found for the rest of AG_O, and their probability distributions and chance of occurrences are also updated.
5. If a part of the AG_O being learned is not present in the AG_M, the AG_M may be updated and learned by adding the unmatched part to the AG_M. This addition starts with the matched vertices of the unmatched segments.

Learning is currently done with an interactive program that uses a graphic monitor. Our philosophy has been to begin with a program in which the user must verify each step, and to incrementally automate the learning process as confidence and experience are gained with each stage.

The screen of the monitor is divided into four windows. In the upper left is a "model" window, in which a copy of the first learning sample is shown. The image of the current learning sample is shown in the upper right window. At the bottom of the screen a set of text fields are maintained that provide information about learning.

Most of learning involves specifying control vertices that match. Control vertices in both the AG_O and the AG_M are indicated by drawing cursors in the overlay plane, over the model window or the learning image window.

4.2 Correspondence Finding in Model Learning

As with matching, the basic problem in learning is to find a correspondence between vertices in an AG_O and vertices in the AG_M. In some ways, the problem is easier than the general matching problem because it is known a priori that the learning sample is an instance of the model, and because restrictions can be made about the "cleanness" of the images used for learning. In other ways, the problem is harder, however, because during learning the model is only partially constructed and may not be useful in finding the best correspondence.

Our initial implementation of the learning stage is based on the assumption that the learning images are "clean," that is, the example of the pattern to be learned is the only thing in the image. In this way, the control vertices and the rest of AG to be learned can be easily found. The user is asked to approve this correspondence. The correspondence for the control vertices determines the pose of the AG to be learned.

In the learning procedure, the statistical attributes are updated after the matching and classification. If a part of the AG_O being learned is not present in the AG_M, the AG_M may be updated by adding the unmatched part to the AG_M. This addition starts with the matched vertices of the unmatched segments.

5 Experimental Results

An experimental preprocessing system was developed in order to demonstrate the possibility of the top-down approach, in which first the global topology of the electrical circuit diagram is investigated and different components in it are separated in advance from each other, and afterwards the different components found in the global analysis are recognized [7]. In the preprocessing system, scanned electrical circuit diagrams are processed to correct shading and remove noise, and components in electrical circuit diagrams are segmented. Detailed description on preprocessing techniques is available on [32].

The symbol recognition system was implemented using C programming language and works on 4.2 BSD UNIX Sun-3/50 workstation. Figure 4 shows an overview of the system.

Three different types of symbol images were used in the experiments:

1. Machine-printed electrical symbols
2. Hand-drawn electrical symbols with templates
3. Hand-drawn electrical symbols without a template

15 different classes of electrical symbols were considered in the experiments: Resistor (RES), capacitor (CAP), inductor (IND), diode (DIO), PNP transistor (PNP), NPN transistor (NPN), inverter (INV), amplifier (AMP), OR-gate (OR), AND-gate (AND), NOR-gate (NOR), NAND-gate (NAND), XOR-gate (XOR), three-state buffer (TSB), and flip flop (FF). Each symbol image is an array of 256 by 256 pixels. Figure 5 shows the standard position of symbols considered throughout this paper.

In Figure 6, the thresholded image for an observed symbol is shown and in Figure 7, the resulting skeletonized image from Figure 6 is given. Figure 8 shows the constructed AG after piecewise approximations and error recoveries from Figure 7. In Figure 9a, a typical AG_M is shown and in Figure 9b, an AG_O to be matched is given. Figure 9c shows the $AG_O{}^N$ based on the estimated pose of the AG_O. The resulting AG's showing the correspondence matching are given in Figure 9d.

The symbol images were scanned by a scanner and processed by a Sun-3 workstation. Each symbol image is an array of 256 by 256 pixels. Most of the processing time in recognition is spent in estimating the pose of the observed symbols.

A set of learning and testing samples was collected from 7 graduate students. By learning and testing samples, we mean that the former are used to construct

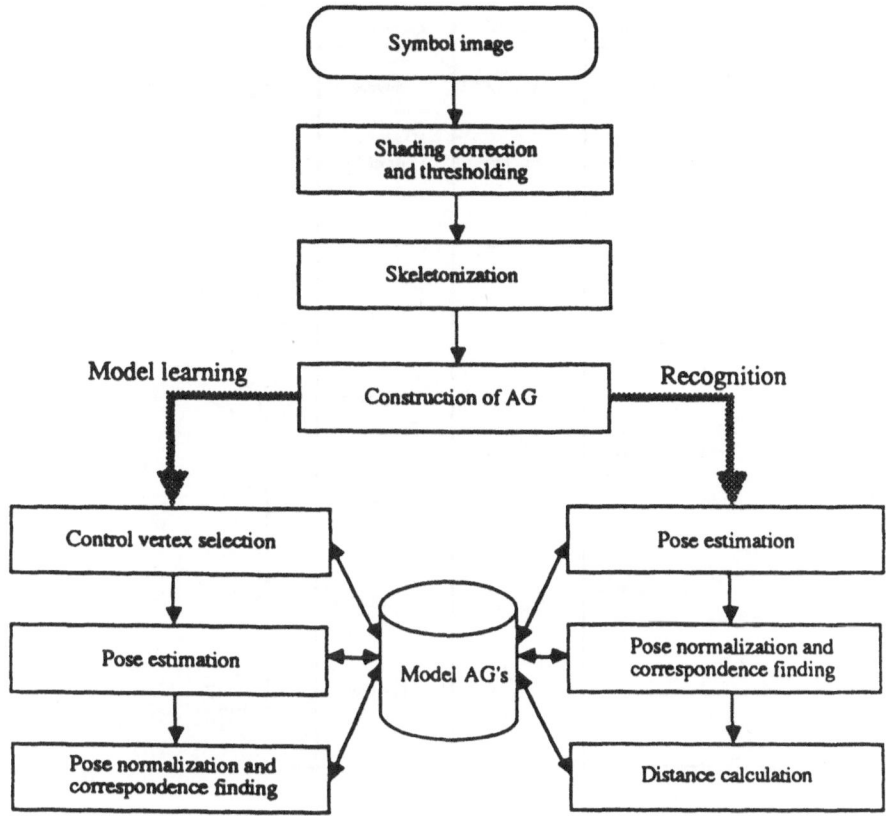

Fig. 4. Overview of symbol recognition system.

the model AG's, while the latter are used to test the system's credibility. That is, the system has never "seen" the member of the testing samples. In our experiments, 10 samples for each class were used for learning. Therefore, there were a total of 450 samples in the learning set for the three different types of symbols. For testing, 20 samples for each class were used in our experiments. Therefore, there were a total of 900 samples in the testing set for the three different types of symbols.

In the experiment for the machine-printed electrical circuit symbols, no errors occurred. In the experiment for the hand-drawn electrical circuit symbols with templates, 8 errors occurred resulting in 2.7% of error rate. In the experiment for the hand-drawn electrical circuit symbols without a template, 58 errors occurred resulting in 19.3% of error rate. In total, 834 images out of 900 images were recognized perfectly and the pose of them were estimated correctly. In other words, average error rate was 7.3%. Most of errors resulted from the incorrect pose estimation and poor skeletonization due to heavy noise.

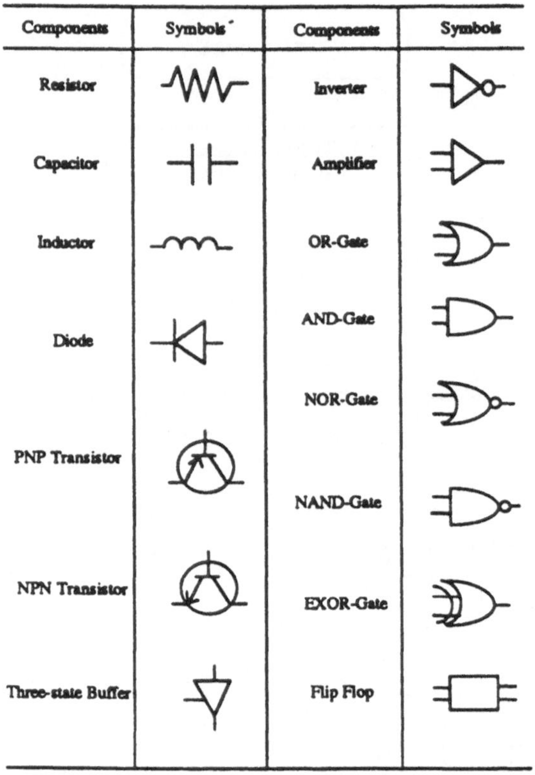

354

S.-W. Lee

Components	Symbols	Components	Symbols
Resistor		Inverter	
Capacitor		Amplifier	
Inductor		OR-Gate	
Diode		AND-Gate	
		NOR-Gate	
PNP Transistor		NAND-Gate	
NPN Transistor		EXOR-Gate	
Three-state Buffer		Flip Flop	

Fig. 5. Standard position of symbols used in the experiments.

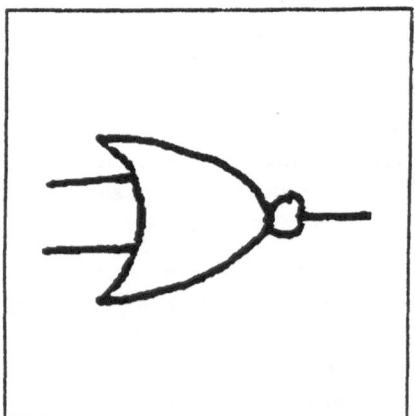

Fig. 6. A thresholded image.

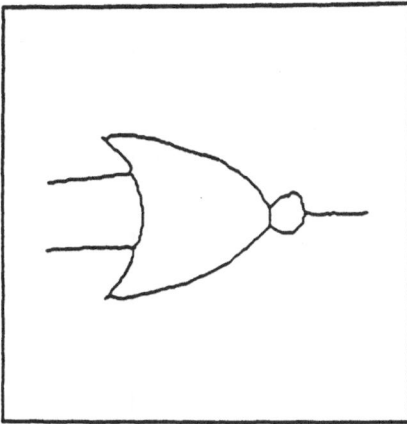

Fig. 7. Skeletonized image from Figure 6.

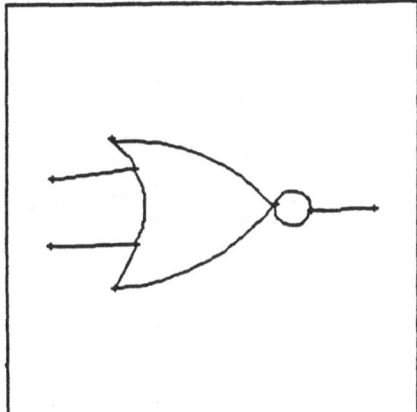

Fig. 8. Graphical representation of the constructed AG after piecewise approximations and error recoveries from Figure 7. "+" sign represents the position of vertex.

6 Concluding Remarks

The contribution of this work may be subdivided into three categories: First, presentation of a model-based scheme for recognizing similar hand-drawn electrical circuit symbols with the AG matching in the absence of any information concerning the pose (translation, rotation and scale) of them. Second, characterization of the distance measuring process between the AG_O and the AG_M from the probabilistic point of view, and approximation of the conditional probability by modeling the probability of some features of a component by a Gaussian distribution. In this way, our distance measure accounts for the statistical characteristics of the distortion process between the AG_O and the AG_M. Third, presentation of a AG_M learning algorithm in which the structural components and their attributes are extracted to construct model.

356

S.-W. Lee

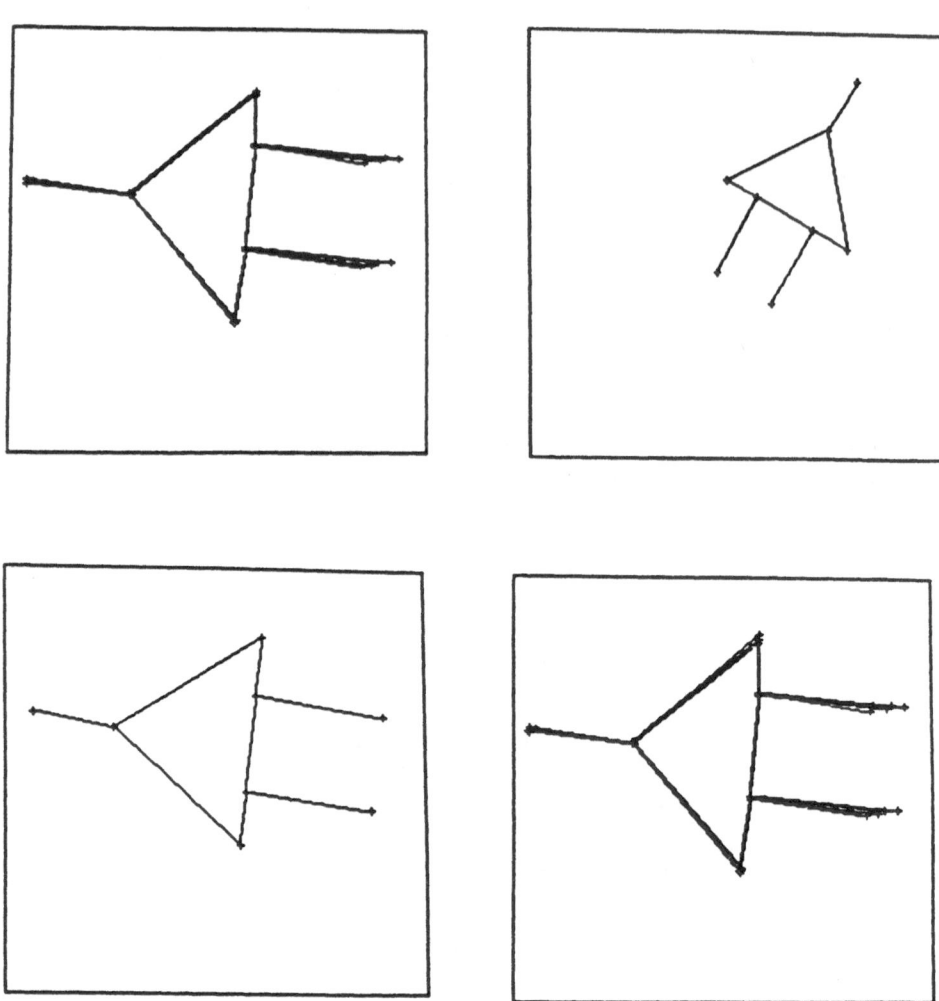

Fig. 9. Graphical representation of AG matching steps.

In order to reduce the computational overhead, our scheme began with an assumption that a particular set of vertices called control vertices are found reliably in the observation. This may not be true in the situations where symbol images contain heavy noise. However, the experimental results confirmed that the assumption was acceptable for most of symbol images, and the proposed scheme might be feasible for practical applications.

References

[1]   A. Okazaki, T. Kondo, K. Mori, S. Tsunekawa, and E. Kawamoto, "An Automatic Circuit Diagram Reader with Loop-Structure-Based Symbol Recognition," *IEEE Trans. Pattern Analysis and Machine Intelligence*, Vol PAMI-10, pp. 331–341, 1988.

[2]   H. Bunke and G. Allermann, "Understanding of circuit diagrams by means of probabilistic relaxation," *Signal Processing* 4, pp. 169–180, 1982.

[3]   H. Bunke, "Experience with several methods for the analysis of schematic diagrams," *Proc. 6th ICPR*, Munich, FRG, pp. 710–712, Oct. 1982.

[4]   H. Bunke, "Attributed programmed graph grammars and their application to schematic diagram interpretation," *IEEE Trans. Pattern Analysis and Machine Intelligence* 4, pp. 574–582, 1982.

[5]   K. Abe, Y. Azumatani, M. Kukouda, and S. Suzuki, "Discrimination of symbols, lines, and characters in flowchart recognition," *Proc. 8th ICPR*, Paris, France, pp. 1071–1074, Oct. 1986.

[6]   M. Minoh, M. Araki, and T. Sakai, "Fair copy reproducing algorithm from roughly sketched diagrams," *Proc. 8th ICPR*, Paris, France, pp. 437–441, Oct. 1986.

[7]   F. C. A. Groen and R. J. van Munster, "Topology based analysis of schematic diagrams," *Proc. 7th ICPR*, Montreal, pp. 1310–1312, Jul./Aug. 1984.

[8]   T. Sato and T. Tojo, "Recognition and understanding of hand-drawn diagrams," *Proc. 6th ICPR*, Munich, pp. 674–677, Oct. 1982.

[9]   Y. Fukada, "A primary algorithm for the understanding of logic circuit diagrams," *Pattern Recognition* 17, pp. 125–134, 1984.

[10] W. Kikkawa, M. Kitayama, K. Miyazaki, H. Arai, and S. Arato, "Automatic digitizing system for PWB diagrams," *Proc. 7th ICPR*, Montreal, pp. 1306–1309, Jul./Aug. 1984.

[11] F. C. A. Groen, A. C. Sanderson, and J. F. Schlag, "Symbol recognition in electrical diagrams using probabilistic graph matching," *Pattern Recognition Letters* 3, pp. 343–350, 1985.

[12] M. Furuta, N. Kase, and S. Emori, "Segmentation and recognition of symbols for handwritten piping and instrument diagram," *Proc. 7th ICPR*, Montreal, pp. 626–629, Jul./Aug. 1984.

[13] P. Kuner and B. Ueberreiter, "Knowledge-based pattern recognition in disturbed line images using graph theory, optimization and predicate calculus," *Proc. 8th ICPR*, Paris, pp. 240–243, Oct. 1986.

[14] H. Bley, "Segmentation and preprocessing of electrical schematics using picture graphs," *Comp. Vision Graph. Image Processing* 28, pp. 271–288, 1984.

[15] J. T. Tou and J. M. Cheng, "AUTOREAD: An Automated Electronic Diagram Reading Machine," *Proc. IEEE Int'l Conf. on CAD*, pp. 19–21, 1983.

[16] J. T. Tou, C. L. Huang, and W. H. Li, "Design of a Knowledge-Based System for Understanding Electronic Circuit Diagrams," *Proc. First Conf. on Artificial Intelligence Applications*, Denver, USA, pp. 652–661, Dec. 1984.

[17] S. Shimizu, S. Nagata, A. Inoue, and M. Yoshida, "Logic Circuit Diagram Processing System," *Proc. 6th ICPR*, Munich, FRG, pp. 717–719, Oct. 1982.

[18] W. C. Lin and J. H. Pun, "Machine recognition and plotting of hand-sketched line figures," *IEEE Trans. Systems, Man and Cybernetics* 8, pp. 52–57, 1978.

[19] R. M. Haralick and D. Queeney, "Understanding Engineering Drawings," *Comp. Vision Graph. Image Processing* 20, pp. 244–258, 1982.

[20] H. Bunke, "Automatic Interpretation of Lines and Text in Circuit Diagrams," In J. Kittler, K. S. Fu, and L. F. Pau (eds.), *Pattern Recognition: Theory and Applications*, pp. 297–310, D. Reidel, 1982.

[21] X. Lin, S. Shimotsuji, M. Minoh, and T. Sakai, "Efficient Diagram Understanding with Characteristic Pattern Detection," *Comp. Vision Graph. Image Processing* 30, pp. 84–106, 1985.

[22] P. Kuner, "Reducing Relational Graph Matching Tasks to Integer Programming Problems, which are solved by a Consistent Labeling Approach," *Proc. 5th Scandinavian Conf. on Image Analysis*, Stockholm, Sweden, pp. 127–134, Jun. 1987.

[23] H. Bunke and G. Allermann, "Inexact graph matching for structural pattern recognition," *Pattern Recognition Letters* 1, pp. 245–253, 1983.

[24] A. K. C. Wong and M. L. You, "Entropy and Distance of Random Graphs with Application to Structural Pattern Recognition," *IEEE Trans. Pattern Analysis and Machine Intelligence* 7, pp. 599–609, 1986.

[25] P. W. Verweek, H. A. Vrooman, and L. J. van Vliet, "Low-level image processing by max-min filters," *Signal Processing* 15, pp. 249–258, 1988.

[26] J. Serra, *Image Analysis and Mathematical Morphology*, Academic Press, London (1982).

[27] K. Preston, *Multicomputers and Image Processing*, Academic Press, London (1982).

[28] L. J. van Vliet and B. J.H. Verwer, "A Contour Processing Method for Fast Binary Neighborhood Operations," *Pattern Recognition Lett.* 7, pp. 27–36, 1988.

[29] C. J. Hilditch, "Linear skeletons from square cupboards," *Machine Intelligence* 4, pp. 404–420, 1969.

[30] S.-W. Lee, J. H. Kim, and F. C. A. Groen, "A fast computational method for minimum square error transform," *Proc. 9th ICPR*, Rome, Italy, pp. 392–394, Nov. 1988.

[31] S.-W. Lee, J. H. Kim, and F. C. A. Groen, "Translation-, rotation-, and scale-invariant recognition of hand-drawn symbols in schematic diagrams," *Pattern Recognition and Artificial Intelligence* 4, pp. 1–25, 1990.

[32] S.-W. Lee, "Line-drawing pattern recognition with attributed graph matching," Ph.D. Dissertation, Dept of Computer Science, KAIST, Seoul, Korea, 1989.

[33] S.-W. Byun, S.-W. Lee, and J. H. Kim, "Extracting basic components for recognizing hand-drawn circuit diagrams," in preparation.

Self-Structural Syntax-Directed Pattern Recognition of Dimensioning Components in Engineering Drawings

Dov Dori

Department of Computer Science,[1]
The University of Kansas,
Lawrence, Kansas 66045, USA

A mechanical engineering drawing is a set of orthogonal 2D views of a 3D object. To establish vision-based communication among CAD/CAM systems and to implement 3D reconstruction, drawings need to be pre-processed to exploit the information conveyed by the annotation before separating it from the geometry. A rationale for a machine drawing understanding system is first argued. A context-free dimensioning grammar provides a basis for a self-structural, syntax-directed pattern recognition scheme. It employs learning the characteristic parameters of arrowheads and text from a detected sample, and using them to detect the entire population. Syntactic considerations that significantly decrease the search space help predict the spatial location and orientation of potential components. The underlying ideas of the scheme may be applicable to a broad scope of tasks involving intelligent recognition.

1 Introduction

The design-and-manufacturing process involves translating designers' ideas into spatial information describing the product, and is predicated upon being able to establish, communicate, use, and maintain product-definition information. Historically, this process has been completely human-based. Product-definition information was created by an engineering drawing — an annotated visual definition of the product's geometry, tolerance, and other characteristics.

Industry makes extensive use of CAD/CAM, but paper drawings continue to prevail as the simplest and most direct means of communication among human designers, producers, subcontractors and consumers [1]. Engineering drawings utilize detailed drafting standards, *e.g.* ANSI [16], which play among humans the same role played by communication protocols among machines, *e.g.* [5]. Engineering drawings have occupied a central position in this human-oriented process, as communication has been accomplished by their physical transfer. Thus,

---

[1] Presently also affiliated with the Faculty of Industrial Engineering and Management, Technion, Israel Institute of Technology, Technion City, Haifa 32000 Israel.

as has been pointed out [11, 13], an automated system for document analysis is highly desirable. The drawing is a graphic product definition consisting of views of the object's geometry, enhanced by annotation. Basic annotation consists of geometric dimensioning and tolerancing, which is a means of specifying engineering design and drawing requirements with respect to actual *function* and *relationship* to part feature [14]. Even with CAD/CAM systems, product definition is still human oriented, with the drawing remaining central to the system [15].

CAD/CAM systems often use dissimilar internal representations, primarily because each system is most productive at one specific application [17]. Nevertheless, they all produce drawings (also referred to as 'hard-copies,' 'plots,' or 'blueprints') for the purpose of interfacing with humans. All these 'interfaces' are similar to each other due to a combination of adhering to an existing drafting standard, such as ANSI, company conventions, and a de-facto common graphic language. Drawings are also the only product representation common to both manual and automated design. The magnitude of the task of converting handmade drawings into computer manipulable representations is evaluated in [2].

The need for understanding engineering drawings is motivated by the following arguments.

(1) **An alternative, human controllable option for product definition exchange will become available.** Currently available systems in the marketplace for the purpose of automating technical documentation are still limited by the extent to which they can really 'understand' the scanned input beyond a mere recognition and digital storage of lines and text [11]. Therefore, inserting a drawing into a CAD database can only be done at the expense of intensive human endeavor. With a system that understands engineering drawings, human control over the correctness of the (hard copy) input is made natural, easy, and immediate. It will contribute to automatic dimensioning procedures [23], and to the development of human-machine interfaces in industrial robotics [17] and image understanding workstations that include multiple levels of representation [19].

(2) **Paper drawings are expected to continue being used in the future.** Standards for symbols for geometric dimensioning and tolerancing are well developed, *e.g.* [5], and symbols are increasingly becoming the 'spoken word' for communicating requirements throughout industry, the military, and internationally, on engineering drawing documentation [14]. New fast thermal color plotters and color scanners are being announced at a high rate [20] to satisfy the ever increasing need for quality paper output. The main reason for the incredible survival of paper documentation is that graphics and text recorded on paper remain the simplest, most immediate means of accessing information by humans. Paper documents are easily carried, read, and understood by humans without any auxiliary equipment whatsoever.

(3) **3-D reconstruction from engineering drawings requires their 2-D understanding.** Ideally, it is possible to recover the three dimensional model

from a proper given set of views. Reconstructing 3-D objects from a given set of 2-D views has been tackled by a number of researchers, *e.g.* [8], [9], [21], [22]. These works tacitly assume an input of a well defined, noise-free set of 2-D projections and do not concern themselves with how they were obtained. Engineering drawings, however, contain many non-geometry, or *annotation* entities, that add information to the geometric entities. As noted in [7], annotation is an extremely tedious area of data exchange. This is true in particular for dimensioning because of the way it is mixed with geometry.

(4) **Overall design productivity is likely to increase.** This will be a result of a significant decrease in the magnitude of manual archives that need to be handled, as the possibility of quickly and reliably converting drawings of interest into a CAD/CAM database will become fairly available [2].

2 Product Data Exchange and Understanding Machine Drawings

Communication among various CAD/CAM systems is presently carried out by means of a neutral format translator. The Initial Graphics Exchange Specification (IGES) [5] is a widely accepted neutral file format. An IGES product definition transfer is a two step process [6, 7]. First, the originating system uses its IGES preprocessor to translate database entities into the 'neutral' IGES format. Then, each receiving system uses its IGES postprocessor to translate the resulting IGES entities into its database format. The Machine Drawing Understanding System (MDUS) proposed in [3, 12, 18] is a potential enhancement for exchange of product information. It also provides an automated means for incorporating manual engineering drawings into CAD/CAM system databases.

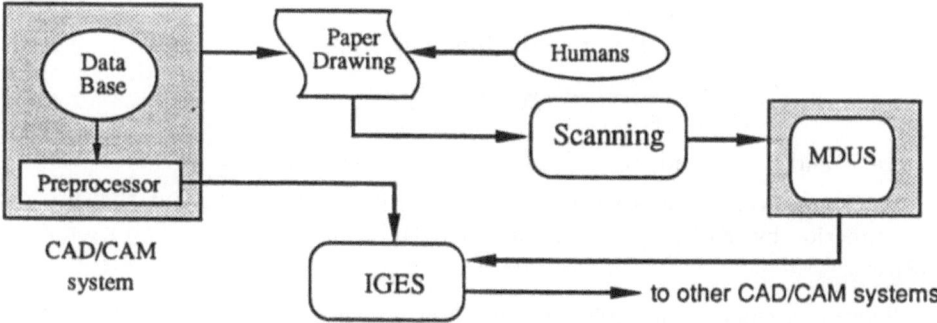

Fig. 1. The MDUS environment.

Figure 1 is a block diagram describing the MDUS environment. The originating CAD system has a preprocessor to translate product data from its internal code into IGES and a plotter to output paper drawings. These, as well as manually prepared drawings, are the input to MDUS, which is expected to analyze the drawings and to output them in IGES format.

The understanding phase of MDUS is preceded by low-level steps that include scanning, optional enhancement, and raster to wire operation. The term *wire* denotes an arc or a straight line segment. A *wire file* is the output of this preprocessing. The wire file is the input to the intermediate level, during which the self, syntax directed pattern recognition takes place.

Adopting IGES conventions, the fundamental unit of information is the *entity*. The DRAWING entity (IGES entity number 404) specifies a drawing as a *"collection of annotation entities and views which, together, constitute a single representation of a part, in the sense that an engineering drawing constitutes a single representation of a part in standard drafting practice"* [5]. It allows a set of views to be identified and arranged for human presentation. The VIEW entity (IGES no. 410) provides characteristics associated with individual views. Dimensioning provides an exact definition of the geometry approximated by the geometry entities in engineering drawings. Therefore, recognition of dimensions is a key component of MDUS.

From a morphological point of view, most annotation and geometry entities are similar, rendering non-syntactic pattern recognition unsuitable for distinguishing between them. A syntactic approach has therefore been proposed [3, 12] that makes use of the spatial relationship among dimensioning annotation entities and formulates them in a two dimensional web grammar. The grammar is used to parse entities in an expert system for engineering drawing interpretation [15], or may serve as a basis for a discrimination vision approach [10], where discrimination graphs are used to prevent the occurrence of a combinatorial explosion in hypothetical interpretations.

3 Dimension-Sets and Their Attributes

A dimension $\mathcal{D}$ may be viewed as the function

$$\mathcal{D} : \mathcal{T} \to \mathcal{G}$$

where $\mathcal{T}$ and $\mathcal{G}$ stand for text and geometry, respectively.

A **dimension-set** is a set of graphical entities that implement the dimension function by denoting the measure (length or angle) between two geometry entities.

The hierarchical structure of of an ANSI, linear type dimension-set is schematically illustrated in Figure 2. The first level building blocks that comprise a dimension-set are termed **components**. These are the *text*, $\mathcal{T}$, one or two

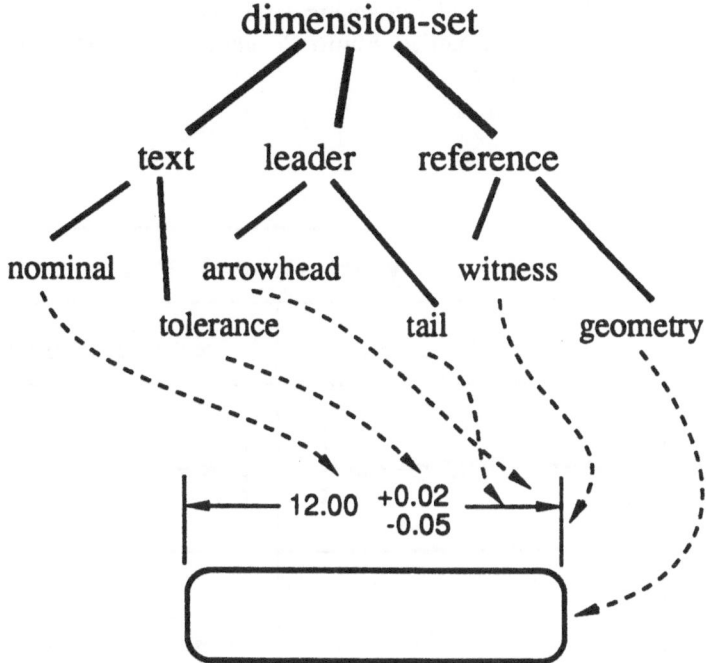

Fig. 2. Schematic hierarchical structure of a dimension-set.

leaders, $\mathcal{L}$, and two *references*, $\mathcal{R}$. As shown in Figure 2, each component usually consists of two *sub-components*. The actual grammar presented below is much more detailed and reflects a somewhat different hierarchy than the one shown here.

Dimension-sets are characterized by five **attributes**: *standard, completeness, type, symmetry,* and *pointing*. The two major standards are ISO and ANSI. **Completeness** refers to the number of leaders in a dimension-set and has the value *complete* if there are two leaders and *incomplete* if it has just one.

Type is characteristic of the object being dimensioned. Four **longitudinal** types, that denote length, are the *linear, cylinder* (a side viewed body of revolution), *diameter* (a top viewed body of revolution), and *radius*. The fifth type, denoting angle, is termed *angular*. Three more types — *chamfer, ordinate,* and *point* — are not considered in this paper.

Pointing pertains to the pointing direction of the two arrowheads with respect to each other. Two values are possible: *out* and *in*, depending on whether the leaders' pointing directions are away from or towards each other, respectively. **Symmetry** pertains to the location of the text with respect to the two arrowheads. Two values are possible: *symmetric* and *asymmetric*, depending on whether the text is located along the wire connecting the arrowheads or not, respectively. As shown in Figure 3, the combination of pointing and symmetry values give rise to four *kinds* of dimension-sets: in-symmetric, in-asymmetric, out-symmetric, and out-asymmetric. Figure 2   shows an ANSI complete linear out-symmetric dimension-set.

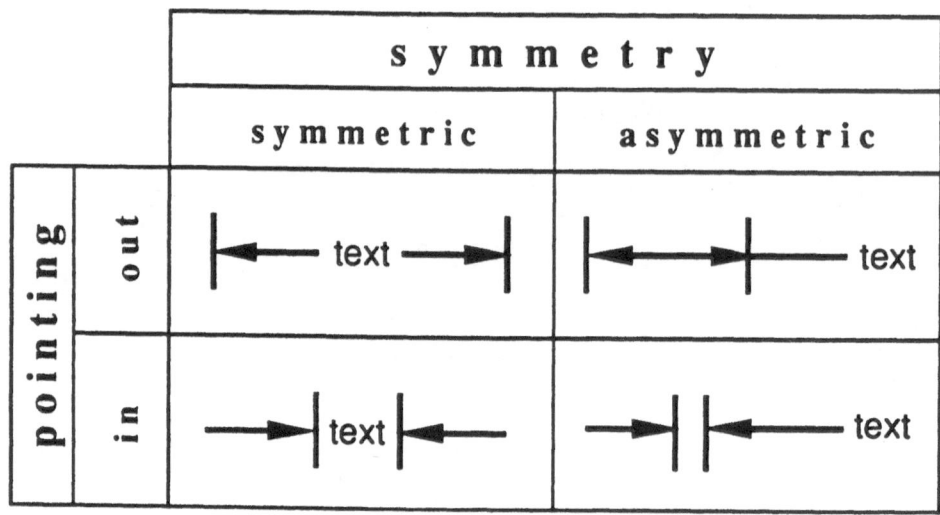

Fig. 3. The four kinds of dimension-sets.

A **normal view orientation** of a complete dimension-set is an orientation of the drawing in which the dimension-set appears to be above the object being dimensioned and the line connecting the two arrowhead tips is (at least approximately) horizontal. The directions *left* and *right* refer to a dimension-set at normal view orientation. The dimension-set in Figure 2   is shown in normal view orientation.

To initiate the detection of dimension-sets we need concrete starting points to hook on to. These are provided by the two components leader and text [3, 12], which are characteristic of annotation and are called **anchors**. Their relative uniqueness makes them suitable candidates for preliminary search by methods which are non-syntactic, but use the grammar below to direct the search so as to reduce the search space from the entire raster file of the drawing to small portions thereof. Once anchors are detected in this intermediate vision stage, syntactic analysis may be applied in the higher level to recover the rest of the components and obtain complete dimension-sets.

4 A Context-free Dimensioning and Tolerancing Grammar

The following grammar is a context-free string grammar that handles dimensioning and size tolerancing. It covers the important and most useful conventions of the first two chapters of ANSI Y14.5M-1982 standard [16]. It is *text-specifying* in the sense that its text-related terminals utilize the same symbols as those that actually appear in the drawing, *e.g.*, the ten digits, $\diameter$, R, °, etc. The grammar uses the following functions, conventions, and notations.

(1) *Customary notations*: 'ϵ' and '$|$' are the customary notations for the empty string and the alternation operator, respectively.

(2) *Reverse string*: for any string S, S^R is the reverse of S. Thus, if $S = abcd$, then $S^R = dcba$. If any of the symbols in the string is directed, *i.e.*, has an arrow on top of it, the direction of the arrow is also reversed. Thus, if $S = \overrightarrow{X} u \overleftarrow{Y} v$ then $S^R = v \overrightarrow{Y} u \overleftarrow{X}$.

(3) *Optional reverse*: for any string S, $S^{(R)} = S \,|\, S^R$, where S^R is the reverse of S. Thus, if $S = abcd$, then $S^{(R)} = abcd \,|\, dcba$.

(4) *Subscript substitution*: all identical subscripts in a given sentential form must be substituted concurrently and by the same symbol. For example, if the subscript c in the sentential form $\overleftarrow{\mathcal{R}}_c \mathcal{T}_c \overrightarrow{\mathcal{R}}_c$ is in $\{\text{L}, \text{C}, \text{D}, \text{A}\}$, then the sentential form may become $\overleftarrow{\mathcal{R}}_{\text{D}} \mathcal{T}_{\text{D}} \overrightarrow{\mathcal{R}}_{\text{D}}$, but not anything like $\overleftarrow{\mathcal{R}}_{\text{L}} \mathcal{T}_{\text{D}} \overrightarrow{\mathcal{R}}_{\text{C}}$. This convention is designed simply to reduce the number of productions in the grammar that need to be written explicitly.

(5) *Positional functions*: the functions $\text{atop}(X, Y)$ and $\exp(X, Y)$ determine the position of grammar symbols X and Y with respect to each other as follows: $\text{atop}(X, Y) = \begin{smallmatrix} X \\ Y \end{smallmatrix}$, and $\exp(X, Y) = X^Y$. The parenthesis that enclose the two parameters of both function are meta-symbols rather than terminals.

The dimensioning grammar G_d is a four-tuple: $G_d = \{N_d, \Sigma_d, P_d, S\}$. N_d is the following set of nonterminals:

$$N_d = \{S, S_{\text{T}}, \overleftarrow{\mathcal{R}}_c, \overrightarrow{\mathcal{R}}_c, \overleftarrow{\mathcal{L}}_c, \overrightarrow{\mathcal{L}}_c, \mathcal{W}, Tail_c, \mathcal{G}_c, \mathcal{T}_{\text{T}}, Num, \ Int,$$
$$I, \ Dig, \ Tol, \ Dev, \ Lim, \ Deg, \ Min, \ Sec, \ Toldeg, \ Devdeg,$$
$$Center, \ Repeat, \ Units, \ Fit, \ Lim\}$$

$S \in N_d$, is the start symbol. $\text{T} \in \{\text{L}, \text{D}, \text{C}, \text{A}, \text{R}\}$ stands for one of the five types: linear, diameter, cylinder, angular, and radial, respectively, while $c \in \{\text{L}, \text{D}, \text{C}, \text{A}\}$ stands for one of the four *complete* types. S_{T} and $\mathcal{T}_{\text{T}}$ denote a dimension-set and a text of type T, respectively. $\overleftarrow{\mathcal{R}}_c$ (or $\overrightarrow{\mathcal{R}}_c$) and $\overleftarrow{\mathcal{L}}_c$ (or $\overrightarrow{\mathcal{L}}_c$) denote a left (or right) reference and leader of type c, respectively.

Σ_d is the following set of terminals:

$$\Sigma_d = \{Bar, Bar_h, Arc, Point, \overleftarrow{\mathcal{A}}, \overrightarrow{\mathcal{A}}, 0, 1, 2, 3, 4, 5, 6, 7, 8, 9,$$
$$., +, -, \ \underline{\quad}, \ -, (,), \diameter, X, R, °, ', '', \text{IN.}, \text{mm}, \text{f}, \text{MIN}, \ \text{MAX}\}$$

All but the first six terminals are text-related and symbolized as they appear in the drawing. *Bar*, *Arc*, and *Point* have their obvious interpretation, Bar_h is a horizontal bar, while $\overleftarrow{A}$ and $\overrightarrow{A}$ are left and right pointing arrowheads.

P_d is the following set of productions (rewriting rules), accompanied by verbal explanations:

$$P_d = \{S \rightarrow S_c \mid S_{\mathbf{R}},$$

$$S_c \rightarrow \overleftarrow{\mathcal{R}}_c \mathcal{T}_c \overrightarrow{\mathcal{R}}_c \mid \overrightarrow{\mathcal{R}}_c \mathcal{T}_c \overleftarrow{\mathcal{R}}_c \mid (\mathcal{T}_c\, Med\, \overleftarrow{\mathcal{R}}_c \overrightarrow{\mathcal{R}}_c)^{(R)} \mid (\mathcal{T}_c\, Med\, \overrightarrow{\mathcal{R}}_c \overleftarrow{\mathcal{R}}_c)^{(R)},$$

> The alternatives stand for out-symmetric, in-symmetric, out-asymmetric, and in-asymmetric kinds, respectively.

$$S_{\mathbf{R}} \rightarrow (Center\, Bar\mathcal{T}_{\mathbf{R}} \overrightarrow{\mathcal{L}}_c \mathcal{G}_{\mathbf{R}})^{(R)} \mid (\mathcal{T}_{\mathbf{R}} Bar_h \overrightarrow{\mathcal{L}}_c \mathcal{G}_{\mathbf{R}})^{(R)} \mid (\mathcal{T}_{\mathbf{R}} Bar_h\, Bar\, \mathcal{G}_{\mathbf{R}} \overleftarrow{\mathcal{L}}_c)^{(R)},$$

> These are the alternatives for the radial type, which is incomplete, and therefore has just one leader.

$$Center \rightarrow Point \mid \epsilon,$$

> The center of the circle whose radius is dimensioned is either a point (cross) or is absent (ϵ).

$$S_{\mathbf{D}} \rightarrow (\mathcal{T}_{\mathbf{D}} Bar_h \overrightarrow{\mathcal{L}}_c \mathcal{G}_{\mathbf{D}})^{(R)},$$

> The diametric type may also be incomplete; when applied to a small circle it may have just one diagonal leader.

$$\overleftarrow{\mathcal{R}}_c \rightarrow \mathcal{G}_c \mathcal{W} \overleftarrow{\mathcal{L}}_c,$$

$$\overrightarrow{\mathcal{R}}_c \rightarrow \overrightarrow{\mathcal{L}}_c \mathcal{W} \mathcal{G}_c,$$

> The reference consists of a leader that points to a witness which guides to a geometry component.

$$Med \rightarrow Bar_h \mid \epsilon,$$

> The mediator, *Med*, is an (optional) horizontal bar which mediates between the text and the leader's tail, if the latter is not horizontal.

$$\mathcal{W} \rightarrow Bar \mid \epsilon,$$

> A witness, if it exists, must be a *Bar*.

$$\overleftarrow{\mathcal{L}}_{\mathbf{T}} \rightarrow \overleftarrow{A} Tail_{\mathbf{T}}; \ c \in \{\mathbf{L}, \mathbf{C}, \mathbf{D}, \mathbf{R}, \mathbf{A}\},$$

$$\overrightarrow{\mathcal{L}}_{\mathbf{T}} \rightarrow \overrightarrow{A} Tail_{\mathbf{T}}; \ c \in \{\mathbf{L}, \mathbf{C}, \mathbf{D}, \mathbf{R}, \mathbf{A}\},$$

> A leader consists of an arrowhead and a tail.

$$Tail_l \rightarrow Bar; \quad l \in \{\mathbf{L}, \mathbf{C}, \mathbf{D}, \mathbf{R}\},$$

> The tail of all but angular leader is a bar.

$$Tail_{\mathbf{A}} \rightarrow Arc,$$

> The tail of an angular leader is an arc.

$$\mathcal{G}_{\mathbf{L}} \rightarrow Bar \mid Arc \mid Point,$$

> The geometry of a linear leader is a bar.

$$\mathcal{G}_b \rightarrow Bar; \quad b \in \{\mathbf{C}, \mathbf{A}\},$$

The geometry of a cylindrical or angular leader is a bar.

$\mathcal{G}_d \rightarrow Arc; \quad d \in \{\mathbf{D}, \mathbf{R}\},$

The geometry of a diametric or radial leader is an arc.

$\mathcal{T}_\mathbf{L} \rightarrow Repeat\ Num\ Units\ Tol \mid \text{atop}(Num, \underline{\quad})$

The text of a linear dimension-set consists of an optional *Repeat*

followed by a number Num (the nominal value), then a tolerance Tol,

$\mid \text{atop}(Num, Num)$

or two numbers on top of each other for upper and lower limits,

$\mid Num\ \text{-}Num$

or two numbers separated by a dash for upper and lower limits,

$\mid (Num)$

or a number in parenthesis for 'reference' ('implied') dimension,

$\mid \text{atop}(\underline{Num}, \underline{\quad})$

or an underlined number for 'dimension not to scale,' or limits and fits.

$\mid Fit,$

$Repeat \rightarrow Int\ \mathsf{X} \mid \epsilon,$

Repeat optionally designates an integer number of repeating features.

$Num \rightarrow Int \mid Int.Int \mid .Int,$

The number is an integer, a decimal number, or a decimal fraction;

in ANSI decimal inch text the zero to the left of the decimal point is omitted.

$Int \rightarrow Dig \mid Dig\ Int,$

$Dig \rightarrow 0 \mid 1 \mid 2 \mid 3 \mid 4 \mid 5 \mid 6 \mid 7 \mid 8 \mid 9,$

$Units \rightarrow \mathsf{IN.} \mid \mathsf{mm} \mid \epsilon,$

Where some inch (millimeter) dimensions are shown on a millimeter- (inch-)

dimensioned drawing, the abbreviation '$\mathsf{IN.}$' ('mm') should follow the number.

$Fit \rightarrow \text{atop}(Num, Num)(Int\ \mathsf{f}\ Int) \mid Int\ \mathsf{f}\ Int(\text{atop}(Num, Num)) \mid Int\ \mathsf{f}\ Int$

These are the three possible notations for metric limits and fits (ANSI B4.2).

$Tol \rightarrow Lim \mid Dev \mid \epsilon,$

$Lim \rightarrow \mathsf{MIN} \mid \mathsf{MAX},$

The MIN (MAX) symbol means the nominal is required as minimum (maximum)

$Dev \rightarrow \text{atop}(+, -)Num \mid \text{atop}(+Num, -Num) \mid \text{atop}(0, -Num) \mid \text{atop}(+Num, 0),$

Deviations are equal and unequal bilateral deviations,

and lower and upper unilateral deviations, respectively.

$\mathcal{T}_t \rightarrow \lozenge \mathcal{T}_\mathbf{L}; \quad t \in \{\mathbf{c}, \mathbf{d}\},$

The text of cylinder and diameter types is like that of the

linear type, preceded by the terminal $\lozenge$.

$\mathcal{T}_\mathbf{R} \rightarrow \mathsf{R} \mathcal{T}_\mathbf{L},$

The text of the radial type is like that of the

linear type, preceded by the terminal R.

$$T_{\mathbf{A}} \rightarrow Deg\ Toldeg \mid atop(Deg, Deg),$$

The text of angular is like that of the linear type,

except for terminals for degrees, minutes, and seconds.

$$Deg \rightarrow Int°Min \mid Num°,$$
$$Min \rightarrow Int'Sec \mid \epsilon,$$
$$Sec \rightarrow Int'' \mid \epsilon,$$
$$Toldeg \rightarrow Devdeg \mid Lim \mid \epsilon,$$
$$Devdeg \rightarrow atop(+, -)Deg \mid atop(+Deg, -Deg) \mid atop(+Deg, 0) \mid atop(0, -Deg)\}$$

To illustrate how the grammar is used to derive sentences in the dimensioning language, consider the two dimension-sets in Figure 4, adapted from ANSI Standard [30].

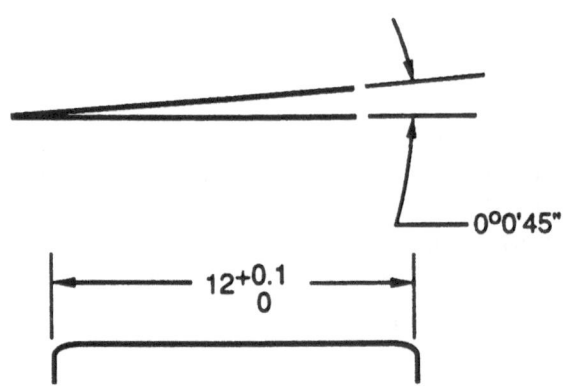

Fig. 4. ANSI standard angular (top) and linear dimension-sets.

As a first example, the sequence of sentential forms obtained by a leftmost derivation that produces the angular dimension-set in the top of Figure 4 is the following:

$$S \Rightarrow S_c \Rightarrow (T_c\ Med\ \overleftarrow{\mathcal{R}}_c\ \overrightarrow{\mathcal{R}}_c)^R = \overrightarrow{\mathcal{R}}_c\ \overleftarrow{\mathcal{R}}_c\ Med\ T_c$$

The reverse string is taken because when rotated to normal view orientation, the text appears to be on the right hand side.

$$\Rightarrow \overrightarrow{\mathcal{R}}_{\mathbf{A}}\ \overleftarrow{\mathcal{R}}_{\mathbf{A}}\ Med\ T_{\mathbf{A}}$$

Here we applied subscript substitution, noting that the dimension-set is of angular type.

$$\Rightarrow \overrightarrow{\mathcal{L}}_{\mathbf{A}}\ W\ \mathcal{G}_{\mathbf{A}}\ \overleftarrow{\mathcal{R}}_{\mathbf{A}}\ Med\ T_{\mathbf{A}}$$

The right reference produces a right leader, a witness, and a geometry component.

$$\Rightarrow Tail_{\mathbf{A}}\,\overrightarrow{A}\,W\,\mathcal{G}_{\mathbf{A}}\,\overleftarrow{\mathcal{R}}_{\mathbf{A}}\,Med\,T_{\mathbf{A}} \Rightarrow Arc\,\overrightarrow{A}\,W\,\mathcal{G}_{\mathbf{A}}\,\overleftarrow{\mathcal{R}}_{\mathbf{A}}\,Med\,T_{\mathbf{A}}$$

The right leader consists of a tail, which is an arc, and a right arrowhead.

$$\Rightarrow Arc\,\overrightarrow{A}\,Bar\,\mathcal{G}_{\mathbf{A}}\,\overleftarrow{\mathcal{R}}_{\mathbf{A}}\,Med\,T_{\mathbf{A}} \Rightarrow Arc\,\overrightarrow{A}\,Bar\,Bar\,\overleftarrow{\mathcal{R}}_{\mathbf{A}}\,Med\,T_{\mathbf{A}}$$

The witness and the geometry component of an angular dimension-set are both bars.

$$\Rightarrow Arc\,\overrightarrow{A}\,Bar\,Bar\,\mathcal{G}_{\mathbf{A}}\,W\,\overleftarrow{\mathcal{L}}_{\mathbf{A}}\,Med\,T_{\mathbf{A}}$$

The left reference is a geometry component, a witness, and a left leader.

$$\Rightarrow Arc\,\overrightarrow{A}\,Bar\,Bar\,Bar\,W\,\overleftarrow{\mathcal{L}}_{\mathbf{A}}\,Med\,T_{\mathbf{A}}$$

$$\Rightarrow Arc\,\overrightarrow{A}\,Bar\,Bar\,Bar\,Bar\,\overleftarrow{\mathcal{L}}_{\mathbf{A}}\,Med\,T_{\mathbf{A}}$$

The geometry and the witness are both bars.

$$\Rightarrow Arc\,\overrightarrow{A}\,Bar\,Bar\,Bar\,Bar\,\overleftarrow{A}\,Tail_{\mathbf{A}}\,Med\,T_{\mathbf{A}}$$

$$\Rightarrow Arc\,\overrightarrow{A}\,Bar\,Bar\,Bar\,Bar\,\overleftarrow{A}\,Arc\,Med\,T_{\mathbf{A}}$$

The left leader is a left arrowhead and a tail, which is an arc.

$$\Rightarrow Arc\,\overrightarrow{A}\,Bar\,Bar\,Bar\,Bar\,\overleftarrow{A}\,Arc\,Bar_h\,T_{\mathbf{A}}$$

The mediator (Med) is a horizontal bar — Bar_h.

$$\Rightarrow Arc\,\overrightarrow{A}\,Bar\,Bar\,Bar\,Bar\,\overleftarrow{A}\,Arc\,Bar_h\,Deg\,Toldeg$$

The text of an angular type dimension-set consists of a number of degrees (Deg) followed by a tolerance of degrees ($Toldeg$).

$$\Rightarrow Arc\,\overrightarrow{A}\,Bar\,Bar\,Bar\,Bar\,\overleftarrow{A}\,Arc\,Bar_h\,Deg$$

In our sentence there is no tolerance, so the production that produces ϵ from $Toldeg$ is used.

$$\Rightarrow Arc\,\overrightarrow{A}\,Bar\,Bar\,Bar\,Bar\,\overleftarrow{A}\,Arc\,Bar_h\,Int°\,Min$$

The degree number is an integer followed by the terminal symbol ° followed by minutes.

$$\Rightarrow Arc\,\overrightarrow{A}\,Bar\,Bar\,Bar\,Bar\,\overleftarrow{A}\,Arc\,Bar_h\,Dig°\,Min$$

$$\Rightarrow Arc\,\overrightarrow{A}\,Bar\,Bar\,Bar\,Bar\,\overleftarrow{A}\,Arc\,Bar_h\,0°\,Min$$

The integer is a digit which is 0.

$$\Rightarrow Arc\,\overrightarrow{A}\,Bar\,Bar\,Bar\,Bar\,\overleftarrow{A}\,Arc\,Bar_h\,0°\,Int'\,Sec$$

The minutes are an integer followed by the terminal $'$, followed by seconds.

$$\Rightarrow Arc\,\overrightarrow{A}\,Bar\,Bar\,Bar\,Bar\,\overleftarrow{A}\,Arc\,Bar_h\,0°\,Dig'Sec$$

$$\Rightarrow Arc\,\overrightarrow{A}\,Bar\,Bar\,Bar\,Bar\,\overleftarrow{A}\,Arc\,Bar_h\,0°0'Sec$$

The integer for minutes is the digit 0.

$$\Rightarrow Arc\,\overrightarrow{A}\,Bar\,Bar\,Bar\,Bar\,\overleftarrow{A}\,Arc\,Bar_h\,0°0'Int''$$

The seconds is an integer followed by the terminal $''$.

$$\Rightarrow Arc\,\overrightarrow{A}\,Bar\,Bar\,Bar\,Bar\,\overleftarrow{A}\,Arc\,Bar_h\,0°0'DigInt''$$

$$\Rightarrow Arc\,\overrightarrow{A}\,Bar\,Bar\,Bar\,Bar\,\overleftarrow{A}\,Arc\,Bar_h\,0°0'4Int''$$

$$\Rightarrow Arc\,\overrightarrow{A}\,Bar\,Bar\,Bar\,Bar\,\overleftarrow{A}\,Arc\,Bar_h\,0°0'45''$$

The final sentential form is the sentence describing an ANSI asymmetric regular angular dimension-set with an angle of $0°0'45''$.

As a second example, consider the second dimension-set, depicted in the bottom of Figure 4. It is a linear regular dimension-set whose text, $12^{+0.1}_{0}$, includes a unilateral tolerancing. The sequence of sentential forms obtained by a leftmost derivation that produces this dimension-set is the following:

$$S \Rightarrow S_L \Rightarrow \overleftarrow{R}_L T_L \overrightarrow{R}_L \Rightarrow G_L W \overleftarrow{L}_L T_L \overrightarrow{R}_L$$

$$\Rightarrow BarW\overleftarrow{L}_L T_L \overrightarrow{R}_L \Rightarrow Bar\,Bar\,\overleftarrow{L}_L T_L \overrightarrow{R}_L \Rightarrow Bar\,Bar\,\overleftarrow{A}\,Tail_L T_L \overrightarrow{R}_L$$

$$\Rightarrow Bar\,Bar\,\overleftarrow{A}\,Bar\,T_L \overrightarrow{R}_L \Rightarrow Bar\,Bar\,\overleftarrow{A}\,Bar\,Num\,Tol\,\overrightarrow{R}_L$$

$$\Rightarrow Bar\,Bar\,\overleftarrow{A}\,Bar\,Dig\,Int\,Tol\,\overrightarrow{R}_L \Rightarrow Bar\,Bar\,\overleftarrow{A}\,Bar\,1\,Int\,Tol\,\overrightarrow{R}_L$$

$$\Rightarrow Bar\,Bar\,\overleftarrow{A}\,Bar\,1\,Dig\,Tol\,\overrightarrow{R}_L \Rightarrow Bar\,Bar\,\overleftarrow{A}\,Bar\,12\,\mathrm{atop}(+Num,0)\,\overrightarrow{R}_L$$

$$\Rightarrow Bar\,Bar\,\overleftarrow{A}\,Bar\,12\,\mathrm{atop}(+Int.Int,\,0)\,\overrightarrow{R}_L$$

$$\Rightarrow Bar\,Bar\,\overleftarrow{A}\,Bar\,12\,\mathrm{atop}(+Int.Int,\,0)\,\overrightarrow{R}_L$$

$$\Rightarrow Bar\,Bar\,\overleftarrow{A}\,Bar\,12\,\mathrm{atop}(+Dig.Int,\,0)\,\overrightarrow{R}_L$$

$$\Rightarrow Bar\,Bar\,\overleftarrow{A}\,Bar\,12\,\mathrm{atop}(+0.Int,\,0)\,\overrightarrow{R}_L$$

$$\Rightarrow Bar\,Bar\,\overleftarrow{A}\,Bar\,12\,\mathrm{atop}(+0.Dig,\,0)\,\overrightarrow{R}_L$$

$$\Rightarrow Bar\,Bar\,\overleftarrow{A}\,Bar\,12\,\mathrm{atop}(+0.1,\,0)\,\overrightarrow{R}_L$$

$$\Rightarrow Bar\,Bar\,\overleftarrow{A}\,Bar\,12\,\mathrm{atop}(+0.1,\,0)\,\overrightarrow{L}_L W G_L$$

$$\Rightarrow Bar\,Bar\,\overleftarrow{A}\,Bar\,12\,\mathrm{atop}(+0.1,\,0)\,Tail_L\,\overrightarrow{A} W G_L$$

$$\Rightarrow Bar\,Bar\,\overleftarrow{A}\,Bar\,12\,\mathrm{atop}(+0.1,\,0)\,Bar\,\overrightarrow{A} W G_L$$

$$\Rightarrow Bar\,Bar\,\overleftarrow{A}\,Bar\,12\,\mathrm{atop}(+0.1,\,0)\,Bar\,\overrightarrow{A}\,Bar G_L$$

$$\Rightarrow Bar\,Bar\,\overleftarrow{A}\,Bar\,12\,\mathrm{atop}(+0.1,\,0)\,Bar\,\overrightarrow{A}\,Bar G_L$$

$$\Rightarrow Bar\,Bar\,\overleftarrow{A}\,Bar\,12\,\mathrm{atop}(+0.1,\,0)\,Bar\,\overrightarrow{A}\,Bar Bar$$

5 Text in Engineering Drawings

Text is an important component in any dimension, because it expresses the value of the measure (length or angle), and tolerance between two geometry entities of the view of the described object. Recognition of text in hand-made drawings may be viewed as a special case of hand-printed character recognition, while computer driven plotted drawings text (as well as arrowheads) may be amenable to printed character recognition techniques.

Shirdhar and Badreldin [24] deal with recognition of isolated and simply connected handwritten numerals, and reports a 99% recognition rate with isolated letters and 93% for connected numerals. Hull [25] has proposed a computational theory of visual word recognition which is based on hypothesis generation, testing, and global contextual analysis. Pavlidis [26] deals with vector and arc encoding on graphics and text.

A robust algorithm for text string separation from mixed text/graphics image, which is relatively independent of changes in text font size, style, and string orientation, has been proposed by Fletcher and Kasturi [27]. Chiu [28] has proposed a reference-line finder for cursive script recognition. Wang [29] addresses the problem of locating address blocks in mail pieces and deals with machine vs. hand generated text blocks. None of [27], [28], and [29] is concerned with actual recognition of the text.

Whereas the clarity which usually characterizes text in drawings should facilitate its recognition, there are several problems that are specific to recognition of text in machine drawings:

(1) The text-specifying grammar is an evidence to the complexity of text in engineering drawings. The characters and accompanying symbols may be aggregated in blocks different than single lines.

(2) The text is scattered in random locations over the paper plane, which may contain elements of geometric descriptions similar to text. It is not necessarily horizontal, especially in drawings which follow the ISO standard, where the text must be parallel to the alignment of the dimension. Random text orientation is addressed by Fletcher and Kasturi [27].

(3) There are usually additional text elements in a drawing which belong to non-geometric annotation, such as production (welding symbols, surface quality) and logistics related annotation (part number tables, title, etc).

(4) The set of terminals contains specific symbols in additional to the Fortran character set (46 characters and digits on Fortran coding sheets).

(5) In manually prepared drawings, text may be drawn either by free hand or by template. Free hand instances of the same character may differ from each other even in the same drawing.

6 Anchor Parameters

A block of dimensioning text is referred to as a **text box**. It is the smallest rectangle enclosing the text block, which, as implied by the grammar, consists of one to three character strings. Adopting IGES notation, the height and width (length) of the text box are denoted HT and WT, respectively (Figure 5). Since we deal only with ANSI standard, the textbox baseline, which is the side of the rectangle, is always horizontal.

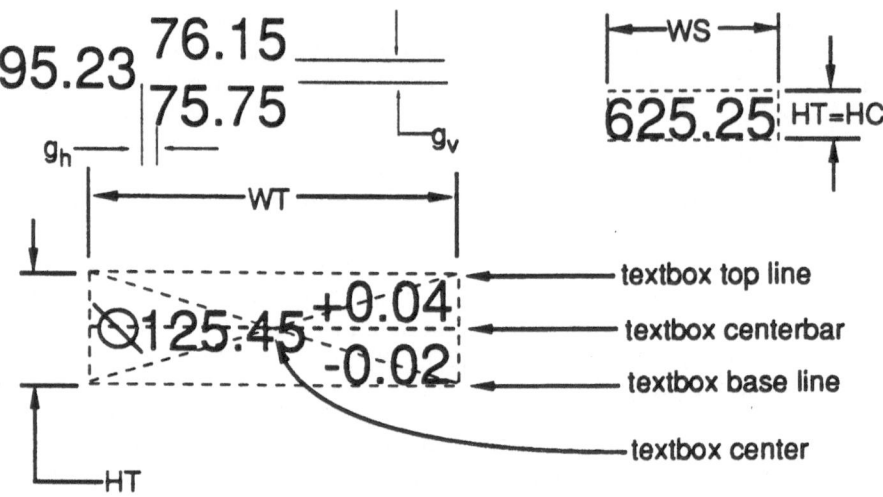

Fig. 5. Parameters of a string and a textbox.

Textbox centerbar is the line passing parallel to, and in the middle between, the text baseline and the text topline. The **textbox center** is a point midway along the textbox centerbar. Ideally, it lies along the continuation of the wire to which the text is attached. Moreover, if the binding wire is a horizontal bar, Bar_h, then the centerbar should coincide with the line on which Bar_h lies, as shown in Figure 6.

Two important text parameters are *character height*, denoted HC(*char*), and *string width*, denoted WS(*string*). HC is typical of a drawing, and is therefore the height of a text string, HS, as well as of a single character. WS, on the other hand, depends on the length of the string, and therefore may vary from one string to another. Unless the string consists of a single character, WS > HC. WT(*textbox*) and HT(*textbox*) designate *textbox width* and *textbox height*, respectively.

If the textbox consists of a single character string, then

$$HC(textbox) = \text{HT}(textbox)$$

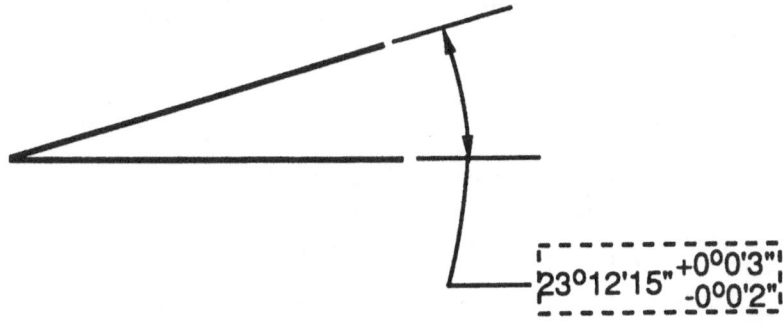

Fig. 6. An angular dimension-set with a three string textbox.

and

$$WT(textbox) = \text{WS}(textbox).$$

If the textbox consists of three character strings, then the following names are used to refer to its strings:

$$TextBox = BaseText\frac{PlusDev}{MinusDev}.$$

In this configuration, the height and width of a textbox are related to the height and width of the comprising text strings as follows (see Figure 5):

$$\text{HT}(TextBox) = 2\times\text{HC}(char) + g_v,$$

where g_v is the vertical spacing gap between two character strings laid on top of each other.

$$\text{WT}(TextBox) = \text{WS}(BaseText) + g_h + \max(\text{WT}(PlusDev), \text{WT}(MinusDev)),$$

where g_h is the horizontal spacing gap between two character strings laid next to each other. Both g_v and g_h are some fraction of HC, typically between 0.20 and 0.75, so HC is the primary text-related parameter to be sought.

As expressed by the grammar, each leader consists of two sub-components: an arrowhead and a tail. IGES permits eleven different forms of arrowheads. Three additional forms are mentioned in [2]. We classify the forms into four groups: triangles, rectangles, circles, and miscellaneous. All 14 forms are depicted in Figure 7 with their form numbers, where a number in parenthesis denotes a non-IGES form.

Of the six possible forms in the triangles group, four are recognized by IGES as wedge (IGES form 1), triangle (form 2), filled triangle (form 3), and open triangle (form 11). The last two forms (12 and 13) appear in [2]. Filled and open rectangles and circles are legal IGES arrowhead forms. Finally, forms of the miscellaneous group, which includes the 'no arrowhead,' 'integral sign,' and 'slash' as legal IGES forms, and the 'cross' that appears in [2], is rarely used in machine drawings and hence are not considered any further. ANSI does not

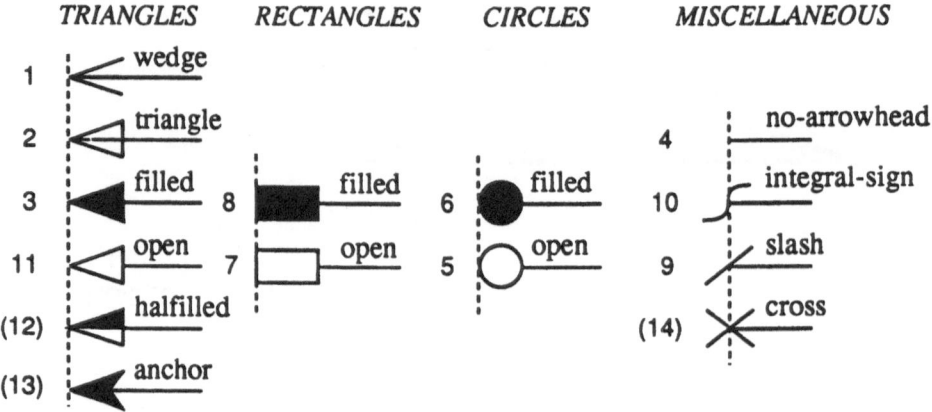

Fig. 7. Arrowhead forms.

specify the arrowhead form, but all the examples in the standard use the filled triangle form.

The tip of the arrowhead is called *arrowhead-front*, while the point in its opposite side is called *arrowhead-back*, as depicted in Figure 8, which also shows the parameters **AD1**, *arrowhead length*, and **AD2**, *arrowhead width*, adapted from IGES [5]. The three arrowhead-related parameters to be sought then, are form, length, and width.

7 Anchor Search

As argued, the possibility of finding arrowheads and text practically anywhere in the drawing plane implies that exhaustive search is prohibitively expensive, and calls for a syntax directed search mechanism to cut down the magnitude of search space. The dimensioning grammar provides the following guidelines:

(1) An arrowhead is always associated with an edge of each leader's tail. This edge is called an **arrowhead edge**, while the other edge is a **non-arrowhead edge**.

(2) The tail's non-arrowhead edge may have one of the following characteristics:

(a) If the tail is horizontal, the edge may be free (*i.e.* not connected to another wire) and may bind a textbox.

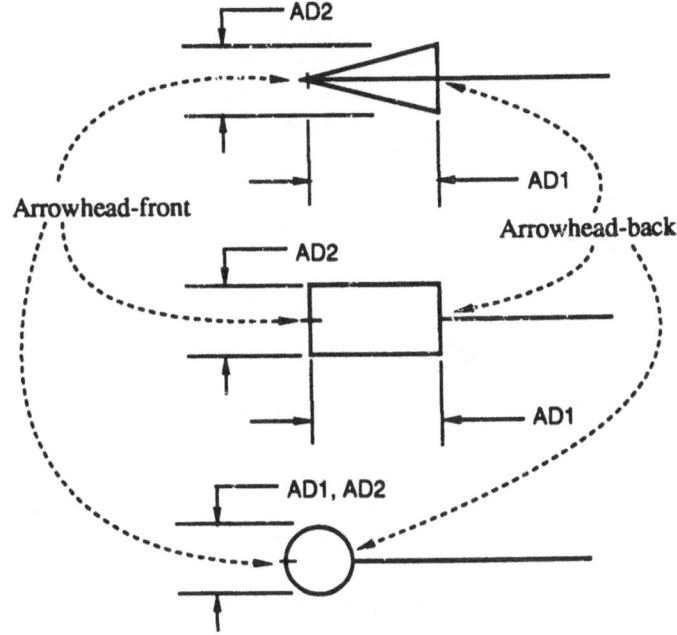

Fig. 8. Triangle, rectangle, and circle arrowhead parameters.

(b) If the tail is not horizontal, the edge may either bind a textbox or be linked to a horizontal bar Bar_h, which, in turn, binds a textbox.

Thus, rather than carry on a blind search for anchors over the entire drawing plane, the syntax directs the search to concentrate around wire edges.

A dimension-set text is always bound to a free edge of a wire. An arrowhead should be attached either to the other edge of that same wire, or to the edge of a connected wire. The latter case occurs if the wire to which the text is attached is a horizontal bar. In that case, the arrowhead is attached to the second edge of the wire whose first edge coincides with the horizontal bar's edge.

Based on the observation that a single drawing uses text and arrowheads of the same form and with substantially equal parameters, the anchor search algorithm has two distinct phases:

(1) *Parameter learning:* a sample of anchors (text boxes and arrowheads) is detected and used to learn (calibrate) anchor parameters.

(2) *Anchor location:* the calibrated parameters are used to effectively locate all detectable anchors in the drawing.

The wires in the wire file serve to limit the search for anchors to **potential-slots** — locations where anchors may potentially be drawn. Thus, even though the search is done on the binary image stored in a relatively big raster file, it is confined to small slots extracted from the wire file. Both phases of the anchor search thus make use of the two files, as conceptualized in Figure 9.

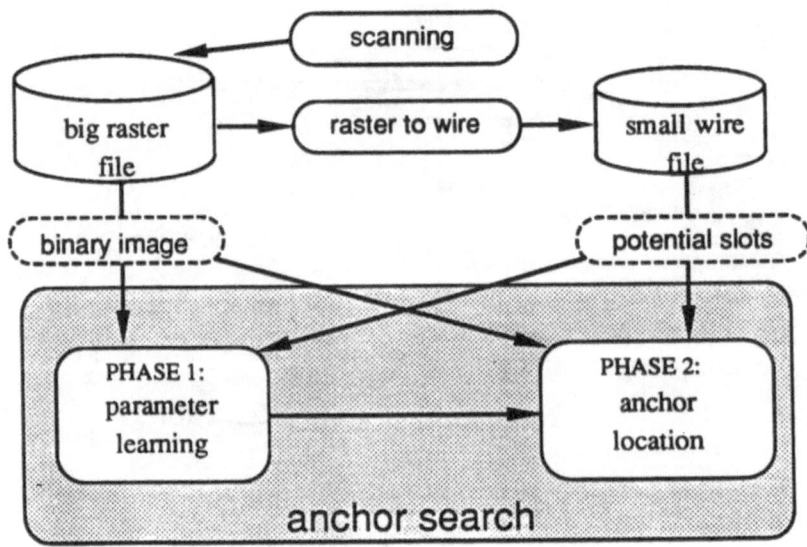

Fig. 9. Relations between sources and phases of anchor search.

8 Arrowhead Parameter Learning

To initiate the parameter learning phase, global anchor parameters are set *a priori*. For arrowheads they are max-AD1 and max-AD2, denoting the maximal possible length (AD1) and width (AD2) of an arrowhead in any machine drawing. Typical values for these parameters may be 8 and 5 mm, respectively. For text, max-HC denotes the maximal possible height (HC) of a text string. A typical value for max-HC may be 10 mm. These *a priori* values are used to define the location and orientation of slots in which anchors are potentially expected to exist. We start by detecting arrowheads. Figure 10 shows a layout of two arrowhead slots with respect to two arrowhead forms.

The slot is a LA×WA rectangular area, whose layout is determined by (1) the location of its center, which coincides with the edge of the wire E_0, and (2) the orientation of its long axis, which is set to potential-tail-direction. The latter is defined as follows:

if potential-tail **is a bar**
then potential-tail-direction **is the direction from** E_1 **to** E_0
else *(the wire is an arc)* potential-tail-direction
     is the direction of the tangent to the arc at E_0. .

A potential-tail is each wire in the wire file which is longer than minimal-tail-length. The latter quantity is taken as

minimal-tail-length = tail-sample-factor×max-A1.

Thus, tail-sample-factor determines the minimal length of wire that should be considered as a potential tail. To limit the number of detected arrowheads in the parameter learning phase, where only a sample is needed, tail-sample-factor may typically be set to 10, which would limit the search for arrowheads to bars which are at least 10 times longer than the maximal length of an arrowhead. Before starting the arrowhead location phase it should be set to $0.7 \times$ average-AD1, assuming that a tail cannot be shorter than 70% of the length of an arrowhead in the drawing. This relatively low limit on minimal-tail-length still saves a lot of computational effort by eliminating the consideration of each wire in the wire file which is shorter than this specified length.

The slot's dimensions are defined as follows: the width WA is set $=$ EF×max-A2. EF is the **enlargement factor** and may typically be set to 1.2. The length LA is taken as LA $=$ 2×EF×max-A1. The multiplication by 2 is needed because for some arrowhead forms, like open triangle, arrowhead-front L_0 (top of Figure 10), does not coincide with E_0. The position of E_0 and the slot's orientation guarantee that if an arrowhead exists in the neighborhood, it will be enclosed within the slot. The possibility that two arrowheads will be captured in one slot is taken care of by the slot's scanning mechanism, explained below.

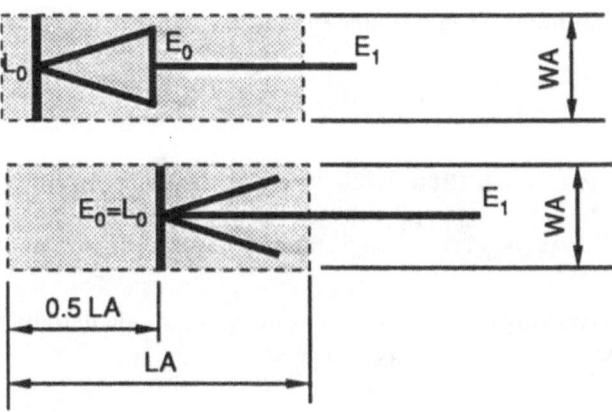

Fig. 10. Potential arrowhead slots.

The slot is scanned by m scan lines that are evenly distributed along, and perpendicular to, the slot's long axis. m is defined such that the gap between two consecutive scan lines is smaller than WL, the width of a line in the drawing, in order that the wire pointed to by an arrowhead will not be missed (skipped). Figure 11 demonstrates each fourth scan line for an ideal wedge.

The lines marked by W and B contain lengths, in pixel-length units, of white and black 'runs,' respectively. The 'runs' here are more general than regular runs of a horizontal scan, as the slot may be tilted. For each scan line, a list of runs, recorded in a column beneath the corresponding scan line, is obtained. Each list should start with a run of white pixels, therefore the list of runs of the second scan line from the left is $(0, 64)$. The line denoted NB is an m-element vector that lists the number of black runs in the scan line. Line BB is another m-element vector that denotes the distance (in pixel units) from the start of the first black run to the end of the last black run. Finally, line DB is an $(m - 1)$-element difference vector whose element DB_i is defined as

$$DB_i = BB_{i+1} - BB_i; \ 1 \leq i \leq m - 1,$$

and may therefore be considered as a crude derivative of BB.

The existence of (at least) two significantly negative elements within DB indicates the presence of an arrowhead in the slot. The arrowhead form is then determined by examining two features: The *Group Feature*, GF, and the *Fill Feature*, FF. GF has three possible values: *triangle*, *rectangle*, and *circle*, and is determined by analyzing the series of elements between the first and last negative elements of DB. Figure 12 summarizes these three possibilities. If DB is (at least approximately) a positive constant (BB increasing), as in Figure 11, then GF=*triangle*. If it is around zero (BB constant), then GF=*rectangle*, and if it is decreasing (BB unimodal) then GF=*circle*.

FF determines which form within the group has been detected. It is defined as the maximal number of black runs in a scan line, *i.e.*

$$FF = max\{NB_i\}; \ 1 \leq i \leq m.$$

If FF=1 then the form is **filled**, while if it is 2 then it is **open** (see Figure 12). For triangles, further analysis of the run lists is needed to distinguish between open and half-filled triangles (forms 11 and 12) and, if FF=3, among forms 1, 2, and 13.

Having determined the arrowhead's form, we now calculate its AD1 and AD2 parameters. AD1 is defined in pixel units as

$$AD1 = (NBN + 1) \times LA/m,$$

where NBN is the number of elements in DB that are between two significantly negative numbers. AD2 is defined as the second largest element of the vector BB, because the largest one corresponds to the wire at which the arrowhead points (*e.g.* the second scan line in Figure 11). The mean and standard deviation of both AD1 and AD2 is calculated, and if the standard deviation does not exceed a predetermined value, the mean is taken as the nominal value.

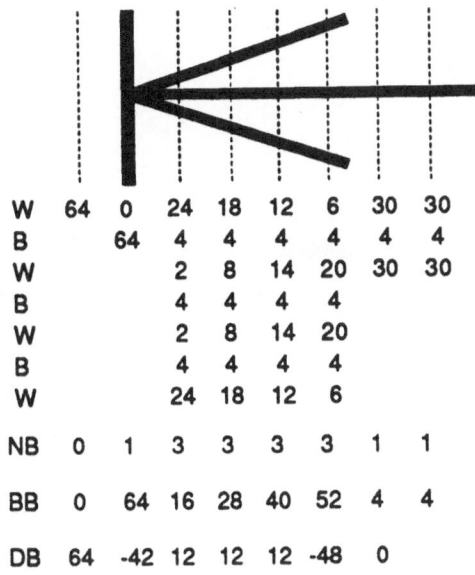

W	64	0	24	18	12	6	30	30
B		64	4	4	4	4	4	4
W			2	8	14	20	30	30
B			4	4	4	4		
W			2	8	14	20		
B			4	4	4	4		
W			24	18	12	6		
NB	0	1	3	3	3	3	1	1
BB	0	64	16	28	40	52	4	4
DB	64	-42	12	12	12	-48	0	

Fig. 11. Ideal wedge scanning results.

9 Arrowhead Location

With arrowhead form and parameters determined, we turn to the second phase of the arrowhead search, which is arrowhead location. For each potential-tail we determine the location of B_0 and B_1 as described in Figure 13.

The presence of an arrowhead is checked in the raster file. We look for black pixels in the circles whose centers are B_0 and B_1, and whose radii are proportional to the standard deviation of AD1. If found — connection from both B_0 and B_1 to L_0, the edge of the presumed arrowhead is tested. This is done by following black pixels along the borderline between black and white areas while moving in the direction that makes with potential-tail an angle of $\phi = \arctan(AD2/(2 \times AD1))$. If nothing is found in the circles B_0 and B_1, a similar test is performed using B_0' and B_1' (also defined in Figure 13) instead. If connectivity is established between B_0 (or B_0'), and the predetermined vicinity of the presumed arrowhead-front, L_0, and between B_1 (or B_1'), and L_0, then we record the location of L_0.

10 Parameter Learning and Location of Text

Each potential tail is expected to bind a text, an arrowhead, both, or none. Therefore, as one edge of a potential tail is examined for the presence of an

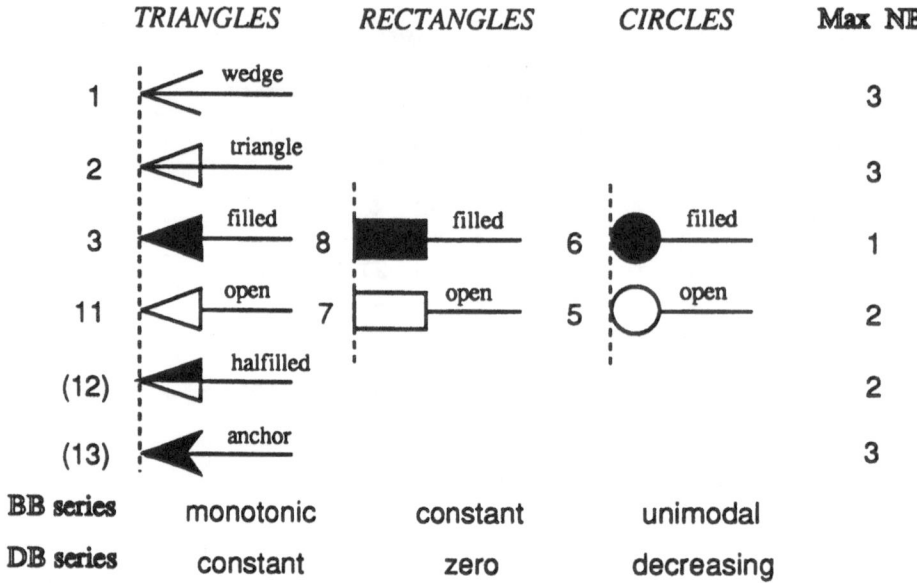

Fig. 12. Determining arrowhead form.

arrowhead, the other edge is examined for binding a textbox. Since the continuation of the tail should pass by the textbox center, as shown in Figure 6, we find the expected location of the textbox center and count the number of times that a horizontal line, passing through that point, crosses wires which are shorter than max-HC. If the number is at least 2, chances are that there is indeed a text there, in which case we apply the *ink stain algorithm*. This algorithm uses one of the detected short wires, which presumably belongs to a text, as a seed (source of the 'ink stain'). The algorithm then looks for additional short wires in the seed's neighborhood. Each detected short wire is used as a new seed to find additional nearby short wires. The process stops when no more short wires can be found in the neighborhood. At that stage, the minimal rectangle that encloses all these wires is defined to be the textbox, and a verification is done as to whether indeed its center is located along the continuation of the potential tail. If so, a textbox is confirmed to exist, and its height is recorded. After accumulating a sufficient number of textboxes, histogramming is done on their heights to determine the value of HC, which completes the text parameter learning phase.

The value of HC is used in the text location phase to determine potential text slots for each potential tail. As in the learning phase, each potential tail is checked for the presence of an arrowhead on one of its edges and a textbox on the other, and *vice versa*. The presence of one increases the probability of

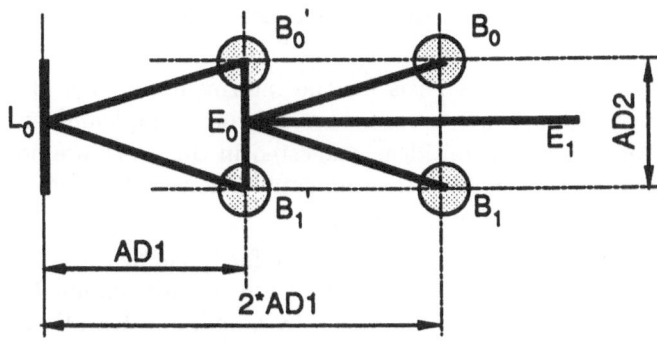

Fig. 13. Determining arrowhead existence.

finding the other at the other edge.

According to the dimensioning grammar, the only two possible cases in which a potential tail has an arrowhead on its one edge but does not have a text box on its other edge are:

(1) When the tail belongs to a leader of an asymmetric dimension-set and the text is bound to the other leader.

(2) When the tail does not have a free edge but is rather linked to a horizontal bar mediator, to which the text is bound.

The only possibility of a text being bound to some wire whose other edge is not bound to an arrowhead is when the wire is a horizontal bar mediator, in which case it is linked to a tail which binds an arrowhead in its other edge. This is the same case as (2) above. For each textbox that has been verified, all the short wires located within the textbox are saved for character/symbol recognition, which is beyond the scope of this paper.

11 Conclusion and Further Work

The scheme presented in this work proposes a two-stage process for recognition and location of sought entities in a given scene. An underlying grammar and an *a priori* knowledge about the possible range of an entity attributes (parameters of anchors in our case) enable reliable and efficient detection of these entities. Learning the parameter values of the sought entities is done in the first stage by a careful examination of a small sample found by applying syntactic considerations. The learned values are then used in the second stage to search for the entire entity population. They quantitatively specify exact potential sites that confine the search space to a manageable size.

The reliability of the search process is obtained by making use of the learned parameter values to characterize the entities. This reduces the rate of false identifications. The efficiency of the process is due to the great reduction in search space, and a concurrent use of the original raster file along with the processed wire file.

The scheme constitutes a basis for the intermediate stage of the Machine Drawing Understanding System, and is currently being implemented on a Sun3/60 Workstation. Since the general ideas suggested in this work are not necessarily implementation dependent, they may be applicable to a broader scope of tasks involved in intelligent recognition systems.

Two recent approaches may prove suitable for the higher level vision tasks of the Machine Drawing Understanding System. One is the Common Lisp Knowledge-Based Computer Vision system approach by Goodman, Haralick, and Shapiro [30]. It seems to be adequate, as it provides for definitions of data types and relations among them at various levels, and takes care of the data base management. Another approach is an object model for image recognition using Thin Line Code by Jagadish and O'Gorman [31], which also employs a hierarchy of four type levels. Future work will pursue the integration of ideas from these approaches with the dimensioning grammar and self, syntax directed pattern recognition for the high level, understanding stage of the drawing analysis.

References

[1] A. Jankel and R. Morton, *Creative Computer Graphic*, Cambridge Univ. Press, 1984.

[2] M. Karima, K. S. Sadhal, and T. O. McNeil, "From Paper Drawings to Computer Aided Design," *IEEE Computer Graphics Applications*, 5, pp. 27–39, 1985.

[3] D. Dori and A. Pnueli, "The Grammar of Dimensions in Machine Drawings," *Computer Vision, Graphics, and Image Processing*, 42, pp. 1–18, 1988.

[4] C. H. Parks, "Solving the Data Exchange Problem — an IGES Update," CAD/CAM: Management Strategies, *Managing the Data Base*, 1, 1986, pp. 1–15, 3.3.5 S29.

[5] B. Smith and J. Wellington, *Initial Graphics Exchange Specification (IGES), Version 3.0*, U. S. Dept of Commerce, National Bureau of Standards, NBSIR 86–3359, April 1986.

[6] J. W. Lewis, "Interchanging Spline Curves Using IGES," *Computer Aided Design*, 13, No. 6, pp. 359–364, 1981.

[7] J. C. Kelly, R. E. Parks, and D. B. Saylors, "CADCAM-005: An Introduction to the Data Exchange Process Using IGES," SANDIA report SAND86–2564.UC–32, 1987.

[8] K. Preiss, Constructing the Solid Representation of Engineering Projections, *Computers and Graphics*, 8, No. 4, pp. 381–389, 1984.

[9] K. Sugihara, *Machine Interpretation of Line Drawings*, The MIT Press, Cambridge, Massachusetts, 1986.

[10] J. A. Mudler, "Discrimination Vision," *Computer Vision, Graphics, and Image Processing*, 43, pp. 313–336, 1988.

[11] S. H. Joseph, T. P. Pridmore, and M. E. Dunn, "Towards the Automatic Interpretation of Mechanical Engineering Drawings," In A. Barrett (ed.), *Computer Vision and Image Processing*, Kogan Page, 1989.

[12] D. Dori, "A Syntactic/Geometric Approach to Recognition of Dimensions in Engineering Machine Drawings," *Computer Vision, Graphics and Image Processing*, 47, 271–291, 1989.

[13] L. A. Fletcher and R. Kasturi, "A Robust Algorithm for Text String Separation from Mixed Text/Graphics Images," *IEEE Trans. Pattern Analysis and Machine Intelligence*, PAMI-10, 6, pp. 910–918, 1988.

[14] L. W. Foster, *Geo-Metrics II–The Application of Geometric Tolerancing Techniques*, Addison–Wesley, Reading, MA, 1986.

[15] A. K. King, "An Expert System Facilitates Understanding the Paper Engineering Drawings," *Proc. IASTED International Symp. Expert Systems Theory and Their Applications*, Los Angeles, California, ACTA Press, Anaheim, Calgary, Zurich, pp. 169–172, 1988.

[16] ANSI Y14.5M-1982 Standard — *Dimensioning and Tolerancing*, The American Society of Mechanical Engineers, NY, 1982.

[17] H. M. Parsons and A. S. Mavor, "Human-Machine Interfaces in Industrial Robotics, Final Report," *Essex Corp.* Alexandria, VA., AD-A200960 HEL-TM-7-88, Avail: NTIS HC A06/MF A01, 1988

[18] D. Dori, "Enhancing CAD/CAM Systems Communication by Understanding Engineering Drawings," *Proc. ACM Seventeenth Annual Computer Science Conf.*, Association for Computing Machinery, Inc., p. 437, Louisville, Kentucky, Feb. 1989.

[19] J. D. Schroeder, "A representational framework and user interface for an image understanding workstation," *Proc. NASA L. B. Johnson Space Center, 2nd Annual Workshop on Space Operations Automation and Robotics (SOAR 1988)*, pp. 4510456. Avail: NTIS HC A22/MF A01, Nov, 1988.

[20] C. Machover, J. C. Dill, and D. L. Peltz, "New Products," *IEEE Computer Graphaphics & Applications*, pp. 111–116, July, 1989.

[21] M. A. Wesley and G. Markowski, "Fleshing Out Projections," *IBM J. Res. Develop.* 25 6, pp. 934–953, 1981.

[22] R. M. Haralick and D. Queeney, "Understanding Engineering Drawings," *Computer Graphics and Image Processing*, 20 3, pp. 242–258, 1982.

[23] D. Dori, "Intelligent Automatic Dimensioning of CAD Engineering Machine Drawings," *Proc. The International Society for Mini and Microcomputers (ISMM) Conf. on Computer Applications in Design, Simulation, and Analysis*, Reno, Nevada, ACTA Press, Anaheim, Calgary, Zurich, pp. 137–140, 1989.

[24] M. Shirdhar and A. Badreldin, "Recognition of Isolated and Simply Connected Handwritten Numerals," *Pattern Recognition*, 19 1. pp. 1–12, 1986.

[25] J. J. Hull, "A Computational Theory of Visual Word Recognition," SUNY at Buffalo, Dept of Computer Sci., *Tech. Rep. 88–07*, 1988.

[26] T. Pavlidis, "Vector and Arc Encoding on Graphics and Text," *Proc. 6th ICPR*, pp. 845–854, 1982.

[27] L. A. Fletcher and Kasturi, R., "A Robust Algorithm for Text String Separation from Mixed Text/Graphics Images," *IEEE Trans. Pattern Analysis and Machine Intelligence*, PAMI-10, 6, pp. 910–918, 1988.

[28] A. L. K. Chiu, "Reference Line Finder for Cursive Script Recognition," *SUNY at Buffalo, Dept of Computer Science Tech. Rep. 88–04*, 1988.

[29] C. H. Wang, "A Framework for Object Recognition in a Visually Complex Environment and its Application to Locating Address Blocks on Mail Pieces," *SUNY at Buffalo, Dept of Computer Science Tech. Rep. 88–22*, 1988.

[30] A. M. Goodman, R. M. Haralick, and L. G. Shapiro, "Knowledge-Based Computer Vision," *Computer*, 22, 12, pp. 43–54, Dec. 1989.

[31] H. V. Jagadish and L. O'Gorman, "An Object Model for Image Recognition," *Computer*, 22, 12, pp. 33–41, Dec. 1989.

Analysis of Technical Documents: The REDRAW System

Dominique Antoine, Suzanne Collin, and Karl Tombre

CRIN — INRIA Lorraine,[1] Campus scientifique,
B.P. 239, 54506 Vandœuvre CEDEX, France

1 Introduction

The automated analysis of technical documents is a problem which has been worked on for several years [19, 37, 16, 18], in many kinds of applications, including flow charts [1], mechanical engineering [8, 23], city maps (plats) [17, 27, 31], electrical circuitry [22, 13], hand-drawn figures [30] and geographical maps [38].

Several commercial systems are available for performing raster-to-vector conversion. However, higher level interpretation, including recognition of entities having a technological meaning, is still out of reach. The current trend is to incorporate as much *a priori* (contextual or domain) knowledge as possible at all stages of the "paper to high level" conversion process [28, 6]. This is especially useful in the area of technical documents, which obey strict representation rules. Our idea is to exploit as much as possible these rules to achieve interpretation at a semantical level [34].

In this paper, we present the REDRAW[2] system, which is currently under development in our group. Its main objective is to build a general, parameterized system for performing analysis of technical documents. For that, we want to integrate into a common environment:

- a module performing *segmentation* into connected components and *vectorization* of the graphics in a document,
- *interpretation* schemes for different kinds of technical documents, using *a priori* and contextual knowledge at all phases of processing,
- a set of general *tools*, such as detection of hatched areas, dotted lines..., available to these different specialized interpretation modules,
- representation of the *models* associated with the different classes of documents.

Figure 1 illustrates the general working of the REDRAW system being developed.

---

[1] This work was partially financed by a "Contrat de stimulation" from INPL (Institut National Polytechnique de Lorraine).
[2] for *REading DRAWings*.

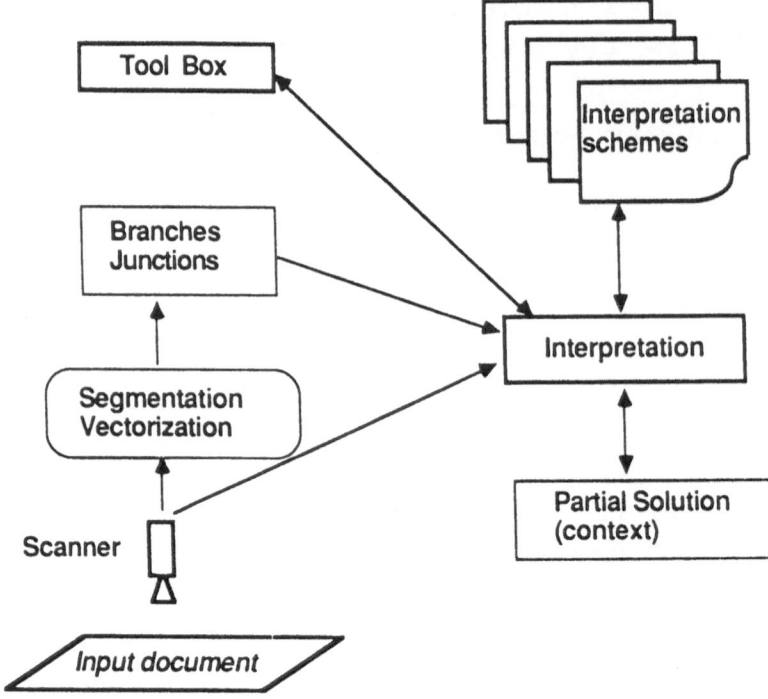

Fig. 1. The REDRAW system.

Presently, we have integrated the segmentation and vectorizing module, as well as interpretation prototypes for two kinds of applications, namely plats and engineering drawings. These parts are described in the next sections. Work is also being done on symbol recognition and other kinds of applications, as we mention in our conclusion.

2 Segmentation and Vectorization

The document image is input *via* a scanner. The resulting bitmap is segmented into a hierarchical tree of connected components; with each component, we associate its chain-coded contour. All this can be done in one single pass over the whole image, processing two lines at a time (Figure 2):

- The black and white runs on the current line are coded with a component label; the equivalence classes between labels are memorized.
- At the same time, we maintain a data structure representing the *border* between two connected components of different colors. These borders are represented using standard chain codes. When we process a line of black and white runs, we add a chain code to the head or to the tail of the associated border, in order to always have the black component on the same "side" of

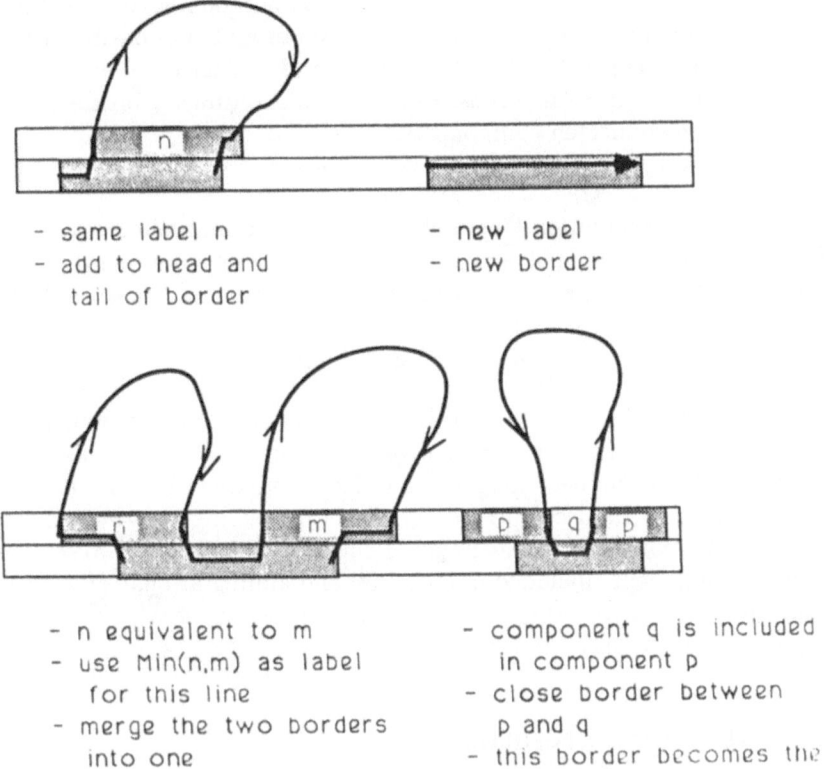

- same label n   - new label
- add to head and   - new border
  tail of border

- n equivalent to m   - component q is included
- use Min(n,m) as label   in component p
  for this line   - close border between
- merge the two borders   p and q
  into one   - this border becomes the
                                    contour of q

Fig. 2. Segmentation into connected components and chaining of contours.

the chain. When we find an equivalence class between two components, we merge the two associated borders into one and we update the whole data structure appropriately.

– When a component is closed, we update the inclusion relation and the border between the closed component and its including component becomes the *contour* of the former.

Figure 2 illustrates the method for some cases which can be found during the processing of the bitmap; of course the same processing is applied to black and to white components. The result of this process is an *inclusion tree* of connected components, each having a contour[3].

The next processing stages all work on this inclusion tree. The advantage is that we have immediate access to topological relation and hence that it is possible to go back to pixel information, retrievable from the contours.

The next phase is to extract *vectors* describing the graphical information present in the document. Whereas vectorization is often done using skeletoniz-

---

[3] Except the "root" component representing the white background.

ing and polygonal approximation, several other methods have been proposed. Among them, one particularly interesting idea is to match opposite parts of the components contours [23, 10, 29]. This is the method we have chosen [32, 33]. One of its advantages is that this processing can be done directly on the previously described tree of connected components.

The main steps of our method are the following:

- polygonal approximation [36] of the previously computed contours,
- matching and following of opposite contour segments, giving a set of *branches* and of *junctions* between those branches; each branch has several parameters, and among them its thickness,
- actual computation of the junction coordinates.

Figure 3 shows the result of vectorizing on an engineering document.

As previously mentioned, use of *a priori* knowledge can tremendously enhance the results of further interpretation. However, there are also cases where such knowledge can be used to guide low-level processing, as we shall see with the analysis of dimensions and as Figure 1 suggests. In the next two sections, we show two developments included in REDRAW and aiming at analyzing city maps and dimensions in engineering drawings. Afterwards, we present the integrated software platform we have designed.

3 City Map Interpretation

In any country, the automated conversion of city maps (plats) to CAD has a strong interest. Entities that appear on such plats are very simple and standardized. Therefore, analysis based on *a priori* knowledge is particularly well suited in this case. Our work consists in interpreting French city maps, with their standard notations and distinctive features (see Figure 4);

however, it can easily be adapted to other features and standards, as they are described in a *model* and each primitive process is applied independently of the others.

Plats mainly consist of buildings, represented by hatched areas, parcels containing these buildings, blocks of parcels, streets, etc. A central part of our method is therefore the efficient extraction of all hatched areas, as it allows to reduce drastically the information and to focus further interpretation on the remaining lines.

As this module is included into the general REDRAW environment, basic processes such as vectorizing are directly available. In the ideal case, text is made of isolated connected components having a small size; thus text/graphics separation is easy to perform. However, we often experience that text actually touches the line graphics. There is no direct way to separate text from graphics in this case; some approaches have been suggested, based on analyzing the straightness of the skeleton of the image [5]. We propose another idea, based on the analysis of the polygonal approximation of the contours, as detailed later.

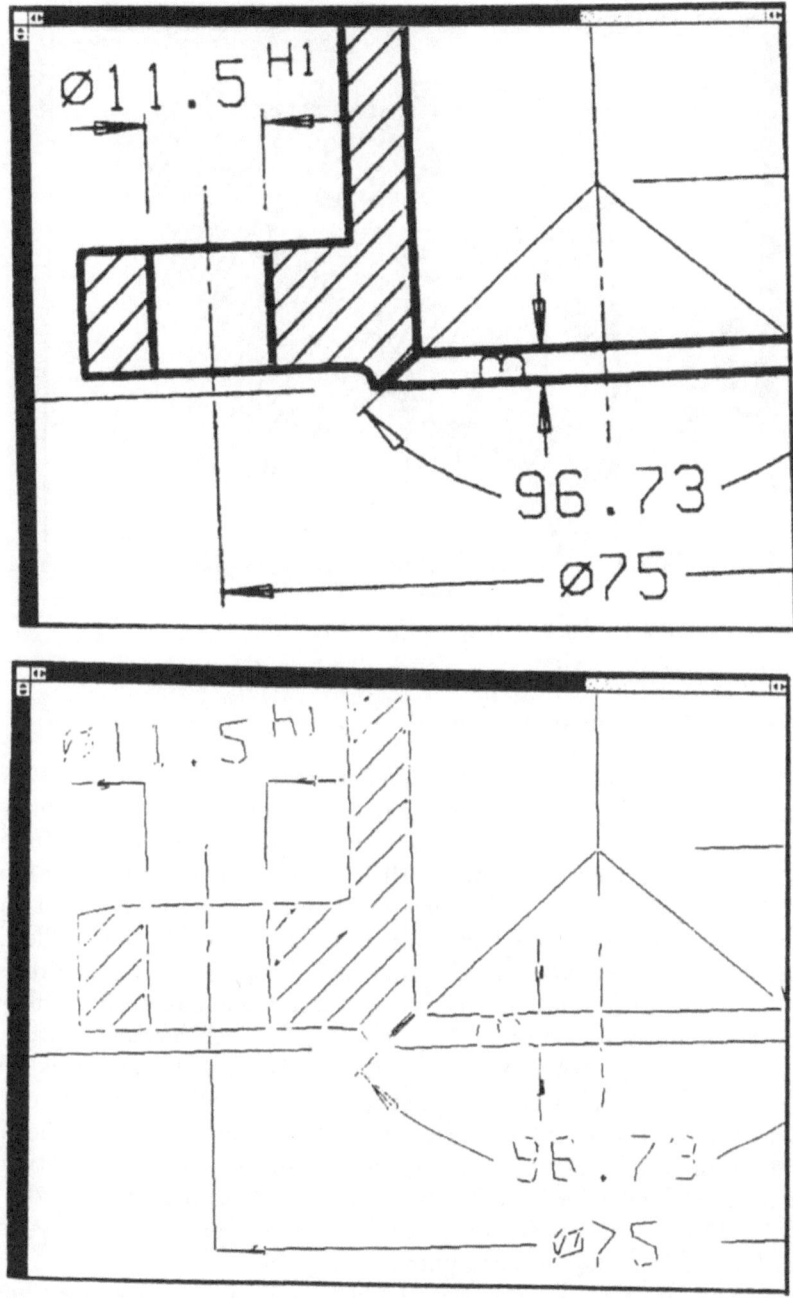

Fig. 3. A document and its vectorization.

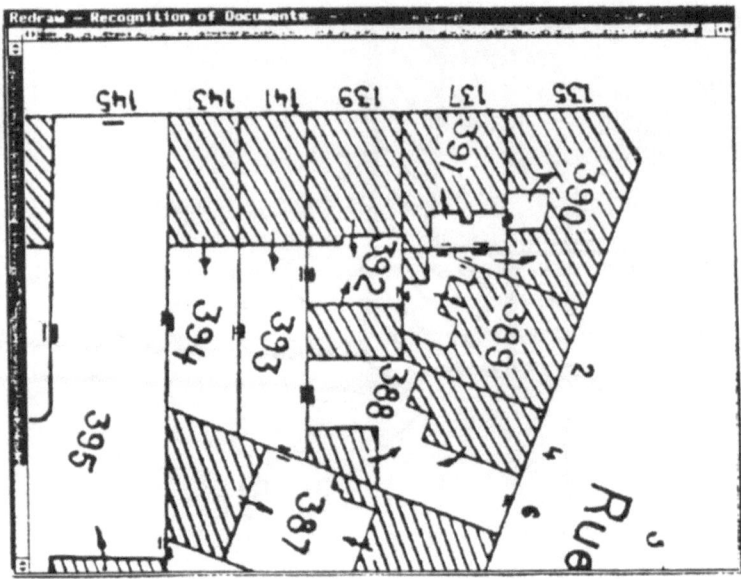

Fig. 4. Example of a French city map.

3.1 Extraction of Parallel Lines

In city maps, more than 70% of the segments represent hatched areas. A good extraction of parallel lines will therefore reduce considerably the number of segments to process. Our first approach was using "brute force": all segments in the document were classified according to their angle, and the "direction families" found in this way were further analyzed for finding adjacencies between lines [3].

Our present method is based on a finer classification of the lines, following an idea given in [25]: a single-scan algorithm in horizontal and vertical directions determinates an order relation for each extremity point of each segment (*i.e.* one for the origin point, another for the end point). A segment is said to be "opened" when the process reaches its origin point, and of course it is "closed" at the end point. It is possible for the same extremity of a given segment to be the origin point in the horizontal direction, and also the end point in the vertical one. In each direction, we can then find some segments to be *open* between the two extrema of another segment; those segments are said to *overlap* the latter (Figure 5). The relation of proximity between the segments and features like the angle of the segments are also computed during this step.

From these relations, we can deduce classes of parallel lines in a same area by assuming that parallel lines from a hatched area must overlap each other in the two main directions (note that the relation of overlapping is defined between two lines, independently of the direction of the relation). Parallel line classes are then merged as much as possible; in the case where there is an included text zone, the two hatched areas on both sides of it are also merged into one.

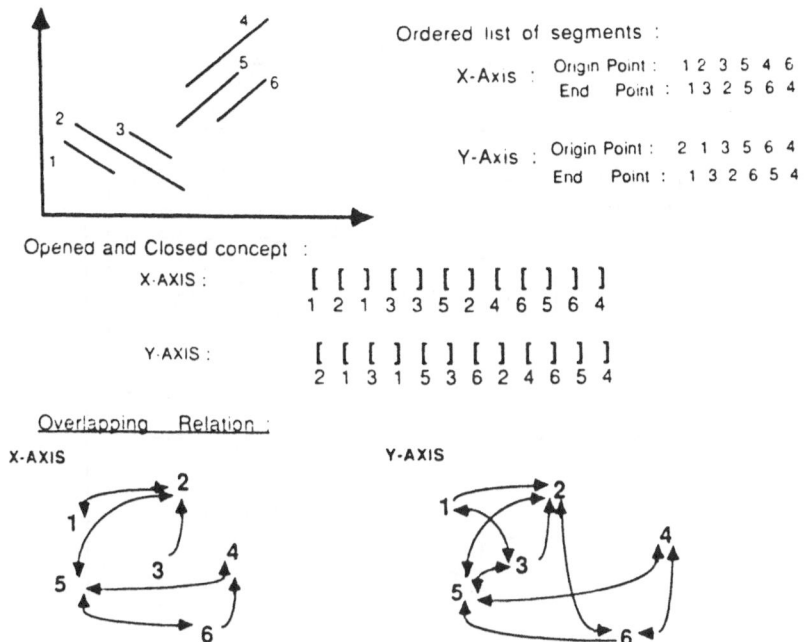

Fig. 5. Overlapping relation between lines.

3.2 Model-Based Analysis

The domain of plats is strongly standardized and can be easily described by a model. In addition, the main relation between entities is the inclusion relation. That means that the model representing city maps is hierarchically structured and contains relations such as proximity, intersection, boundary between entities (Figure 6). The main idea in this part of the interpretation process is to use the features such as the location and type of junction points, the proximity between connected components [2].

Knowledge about the domain leads us to choose extraction of parallel lines as a first step in the interpretation strategy. As a matter of fact, as hatched areas represent houses, we can deduce houses from a class of parallel lines which are close to each other. After that, parcels around them, districts around neighboring parcels, streets bordering districts, and so on, can be extracted by progressive grouping (Figure 7).

The extraction of houses is based on line following starting at the end points of a set of parallel lines previously recognized as a hatched area. In this way, a closed curve is constructed around this area (Figure 8). Once this house area has been located, the system can add to the hatched area the lines which were previously missed because of vectorization mistakes, for instance.

From the junction points between segments which constitute a house, we follow lines by progressive labeling, applying the following rules:

— If, at an intersection, we have the choice between different segments, we

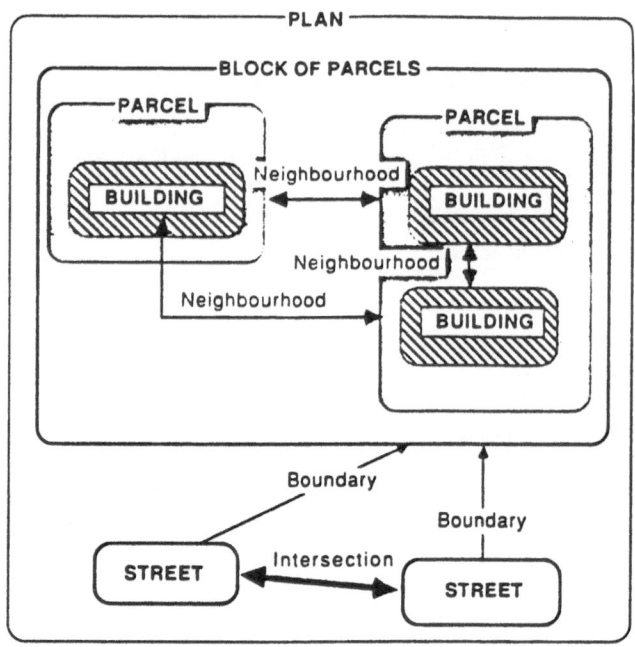

Fig. 6. A hierarchical model of French city maps.

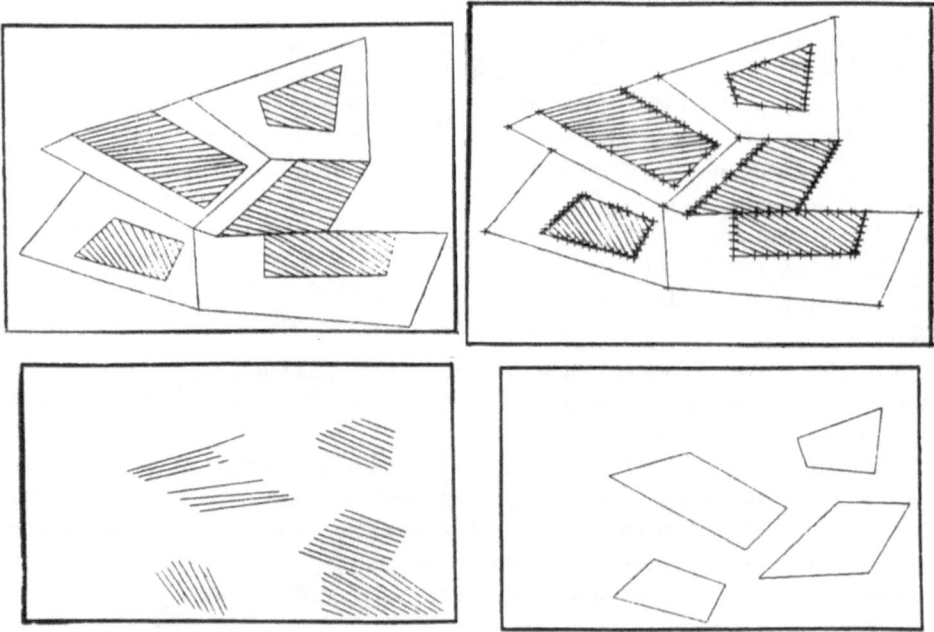

Fig. 7. An example of house detection in an artificial image.

always adopt as strategy to move as little as possible from the house.

- If a house is strictly enclosed in a parcel, without any common border with it, we use the overlapping relation between segments, computed during the lower level process, to make hypotheses about the parcel contours. However, it is quite evident that these hypotheses will not be as reliable as those made about the location of houses.

- We keep the possibility of backtracking by invalidating a parcel previously detected, if further exploration leads to inconsistencies in the relations between the various entities given in the model.

After having detected a closed curve, its lines are marked as being the borders of a parcel. The identification of blocks of parcels follows the same kind of strategy, this time applied to the individual parcels.

3.3 Text Areas

Character localization can validate hypotheses about graphical entities which are closely linked to text, such as streets which may contain their name. Characters are usually small connected components lined up to make words. To detect possible text areas, we search in the proximity of an already localized character, or in a complex set of small segments yielded by the polygonal approximation of the components contours. A set of connected segments is considered as being complex when many direction changes occur between the segments.

A character recognition process can be applied directly after this segmentation, in order for very small segments not to be introduced in the processing of the lines. Such a module, although not implemented yet, will be very useful. The characters in such documents tend to be normalized, well written, and thus relatively easy to identify. Therefore, the recognition module does not need to be very sophisticated, but it remains essential in order to build a complete technical document interpretation system.

3.4 Towards a General Strategy

The model used for city plans is hierarchical, with great importance given to the inclusion relation. In other domains, this relation may be less frequent, whereas other relations may play a bigger role. More generally, such relations (in our case proximity and inclusion) are very useful as they allow to reduce the search space when interpreting the document. The interpretation strategy must therefore take into account the fact that it may be best to process the graphical primitives in a given order, and also that recognition is strongly based on the *context* of the already extracted primitives.

In the case of city maps, we can make a difference between the *house* entity, defined as a contour of a hatched area, and the *parcel* entity, a closed curve containing a house. As a matter of fact, some relations are used to extract entities (the *around* relation applied to a hatched area, for instance), whereas others have no use before some objects have been detected (the *neighboring* relation between two houses, for instance).

The extraction of hatched areas is typically a *tool-box* module, which can be applied whenever it is needed, at different steps of the analysis process. The input data is a set of segments and junction points between these segments, the result consisting in a family of parallel lines.

In a general structural model, it is necessary to define operators bound to relations, which induce activation of specific procedures working on some entities. The operator called *around* is applied to a hatched area and consists in searching segments which have a junction with one of the parallel line extremities. The *included-in* operator follows a contour, searching for the inclusion of a hatched area in another curve (Figure 8). Its strategy is: move off the origin curve as little as possible, taking only into account junction points with lines which are not yet marked as belonging to a hatched area. When houses are strictly inside a parcel, the inclusion relation between connected components can also help in focusing attention on a restricted set of segments. Finally, the *neighboring* concept is represented by an operator which is only applied to entities already localized, and takes into account the fact that there is at least one common segment between these two entities.

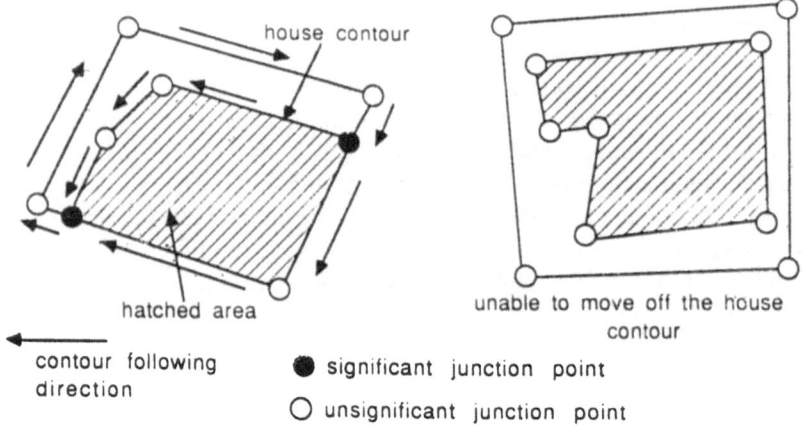

Fig. 8. Two different types of inclusion relation between a house and a parcel.

The definition of a model as a set of primitives, higher-level entities and relations between them is an important part of a general technical document interpretation system. As we have seen, this model must also include *operators*, associated with the structural relations present in the model, which are specific procedures for detection of the primitives, entities and relations. In the case of city maps understanding, we have developed a hierarchy of operators and primitives, formalized into the model. It can be easily transferred to architecture plans for instance, where hatched areas are very significant. But there is still an open problem: how can we define a general language for representing the model, in order to transfer knowledge from the model to the interpretation system?

4 Analysis of Dimensions in Mechanical Engineering Drawings

Engineering applications use a lot of technical documents. Many paper drawings are still used and there is a demand for reliable means of transforming and converting them to a suitable CAD format. By doing this, it becomes possible to match several views of the same mechanical part in order to build a 3D model [15], which can then be manipulated by a CAD system. Even if one could wish to have a completely automatic system, it is reasonable to provide user interaction at this stage, in order to correct errors and solve ambiguities [7].

However, if the exact dimensions of the 2D drawings are known, the building of the 3D model can be much more precise and automatic [21], as the lines and curves yielded by vectorization, which may have been distorted by the various processing steps, can be corrected again. This motivates our work on localization and analysis of the dimensions in engineering drawings. This is a typical case where *a priori* knowledge can be introduced, as well in low-level processing (image segmentation, edge detection, feature extraction) as at higher levels (object recognition, line drawing interpretation). Knowledge rules are used to control the recognition of components on the basis of their geometric, topologic and topographic structure.

4.1 Low Level Processing

The basic vectorization process is provided by the REDRAW system, as previously described. However, we must add more specific processing steps for taking into account the specificities of dimensions, which are basically made of thin lines (witness lines), arrows and text. The line thickness is provided directly by the general vectorization process, but the other two features have to be looked for explicitly. Figure 9 shows the different parts of a dimension line.

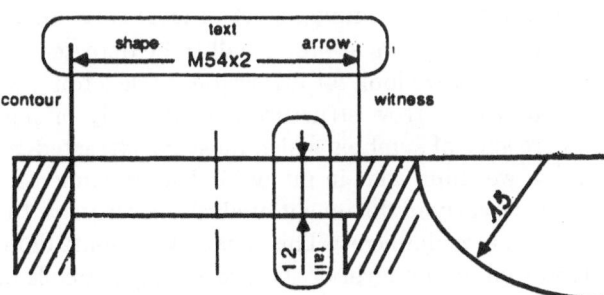

Fig. 9. The parts of a dimension.

4.1.1 Separation of text and graphics. The digitized image, consisting of a mixture of text and graphics, must be segmented in order to represent more efficiently the areas containing respectively text and graphics. The method described in [14] is well adapted for this kind of documents. The algorithm performs automated text string separation, independently of changes in text style, size and orientation. It doesn't require actual recognition of the individual characters. The algorithm is based on the analysis of the connected components and on the application of the Hough transform, in order to group components into character strings which are separated from the graphics. Thus, the method separates the image into text and graphics parts.

We have adapted the previous method to our case. In order to generate text components and separate them from graphics components, we build a histogram of their attributes (surface and density). The larger components represent graphics; which are discarded before further analysis. On the remaining components, labeled as text, strings are looked for by applying the Hough transform to the center of each surrounding rectangle, to detect text alignment. It may sometimes be difficult to extract a string composed of only two characters, as the Hough local maximum is low. Another method can be used in this case: grouping text components by considering the proximity relations between them [9]. This method yields text lines even when they are slightly slanted.

The results of the text/graphics separation process is a set of text strings having the following features: position, orientation, size and height.

4.1.2 Extraction of arrows. This problem is a "classical" pattern matching problem. In general, structural matching consists of two processes:

1. *extraction of local image features* with properties such as edges, corners, segments, intersection points,
2. *local matching*, *i.e.* finding all possible matches between image features and parts of the model, basing oneself on local consistency.

Sometimes, a third process is applied: *global matching*, *i.e.* using global geometric relations of the local features for finding a set of local correspondences.

It must be noticed that arrows are too small to be detected after line extraction. As a matter of fact, if we look for arrows on a "skeleton", we have lost too much information, and the arrow structure is completely or partially missing. Therefore, arrows are special symbols which must be extracted *before* vectorization. More generally, we think that in many kinds of documents, some symbols must be looked for very early in document analysis, as they are too small to pass vectorizing without "major damage". This means that some domain knowledge must also be introduced at the level of the processing of pixels or of connected components. Of course, all the information extracted at this level must be passed on to the interpretation phase.

We chose to work on the polygonal approximation of the component contours, in order to identify the arrow symbols. There are many ways to extract arrows:

- finding a *subgraph isomorphism* [20, 35], which is a good but expensive method,
- applying the *Hough transform* to detect this particular shape,
- taking into account all segments and trying to find small "triangular" configurations,
- looking at the *extremity* of each segment, to detect triangles.

We have chosen the third solution, and have selected the *main feature* of an arrow, *i.e.* the triangle shape. Because of the great variety of possible arrows, it is impossible to know in advance what kind of arrow we have to look for in a given document. Therefore, we choose interactively a model arrow in the document. We compute the angle between the two lines of the model arrow's head. We then process the whole image looking for pairs of connected "small" segments which have a similar angle with each other. Notice that local configurations with such an angle are not very current in document images; thus there will not be many false candidates. We obtain a set of possible arrows and confirm the hypothesis *arrow* by looking at its neighborhood, using *a priori* knowledge, for example, contact of the head with a line in the drawing, presence of a segment stemming from the head.

4.2 Drawing Analysis

4.2.1 Extraction of dimensions. A dimension is a set of components such as text, arrows, witnesses and shape. To build association between these components, we use information about text and arrows, and technical drawing normalization. In the first step, we don't deal with character recognition, which will be done later, in the *dimension/line drawing* association stage.

At this level, we have a set of arrows and segments with their properties. The main idea is to gradually build a set of dimensions from these isolated components, using domain knowledge about dimensions. Dori has shown that this domain knowledge can be described by a grammar [12, 11]; our work is strongly based on his method. Typical knowledge rules are:

- dimension lines are thinner than drawing lines;
- the arrow's head is in contact with a line, witness or drawing line;
- two arrows that are in a same dimension have the same orientation and opposite directions; they can point "inwards" or "outwards" with respect to the dimension text;
- if two arrows point inwards, they are connected to two different shape lines.

The strategy we chose is to build sets from arrows and witness lines (or drawing lines), then shape lines, then associations with text. We generate hypotheses, confirm them with the knowledge rules, and cancel the hypotheses if the whole correspondence is not consistent (no text found, or text not suitable because of its orientation...). Backtracking to lower levels is possible, by applying for example template matching on the pixel image in the vicinity of a line extremity when no arrow has been detected by the other strategy.

The aim of this process is to build a dimension classification based on line properties such as straight, circular or broken line, with one or two arrows, long or short lines... and on arrow characteristics, such as inwards or outwards pointing, contact with line drawing or not, etc. Dori defines a dimension grammar with rewriting rules to detect the tree structure of the corresponding dimension set, by applying successively these rewriting rules.

Figure 10 shows the results of arrows and dimension text detection.

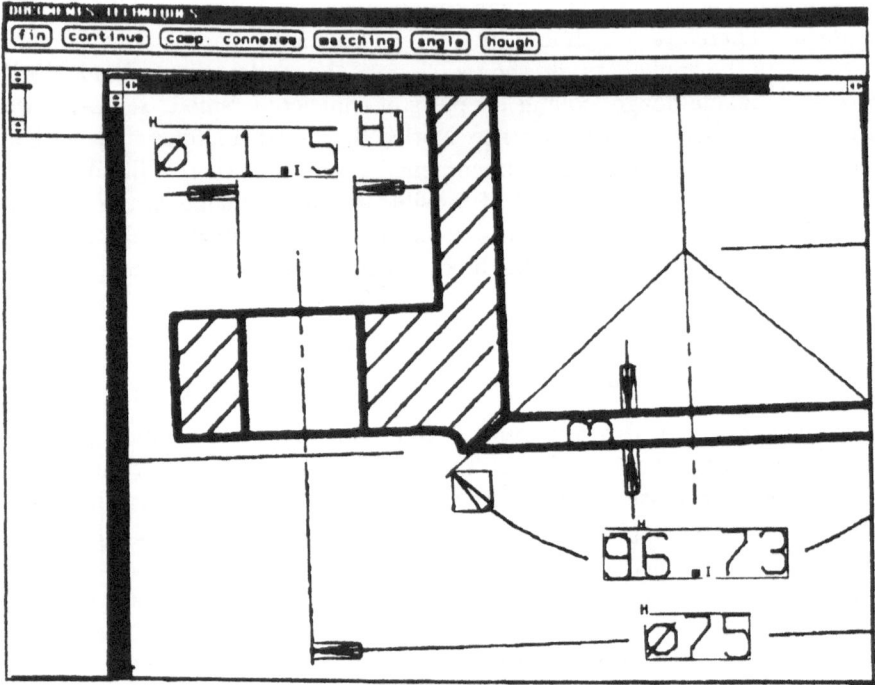

Fig. 10. Arrows and dimension text extracted from a technical drawing.

4.2.2 Line drawing and dimension association. This module, on which we are working now, is the second stage of the interpretation process. We must associate one dimension with one drawing line. The previous stage provided a dimension classification (linear, radial, angular, diametric, circular, chamfer dimension). Here, we have to use all information about arrows, text, witness and shape lines, and build some decision rules between these objects, essentially based on the technical drawing normalization. The main idea of this process is to follow the witness or drawing lines and to look for contact with arrows. The presence of a dotted line provides extra information, such as the detection of an axis or of a hidden line. All these data are expressed by knowledge rules which control the recognition.

Figure 11 gives a global view of the interpretation system.

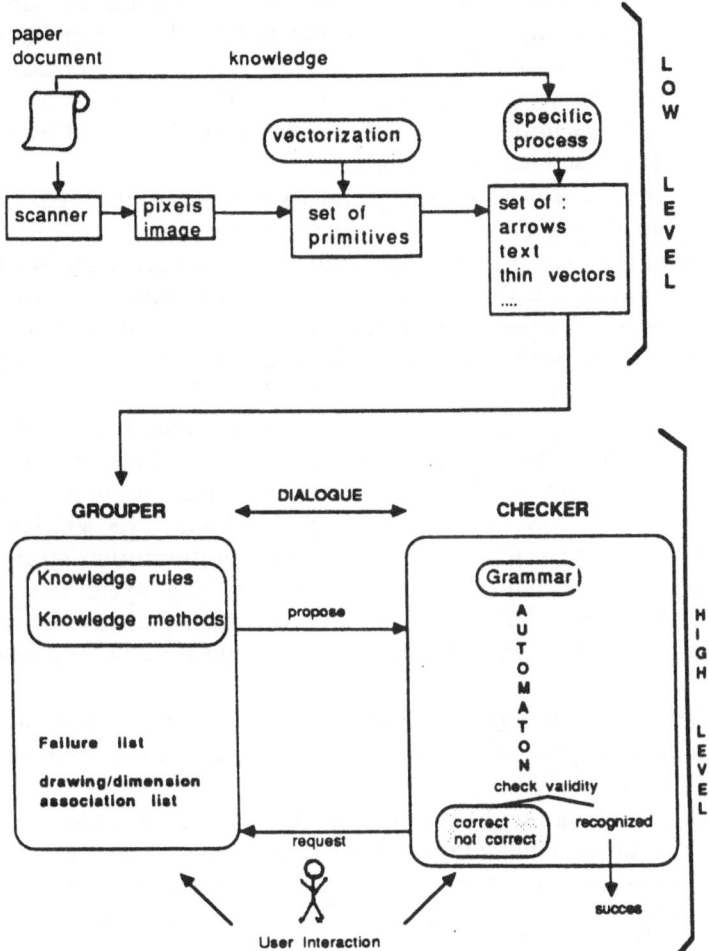

Fig. 11. Global view of the system.

5 Other Applications and Perspectives

In addition to the modules described in this paper, we are also working on other tools which are going to be integrated in REDRAW. Among them, let us mention the use of discrete relaxation for reducing the number of hypotheses on each graphical primitive, when interpreting city maps [24]. We have also started developing a general tool for *symbol location and recognition*, based on contextual search for the location and subgraph isomorphism for the recognition, and another tool for segmentation of printed musical scores, by adding domain knowledge to the general connected components segmentation.

At the lower level, the vectorization process can be improved by going from polygonal approximation to approximation in lines and circular arcs. We can assume that polygonal approximation is sufficient for documents like city maps, which don't contain many circular primitives. But in other domains like mechanical engineering, or when there are many symbols as in phone or electrical wiring, it can be very important to have precise recognition of at least two types of primitives (lines and circular arcs).

Another module which needs refinements is text/graphics recognition. We have already mentioned that serious problems arise when text touches line graphics, as is often the case in city maps. But even more generally, we think that a good segmentation must once more use extensively domain knowledge, as we saw in engineering drawings, where the location of text above dimension lines is a very precious information. More general segmentation tools, such as those used for office documents [4, 26], cannot be of immediate help in most technical documents, where text is sparse and disseminated among the graphics.

Actually, technical documents often consist of several *layers*: text, hatching, dimensions, small isolated symbols, the actual drawing, etc. In several cases, the superposition of these layers in a single document leads to recognition problems; for instance, when text touches graphics. The interpretation strategy should therefore allow for the independent processing of these layers, in the most appropriate order. When one layer has been identified and processed, it might be "removed" from the original image, which would then be re-processed from "scratch" again.

As satisfying results cannot be achieved only by automatic ways, we also must add *interactivity* at all stages, to let the user easily correct and enhance the interpretation results.

Generally speaking, we believe that REDRAW can be a useful test lab for several tools using domain knowledge to perform interpretation of technical documents. In Section 3.4, we showed how a global interpretation system, based on a set of recognition strategies, may work. We hope that we will be able to report further progress in the coming years.

References

1. K. Abe, Y. Azumatani, M. Mukouda, and S. Suzuki, "Discrimination of Symbols, Lines, and Characters in Flowchart Recognition," *Proc. 8th ICPR*, pp. 1071–1074, Paris, 1986.

2. D. Antoine, "A Technical Document Understanding System Based on *a priori* Knowledge," *Proc. 6th Scandinavian Conf. on Image Analysis*, pp. 843–846, Oulu, Finland, 1989.

3. D. Antoine, "Interprétation des parties graphiques dans un document technique," Rapport de DEA, Centre de Recherche en Informatique de Nancy, Vandœuvre-lès-Nancy, 1987.

4. H. S. Baird, "Global-to-Local Analysis," In R. Mohr, T. Pavlidis, and A. Sanfeliu (eds.), *Structural Pattern Analysis*, pp. 181–196, World Scientific, Singapore, 1990.

5. G. Bauer, "Following Lines in Vector Data Using Smoothness or Straightness Criteria and Applications," *Proc. International Seminar on Symbol Recognition*, pp. 9–15, Oslo, 1985.

6. D. Benjamin, O. Forgues, E. Gulko, J. B. Massicotte, and C. Meubus, "The Use of High-Level Knowledge for Enhanced Entry of Engineering Drawings," *Proc. 9th ICPR*, pp. 119–124, Rome, 1988.

7. O. Bergengruen, "Generating and Manipulating Solid Models from Images," *Proc. 6th Scandinavian Conf. on Image Analysis*, pp. 660–667, Oulu, Finland, 1989.

8. V. Cappellini, F. Flamigni, and A. Mecocci, "A System for Automatic Drafting Encoding," *Proc. IAPR Workshop on Computer Vision*, pp. 173–178, Tokyo, 1988.

9. S. Collin and K. Tombre, "Image Segmentation Using Connected Components for Document Analysis," *Proc. IFACS/IMACS/IFORS International Symp. on Advanced Information Processing in Automatic Control*, pp. 166–170, Nancy, France, 1989.

10. U. Cugini, G. Ferri, P. Mussio, and M. Protti, "Pattern-directed Restoration and Vectorization of Digitized Engineering Drawings," *Computers and Graphics*, 8(4):337–350, 1984.

11. D. Dori, "A Syntactic/Geometric Approach to Recognition of Dimensions in Engineering Drawings," *Computer Vision, Graphics and Image Processing*, 47:271–291, 1989.

12. D. Dori and A. Pnueli, "The Grammar of Dimensions in Machine Drawings," *Computer Vision, Graphics and Image Processing*, 42:1–18, 1988.

13. C. S. Fahn, J. F. Wang, and J. Y. Lee, "A Topology-Based Component Extractor for Understanding Electronic Circuit Diagrams," *Computer Vision, Graphics and Image Processing*, 44:119–138, 1988.

14. L. A. Fletcher and R. Kasturi, "A Robust Algorithm for Text String Separation from Mixed Text/Graphics Images," *IEEE Trans. on PAMI*, 10(6):910–918, 1988.

15. R. H. Haralick and D. Queeney, "Understanding Engineering Drawings," *Computer Graphics and Image Processing*, 20:244–258, 1982.

16. J. Hofer-Alfeis and G. Maderlechner, "Automated Conversion of Mechanical Engineering Drawings to CAD Models: Too Many Problems?," *Proc. IAPR Workshop on Computer Vision*, pp. 206–209, Tokyo, 1988.

17. T. Hoshino and S. Suzuki, "Automatic Input Method For Large-Scale Maps," *Proc. 8th ICPR*, pp. 449–453, Paris, 1986.

18. S. H. Joseph, T. P. Pridmore, and M. E. Dunn, "Towards the Automatic Interpretation of Mechanical Engineering Drawings," In A. Barrett (ed.), *Computer Vision and Image Processing*, Kogan Page, 1989.

19. M. Karima, K. S. Sadhal, and T. O. McNeil, "From Paper Drawings to Computer-Aided Design," *IEEE Computer Graphics and Applications*, 5(2):27–39, 1985.

20. P. Kuner, "Efficient Techniques to Solve the Subgraph Isomorphism Problem for Pattern Recognition in Line Images," *Proc. 4th Scandinavian Conf. on Image Analysis*, pp. 333–340, Trondheim, Norway, 1985.

21. R. Lequette, "Construction automatique de solides à partir de vues orthogonales de type dessin industriel," Doctoral Thesis, Univ. Grenoble, 1987.

22. X. Lin, S. Shimotsuji, M. Minoh, and T. Sakai, "Efficient Diagram Understanding with Characteristic Pattern Detection," *Computer Vision, Graphics and Image Processing*, 30:84–106, 1985.

23. W. Lu, Y. Ohsawa, and M. Sakauchi, "A Database Capture System for Mechanical Drawings Using an Efficient Multi-dimensional Graphical Data Structure," *Proc. 9th ICPR*, pp. 266–269, Rome, 1988.

24. G. Masini and K. Tombre, "Discrete Relaxation Applied to Interpretation of Technical Documents," *Proc. 10th ICPR*, pp. 706–708, Atlantic City, NJ, 1990.

25. T. Matsuyama, H. Arita, and N. Nagao, "Structural Matching of Line Drawings Using the Geometrical Relationship between Line Segments," *Computer Vision, Graphics and Image Processing*, 27:177–194, 1984.

26. E. Meynieux, W. Postl, S. Seisen, and K. Tombre, "Office paper document analysis," In G. Bracchi and D. Tsichritzis, editors, *Office Systems: Methods and Tools*, pp. 267–285, North–Holland, Pisa, 1987.

27. T. Nagao, T. Agui, and M. Nakajima, "An Automatic Road Vector Extraction Method from Maps," *Proc. 9th ICPR*, pp. 585–587, Rome, 1988.

28. J. W. Roach and J. E. Tatem, "Using Domain Knowledge in Low-level Visual Processing to Interpret Handwritten Music: An Experiment," *Pattern Recognition*, 21(1):33–44, 1988.

29. C. C. Shih and R. Kasturi, "Extraction of Graphical Primitives from Images of Paper Based Line Drawings," *Machine Vision and Applications*, 2:103–113, 1989.

30. S. Shimotsuji, A. Okazaki, O. Hori, and S. Tsunekawa, "A High Speed Raster-to-Vector Conversion Using Special Hardware for Contour Tracking," *Proc. IAPR Workshop on Computer Vision*, pp. 18–23, Tokyo, 1988.

31. S. Suzuki and T. Yamada, "MARIS: Map Recognition Input System," *Proc. IAPR Workshop on Computer Vision*, pp. 421–426, Tokyo, 1988.

32. K. Tombre, "Finding and Coding Graphics in a Composite Document," *Proc. 5th Scandinavian Conf. on Image Analysis*, pp. 589–596, Stockholm, 1987.

33. K. Tombre, "La saisie automatisée de documents composites : reconnaissance, codage et interprétation des parties graphiques," Doctoral Thesis, INPL, Centre de Recherche en Informatique de Nancy, Vandœuvre-lès-Nancy, 1987.

34. K. Tombre and D. Antoine, "Analysis of technical documents using *a priori* Knowledge," In R. Mohr, T. Pavlidis, and A. Sanfeliu, editors, *Structural Pattern Analysis*, pp. 229–241, World Scientific, Singapore, 1990.

35. J. R. Ullmann, "An Algorithm for Subgraph Isomorphism," *J. of the ACM*, 23(1):31–42, 1976.

36. K. Wall and P. Danielsson, "A Fast Sequential Method for Polygonal Approximation of Digitized Curves," *Computer Vision, Graphics and Image Processing*, 28:220–227, 1984.

37. L. S. Wolfe and J. de Wyze, "An Update on Drawing Conversion," *Computer Aided Design Report*, 8(6):1–11, 1988.

38. J. Ylä-Jääski and H. Ahonen, "Knowledge-based Analysis of Line Drawings," *Proc. 6th Scandinavian Conf. on Image Analysis*, pp. 774–777, Oulu, Finland, 1989.

Music Notation

A Critical Survey of Music Image Analysis

Dorothea Blostein[1] and Henry S. Baird[2]

[1] Department of Computing and Information Science,[3]
   Queen's University, Kingston, Ontario, Canada K7L 3N6
[2] AT&T Bell Laboratories, Computing Science Research Center,
   600 Mountain Avenue, Murray Hill, NJ 07974, USA

The research literature concerning the automatic analysis of images of printed and handwritten music notation, for the period 1966 through 1990, is surveyed and critically examined.

1 Introduction

Printed and handwritten music notation is intended to document musical information in a legible, archival form. Both recognition and generation of music notation can of course be modeled as mappings between the printed notation and the information it represents (Figure 1).

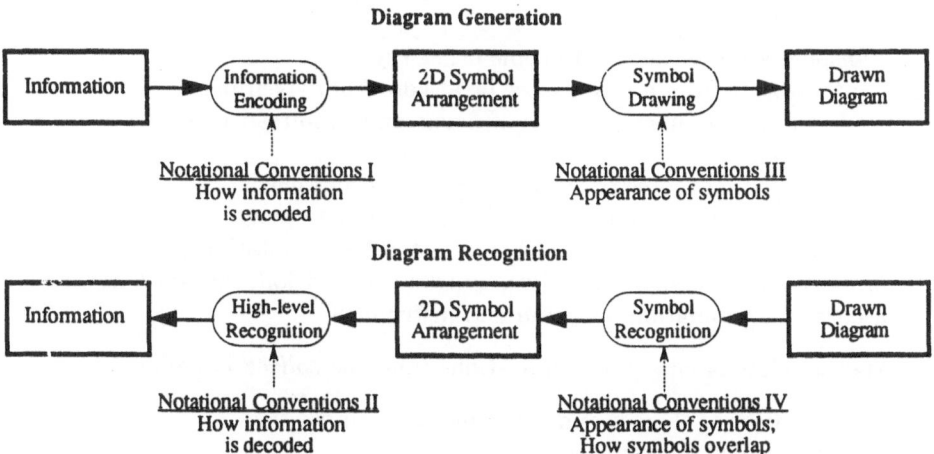

Fig. 1. Recognition and generation of music notation.

While many important details of the appearance of machine-printed music notation are effectively standardized, the information to be recovered during mu-

---

[3] This work was supported in part by the Natural Sciences and Engineering Research Council of Canada.

sic recognition is much less well formalized, and furthermore depends strongly on the application (Section 1.1). As a result, agreement is elusive on uniform standards for success: existing music recognition systems are able to extract information sufficient for some applications but not for others. Most work through 1990 has concentrated on locating staves and isolating and recognizing symbols. Outstanding problems include effective algorithms to interpret the resulting 2-D arrangement of symbols, and precise formalisms for representing the results of interpretation.

1.1 Goals and Applications

Automatic recognition of machine-printed music has been undertaken for a variety of reasons, and as a result, technical goals vary also. For example, for the analysis of musical style, it may be sufficient to extract the pitch, duration, and simultaneity of all notes. It is harder to produce parts from a score (or *vice versa*), since all musical symbols, not only the notes, must be recognized and associated correctly with voices. The following list of applications for printed music recognition is compiled from various authors' lists, including [Kas70, Pre75, Fuj88].

One important class of applications concerns *editing of scores* for reprinting, revision, and preparation of performance materials:

1. adapt existing works to other instrumentations: for example, reduce full scores to piano scores;
2. read various works in old editions and produce a new printing;
3. make critical editions of musical compositions given different printed versions of the 'same' composition;
4. transpose a music sample to some other key;
5. produce parts from a given score or a score from given parts;
6. read in a newly engraved piece of music and proofread it for syntactic and other errors;
7. convert existing scores to Braille to aid blind musicians;
8. print newly written music automatically (if the recognition program were extended to the recognition of handwritten music notation); and
9. produce audio versions of a given written composition; the computer can be used as a combination musician and instrument.

Another class of emerging applications concerns *collecting databases*:

1. create indices of themes and other music features;
2. analyze musical structure and style;
3. test theories of music; and
4. evaluate algorithms for the automatic analysis or composition of music.

1.2 Non-optical Input Methods

In the absence of optic music reading capabilities, non-optical input methods have been used. [CBM88] contains an extensive survey of music input methods;

see also ([Fuj88], pp. 4-6). Alphanumeric entry of a music-description language is common, but this method is slow and error prone. Music editors with graphical user interfaces can be used; this reduces errors and speeds up entry, particularly if MIDI input devices can be used to enter pitch and rhythm information directly. Attempts have been made to recognize music from audio input; some success has been obtained with monophonic music, but extension to polyphonic music seems very difficult.

1.3 Terminology

Here is a summary of commonly occurring terminology:

staff line A long thin horizontal line which defines a coordinate system for music notation. Typically five parallel staff lines are drawn to form a staff, but only one or two staff lines may be used for percussion music.

staff-line sections The *covered* sections of a staff line are those sections where other music symbols intersect the staff line; the remaining sections of the staff line are *bare*.

staff The staff lines plus all associated symbols, including music symbols, lyrics and textual annotations.

staff space The distance between the staff lines within a single staff. The staff space provides a normalized unit of measurement for expressing distances.

system A set of staves that are played in parallel; in printed music these staves are connected by braces, and bar lines may be drawn through from one staff to the next. A page of an orchestra score may contain only a single system. (Some authors prefer the term *paragraph*.)

staff nucleus The area of a staff that contains the staff lines and the musical symbols (we introduce this term for lack of any existing term). Many music recognition systems restrict their attention to symbols in the staff nucleus. In order to avoid missing symbols on ledger lines, the staff nucleus can be defined to extend vertically one or two staff spaces above the top staff line and one or two staff spaces below the bottom staff line.

voice A musical line. A voice may correspond to a single instrument; a piano part is usually notated as two and sometimes more voices. Several voices may be printed together on one staff: in an orchestra score, the Flute 1 and Flute 2 voices are printed on the same staff (with opposite stem direction), but they are printed separately to make the individual instrumental parts.

monophonic Music consisting of a single voice, where this voice contains no chords.

X projection A projection of an image onto the X axis, that is, downwards forming a horizontal distribution. The result is a vector whose ith component is the sum of all black pixels in the ith column of the image. (Some authors refer to this as a *vertical projection*, since the projection is in the vertical direction.)

Y projection A projection of an image onto the Y axis. The result is a vector whose ith component is the sum of all black pixels in the ith row of the image. (Some authors refer to this as a *horizontal projection*.)

digitizing resolution The spatial resolution of the document scanner during image acquisition, usually expressed in units of *dots per inch* (dpi). (Some authors prefer *pixels per inch* (ppi).)

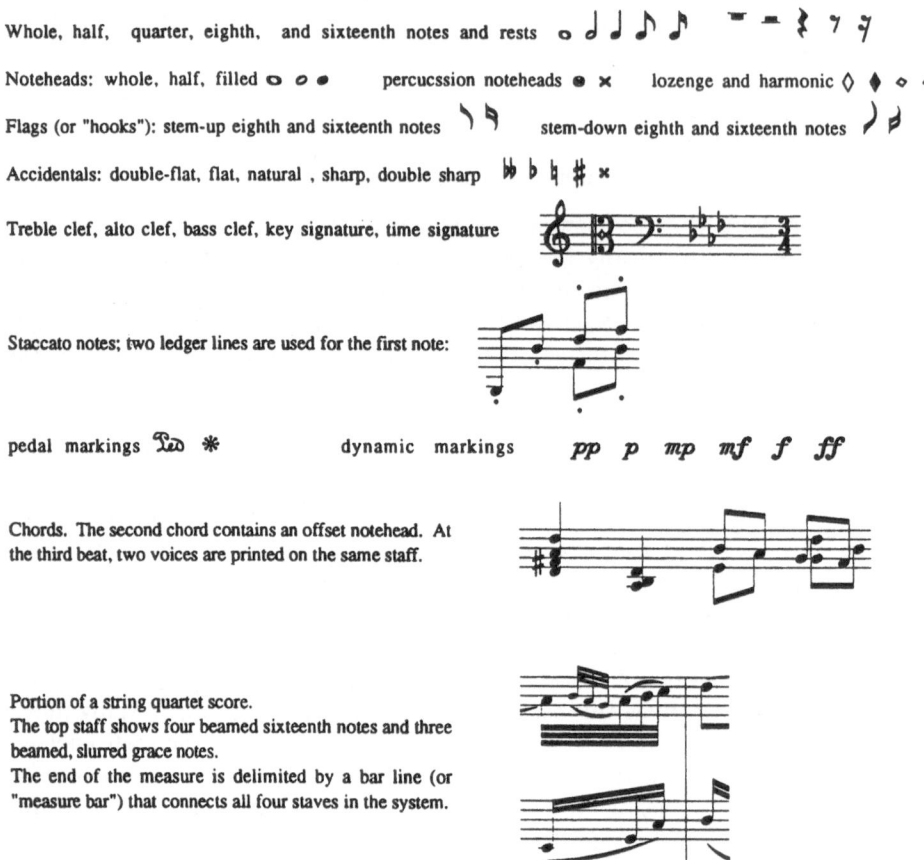

Fig. 2. Illustration of some terms for musical notation.

2 Problem Statement

Common music notation does not have a unique, precise definition. Four particularly useful publications in English that attempt to codify printing standards for music notation are [Gro90, Rea79, Ros70, Sto80]. All of these admit that, in practice, composers and publishers often feel free to adapt old notation to new uses, and invent new notation, as they see fit. There are in fact national "dialects" of music notation, and musical works use many different levels of notational complexity. Thus it may not be possible to devise a single recognition system capable of recognizing all music notation. [Pru66] states that a complete solution to the music recognition problem is "the specification of: which notes are present, what order they are played in, their time values or durations, and volume, tempo, and interpretation." This level of recognition suffices for only some of the applications listed in Section 1.1.

[Kas70] gives a musician's view of the desired I/O behavior of a music-reading machine. The proposed output language is somewhat clumsy and dated due to its emphasis on binary and octal codes. However, it is interesting to see a musician's list of the information that would be desired from a music-reading machine. In addition, Kassler's definition of a *scanning unit* may be useful. A scanning unit is composed of a subset of music symbols found on one staff and forming an unbroken X projection. The following music symbols are not included in scanning units: staff lines, beams, slurs, ties, brackets, text, and crescendo or decrescendo signs. Thus the scanning units are generally quite small, for example, a clef, one or more key-signature accidentals, a time signature, note heads in a chord. These scanning units are used to delimit the extent of parameterized symbols such as slurs and beams.

2.1 Music Symbols: Primitives, Parameterized Symbols, and Characters

The definition of a "music symbol" varies, although all authors agree that staff lines are symbols in their own right, separate from all other symbols that appear on the page. Some authors (*e.g.* [Pre70]) define music symbols as all four-connected regions that remain after staff lines have been removed. Thus a beamed note sequence is called a single symbol. Other authors (*e.g.* [Mah82, KI91]) consider such symbols to be composed of pattern primitives such as stems, beams and note heads.

Many authors [Pre70] distinguish between *characters*, which are size invariant, and other malleable symbols such as beams and slurs, which have a parameterized shape. Traditional character recognition methods such as template matching can be applied to music characters, but not to parameterized symbols. [Mah82] distinguishes between the music symbols that describe what is to be played and the music symbols that describe how things are to be played. The recognition of the "what" symbols (notes, clefs, key signatures, and so on) forms the basic music recognition problem. Extending this to the "how" symbols (which occur in great variety, often in the form of text phrases) compounds the basic music recognition problem with that of reading printed alphanumeric text. Note that recognition of the "what" symbols would be sufficient for many of the applications listed in Section 1.1.

2.2 Recognition of Music Symbols

A good introduction to the difficulties of symbol recognition in music is given in [Fuj88], Chapter 4. This thesis provides a well-illustrated introduction to music printing methods — typography, engraving, lithography, and modern methods.

Examples are given of the widely varying appearance of symbols such as the treble clef. Music symbols vary in orientation, appearance and positioning. Typical music symbols are much less regular in appearance and positioning than are the characters in printed text. Adjacent and overlapping symbol placements are used, further complicating the recognition process.

3 Thresholding and Noise Reduction

A common first operation in a music recognition system is thresholding to convert a gray-scale image into a binary image. Other forms of preprocessing are sometimes used for noise reduction. The early work of Prerau is typical: [Pre71] works with 512×512 images with 8 gray levels, scanned at 225 dpi . A threshold is chosen (apparently manually) to convert to a binary image. Prerau claims that since most points in the image are not near the threshold, the choice of threshold-level is not critical. In [CB91], the scanner performs automatic thresholding. A horizontal low-pass filter is used to remove short breaks in staff lines and symbols. In images scanned at 400 dpi, isolated or singly connected black sections of less than 5 pixels are removed as noise. (The division of the image into sections is described in Section 4.6.)

[LC85] describes the use of preprocessing for noise reduction. A three-by-three mask is used to eliminate isolated black pixels and to fill in isolated white pixels. Also, a simple filter is used to control the amount of light in the CCTV camera image; details about this filter are not given. In the vision system for the Wabot-2 robot [Mat85] (Section 5.4), the image is subdivided and each region separately thresholded to allow for uneven illumination. The image is then rotated as required and normalized to compensate for distortions introduced in scanning.

4 Staff Lines

Staff lines play a central role in music notation. They define the vertical coordinate system for pitches, and provide a horizontal direction for the temporal coordinate system. The staff spacing gives a size normalization that is useful both for symbol recognition and interpretation. Almost universally, sizes and distances are measured in units that are normalized to the staff spacing. Many authors implicitly make an assumption that was explicitly stated by [Fuj88]: the size of musical symbols is linearly related to the staff spacing. This assumption has not been rigorously tested, but appears to hold at least approximately.

Recognition of staff lines is one of the first steps in most music recognition systems. Since recognition of music symbols is confounded by the existence of horizontal lines through the symbols, a common goal is to identify staff lines and remove the bare staff-line sections. [Pre70] identifies three ways in which staff lines interfere with symbol recognition: (1) the staff lines graphically connect symbols that would normally be disconnected, (2) the staff lines camouflage the contour of a symbol, and (3) the staff lines fill in symbol areas that would normally be blank. Staff line identification is complicated by noise and distortion. [Pre70] notes that the five staff lines found on a piece of sheet music are not exactly parallel, horizontal, equidistant, of constant thickness, or even straight; scanning noise and quantization noise compound these problems. [Car89] notes that staff-line analysis techniques must be able to cope with staff-line inclination and curvature, as well as with the interfering effects of beams and other linear elements in the score. In some cases, staff lines may be obscured to a significant extent by multiple beams, particularly when these are horizontal. Thus standard image-processing techniques for line-finding often do not suffice for locating staff lines.

4.1 Pruslin

Two early MIT PhD theses, one by Pruslin [Pru66] and the other by Prerau [Pre70, Pre71, Pre75] addressed the removal of staff lines in images of sheet music. Both of these theses were reviewed in [Kas72]. [Pru66] preprocesses the music image by eliminating all thin horizontal and vertical lines, including many bare staff-line sections and stems. This results in an image of isolated symbols, such as note heads and beams, which are then recognized using contour-tracing methods. This drastic preprocessing step erases or distorts most music symbols other than quarter notes and beamed note groups, so extension of this work seems infeasible [Pre70].

4.2 Prerau: Contour Tracing

In his PhD thesis, Prerau [Pre70] describes a "fragmentation and assemblage" method for treating staff lines and isolating music symbols. In the fragmentation step, the system scans along the top and bottom edges of staff lines to identify parts of symbols lying between/above/below the staff lines; a new symbol fragment is begun whenever a significant change in slope is encountered. Fragments from a single symbol are separated by the gaps left from crossing staff lines. In the assemblage step, these symbol fragments are recombined. A simple connection rule is used in the assemblage step: two symbol fragments that are separated by a staff line are connected if they have horizontal overlap. As noted by [CB91], symbols which merge with staff lines do not always have horizontal overlap, and would be disconnected by Prerau's method. For example, the top portion of a bass clef would be disconnected, as would shallow slurs tangent to a staff line.

4.3 Andronico and Ciampa: Bare Staff-line Removal

[AC82] mentions an alternate treatment of staff lines, which attempts to remove staff lines only in bare sections where the staff lines are not crossing symbols. Three additional hypothetical staff lines (2 above and one below) are traced to remove ledger lines. Successive trials are used to search for staff lines, using a number of iterations proportional to the amount of background noise. The method used is not described, but the figures show creditable results on simple examples. Not surprisingly, gaps are left in symbols that are tangent to staff lines, and staff lines are not removed when they pass through small holes in symbols. The crossing of beams and staff lines is a problem: the staff-line removal results "in the suppression of some particulars that ... prevent the identification ... of the linking of the notes" ([AC82], p. 255).

4.4 Mahoney: Line Removal for Region Isolation

[Mah82] distinguishes between two types of line removal, removing real lines (bare staff-line sections) and removing ideal lines (complete staff lines). The goal in real line removal is to remove only those parts of the line that do not overlap other symbols; this is accomplished by removing only those portions of the line satisfying the line's allowed thickness range. This type of removal is generally desirable for staff lines. Ideal line removal involves removing the line everywhere along its length. This can be used to split adjacent symbols; for example, performing ideal removal of a staff line can be used to separate note heads that are located on adjacent spaces. In some cases, ideal stem removal splits note heads that are a half-step apart and on opposite sides of the stem. In other cases, a different region segmentation approach would be needed — one that is not provided in [Mah82]. Mahoney repeatedly uses the following strategy for symbol identification: first construct a set of candidates for one or more symbol types, then use symbol-type descriptors to select the matching candidates ([Mah82], pp. 39 ff). For example, to identify staff lines, staff-line candidates are constructed; these include all thin horizontal lines in the image. Next, the staff-line descriptor (specifying allowable thicknesses, lengths, and gap-lengths) is used to classify staff lines. Similarly, the ledger-line descriptor is used to classify ledger lines. Good extraction of staff lines and ledger lines is achieved even though the initial construction of horizontal lines contains unwanted segments, such as the tops and bottoms of half-note heads.

The treatment of vertical lines is similar, with descriptors for stems and bar lines used to classify the vertical lines. The note stems are removed to preserve beam continuity, and then beams are constructed and classified. Once the classification of lines is completed, symbol classification begins. First, loop interiors are found: this detects the whole- and half-note heads that do not have a staff line running through them. (Other regions are also detected; for example, the top half of a "3" used for fingering.) Then the bare staff lines and ledger lines are removed from the image (the lines are removed only where they are within the allowable thickness range, so line removal does not cause gaps in superimposed symbols).

. The detection of loop interiors is repeated to find the loops on staff lines. Then the descriptors for half- and whole-note heads are used to classify these regions. (Erroneous regions, such as the top half of the "3" are left unclassified.) Candidate regions for other symbols are constructed by removing all staff lines, ledger lines, stems, bars and beams, and then finding connected regions. All other symbols, such as solid note heads, accidentals and flags, are found by matching symbol descriptors to this set of candidate regions. Special processing, such as removal of complete staff lines, is performed to separate vertically connected note heads. Section 5.3 contains further details of Mahoney's methods for primitive extraction. Mahoney concludes that this system "goes a long way toward correct isolation of characters in the image, but more work is needed for dealing with the more difficult cases of line-region overlap. This is a challenging problem."

4.5 Roach and Tatem: Staff-line Identification Via Line Angle and Thickness

Roach and Tatem [RT88] discuss a knowledge-based system for segmenting images of music notation. Their processing of staff lines is reviewed here; symbol processing is reviewed in Section 5.6. Roach and Tatem worked with images of hand-drawn sheet music — the staff lines themselves were machine printed, but all other music symbols were hand drawn. Traditional general-purpose methods for line-detection, such as the Hough transform or line tracking, did not perform well on these images; the need to introduce domain specific knowledge was identified. In order to isolate musical symbols, only the bare sections of staff lines should be removed. Staff lines are detected using measures of line angle and thickness. A window is passed over the image to compute a line-angle for every black pixel. The line angle is measured from the center of the window to the furthest black pixel in that window; this furthest black pixel is chosen so that the path from it to the center does not cross any white pixels. To detect staff lines, a large window radius is used. This causes covered staff-line sections to be labeled with a horizontal line-angle despite the interference of the superimposed musical symbols. Once a line angle has been determined, a line-thickness can be measured. These two measurements, combined with adjacency information, are used to identify horizontal lines, and "questionable pixels" which occur at the intersection of a line and a figure. It would be interesting to perform a comparison of this algorithm with the LAG-based methods used by Carter (Section 4.6).

4.6 Carter: LAG-based Staff-line Identification

[Car89, CB91] discuss a comprehensive system for segmentation in images of music notation, using processing based on a Line Adjacency Graph (LAG). A common problem in staff-line identification is to distinguish the bare staff-line sections from the sections where the staff is intersected by a music symbol. Particularly difficult is to detect places where a thin portion of a symbol tangentially intersects a staff line. Examples of this include the highest part of a bass clef, as well as the intersection of the treble clef with the lowest staff line. Under these conditions, many other methods of staff-line processing create gaps in symbols, but Carter's LAG-based analysis successfully identifies such tangential intersections of symbols with staff lines. Other goals of this work are (1) to locate staff lines despite image rotation of up to 10 degrees, (2) to cope with slight bowing of staff lines, and (3) to cope with local variations in staff-line thickness. Region information, derived from the LAG, is used to determine whether a symbol has merged with a staff line.

The Line Adjacency Graph is formed directly from a vertical run-length encoding of a binary image. An individual vertical run of pixels is called a segment. A transformed LAG is formed by linking together neighboring segments to form sections. Sections are formed using a left-to-right scan, in which neighboring vertically overlapping segments are linked. Junctions occur when a segment in one column overlaps several segments in an adjacent column; sections are terminated at these junctions. In the transformed LAG, each section is represented by a node in a graph, and junctions are represented by edges in the graph. The nodes in the transformed LAG should correspond to structural components of musical symbols. A rule limiting the rate of change in section thickness helps accomplish this. The rule states that the current section is terminated if its average height differs from the height of the next segment by more than a factor of 2.5. This rule ensures that staff lines and ledger lines are assigned to different sections than are portions of music symbols. Similarly, a note head is assigned to a different section than the note stem. Section formation is insensitive to small rotations: [CB91] shows consistent sections obtained from an image at two different orientations. The use of a LAG is also efficient, since subsequent processing operates on section data rather than on individual pixels. [Car89] found the LAG preferable to other common methods of data reduction and feature extraction, such as thinning to form skeletons. The LAG is equally effective describing blobs as well as lines.

Noise removal on the transformed LAG proceeds by removing isolated or singly connected sections with small area (5 pixels or less in a 400 dpi image). If removal of these noise regions turns a multi-way junction into a two-way junction, then the two remaining sections are merged provided their heights differ by less than a factor of 2.5.

The transformed LAG is searched for potential staff-line sections (filaments): sections that satisfy criteria related to aspect ratio, connectedness and curvature. Long beams may be included as filaments; these are filtered out using a histogram of filament thickness to determine a threshold for maximum staff-line thickness. Roughly collinear filaments are concatenated together into filament strings, thereby bridging the gaps introduced by superimposed music symbols. The occurrence of five horizontally overlapping and roughly equally spaced filament strings is recognized to form a staff. After staff lines are identified, the transformed LAG is restructured: further merging of non-staff sections takes place, now that junctions with staff-line sections have been specially marked. At this point, musical symbols are effectively isolated from the staff lines. Connected non-staff-line sections are combined to form objects, which correspond to music symbols or to connected components of music symbols.

4.7 Kato and Inokuchi: Run-length Histograms and Projections

In [KI91], the spacing of staff lines is estimated by scanning 10 evenly spaced columns in the image. Run-lengths are measured in each of these columns, and histograms of run lengths are calculated. The maximum in the 0-pixel histogram is interpreted as the staff spacing, and the maximum in the 1-pixel histogram is interpreted as the staff-line width. Once the staff size has been established, the staff lines themselves are located. Run-lengths in 10 evenly spaced columns are used to get accurate local estimates of staff-line spacing and width. Next, small rectangular sections of the staff are analyzed, near the left and right ends of the staff. Short horizontal runs are eliminated; this eliminates most music symbols, but beams and portions of note heads and clefs remain. Next an X projection is used to estimate the locations of the ends of the staff, and a Y projection is used to obtain an accurate height estimate. If the edge of the staff is not found, the window is moved further toward the margin of the page. Bar lines are found using similar methods, tailored to the recognition of piano music. Rectangular masks are placed on the right-hand staff (top staff), the left-hand staff, and between the staves. Then short vertical runs are eliminated, and hypothesized bar-line locations are extracted from an X projection. The existence of a bar line is established if all three masks hypothesize a bar line at the same X location.

In this system, the distance between staff lines is used to restrict the size of symbols, and the width of the staff lines is used to set thresholds for symbol recognition. Staff lines are eliminated from the image before recognition of music symbols begins. The staff lines are tracked from the left, based on initial estimates of their location. A staff line is eliminated wherever the staff width is below a threshold. The methods used for symbol recognition are described in Section 5.9.

4.8 Staff-line Identification Without Staff-line Removal

So far we have surveyed techniques for detecting and removing staff lines from an image of music notation. Some researchers have developed alternate analysis techniques that that involve staff-line identification, but not staff-line removal.

4.8.1 Template matching in the presence of staff lines. [Mah82], p. 21, suggests that template-matching could be applied to characters such as time-signature numerals without actually separating them from the background lines; no attempt is made to implement this.

The Wabot-2 system [Mat85] does perform template matching in the presence of staff lines (Section 5.4). Staff lines are detected and used to normalize the image, to determine the score geometry, and also to restrict the search area for music symbols. Staff lines are detected in hardware by a horizontal line filter. In order to tolerate skew, a short filter is used: the filter size can be between 8 and 80 pixels long. Where five equally spaced lines are found, a staff is deemed to exist. Normalization parameters are calculated for each staff; these parameters include staff location, staff inclination, area covered by staff, and note-head size. In preparation for further processing, the image of each staff is normalized according to these parameters.

4.8.2 Projection methods for staff-line identification. Various authors
have used projection methods for staff-line identification; some of these methods
operate without removing the staff lines from the image. Here we concentrate
on the work of Fujinaga *et al.* [Fuj88, FAP89, FAPB89]. Other systems using
projections are mentioned in Sections 4.7 and 5.5. In Fujinaga's work, a Y projection of the entire page of music is used to locate staves. The mean of the entire
projection is used as a threshold value; then groups of five peaks are sought. Staff
lines are rarely perfectly horizontal. In a Y projection, individual staff-line peaks
cannot be resolved if the staff is skewed so that delta-y for a single staff line is
greater than than half of a staff space. ([CB91] performed projection experiments
and states that a rotation of less than 30 minutes of arc can cause the peaks
of the Y projection to merge.) Nevertheless, the staff as a whole projects to a
region of high values, and can be distinguished from the relatively empty space
between staves.

Fujinaga accepts a cluster of five or more peaks as a staff; extra peaks can
result from ledger lines, horizontal beams, or skew. A minimum-staff-separation
parameter is used: a cluster of five or more peaks must be separated from other
clusters of peaks by a certain distance to be recognized as a staff. This method
successfully locates most staves, except for percussion staves using only a single
staff line. An underlying assumption is that a horizontal line can be used to
separate neighboring staves and their associated symbols. This is true in most
music printed for single monophonic instruments, but it is not true for dense
orchestral scores. Fujinaga's method does not solve the problem of separating
staves that occupy overlapping y intervals. Once the area occupied by a staff has
been located, localized Y projections are used to accurately locate the staff lines:
series of Y projections are taken starting at the right margin, moving leftward
until five clear peaks appear.

5 Symbol Classification

After staff lines, have been identified and/or removed from the image, the next
major processing step is to classify music symbols. A great variety of techniques
have been applied to this problem.

5.1 Pruslin

[Pru66] uses contour tracing to describe connected binary image regions that
remain after removal of thin horizontal and vertical lines. Classification depends
both on trace properties as well as on inter-trace measurements. A method for
performing template matching using contour traces is developed.

5.2 Prerau: the Height/Width Symbol Space

Prerau recognizes a subset of music symbols using simple measures. Relative
symbol size is used for an initial classification. [Pre75], p. 27, states "A property

of standard music notational symbols ... is that each type of music symbol is significantly different in overall size from almost all other types of music symbols." To exploit this, the bounding-box dimensions of each symbol are expressed in staff-space units. The height and width of the bounding box are used to look up a list of possible matches; this is done via a precomputed table containing the areas where each symbol can occur in a height/width space. (This height-width table was constructed by hand-measurement of the size of many samples of each type of notational symbol. The measurements obtained for each type of symbol form small regions in the height/width space; these regions are enlarged to accommodate printing errors and variations.) Typically there are three to five possible matches for each symbol, given the fairly small subset of music symbols being analyzed. Heuristic tests are used to distinguish symbols that overlap in the height/width space; these tests take advantage of the syntax, redundancy, position and feature properties of each music symbol type. [Pre70] states that this classification scheme is specific to one publisher, but could easily be adapted. [Pre71] presents examples of syntactic redundancy and positional redundancy, and also discusses representative symbol-discrimination tests.

5.3 Mahoney: Pattern Primitives and Composite Symbols

[Mah82] deals with the extraction of pattern primitives in music. Section 4.4 reviewed Mahoney's use of line removal for region isolation; here we discuss his primitive-recognition methods. The goal of Mahoney's work is to design an approach on the basis of which a real recognition system might be developed. Some approaches he suggests are probably infeasible in practice, but others may prove useful. Pattern primitives, such as note heads, stems, beams and flags, can be combined to form "composite music symbols," such as notes, chords, and beamed note sequences. This distinction between pattern primitives and composite symbols subdivides and simplifies the recognition task. The primitive lines accommodate the variable parameters of the composite symbols: a parameterized composite symbol such as a beamed note sequence is made up of (unparameterized) characters and parameterized lines. [Mah82], p. 24, states that "It is simpler to give a variable description for a beam than for a beamed note sequence, and it is easier to design flexible recognition procedures around simple descriptions."

Mahoney envisions a system that does not use context for the recognition of primitives. Knowledge about the structure of standard music notation is needed to infer musical symbols from the relationships between the various kinds of primitives; this topic is beyond the scope of [Mah82]. The pattern primitives Mahoney uses are lines, dots and characters. Classes of primitives are described using ranges of values for parameters. For example, lines typically have ranges for length, thickness and orientation. These ranges can be used to characterize the difference between stems, beams and staff lines. The thickness ranges are also useful for removing the bare portions of lines: in order to remove a staff line without leaving holes in the symbols superimposed on the staff line, Mahoney suggests removing the line only in places where the measured thickness is within the allowable thickness range for the line. The "dot" primitives are not extracted until after line primitives have been processed and removed. [Mah82], p. 22, states that "It is clear from these examples that the actual process of breaking a PSMN [Printed Standard Music Notation] image up into its simple components requires having some knowledge about the structure of the notation. One could not, for instance, successfully extract all primitive symbols, as we have defined them, by simply extracting all lines and then extracting all regions." On the other hand, [Mah82], p. 24, says "There is no reliance on context for the recognition of primitives... All syntactic considerations are left to the analysis routine, whose sole task is to find specified relationships between already classified symbols and build corresponding objects."

Mahoney's processes are initially used in an interactive mode to develop object descriptions and to tailor predefined descriptions to new music samples for which the old descriptions do not work well. A "correct and redisplay" loop is used to refine the descriptions. All measures of distance are normalized on either the staff-line or staff-space thickness. Region masses are normalized on the mass of whole-note interiors (the white space inside the whole-note head). Sample line parameters for describing staff lines, ledger lines, beams, note stems and bar lines are: principal direction (horizontal, vertical); angle (permitted deviation from horizontal or vertical); thickness (lower and upper bound), length (lower and upper bound), maximum permitted gap. Sample region parameters for describing whole-, half-, and quarter-note heads, flags, sharps and dots are: mass (lower and upper bound), width (lower and upper bound), height (lower and upper bound), inclination angle (used only for selected symbols).

5.4 Wabot-2: Symbol Detection in a Two-level Hierarchy

In the early 1980s an impressive keyboard-playing robot was developed in Japan. [Gro85] provides a description of the whole system; [Roa86] is a short, easily available overview. For a detailed description of the vision system, see [Mat85]. [SHM+85] is a reference suitable for readers of Japanese. [MOH89, IIHO91] describe extensions to form the PBS (Performance, Score, Braille) system. Among its other capabilities, the Wabot-2 robot has a vision system capable of interpreting images taken of sheet music placed on a music stand. For an anthropomorphic effect, the CCD camera is placed on the robot's shoulders; thus, while the robot plays the keyboard, vibrations prevent the CCD camera from being used for score reading. The sheet music must be read and interpreted before the robot begins to play. Very fast image interpretation is achieved in the Wabot design — approximately 10 to 15 seconds are needed to interpret one page of music. Special purpose hardware and parallel processing are used to achieve such high speed. For the simple scores used, the recognition rate is nearly 100%.

The robot plays three-part organ scores, containing relatively simple notation. There are three staves per system: the top staff is for the right hand, the middle staff is for the left hand, and the bottom staff is for the feet. The robot's video camera captures images of organ scores that have been placed on a music stand. The following attributes of the imaging must be taken into consideration:

(1) distortions occur when the page of music sags on the music stand, (2) some rotation may be present, (3) distance to the page may vary, and (4) the illumination is uneven. (Images captured using a flatbed scanner or drum scanner avoid some of these problems.) The image is subdivided and each region separately thresholded to allow for uneven illumination. After staff detection, the image is rotated and normalized to compensate for distortions introduced in scanning.

Musical symbols are recognized according to a two-level hierarchy, where the upper level is implemented in hardware and the lower level in software. Staff lines, note heads and bar lines, which can occur in many places in the image, belong to the upper level. These are searched for using hardware-implemented template-matching. The template matching is done using an AND operation rather than an EXCLUSIVE-NOR operation; that is, the number of coincident black pixels are counted. Eight standard templates for note heads are used. Each template comes in nine different sizes, ranging from 8 × 8 to 16 × 16 pixels. The correct template size is selected on the basis of the normalization parameters resulting from staff-line detection. The lower level of the hierarchy contains symbols whose possible locations are constrained by the recognition results for the upper level symbols; these symbols are found using software-implemented localized search. Lower level symbols include rests, stems, flags, repeat signs, staccato and marcato marks, accidentals, prolongation dots, clefs and time signatures.

Template matching to detect filled note heads leads to incorrect matches. These are eliminated at a later stage, using knowledge about the syntax of music notation. If this method were applied to more complex notation, the problem of spurious matches might become more serious. As it stands, excellent recognition results are achieved on organ scores containing relatively simple notation.

5.5 Symbol Recognition Using Projections

Various researchers have used projections for symbol recognition. [Pru66] mentions that a function "thickness in points versus x coordinate" could be used to yield equivalent information to the transition information he stores for each symbol-trace. [NSI78] and [Tøn86] both use projections (Section 8). [Taw86, HO87] use projection methods for analyzing Labanotation, a dance notation (Section 9). We now discuss two projection-based methods in more detail.

5.5.1 Lee and Choi. [LC85] describes a microcomputer-based music recognition system that uses projection methods to first recognize staff lines, then recognize bar lines and finally recognize notes, including chords and rests. The images have severe noise problems, particularly near the image border; this is due to the imaging method and to lighting problems. Preprocessing is performed to reduce noise.

Staff lines are found in a Y projection. A threshold of 0.7 × (maximum projection value) is used to select projections strong enough to be candidate staff lines. These candidates are searched to find groups of five equally spaced lines.

Next an image area containing only a staff nucleus is formed, and X and Y projections are used to find bar lines. Notes are recognized using X and Y projections from a small window around the symbol. Characteristic points in the projections are used for classification; a comparison is made with stored projections for known symbols. The examples contain chords and horizontal beams. Pitch and duration of notes is recognized. The authors state that the method is rather rotation-sensitive, so that recognition fails if the image is tilted.

5.5.2 Fujinaga, Alphonce and Pennycook. [Fuj88] and [FAP89] describe work that makes extensive use of X and Y projections both for segmentation and for symbol recognition. The system was initially designed on an IBM PC but is being transported to a Sun workstation [FAP89]. [Fuj88], p. 2, defines "The basic task of an OMR [Optical Music Recognition] system is to convert the score into a machine-readable format by means of an optical scanner; the digitized image is then analyzed to locate and identify the musical symbols." Thus, the emphasis of this thesis is on symbol recognition, not on higher-level analysis of 2-D arrangements of music symbols.

There is great variation in shape and size among music symbols. Thus X and Y projections suffice for identification of many music symbols even though they can only establish the approximate shape and size of symbols. The basic strategy employed by [Fuj88] is to locate symbols using projections or syntactic knowledge, and to then calculate local projections for detailed symbol classification. Heavy reliance on properties of monophonic music are made in this process. Fujinaga makes interesting comments regarding system development [Fuj88], p. 53: "Many different algorithms and threshold values were tried until a satisfactory recognition rate was achieved with the training samples...The most frustrating aspect of developing this system was the difficulty of monitoring progress. Because there are several steps involved before any decision is made about the symbols, it was extremely hard to locate problem areas. It was particularly difficult to determine whether misrecognitions occurred because of segmentation errors or because of classification errors." Section 4.8.2 describes how a global Y projection is used to roughly locate the staves, followed by localized Y projections which accurately determine the position of staff lines.

Next, an X projection of the staff is used to locate the individual musical symbols. (Only monophonic music is being analyzed.) An X projection of the entire staff is difficult to analyze due to interference from associated symbols such as expression marks, measure numbers, and lyrics. Instead, [Fuj88] uses a projection of the staff nucleus, the area between the top and bottom staff lines. While this projection cuts off symbols that protrude above or below the staff, it is sufficient for locating symbols. The staff lines themselves give a background projection value in the X projection; symbol-locations are identified whenever the X projection value exceeds the background value by one staff space. At this point a local Y projection is taken, covering the full height of the staff rather than just the staff nucleus. This Y projection is used to determine the vertical extent of the symbol; finally, an X projection is taken using these vertical bounds. The contribution due to staff lines is subtracted from this X projection, and then the following features of the symbol are calculated: width, height, area, and number of peaks in the X projection.

These features are used in conjunction with syntactic knowledge for symbol classification. Examples of syntactic knowledge include (1) the first symbol in the staff projection is expected to be one of four clefs, (2) the next group of symbols, containing no horizontal gaps greater than a staff space, are expected to be a key signature, (3) within beamed note groups, notes and accidentals are the only expected symbols and (4) dots of prolongation only occur following notes and rests. In some cases localized projections are used to distinguish symbols; for example, a Y projection of the bottom staff space is used to distinguish between treble and bass clefs, and Y projections on either side of a note stem are used to detect flags and beams. Classification of other symbols relies on a width-height space similar to that used by Prerau (Section 5.2). Some classifications are difficult to perform reliably using projection methods. For example, time signatures are not recognized, and the distinction between a sharp and a natural is not made. However, this work demonstrates that projections provide an efficient means for performing initial classifications.

In [Fuj88] a series of ad-hoc tests are used for symbol recognition. [FAP89] reports on a more general and extensible treatment of symbols, based on classification in a feature space. Symbol recognition is done using features extracted from the projection profiles and their first and second derivatives. (No mention is made of noise problems being encountered when taking a second derivative of a projection profile.) Features include width, maximum height, area, aspect ratio and rectangularity. Classification using the k-nearest neighbor rule was found to be prohibitively time-consuming. Offline optimization is used to address this problem; for example, an attempt is made to calculate the most effective subset of features to use.

5.6 Roach and Tatem: Rule-based System for Handwritten Music

All of the systems that we have surveyed make some use of knowledge about music notation: the existence and properties of staff lines, note stems and note heads, the syntax of music notation, etc. The work of Roach and Tatem [RT88] proposes that such information should be represented in a rule-based system, and that the information should be applied starting with the earliest steps of symbol segmentation and recognition. Tatem and Roach describe the segmentation portion of a prototype system that processes hand-written music notation.

Unfortunately, the input chosen was of such poor quality and such low resolution that it is difficult to judge the effectiveness of the system. The experiments reported in [RT88] use sloppy hand-written sheet music as input. The music is digitized at 100 dpi, which means that the distance between staff lines is six rows of pixels. The staff lines themselves occupy one or two pixels, leaving only four or five pixels for the gap between neighboring staff lines. One of us (Blostein) has found that such resolution is barely satisfactory for displaying legible music on a terminal screen, even when hand-tuned bit maps are designed for each music character. Thus it may not be realistic to attempt to recognize music at such low resolution. [RT88] states that the results obtained were "quite good." Indeed, the low-level processing does capture some of the important features of the poor-quality input. However, it is not clear that further processing of such low-quality segmentation results will succeed. To better illustrate the performance of this system, tests with good-quality machine-printed and hand-written music are needed.

The following primitives are recognized: circular blobs (for closed note heads), circles (open note heads), horizontal lines, non-horizontal line segments, and arcs. (Symbols such as clefs do not occur in any of the test examples.) The location and orientation data for each primitive are intended to form the input to a high-level visual expert system. Primitive identification is coded as several passes, with procedural Fortran code in the first passes and "knowledge-based" Prolog code in the last pass. Staff-line detection has been reviewed in Section 4.5. Note-head detection is extremely difficult in these handwritten images, and a general-purpose blob detector is often fooled. Thus note heads are searched for in constrained locations. Vertical lines, which might be note stems, are located. Then a thickness measure is used to test for wide spots at the ends of each potential stem. Finally, if there is a wide spot, it is accepted as a note head if it has a circularity measure greater than some threshold. The authors claim to have benefited from writing most of their code using a rule-based approach. Unfortunately, no comparison is made with other techniques that have been used for incorporating knowledge of music-notation into a recognition system.

5.7 Clarke: Score Reading on a Microcomputer

Work by Clarke *et al.* [CBT88a, CBT88b, CBT89] is directed at performing optical score reading on a microcomputer. Thus much of their effort is directed at dealing with the main-memory-size restrictions on IBM PCs, and at developing computationally inexpensive methods for symbol identification. Staff lines are identified and removed before the remaining symbols are classified. The staff lines are located by looking for long horizontal runs of black pixels. Then the neighborhood of each staff-line pixel is examined to determine whether a music symbol intersects the staff line at this point [CBT88a]. It is not clear how much this method has been tested; the authors claim that this "relatively simple algorithm has proved to be satisfactory in removing the stave lines from the image."

The image is processed one staff at a time, to accommodate the memory limitations on a PC. Staves are located by examination of a single column of pixels near the left end of the system. Large blank sections indicate gaps between staff lines, and are used to divide the image into individual staves. Complete staff separation is not always achievable — parts of symbols belonging to the staff above or the staff below may be included; these have to be ignored in processing.

For symbol recognition, an initial classification is obtained from the symbol height and width, as in Prerau's system (Section 5.2). Further classification is performed by examining the pixels in a few particular rows and columns of the symbol-image. (Complete template matching was judged to be too computationally expensive.) For example, three rows of pixels, near the top, middle and bottom of the symbol, are used to identify an accidental as a flat, a sharp or a natural. Individual notes in a beamed group of notes may be identified by examining top and bottom profiles of the beamed-note symbol.

Work on chord recognition is beginning. Chord recognition is complicated because note heads are not constrained to occur only at the end of a stem. Starting with a quarter-note or half-note chord that has been perfectly segmented, stem direction can be determined by checking a row at the top and bottom of the symbol: one of the rows should intersect a note head and the other row should intersect a stem. The note heads themselves are found by checking a vertical column of pixels that is offset from the stem. If the stem x location is in the middle of the chord, then two vertical columns of pixels are checked to look for note heads on either side of the stem. No mention is made of how beams or flags are handled.

This system is not yet complete. Many of the proposed techniques are not robust; noise sensitivity may turn out to be a significant problem. [CBT88a] mentions that "other problems that need to be solved include that of recognizing symbols that coalesce together, and the complications that spurious points or noise can cause during the recognition process."

5.8 Carter: LAG-based Symbol Segmentation

[Car89, CB91] discuss a comprehensive system for segmentation in images of music notation. Section 4.6 reviewed the use of the transformed LAG to separate staff lines from music symbols, and to describe objects which correspond to music symbols or connected components of music symbols. These segmentation results are interpreted by a recognition system; compared to the segmentation system, the recognition system is in an early stage of development. The objects resulting from the segmentation are classified according to bounding-box size, and according to the number and organization of their constituent sections. [CB91] notes that "overlapping or superimposed symbols will need to be separated out by a specific algorithm. This is similar to the not insignificant problem of character separation, but far more complex due to the 2-D organization of music notation."

5.9 Kato and Inokuchi: Layered Working Memory

Kato and Inokuchi describe a sophisticated recognition system for printed piano music [KI91]. Musical knowledge is required to deal with the connections and overlaps between music symbols, and to handle ambiguities. A top-down approach is used, recognizing one measure of music at a time. The system is designed to handle both simple and complex notation. Simple, monophonic notations can be interpreted uniquely by means of simple rules. Complex notations have higher symbol density, with more connections, overlaps and complicated placement of symbols. These complex notations may be ambiguous, so proper knowledge is required for their interpretation.

Music symbols differ greatly in size and position, frequency of appearance, importance and so on. Thus it is difficult to devise a single method for recognizing all symbols. It may be necessary to use a variety of recognition methods. A flexible control structure is required to make this possible. Kato and Inokuchi use a collection of processing modules that communicate by operating on a common working memory. The working memory represents information about the current bar of music at five levels of abstraction. The first layer is the pixel image. The second layer contains primitives, including stems, note heads, beams, flags, accidentals, duration dots, and rests. The third layer contains music symbols: notes and rests which are synthesized as combinations of primitives from the second layer. The fourth layer contains the meaning of each symbol, such as the pitch and duration of a note. The fifth layer contains possible interpretations of the bar as a whole; these are formed by time-order combinations of the hypotheses in the fourth layer.

The four processing modules are (1) primitive extraction, (2) symbol synthesis, (3) symbol recognition, and (4) semantic analysis. These processing modules are made up of one or more recognition and verification units. The primitive extraction module contains units for recognizing items such as stems, beams and note heads. Hypothesized primitives are removed from the pixel image; thus the order of execution of units influences the result. Execution of units occurs in a heuristically determined order.

The operation of the processing modules is governed by a variable threshold that controls the strictness of matching. Tight thresholds mean that extracted primitives are faithful to the primitive model, whereas looser thresholds mean that regions whose shape are far from the primitive model are also extracted as primitives. Unacceptable hypotheses are rejected at higher layers, and sent back to lower layers for further processing. (For example, rejected primitives are restored in the pixel image.) Thus results are obtained quickly for high-quality images, but the analysis of noisy images takes much longer.

High-quality parts of the image are recognized first, with tight thresholds. Once these extracted primitives have been eliminated from the image, further recognition is performed with looser thresholds. Recognition consists of pattern processing (symbol recognition) and semantic analysis. The pattern processing has to cope with overlap between symbols, breaks in thin lines, and unexpected ink spots. The processing modules use knowledge about music notation to constrain the pattern processing task. For example, the distance between staff lines is used to restrict the size of symbols. The width of the staff lines is used as an indicator of the image quality, and is used to set some thresholds for symbol recognition.

Recognition proceeds one measure at a time. In the preprocessing stage, staff lines and bar lines are detected (Section 4.7). Next, subimages containing single measures are processed. This processing consists of staff-line elimination, recognition of attributive symbols (clefs, key signatures and time signatures), and recognition of note symbols. Finally, the postprocessing stage performs recognition of symbols that span measure boundaries. The final image interpretation is formed by combining the partial results from each measure. Good recognition results are obtained on complicated piano music, as discussed in Section 11.

6 Relative Positions of Symbols

In music notation, a two-dimensional arrangement of symbols is used to transmit information. Thus in addition to recognizing the identity of individual symbols, it is necessary to analyze the relative positions of symbols. A variety of methods have been devised for describing and testing relative symbol positions. Non-syntactic methods are reviewed here; syntactic methods will be discussed in Section 7. [Pre70] places the minimum and maximum x values for recognized symbols into a sorted list. This permits overlapping symbols to be easily identified. [Mah82] treats musical symbols as being made up of simple component primitives. Spatial relationships between musical symbols are expressed as simple relationships between their component primitives. For example, if the second note in a beamed note sequence is preceded by a sharp, then the important relationship is that between the sharp and the note head to its right. This is a simpler description than that which results by viewing the beamed note sequence as a single symbol which "surrounds" the sharp.

It is hoped that the use of simple relationships between component primitives will simplify syntactic description and analysis. Mahoney suggests describing relationships as an absolute distance combined with a relative position (left, right, above, below). The distance between two primitives can be defined in a variety of ways. For example, one could designate distinguished locations on each primitive, such as the center of a dot and the midpoint of a line, and measure distances between these distinguished points. Alternatively, one could measure the distance between the closest points on two symbols.

7 Syntactic Methods

Music notation consists of symbols related to each other in a two-dimensional way, and these two-dimensional relationships often carry information. The significance of these relationships must be captured in a syntactic description of music. Various methods have been suggested for extending grammatical methods which were developed for one-dimensional languages. While many authors suggest using grammars for music notation, their ideas are only illustrated by small grammars that capture tiny subsets of music notation.

[AC82] uses a high-level grammar for describing the organization of music notation in terms of music symbols. Lower level grammars are used to describe the structure of individual music symbols; these grammars are used for music symbol recognition. The high-level grammar is strict and very simple, describing a piece as a sequence of staves, where a staff starts with a clef, then a key signature then a sequence of measures. The lower level grammars are only briefly described in the paper. They use 5 adjacency operators (above, below, right of, above-right of, and above-left of) to relate terminal and nonterminal grammar symbols. The terminal grammar symbols are geometric figures such as white dots, black dots, and oriented lines of various lengths.

[Pre70] mentions grammars for music notation but restricts his work to the development of algorithmic implementations of syntax rules. Prerau makes a distinction between notational grammars and higher-level grammars for music. Notational grammars allow the computer to recognize important music relationships between the symbols of the music sample. The higher-level grammars are concerned with phrases and larger units of music. [Pre75], p. 27, says "to recognize music notation, however, a computer must find an algorithmic description of the music notation syntactical system." His research concentrated on algorithmic syntax rules, used to constraint the possible locations of various symbols. He concludes "The determination of this algorithmic description, a major phase of the solution of the recognition problem, ... may be the first detailed algorithmic description of the grammar of even a subset of the standard music notation symbol system." This algorithmic description is directed at recognition of music notation; other researchers have developed algorithmic descriptions of music syntax directed at generation of music notation (e.g. [Rou88, BH91]).

[Fuj88], p. 16, states that "Music notation grammar is context-free and LL(k); this is in effect what allows musicians (top-down parsers) to read the music as efficiently as they do." A small context-free grammar for simplified, monophonic music is presented; this ambiguous grammar does not contain any positional information other than left-to-right ordering. The author notes the limitations of the purely syntactic approach where context is not taken into account, and suggests that attributes could be used to introduce semantic considerations into the grammar.

[Mat85], p. 481, mentions the use of a musical grammar to correct errors such as missing beats or contradictory repeat signs. The following grammar constraints are given, to be applied to three-part organ music: each of the three parallel voices have the same total note duration; a fat double bar appears only at the end of each part; a treble or bass clef always appear right at the start of each staff; the time and key signatures almost never change within a system, and can be determined by majority rule; and, except for pickup measures, the number of beats in each bar should match the time signature.

8 Miscellaneous Papers

In spite of our best efforts, we were unable to locate copies of all known publications on this subject; for completeness, however, we wish to mention [Mar87], an undergraduate research project, [Wit73], a one-page abstract touching on the subject, and [NP73], a two-page summary of remarks.

Music image analysis is an international research field, and English translations or summaries are not always available. Here we offer brief comments on several foreign-language publications, with apologies for our inability to understand them fully.

[Tøn86] describes an extensive project at the University of Oslo to read sheet music from video camera images with variable lighting, scale, and orientation. Histogramming, skeletonization, projections and template matching are used, resulting in a system that can recognize staff lines and some of the most common music symbols. [Øst88] and [Tho88] describe a second music-reading project at the University of Oslo. In [Øst88], after staff-line removal, a polygonal approximation is constructed by tracing the contours of the music symbols. An analysis of concavities is performed to segment the symbols into constituent components. [Tho88] performs symbol classification using statistical and syntactic methods. Features used include height, width, area, perimeter, and number of holes. Feature analysis was combined with the use of syntactic rules about music symbols.

The music reading system of [NSI78] is aimed at constructing a database of Japanese folk music. This music is monophonic. Projection methods appear to be used. [AT82] reports on another Japanese score-reading effort; [TA82] is a one-page English summary of this work. The motivation for this work is the creation a music data base. The system is designed to recognize both monophonic and polyphonic music, including music with chords as well as music where two voices are printed together on a single staff. A series of passes are used to detect staff lines, to form a coarse segmentation by removing portions of staff lines, to perform fine segmentation, to classify segments into 10 categories, to perform symbol recognition using decision trees designed for each category, and finally, to perform a syntax check and interactive correction of erroneous or ambiguous interpretations. Preliminary experiments are reported to be quite promising.

Other publications available only in Japanese include [OIT79].

9 Dance Notation

Music notation is one of many graphical notations used for transmitting information. The problem of automatic score reading is related to the problem of reading other graphical notations. Some notations are more similar to music notation than others; perhaps dance notation is particularly closely related. [HO87] describes a recognition system for Labanotation, one of the common notations for dance [Hut70]; a more detailed account of this work, in Japanese, is given in [Taw86]. Labanotation is similar to music notation in that information is transmitted by symbols drawn on a background of lines, with one axis denoting the passage of time. A Labanotation score is written in vertical runs, with time increasing from bottom to top. Vertical "base lines" subdivide each run into columns, where each column represents the movement of a body part such as the head, an arm, or a leg. The base lines are somewhat analogous to staff lines in music. Horizontal "separation lines" provide synchronization points; these are roughly analogous to bar lines in music. Body movements are indicated by polygonal symbols drawn in the column corresponding to the body part. Duration of a movement is indicated by the vertical length of a symbol, direction is indicated by the shape of the symbol, and vertical motion is indicated by the shading of the symbol. The principal goal in [HO87] is to recognize the shape, size, shading and position of each Labanotation symbol. X and Y projections of a reduced-resolution image are computed; prominent peaks in these projections are used to detect base lines and separation lines. Next, skeletonization is used to split the image into two images, one consisting of line components and the other consisting of solid blob-like component. The base and separation lines are located in the line-image, and then removed. The resulting line image and blob image contain candidate figures for Labanotation symbols. Touching and incomplete symbols are processed using knowledge of the notation.

10 Open Problems

Many open problem must be solved before optical score reading becomes reliable enough to accomplish many of the goals mentioned in Section 1.1. We briefly mention two problem areas: problems of system organization, and problems of image noise.

10.1 System Architecture: Scaling Up a Prototype

In music reading, as in other applications, it is difficult to scale up a small working prototype into a large, complete system. For example, in syntactic methods, a grammar organization that is intellectually manageable when it contains 30 production rules may be come unmanageable if it is expanded to hundreds of production rules. It is hard to predict the difficulty of extending a system that can analyze monophonic music to one capable of analyzing polyphonic music. Thus, methods of structuring and organizing systems to be expandable are of great interest. In this section we summarize various approaches to the organization of a music-recognition system.

[RT88] describes the use of a rule-based system (Section 5.6). Various researchers have experimented with syntactic methods (Section 7). Also, multiple passes are often used to break the music-recognition task into smaller subtasks [AT82, RT88]. The projection methods (Section 5.5) have the advantage of great simplicity. They are able to recognize simple monophonic music efficiently. However, it may be difficult to extend these methods to polyphonic music, which contain more symbols that are connected or in vertical alignment. [Fuj88], p. 3, states that the restriction to monophonic music "is not critical since a complete OMR [Optical Music Recognition] system will contain a number of subprograms, each specifically designed to analyzed a certain type of score."

[KI91] describes a flexible control structure and data flow for a recognition system. A variety of recognition methods can be accommodated. These methods communicate their results via a working memory that contains hypotheses at various levels of abstraction, ranging from the pixel image at the bottom to the abstract interpretation at the top. Kato and Inokuchi argue that a top-down approach to recognition is useful: high-level knowledge about music notation can be used to constrain low-level pattern processing tasks. In the system described in [KI91], information in the working memory is generated primarily in a bottom-up fashion, but upper levels can reject the results produced from lower levels,

thereby providing top-down feedback for error correction and data disambigua-
tion. This approach provides a promising method for subdividing a recognition
system into intellectually manageable tasks. The modularized knowledge organization and control structure provide a good basis for scaling up from a small
system to a large system.

10.2 Image Defects and Broken Characters

Robust methods must be developed for interpreting music notation despite image noise. [Mah82], p. 27, discusses problems with image noise, and says that
"The worst case is when a primitive of character pattern, which is expected to be
connected for extraction purposes, is actually broken up into two or more fragments in the image." His work does not address this problem. [Car89] mentions
difficulties that arise from fragmentation of symbols due to poor print quality.
Carter's processing methods (Section 5.8) are designed to minimize these problems. He states that "Severe break-up of symbols will, however, continue to be a
problem for a topology-based approach and will probably necessitate the use of
artificial intelligence based techniques in order to take advantage of higher level
musical information." [Car89], p. 153.

11 Working Systems and Experimental Results

Various systems for music recognition have been implemented. Comparing these
systems is difficult because of the variety of input data used, and because it is
difficult to judge how much each system is tuned to the particular examples for
which results are reported. Thus we simply present a list of systems, approximately in chronological order. The system described in [Pru66] recognizes quarter
notes and beamed note groups (Sections 4.1 and 5.1). Up to four-note chords
are allowed, provided the note heads are physically adjacent, forming "note clusters." Other music symbols, such as rests, flags, hollow note heads, accidentals
and clefs, are not treated. All tests were drawn from one musical publication. On
this small experimental sample, good recognition results were achieved. [Pre70]
describes a system that recognizes a more complete set of symbols (Sections
4.2 and 5.2). Work-in-progress towards this system was mentioned in [Ede68].
The system was only tested on four small examples drawn from the same piece
(Mozart duets for two wind instruments, scanned at 225 dpi). [Pre71] reports a
total of 137 components in all of the tests; these components were constructed
from 527 fragments (Section 4.2). Good recognition rates were achieved, but the
recognition system was tuned to these examples. Recognized symbols include
clefs, accidentals, half quarter and eighth notes; flagged sixteenth notes are not
recognized but multiple beams are permitted. No chords were recognized. [AC82]
describes a system that recognizes clefs, key signatures, notes, rests and accidentals in simple monophonic music. Hand-chosen thresholds are used to binarize
the images (force to bilevel). Staff-line removal is used for symbol segmentation
(Section 4.3) and syntactic methods are used for symbol recognition (Section 7).
Examples of successful and unsuccessful recognition are given. [Mah82] reports

on a partial implementation of a system to recognize primitive patterns in music; the inference of musical symbols from these was not attempted (Sections 4.4 and 5.3). His examples show the effect of removing the bare parts of lines (those portions where the measured line width lies within a given range); the successive removal of staff lines and stems is used to isolate the remaining symbols. The primitive-extraction system, written in Zetalisp, is capable of extracting roughly vertical or horizontal lines or shallow arcs and elementary 4-connected regions from a binary image. Interactive facilities are used for determining normalization factors, building and refining line and region descriptions, and constructing and classifying pattern objects. Small tests have been done, including a few measures of polyphonic guitar music, scanned at 250 dpi. The detection of curved lines (slurs and ties) was not tested. This method emphasizes human interaction in the "pre-calibration" stage used to construct symbol descriptions; thus the system is fine-tuned to the examples it was tested on. Even though good results were achieved on the small tests shown, no conclusions can yet be drawn about the generality of the method.

The vision system for the Wabot-2 robot [Oht84, Gro85, Mat85, SHM+85, Roa86, MOH89] can perform fast, accurate recognition of simple three-part organ scores (Sections 4.8.1 and 5.4). Images are 2000 by 3000 pixels, which provides about 250 dpi for a standard page of music. A page of music is processed in 10 or 15 seconds, using special correlation hardware and parallel processing to achieve such speed. Basic music symbols are recognized, including clefs, accidentals, time signatures, bar lines, notes, beams, rests, staccato and marcato marks. Symbols such as words, slurs, ties, expression marks, ornaments and tempo indications are not recognized. [Gro85] reports on recognition results for ten simple scores, with 15 second recognition time and nearly 100% recognition rate. This system has been successfully used in live demonstrations. It is not clear whether this system could be easily extended to handle more complex music notation. [LC85] describe a system that recognizes staff lines, bar lines, notes, chords and rests. Projection methods are used. Processing time for a 237×192 image was eight minutes on an Apple II. These efforts were hampered by poor imaging conditions. A recognition rate of over 90% was obtained on some inputs.

[Fuj88, FAP89, Pen90] describe music-recognition systems that use X and Y projections for symbol identification (Sections 4.8.2 and 5.5.2). [Fuj88] reports on an IBM PC implementation whose symbol extraction capabilities were well-tested on a variety of monophonic music taken from various publishers. (Seventeen monophonic works were tested; the code for staff-locating was tested on an additional 12 polyphonic works.) The music is scanned at 200 dpi; each page takes about two minutes of processing time on a PC (fifteen seconds per staff). A symbol recognition rate of 70% was achieved on new samples; 100% recognition was achieved on the development samples. Recognized symbols include four types of clefs, key signatures, half notes, quarter notes, beamed notes, flagged notes (the type of flag is not recognized), two classes of accidentals (flat and sharp/natural), quarter and eighth rests, duration dots and bar lines. The projection methods as implemented in [Fuj88] rely heavily on properties of monophonic music for separating and isolating musical symbols. [FAP89] reports on a second implementation, on a Sun workstation. This music recognizer presents the user with a split screen, showing both the original music and the recognized score. The user then interactively corrects the recognized version. [FAP89] states that the initial target is simple polyphonic music with one note per stem. The next target will be the recognition of traditional piano music.

[RT88] describes a system for primitive extraction in hand-written sheet music (Sections 4.5 and 5.6). Few performance results for this system have been given. Extremely difficult input was used: sloppy handwritten music, digitized at only 100 dpi. Analysis results for a few short sections music were described. In these tests, a total of 17 solid note heads were recognized; 7 of these had mistaken pitch, and 9 extra blobs were detected. It is difficult to estimate how this method would compare to other methods when applied to higher-resolution, better-quality input. The authors state that "The results obtained using these techniques were quite good — certainly far above expectations."

Clarke *et al.* [CBT88a, CBT88b, CBT89] describe a partial implementation of a score-reading system written in Turbo C and running on an IBM PC (Section 5.7). Digitization occurs at around 200 dpi. A user-chosen threshold converts the scanned gray-level image into binary. Preliminary results have been reported but no details about testing are supplied. [CBT88b] states that "At present, the system will correctly recognize single line melodies of a subset of musical notation, with about 90% accuracy."

[Car89, CB91] describe a promising system for segmentation of musical symbols in images of music notation (Section 4.6 and 5.8). It produces a natural, stable segmentation under difficult imaging conditions, without an excess of ad hoc rules. A complete recognition system using these segmentation results is under development. The implementation is in C, running under Unix. The results currently available do not include figures on recognition accuracy. The test data consisted of nine images sampled at 400 dpi (4680 × 3344 pixels for an A4 size page) and a tenth image sampled at 200, 300 and 400 dpi. Various layouts and font sizes were used, including solo instrument parts, solo instrument with piano accompaniment, and orchestra score. The results shown in [CB91] demonstrate a clean separation of music symbols from staff lines. The system shows good tolerance of noise, limited rotation, broken print and distortion.

[KI91] is a sophisticated system for recognizing images of piano music (Sections 4.7 and 5.9). This system handles complex music notation, including two voices per staff with chords and shared note heads. Symbol recognition is fairly complete, including slurs and pedal markings. Grace notes are not recognized. The system is written in C, running on an APOLLO workstation. Scanning is at 240 dpi. Four works were selected for experimentation, with the indicated recognition rates: Beethoven's "Für Elise" (95.6%), Mozart's Turkish March (91.5%), a Chopin etude (87.1%), and a movement of a Beethoven sonata (83.3%). The recognition rate is calculated by counting the words that are modified or appended in the process of correcting the output of the system. These words correspond to information such as note pitch and duration, or the presence of a slur or pedal marking. These are impressive recognition rates, given the complexity of the notation and the completeness of the recognition.

References

[AC82]   A. Andronico and A. Ciampa. On automatic pattern recognition and acquisition of printed music. In *Proceedings, International Computer Music Conference*, pages 245–278, Venice, Italy, 1982. Computer Music Association Publications.

[AT82]   H. Aoyama and A. Tojo. Automatic recognition of printed music. *TG*, PRL82-5:33–40, 1982. In Japanese.

[BH91]   D. Blostein and L. Haken. Justification of printed music. *Communications of the ACM*, 34(3):88–99, March 1991.

[Car89]   N. P. Carter. *Automatic Recognition of Printed Music in the Context of Electronic Publishing*. PhD thesis, Univ. of Surrey, Depts. of Physics and Music, February 1989. 174 pages.

[CB91]   N. P. Carter and R. A. Bacon. Automatic recognition of printed music. In this volume.

[CBM88]   N. Carter, R. A. Bacon, and T. Messenger. The acquisition, representation and reconstruction of printed music by computer: A survey. *Computers and the Humanities*, 22:117–136, 1988.

[CBT88a]   A. Clarke, B. M. Brown, and M. P. Thorne. Inexpensive optical character recognition of music notation: A new alternative for publishers. In *Proceedings, Computers In Music Research Conference*, Bailrigg, Lancaster LA1 4YW, U.K., 11-14 April 1988. Sponsored by Ctr for Res. into the Applications of Computers to Music, Dept. of Music, Univ. of Lancaster; 6 pages.

[CBT88b]   A. T. Clarke, B. M. Brown, and M. P. Thorne. Using a micro to automate data acquisition in music publishing. *Microprocessing and Microprogramming*, 24:549–554, 1988.

[CBT89]   A. T. Clarke, B. M. Brown, and M. P. Thorne. Coping with some really rotten problems in automatic music recognition. *Microprocessing and Microprogramming*, 29:547–550, 1989.

[Ede68]   M. Eden. Other pattern-recognition problems and some generalizations. In P. Kolers and M. Eden, editors, *Recognizing Patterns*, pages 196–225. MIT Press, Cambridge, Massachusetts, 1968.

[FAP89]   I. Fujinaga, B. Alphonce, and B. Pennycook. Issues in the design of an optical music recognition system. In *Proceedings, 1989 International Computer Music Conference*, Columbus, Ohio, 2-5 November 1989. 4 pages.

[FAPB89]   I. Fujinaga, B. Alphonce, B. Pennycook, and N. Boisvert. Optical recognition of musical notation by computer. *Computers in Music Research Newsletter, No. 1*, 1989. 4 pages.

[Fuj88]   I. Fujinaga. Optical music recognition using projections. Master's thesis, McGill University, Faculty of Music, Montreal, CANADA, September 1988. For an M.A. in Music Theory; 67 pages.

[Gro85]   Mu Research Group. Automated recognition system for musical score. Bulletin 112, Science and Engineering Laboratory, Waseda University, 6-1 Nishiwaseda 1-chome, Shinjuku-ku, Tokyo 160, 1985. 28 pages.

[Gro90]   J. Groever. A computer-oriented description of music notation. Technical report, MUSIKUS, Department of Music, University of Oslo, P.O.Box 1017, Blindern, N-0315 Oslo 3, Norway, 1990. Contact: Arvid Vollsnes arvid@ifi.uio.no.

[HO87]   K. Hachimura and Y. Ohno. A system for the representation of human body movement from dance scores. *Pattern Recognition Letters*, 5:1–9, January 1987.

[Hut70]   A. Hutchinson. *Labanotation*. Theater Art Books, New York, NY, 1970.

[IIHO91]   T. Itagaki, M. Isogai, S. Hashimoto, and S. Ohteru. Automatic recognition of several types of musical notation. In this volume.

[Kas70]   M. Kassler. An essay toward specification of a music-reading machine. In B. S. Brook, editor, *Musicology and the Computer*, pages 151–175. City University of NY Press, New York, NY, 1970.

[Kas72]   M. Kassler. Optical-character recognition of printed music: A review of two dissertations. *Perspectives on New Music*, 11(1):250–254, Fall-Winter 1972.

[KI91]   H. Kato and S. Inokuchi. A recognition system for printed piano music using musical knowledge and constraints. In this volume.

[LC85]   Myung Woo Lee and Jong Soo Choi. The recognition of printed music score and performance using computer vision system. *Journal of the Korean Institute of Electronic Engineers*, 22(5):429–435, 5 September 1985. In Korean; English translation available from H. S. Baird.

[Mah82]   J. V. Mahoney. Automatic analysis of musical score images. B. S. thesis, Dept of Computer Science and Engineering, Massachusetts Institute of Technology, Cambridge, Massachusetts 02129, May 1982.

[Mar87]   N. Martin. Towards computer recognition of the printed musical score. B.sc. project report, Thames Polytechnic, Woolwich, London, May 1987.

[Mat85]   T. Matsushima. Automated high speed recognition of printed music (Wabot-2 vision system). In *Proceedings, 1985 International Conference on Advanced Robotics*, pages 477–482. Japan Industrial Robot Association (JIRA), 3-5-8, Shiba Koen Minato-ku, Tokyo, 1985.

[MOH89]   T. Matsushima, S. Ohteru, and S. Hashimoto. An integrated music information processing system: PSB-er. In *Proceedings, 1989 International Computer Music Conference*, pages 191–198, Columbus, Ohio, November 1989.

[NP73]   G. Nelson and T. R. Penney. Pattern recognition in musical score - project no. m88. *Computers and the Humanities*, 8:50–51, 1973.

[NSI78]   Y. Nakamura, M. Shindo, and S. Inokuchi. Input method of [musical] note and realization of folk music data-base. *TG*, PRL78-73:41–50, 1978. In Japanese.

[Oht84]   S. Ohteru. A multi processor system for high speed recognition of printed music. *Natl. Conv. (Rec.)*, 1984.

[OIT79]   M. Onoe, M. Ishizuka, and K. Tsuboi. Experiment on automatic music reading. In *Proceedings, 20th IPSJ National Conference*, volume 6F-5, 1979. In Japanese.

[Øst88]   B. Østenstad. Oppdeling av objektene i et digitalt notebild i klassifiserbare enheter. Rapport 31, Bildebehandlingslaboratoriet, Institutt for informatikk, Universitetet i Oslo, Oslo, Norway, October 1988. In Norwegian; 57 pages.

[Pen90]   B. Pennycook. Towards advanced optical music recognition. *Advanced Imaging*, April 1990. 3-page magazine article.

[Pre70]   D. S. Prerau. *Computer Pattern Recognition of Standard Engraved Music Notation*. PhD thesis, Massachusetts Institute of Technology, Cambridge, Massachusetts, September 1970. 240 pages.

[Pre71]   D. S. Prerau. Computer pattern recognition of printed music. In *Proceedings, Fall Joint Computer Conference*, volume 39, pages 153–162, Montvale, NJ, November 1971. A.F.I.P.S. Press.

[Pre75]   D. S. Prerau. Do-re-mi: A program that recognizes music notation. *Computers and the Humanities*, 9:25–29, 1975.

[Pru66]   D. H. Pruslin. *Automatic Recognition of Sheet Music*. PhD thesis, Massachusetts Institite of Technology, June 1966. Sc.D. dissertation; 94 pages.

[Rea79]   G. Read. *Music Notation: A Manual of Modern Practice (2nd Edition)*. Taplinger Publishing, New York, NY, 1979.

[Roa86]   C. Roads. The Tsukuba musical robot. *Computer Music Journal*, 10(2):39–43, Summer 1986.

[Ros70]   T. Ross. *The Art of Music Engraving and Processing (2nd Edition)*. Hansen Books, Miami, FL, 1970.

[Rou88]   D. Roush. Music formatting guidelines. Technical Report OSU-3/88-TR10, Department of Computer and Information Science, The Ohio State University, 1988.

[RT88]   J. W. Roach and J. E. Tatem. Using domain knowledge in low-level visual processing to interpret handwritten music: an experiment. *Pattern Recognition*, 21(1):33–44, 1988.

[SHM⁺85]   I. Sonomoto, T. Harada, T. Matsushima, K. Kanamori, M. Konuma, A. Uesugi, Y. Nimura, S. Hashimoto, and S. Ohteru. Automatic recognition system of printed music for playing keyboards. *TG*, MA84-22:17–22, 1985. In Japanese.

[Sto80]   K. Stone. *Music Notation in the Twentieth Century: A Practical Guidebook*. W. W. Norton & Co., New York, NY, 1980.

[TA82]   A. Tojo and H. Aoyama. Automatic recognition of music score. In *Proceedings, 6th International Conference on Pattern Recognition*, page 1223, Munich, W. Germany, 1982. Short English version of longer Japanese [AT82].

[Taw86]   S. Tawada. Dance score input system for the representation of human body movement. B.S. thesis, Educational Center for Inf. Proc., Kyoto University, Kyoto 606, Japan, 1986. In Japanese; 59 pages.

[Tho88]   E. Thorud. Analyse av notebilder. Rapport 28, Bildebehandlingslaboratoriet, Institutt for informatikk, Universitetet i Oslo, Oslo, Norway, August 1988. In Norwegian; 63 pages.

[Tøn86]   S. Tønnesland. SYMFONI: System for notekoding. Technical report, Institute of Informatics, P.O. Box 1080 Blindern, N-0316 Oslo 3, Norway, November 1986. In Norwegian; generously illustrated; 90 pages.

[Wit73]   G. Wittlich. Project SCORE. *Computational Musicology Newsletter*, 1(1):6, 1973. Abstract of paper from *International Conference on Computers in the Humanities*, University of Minnesota, 1973.

A Recognition System for Printed Piano Music Using Musical Knowledge and Constraints

Hirokazu Kato and Seiji Inokuchi

Department of Control Engineering,
Faculty of Engineering Science,
Osaka University, Toyonaka, Osaka 560, Japan

We describe a recognition system for printed piano music, which presents challenging problems in both image pattern matching and semantic analysis. In music notation, the shape of symbols is simple, but confusing connections and overlaps among symbols occur. In order to deal with these difficulties, proper knowledge is required, so our system adopts a top-down approach based on bar-unit recognition to use musical knowledge and constraints effectively. Recognition results, described with a symbolic playable data format, exceed 90% correct on beginner's piano music.

1 Introduction

The advancement of computer technology has a great influence on the musical field. Automatic musical performance using electronic instruments has already received practical application. Analysis and comparison of musical style, automatic composition and arrangement system and music information processing system unifying these systems has been studied [1]. The more these subject is studied, the more important musical database becomes.

A music notation represents musical information by symbolic form. It includes much information that is important for many other music information processing studies, so music notation has been input in most laboratories where music information processing is studied. In most cases, this is done manually by use of the computer keyboard or the mouse. Automatic recognition would be preferable.

Some automatic recognition systems for music notation have been developed. Nakamura [2] and Fujinaga [3] has proposed using projection profiles, the type and position of each symbol are recognized by means of the extraction of the feature of the shape and position from horizontal or vertical projection, because a certain point in the pattern of symbol has an important feature. The advantage of these methods is simplicity. If symbols are connected or drawn in vertical alignment, however, recognition is difficult. These methods are able to recognize only simple music notation of monophony such as children's songs.

Tojo [4] has proposed a recognition method using the classification of symbols into large groups according to the shape of the rectangle circumscribed with symbols and the discrimination of symbols from the structure analysis. In order for this method to be carried out, a careful elimination of the staff lines as a preprocessing and a fine segmentation of symbols are required. Matsushima [5] has developed a high-speed recognition system for real time musical performance with a robot. This system has hardware to detect symbols in about 10 seconds, and is too inflexible to handle complex notations.

Difficulties of the recognition of music notations are various. In simple notations, the density of symbols is low, so the connection between symbols doesn't need to be considered. In complex notations, symbols are drawn with high density, so connection, overlap and containment of symbols appears everywhere. The segmentation of symbols is very difficult for this feature in addition to the overlap with staff lines. Considering from the viewpoint of semantics, simple notations can be interpreted uniquely by means of simple rules. In complex notations, there are ambiguous descriptions, so the proper knowledge is required to interpret such description. Existing recognition system of music notations cannot deal with complex notations for these difficulties.

We have studied the translation system of complex music notation into a playable musical data as a part of intelligent music information processing system [6, 7, 8]. This paper describes the recognition system of the printed notation for piano music using knowledge and constraints related to the music notation in order to overcome the above difficulties.

2 Overview

Symbols in the music notations differ remarkably from each other in conditions of size and position, frequency of appearance and importance, and so on. For this reason, it is difficult to recognize all symbols by a certain specific method. There are various methods of pattern recognition, so we may adopt the proper recognition methods for each symbol. The kinds of symbols in music notations are few enough that the proper specific recognition methods for each symbol can be utilized. Top-down approach to recognition is also useful.

In order to use musical knowledge effectively, we take notice of the bar. Most symbols are able to be interpreted in the process of the bar-unit recognition. This is a basic idea. Naturally there are some symbols whose recognition is difficult in this idea. We deal with them by the other approaches, but they are few.

The recognition process consists of a pattern processing task and a semantic analysis task. In order for the recognition process to be preformed successfully, the pattern processing task has to cope with the various unexpected states, for examples: overlap between symbols, breaks of thin lines, unexpected ink spots, etc. Then, we prepare the pattern processing units with top-down approach using the knowledge and the constraints of music notations for each symbol. Especially, musical notes are regarded as the combination of some primitives as shown in Figure 1. Although the shape of musical notes varies from simple to complex, the shape of primitives is simple and the position and the size can be expected from the relation between each other. In the primitive level, the pattern processing deals with musical notes.

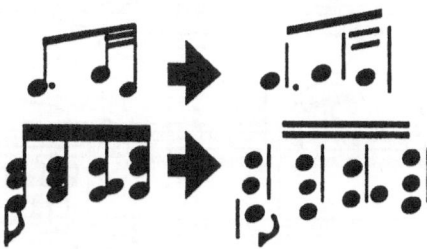

Fig. 1. Examples of musical notes.

The semantic analysis task interprets the results which the pattern processing task produces and translates them into the playable musical data format using musical knowledge. If a contradiction is found in the result of pattern processing task, this task rejects it and queries the pattern processing task for results to resolve the contradiction.

2.1 Processing Flow

This system deals with the printed notation for piano music. They are typical examples of the musical notations and range from the simple to the complex, so we choose them as objects of study. An example of printed notation for piano music is shown in Figure 2.

The processing flow of this system is shown in Figure 3. As the preprocessing, the detection of staff lines and bar lines are applied to the notation image input with a optical scanner, after the estimation of the average width of staff lines and the distance between each staff lines. This processing enables separation of the image into bar-units. Most recognition processing is applied to images of bar-unit. The recognition processing of some symbols whose recognition is difficult in the bar-unit processing and the unification processing of the results from the each bar-unit processing are applied in the postprocessing.

3 Preprocessing

Music notation is built around staff lines, so the position and size of symbols are restricted by the staff lines. In addition, music notation represents the time series of the musical data with symbolic format and the bar divides the staff by the constant number of the beat. Bar-unit processing, therefore, is reasonable. In the preprocessing, music notations are divided into the bar-units by the detection of the staff lines and bar lines.

Fig. 2. An example of printed notation for piano music.

3.1 Estimation of the Size of Staff Lines

The size of the staff in the notation image input by an optical scanner is unknown. The average width of the staff lines and the distance between staff lines have to be estimated before the recognition processing. The distance between staff lines restricts the size of symbols. The width of the staff lines, which is thin in most case, determines the quality of the notation image, so it is used in setting some thresholds in later recognition processing.

The run-lengths of 0-pixel and 1-pixel is measured by scanning on 10 vertical lines which separate the image into small plots of the equal area. In Figure 4, histograms of these run-lengths are shown. The maximum values of these histograms is regarded as the distance and the width of the staff lines.

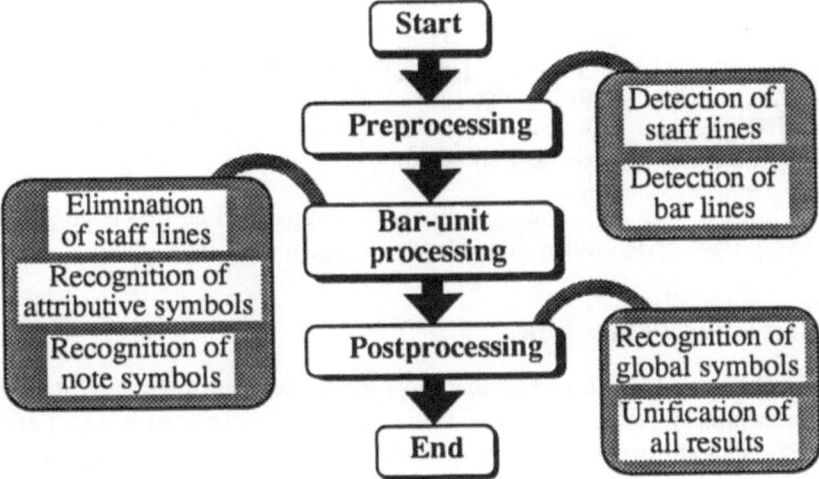

Fig. 3. The processing flow.

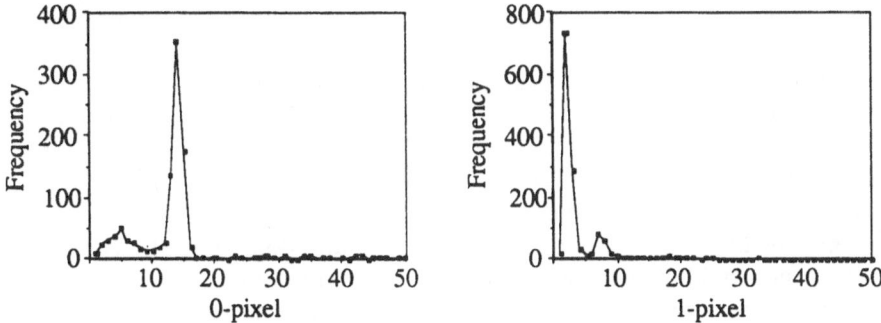

Fig. 4. Histograms of run-lengths.

3.2 Detection of the Staff Lines

In the notation image, it is not guaranteed that the staff lines lie horizontally. It seems that they have a little slope but they keep straight. Then, the staff line is represented as the straight line connecting the 2 coordinates of edge points. The detection of the staff lines works out as follows.

Step 1: An image is vertically scanned on 10 lines which separate the image into small plots of the equal area. In the each scan, the height of staff lines is estimated by using the distance and width of the staff lines which has been estimated in the above processing.

Step 2: After unifying all results from the each scan, the height with highest frequency is chosen as the height of the staff lines.

Step 3: The rectangular mask is put where height is the estimated point at Step 2 and side is the most sideward scan line including the estimate.

Step 4: After short components in the horizontal direction are eliminated, projections in the horizontal and vertical directions are formed.
Step 5: The accurate height of the staff line is obtained from the horizontal projection. The accurate edge point is obtained from the vertical projection.
Step 6: If the edge point is not found in the mask, the window mask is moved in the horizontal direction and Step 4 and 5 is repeated.

An example of this processing is shown in Figure 5. The processing to Step 3 from Step 6 is carried out independently for each staff lines.

3.3 Detection of Bar Lines

The symbols recognized as the bar lines in this system are shown in Figure 6. This system also deal with piano music notations constructed from 2 parts, that is, the right-hand part and the left-hand part. Bar lines are drawn through from the right-hand part to the left hand part. This property is used for the detection of the bar lines as follows.

Step 1: Rectangular masks are placed about three domains: the right-hand (upper) staff; the left-hand (lower) staff; and and the "middle domain" between the two staves.
Step 2: In each domain, short components in the vertical direction are eliminated and hypotheses of bar lines are extracted from the projection in the vertical direction.
Step 3: If the positions of three hypotheses in each domain are identical, they are detected as the bar line.
Step 4: The lines are classified into single bar and double bar by the distance from the neighbor bar line. In double bars, repeat marks are discriminated from the line width and the presence of the spots in the second space and the third space.

"? is this the correct end of the description?" An example of this processing is shown in Figure 7. This processing is also carried out independently for each staff.

4 Bar-Unit Recognition

Recognition processing is carried out in each bar-units separately, as follows.

1. Elimination of staff lines.
2. Recognition of attributive symbols.
3. Recognition of note symbols.

In these tasks, recognized symbols are eliminated one after another from the original notation image. Some symbols which can not be recognized may remain at the end.

 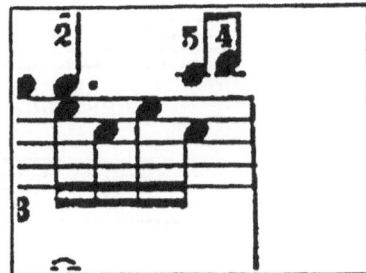

(a) An original image in the rectangular mask.

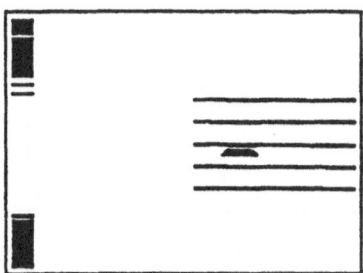 

(b) Elimination of short components in the horizontal direction.

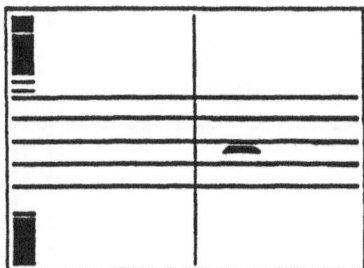 

(c) Detection of edge points of staff lines.

Fig. 5. An example of detection of staff lines.

4.1 Elimination of Staff Lines

The staff lines are the most important in the music notation, for they play a part of the criteria for the position of all other symbols. But they disturb the recognition of the other symbols for the overlap, so it is eliminated from the notation image before the recognition task.

The edge points of the staff lines in the bar image are estimated from the one in the original notation image. The staff lines are tracked from the left based on

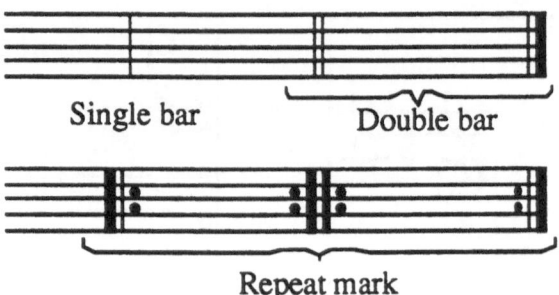

Fig. 6. Symbols recognized as bar lines.

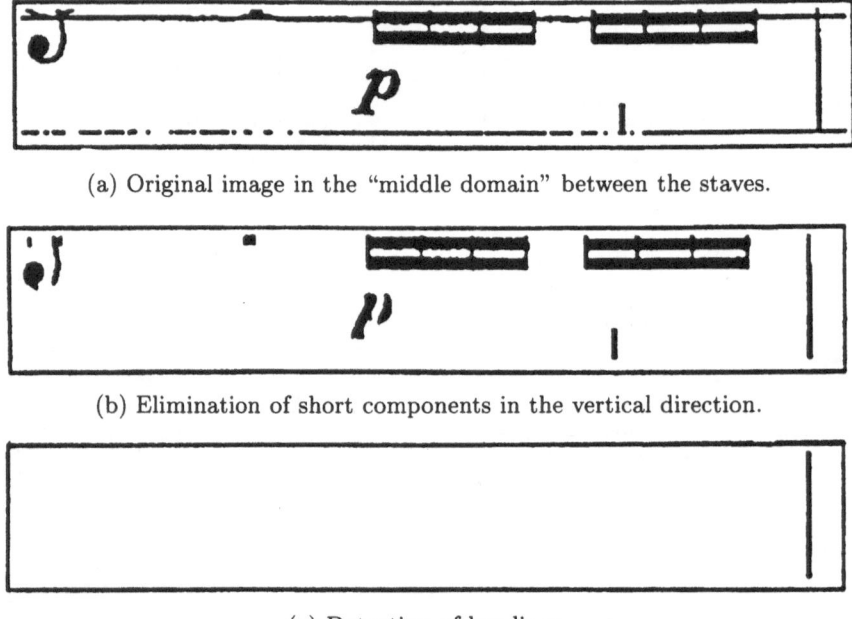

(a) Original image in the "middle domain" between the staves.

(b) Elimination of short components in the vertical direction.

(c) Detection of bar lines.

Fig. 7. An example of detection of bar lines.

these estimates. Then, if the staff width at each point is thinner than a threshold, the staff line under the point is estimated. This threshold is decided from the staff width estimated in the preprocessing. Figure 8 explains this process, which isn't quite perfect: a few symbols are fragmented unexpectedly. This problem is coped with in each recognition task. As top-down approach based on the knowledge for each symbols is available, it is easy.

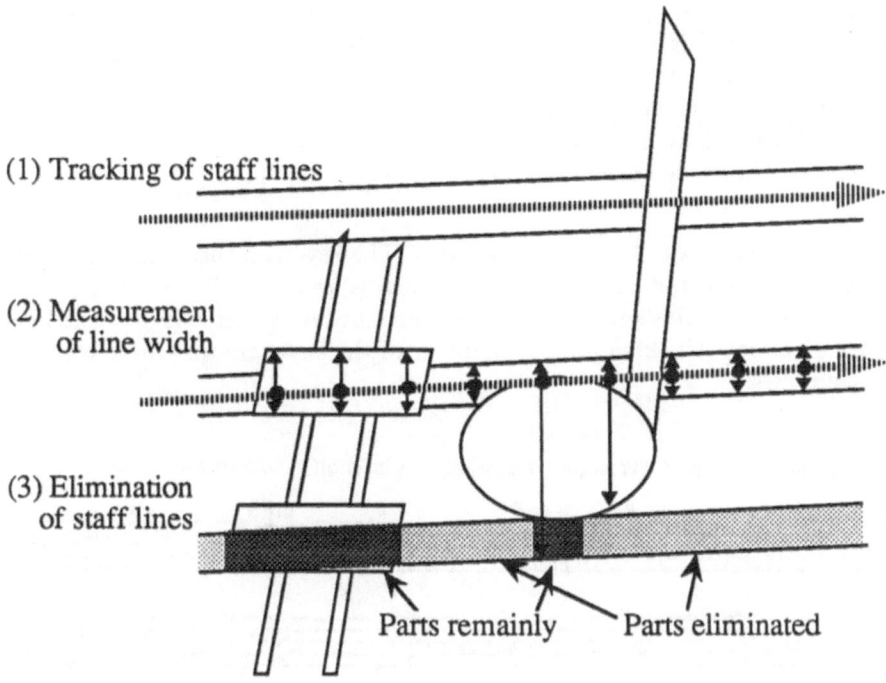

(1) Tracking of staff lines

(2) Measurement
of line width

(3) Elimination
of staff lines

Parts remainly   Parts eliminated

Fig. 8. Elimination of staff lines.

4.2 Recognition of Attributive Symbols

In this system, an attributive symbol is one that is recognizable during bar-unit
processing and influences the interpretation of other symbols, that is: clef, key-
signature and time signature. The position where these symbols are drawn is
restricted, as follows.

1. The clef has to be drawn on the left edge of the staff lines.
2. The presence of key-signatures is restricted to the part behind the clef or
   the double bar.
3. The time signature has to be drawn behind the first clef in music notations.
   In addition, it is allowed to be drawn behind a double bar.

Based on the above rules, the bar where processing is carried out can be limited
from the position of the bar and the kind of a bar line in front of the bar, so these
symbols are recognized only in the bar limited by the rules. This processing is
enabled to cope with changes of key or meter.

4.2.1 Recognition of the clef. The recognized clefs are the G clef or the F
clef. The connected region estimated as the clef is extracted. It is classified into
the G clef and the F clef from the size of the rectangle circumscribing it.

Besides the clefs keeping the above rules, there are some clefs as shown at the 1st and 8th bar in Figure 2. The recognition of these clefs has to be carried out for all bars in a different method from the above. The presence of such clefs is verified by the top-down structural analysis using the following knowledge: "The kind of clef which may be drawn next is different from the one drawn last." and "The height where such clefs may be drawn is constant for staff lines."

4.2.2 Recognition of the key signature. The key-signature consists of some sharps, flats or naturals. The position of them is known as Figure 9. The kind and the number of the key-signature of the right-hand part and the left-hand part are identical. The kind and the number of the key-signature are recognized using this rules.

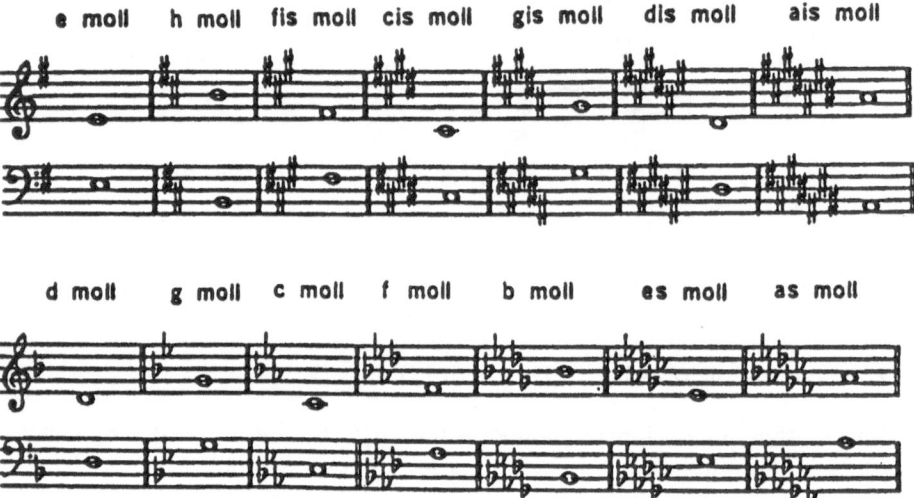

Fig. 9. The position of the key-signature.

4.2.3 Recognition of the time signature. The time signature consists of 2 numbers. The combination of them is restricted by musical knowledge. They are recognized by top-down structural analysis.

4.3 Recognition of Note Symbols

The note symbols are the most fundamental symbols to describe sounds. In this system, notes, rests and accidentals are treated as note symbols. The recognition of them has the following difficulty.

1. The note symbols have some connections, overlaps and containments with other symbols very often, so the segmentation of them is not easy.

2. Shape and Size of some symbols are not kept constant.

3. Some space in a symbol are filled with the staff lines. In the elimination of the staff lines, some symbols are fragmented.

4. Symbols include many thin regions. In such regions, there are some breaks.

5. Some symbols are ambiguously.

6. The semantic relationship between symbols is described ambiguously.

The difficulties from 1 to 4 affect the pattern processing. The ones from 5 to 6 affect the semantic analysis. The Recognition method of note symbols has some features to deal with them. In the pattern processing, notes are regarded as the combination of primitives and they are extracted from an image. Primitives have so simple shape that the segmentation of them is easier than the one of a whole note. In the semantic analysis, various knowledge are prepared to enable various interpretations, and the processing strategy which drives processing modules in variable threshold based on the condition of hypotheses in a working memory is adopted.

The outline of the recognition is shown in Figure 10. It consists of the working memory with 5 layers to describe some hypotheses and 4 processing modules which have access to the working memory. In the initial condition, only the bottom layer has a data, that is, the bar image eliminated staff lines and attributive symbols. The working memory is modified by the execution of a processing module. One of the hypotheses written in the top layer becomes the result of this recognition processing. The following describes the detail about the working memory, processing module and processing strategy.

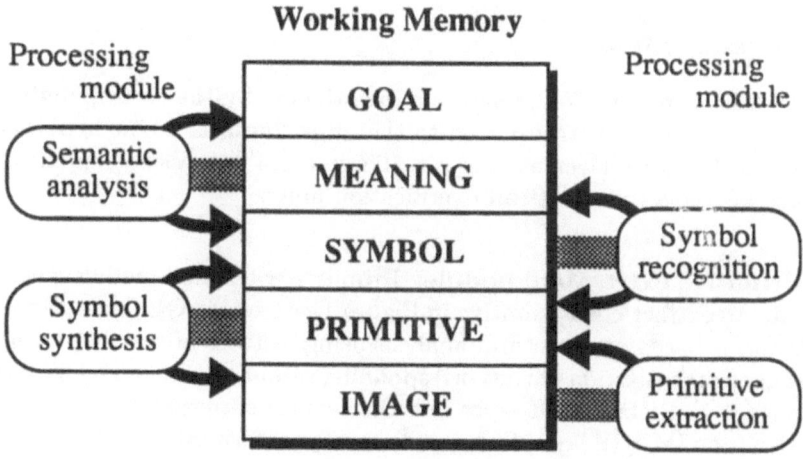

Fig. 10. Outline of recognition of note symbols.

4.4 Layered Working Memory

4.4.1 The IMAGE layer. This is the bottom layer. The data in it is the bar image to be recognized. When the recognition is performed, the region extracted as a primitive is eliminated from IMAGE layer as shown in Figure 11.
  (a) original image.
  (b) initial condition.
  (c) intermediate condition.
  (d) final condition.

4.4.2 The PRIMITIVE layer. Primitives, which construct notes or rests, are described in PRIMITIVE layer. Accidentals and dots are treated as primitives. Examples of the primitives are shown in Figure 12.

4.4.3 The SYMBOL layer. Notes and rests which are synthesized from the combination of some primitives are described in the SYMBOL layer.

4.4.4 The MEANING layer. The meaning of each symbol described in the SYMBOL layer, that is, information about the pitch and the beat, is described in the MEANING layer. The rest are regarded as notes without pitch.

4.4.5 The GOAL layer. The result obtained by means of time-sequentially connecting all hypotheses in MEANING layer based on musical knowledge is described in GOAL layer. One of hypotheses in this layer becomes the result as the bar-unit recognition processing.

4.5 Processing Module

A hypothesis in the working memory is investigated by the corresponding processing module, and it is transferred to the upper layer as a new hypothesis or returned to the lower layer as a reject. There are 4 processing modules: each consisting of recognition units and verification units.

4.5.1 Primitive extraction module. Primitive extraction module consists of some units to extract each primitive in Figure 11 from IMAGE layer. Processing in each unit is based on structural analysis using features of the shape and constraints about the position of the corresponding primitive. Extracted hypotheses are described in PRIMITIVE layer and the regions corresponding to them are eliminated from IMAGE layer. Some units also use information of the hypotheses in PRIMITIVE layer. For example, units to extract accidentals uses information of the position of heads described in PRIMITIVE layer.

  The executing order of the units influences a result, as some units use information in PRIMITIVE layer, and the regions corresponding to the extracted

(a) Original image.

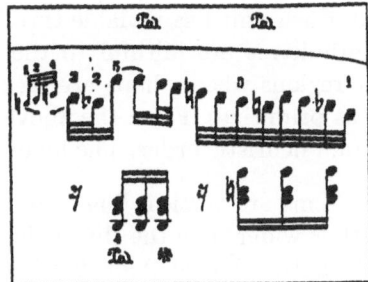

(b) Initial condition.

(c) Intermediate condition.

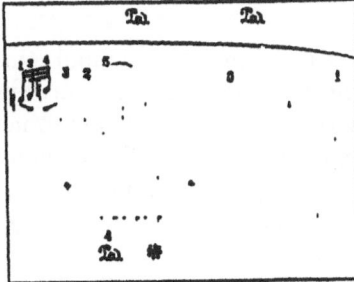

(d) Final condition.

Fig. 11. IMAGE layer.

Fig. 12. Examples of the primitives.

hypotheses are eliminated. Each unit has variable thresholds. When the threshold is severe, extracted primitives are faithful to the primitive model. When the threshold is loose, the regions whose shape are far apart from the primitive model are also extracted as primitives. From the above mentioned, the units in this module work in a certain heuristic order. The following is examples of units.

Stem extraction unit. Stems are vertical line components. After the regions where horizontal length is wider than the threshold are eliminated, the component whose vertical length is longer than threshold is extracted as a stem. These two thresholds are variable in the recognition processing.

Continuous hook extraction unit. Continuous hooks are long components in the horizontal direction. The regions where vertical width is not satisfied with thresholds are eliminated, then the components whoes horizontal length is longer than the threshold is extracted as a continuous hook. These thresholds are also variable in the recognition processing.

Black head extraction unit. Black heads have a very simple shape, and they are often connected with each other in case of the chord. Therefore, the feature of shape is not useful. This unit utilizes information of the hypotheses of stems, hooks and heads which have been extracted in the PRIMITIVE layer. As the position of head is restricted by them, the regions where the presence of head is expected are only verified. The components whose position and size are satisfied with some thresholds are extracted as a black head.

4.5.2 Symbol synthesis module. The symbol synthesis module consists of the note synthesis unit and the rest synthesis unit. Symbol hypotheses are synthesized from the combination of some primitives. A note fundamentally consists of heads and a stem except a whole note. The combination of them is searched in PRIMITIVE layer and the presence of hooks, dots and accidentals is verified. Then, the following are examples of rules used to reject primitives with illegal combinations.

1. Only one side of a stem must be connected with heads.
2. Only one side of a stem is allowed to have hooks.
3. A single hook must be connected with only one stem.
4. A continuous hook must be connected with more than 2 stems.

5. A head can be connected with each one stem with both up and down side.

In addition, there are some rules to limit the relative sizes of primitives. The primitives failing these checks are rejected back into the IMAGE layer. A note synthesized from primitives without inconsistency is transferred into SYMBOL layer. A rest is a symbol by itself, so it is transferred easily into SYMBOL layer. The rest with dots is synthesized as a dotted rest. Each unit in this layer also uses variable threshold to synthesize symbols.

4.5.3 Symbol recognition module. The task of the symbol recognition module is interpretation of notes and rests in the SYMBOL layer. A rest is regarded as a note without pitch. The pitch can be interpreted uniquely from the relative position of a head and staff lines, key-signature, the presence of accidentals and the kind of a clef. Information of the ledger lines, which is not extracted, is also used effectively to verify the pitch. The beat number, however, cannot be interpreted uniquely. The interpretation of the beat number can be divided into the fundamental interpretation and the exceptional interpretation. The exceptional interpretation results from semantic ambiguity or noises in the image. Semantic ambiguity mainly occurs in the interpretation of triplets or quadruplets. Noise in the image has a great influence on the detection of the number of hooks connected with a stem. The thin space between hooks is often filled due to overlaps with staff lines and the blur of ink, so some possibilities are expected on the detection of the number of hooks.

In processing of this module, the fundamental interpretation is applied first to the hypotheses in SYMBOL layer and the interpreted results are transferred into MEANING layer. As often as the hypothesis is rejected from MEANING layer, exceptional interpretation is applied to it in order.

4.5.4 Semantic analysis module. The result of the bar-unit is obtained from the connection of all hypotheses in MEANING layer by the semantic analysis module. In this task, the following have to be noticed.

1. When various notes are struck at the same time, some note symbols are sometimes drawn on the different position back and forth as shown in Figure 13.
2. In the case of polyphony, the connection of notes or rests is sometimes uncertain.

The result is verified by the total beat number in the bar. If the total beat number of the result is illegal, it is rejected. In the music with auftakt, however, the total beat number in some bars as a first bar is unknown by itself. In such bars, all results are left without rejects and unique result is determined in the postprocessing.

4.6 Processing Strategy

As often as a processing unit in the each module is carried out, intermediate hypotheses are generated or modified in the working memory. At the end the

Fig. 13. Bars in which notes are struck at the same time.

result is generated in GOAL layer. Most units in the low level modules include binary image processing as a labeling processing, so they take more CPU time than units in the high level modules which treat symbolic data. The units in the low level modules are carried out in a certain order determined heuristically. In the high level modules, a priority is attached to each rule and the rules are applied in order of priority until the result is generated in GOAL layer. If the result is not generated, processing in the low level module is retried with looser thresholds. Once hypotheses are transferred in SYMBOL layer, they are allowed to be rejected in PRIMITIVE layer but not allowed to be rejected in IMAGE layer.

In this method, a result is obtained quickly for high quality images, but for noisy images, it takes a long time. Symbols are extracted from the image in order of clearness, so the mistaken extraction of clear parts caused by loosing thresholds can be inhibited.

An imperfect result is sometimes obtained before a perfect one. For example, if only the symbols shown in Figure 14 are extracted in the case of the recognition of the first bar in Figure 2, this hypothesis is satisfied with the condition of total beat number and it is transferred into GOAL layer as the result. But, this result does not include expected 2 quarter notes. Even if a result is obtained, therefore, it is unknown weather it is a perfect result. In this method, when the result is obtained, it is saved and recognition processing is continued in a certain range with looser thresholds. if more excellent result is obtained, the saved result is modified to the new result and processing is continued further. Otherwise the saved result is regarded as the perfect result and processing is finished.

5 Postprocessing

The postprocessing is consists of 2 tasks, that is, the recognition of the global symbols and the unification of all results. The following describes each task.

5.1 Recognition of the Global Symbols

The symbols shown in Figure 15 are recognized in the postprocessing. The symbols whose recognition is difficult in the bar-unit recognition belong to the group 1. The symbols whose recognition has no meaning in the bar-unit recognition

Fig. 14. Imperfect results for the first bar in Figure 2.

belong to the group 2. These symbols are called global symbols in this system. The recognition of these symbols is applied to the every column images in the notation treated by the bar-unit recognition. In Figure 16, an example of such images is shown.

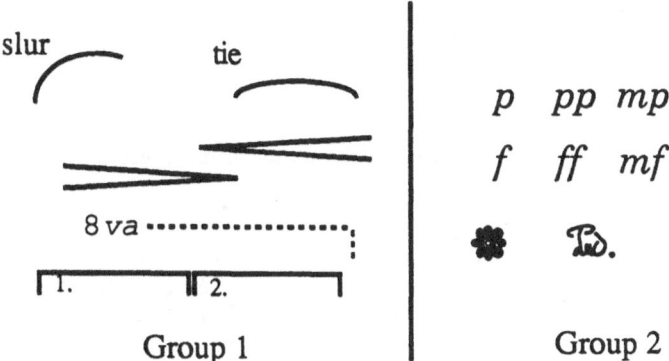

Fig. 15. Symbols recognized during postprocessing.

The recognition is carried out by recognition units for each symbol by means of utilizing the results of the bar-unit recognition. Staff lines and most symbols are eliminated in the bar-unit recognition, so the segmentation of symbols is easy. At first, bar lines and ledger lines are eliminated from the image. The position of ledger lines can be estimated from information of the position of heads. The symbols like letters are recognized by means of the adaptive template matching and the other symbols are recognized by means of the structural analysis method. Most part of ties overlapping with staff lines are eliminated in the elimination processing of the staff lines. They also can be recognized by the analysis from top-down approach based on information of the position of the heads.

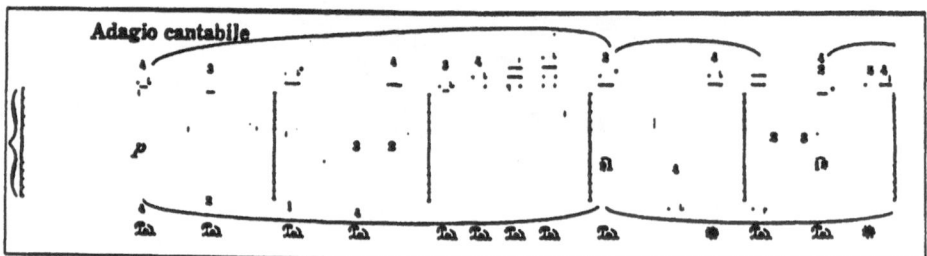

Fig. 16. A column image treated by bar-unit recognition.

5.2 Unification of All Results

In this task, for the bar with some results as the first bar of auftakt, unique result is determined using the results of the other bars and the results in the all bars are unified. In addition, the results obtained in the postprocessing are also appended to the result.

The final result is obtained by the processing as described above. In Table 1, a part of the final result is shown. This is a playable data. But fixed values are assigned for the length and the power of the sound, so the performance is felt monotonously. We have been developing the music interpretation system for performances "with feeling" [8].

Table 1. Selection from final results on the notation in Figure 2.

```
Flat : 4
2/4
==<1>== : 4 * 2              ==<2>== : 4 * 2
C3   0 4 (right, slur,       Eb3 0 6 (right, pedal)
            p, pedal)        Ab2 0 1 (right)
Ab2  0 1 (right)             C2   0 4 (left)
Ab1  0 4 (left, slur)        Eb2 1 1 (right)
Eb2  1 1 (right)             Ab2 2 1 (right)
Ab2  2 1 (right)             Eb2 3 1 (right)
Eb2  3 1 (right)             Bb2 4 1 (right, pedal)
Bb2  4 4 (right, pedal)      G1   4 4 (left)
G2   4 1 (right)             Eb2 5 1 (right)
Db2  4 4 (left)              Bb2 6 1 (right)
Eb2  5 1 (right)             Db3 6 2 (right)
G2   6 1 (right)             Eb2 7 1 (right)
Eb2  7 1 (right)
```

6 Experimental Results

This system was developed on APOLLO workstations using the C programming language. An optical scanner with a digitizing resolution of 240 dpi was used to acquire binary images of A4 pages.

The following scores were selected for testing:

1. Für Elise (Beethoven, Op. 173);
2. Turkish March (Mozart);
3. Etude (Chopin, Op. 10 No. 3); and
4. Sonata Pathetic, 2nd movement (Beethoven, Op. 13).

The 1st and 2nd scores are somewhat complex; the 3th and 4th are very complex. The recognition results are shown in Table 2.

Table 2. Recognition accuracy results.

Name of piece	Recognition rate
For Elise (L.V.Beethoven Op.173)	95.6%
Turkish March (W.A.Mozart)	91.5%
Etude (F.Chopin Op.10 No.3)	87.1%
Sonata Pathetic 2nd movement (L.V.Beethoven Op.13)	83.3%

The recognition rate is calculated from the count of modified and appended words in repairing the obtained result to the correct musical data. In the 1st or 2nd notations, there are several triplets and accidentals. Especially in the 2nd notation, many small notes, which represent ornaments and which are not recognized by this system, are drawn. Most mistakes result from them. In the 3th and 4th notations, many symbols are drawn with high density and there are many connections and overlap between symbols. Most mistakes result from many chords and accidental which are drawn with high density.

Processing time, which is different by the count of bars and the quality of image, take about 90 minutes for one page of A4 on APOLLO DN3000. Bar-unit processing consumes most of the processing. It is able to be carried out in parallel every bar-units. It means a possibility of the reduction of the processing time. In Figure 17, A result of the reduction of the processing time by parallel processing is shown. For this experiment, two DN3000s, DN570, DN3500 and DN4000 were used.

7 Conclusion

In this paper, a recognition system for printed piano music is described. The notation image input by an optical scanner is translated into a playable symbolic

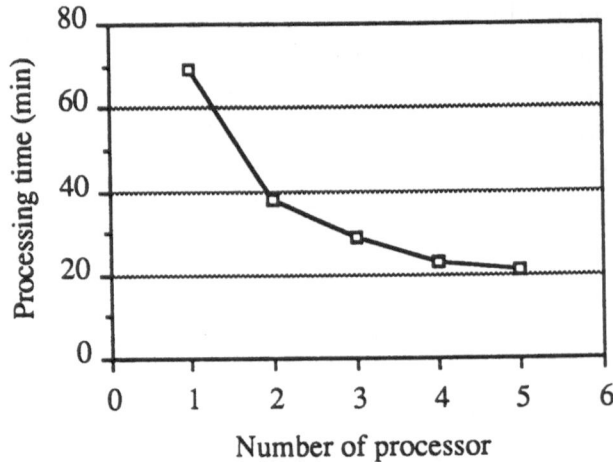

Fig. 17. Reduction of CPU time by parallel processing (Für Elise, 1st page)

data format. There are some difficulties both in the pattern signal processing and in the semantic analysis. In order to deal with these difficulties, this system adopts a top-down approach based on bar-unit recognition to use musical knowledge and constraints effectively. The recognition rate of simple beginner music is over 90%. The recognition rate on expert music is a little less. But, the results can be modified easily by means of the graphical editor.

Not all symbols in music are treated by this system, so the recognition of the remaining symbols is the subject for future study. But, all important symbols have been already recognized. Even if the kind of symbols which are not treated is many, the total number of them will be a few. Then, it is easy to append information about them into the data by the manual operation.

The recognition of the music notations is interesting as the object of the syntactic and structural pattern recognition. Described system has been developed for the automatic recognition system without human assistance, so it takes too much time to recognize the notation. If the system for practical use is wanted, more simple recognition method and intelligent human interface will be required to reduce the processing time.

References

[1]   C. Roads, *The Music Machine*,MIT Press (1989).
[2]   Y. Nakamura *et al.*, "Input Method of Note and Realization of Folk Music Data-Base," *TG PRL78–73*, pp. 41–50, Institute of Electronics and Comm. Engineers of Japan (IECE), (in Japanese)(1978).
[3]   I. Fujinaga *et al.*, "Issues in the Design of an Optical Music Recognition System," *Proc. 1989 International Computer Music Conf.*, Columbus, Ohio.
[4]   A. Tojo and H. Aoyama, "Automatic Recognition of Music Score," *Proc. 6th ICPR*, Munich, W. Germany, p. 1223.

[5]   T. Matsushima *et al.*, "Automated High Speed Recognition of Printed Music (WABOT 2 Vision System)," *Proc. Int'l Conf. on Advanced Robotics*, Tokyo, pp. 477–482, (1985).

[6]   H. Katayose *et al.*, "An Approach to an Artificial Music Expert," *Proc. 1989 International Computer Music Conf.*, Columbus, Ohio, pp. 139–146, (1989).

[7]   H. Kato and S. Inokuchi, "Automatic Recognition of Printed Piano Music Based on Bar Unit Processing," *Trans. of IECE*, J71–D, 5, pp. 894–901, (in Japanese)(1988).

[8]   H. Katayose *et al.*, "Music Interpreter in the Kansei Music System," *Proc. 1989 International Computer Music Conf.*, Columbus, Ohio, pp. 147–150, (1989).

Automatic Recognition of Printed Music

Nicholas P. Carter and Richard A. Bacon

Department of Physics,[1] University of Surrey,
Guildford, Surrey GU2 5XH, U.K.

There is a need for an automatic recognition system for printed music scores. The work presented here forms the basis of an omnifont, size-independent system with significant tolerance of noise and rotation of the original image. A structural decomposition technique is used based on an original transformation of the line adjacency graph. An example of output is given in the form of a data file and its score reconstruction.

1 Introduction

The existence of an automatic recognition system for printed music would make practical the conversion of large quantities of printed music into computer-readable form. This is similar to the requirement for automatic entry of engineering drawings, circuit diagrams, etc. from existing documents. Once the music is stored electronically, using some music representational language, it can be manipulated freely, enabling applications such as musicological analysis, point-of-sale printing, production of new editions, and production of braille or large format scores. For further background information regarding the field of acquisition, representation and reconstruction of printed music, the reader is referred to Carter ([1988]) and Hewlett ([1990]).

Work on automatic recognition of printed music began in the late 1960s and early 1970s, with the research of Pruslin and Prerau at the Massachusetts Institute of Technology (Pruslin [1967], Prerau [1970]). The limitations of the hardware available at that time for acquiring and manipulating images restricted the possibilities of the work, but some progress was made using techniques including low-pass filtering and contour tracing. More recent work has involved Japanese research teams (Matsushima [1985], Katayose [1989]). At Waseda University the WABOT–2 keyboard-playing robot has a vision system which uses mask-matching implemented in hardware in conjunction with localized measurements to read nursery song sheets. The work of the team at Osaka University is aimed at a recognition system for keyboard music as part of an overall 'music information processing system'. This system also tackles the problems of automatic

---

[1] This research was undertaken with support from Oxford University Press.

transcription of music (producing a score from a soundtrack) and sentiment extraction. Other research into automatic recognition of printed music is currently being undertaken at the University of Ottawa (Fujinaga [1988]), and at University College Cardiff (Clarke [1988]). The former makes use of projection profiles in order to recognize the music symbols in an image, whilst the latter is aimed at producing a system which uses simple tests on the input image so that a low-cost solution to the automatic input problem can be provided for widespread use by publishers and engravers. Several short term projects in this field have also been undertaken recently including work by Tojo ([1982]), Roach and Tatem ([1988]), Mahoney ([1982]), Martin ([1987]), and Tønnesland ([1986]).

2 Image Acquisition

The basis of the recognition system described here is a structural decomposition technique which makes use of an original transformation of the line adjacency graph. Input is provided by a Hewlett Packard ScanJet flatbed CCD scanner at a resolution of 300 dots per inch, with maximum image size of A4 and automatic thresholding, providing approximately 1Mbyte of binary data per page. A form of horizontally oriented low-pass filter was developed initially for pre-processing, filling gaps up to five pixels wide in sets of black pixels, but it was found to be superfluous due to the robust nature of the staff-line-finding algorithm. No other pre-processing is used.

3 Segmentation

Although all music scores using conventional music notation contain staves of five lines, it should be stressed that although these five lines are supposedly parallel, equally spaced, horizontal, unbroken and of constant thickness, this is often not the case. Staff lines may be skewed, bowed, fragmented, of varying thickness and, perhaps most significantly, substantially obscured by superimposed musical symbols. As a consequence of this, many of the more obvious methods for finding the staff lines (such as forming a horizontal histogram of black pixels) are rendered impractical. A means of segmenting the image is thus required which would facilitate staff-line recognition and hence permit isolation of the musical symbols, whilst also coping with the possibility of slight rotation or skewing of the image, together with the other attributes of the staff lines mentioned above. The technique which has been adopted uses an original transformation of the line adjacency graph (Pavlidis [1982]) and is derived using two passes over the binary image. The first pass run-length encodes the image with the continuous runs of black pixels (termed 'segments') oriented vertically. The second pass constructs the transformed line adjacency graph by proceeding across the image examining pairs of columns of run length encoded data and, where appropriate, agglomerating segments to form 'sections' (the nodes of the transformed line adjacency graph). As can be seen in Figure 1, some of the sections correspond to structural components of the music image, including note heads and staff-line fragments.

For further details of the specific rules used to achieve the transformation, the reader is referred to Carter ([1989]).

Fig. 1. A fragment of an image showing the boundaries of the sections.

The advantages of this technique include a consistency in the breakdown of the image regardless of small amounts of rotation or skewing of the original, and significant data reduction, *i.e.* subsequent processing can refer to the section data rather than the original bit-map image. The data structure which is used to store section information contains values such as maximum and minimum x and y, area, aspect ratio (length/average thickness), lists of connections to sections to left and right, and a least-squares fit line through the mid-points of constituent segments.

Where a section exists which has a sufficiently small area (currently five pixels or less) and is not connected or has just one connection to another section, then it is removed as noise. Appropriate adjustments are then made to the transformed line adjacency graph in situations where the noise section was attached to another section, including the merging of sections where necessary.

4 Staff-Line Finding

The aim of the staff-line-finding process is to categorize all sections which remain after noise-removal as either staff-line or non-staff-line. The first stage in finding staff-line sections is to extract those which have a high aspect ratio, low curvature (currently indicated by the variance figure of the least-squares fit line) and are single-connected. These sections, which are relatively long and thin are termed filaments. The avoidance of absolute measurements in extracting filaments leads to the inclusion of some sections which are not part of a staff line (long beam fragments for example), but these are removed by establishing a threshold for the maximum permitted filament thickness based on the mean thickness of the initial set of filaments. Other sections which have high aspect ratio, such as portions of crescendo or diminuendo markings (known as 'hairpins'), are removed from the filament list by establishing limits for permitted angle with the respect to the staff lines (which may not themselves be horizontal).

Having found the filaments in an image, these must be combined in order to locate possible fragments of complete staves, *i.e.* a set of five horizontally over-lapping, roughly equally spaced and parallel filaments. Initially, vertical links are established between filaments which overlap horizontally. By finding the closest vertical spacing between each filament and those to which it is linked, and finding the mean for this figure over all filaments, a distance is established for the inter-staff-line spacing (or staff space height). This dimension is used later in order to maintain the use of relative measurements, which is particularly important when examining section characteristics for recognition purposes. For example a section may be part of a solid note head if the height of its bounding rectangle is approximately equal to the staff-space height. Similarly, a half-note rest will have average thickness equal to roughly half of the staff-space height. The staff-space height is also used to threshold the vertical links between filaments. This is because the maximum distance between filaments which are part of the same staff will occur between the top and bottom staff lines — consequently any links between filaments which are spaced by more than a multiple of 4.5 times the staff-space height cannot be between filaments from the same staff and are therefore removed. A test is also made to examine the degree of parallelism between two horizontally overlapping filaments. This involves testing the ratio of the spacings at the extremes of the region of overlap to prevent a link being established if inappropriate. This prevents inclusion of those non-staff-line line fragments which are not parallel with a staff line. Having found vertical links, right and left links are then determined by projecting each filament by a proportion of its length and searching for the existence of another filament within a fixed vertical tolerance of the staff-space height either side of the projected line.

The next operation examines the list of filaments to find sets of five which are all concurrent, *i.e.* for which there is a common region of horizontal overlap, and whose vertical spacing is, in the case of adjoining filaments, roughly equal to the staff-space height. Each set of five filaments is stored as a 'staff fragment' in a data structure which holds the horizontal and vertical position of the region of overlap and the gradient and intercept of a line based on the average of the least-squares fit lines of the five filaments. Other information can be contained within the structure, including a staff number and links to other staff fragments to right and left, when these are established.

Once all the staff fragments have been found, they are checked to detect those which are erroneous (for example where a filament which consists of a thin ledger line forms a staff fragment with four true staff-line filaments). This is done by projecting the fitted line for each staff fragment across the page in both directions and confirming that, if it intercepts the vertical extent of another staff fragment, it does so within the correct region. Currently, this procedure assumes that the leftmost staff fragment of any particular staff is correct in order to avoid a sequence of incorrect staff fragments being classified as the staff. Ledger lines and other linear markings are much less likely to appear at the start of a staff so this appears to be a safe assumption. As part of the above testing, a staff number is allocated to all those staff fragments which are found to form part of the same staff. At this stage, the number of staves present in the image has been found and a linked list of staff fragments established for each staff. Now, each of the sections which constitute a staff fragment can be labeled as staff-line sections by storing the appropriate staff number and staff-line number in the associated data structure. The next stage is to interpolate between all pairs of staff fragments, and extrapolate beyond those at the horizontal extremes of a staff, in order to locate those sections which can also be categorized as staff-line sections.

The interpolation procedure examines each linked pair of staff fragments and attempts to find a path between corresponding staff lines which constitute the two staff fragments. Firstly, it tests whether a particular section is common to the pair of staff fragments, if not then it tracks the right and left links of the appropriate pair of filaments in an attempt to find a path between them, and if this fails it interpolates to bridge the gap where there is no filament link. As part of this process, thin sections which fall within a search region between filaments are also categorized as staff line and allocated the relevant staff and staff-line numbers. The thickness threshold which is used is that previously established as the maximum permitted filament thickness. Similarly, the extrapolation procedure makes use of filaments links where these exist, in addition to the projection of the appropriate fitted line until the edge of the image is reached. Again, thin sections which are found in the course of this tracking are classified as staff-line sections. The staff-line-finding technique described above typically results in clean isolation of the musical symbols in an image, as can be seen in Figure 2. One problem which exists with the approach is commonly illustrated by the uppermost portion of the bass clef, which is normally classified as staff-line because it coincides with the top staff line and is below the thickness threshold. A similar effect occurs with the portion of the treble clef which coincides with the lowest staff line. The resulting breaks in isolated symbols are similar to those which may occur in the original image due to low print quality, so will still fall within the scope of the recognition system. Additionally, avoiding the misclassification of such a symbol fragment as part of a staff line would necessitate the use of a significant quantity of contextual knowledge which would seem unwarranted.

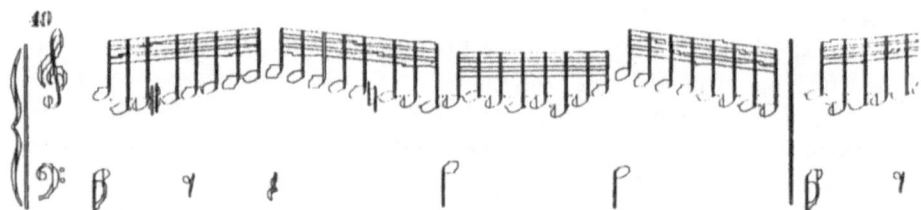

Fig. 2. An example of symbol isolation.

After all staff-line sections have been classified as such, a reorganization of the transformed line adjacency graph is undertaken in order to separate each section's connections into staff-line and non-staff-line. Where appropriate, sections are then merged, resulting in a closer correspondence between sections and the underlying structure of the musical symbols.

5 Object Formation

Each group of connected non-staff-line sections is formed into an 'object'. This object may consist of a complete musical symbol, a fragment of a symbol or a number of touching or overlapping symbols. Object formation is achieved by stepping through the list of non-staff-line sections and undertaking a depth-first traversal of the transformed line adjacency graph, commencing with the next section which has not already been included in an object. A further type of data structure is used to store individual objects and this contains information such as the dimensions of the bounding rectangle, a list of constituent sections, area, etc.

As a result of deriving the objects from the section list, their ordering bears no real relation to their musical sequence. The objects are, however, associated with one or more staves by using the staff numbers of any staff-line sections connected to the object's constituent sections. When recognition is attempted, each staff's objects are examined in order from left to right, with those objects which are 'floating' in space in the original image (dots for example) being processed separately. The spatial layout of musical symbols, although basically organized around two orthogonal axes of time and pitch, has numerous subtle contradictions and complex variations of this structure. This can be illustrated by simultaneously sounding pitches, which are not always vertically aligned. Also multiple voices (melodic lines) may share one staff and be mixed with chords. The ultimate aim of this work is to produce a system which can cope with at least two voices per staff, with the presence of chords and with multiple staff systems (a system is formed from a group of staves bracketed together to indicate that they are to be performed simultaneously). The example given in the following section shows results on an example consisting of multiple staff systems with a single voice per staff. Work is underway to expand the system to cope with chords and multiple voices per staff.

6 Recognition

A number of models have been derived which are used in conjunction with a limited set of parameters in order to achieve object recognition. For example, a small symbol such as a dot or staccatissimo marking can be recognized as a single section with a bounding rectangle with appropriate maximum side length and aspect ratio. A further test is required to identify the triangular shape of a staccatissimo mark. A more complicated symbol type such as the beamed group requires its own processing routine to cope with the many permutations of pitch and rhythm values, together with ledger lines, which it may contain. Beamed groups are examined for the presence of vertical lines, again by making use of the transformed line adjacency graph but in this instance based on horizontally oriented segments. Sections of high aspect ratio are identified as vertical lines (*i.e.* the note stems) and a collinearity test finds those thin sections which form stem fragments. A search is then undertaken either side of each note stem in order to find candidates for note-head sections, including multiple note heads clustered together. A vertical extent is established for each note head or note-head cluster and local staff-line sections are found in order to ascertain the relevant pitch values. The beaming complex itself is isolated and its thickness measured at the end of each note stem in order to establish the rhythm value for each note.

Objects which are not physically attached to a staff require more effort to achieve full recognition. For instance, once a dot is found it has to be associated with a note or rest, and its role categorized as rhythm augmentation or staccato. Similarly, a slur has to be associated with two notes if possible, although it may start or end beyond the horizontal extremes of a staff in order to indicate phrasing across a line break. The latter situation has to be identified so that it can be represented in the output file. The current system provides output in the form of an ASCII file compatible with the SCORE [1] desktop music publishing package (the output which results from processing Figure 3 is shown in Figure 4). The format consists of blocks of five data categories — pitch, rhythm, markings, beams and slurs — each separated by a semi-colon. The pitch representation uses a letter and octave number, rhythm uses the denominator of the fractional representation of the rhythm (for example 8 is an eighth note) and the last three categories contain the note numbers to which they apply. The reconstruction seen in Figure 5 is output from SCORE (based on the file shown in Figure 4), using its default settings for size and spacing. SCORE was chosen because it includes a wide variety of symbols, permits editing in a variety of ways (including transposition), provides complete control over symbol placement, has a playback facility for proof-hearing and produces high-quality hard-copy.

Fig. 3. Two systems from a keyboard sonata by C.P.E. Bach.

7 Conclusions

Further work needs to be done in order to cover a larger vocabulary of symbols, but the foundations of a robust, omnifont and size-independent system which

---

[1] SCORE is a trademark of Passport Designs, Inc.

```
IN 1
0 200
M2/BA/E3/R/F3/R/M2/G3/R/A3/A2/A3/F3/M2/G3/A3/B3/B2/M2/R/M2/M2;
4/8./4/8./4/8./8./16/8./16/4/4/4/4/2;
HW 2/HW 3;
4 5/6 7;
;
IN 2
0 200
TR/G5/A5/G5/F5/G5/E5/D5/E5/A5/B5/A5/G5/A5/E5/D5/E5/B5/C6/B5/A5/B5/E5/D5/E5/
C6/C5/E5/B4/A4/B4/C5/B4/A4/E4/G4/B4/E5/B4/E5/B4/G4/E4;
16/16/16/16/16/16/16/16/16/16/16/16/16/16/16/16/16/16/16/16/16/16/16/16/
4./4/16/16/16/16/8/16/16/16/16/16/16/16/16/16/16/4;
;
1 4/5 8/9 12/13 16/17 20/21 24/27 30/31 33/34 37/38 41;
;
IN 3
0 200
M2/BA/B3/B2/D3/M2/E3/G3/F3/G3/E3/M2/B3/B2/D3/M2;
4/4/4/4/8./16/4/4/4/4/4;
;
5 6;
;
IN 4
0 200
TR/D5/B5/A5/G5/F5/E5/D5/C5/B4/C5/D5/E5/F5/G5/A5/F5/G5/B4/C5/D5/E5/F5/G5/A5/
B5/C6/B5/A5/B5/G5/F5/E5/D5/B5/A5/G5/F5/E5/D5/C5/B4/C5/D5/E5/F5/G5/A5/F5;
16/16/16/16/16/16/16/16/16/16/16/16/16/16/16/16/16/16/16/16/16/16/16/16/
16/16/16/16/16/16/16/16/16/16/16/16/16/16/16/16/16/16/16/16/16/16/16/16;
;
1 4/5 8/9 12/13 16/17 20/21 24/25 28/29 32/33 36/37 40/41 44/45 48;
;
```

Fig. 4. The data file resulting from processing Figure 3.

Fig. 5. The reconstruction of Figure 3.

has significant tolerance of noise and rotation, are in place. Some of the problems which require special attention in the future include the processing of multiple voices on one staff and recognition of overlapping or touching symbols. Both of these problems will need an algorithm which can break down a composite object (which consists of more than one musical symbol) into its constituent parts so that these can be recognized by existing techniques. A comprehensive music recognition system must also cope with text of various fonts and point sizes. Our approach is to isolate the text from the initial mixed text and graphic image. Preliminary work which we have undertaken in this area has been successful, with the ultimate aim being to pass the isolated text to existing character recognition software, before finally reassembling the text and music.

With regard to printing defects, a significant amount of tolerance to noise, including breaks in staff lines, is built into the system, but coping with extreme cases of fragmentation will require new techniques. These will be based on cluster analysis and make further use of graph structures in order to establish the spatial relationships between portions of a fragmented symbol necessary to achieve reconstruction.

Acknowledgements

The authors would like to thank Oxford University Press for supporting this research and for permitting the processing and reproduction of the musical examples.

References

[1988] N. P. Carter, R. A. Bacon, and T. Messenger, "Acquisition, Representation and Reconstruction of Printed Music by Computer: A Review," *Computers and the Humanities*, 22 (2), pp. 27–46, 1988.

[1989] N. P. Carter, *Automatic Recognition of Printed Music in the Context of Electronic Publishing*, Ph.D. dissertation, Univ. Surrey, 1989.

[1988] A. T. Clarke, "Inexpensive Optical Character Recognition of Music Notation: A New Alternative for Publishers," *Proc. Computers in Music Conf.*, Lancaster, 1988.

[1988] I. Fujinaga, *Optical Music Recognition using Projections*, M. A. thesis, McGill Univ., Montreal, 1988.

[1990] W. B. Hewlett and Selfridge-Field, E., *Computing in Musicology: A Directory of Research*, Center for Computer Assisted Research in the Humanities, Menlo Park, CA, 1990.

[1989] H. Katayosea and S. Inokuchi, "The Kansei Music System," *Computer Music J.*, 13 (4), pp. 72–77, 1989.

[1982] J. V. Mahoney, *Automatic Analysis of Music Score Images*, B. Sc. dissertation, MIT, Cambridge, MA, 1982.

[1987] N. G. Martin, *Towards Computer Recognition of the Printed Musical Score*, B. Sc. dissertation, Thames Polytechnic, London, 1987.

[1985] T. Matsushima *et al.*, "Automated recognition system for musical score," *Bulletin of Science and Engineering Research Laboratory*, Waseda Univ., 112, pp. 25–52, 1985.

[1982] T. Pavlidis, *Algorithms for Graphics and Image Processing*, Computer Science Press, Rockville, MD, 1982.

[1970] D. S. Prerau, *Computer Pattern Recognition of Standard Engraved Music Notation*, Ph.D. dissertation, MIT, 1970.

[1967] D. H. Pruslin, *Automatic Recognition of Sheet Music*, Sc.D. dissertation, MIT, 1967.

[1988] J. W. Roach and J. E. Tatum, "Using domain knowledge in low-level visual processing to interpret handwritten music: an experiment," *Pattern Recognition*, 21 (1), pp. 33–44, 1988.

[1982] A. Tojo and H. Aoyama, "Automatic recognition of music score," *Proc. 6th ICPR*, p. 1223, 1982.

[1986] Tønnesland, S., *SYMFONI: System for Notekoding*, Ph.D. dissertation, Institute of Informatics, Oslo, Norway, 1986.

Automatic Recognition of Several Types of Musical Notation

Takebumi Itagaki,[1] Masayuki Isogai,
Shuji Hashimoto, and Sadamu Ohteru

Department of Applied Physics, School of Science and Engineering,
Waseda University, 3-4-1 Okubo, Shinjuku-ku, Tokyo 169, Japan

This paper describes recent progress towards systems for automatic recognition of several different types of musical notation, including printed sheet music, Braille music, and dance notation.

1 Introduction

Previously we reported on a human type musician robot "WABOT-2" [1]. Using a CCD camera its vision system could in real time read a score placed on a music stand. In this case, positioning and optical adjustments of the camera were required to obtain a result due to the camera being situated about one metre from the score.

Our Automatic Score Recognition System, which used an image scanner, has been developed as a part of "An Integrated Music Information System: PSB-er" [2] as a music score information entering device. "PSB-er" is an acronym for "Performance Score and Braille music system for Education and Research." Music performance, printed score, musical braille and dance score are ways of representing which are used like universal languages.

2 A Common Language for Different Types of Musical Notation

There are various representation of musical information; performance, printed score, braille score and dance notation. These expressions are quite different; performance is time-dependent and demands analogue acoustic information; printed score is a two dimensional graphic image presenting analogue and digital information; dance notation is a two dimensional graphic image presenting analogue movement information; and braille score is a digital one dimensional sequence of braille characters.

---

[1] Presently at City University, London, Department of Music, City University, Northampton Square, London EC1V 0HB, U.K.

Accordingly, at first, we had to contrive a new common representation of musical data, named SMX (Standard Music eXpression) [3], which is based on score information and which is used to exchange information between sub-systems, *e.g.* from braille scores to printed scores and *vice versa*. The system configuration and data flow within PSB-er is shown in Figure 1.

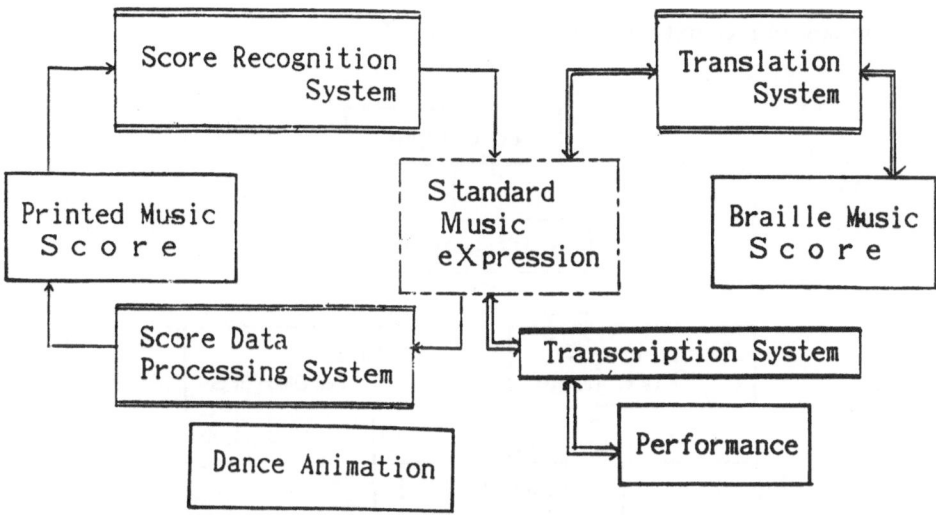

Fig. 1. Configuration of PSB-er.

Music information can be input to "PSB-er" by automatic music score recognition and dance notation recognition, as optical image data, or from keyboard instrument, as a performance. In addition, information entered from a computer keyboard also can be used for correcting or editing.

The following sections describe about each sub-system on PSB-er.

3 Automatic Recognition of Music Scores

3.1 Outline of the System

In the "WABOT-2" system, its visual system was required to recognize a score placed on a music stand situated about one metre from the CCD camera. However in this system, to reduce the time for preparation (optical and positional adjustments), we now use an image scanner instead of a CCD camera. Furthermore, the concept of the system has been changed from "real time score reading" on the WABOT-2 system to a "score data entering device" on this PSB-er system. The target music scores were piano scores, ranging from beginners' studies to a Chopin Etude, and including some popular songs. The system comprises an image scanner [NEC PC-IN503H] and a 32bit workstation [Apollo Domain DN3000] to analyze the image data from the scanner and control it. The scanner

scans an A4 sheet in one minute at 240 DPI resolution and the image data is
analyzed in about three to four minutes, depending on the complexity of the
score. Its recognition rate is nearly 100% on a beginner's score, and 85% to 95%
on a score of moderate complexity.

3.2 Recognition Sequence

The process of recognition is shown as Figure 2.

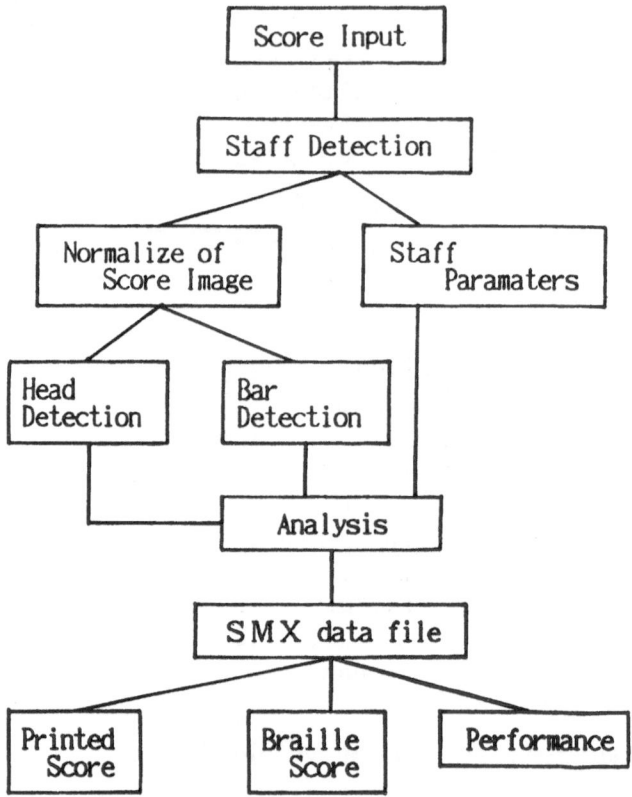

Fig. 2. Recognition sequence for printed music scores.

From the scanned image data, first, the staffs are detected. The location and
size of the staffs are very important since they will be used to determine the
score geometry and to restrict the search area. Therefore, the initial detection
of staffs should be accurate.

The staff lines do not always lie horizontally, and for that reason, staff candidates are detected at a number of points. This location information is used for
the normalization, inclination correction of the score image and the threshold
setting for pattern discrimination. After that, the score image is divided into

individual staffs and note head detection and bar detection are performed on each divided image.

The note heads are detected by correlating the patterning of black head and the two patterns of white heads (half notes and whole notes). The size of these patterns is determined by spacing of staff lines is used. First of all, the symbols, located at left end of the staves (clef, time signature and key signature) are detected and discriminated. Next, the note heads are discriminated by checking for four types of tail, and looking for three other attributes: dots, tenuto and staccato marks.

Finally, using the musical syntax and location data of staffs, the symbols are analyzed and the recognition results, as an SMX data file, is generated.

4 Recognition of Braille Scores

The Automatic Translation System of Printed Music to and Braille [4] can translate printed music, which includes almost all score symbols for piano, into braille music within a few seconds. Also the system can analyze a complex braille score and generate score data, in the form of an SMX file, in about two CPU minutes.

4.1 Bilateral Translation System

A few years ago, the system was tested for practical use in a library for the blind. Following this practical test, the system was simplified to work on a desk top PC without any special equipment and to be used it by any person in any location. The system can translate score data, an SMX file, written by our Automatic Score Recognition System, or a score data processor for commercial printing in to a braille score. The results of translation were output as NABCC (North American Computer Code). After then, the data are amended to include several symbols which could not be translated automatically.

According to users' suggestions, a person who had no knowledge of a braille score should be able to participate in a part of the translation. In addition, the users wanted to improve the translation system from a braille score to a printed score to aid publishing the work of blind composers.

4.2 Data Entry from Braille Scores

As a practical testing system, we made the reverse translation system from NABCC, using a word processor for blind, to SMX data. This system can be used not only for direct braille music acquisition but used for translation verification on an existing workstation.

In early experiment at recognizing a braille score, we entered a printed braille score, instead of ordinary embossed braille symbols.

As for the practical execution of data entry, using an image scanner, the two methods were attempted; one is the direct reading of embossed braille score [8]

FANTAISIE-IMPROMPTU

Fig. 3. An example of a music score.

```
$score
        @title "IMPROMPTU Op.29 1"
        @size     A4
        @format p2*d5
        @staff_width    64
        @staff_len      1781
        @staff_location (252,414) (251,590) (139,869) (137,1046) (138,1303) (138
,1481) (139,1741) (139,1920) (137,2178) (135,2358)
$measure 1
        @bar 2
        @position left_end
$bar 1
        @voice 1
        !front_bar      #type normal_bar (0,)
$voice 1
        ?clef   #type G
        !key    #type flat 4 (98,)
        !time   #type 2/2 (150,)
        !note   #pitch E (215,)
                #duration 8
                #stem up ((232,11),(232,72))
                #beam 0 1
        !note   #pitch nD (277,)
                #duration 8
                #stem up ((294,11),(294,79))
                #beam 1 1
        !note   #pitch E (329,)
                #duration 8
                #stem up ((346,11),(346,70))
                #beam 1 0
        !note   #pitch 'C (391,)
                #duration 8
                #stem down ((391,24),(391,70))
                #beam 0 1
        !note   #pitch B (446,)
                #duration 8
                #stem down ((446,33),(446,98))
                #beam 1 1
        !note   #pitch A (499,)
                #duration 8
                #stem down ((499,41),(499,85))
                #beam 0 1
        !note   #pitch G (551,)
                #duration 8
                #stem down ((551,50),(551,93))
                #beam 0 1
        !note   #pitch 'F (608,)
                #duration 8
                #stem down ((608,-1),(608,81))
                #beam 1 1
        !note   #pitch n'E (672,)
                #duration 8
                #stem down ((672,8),(672,67))
                #beam 1 0
        !note   #pitch f'E (737,)
                #duration 4
                #stem down ((737,8),(737,58))
```

Fig. 4. Results of recognition (SMX data).

and the other is indirect reading of a copy of real embossed braille. The latter can be easily produced, similar to a credit card receipt.

In order to improve the signal-noise ratio, the following pre-processing is effective. At first, we entered the score through an image scanner and then took projections of the horizontal and the vertical axis of the image data. As a result of the projections, we obtained a grid of the braille score and the nodes on a CRT. At the end points correction could be achieved by considering the musical context represented in the grid.

The former system, which using a small laser surveyor and a plotter printer, was produced for direct reading without any contact with an embossed paper. The laser surveyor was situated on a plotter printer, instead of a pen, and the printer was controlled by a PC. Scanning the surface of an embossed braille, the surveyor measured the distance between itself and the paper. As a result, the embosses were recorded as distance data and their analysis was almost similar to the latter method, carbon copied.

5 Automatic Recognition of Dance Notation, "Labanotation"

5.1 Description of Body Movement

Music and dance or human body movement have been closely related. Music has created new dances and dances have produced new music. Many varieties of dance notation have been reported since ancient times [6, 7], but its automatic recognition using a computer has scarcely been reported, except for Hachimura's work [9]. We have been studying Automatic Recognition of Dance Notation together with the actual body movement of dance [10, 11] in an Integrated Music Information Processing System, PSB-er.

Labanotation is a well known dance notation, and it can describe the direction of the action, level, timing and the part of the body moving. And in many cases, its time scale is expressed by the corresponding music score.

5.2 Automatic Recognition of Labanotation

Using an image scanner, Labanotation is entered into a workstation as image data. The inclination of the dance score sheet is detected, and the image is divided into main symbols and sub symbols. Bars and lines are detected to restrict the scanning area. After that, the main symbols are distinguished (solid symbols, symbols with a dot and hatched symbols) by scanning along the three parallel lines which contain the critical information. Once identified, the symbols are extracted from the score image. The recognition of sub symbols is done separately.

The result of recognition can be displayed on a CRT or printed out as animated graphics or as text which describes the meaning of the dance score, corresponding to body movements in the graphics.

This system will be applied not only to the recognition of dance notation, but also the understanding of body movement from a data-glove [12] the output of which should be a notation like Laban's.

6 Conclusion

In this paper, we described three automatic music notation recognizing systems; printed music, braille music and dance notation. These notations are worldwide

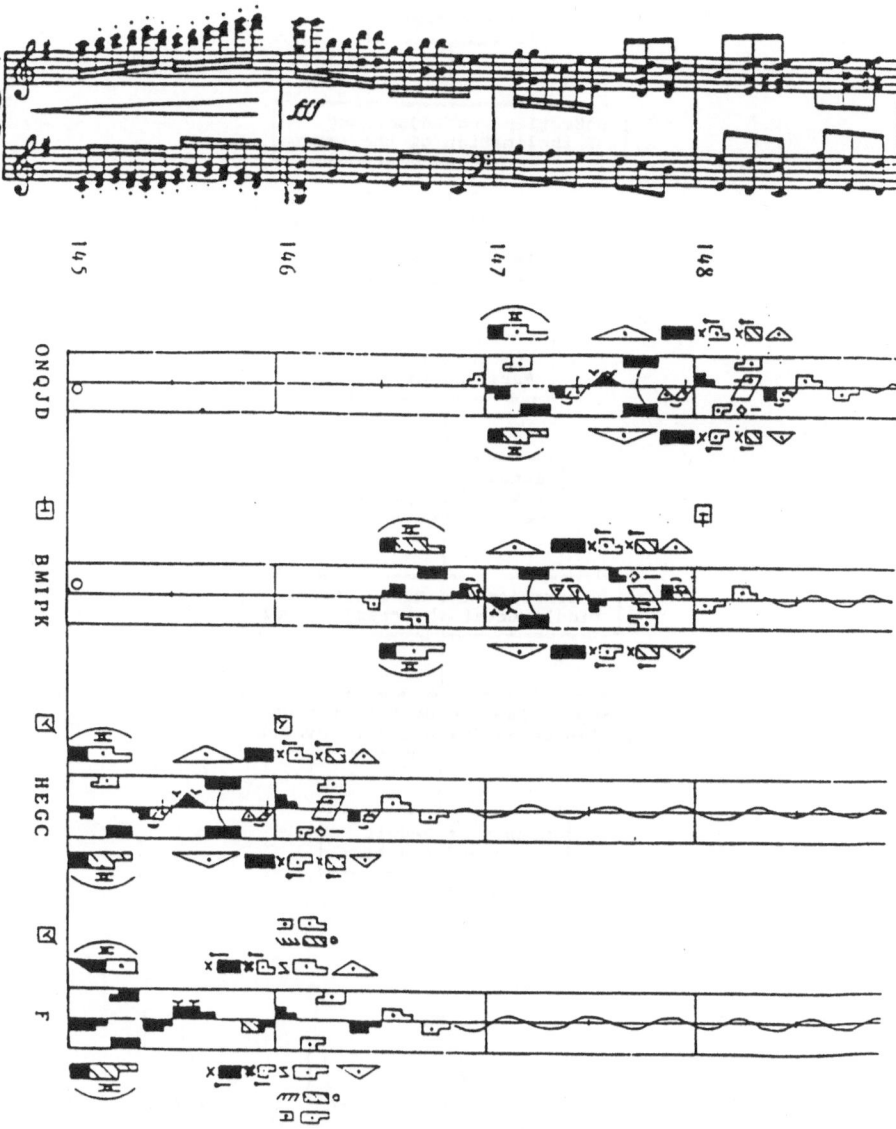

Fig. 5. Example of Labanotation, including a music score.

systems. However not all notations are acceptable to a single individual. Our system can perform conversions of medium complexity scores with an 80% to 90% accuracy in a few minutes. In addition, irrespective of the musical notation, printed or braille, a common SMX file is generated which describes almost all piano performance symbols. This can be used to modify a piano performance by a machine.

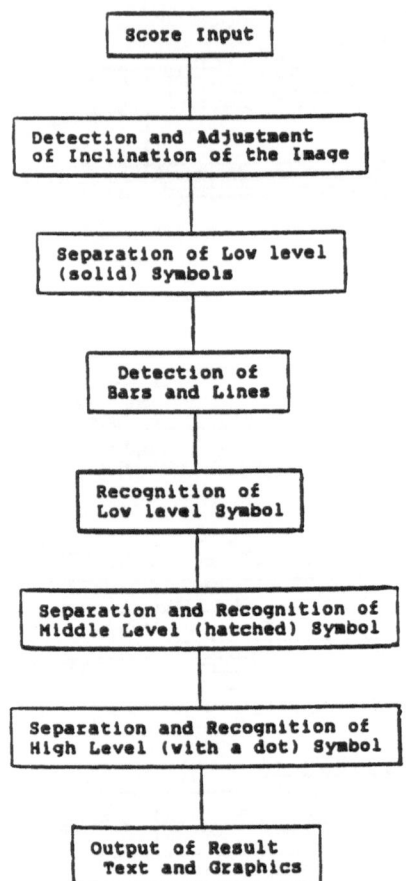

Fig. 6. Recognition sequence for Labanotation.

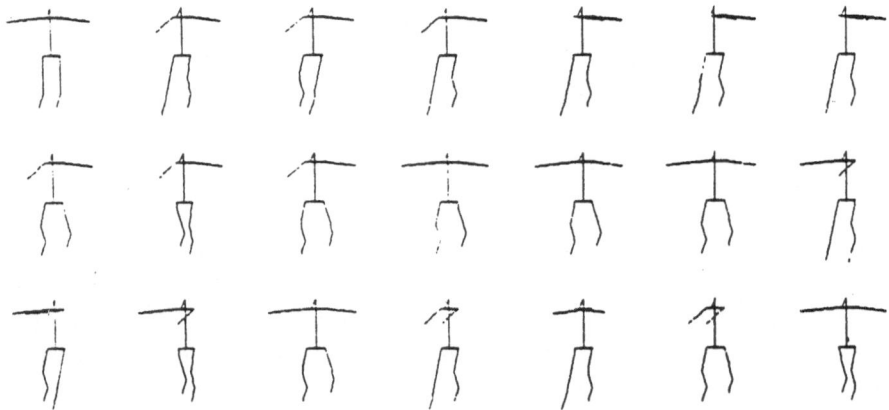

Fig. 7. Result of Labanotation recognition: graphics.

```
=========================================================
Middle level:  move forward for 2.0 secs
Middle level:  right arm swing forward for 4.0 secs

Middle level:  move forward for 2.0 secs


=========================================================
Middle level:  move forward for 2.0 secs
Middle level:  right arm swing to left side for 3.0 secs
```

Fig. 8. Result of Labanotation recognition: text.

Each system was designed to recognized only one type of notation. Work is in progress towards the recognition of song scores and orchestral scores. Problems yet to be overcome are the distinction between musical symbols and lyrics. This problem will probably be resolved by the inclusion of extended character recognition capabilities within the score recognizer.

References

[1]   S. Ohteru *et al.*, "Automated High Speed Recognition System (WABOT-2 Vision System)," in *Proc. Int'l Conf. on Advanced Robotics*, Tokyo, Japan, September 1985.

[2]   T. Matsushima, S. Ohteru, and S. Hashimoto, "An Integrated Music Information Processing System: PSB-er," in *Proc. 14th International Computer Music Conf.*, Cologne, September 1988.

[3]   S. Ohteru, K. Oka, *et al.*, "A Musical Data Expression for Integrated Music Information System :SMX," in *Proc. 36th Annual Convention IPS*, Japan, March 1988 (in Japanese).

[4]   H. Sawada, T. Matsushima, T. Itagaki, and S. Ohteru, "A Practical Bilateral Translation System Between Printed Music and Braille," in *Proc. 6th International workshop on Computer Applications for the Visually Handicapped*, Luven Belgium, September 1990.

[5]   T. Itagaki, T. Matsushima, S. Ohteru, *et al.*, "Practical Testing of Automated Printed Music to Braille Translation System," in *Proc. The 15th Sensery Substitution Symp.*, Tokyo, Japan, December 1989 (In Japanese with English abstract).

[6]   A. Hutchinsons, *Labanotation*, Theatre Arts Books, London.

[7]   A. Hutchinsons, *Dance Notation*, Dance Horizon, New York.

[8]   T. Miyazawa, S. Ohteru, and S. Hashimoto, "The Performing System of Music Through Braille Transaction," in *National Convention Record 1991 Information Processing Society of Japan* (in Japanese).

[9]   K. Hachimura and Y. Ohno, "A System for the Representation of Human Body Movement for Dance Scores," In *Pattern Recognition Letters*, Vol. 5 1–9, North-Holland, Amsterdam, 1987.

[10] M. Isogai, N. Namekawa, S. Ohteru, and S. Hashimoto, "Automatic Recognition of Dance Notation," in *National Convention Record 1990 The Institute of Electronics, Information and Communication Engineers*, (in Japanese).

[11] N. Namekawa, D. Shin, K. Naoi, H. Morita, S. Ohteru, and S. Hashimoto, "Computerized Dance-Step Recognition for Representations of Body Movement," In *Information Processing Society of Japan Technical report* PRU 89–63 (1989) (in Japanese).
[12] H. Watanabe, H. Morita, S. Ohteru, and S. Hashimoto, "Hand Movement Understanding using the Data Glove," in *National Convention Record 1990 The Institute of Electronics, Information and Communication Engineers* (in Japanese).

Methodology

Syntactic and Structural Methods in Document Image Analysis

Alberto Sanfeliu

Instituto de Cibernética, Universidad Politécnica de Cataluña
Diagonal 647, 2, 08028 Barcelona, Spain

We survey applications of syntactic and structural pattern recognition (SSPR) methods to the field of document image analysis, analyze the strengths and weakness of these methods for document image analysis, and discuss other complementary techniques.

1 Introduction

Document image analysis is a growing field with a wide spectrum of applications whose objective is to create higher level descriptions of the contents of paper-based documents. These high level descriptions will permit the use of efficient algorithms for archiving and retrieving documents, for reducing the storage of mixed text and graphics documents and, in general, for doing intelligent interpretation of document image information.

A conservative list of applications where document image analysis is required at present is shown below:

1. Magazine and journal storage and retrieval
2. Book storage and retrieval
3. Business letters and document storage and retrieval
4. Technical documentation for storage, retrieval, manipulation, integration or edition:
   - Flow charts
   - Mechanical engineering drawings
   - City maps
   - Electrical circuits
   - Hand-drawn figures
   - Geographical maps
5. Printed music storage, retrieval and manipulation

As with much other work on image analysis (image processing and computer vision), many authors choose to partition the stages of processing required for document images as follows:

1. Image acquisition and preprocessing
2. Region segmentation
3. Extraction of primitives: lines and regions
4. Extraction of features and symbolic representations
5. Analysis and interpretation

1.1 SSPR Methods in Document Image Analysis

Structural and Syntactic methods ([BUSA90, FU82, GOTH78, MIC86, PAV77]) are being used in many image-analysis-related fields and they are often suitable for document image analysis, with the possible exception of the first stage. However, document images have special properties which can make SSPR techniques particularly attractive:

1. A document has several levels of information — chapter, section, subsection, etc. — which can be described by means of structural information or a grammar. These formal pattern representations can be used to verify, organize and compact the data.
2. Every subsection contains headings, a set of paragraphs, mathematical formulas, figures, images, etc, which follows some kind of structure. These structures can be represented by strings, trees or graphs.
3. The texts of every sentence of a paragraph are generated by a grammar which can be used to verify the words and their syntax. In the same way the words can be verified by matching the input word with a dictionary of words.
4. The layout of a document image is essentially structured and can be described by a tree or a graph, or a grammar. For example, a letter can be described by several blocks spatially located, the block of the sender, the receiver, the theme, the date and the signature. The analysis of the layout can be done through SSPR techniques.
5. The layout of engineering drawings, graphics, printed music, etc. is also structured and contains a series of blocks which can be described by strings, trees or graphs. The analysis and verification of the contents of these blocks can be done through the analysis of the layout structure.
6. The organization of the key information for data base retrieval can be done by using the structural information of the document.

In summary, the document image information is often essentially structured and for this reason SSPR techniques may be appropriate for document image analysis.

2 Formal Grammars and Prototype Structures for Document Image Analysis

Formal grammars and prototype structures are tools for representing structured information. They can be used alone or in combination with other type of pattern representation, for example logic based. The use of one or the other type of pattern representation depends mainly on two issues:

1. The pattern representation descriptive power and compactness
2. The efficiency and flexibility of the analysis procedures

The pattern representation issue permits us to describe the structures in a formal way. There are two types of pattern representation methodologies in SSPR: formal grammars and prototype structures. Both pattern representations have different descriptive power and space occupancy. Moreover the efficiency and flexibility of the analysis depends also on the type of methodology chosen. Figures 1-4 show pages of a document, and Figures 5 and 6 show representations of the document by means of formal grammars and prototype structures.

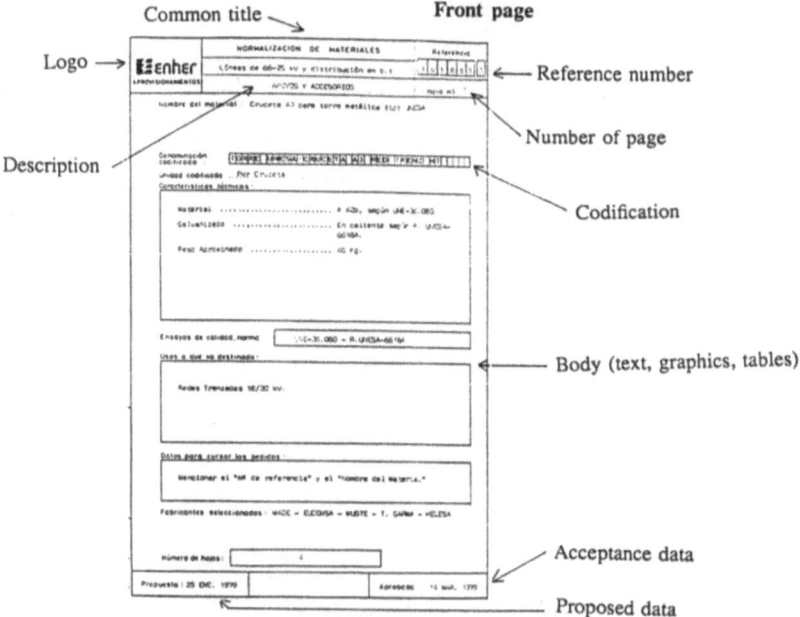

Fig. 1. Example document: textual cover page.

2.1 Formal Grammar Pattern Representation

The use of formal grammars are based on a very well established formal language theory ([HOUL79, AHUL73]) which has been proved useful in many subfields of computer science. The formal grammar pattern representation describes a structure recursively through production rules. Every production rule generates a subset of the elements of the grammar, nonterminals and terminals. The terminals are the constituents or primitives and the nonterminals are the subsets

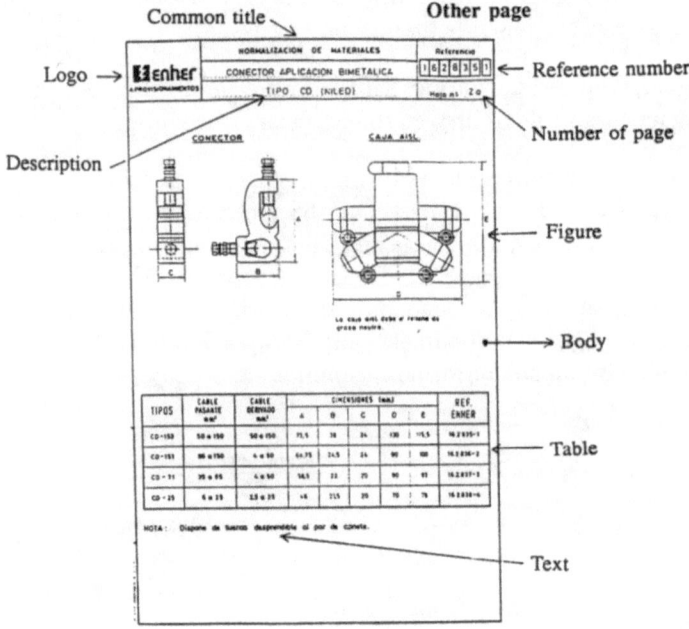

Fig. 2. Example document: technical drawings and tabular data.

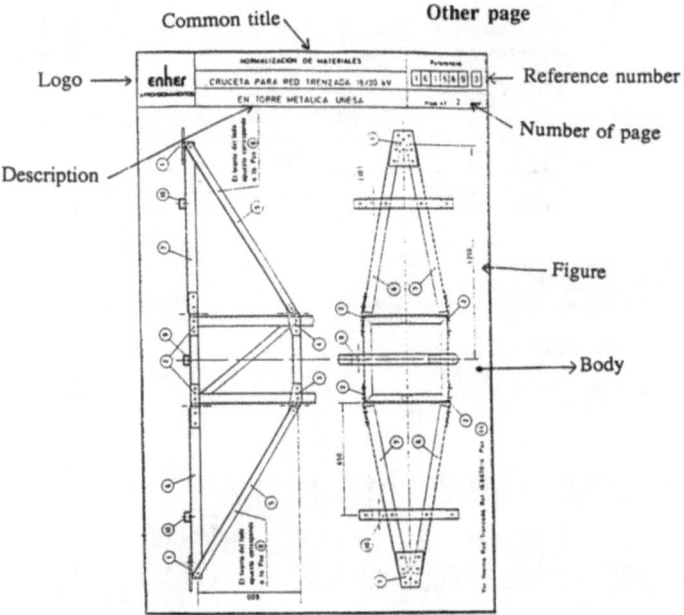

Fig. 3. Example document: mechanical drawings.

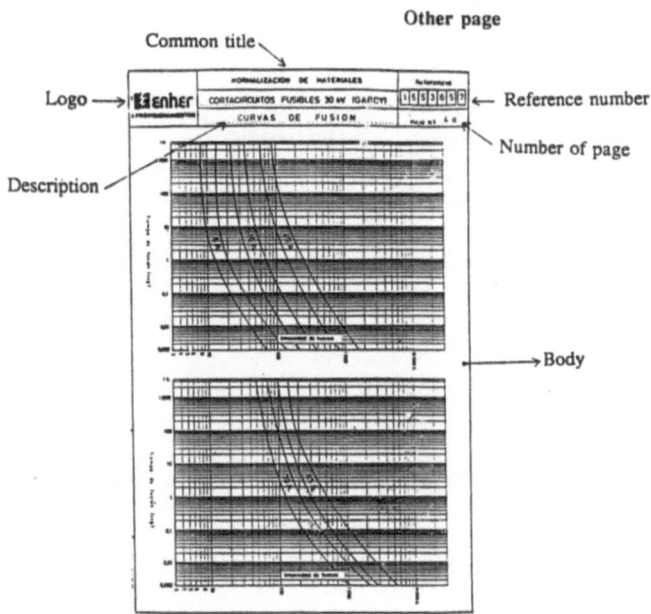

Fig. 4. Example document: data graphs.

of the grammar. If the terminals are the simpler elements of the structure, the grammar will able to generate the complete structure. A grammar can generate one structure, a set of structures or an infinite number of structures. Figure 5 shows a grammar which generates a document image.

Grammars are classified according to the type of structure which they generate. The grammar categories are: string grammars (generating strings over an alphabet), matrix and array grammars (generating two-dimensional arrays) and graph and tree grammars (generating graphs or trees). There are other special type of grammar which are actually graph grammars but that are generally known as higher-dimensional extensions of string grammars, for example the Picture Description Language (PDL) or the Plex grammar. Examples of these grammars applied to pattern representation can be seen in [BUSA90, FU82, GOTH78, MIC86, PAV77, ROS79, ENRR87]

Let us begin with string grammars. A *string grammar* is a 4-tuple $G \equiv (V_N, V_T, S, P)$ where

- V_N is a nonempty, finite set of symbols, called *nonterminal vocabulary* of G
- V_T is a nonempty, finite set of symbols, called *terminal vocabulary* of G
- $S \in V_N$ is the *start symbol*
- P is a nonempty, finite set of pairs (α, β), where α, β are non-null strings of elements of $V_N \bigcup V_T$.

The pairs of P are called the production rules of G and are written in the form of $\alpha \to \beta$. A production rule is the mean of generating the strings of the

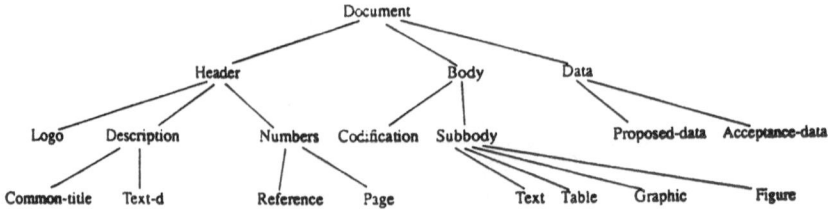

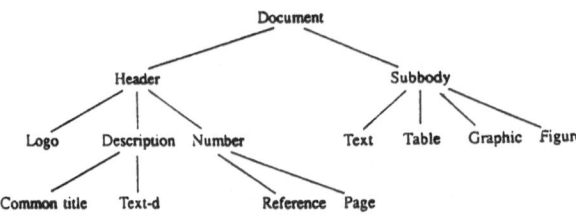

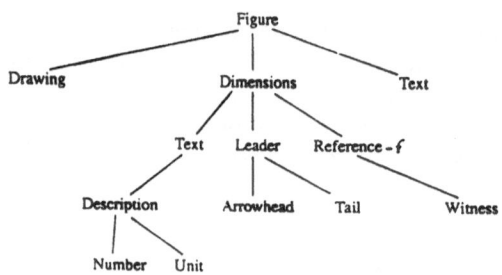

Fig. 5. Tree pattern representations of images in Figures 1-4.

language of G $(L(G))$. In order to define $(L(G))$ we must introduce the notion of *derivation*. We say that a the string w is directly derived from the string δ in G $(\delta \Rightarrow w)$ if there exists a rule $\alpha \rightarrow \beta$ in G such that w is the result of replacing α (a substring of δ) by β in δ. In general we say that w is derived from the initial symbol of G, S, if there exists a sequence of strings from which we can derive w from S (the notation is $S \overset{G}{\Rightarrow} w$).

Grammars can be used for generating the structures (the document images) and for accepting them, *i.e.*, to know if a structure belongs to a grammar. This mechanism is known in formal language theory as the grammar *parser*. For the analysis of document images the parser is an essential tool since that permit us to know if an input structure belongs to one of the pattern classes (in this case,

$G \equiv (V_N, V_T, \triangle, P, S)$

V_N = {S, Doc-fp, Doc-op, Header, Body, Data, Subbody, Logo, Description, Numbers, Codification, Subbody, Comm-title, Text-d, Reference, Page, Text, Table, Graphic, Figure, Prop-data, Acc-data, Drawing, Dimension, Text-f, Leader, Reference-f, Description-f, Unit, Number, Arrowhead, Tail, Witness }

V_T = { (NORMALIZACION DE MATERIALES), text, digits, drawing, table, (Referencia), (Hoja n), graphic, (Aprobada :), (Propuesta :), logo, tail, witness, arrowhead }

P :

S	→	Doc-fp		
S	→	Doc-op		
Doc-fp	→	Header	Body	Data
Doc-op	→	Header	Subbody	
Header	→	Logo	Description	Numbers
Body	→	Codification	Subbody	
Description	→	Comm-title	Text-d	
Numbers	→	Reference	Page	
Subbody	→	Text Table	Graphic	Figure
Data	→	Prop-data	Acc-data	
Comm-title	→	{1-tx}		
Text	→	< text(40) >		
Text-d	→	< text(30/30) >		
Reference	→	{4-tx} < digits(7) >		
Page	→	{5-tx} < digits(3) >		
Table	→	< table(9,5) >		
Graphic	→	< graphic >		
Acc-data	→	{2-tx} < digits-text-digits(2,3,4) >		
Prop-data	→	{3-tx} < digits-text-digits(2,3,4) >		
Logo	→	< logo >		
Figure	→	Drawing	Dimension	Text
Drawing	→	< drawing >		
Dimension	→	Text-f	Leader	Reference-f
Text-f	→	Description-f		
Description-f	→	Number	Unit	
Leader	→	Arrowhead	Tail	
Reference-f	→	Witness		
Number	→	< digits >		
Unit	→	< text >		
Tail	→	< tail >		
Witness	→	< witness >		
Arrowhead	→	< arrowhead >		

1-tx	≡	NORMALIZACION DE MATERIALES
2-tx	≡	Aprobada :
3-tx	≡	Propuesta :
4-tx	≡	Referencia
5-tx	≡	Hoja n

Fig. 6. Some production rules of a context-free grammar for the images in Figures 1-4.

every pattern class is defined by the language generated by a grammar).

Parsing is the inverse process of generation, which permits us to find a sequence of substructures $w = \delta_n, \delta_{n-1}, ..., \delta_o = S$ such that δ_i is directly derivable from δ_{i-1} in G, for $1 \leq i \leq n$. The parsing process is a very time and space consuming task which time and space complexity depends on the category and type of grammar. For this reason only few types of grammars are eligible for practical applications.

In Pattern Recognition the grammars which are mainly used are those which have a parser which time complexity is at most of polynomial degree ($O_T = (n^k$ where k is of low order and $k > 0$).

Let us going to present a brief description of the most well known grammars used for pattern representation ([BUSA90, FU82]):

2.1.1 String grammars

Context free grammars

A context free grammar is a 4-tuple $G \equiv (V_N, V_T, S, P)$ where V_N, V_T and S have been defined previously and P has the following structure:

The production rules are of the form $A \rightarrow \beta$ where $A \in V_N$ and $\beta \in V_N \bigcup V_T$.

Finite state grammars

A finite state grammar is a 4-tuple $G \equiv (V_N, V_T, S, P)$ where V_N, V_T and S have been defined previously and P has the following structure:

The production rules are of the form $A \rightarrow aB$ or $A \rightarrow a$ where $A, B \in V_N$ and $a \in V_T$.

2.1.2 Tree grammars

Regular tree grammars

A regular tree grammar over $< V_t, r >$ is a 4-tuple $G_t \equiv (V, r', S, P)$ satisfying the following conditions:

- $< V, r' >$ is a finite ranked alphabet with $V_T \subset V$ and $r'/V_T = r$ and $V - V_t = V_N$
- P is a finite set of production rules of the form $\phi \rightarrow \psi$ where ϕ and Ψ are trees over $< V, r' >$
- S is a finite subset of T_r, where T_r is the set of trees over alphabet V

In this case P works as follows: $\alpha \overset{a}{\Rightarrow} \beta$ is in G_t if and only if there exists a production rule $\phi \rightarrow \psi$ in P such that ϕ is a subtree of α at a and β is obtained by replacing the occurrence of ϕ at a by ψ.

2.1.3 Transition network grammars

Transition network grammars

A basic transition network (BTN) is a direct graph with labeled states and arcs, a start state and a set of final states. The basic transitions network is a generalized pushdown automaton equivalent to a context free grammar. If some facilities are added to each arc, for example a set of register-setting actions to be executed if the arc is followed, then the transition network is denominated Augmented Transition Network (ATN). An ATN could achieve the power of a Turing machine and can be modified to any kind of application by changing the conditions and restrictions of the arcs.

2.1.4 Generalizations of grammars

Programmed grammars

A programmed grammar differs from the conventional ones in that every production rule have associated the following production rule which may be applied next. Each production rule consists on a label, a regular production rule and two associated fields — $S(U)$ (success field) which tell us which is the next production rule to be applied, and $F(W)$ (failure field) which tell us which production rule is applied next if the production rule of $S(U)$ can not be applied -.

A programmed grammar G_P is a 5-tuple $G_P \equiv (V_N, V_T, J, S, P)$ where V_N, V_T and S have been defined previously, J is a set of production labels and P is of the form:

$$\alpha \to \beta \quad S(U)\ F(W)$$

where $\alpha \to \beta$ is a production rule, $\alpha, \beta \in V_N \bigcup V_T$, (r) is the label, $r \in J$, U is the success field and W is the failure field.

Programmed grammars can be extended to any of the aforementioned grammar categories and they are very useful for practical applications.

Attributed grammars

A powerful extension of grammars is the association of numerical-value parameters (or attributes) with the symbols. We can assign a set of initial parameter values to the initial symbol S and a set of functions to every production rule $\alpha \to \beta$ that permit us to compute the values for the symbols in β from the symbols in α. In the same way the parameters can be associated to the terminals and for every production $\alpha \to \beta$ we can have a set of functions which permit to compute the parameters of α from the ones of β. Attributed grammars have also many applications and are specially suitable for document image analysis.

Stochastic grammars

A stochastic grammar is a 4-tuple $G_s \equiv (V_N, V_T, S, P_s)$ where V_N, V_T and S have been defined previously and P is a finite set of stochastic production rules of the form:

$$\alpha_i \overset{p_{ij}}{\to} \beta_{ij} \quad j = 1, ..., n_i \ \ i = 1, ..., k$$

where $\alpha_i \in (V_N \bigcup V_T)$, $\beta_{ij} \in (V_N \bigcup V_T)$ and p_{ij} is the probability associated with the application of this stochastic production

$$0 < p_{ij} \leq 1 \quad \text{and} \quad \sum_{j=1}^{n_i} p_{ij} = 1$$

The global probability of a derivation from $\delta \overset{P}{\to} w$ is

$$P = \prod_{i=1}^{n} p_i$$

2.2 Prototype Pattern Representation

The use of prototype structures for pattern representation is another way of describing structures. There are basically tree types of structures: strings, trees and graphs. For the graph case there are two basic types of representation: hierarchical and non-hierarchical.

In prototype pattern representation a pattern class is formed by a set of structures — strings, trees or graphs — instead of a grammar.

The structures can incorporate additional information, attributes, relational or procedural information. Usually attributes refer to numerical information. The other two have the following meaning,

- *Relational information*, which permits to describe structures in terms of its properties, its parts and its interrelations among its parts, for example *Part-of* or *Subset-of*. The relational information is very useful in graphs and they can be used for guiding the analysis of a document. Usually these type of graphs are denominated *Relational graphs*.
- *Procedural information* which include algorithmic and rule based mechanism in the symbols (for example the nodes of a graph) or in the interrelation of symbols (for example the branches of a graph). When the procedural information is included in the nodes of a digraph and some mechanism of inherence is included, then the structure is called frame-based system ([MIN75]). Other types of structures are also possible, for example semantic nets ([FIN79]).

2.3 Comments on Pattern Representation

The formal grammar pattern representation although is a powerful tool has some restrictions which have to be taken into account in practical applications:

1. The descriptive power of the string and tree grammars described before is limited. This implies that some complex patterns can not be generated and in others is not trivial to find the grammar. In some cases neither it is easy to modify a grammar to include new patterns which structure differs slightly from the basic typical structure. For these cases is recommended to use attributed grammars which permits to solve many of the aforementioned problems. Other way of solving the problem is including functions in the grammar rules which allow to expand the power of the grammar. Examples of these types of grammars are the ATN and programmed grammars.

2. The design of a pattern analysis system implies the consideration of hundred and thousand of prototype patterns. Since there are not yet available inference procedures for generating the optimal grammar, some times becomes almost impossible to create such a grammar. On the other side, the use of a grammar which generates an infinite language can become a problem since it can derive structures which do not belong to the pattern class. The first enumerated problem has not been solved at present. The second problem can be solved through attributed and programmed grammars.

The use of prototype pattern representation has also some issues which have to be taken into account for practical applications.

1. The design of a pattern analysis system implies the generation of all the prototype patterns which must be used to analyze the pattern class. If the number of patterns is high or almost not enumerable, which is not rare in document analysis, there is not possible to generate all patterns. This problem can be solved by using *procedural information* in the structures.

2. Document images have not a fixed structure, as opposite in case of physical objects, but contain substructures which can differ slightly in information, position and orientation. Moreover, as in the case of text information, the structures (for examples words) are related through a grammar. The first problem requires the use of *procedural information*. The second problem can not be solved through prototype structures and requires the combination of other techniques.

3 Methods of Analysis

Document analysis requires the use of different techniques depending on which information is going to be processed. The basic analysis techniques which are related to SSPR methods are:

1. *Matching:* These methods ([BU90, SA90, SHHA90, BUSA90, FU82]) are used for finding a similarity measure between two structures, an unknown input pattern and the prototype pattern. They can be also used to find a substructure into structure. If both structures are identical the similarity measure is zero, otherwise is higher than zero. The methods can be used in several stages of the analysis and can be applied basically for classification and verification.

2. *Parsing:* These methods ([BUSA90, FU82]) are used for finding if a structure
or substructure belongs to the language generated by the pattern grammar
and for finding a similarity measure between an unknown input pattern and
the pattern grammar. They can also be used for guiding a search through
the pattern grammar. The methods can be used in several stages of the
analysis and can be applied in the classification of structures with respect to
a pattern grammar, in the verification of structures and in the verification
of a substructure into a grammar language.

3. *Heuristic search:* These methods ([PEA84, NIL80]) are used for decision
making, interpretation, classification, etc. They can be applied in several
stages of document analysis. These methods are based on looking one of the
solutions in the space of search.

4. *Decision trees:* These methods ([PEA88]) are used for classification purposes
and for guiding a search. They can also be applied in several stages of document analysis. Tree search is a special case of *search* where the control is
irrevocable and the there is not backtracking.

5. *Constraint propagation:* These methods ([WAL75], [RHZ76], [HAR83],
[HUZU83], [PEA88]) are used for verification, interpretation, etc. They can
be applied in several stages of document analysis. These methods are based
on the propagation of local constraints among the neighbor nodes of the
studied node.

These are not the only methods at hand, but they are the best known SSPR
methods. We have not discussed here *statistical methods in pattern recognition*,
neither *logic based methods*.

Let us review briefly some of the best known algorithms in each one of the
aforementioned methodologies and discuss their main advantages and disadvantages.

3.1 Matching

The process of comparing two structures, an unknown input pattern and a prototype pattern, to obtain a similarity measure between both is called matching.
The similarity measure value ranks usually between 0 and 1, where 0 implies a
perfect match between both structures and 1 means no match at all. Matching
can be done between strings, trees and graphs and several methods exists. Let
us review some of them.

3.1.1 String to string matching

Matching based on edit operations

The basic method ([LEV66, AHPE72]) consists on computing the minimum
number of edit operations — insertion of a symbol $a \in V_T$ in y, deletion of a
symbol $a \in V_T$ in x and substitution of a symbol $a \in V_T$ by a symbol $b \in V_T$

in y, $a \neq b$, where x and y are the strings — to transform x into y. The formal expression is:

$$d(x,y) = \min \{\ c(s) : s \text{ is a sequence of edit operations}$$
$$\text{which transforms } x \text{ into } y\ \}$$

The method uses dynamic programming to optimize the computation and the time complexity of the computation is $O(nm)$ where n and m are the lengths of x and y.

Modifications of the basic method can be found in [BUSA90]. Let us comment some of them. A simplified approach where the distance is taken in relation to the number of identities, has a reduced computational complexity, $O(max(n,m))$, however the applicability of the method is very restricted. Warping and elastic matching is another modification of basic method. In this case, the method incorporate the stretching and the expansion of a single symbol a into k consecutive symbols $a_1...a_k$ as well as the compression of $a_1...a_k$ into a without any cost, where $a_1 = a_2 = ... = a_k = a$ and $k \geq 1$. The time complexity is the same as in the basic case.

The basic method can be extended by introducing as elementary edit operations, the generalization of substitutions $u \rightarrow v$ where both u and v are arbitrary strings of length greater than or equal to zero. The generalization of the substitutions have time complexity of $O(n^2 m^2)$ and $O(nm)$ depending on the approach selected to compute the similarity measure.

If the cost associated to each edit operation is dependent of the context (in the other cases we have assumed context independence), then we will have a new distance measure. The approach is similar to the previous ones and the time complexity is $O(nm)$.

Matching of attributed strings

The symbols of the strings can have an associated attributed vector, *i.e.*, for every $x_i \in V_T$, $\mathbf{a} = (a_1^i, ..., a_k^i) \in R^k$ with $i = 1, ..., n$, where a_j^i are numerical quantities. In this case we can determine a similarity measure ([FU83, TSFU85]) where the cost of modifying the attributes is included. For example the computation of the distance measure $D(x,y) = d(x,y) + d_a(x,y)$ includes the differences between the symbols where $d_a(x,y)$ is computed as follows

$$d_a(x,y) = \sum_{r,s} \sum_{l=1}^{k} w_l \mid a_l^r - a_l^s \mid$$

w_l are the weight coefficients and the attributed distance measure is calculated only for those symbols that are not changed when x is transformed into y.

3.1.2 Tree to tree matching

Matching based on three edit operations

As in the case of strings, these methods are based on the computation of the number of modifications to transform the unknown tree T_α into the prototype tree T_β. The similarity measure can be formulated as follows:

$$d(T_\alpha, T_\beta) = \min\{r(s) \mid s \text{ is a sequence of edit operations}$$
$$\text{to transform } T_\alpha \text{ into } T_\beta\}$$

The three edit operations are node label substitution, node deletion and node insertion. The basic method ([TAI79]) to compute the similarity measure was developed by Tai and is based on reordering the trees and using dynamic programming. The time complexity of Tai's similarity distance is $O(N_\alpha N_\beta D_\alpha^2 D_\beta^2)$ where N_α and N_β are the number of nodes of the trees and D_α and D_β are the depths of the trees.

There have been developed several methods faster than the previous method. One efficient method was developed by Tanaka ([TAN88]) which uses two strategies to reduce the number of computed subtree distances. By rearranging one of the steps of Tai method by dynamic programming and using the restrictions imposed by the leaves of one of the trees, the time complexity is reduced to $O(N_\alpha N_\beta L_\alpha)$ or $O(N_\alpha N_\beta L_\beta)$ where L_α and L_β are the number of leaves of the trees.

Matching based on node splitting and merging

The three operations described before sometimes are not enough to calculate a similarity measure between two trees. A method ([LU84]) that incorporates node splitting and node merging will able to distinguish better the similarities between some trees. Lu developed a method for unlabeled trees which takes into account node deletion, node insertion, node splitting and node merging. This method uses a divide and conquer strategy for computing the similarity measure and the time complexity is $O(nm^2)$ where n and m are the respective sizes of both trees.

3.1.3 Graph to graph matching

Matching relational graphs using discrete relaxation

The matching of relational graphs ([SHHA90]) is doing by computing how many tuples in R_i (where R_i indicate the various relationships among the parts of the graph G_α) are not mapped by f (the mapping function between G_α and G_β) to tuples in S_i (where S_i indicate the various relationships among parts of the graph G_β), and how many tuples in S_i are not mapped by f^{-1} to tuples in R_i. The similarity measure between G_α and G_β is

$$d(G_\alpha, G_\beta) = \min\{\sum_{i=1}^{I} E_s^i(f)\}$$

where

$$E_s^i(f) = \mid R_i \circ f - S_i \mid + \mid S_i \circ f^{-1} - R_i \mid$$

An extension of this method includes attributes to the relational graphs and the similarity measure includes this information in the computation of $d(G_\alpha, G_\beta)$. The method to compute the similarity measure is based on a tree search which time complexity is reduced by using discrete relaxation methods. However, since the method is based on a tree search the time complexity is exponential.

Matching attributed relational graphs using cost functions

The matching of attributed relational graphs ([SAFU83]) is done by computing the cost of node recognition and the cost of error transformation. The local features of the graph are included in the first cost and the general structure is considered in the second cost. The cost functions are computed as follows:

$$C_{xy} = \sum_{k=1}^{m} w_{xyk} g_{xyk} \qquad \sum_{k=1}^{m} w_{xyk} = 1$$

where g_{xyk} is the cost of xy (for example, node insertion) for each one of the graphs and w_{xyk} are the partial weights. The computation of the global similarity measure is:

$$d(G_\alpha, G_\beta) = min_{config.}(w_{nr}C_{nr} + w_{ni}C_{ni} + w_{bi}C_{bi} + \\ w_{bd}C_{bd} + w_{ns}C_{ns} + w_{bs}C_{bs})$$

where *nr*, *ni*, *nd*, *bi*, *bd*, *ns* and *bs* are node recognition, node insertion, node deletion, branch insertion, branch deletion, node label substitution and branch label substitution. The method is based on a tree search which time complexity is exponential.

3.2 Parsing

The parsing methods are used to know if an unknown input pattern belongs to one of the class grammars or which is the similarity measure with it. Basically there are two general group of methods: the grammar parsers and the error correcting parsers. The first group are the parsers developed in the formal language theory to accept or reject a structure by a grammar. The second group is based in the same parsers commented before but the grammars are expanded versions of the previous ones. Let us briefly review them:

3.2.1 Grammar parsers

String grammars

For finite state grammars there exist parsers ([AHUL73]) which time and space complexity is lineal, $O(n)$, where n is the number of symbols of the string. For binary finite state grammars the time complexity is reduced to $O(lnn)$.

For context free grammars there exist two parsers ([AHUL73]), Cocke-Younger-Kasami and Early parsers, which time complexity is $O(n^3)$. If the grammars are unambiguous the parsing complexity time for Early parser is $O(n^2)$.

Tree grammars

For regular tree grammar there exist parsers ([BA78, FU82])which time complexity is polynomial with respect to the number of nodes of the tree.

3.2.2 Error-correcting parsers

Error correcting string parsers

The method ([TAN90, TAFU82, LYON74, GHR80]) is based on incorporating the edit operations described in the previous subsection into the grammar rules. In this way we can expand the grammar to include the edit operations in the form of production rules (we will call them error productions). The parser for strings is modified to be able to count the number of error productions required to derive the unknown structure by the grammar. The derivation which have the smallest number of error productions will be the result of the similarity measure. The computation of the similarity measure is:

$$d(x,y) = min_z\{d(z,y) \mid z \in L(G)\}$$

For context-free grammars the computation of the similarity measure is done in a modified version of the Early's parser. In this way the time complexity depends only on the parser used.

Several approaches for context-free error correcting parsers have been developed.

Error correcting tree automata

The method ([LUFU78]) is based on incorporating five types of edit operations — substitution, stretch, branch, split and deletion of nodes — into the grammar rules to obtain the error production rules. As before the tree grammar is expanded to incorporate the error productions and the tree parser or acceptor is modified to be able to count the number of error productions rules used to derive the unknown input tree.

3.2.3 Heuristic search

Depth-first search and backtracking

A depth-first search ([PEA84, NIL80]) is a search procedure applied to a graph of search. A graph of search consists of a *root node*, the start node (the initial state from where the search starts), and a set of nodes which represent encodings of subproblems. In the graph certain pairs of nodes are connected by directed *arcs* which represent operators available to the problem solver. If an arc is directed from node n to node n', node n' is said to be a *successor* (or *child*) of n and node n is said to be a *parent* (or a *father*) of n'. If each node of this graph has only one parent the graph is called a *tree*. A *leaf* in this tree is a node without successors and a *path* of length k is a sequence of nodes $n_1, n_2, ..., n_k$ where each n_i is a successor of n_{i-1}. We will denominate *tree search* to the procedure of searching a path from the root node to one of the solution nodes.

The depth-first search, in the process to find a path to one of the node solutions, expands each chosen node by generating all its successors. After each node expansion one of the newly generated children is again selected for expansion and this forward exploration is pursued until, for some reason, progress is blocked. Once blocked occurs, the process resumes from the deepest of all nodes left behind, *i.e.*, from the nearest decision point with unexplored alternatives. Depth first search works well when the solutions are plentiful and equally desirable.

The tree search procedure denominated depth-first search based on *backtracking* follows the strategy of generating only one of the successors of a node to be explored, and this newly generated node, unless is found to be terminal (a leaf of the tree) or dead end, is again submitted for exploration. If the generated node meets some stopping criterion, the program backtracks to the closest unexpanded ancestor, *i.e.*, an ancestor which have not been generated successors.

The time complexity of depth-first search is often exponential.

Breadth-first

Another way of doing a tree search procedure ([PEA84, NIL80]), as opposed to depth-first, is by progressively exploring sections of searched graph in layers of equal depth. In this case the priority is to explore the nodes of the same layer before start exploring the nodes of the following layer. The breadth-first search of locally graphs is guaranteed to terminate with a solution if the solution exists and moreover it is also guarantee to find the shallowest possible solution. The price paid is a huge storage of the generated search graph.

The time complexity of the method is also often exponential.

Heuristics in the search control

In order to reduce the huge search to be done in the depth-first search it is possible to introduce an evaluation function when it is required to expand a node ([PEA84, NIL80]). If the evaluation function guarantees to find the solution, then the search will be reduced drastically, since there will be no backtracking of nodes, always we will select the right node until to reach the solution. However, in very few cases there exist such optimal evaluation function and usually we will have an evaluation function which is suboptimal. In this case, to find one solution is not guarantee, however in well known problems we will able to reduce the space of search. A very well known evaluation function for A^* algorithm is:

$$f(n) = g(n) + h(n)$$

where $g(n)$ is the cost to reach the node n from the root node and $h(n)$ is a heuristic function which computes the cost from the node n to the solution node.

If the evaluation function guarantees one solution, the time complexity only depends on the depth to reach the solution. In the other cases the time complexity is exponential.

3.2.4 Decision trees

Decision trees

A decision tree ([PEA88, BE78, YOFU76]) is a restricted version of a tree search where the leaves are the solutions and there are not backtracking in the search procedure. In a decision tree, an evaluation function is used to select the successor of a chosen node, but once has been selected the new node there is not backtracking, *i.e.*, the next move in the path is irrevocable. Moreover, each layer of the same depth can have a different own evaluation function which is very useful for the analysis procedures. The evaluation function can be an heuristic function, a cost function or a procedural method. The time complexity of a decision tree depends only on the maximum number of layers (the depth) to reach a leaf.

3.2.5 Constraint propagation

Constraint propagation

One way of analyzing a structure is by means of propagating some local constraints among the directed connected nodes to a given node ([WAL75, RHZ76, HAR83, HUZU83, PEA88]). The propagation mechanism is based on modifying the present state of the node — the probabilities, the label, etc. — depending on the information received from its neighbor nodes, by using some local function. The propagation proceeds to all the nodes until there is not change in any of the nodes. Some propagation schemes, as for example relaxation, can not guarantee that the process will converge.

Constraint propagation mechanisms have a time complexity which depends on the mechanism used and whether the process converges.

3.3 Comments on the Analysis Methods

We have touched on several well known methods of analysis some of them mainly oriented to classification and verification — *matching, parsing* and *constraint propagation* — and others oriented to decision making and interpretation — *heuristic search, decision trees*. However, the two last can also be applied to classification and verification and *constraint propagation* can also be applied to decision making and interpretation.

For classification and verification, the most efficient methods are matching and parsing since their time complexity is polynomial in the number of symbols of the structure. Between these two, matching methods are more efficient than the parsing ones. However, when the similarity measure is between an unknown structure and a language generated by a grammar, parsing methods are the only ones which can be applied. Decision trees can be faster than either matching or parsing, but they require perfect knowledge in advance of all possible solutions, and may be extremely space-intensive.

For interpretation and decision making, heuristic search methods are the best ones, but they are very expensive in computational time, and they only can be applied when there is an optimal evaluation function or the space of search is reduced. However, there are methods based on heuristic search which share irrevocable strategies with heuristic search which are being applied to real problems.

For classification, verification, decision making and interpretation, constraint propagation methods are also used. These methods are in general very expensive in computational time since they require a very large number of local computations. At present, these methods are restricted to parallel processors.

4 Conclusions

We have argued that document images are often structured at different levels of detail in ways that invite the use use of SSPR methods. We have also reviewed the basic methods of representing a document image using these methods and discussed several of their most successful applications.

References

[AHPE72]   A. V. Aho and T. G. Peterson, "A minimum distance error-correcting parser for context-free languages," *SIAM J. Computing*4, pp. 305–312, 1972.

[AHUL73]   A. V. Aho and J. D. Ullman, *The theory of parsing translation and compiling.*Prentice–Hall, Englewood Cliffs, NJ, 1973.

[BA78]   B. S. Baker, "Tree transducers and tree languages.," *Inf. Control*37, pp. 241–266, 1978.

[BE78]   D. A. Bell, "Decision trees, tables and lattices," In B. G. Batchelor (ed.), *Pattern Recognition,*Plenum Press, 1978.

[BU90]   H. Bunke, "String matching for structural pattern recognition," In H.
           Bunke & A. Sanfeliu (eds), *Syntactic and structural pattern recognition:
           theory and applications*, World Scientific, Singapore, pp. 119–144, 1990.

[BUSA90]   H. Bunke and A. Sanfeliu (eds), *Syntactic and structural pattern recog-
           nition: theory and applications.* 1990.

[ENRR87]   H. Ehrig, M. Nagl, G. Rozenberg, and A. Rosenfeld (eds.), *Graph gram-
           mars and their application to computer science.* Lecture Notes Computer
           Science 297. Springer–Verlag, Berlin, 1987.

[FIN79]   N. V. Findler (ed,), *Associative networks: the representation and use of
           knowledge by computers.* Academic Press, New York, 1979.

[FU82]   K. S. Fu, *Syntactic pattern recognition and applications.* Prentice–Hall,
           Englewood Cliffs, NJ, 1982.

[FU83]   K. S. Fu, "A step towards unification of syntactic and statistical pattern
           recognition," *IEEE Trans. PAMI* 5, pp. 200–205, 1983.

[GOTH78]   R. C. Gonzalez and M. G. Thomason, *Syntactic pattern recognition.*
           Addison–Wesley, Reading, MA, 1978.

[GHR80]   S. L. Graham, M. A. Harrison, and W. L. Ruzzo, "An improved context-
           free recognizer," *ACM Trans. Program Lang. and Syst.*, pp. 415–449,
           1980.

[HAR83]   R. M. Haralick, "An interpretation for probabilistic relaxation," *Comp.
           Vision, Graphics and Image Processing* 22, 1983.

[HOUL79]   J. E. Hopcroft and J. D. Ullman, *Introduction to automata theory, lan-
           guages and computation.* Addison–Wesley, Reading, MA, 1979.

[HUZU83]   R. Hummel and S. Zucker, *On the foundations of relaxation labeling
           processes.* IEEE Trans. PAMI 5, pp. 267–287, 1983.

[LEV66]   V. I. Levenshtein, "Binary codes capable of correcting deletions, inser-
           tions and reversals," *Sov. Phys. Dokl.* 10 (8), pp. 707–710, 1966.

[LU84]   S. Y Lu, "A tree matching algorithm based on node splitting and merg-
           ing," *IEEE Trans. PAMI* 6, pp. 249–256, 1984.

[LUFU78]   S. Y. Lu and K. S. Fu, "Error-correcting tree automata for syntactic
           pattern recognition," *IEEE Trans. Computers* 27, pp. 1040–1053, 1978.

[LYON74]   G. Lyon, "Syntax-directed least-errors analysis for context-free lan-
           guages: a practical approach," *CACM* 17, pp. 3–14, 1974.

[MIC86]   L. Miclet, *Structural methods in pattern recognition.* North-Oxford Aca-
           demic, 1986.

[MIN75]   M. Minsky, "A framework for representing knowledge," In P. Winston
           (ed), *The psychology of computer vision*, McGraw-Hill, New York, 1975.

[NIL80]   N. J. Nilsson, *Principles of artificial intelligence.* Tioga, Palo Alto, Cal-
           ifornia, 1980.

[PAV77]   T. Pavlidis, *Structural pattern recognition.* Springer Series Electrophysics
           1, Springer–Verlag, Berlin, 1977.

[PEA84]   J. Pearl, *Heuristics : intelligent search strategies for computer problem
           solving.* Addison–Wesley, Reading, MA, 1984.

[PEA88]   J. Pearl, *Probabilistic reasoning in intelligent systems: networks of plau-
           sible inference.* Morgan Kaufmann, 1988.

[ROS79]   A. Rosenfeld, *Picture languages: formal models for picture recognition.*
           Academic Press, New York, 1979.

[RHZ76]   A. Rosenfeld, R. A. Hummel, and S. W. Zucker, "Scene labeling by
           relaxation operations," *IEEE Trans. SMC* 6, pp. 420–443, 1976.

[SA90]   A. Sanfeliu, "Matching tree structures," In H. Bunke and A. Sanfeliu
            (eds), *Syntactic and structural pattern recognition: theory and applica-
            tions*, World Scientific, Singapore, pp. 145–178, 1990.

[SAFU83]   A. Sanfeliu and K. S. Fu, "A distance measure between attributed rela-
            tional graphs for pattern recognition," *IEEE Trans. SMC* 13, No.3, pp.
            353–362, 1983.

[SHHA90]   L. G. Shapiro and R. M. Haralick, "Matching relational structures using
            discrete relaxation," In H. Bunke & A. Sanfeliu (eds), *Syntactic and
            structural pattern recognition: theory and applications*, World Scientific,
            Singapore, pp. 179–196, 1990.

[TAI79]   K. C. Tai, "The tree to tree correction problem," *J. ACM* 26, pp. 422–
            433, 1979.

[TAN88]   E. Tanaka, "Efficient computing algorithms for the Tai metric," *Int'l J.
            Pattern Recognition and Artificial Intelligence*, 1988.

[TAN90]   E. Tanaka, "Parsing and error-correcting parsing for string grammars,"
            In H. Bunke & A. Sanfeliu (eds), *Syntactic and structural pattern recog-
            nition: theory and applications*, World Scientific, Singapore, pp. 55–84,
            1990.

[TAFU82]   E. Tanaka and K. S. Fu, "Error correcting parsers for formal languages,"
            IEEE Trans. Comp. 31, pp. 327–328, 1982.

[TSFU85]   W. H. Tsai and K. S. Fu, "Attributed string matching with merging for
            shape recognition," *IEEE Trans. PAMI* 7, pp. 453–462, 1985.

[WAL75]   D. Waltz, "Understanding line drawings of scenes with shadows," In P.
            Winston (ed), *The psychology of computer vision*, McGraw–Hill, New
            York, pp. 19–91, 1975.

[YOFU76]   K. C. You and K. S. Fu, "An approach to design of a linear binary
            classifier," *Proc. Symp. of Machine Processing of Remotely Sensed Data*,
            Purdue Univ., 1976.

Syntactic Analysis of Context–Free Plex Languages for Pattern Recognition

Horst Bunke and Bernhard Haller

Universität Bern, Institut für Informatik und Angewandte Mathematik
Länggassstr. 51, CH-3012 Bern, Switzerland

Plex languages are a generalization of string languages into two dimensions. In this paper we describe an algorithm for the syntactic analysis of plex languages. The algorithm is an extension of Earley's parser which was originally developed for context free string languages. Our algorithm is able to recognize not only complete two–dimensional structures generated by a plex grammar but also partial ones.

1 Introduction

In syntactic pattern recognition, formal grammars are used for pattern class representation. The terminals of the grammar correspond to primitive patterns which are directly extractable from an input by means of preprocessing and segmentation. The set of grammar nonterminals corresponds to patterns and subpatterns of greater complexity which are hierarchically built up from primitive elements. The process of building up complex subpatterns and patterns is modeled by the grammar productions. Finally, the most important part of a syntactic pattern recognition system is the parser which analyzes the unknown input according to the grammar productions, thus providing a classname and a structural description (the derivation tree) of the input. Various representation formalisms, grammar models and parsing algorithms for a great number of different applications have been proposed within this framework in the past. Standard textbooks in syntactic pattern recognition are [1, 2, 3, 4]. Further work is reported in [5, 6, 7].

The most fundamental model for syntactic pattern recognition is string grammars. A string grammar operates on sequences of symbols, *i.e.* words over a finite alphabet. There are some advantages in using string grammars. For example, the underlying mathematical concepts from formal language theory are very well understood and there are standard parsing algorithms with a low computational time complexity (linear or low order polynomial depending on the type of the grammar). On the other hand, string grammars are limited in their representational power, particulary in representing two–dimensional patterns as they may occur, for example, in images. Therefore, more effective two–dimensional representation formalisms have been proposed. The most powerful of those approaches is graph grammars. Conceptually, a graph grammar is similar to a string grammar. The rewriting steps, however, operate on graphs instead of words over an alphabet. Thus the various relations between the components of a two– or more–dimensional structure can be modeled much more naturally and effectively. In the past, a number of different graph grammar formalisms have been proposed. For an overview see [8]. Applications of graph grammars in pattern recognition are reported in [1, 2, 3, 4, 5, 6, 7]. For further applications see [9, 10, 11].

A serious obstacle in using a graph grammar in a syntactic pattern recognition system comes from the fact that parsing, *i.e.* syntactic analysis, of graph languages is quite complicated. Although many different models of graph grammars and a variety of applications have been reported in the literature, only little attention has been paid to the parsing problem. Franck was the first who had developed a parser for graph languages [12]. For reasons of efficiency, he restricted his considerations to a special subclass of graph languages which are parsable in linear time. Later on, the work of Franck was extended by Kaul [13, 14]. Another early paper on parsing of graph languages is [15]. In the beginning of the 1980's Fu and his collaborators studied special subclasses of graph languages and developed corresponding parsers [16, 17]. Similar classes of graphs have been studied by Brandenburg [18]. Recently, a parser for a subclass of node label controlled (NLC) graph grammars has been proposed [19]. The relationships between hyperedge replacement systems and NLC graph grammars have been studied in another recent paper [20] which also introduces a polynomial time parsing algorithm for a special subclass of graphs generated by hyperedge replacement systems.

In this paper we consider plex grammars according to [21] as a special type of grammar formalism generating two–dimensional structures. Applications of plex grammars in syntactic pattern recognition include analysis of circuit diagrams and chemical structures [21]. A more recent application is three–dimensional scene analysis [25]. Although plex grammars have been known for quite a long time, only one parser for plex grammars has been reported in the literature to our knowledge [22]. This parser works top-down with backtracking and is restricted to context free plex grammars without left-recursions. In this paper we describe another parsing algorithm for context free plex grammars without any restriction. In contrast with the parser by Lin and Fu [22], our approach is based on a generalization of Earley's algorithm for context free string grammars [23]. It is able to recognize not only complete structures generated by a plex grammar but also partial ones. This ability makes our algorithm interesting for applications in pattern recognition and scene analysis, where, due to occlusions and other types of distortions, parts of an input structure may be missing. Other potential applications of our parser include syntactic analysis of two-dimensional, *i.e.* graphical or visual, programming languages [24].

2 Basic Concepts

The basic constituents of plex grammars and languages are napes (n-attaching point entities). As a generalization of a symbol occurring in a string, a nape may have any number of points where it can be connected to one or more other napes. Thus, particular two-dimensional structures called plex structures are obtained. In this paper, we will restrict our considerations to context free plex grammars, *i.e.* plex grammars with only one nape in the left-hand side of any production. The following basic definitions are included in this paper for the purpose of self-containedness. For more details the reader is referred to the original paper on plex grammars [21].

Definition 1 *A **plex structure** is a triple $\Pi = (\mathcal{X}, \Gamma, \Delta)$ where*

- $\mathcal{X} = (\chi_1, \ldots, \chi_{n_\chi})$ *is a list of napes; each nape χ_i has $n_{\chi_i} \geq 0$ connection points*
- $\Gamma = (\gamma_1, \ldots, \gamma_{n_\Gamma})$ *is a list of internal connections*
- $\Delta = (\delta_1, \ldots, \delta_{n_\Delta})$ *is a list of external connections*

such that each connection point of each nape belongs to exactly one internal or external connection.

We write $a(\chi_i, j) = \gamma_k$, or $a(\chi_i, j) = \delta_k$ iff the connection point j of the nape χ_i belongs to the connection γ_k, or the connection δ_k.

Definition 2 *A **context free plex grammar** is a 4-tuple $G = (V_T, V_N, P, S)$ where*

- V_T *is a finite, nonempty set of napes, called the set of terminal napes; each terminal nape has a nonempty set of connection points*
- V_N *is a finite, nonempty set of napes, called the set of nonterminal napes where $V_T \cap V_N = \emptyset$; $V = V_N \cup V_T$*
- P *is a finite set of context free productions*
- $S \in V_N$ *is the starting nape; this nape is the only one with an empty set of connection points.*

Definition 3 *A **context free production** is an entity $A\Delta \to \mathcal{X}\Gamma\Delta$ where*

- $(\mathcal{X}, \Gamma, \Delta)$ *is a plex structure according to Definition 1*
- A *is a single nonterminal nape and Δ is the list of its connections*

The components $A\Delta$ and $\mathcal{X}\Gamma\Delta$ are called the left-hand and right-hand side of the production, respectively. Notice that the list Δ of external connections in the right-hand side is identical to the list of (external) connections of the single nonterminal nape A in the left-hand side. The left-hand side can be interpreted as a plex structure consisting of only one (nonterminal) nape with an empty list of internal connections.

The derivation of a context free plex grammar proceeds by replacing the nonterminal nape in the left-hand side of a production by the plex structure in the right-hand side. Such a replacement usually occurs in a larger context. The list Δ plays the role of the embedding transformation [8]. That is, the role of the connections of the nonterminal in the left-hand side is taken over by the (identical) external connections of the right-hand side, which are both given by Δ. The language L(G) generated by a plex grammar G consists of the set of all terminal plex structures which can be derived from the starting nape by successive application of productions.

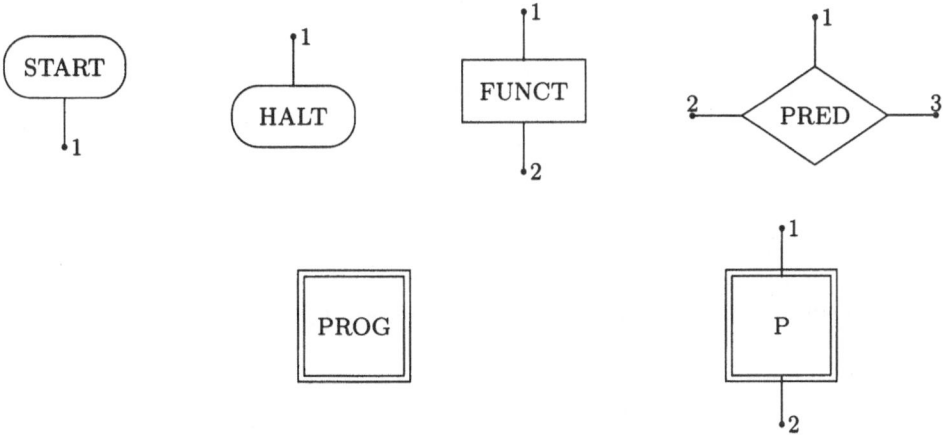

Fig. 1. Napes of a sample plex grammar, terminals above and nonterminals below

As an example, consider the two nonterminal napes PROG and P and the four terminal napes START, HALT, FUNCT, and PRED in Figure 1. For instance, PRED has three connection points 1, 2, and 3, while P has only two connection points 1 and 2. In this paper we represent nonterminals by double-bordered boxes while terminals are represented by graphical symbols with a single border line.

A graphical representation of a plex structure is given in Figure 2. Its description according to Def. 1 is $\Pi = (X, \Delta, \Gamma)$ with

$$X = (t_1 = \text{PRED}, t_2 = \text{START}, t_3 = \text{FUNCT}, t_4 = \text{HALT}, t_5 = \text{FUNCT})$$
$$\Gamma = (c_1, \ldots, c_4)$$
$$\Delta = ()$$

The connections are:

$a(t_1, 1) = c_1,$ $a(t_1, 2) = c_2,$ $a(t_1, 3) = c_3,$
$a(t_2, 1) = c_1,$ $a(t_3, 1) = c_2,$ $a(t_3, 2) = c_4,$
$a(t_4, 1) = c_4,$ $a(t_5, 1) = c_3,$ $a(t_5, 2) = c_4.$

Three productions of a context free plex grammar are shown in Figure 3. The graphical representation for each production is such that the outermost box

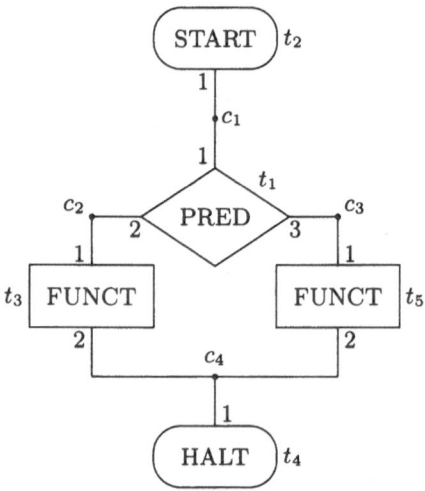

Fig. 2. A sample plex structure

corresponds to the nonterminal in the left-hand side while the right-hand side
is drawn inside this box. For example, production p_2 replaces the nonterminal
nape P by a plex structure consisting of one terminal PRED, two nonterminals
P, two internal connections γ_{21} and γ_{22}, and two external connections 1 and 2.
According to Def. 3, the productions p_1, p_2 and p_3 can be written as

- $p_1: A_1() \rightarrow (\chi_{11}, \chi_{12}, \chi_{13})(\gamma_{11}, \gamma_{12})()$
  $= \mathrm{PROG}() \rightarrow (\mathrm{START}, \mathrm{P}, \mathrm{HALT})(\gamma_{11}, \gamma_{12})()$
  connection points:

  $a(\chi_{11}, 1) = \gamma_{11}, \quad a(\chi_{12}, 1) = \gamma_{11}, \quad a(\chi_{12}, 2) = \gamma_{12}, \quad a(\chi_{13}, 1) = \gamma_{12}$

- $p_2: A_2(\delta_{21}, \delta_{22}) \rightarrow (\chi_{21}, \chi_{22}, \chi_{23})(\gamma_{21}, \gamma_{22})(\delta_{21}, \delta_{22})$
  $= \mathrm{P}(\delta_{21}, \delta_{22}) \rightarrow (\mathrm{PRED}, \mathrm{P}, \mathrm{P})(\gamma_{21}, \gamma_{22})(\delta_{21}, \delta_{22})$

  $a(\chi_{21}, 1) = \delta_{21}, \quad a(\chi_{21}, 2) = \gamma_{21}, \quad a(\chi_{21}, 3) = \gamma_{22}, \quad a(\chi_{22}, 1) = \gamma_{21},$
  $a(\chi_{22}, 2) = \delta_{22}, \quad a(\chi_{23}, 1) = \gamma_{22}, \quad a(\chi_{23}, 2) = \delta_{22}$

- $p_3 : A_3(\delta_{31}, \delta_{32}) \rightarrow (\chi_{31})()(\delta_{31}, \delta_{32}) = \mathrm{P}(\delta_{31}, \delta_{32}) \rightarrow (\mathrm{FUNCT})()(\delta_{31}, \delta_{32})$

  $a(\chi_{31}, 1) = \delta_{31}, \quad a(\chi_{31}, 2) = \delta_{32}$

If we use the nonterminal PROG as starting symbol, then the productions
shown in Figure 3 generate a language which represents a special subclass of
flowchart diagrams. One element of this language is given in Figure 2. (A more
complex plex grammar generating the class of all well structured flowchart diagrams is given in the Appendix.)

There are some slight changes in the definitions of this section as compared
to [21]. These changes have been made for the purpose of notational convenience

PROG

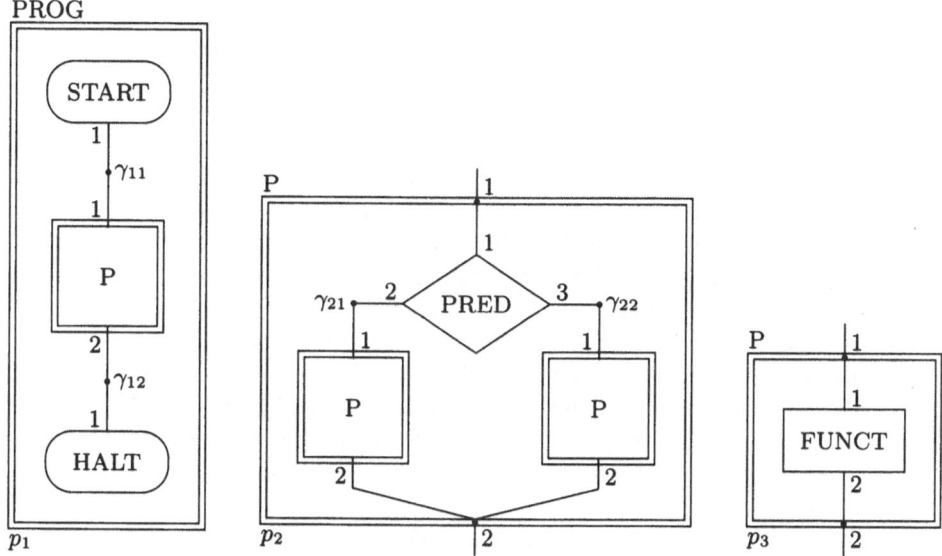

Fig. 3. Productions of the sample plex grammar

only. From a theoretical point of view, the above definitions are equivalent to the original ones. For the parsing algorithm described in the following sections of this paper we assume that any plex structure to be analyzed is connected and that the starting symbol doesn't have external connections. It is furthermore supposed that any internal connection consists of at least two connection points and that not more than one connection point of the same nape participates in any internal or external connection. We want to point out, however, that these restrictions aren't essential and could be overcome by slight modifications to the parsing algorithm described in the following section.

3 The Algorithm for Syntactic Analysis

Given a terminal plex structure $\mathcal{X}$ and a context free plex grammar G, the task of our algorithm for syntactic analysis is to determine if $\mathcal{X} \in L(G)$, *i.e.* if $\mathcal{X}$ can be generated by G. If $\mathcal{X} \in L(G)$ then it also has to report how $\mathcal{X}$ can be generated, *i.e.*, which rules have to be applied to which nonterminal napes in which order. Our algorithm is based on the same idea as Earley's parser [23]. I.e., we sequentially read one terminal nape after the other from the plex structure to be parsed and construct a list for each terminal. In the list belonging to the terminal read in the j-th step we keep entries describing all possibilities to derive a nonterminal into a plex structure which is compatible with all the terminals read up to step j. The construction of the lists is done by three different subroutines called scanner, completer, and predictor.

An entry in a list consists of a production and additional information concerning the degree to which this production has been recognized. Consider the list I_j and the production $p : A\Delta \rightarrow \mathcal{X}\Gamma\Delta$. If p is contained in I_j then the additional information consists of

- an injective mapping from the terminals in the right-hand side $\mathcal{X}$ to the terminals $t_1, \ldots, t_j$ read by the parser so far. This mapping contains the information which of the terminals $t_1, \ldots, t_j$ in the input plex structure can be recognized as instances of the terminals in $\mathcal{X}$. It also indicates whether or not the right-hand side of p has been completely recognized. This mapping is a straightforward generalization of the "dot" in Earley's parsers.
- a mapping similar to the above one for external and internal connections.
- all productions which contain, in their right-hand side, the nonterminal A in a way consistent with the terminals $t_1, \ldots, t_j$ read as far.
- for each nonterminal nape A' in the right-hand side $\mathcal{X}$ all productions $p' : A'\Delta' \rightarrow \mathcal{X}'\Gamma'\Delta'$ which derive A' into a plex structure $\mathcal{X}'$ compatible with $t_1, \ldots, t_j$.
- a pointer to production p'' in list I_{j-1} if the entry concerning the production p in I_j has been generated from p'' in I_{j-1} (see also steps 2c and 2d of the parsing algorithm).

In the rest of this paper we will use only the word "production" in order to refer to an entry in any of the lists $I_j; j = 1, \ldots, n$. However, the reader should keep in mind that for each production, $i.e.$ each entry, the additional information described above is always present in I_j, too. Two productions in a list are identical if and only if they are identical with respect to their left-hand and right-hand side, and their additional information.

Algorithm: syntactic analysis for context free plex grammars
Input: a context free plex grammar and a terminal plex structure with terminal napes $t_1, t_2, \ldots, t_n$ and internal connections
Output: a list I_j for each terminal nape $t_j; j = 1, \ldots, n$

1. **Construction of the list I_1:**
   (a) Select a terminal nape t_1.
   (b) *Scanner:* Add each production which contains t_1 in its right-hand side to I_1.
       /* After completion of the scanner, I_1 shows all possibilities to derive t_1, and perhaps additional terminal napes, in one derivation step */
   (c) *Completer:* If there is a production p_1 contained in I_1 which has a nonterminal N in its left-hand side, and if there exists another production p_2 with the same nonterminal N in its right-hand side, then add p_2 to I_1. Repeat this step as long as new entries are generated.
       /* After completion of the completer, I_1 shows all possibilities to derive t_1, and perhaps additional terminal napes, in $n \geq 1$ derivation steps from a nonterminal. */

(d) *Predictor:* If there is a production p in I_1 and if the right-hand side of p contains a nonterminal N which shares a connection with t_1, then add any production to I_1 which replaces the nonterminal N. Repeat this step as long as new entries are generated.

/* The predictor prepares the processing of the next terminal t_2 by the scanner. It enters all those productions to I_1 which derive, in $n \geq 1$ steps, a terminal in the immediate neighborhood of t_1. I.e. the predictor predicts all terminals which can share a common connection with t_1. */

2. **Construction of the list I_j based on I_{j-1} for $j = 2, \ldots, n$:**

(a) Select a new terminal nape t_j which has at least one connection in common with the connection points of the terminal napes $t_1, \ldots, t_{j-1}$.

(b) *Scanner:* Select a production p from I_{j-1} which contains t_j in its right-hand side in such a way that it is compatible with $t_1, \ldots, t_{j-1}$. Modify it (*i.e.*, update its additional information) in order to take into account that t_j has been read, and add it to I_j. Repeat this step for all productions having t_j in their right–hand side.

/* The productions in I_{j-1} which possibly fulfill this condition have been added to I_{j-1} by the predictor. After completion of the scanner, I_j shows all possibilities to derive t_j, and perhaps additional terminal napes, in one derivation step */

(c) *Completer:* If there is a production p in I_j with a nonterminal N in its left-hand side, select the corresponding production p' in I_{j-1} from which p in I_j has been generated. (This production p' also has the nonterminal N in its left-hand side.) Take each production p'' in I_{j-1} which contains this nonterminal in its right-hand side, update it by the information about t_j, and add it to I_j. Repeat this procedure for all productions which have been added to I_j by the scanner, and for all productions which have been added to I_j by the completer.

/* After completion of the completer, I_j shows all possibilities to derive t_j, and perhaps additional terminal napes, in $n \geq 1$ derivation steps form a nonterminal. */

(d) *Predictor:* If there is a production p_1 in I_j which contains a nonterminal nape N in its right-hand side, consider all productions p_2 which contain N in their left-hand side, and distinguish between the following cases:

(a) p_2 is contained in I_j: do nothing;

(b) p_2 isn't contained in I_j, but in I_{j-1}: in this case update p_2 by information about t_j and add it to I_j;

(c) p_2 is contained neither in I_{j-1}, nor in I_j: if the nonterminal N shares a common connection point with t_j then add p_2 to I_j, else do nothing.

Repeat this procedure for all productions which have been added to I_j by either the scanner or completer, and for all productions which have been added to I_j by the predictor.

/* The predictor updates all information which is relevant with respect to t_j and transfers it from I_{j-1} to I_j (case b). It also prepares the processing of the next terminal t_{j+1} by the scanner (case c). After completion of the predictor, I_j shows all possibilities to derive one or more of the terminals $t_1, \ldots, t_j$ and / or one or more of the terminals in the immediate neighborhood of $t_1, \ldots, t_j$, and perhaps additional terminals. Thus, it predicts the neighborhood of $t_1, \ldots, t_j$, *i.e.* all terminals which share a common connection with at least one of the terminals $t_1, \ldots, t_j$. */

End of Algorithm

The behavior of the above parsing algorithm can be characterized by the following theorem.

Theorem: Let G be a plex grammar and Π a terminal plex structure consisting of napes $t_1, t_2, \ldots, t_n$ and internal connections $c_1, c_2, \ldots, c_m$.

1. The plex structure Π is generated by G, *i.e.* $\Pi \in L(G)$, if and only if the list I_n constructed by the parsing algorithm contains an instance of a production p such that
   (a) the left–hand side of p is the starting nape;
   (b) all terminals and all connections of Π either directly occur in the right–hand side of p, or can be derived by means of productions from nonterminals occurring in the right–hand side of p;
   (c) the right–hand side of p has been completely recognized.
2. The plex structure Π is a substructure of another plex structure $\Pi' \in L(G)$, *i.e.* $\Pi \subseteq \Pi'$, if the conditions (a) and (b) above are fulfilled.   □

The proof of this theorem can be done by induction on the number of terminal napes in Π. All details are given in [28]. Each of the conditions (a) — (c) in the theorem can be easily checked using the additional information which is associated with the productions in the list I_n. Similar to Earley's parser for string grammars it is possible to reconstruct, from the list entries, the sequence of derivation steps leading from starting nape to the plex structure to be parsed. This sequence is equivalent to the derivation tree. In contrast with Earley's parser we need only the entries in I_n. More specifically, the sequence of derivation steps directly corresponds with the order in which the productions are added to I_n by the scanner, completer and predictor. This order, again, follows immediately from the additional information associated with each list entry.

The second part of the theorem says that our parser is able to recognize not only complete structures but also partial ones. In this case there is no production p in I_n with the initial nape in its left–hand side and its right–hand completely recognized. However, the terminals $t_1, t_2, \ldots, t_n$ and the connections $c_1, c_2, \ldots, c_m$ can be consistently interpreted as a part of the right–hand side of p.

4 An Example

Consider the productions in Figure 3 and the terminal plex structure in Figure 2. The construction of the list I_1 proceeds as follows:

1. The terminal t_1 is read. (The order of the terminals in the example has been arbitrarily assumed. The parser can process any plex structure independent of the order of the terminals.)
2. The scanner adds p_2 to the (empty) list I_1 and adds the following information:
   - the terminal PRED in the right–hand side of p_2 is mapped to t_1, *i.e.*, t_1 is recognized as PRED in the right-hand side of p_2;
   - c_1 is recognized as external connection 1 in Δ; external connection 2 in Δ is not recognized; c_2 and c_3 are recognized as internal connections γ_{21} and γ_{22}, respectively.

   (This instance of p_2 in I_1 will be referred to as $p_{2,1}$ in the following.)
3. The completer adds one instance of p_1 and two instances of p_2 to I_1. (These instances will be referred to as $p_{1,1}, p_{2,2}$, and $p_{2,3}$ in the following.) They describe how the nonterminal P in the left-hand side of $p_{2,1}$ can be derived by means of other productions. Notice that the completer generates two instances of p_2 since the nonterminal P in the left-hand side of $p_{2,1}$ may correspond to either the nonterminal in the left or in the right branch of the right-hand side of p_2.
   The completer adds one more instance of p_1 and two more instances of p_2 (being referred to as $p_{1,2}, p_{2,4}$, and $p_{2,5}$ in the following), which describe how the nonterminal P in the left-hand sides of $p_{2,2}$ and $p_{2,3}$ can be derived by means of other productions. (Notice that $p_{2,4}$ and $p_{2,5}$ are different from $p_{2,2}$ and $p_{2,3}$ because the connection point 1 of the nonterminal P is unknown in both $p_{2,4}$ and $p_{2,5}$ while it is known in $p_{2,2}$ — identical with c_2 — and $p_{2,3}$ — identical with c_3. Similarly, the connection point 1 of the nonterminal P is unknown in $p_{1,2}$ while it is identical with c_1 in $p_{1,1}$.) By recursion, the productions $p_{1,2}, p_{2,4}$, and $p_{2,5}$ describe how the nonterminal P in the left-hand sides of $p_{2,4}$ and $p_{2,5}$ can be generated by means of a sequence of derivation steps of any length.
4. The predictor adds two instances for each of the productions p_2 and p_3. (They will be referred to as $p_{2,6}, p_{2,7}, p_{3,1}$, and $p_{3,2}$ in the following.) They are for predicting the neighborhood shared by the terminal t_1 at c_2 and c_3, respectively.

Now the list I_1 is complete and we proceed by constructing I_2.

1. The terminal t_2 is read.
2. The scanner selects $p_{1,1}$ from I_1 and adds to it the information that the terminal START in the right–hand side represents the terminal t_2 in the structure. This updated instance of p_1 is added to the (empty) list I_2 and will be referred to as $p_{1,3}$ in the following.
3. The completer selects $p_{1,3}$ from I_2 and gets to $p_{1,1}$ from which $p_{1,3}$ has been generated by the scanner. Because the nonterminal PROG — the left–hand side of p_1 — doesn't occur in the right–hand side of any production, the list of such productions in I_1 is empty. So the completer adds no productions to I_2.

4. The predictor selects $p_{1,3}$ from I_2 and finds that the nonterminal P in the right-hand side is described by the production p_2, *i.e.* by its instance $p_{2,1}$, which is contained in list I_1 (case b). So the predictor updates $p_{2,1}$ by the information that the nonterminal P in its left-hand side corresponds to the nonterminal P in the right-hand side of $p_{1,3}$ and adds it to I_2 as instance $p_{2,8}$ of p_2. Furthermore, the predictor selects $p_{2,6}, p_{2,7}, p_{3,1}$ and $p_{3,2}$, updates them analogously, and adds them to I_2 for predicting the neighborhood of t_1.

Now the list I_2 is complete and the parser continues by constructing I_3. The detailed steps which follow are omitted. After the last terminal t_5 has been read and the list I_5 has been completely constructed, I_5 contains an instance of p_1, an instance of p_2 for replacing the nonterminal P in the right-hand side of p_1, and two instances of p_3 for replacing the two nonterminals P in the right-hand side of p_2.

There are pointers in the additional information of each production indicating for each nonterminal in the right–hand side the production by which it is replaced, and *vice versa*. The terminals START and HALT in the right–hand side of p_1 are mapped to t_2 and t_4, respectively. Similarly, the terminal PRED in the right–hand side of p_2 is mapped to t_1. Finally, the terminals FUNCT in both instances of p_3 are mapped to t_3 and t_5, respectively. Analogously to the napes, the connections $\gamma_{11}, \gamma_{12}, \gamma_{21}$ and γ_{22} are mapped to c_1, c_4, c_2 and c_3, respectively. The information contained in I_n can be graphically represented by means of Figure 4. In Figure 4, boxes with a double border line represent nonterminals. So the representation in Figure 4 is equivalent to the derivation tree of the plex structure in Figure 2 according to the productions shown in Figure 3.

5 Computational Complexity

In the worst case, the parser described in section 3 has an exponential time and space complexity. As an example, consider the flowchart shown in Figure 5. This flowchart can be generated by the productions given in Figure 3. In Figure 5 there are n successive layers of conditions each having two exits. In layer $n + 1$ we observe 2^n terminals FUNCT. Let $m = 2^{n-1} + 1$ and assume that the parser reads the terminals in order $t_1, t_2, \ldots, t_m$ (see Figure 5). In I_1 the parser enters instances of p_1, p_2 and p_3. (Notice that the terminal PRED in the right-hand side of p_2 corresponds to the terminal in the topmost layer in Figure 5.) After reading t_2, the parser can conclude that t_2 belongs to the nonterminal P in either the left or ther right branch of the right-hand side of p_2 in I_1. Since there isn't any further information which case is the correct one, both alternatives are entered in I_2. The same happens independently to all the terminals $t_3, t_4, \ldots, t_m$. For example, in list I_3 the parser has to take into account four possibilities: both t_2 and t_3 in the left branch; both t_2 and t_3 in the right branch; t_2 in the left and t_3 in the right branch; t_2 in the right and t_3 in the left branch. Therefore, the number of entries in the list I_j exponentially grows with $j = 1, \ldots, m$. So both the space and time complexity are exponential.

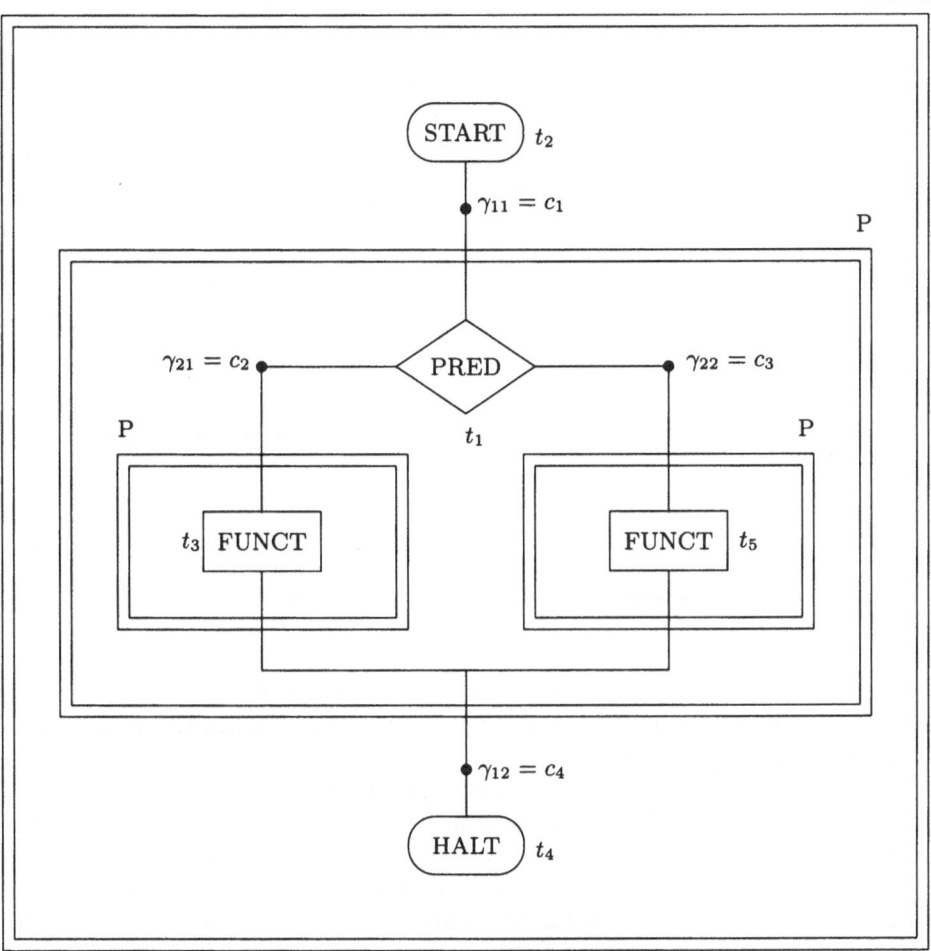

Fig. 4. Result of parsing the plex structure shown in Figure 2 according to the plex grammar given in Figure 3.

The exponential time complexity of our parser is not surprising because of the equivalence of plex grammars and so called hyperedge replacement systems, which have been introduced recently [26]. As one can trivially see from the definitions given in [26], hyperedge replacement systems use just another terminology, but are conceptually identical with plex grammars. Hyperedge replacement systems are known to generate graph languages with an NP–complete membership problem [20, 29]. Notice, that there are subclasses of graph languages generated

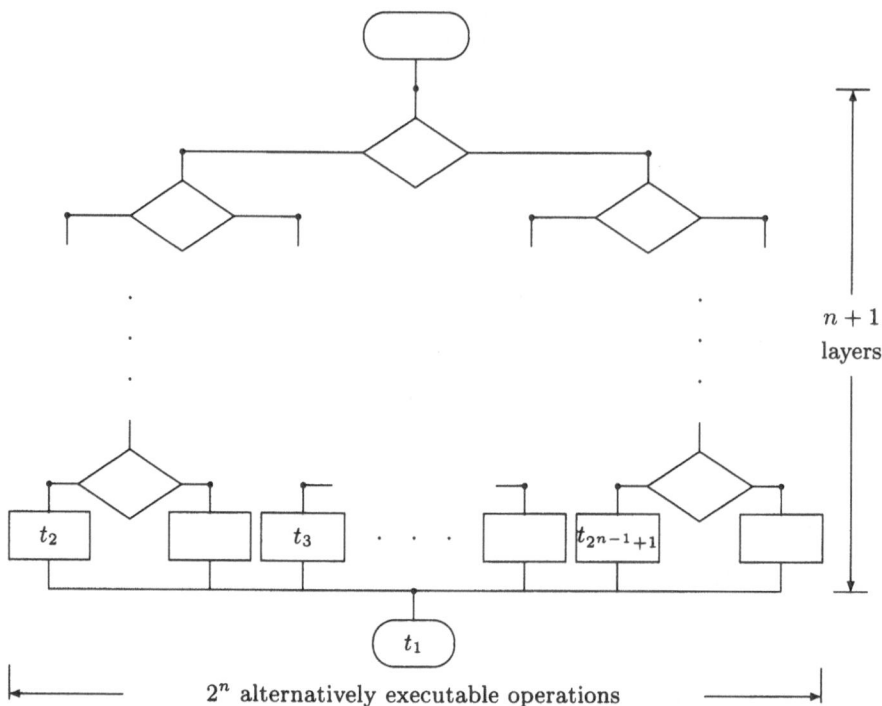

Fig. 5. A plex structure with exponential parsing time and space complexity.

by hyperedge replacement systems which are parsable in polynomial time [20]. It is an open question at the moment if the parser described in this paper works in polynomial time on this subclass.

However, there is another subclass of plex languages where our parser as described in section 3 — without any modifications — works in polynomial time. It is the class of context free string languages which can be considered as a special subclass of plex structures if we interpret each symbol of an alphabet as a nape with two external connection points. Earley's parser for string grammars [23] has a time complexity of $O(n^2)$ if the underlying grammar is unambiguous and $O(n^3)$ otherwise, where n gives the length of an input string. A simple analysis shows that our parser, which is an extension of Earley's algorithm, has a polynomial time complexity of $O(n^5)$ for plex languages representing string languages. Let $I_{E,j}$ and $I_{P,j}$ denote the lists generated by Earley's parser and our parsing algorithm, respectively, when the j-th terminal is read. The entries in list $I_{P,j}$ correspond to a subset of all the entries which are generated in $I_{E,1}, \ldots, I_{E,j}$. The number of entries in each list $I_{E,i}$ grows linearly with $i = 1, \ldots, n$ (see [23]). So the number of entries in $I_{P,j}$ is of order $O(j^2)$. Notice that the length of each entry in $I_{p,j}$ is linearly dependent on j. Since our parser has to keep only the lists I_{j-1} and I_j in step j, the space complexity is $O(j^3)$. For each new entry in $I_{P,j}$ the parser has to check if an identical entry is already contained in

$I_{P,j}$. Since this check can be done in constant time, we get a time complexity of $O(j^2) \cdot O(j^2) = O(j^4)$ for each list $I_{P,j}$. Summing over $j = 1, \ldots, n$ a time complexity of $O(n^5)$ results.

6 Experimental Results

The parser described in section 3 has been fully implemented in C under UNIX on a Nixdorf Targon (a 4 MIPS machine, approximately). The length of the program code is about 6000 lines, including a number of input and output routines. As executable code, the program takes about 60 Kbyte. We did a number of experiments primarily concerned with the computation time needed by the parser. For these experiments we used grammars describing line drawings. One of these grammars is given in the Appendix. It is a generalization of the three productions shown in Figure 3. The generalized grammar generates the set of all well structured flowchart diagrams composed of the primitive elements shown in Figure 1.

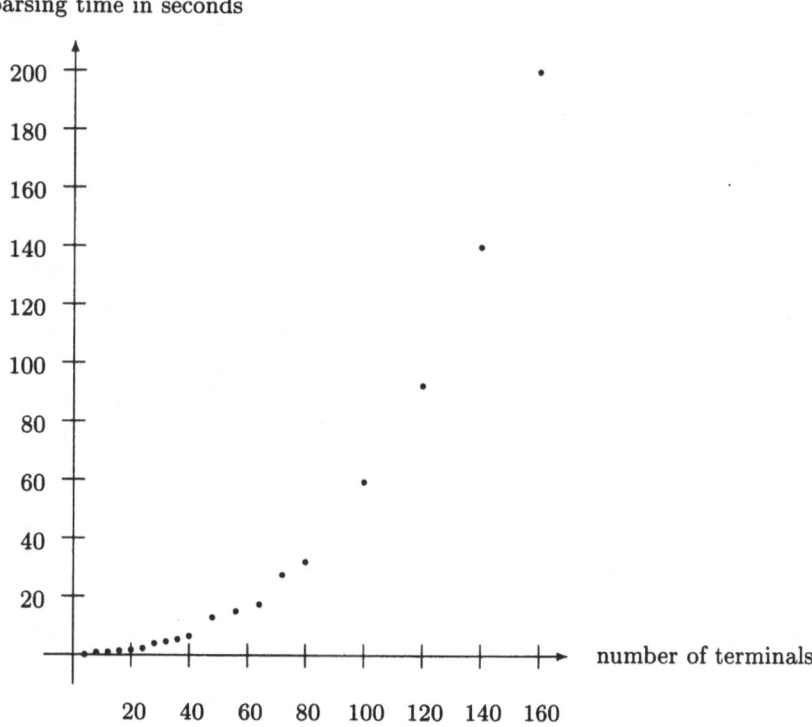

Fig. 6. Parsing time for plex structures.

From our experiments we found out that the actual runtime of the program depends on a number of factors like the order in which the terminals are read, and particular characteristics of the underlying grammar. An example is shown in Figure 6. In this example, we used the grammar given in the Appendix. As heuristics for determining the order in which the terminals are read we used two rules. First, we prefer that terminal which has the least number of "unknown" and the maximum number of "known" connection points. A connection point is called unknown if it is not connected to any connection point of a terminal already read, otherwise it is a known connection point. If there are ties, we use a second rule and prefer that terminal which has the minimum number of neighboring terminals not yet inspected and the maximum number of neighboring terminals already read. Informally speaking, this strategy keeps the structure inspected during the course of the analysis in a "compact" form and thus reduces the degree of uncertainty. The strategy has not been developed particularly for the grammar given in the Appendix. It has proven useful for other grammars, too. The planarity of the graphs in this example doesn't have any direct influence on the performance of the parser.

As one can conclude from Figure 6, there is a subexponential growth of the computation time (less than cubic) in the considered range. Generally, we believe that there are many applications where it is possible to find suitable heuristics such that the computation time actually needed in the average case is better than exponential.

7 Conclusions

An algorithm for parsing plex structures generated by context free plex grammars is proposed in this paper. It follows the same strategy as Earley's parser does for context free string languages. For the string case, a number of different versions of Earley's parser have been developed like an error correcting parser [30] or parsers which can handle probabilistic information, either in the productions [31] or in the input string [32]. Such extensions potentially have a number of interesting applications, primarily in the domain of pattern recognition and image analysis. The clear logical structure of the plex grammar parser described in this paper and its similarities with Earley's algorithm seem to be a promising basis for similar extensions. They would certainly further enhance the applicability of our proposed parser to problems in pattern recognition and image analysis.

Perhaps the most critical problem with our parser is its high computational complexity. As mentioned in section 6, however, there seems to be a potential for incorporating heuristics for speeding up the parsing time actually needed. Such heuristics may be put into the grammar itself or into the order in which the terminals of the plex structures under consideration are read. Furthermore, as already discussed in section 5, there exist subclasses of plex structures with a lower time complexity. A detailed investigation of the properties of such subclasses will be an interesting topic for further research, from both a practical and theoretical point of view.

Acknowledgements

The implementation of the parser was done on a Nixdorf Targon which was made available to us by Nixdorf AG, Switzerland. We gratefully acknowledge their generous support. We also want to thank A. Ueltschi, who provided help in typing the paper.

References

1. K. S. Fu (ed.), *Syntactic Pattern Recognition Applications*, Springer–Verlag, Berlin, 1977.
2. K. S. Fu, *Syntactic Pattern Recognition and Applications*, Prentice–Hall, Englewood Cliffs, NJ, 1982.
3. R. C. Gonzales and M. G. Thomason, *Syntactic Pattern Recognition*, Addison–Wesley, Reading, MA, 1978.
4. L. Miclet, *Structural Methods in Pattern Recognition*, North–Oxford Academic, 1986.
5. H. Bunke and A. Sanfeliu (eds.), "Advances in Syntactic Pattern Recognition," Special Issue of *Pattern Recognition* 19, No. 4, 1986.
6. G. Ferrate, T. Pavlidis, A. Sanfeliu, and H. Bunke (eds.): *Syntactic and Structural Pattern Recognition*, NATO ASI F45, Springer–Verlag, Berlin, 1988.
7. H. Bunke and A. Sanfeliu (eds.), *Syntactic and Structural Pattern Recognition — Theory and Applications*, World Scientific, Singapore, 1990.
8. M. Nagl, "A tutorial and bibliographical survey on graph grammars," in [9], pp. 70–126.
9. V. Claus, H. Ehrig, and G. Rozenberg (eds.), "Graph-grammars and their application to computer science and biology," *Proc. 1st Int'l Workshop*, Lecture Notes Computer Science 73, Springer–Verlag, Berlin, 1979.
10. H. Ehrig, M. Nagl, G. Rozenberg (eds.), "Graph-grammars and their application to computer science," *Proc. 2nd Int'l Workshop*, Lecture Notes Computer Science 153, Springer–Verlag, Berlin, 1982.
11. H. Ehrig, M. Nagl, G. Rozenberg, and A. Rosenfeld, "Graph-grammars and their application to computer science," *Proc. 3rd Int'l Workshop*, Lecture Notes Computer Science 291, Springer–Verlag, Berlin, 1987.
12. R. Franck, "A class of linearly parsable graph grammars," *Acta Informatica* 10, pp. 175–201, 1978.
13. M. Kaul, "Syntaxanalyse von Graphen bei Präzedenz–Graph–Grammatiken," Techn. Report MIP–8610, Univ. Passau, FRG, 1986.
14. M. Kaul, "Computing the minimum error distance of graphs in $O(n^3)$ time with precedence graph grammars," in [6], pp. 69–83.
15. P. Della Vigna and C. Ghezzi, "Context-free graph grammars," *Information and Control* 37, pp. 207–233, 1978.
16. A. Sanfeliu and K. S. Fu, "Tree graph grammars for pattern recognition," in [10], pp. 349–368.
17. Q.-Y. Shi and K. S. Fu, "Parsing and translation of (attributed) expansive graph languages for scene analysis," *IEEE Trans. PAMI*, PAMI-5, pp. 472–485, 1983.
18. F. J. Brandenburg, "On partially ordered graph grammars," in [11], pp. 99–111.
19. M. Flasinski, "Parsing of edNLC–grammars for scene analysis," *Pattern Recognition* 21, pp. 623–629, 1988.

20. C. Lautemann, "Efficient algorithms on context–free graph languages," In T. Lepistö and A. Salomaa (eds.), *Automata, Languages and Programming, Proc. 15th Int'l Coll.*, pp. 362–378, Lecture Notes Computer Science 317, Springer–Verlag, Berlin, 1988.

21. J. Feder, "Plex languages," *Information Sciences* 3, pp. 225–241, 1971.

22. W. C. Lin and K. S. Fu, *A syntactic approach to 3D object representation and recognition*, TR – EE pp. 84–16, Purdue Univ., West Lafayette, Indiana, June 1984.

23. J. Earley, "An efficient context-free parsing algorithm," *Comm. ACM*, Vol. 13, No. 2, pp. 94–102, Feb. 1970.

24. S. K. Chang *et al.*, *Visual programming*, Plenum, 1986.

25. W. C. Lin and K. S. Fu, "A syntactic approach to 3-D object representation," *IEEE Transaction on Pattern Analysis and Machine Intelligence*, Vol. PAMI-6, No. 3, pp. 351–364, May 1984.

26. A. Habel and H.–J. Kreowski, "May we introduce to you: hyperedge replacement," in [11], pp. 15–26.

27. B. Courcelle, "Some applications of logic of universal algebra and of category theory to the theory of graph transformations," *Bulletin of the EATCS 36*, pp. 161–213, 1988.

28. B. Haller, "A parser for context-free plex grammars," Diploma Thesis, Institute of Informatics and Applied Mathematics, Univ. of Bern, Switzerland, 1989 (in German).

29. J. Y.–T. Leung, J. Witthof, and O. Vornberger, "On some variations of the bandwidth minimization problem," *SIAM J. Comp.* 13, pp. 650–667, 1984.

30. A. V. Aho and T. G. Peterson, "A minimum distance error–correcting parser for context–free languages," *SIAM J. Computing*, Vol. 1, No. 4, pp. 305–312, Dec. 1972.

31. S. Y. Lu and K. S. Fu, "Stochastic error–correcting syntax analysis for recognition of noisy patterns," *IEEE Trans. on Systems, Men, and Cybernetics*, Vol. SMC-8, pp. 380–401, 1978.

32. H. Bunke and D. Pasche, "Parsing multivalued strings and its application to image and waveform recognition," In R. Mohr, T. Pavlidis, and A. Sanfeliu (eds.), *Structural Pattern Analysis*, pp. 1–15, World Scientific, Singapore, 1990.

Appendix

The following plex grammar G generates the set of all well structured flowchart diagrams.

Initial nape:

Terminal napes:

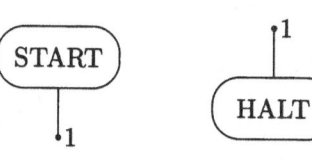 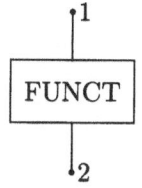 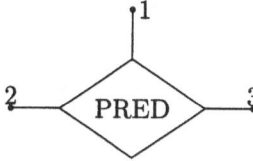

Nonterminal napes:

  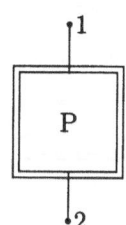

Productions:

PROG

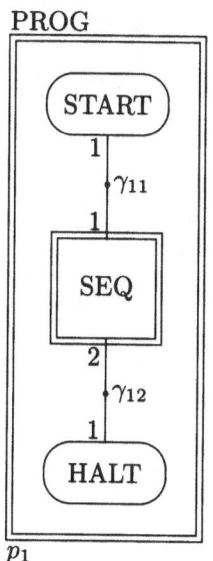 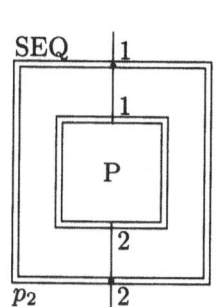 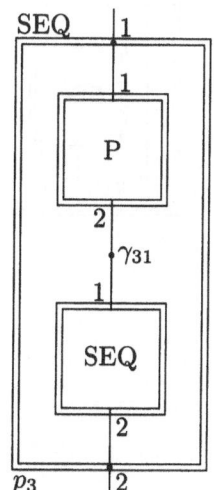

Productions (continued):

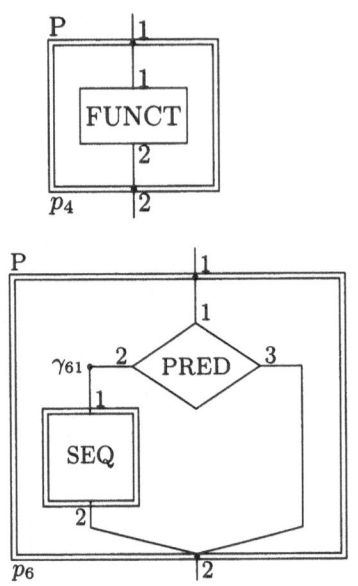

p_4

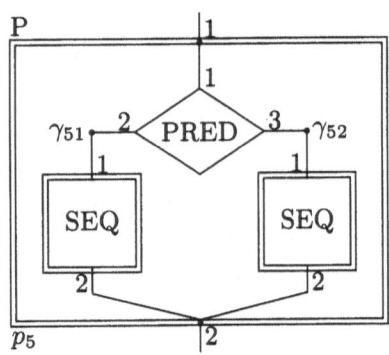

p_5

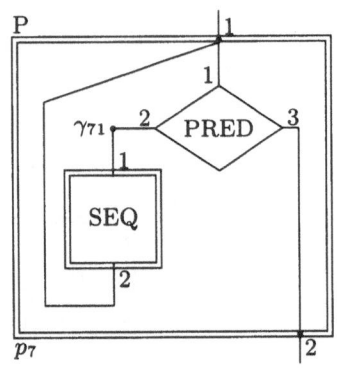

p_6

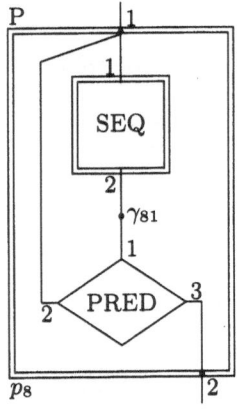

p_7

p_8

An example of a plex structure generated by G:

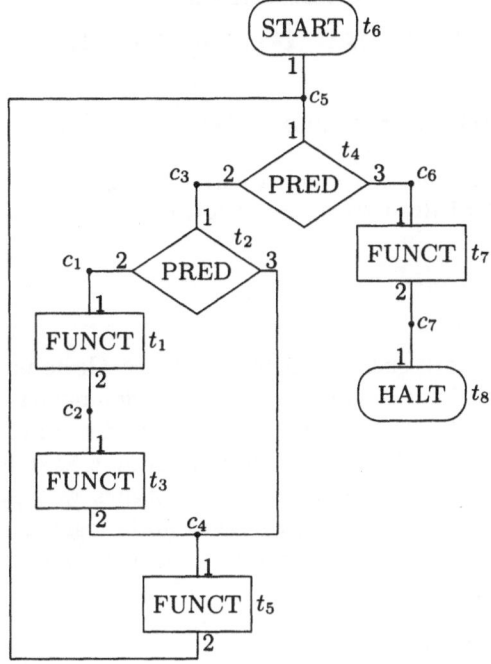

Document Image Analysis Using Logic-Grammar-Based Syntactic Pattern Recognition

David B. Searls and Suzanne Liebowitz Taylor

Unisys Center for Advanced Information Technology,
70 East Swedesford Road, Paoli, PA 19301, USA

Logic grammars such as Definite Clause Grammars — linguistic formalisms closely associated with the Prolog language — are powerful and highly versatile systems for specifying and detecting patterns not only in natural language, but in any suitably organized string, signal, or image. This paper reviews several such prototypes we have developed, which demonstrate the characteristics that make logic grammars a good vehicle for many Syntactic Pattern Recognition applications.

1 Introduction

Syntactic Pattern Recognition (SPR) makes use of the tools and techniques of computational linguistics, or other means of "structural" specification of a pattern, in order to detect that pattern in data which has been encoded in a suitable form for input[Fu82]. Because of the wide variety of types of input, ranging from strings to waveforms to images, many specialized grammar formalisms have been developed, together with *ad hoc* parsers to apply them. This proliferation of techniques and systems, however, may in some cases inhibit the more general use of SPR approaches. For example, such grammar and parser frameworks may require considerable initial effort to create, discouraging rapid prototyping and free experimentation. Also, specialization of SPR implementations may make it difficult to combine them into much more comprehensive, "layered" systems that are typical of many applications. The latter point, in particular, is unfortunate, insofar as SPR by its nature is hierarchical and should promote tight integration from very high-level application specifications down to very low-level implementation details.

We believe that the Definite Clause Grammar (DCG) formalism[PW80] can address these issues. We have found it to be a very convenient, versatile, and powerful framework for the development of SPR systems, largely because it is essentially a syntactic variant of the logic programming language Prolog. As such, it not only provides Turing power computation *within* an otherwise context-free grammar form, but also offers all the advantages of a symbolic programming language, especially the ability to rapidly prototype new applications and forms of input.

This paper illustrates our experiences by giving a series of examples of the use of DCGs in SPR applications, ranging from address block grammars (Section 3), to text processing (Section 5), to more *ad hoc* image analysis problems (Section 4). We also present examples that illustrate the ability of DCGs to deal with noisy data (Section 7) and to perform other kinds of signal processing (Section 8) in a prototyping mode. Finally, we show how parse *visualization* may be used as an aid to prototyping multidimensional grammars (Section 6).

2 Logic Programming and Definite Clause Grammars

The Definite Clause Grammar (DCG) formalism[PW80] is currently one of the most popular tools available for capturing in computational form a variety of linguistic phenomena[DA84, Per81, Sta87]. Our group has used DCGs extensively, not only as the foundation of a major DARPA-sponsored natural language processing program[HP86], but also as a starting point in creating linguistically based approaches to pattern-matching search and analysis in biological systems[SN91, Sea89], as well as in signal processing applications[Sea90].

Prolog is a programming language that implements a procedural interpretation of a subset of first-order predicate logic[Bra86]. It represents knowledge by means of a particular clausal form of logic (using *Horn*, or *definite* clauses) which allows programs to be written as databases containing atomic predicates called *facts*, *e.g.* `numeral(4)`, and *rules* which are Horn clauses written in the form

```
mailpiece(X) :- letter(Y), has_postage(X,P), P >= 0.30.
```

This can be read "X is a mailpiece *if* X is a letter *and* X has postage P *and* P is at least 0.30". Prolog's rules and facts, together called *relations*, can be queried to perform inferences by backward-chaining proof, using a mechanism called *resolution*; the resulting system is able to perform computation as controlled deduction, following a pattern of depth-first search.

Prolog's history is closely linked with the formalism of DCGs, and the notion that grammars can be expressed as rules of a Prolog program. The process of parsing a string then becomes that of proving a theorem given an input string and the "axioms" or rules of a grammar. Grammar rules occurring in a context-free form can be given as input to a Prolog compiler, exactly as shown below in a highly simplified natural language grammar:

```
sentence --> noun_phrase, verb_phrase.

noun_phrase --> determiner, nominal.
noun_phrase --> nominal.
noun_phrase --> pronoun.

nominal --> noun.
nominal --> adjective, nominal.
```

```
nominal --> noun, prepositional_phrase.
nominal --> noun, conjunction, nominal.

prepositional_phrase --> preposition, noun_phrase.

verb_phrase --> verb.
verb_phrase --> verb, prepositional_phrase.
verb_phrase --> verb, noun_phrase.
```

Note that in Prolog, logical predicates begin with a lower-case letter, and in DCGs these correspond to nonterminals. However it can be seen that DCGs require a translation step to become Prolog clauses, because Prolog must have a mechanism for manipulating the input string, which it does by maintaining the string in parameters added to the nonterminals. For instance, the last rule would be translated to:

```
verb_phrase(S0,S) :- verb(S0,S1), noun_phrase(S1,S).
```

Variables in Prolog are represented by atoms beginning with upper-case letters. When nonterminals are translated, they have two variable parameters added — sometimes called *difference lists* — corresponding to the lists that will be passed in and then back out, *i.e.* the input string (S0) and what is left of it (S) after the nonterminal consumes some initial string from it. The difference lists are arranged so that the span of the left hand side nonterminal is that of the entire right hand side. This rule can thus be paraphrased as "a verb phrase spans the input from S0 to S *if* a verb spans S0 S1 *and* a noun phrase spans S1 to S."

Grammar terminals are denoted using the Prolog list notation, in which list elements appear within square brackets and are separated by commas (*e.g.* [a,b,c]). This is illustrated in the following sample lexicon for our simple natural language grammar:

```
determiner --> [the].
pronoun --> [he] | [she] | [it].
noun --> [man] | [woman] | [house] | [dog].
adjective --> [old] | [nice].
preposition --> [with] | [in] | [from].
conjunction --> [and].
verb --> [walked] | [sang].
```

The vertical bars signify the logical "or", indicating rule disjunction; this convention is common in BNF specifications of programming language syntax. Grammar terminals must be translated to some representation that establishes that the input string consists of that terminal at the head of the remainder list. This is done with the Prolog list constructor, which is a vertical bar appearing *inside* list brackets (not to be confused with disjunction). Thus, [H|T] denotes a list with H as its head element and T as the tail or remainder of the list. The first rule above could thus be translated to

```
determiner(S0,S) :- S0=[the|S].
```

which indicates that "a determiner spans S0 to S *if* S0 consists of the list with the token **the** at its head and S as its tail."

Actual top-level calls to **sentence(S0,S)** would succeed when S0 is bound to a valid sentence and S is the empty list **[]** (this being the necessary remainder to indicate that the span is exact). However, our top level calls will use a *derivation* operator in the form **sentence --> *input*. An actual Prolog interaction might be

```
| ?- sentence ==> [the,old,man,and,woman,walked,the,dog].
yes
```

where, in response to a query typed at the Prolog prompt, a valid parse is found and Prolog indicates success with the answer "yes." Similarly, a grammatically incorrect sentence is rejected:

```
| ?- sentence ==> [old,walked,man,nice,dog,and,the].
no
```

An initial substring can be parsed by appending to the input a slash and a variable, which then is bound to the remainder of the input string:

```
| ?- noun_phrase ==> [the,nice,old,man,walked,the,dog]/Rest.
Rest = [walked,the,dog]
```

(This form of input actually represents the difference lists of the top level call, *i.e.*, the Prolog query **sentence --> S0/S** is equivalent to **sentence(S0,S)**).

Logic grammars can also be used generatively, to produce valid phrases given a specification:

```
| ?- sentence ==> X.

X = [the,man,walked] ;
X = [the,man,sang] ;
X = [the,man,walked,with,the,man] ;
...

X = [the,man,walked,with,the,old,dog] ;
X = [the,man,walked,with,the,old,old,man] ;
...
```

The semicolon entered by the user after every successful parse forces the parse to fail, backtrack, and find another answer.

Thus, it can be seen that DCGs provide an immediately executable top-down, backtracking parser for context-free grammars in a suitable form. However, underlying this is the powerful logic programming language Prolog, and it will be seen that DCGs can use this symbolic processing capability to extend their linguistic power and utility in a number of ways that are particularly appropriate for SPR applications.

3 Address Block Grammars

Document processing is one of the more significant potential applications of SPR techniques, and one which perhaps has the most to gain from an approach that encourages a fully integrated, hierarchical organization. This is because models of the underlying "signal" — that is, human natural language — are being actively developed, in most cases using grammar-based systems at their lowest (syntactic) level. Our own Prolog-based PUNDIT natural language processing system[HPD+89] is now being integrated with speech understanding technology, in the expectation that the latter field will benefit from an increased "understanding" of the underlying domain, providing greater discrimination over the contents of the speech waveform. The same principle could apply to machine reading of written text, and the easiest way to accomplish this might well be to push the natural language grammars down to lower levels than word tokens, allowing them to drive SPR-based character recognition.

While text understanding in its full generality is not yet a "solved" technology, this same principle may be applied in isolation to better-specified subdomains of language. Such an application is the interpretation of address blocks on mail, with the goal of determining a ZIP code for the destination. We are addressing this with SPR techniques, but rather than imposing knowledge of the address block as a contextual *post-processing* step on character or word recognition[Hul87], we hope to use logic grammars to establish a uniform top-down approach to the greatest extent possible.

The structure of an address block by its nature obeys rules, just as natural language does, regarding the order and grouping of words and numerals. For example, a high-level rule for an address block might be given in DCG form as

```
address_block(Zip,Plus4) --> addressee, newline,
       street_address(BlockFace), newline,
       city_state_zip(BlockFace,Zip,Plus4).
```

where parameters would be used not only to pass important information to the top level but also to relay information *between* rules.

To illustrate this and other aspects of DCGs in this regard, we concentrate on a partial grammar for addressees:

```
addressee --> person_s | organization.

person_s --> person | list(person).
person_s --> "Mrs.", full_name(male).
person_s --> title(male), conj, "Mrs.", full_name(male).
person_s --> titles, list(full_name(_)).
person_s --> ( titles | "" ), list(first_name), last_name.

list(NT) --> NT, conj, NT | NT, ",", list(NT).

person --> title(Gender), full_name(Gender).
```

```
person --> full_name(_), ( post_title | "" ).

full_name(G) --> first_name_s(G), last_name.

first_name_s(_) --> initial.
first_name_s(G) --> first_name(G), ( initial | "" ).

initial --> upper_case_letter, ".".

titles --> "Drs." | "Messrs".

post_title --> ",", ( "MD" | "PhD" | "LLD" ).

title(male) --> "Mr." | "Mister".
title(female) --> "Mrs." | "Ms." | "Miss".
title(_) --> "Dr." | "Doctor" | military_title.

military_title --> "Private" | "Corporal" | "Sergeant"
        | "Lieutenant" | "Captain" | "Major"
        | "Lieutenant Colonel" | "Colonel" |
        ("Brigadier" | "Major" | "Lieutenant"),
        "General".

conj --> "and" | "&".
```

The *lexical* entries here are again strings of characters (e.g. "Drs." or "Messrs."
would be valid string expansions for the nonterminal titles); however, these
would eventually be *nonterminals* as the grammar would extend further downward below the level of characters, to specify at a "lexical" level stroke features
or even (as will be seen) individual pixels. In any case, note that the grammar
representation not only promotes a highly modular description, but also allows
detail to always be presented at its appropriate level.

This grammar again attaches parameters to nonterminals, as in the rules for
title(Gender), where the parameter identifies any gender-specifics inherent in
the lexical entries (*e.g.* "Mr." is male). Note that an "anonymous" variable is
returned when there is no specific gender associated with a title. DCG parameters
may share all the characteristics of Prolog variables, *e.g.* they can stand for
arbitrary types or even complex term structure — most DCGs, in fact, are
written so as to build up a parse tree and return it — which can be fully or
partially instantiated at any point in the parse. For example, in the first rule for
person, the parameter Gender may or may not be bound by the subparse of the
nonterminal title; if it is, that gender will be *imposed* on the subparse of the
nonterminal full_name. This technique is commonly used in natural language
DCGs to impose agreement as to gender, number, tense, etc.

Logic grammars in general also allow for powerful *meta-programming* techniques [Abr88], as in the rule for list(NT). A metarule is a rule *about* rules,

which allows for very economical descriptions of general patterns of rule application. The example rule is used to create lists of other nonterminals in which each item is separated by a (lexical) comma, and the last two items are separated by a conjunction. The rule can be logically read as "a list of nonterminals is an example of that nonterminal followed by either a conjunction and a final instance of that nonterminal, or a comma and a remaining list of those nonterminals." (While the example given in this grammar was hand-compiled, our group has investigated the use of metarules in DCGs for natural language processing extensively[Hir86, Hir88]).

As noted in Section 2, another important aspect of grammars and logic programming is the fact that appropriately written rules may be "run backwards" to *generate* as well as *accept* input. Thus, we can enter a few typical names at the lexical level

```
first_name(male) --> "John".
first_name(female) --> "Mary".

last_name --> "Smith" | "Jones".
```

and use the grammar to generate a wide range of forms of individual addressees, among them:

Mr. A. Smith	Mr. John A. Jones	Mr. John Smith
Mrs. Mary A. Smith	Mary Jones, MD	Dr. John A. Jones
Mrs. A. Smith	Major General A. Smith	Mrs. Mary Jones
Dr. Mary Smith	Colonel Mary A. Jones	John Smith, PhD
Drs. John & Mary Jones	Dr. and Mrs. John Smith	

This feature is particularly useful in the testing phase of grammars under development. More importantly, the fact that generative grammars essentially function in a "generate-and-test" fashion can greatly prune the search in lower levels of the parse, *e.g.* character recognition. For example, consider a few additional rules for the last line of our simplified address block:

```
city_state_zip(BlockFace,Zip,Plus4) -->
        city_state(City,State),
        zipcode(BlockFace,City,State,Zip,Plus4).

city_state('Philadelphia','PA') -->
        ("Philadelphia" | "Phila."), state('PA').
city_state(C,S) --> city(C), state(S).

state('PA') --> "PA" | "Pa." | "Penna." | "Pennsylvania".
state('MA') --> "MA" | "Ma." | "Mass." | "Massachusetts".
```

In the rules for **state**, for example, when a state is expected in the address block it is only necessary to try to parse a limited number of initial upper-case letters; following this, the search space narrows rapidly on subsequent letters, even given the large degree of disjunction for various potential forms of abbreviation.

Although in a purely declarative reading of grammars there is no implicit ordering of the rules or their disjuncts (or for that matter of their conjuncts), in Prolog's procedural interpretation those rules and disjuncts are in fact tried in the order in which they occur in the rule database. One consequence of this is that an intrinsic bias may be put on which readings of the input are tried first. Thus, in parsing the `city_state` position, it would be economical to have the largest population centers "hard-wired" into the grammar, narrowing the character search significantly, before resorting to simply reading the string character by character and performing a lookup in a more complete directory. This principle, of course, also extends to the character level, insofar as alphanumerics may be tried in the order of the frequency in which they occur, e.g.

```
upper_case_letter --> "E" | "T" | "A" | "I" | "O" | "N" |
                      "S" | "H" | "R" | "D" | "L" | ...
```

Moreover, it is possible to use *context sensitive* grammar features (referring to rules which have more than one element on the left hand side) in order to account for association frequencies of letters, in the manner of Markov models[KHB89]. In logic grammars, it is possible to write rules like

```
lower_case_letter, "h" --> "th" | "sh" | "wh" | "ch".
```

which asserts that a lower-case letter followed by an "h" is likely to be a "t", "s", "w", or "c" (in that order); typically, these rules would be tried before the single-letter rules for `lower_case_letter`, which would be ordered simply by single-letter frequencies. Such rules can be intermixed freely with others of varying Markov "order" (i.e. size of context). Not only can rule ordering be used to accelerate search, but when there is uncertainty as to a letter's identity (as, for instance, if there is a variable in the input stream for the grammars shown so far) it can be used to postulate letters to be inserted. In combination with stochastic grammars, this can allow for a statistical model embedded in the declarative grammars.

The ordering of the procedural interpretation of the declarative grammars can also lead to inefficiencies. For instance, when a very nondeterministic feature occurs *before* a very deterministic one on the input, the grammar will nonetheless try to parse the former before the latter, however inefficiently. In the top-level rule, the `street_address` is parsed before the `city_state_zip` line, despite the fact that the `BlockFace` parameter cannot in fact be determined unless the city and state are first passed to the former nonterminal. We have addressed this in other domains by disconnecting the order of parsing from the positional order expressed in declarative grammars, by, for instance, allowing repositioning of the parse (see Section 5 and [Sea89]). We are also investigating the simultaneous use of pure declarative grammars and procedural grammars (or annotations to the declarative grammars) that give directions as to the most efficient order of parsing while preserving the virtues of a straightforward, high-level description of the domain.

We hope to use sub-domain grammars such as this to drive lower levels of analysis and thus impose domain knowledge of the sort that assists human

reading. The importance of this has been shown in applications such as reading hand-printed FORTRAN coding sheets, where knowledge of the syntax and
semantics of the FORTRAN language itself can help to disambiguate isolated
characters[BW79, Hul87].

4 Two-Dimensional Grammars

DCGs can be readily generalized to accept 2-dimensional input, rather than a
1-dimensional string of input tokens, using techniques from SPR such as linear
encodings of images as connected series of directional "strokes", or by use of
higher-dimensional systems such as web or graph grammars[Fu82]. A technique
which is promoted by our logic-based approach is to view the input as an unin-
stantiated list of logic variables, for which bindings are generated by drawing
from an alphabet which is a gradually decreasing set of available primitives *and*
their locations — that is, the description of the image.

This is illustrated below, where we show the major portion of a grammar
developed to graphically describe the sail plans of small sailing craft. (This was
developed as a prototyping domain for a much more complex military application
involving the identification of ships from radar images that roughly approximate
the silhouettes of the ships.)

```
sailboat(SailTypes,HullType,JibType) --> hull(Aft), ...^Aft,
        jib(Aft,JibHeight,JibType), ...^Aft,
        sails(Aft,JibHeight,SailTypes,HullType).

hull(Aft) --> @Bow, line, horizontal^Aft#Waterline,
        line, line#Deck, @Bow?, {Deck>Waterline}.

jib(Aft,Height,working_jib) --> @Tack, horizontal^Aft,
        @Clew, vertical#Height, line, @Tack?, @Clew.
jib(Aft,Height,genoa_jib) --> @Tack, horizontal^Aft,
        @Clew, line, @Head, line, @Tack?,
        {Tack-Clew/Head#Height}.

sails(Aft,Jib,Rig,sloop) -->
        ...^Aft, sail(Rig,Aft,Main), {Main>Jib}.
sails(Aft,Jib,Rig,yawl) --> ...^Aft, sail(Rig,Aft,Main),
        {Main>Jib}, ...^Aft,
        sail(Rig,Aft,Jigger), {Jib>Jigger}.
sails(Aft,Jib,Rig,ketch) --> ...^Aft, sailRig,Aft,Main),
        ...^Aft, sail(Rig,Aft,Mizzen),
        {Main>Mizzen, Mizzen>Jib}.
sails(Aft,Jib,Rig,schooner) --> ...^Aft, sail(Rig,Aft,Fore),
        {Fore>Jib}, ...^Aft, sail(Rig,Aft,Main),
        {Main>Fore}.
```

```
sail(jib_headed,Aft,Height) --> @Tack, horizontal^Aft,
        @Clew, line, vertical#Height, @Tack?, @Clew.
sail(gaff_headed,Aft,Height) --> @Tack, horizontal^Aft,
        @Clew, line, @Peak, line, vertical#Luff, @Tack?,
        @Clew, {Tack-Clew/Peak#Height, Height>Luff}.
```

This grammar takes as its starting alphabet a set of line segments, represented as pairs of X-Y coordinates, and generates a "string" from this alphabet
which is required to satisfy the description of a sailboat. In the process, a specific such description is derived, returned as parameters through the parse to the
top-level nonterminal. The system can classify sail plans such as those shown in
Figure 1.

[jib_headed, sloop]   [gaff_headed, yawl]   [staysail, schooner]

Fig. 1. Typical sail plans.

Prolog allows new syntactic operators to be defined with ease, and we use
this feature freely in developing domain-specific grammar systems. One such
operator which has proven to be useful in a large variety of applications is the
positional operator ('@'). This prefix operator binds to its variable argument an
indication of the current position in the parse — in the case of images, a physical
position in 2-space. If the argument is already a bound variable, the position in
the parse (or image) *reverts* to the indicated binding. Alternatively, appending
a question mark allows for *testing* position, *i.e.* @Posn? will only succeed if the
current position in the parse is Posn. We have previously given an extensive
treatment of the theoretical underpinnings of this simple but extremely versatile
operator[Sea89], which essentially allows for grammars to treat position as a
"first-class object", subject to examination and alteration at will.

An example of the use of '@' can be seen in the following simple rule:

```
triangle --> @Start, line, line, line, @Start? .
```

The first @Start records the current position in the variable Start, after which three lines are "consumed" from the database of line segments, after which the @Start? tests to be sure the parse has returned to the starting position, *i.e.* that the three lines form a closed triangle. Just such rules are used in the example to describe sails, for instance, albeit with additional constraints.

These constraints, which are again domain-specific features, are also annotated using special operators. The *directional* operator ('^') behaves in a similar fashion to the positional operator, but in this case requires its variable to be an indication of the current direction of motion. Similarly, the *length/distance* operator ('#') is used to bind the length of a line, or the distance of a point from another point or line.

Gaps may also be constrained by the directional operator to scan in a particular direction in two dimensions. For example, in the top-level rule for sailboat, the subparse for hull leaves the parse sitting at the bow of the boat and also returns a parameter indicating the aft direction; then, in parsing for the sails, the

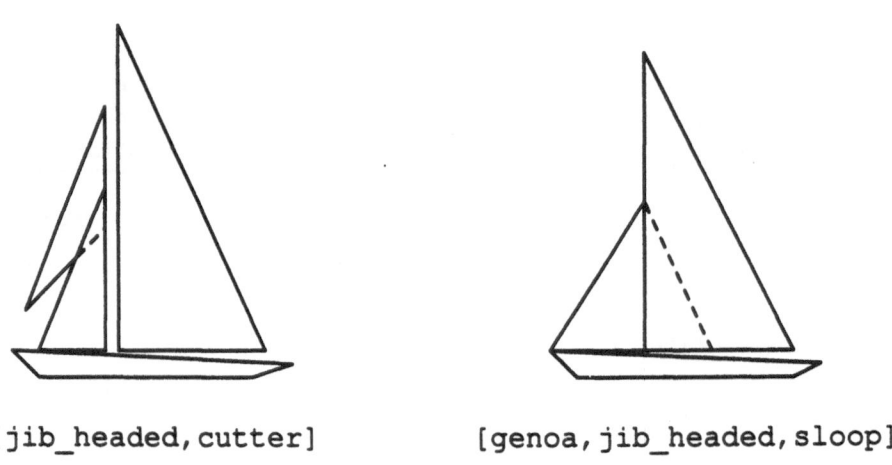

[jib_headed, cutter]   [genoa, jib_headed, sloop]

Fig. 2. Overlapping sail plans.

embedded gaps are required to scan from fore to aft by the directional operator attached to the gaps, ...^Aft. We have also shown how other limitations of traditional grammars, such as an inability to represent *superposition* of features, can be overcome in DCGs by simple expedients[Sea89] (In particular, we have demonstrated that Allen's interval calculus, which allows arbitrary relationships between and among features — *i.e.* one may contain the other, or overlap it, or exactly meet it, etc. — can be subsumed by the grammar features we have developed[Sea90]. Thus, these grammars are able to deal with input such as that in Figure 2.

The rule for `hull` exhibits several more important features. The rule starts by binding a position to the variable `Bow`. (By convention, if there is no current position, one is chosen at random from the database.) It then parses a line, and then another line using a higher-level non-terminal called `horizontal`, which is required to have the same Y-coordinates at its endpoints. This nonterminal also serves to bind a direction to the variable `Aft` which until now is unbound, as well as a length to the variable `Waterline`, using the '#' operator. Another line is then parsed, and then a fourth line whose length is assigned to the variable `Deck`. Then, the `@Bow?` checks that a closed quadrilateral has been parsed, *i.e.* that the parse has returned to its starting point. We now wish to use the measurements of the lengths of the putative waterline and deck of the hull to further constrain the parse; that is, we will require that the deck be longer than the waterline. This is done by simply stating this inequality inside curly braces, which is a DCG convention indicating a call to arbitrary Prolog code within the body of a rule. This is another feature (in addition to unrestricted use of parameters) which gives DCGs greater than context-free power, and in fact gives them access to the full Turing power of Prolog. Not only can constraints and code fragments be embedded in rules inside curly braces, but entire expert systems, or even subroutine calls to foreign functions in 'C', FORTRAN, Pascal, or assembler. The utility of this to the proposed application will be discussed further below.

The ability to apply constraints in the course of a parse and to bind and pass variables as parameters allows grammars to be written which are able to extract "cues" (such as distances and directions) from the image on the fly, and to propagate those cues through the remainder of the parse. This leads to some useful properties of invariance. For example, there is no particular predilection for an overall size or a fore-to-aft direction; these are bound to variables where necessary so that the remainder of the parse is *relative* to those bindings. This means that the grammar is invariant to scale, and to inversion or vertical compression of the image — invariances which happen to be very important to the radar domain for which this system was developed — as illustrated in Figure 3(c). In character recognition, grammars could be tailored to possess suitable invariances, such as scale, and a limited degree of rotation or horizontal shear (slant).

These grammars are of the same order of complexity as previous efforts to apply SPR to character recognition based on similar primitives[Fu82], and we have achieved reasonable efficiency in this domain with little attempt at optimization — a set of 20-odd sail plans can be parsed in under a second each. This level of application of DCGs is a viable possibility, making use of other technology to segment and extract features.

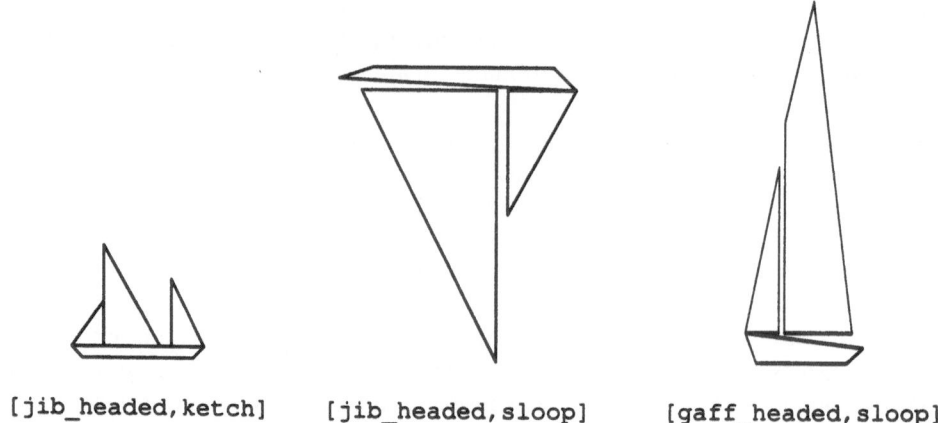

[jib_headed,ketch]   [jib_headed,sloop]   [gaff_headed,sloop]

Fig. 3. Invariances.

5 Pixel-Level Grammars

We are currently investigating the design of grammars at the level of individual pixels, rather than of higher-level features segmented and extracted by other means. Our prototype uses actual grayscale images (selected from a US Postal Service database of address block images), such as the ZIP code in Figure 4.

Fig. 4. ZIP code: (a) grayscale image (top); and (b) after preprocessing (bottom).

These images are first preprocessed to a form suitable for parsing, using programs written in 'C'. The images are binarized and decimated by a factor of two, and then thinned to a one-pixel thickness using a modification[ASM88,

ZS84]. The thinning was a crucial preprocessing step to accelerate the parse of a character for several reasons. First, for every point in the image, the parser can travel in one of eight compass-point directions. The amount of time necessary to consume the entire image parse is directly related to the number of points in the image. Therefore, it is advantageous to eliminate as many character pixels as possible and still retain the shape information. Second, our parsing method depends on the location of distinguished points such as *branch-points* in the image. A branch-point is defined as a point with more than two neighbors and, if the image is not thinned, many spurious points will be classified as branch-points.

Thinning, noise in the original image, and writer style cause gaps to appear in the characters. Gap filling is currently performed as a preprocessing step in 'C'. In the future, we will determine whether this could be incorporated into the Prolog parsing process, taking advantage of the potential for a grammar to *generate* points as necessary, driven by context[Hul87]. The advantage of incorporating gap filling into the grammar is that it will only fill gaps when needed to successfully complete a parse, eliminating the current problem of some erroneously filled gaps. Other preprocessing algorithms can be incorporated readily due to most Prologs' convenient interfaces to other languages such as 'C' (*e.g.* Quintus Prolog, used in this work).

The rest of the preprocessing done in 'C' prepares the remaining data for input to the Prolog code. The result is a database of points as shown in Figure 4(b). While the grammar can simply use data in the form of a database of coordinates (*e.g.* in the form pt(X,Y)), we have found that the parser is accelerated by precompiling an adjacency list for each point as well, specifying all its nearest neighbors. Thus, the actual lowest level of the Prolog code is a database of predicates in the form adj(pt(X,Y),[pt(X1,Y1),pt(X2,Y2),...]) where the listed points are adjacent to the main (X,Y) point. Our current prototype has rules such as:

```
numeral(4) --> @branch, @P, 4<lineseg~n, @P, 4<lineseg~s,
               @end?, @P, 3<lineseg~w, 4<lineseg~n,
               @end?, @P, line~e, @end?.
numeral(3) --> @end~sw, 4<curve(cw)~ne, move~sw, @branch?,
               4<optional_loop, move, 4<curve(cw)~e, @end~nw?.
numeral(2) --> @end, 8<curve(cw)~ne, @edge~w?,
               line~s, 6<lineseg~e, @end?.
numeral(2) --> @end, 10<curve(cw)~ne, move~ne, @direction^D,
               curve(cw)~D, cross-back(6), 4<line~=e, @end?.
numeral(X) --> @edge~n, line~se, line~sw, @[H1|T1], line~nw,
               @[H2|T2], line~ne, cross,
               {append(Edge,[H1|T1],[H2|T2])}, !,
               @backtrack([]), @start, add_loop(Edge,X).

add_loop([],0) --> stop.
add_loop([H|_],8) --> @H, @branch?, line~se, line~sw,
```

```
                        line~nw, line~ne, cross.
        add_loop([_|T],X) --> add_loop(T,X).


        optional_loop --> @P, line~w, @end~w?, @P .
        optional_loop --> @P, curve(cw)~w, cross, @P.


        line~Dir --> move~Dir, (stop | line~Dir).
```

As before, this DCG makes extensive use of domain-specific operators for a more economical syntax. The positional operator ('@'), in particular, has been generalized to accept as arguments a series of keywords that greatly facilitate positional testing and translocation within the image. For example, each rule begins with a command to select a point from the image which fulfills certain criteria, *e.g.* @branch means select any point which has more than two neighbors, while @end selects points with only one neighbor. The latter points are qualified with directional operators, which have also been generalized somewhat; @end^n signifies an endpoint facing due north, *i.e.* its sole neighbor must be directly south, whereas @end~n means "approximately" northerly, *i.e.* its sole neighbor must be south, southeast, or southwest. We have also incorporated length constraints directly as annotations to nonterminals, rather than as curly-bracketed embedded calls; these are in the forms of inequalities such as 4<lineseg~n, which means "consume a line segment running at least four pixels in a northerly direction." As always, these operators may make use of Prolog variables in order to "read" and transmit cues through the parse.

The following is an (abbreviated) interaction showing a parse of the image given above, using a higher-level rule which scans the image for digits and assembles them into a ZIP code:

```
        | ?- zipcode(Z) --> file('zip63101.bit').
        trying 4... 5... 6... found 6
        trying 6... 9... 7... 3... found 3
        trying 3... 2a... 2b... 1... found 1
        trying 1... found 1
        trying 1... trying 0/8... found 0
        Z = 63101
```

Many other features have been added to this DCG, which are beyond the scope of this paper to describe in detail. This prototype grammar is already quite dense, yet is still far from completely general; however, it is our belief that the required generality can be added to the grammar in a clear, hierarchical manner, preserving its declarative nature.

Part of our future effort will be involved in developing fast parsing techniques within the logic grammar formalism in order to make the SPR approach tractable. We will incorporate known techniques from other fields, such as chart parsing from natural language processing (see the following section), as well as approaches suggested by the domain at hand. Among these may be the use of existing algorithms, which should easily be integrated into the grammars using foreign function interfaces. We also plan to explore optimization of the data representation using external 'C' data structures, with which we have experience in the domain of DNA sequence analysis[SN91]. In general, part of the "tuning" process will be conversion of aspects of the grammars and parsing to fast 'C' programs, where such conversion will have no ill effect on the modularity, versatility, maintainability, and overall declarative flavor of the SPR approach.

Another future direction might be parallel execution of SPR parses. Grammars by their nature present opportunities for OR-parallelism, and we have studied this in the case of natural language processing[HHS88]. Logic grammars would have a particular advantage in this regard, insofar as OR-parallel implementations of Prolog exist (e.g. the Aurora system[LBD+88] which provide automatic detection of concurrency, with no change to the serially executable Prolog code. (In recent tests using an Encore multiprocessor machine, we have achieved excellent processor utilization and speedup with DCG-based parsing on Aurora.)

6 Parse Visualization

Since the grammar is implemented with a parser which, at the lowest level, operates on the pixels in the image, conventional debugging tools are nearly useless due to cognitive overload and the inability to easily relate the progress of the parse to the image itself. Accordingly, we have developed a visualization environment, GASPR (Graphical Aid for Syntactic Pattern Recognition), to provide a computational tool for rule development, debugging and refinement, as well as a visual abstraction of the parser operation at the pixel level.

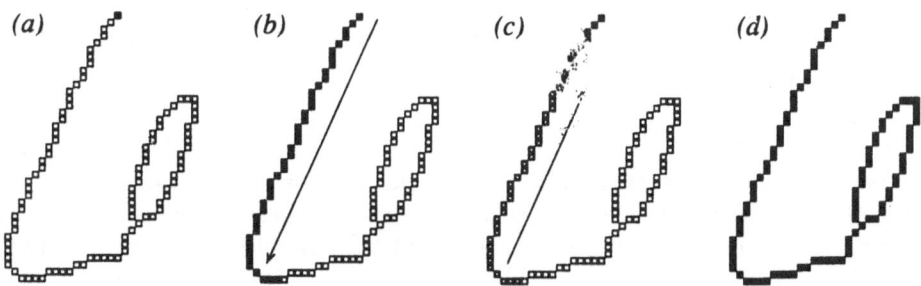

Fig. 5. Parser path in graphical debugger.

GASPR was developed from XWIP, a public domain Prolog interface to the X Window System, and is currently implemented on a SUN 3/160 color workstation. At the beginning of each inquiry, the image pixels are represented in a separate graphics window by outlined rectangular regions. These pixel regions change state as the parser applies the grammar rules, and GASPR produces a corresponding change in the appearance of the pixel (shape, color, etc...). Thus, GASPR traces the "movement" of the parser through the image as it attempts to satisfy the rules. The possible states of the image pixels we have thus far implemented are: pixels in the image not yet considered, retracted pixels (pixels which were considered part of an object, but were later rejected upon backtracking) and pixels presently on the parse path. Figure 5 shows a succession of images of the number "6" in the course of parsing part of a ZIP code image. An outlined pixel represents one that is in the ZIP code, but has not been considered yet, a filled-in pixel represents a pixel on the current path or part of a completed numeral, and the heavily outlined pixels represent those which have been backtracked over. Thus, Figure 5(a) shows the state at the beginning of a parse, where an end-point at the top of the numeral has been selected; 5(b) shows a point at which a long southwesterly line has been consumed; at 5(c), the current attempt has failed, and the parse is backtracking up the diagonal; and at 5(d), a new subparse discovered a complete "6" and filled in the figure. The entire ZIP code image is represented in the GASPR window image of Figure 6.

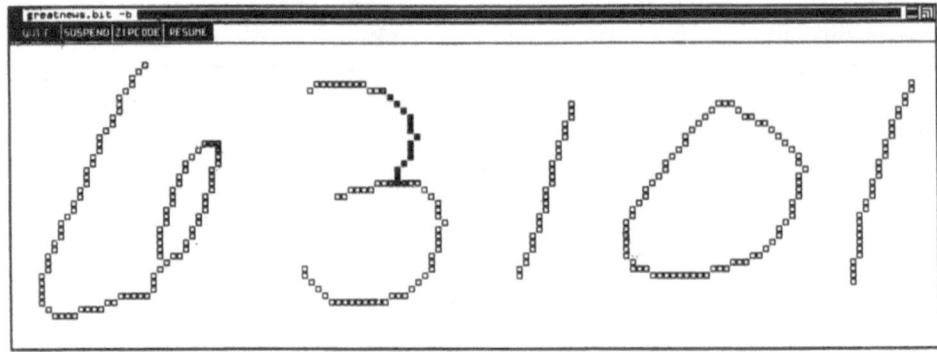

Fig. 6. GASPR window.

We have added the capability for the user to suspend the parse, with the click of a button in the window, remove or add pixels from the database (by clicking the mouse in appropriate regions of the graphics window), and then to click another button in the graphics window to continue the parse with the changes. This creates a mechanism for a greater understanding of the parsing process as well as the capability to experiment with the grammar in order to develop more efficient grammar rules. Eventually, more sophisticated versions of this grammar writer's "assistant" may also include semi-automated learning tools, whereby grammars would be produced by induction, under the interactive control of the user. This might involve the selection of a set of image subregions as a training set, to be used in generating an abstracted rule set, using *gram-*

matical inference[Fu82]. Although GASPR has been developed for our character recognition application, it may be easily enhanced and adopted to other SPR applications where visualization will be an essential aid for algorithm development and analysis.

7 Error-Correcting Grammars

Grammars typically suffer another shortcoming when compared to other approaches, and that is their inability to capture statistical information in order to deal with data that is noisy, incomplete, or simply wrong. This problem has been addressed by the development of *stochastic* grammars[Fu82], and we believe that not only these but other solutions to this problem can be encompassed within DCGs, with their flexibility to pass parameters and to perform arbitrary embedded computations. Grammars do possess characteristics that make them

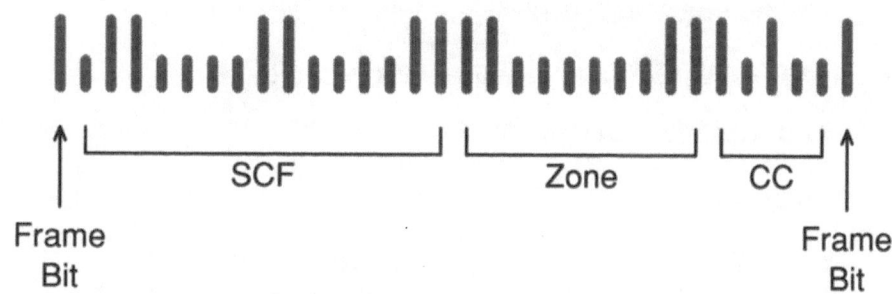

Fig. 7. POSTNET barcode for "63101".

immediately suitable for certain kinds of error correction. Consider a classic example of an error-correcting system: that for reading bar codes such as the POSTNET system used for encoding ZIP codes on mailpieces. This is illustrated in Figure 7.

While algorithms already exist which read barcodes quite efficiently, we have rapidly prototyped one in grammar form simply for demonstration purposes. Given a "bar code" input represented as a string of ':'s (denoting full bars) and '.'s (half bars), this grammar parses a zipcode in any of the three standard formats (52-bit, 32-bit, or 69-bit) in the POSTNET specification[pos85]:

```
zip_bar_code(Bits,D) --> std_format(Bits,D).

std_format(52,D) --> field(c,D).
std_format(32,D) --> field(a,D).
std_format(69,D) --> field(a,A), field(b,B),
```

```
                        {append(A,B,D)}.

field(Type,Digits) --> frame_bit, pattern(Type,Digits),
                       correction_character(Digits),
                       frame_bit.

pattern(a,D) --> scf(D/Z), zone(Z/[]).
pattern(b,D) --> zone(D/SS), sector(SS/[]).
pattern(c,D) --> scf(D/B), pattern(b,B).

scf([D1,D2,D3|R]/R) --> digit(D1), digit(D2), digit(D3).
zone([D4,D5|R]/R) --> digit(D4), digit(D5).
sector([D6,D7,D8,D9|R]/R) -->
       digit(D6), digit(D7), digit(D8), digit(D9).

correction_character(Digits) --> digit(D),
       {check_sum(0)-->[D|Digits]}.

check_sum(Sum0) --> [Digit], {Sum is Sum0+Digit},
                    check_sum(Sum).
check_sum(Total) --> {(Total mod 10)=:=0}.

digit(D) --> code(D).

frame_bit --> ":".

code(0) --> "::...".          code(5) --> ".:.:.".
code(1) --> "...::.".         code(6) --> ".::..".
code(2) --> "..:.:.".         code(7) --> ":...:.".
code(3) --> "..::..".         code(8) --> ":..:..".
code(4) --> ".:...:".         code(9) --> ":.:...".
```

The grammar exhibits the characteristic hierarchical abstraction of SPR systems, expressing the breakout of bit fields into patterns which are combinations of SCF, zone, and sector-segment information within the zipcode. At the next lowest level, digits are read and returned as parameters, using the 5-bit lexical code rules. This grammar correctly parses a "good" bar code input:

```
| ?- zip_bar_code(Bits,Z) -->
            ":...::.:....::.::.....::.::..:".

Bits = 32,
Z = [1,9,3,0,1]

no
```

Note that an attempt to find another answer fails, as it should. We can also use the Prolog *bagof* command to find a list of all possible answers:

```
| ?- bagof(Z,zip_bar_code(_,Z) -->
              ":.::....::...:::::......:::.:..:",Zs).

Z = _57,
Zs = [[6,3,1,0,1]]
```

Again there is a unique reading. In case an error should occur, the specification allows the offending digit to be detected in general, since each digit code is required to have two full bars and three half bars. Where this rule is violated, typical bar code reading algorithms attempt to recover using a final checksum digit.

We can also implement error correction in our grammar by adding the following rules:

```
digit(X) --> change_digit(1-5), code(X).

change_digit(_) --> change_bar.
change_digit(N-M), [B] -->
            {N<M, N0 is N+1}, [B], change_digit(N0-M).

change_bar, ":" --> ".".
change_bar, "." --> ":".
```

These rules change a single bar anywhere in the range 1 to 5 bars ahead, using the context-sensitive rule **change_bar** to switch readings. This allows the digit rule to retry bad codes if the original rule for **digit** fails. We test this by introducing first one and then two errors into a good bar code, requiring a unique reading by coercing the answer from *bagof* to be a singleton list:

```
| ?- bagof(Z,zip_bar_code(_,Z) -->
              ":.::....::.:.:.:::....:::.:..:",[Z]).

Z = [6,3,1,0,1]

| ?- bagof(Z,zip_bar_code(_,Z) -->
              ":.:.....::.:.:.:::....:::.:..:",[Z]).

Z = [6,3,1,0,1]
```

This grammar-based approach differs from the usual algorithms in one essential respect. If erroneous digits are encountered, the grammar will immediately "postulate" changes to individual bars that would allow the parse to proceed, and the overall parse can succeed only if the **correction_character** checks; if it doesn't, the parse will backtrack and try alternative readings. This is a purely declarative statement as to what constitutes a valid zipcode, as opposed to the procedural algorithms which would calculate what the erroneous digits must be at the end using mathematical formulas and reasoning about numbers of bars of each height.

The use of non-determinism for error-correction would appear to be wasteful, since backtracking to try different readings of erroneous digits will require re-parsing all the intervening "good" digits. However, it need not be expensive, since there are well-known parsing techniques (including *chart parsing* from the natural language field) that store intermediate subparses in a table, which saves them from being reparsed. We have implemented such a system in the DNA domain, producing dramatically reduced parse times in cases of highly non-deterministic pattern matching grammars[SN91].

On the other hand, one significant advantage of the declarative approach in general is that it does not require an early commitment as to the form and function of an algorithm — it is merely descriptive (at least in spirit). This is illustrated by the use of the grammar to correct a wider range of errors than the POSTNET specification deals with. In the latter, the error-correction algorithm is required to correct 100% of single-digit errors, and it happens that it can also correct about half of two-digit errors (42%, in our tests of a few typical ZIP codes). However, because the grammar makes no assumptions about the total number of errors, it is able also to parse the additional 1.4% of three-digit errors that are correctable in theory. (Because the grammar is again generative by nature, the experimentation that led to this result made use of the grammar to both *generate* all possible bar codes from a given zipcode with one error per digit and a given number of digits in error, and to *accept* only those parses that still led to a unique, correct reading.)

Note that the rule for `correction_character` makes use of a *recursive derivation* — that is, a call to the derivation operator within curly braces, in effect a parse within a parse — in this case to determine if the list of digits about to be returned has the appropriate modulo-10 checksum. We have described recursive derivation at length from a theoretical standpoint[Sea89], and have also found it to be a powerful practical method for performing "layered" operations in grammars, and for accomplishing superposition of features, as described in Section 4.

Stochastic grammars attach probabilities to rules in a grammar and multiply them as rules are applied to return a final likelihood for an entire parse[Fu82]. Such probabilities are easily attached to nonterminals in DCGs as parameters, and in more sophisticated DCG translators may be passed as hidden parameters (like the difference lists) in order to hide this overhead from the grammar writer. We have implemented mechanisms such as this in dealing with specifications of signal sequences in DNA which are typically specified as a "weighted matrix" of frequencies of occurrence of individual terminals[SN91]. Moreover, we have implemented in grammar form dynamic programming algorithms that are used in biology, signal processing, and other fields to find the best match to a given specification, allowing for errors of substitution, deletion, and insertion, and minimizing distance metrics such as Levensheim distance[Kru83]. In general, the use of DCGs will make available to SPR a wide range of research and established techniques in logic-based approaches to uncertainty, *e.g.* "fuzzy" logic.

8 Signal Processing Grammars

Grammar-based approaches would never replace fast, deterministic algorithms for any operation as "standardized" as bar code reading. Rather, we have argued that a useful system development methodology is to rapidly prototype algorithms in grammar form, using DCGs as a kind of high-level specification language, and then to "tune" the grammars by porting appropriate computations to more efficient languages or even hardware[Sea90]. For instance, we have used grammars for writing executable specifications of complex dynamic programming algorithms in the DNA domain. Just as, in text processing applications it is possible to use grammars even at the lowest levels of feature extraction, and to later incorporate more conventional algorithms as appropriate, so it is possible to prototype even low-level numeric algorithms with DCGs.

We can illustrate this with grammars that deal with one-dimensional signals. Electrocardiograms, such as those shown in Figure 8, can clearly be modeled as strings of millivoltages over time. As such, this domain has been the subject of previous efforts using SPR[Hul87, PS87], and it is possible to quickly prototype DCGs that detect both normal and pathological patterns in such signals. The top level of such a working grammar is summarized below:

```
normal_sinus_rhythm --> ..., p_wave, ..., qrs_complex,
    ..., t_wave(normal).
myocardial_infarction(Age) --> ..., p_wave, [PQlevel], ...,
    bizarre_qrs, [STlevel], ..., t_wave(Polarity),
    {STlevel>PQlevel+10},
    {Polarity=inverted -> Age=recent; Age=old}.
p_wave --> wave(4,8,up). % width>4, height>8

t_wave(normal) --> wave(15,20,up).
t_wave(inverted) --> wave(15,10,down).

qrs_complex --> segment(Q,50,30),
    segment(R,-50,30), segment(S,50,30),
    {QRSwid is Q+R+S, QRSwid>6, QRSwid<12}.

bizarre_qrs --> segment(Q,50,45), segment(R,-50,45),
    segment(S,50,45), {QRSwid is Q+R+S, QRSwid>12}.
```

This grammar was able to parse the sample data given in Figure 8, and in fact the notations labeling each of the "landmarks" were actually generated by the parse.

However, such signals need not be thought of strictly as patterns, in using grammars for their analysis. We have demonstrated the use of DCGs for a

normal_sinus_rhythm

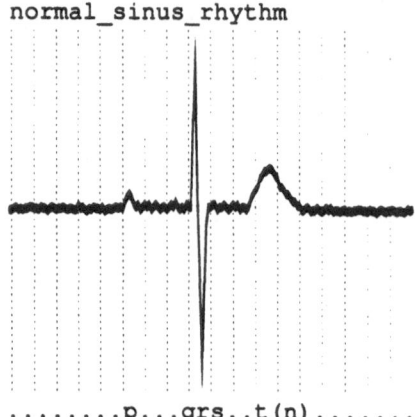

........p...qrs..t(n).......

myocardial_infarction(recent)

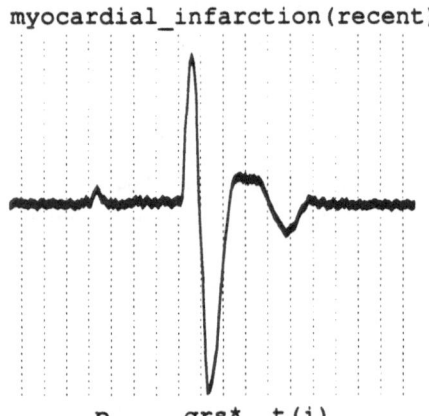

......p.....qrs*..t(i)......

Fig. 8. Simulated electrocardiograms.

number of "preprocessing" style computations[Sea90], such as the low-pass filter captured in the following code:

```
low_pass(RC,Last), [Out] --> [In],
                            {Out is (In+RC*Last)/(1+RC)},
                            low_pass(RC,Out).
low_pass(_,_) --> [].
```

This rule takes as parameters an RC time constant and the most recent output; it consumes a point from the input, calculates an output, and replaces that output on the input stream (by virtue of the context-sensitive left hand side of the rule) *after* calculating and replacing the remainder of the outputs recursively. This style of grammar, in which each point consumed is replaced, amounts to preprocessing of the input string with no net consumption of input; invocations of such rules involve a "reinterpretation" of the derivation operator, as follows:

```
operation --> Input/Output.
```

(Here, the infix slash separates the input list from an output that is simply the "remainder" list of the top-level DCG call.) Alternatively, such operations can be compositionally applied to the input by simply listing them in a rule body, perhaps to be followed uniformly by more typical pattern recognition grammar nonterminals[SN91], for instance:

```
electrocardiogram --> low_pass(5,0),
   ( normal_sinus_rhythm | myocardial_infarction(_) | ... ).
```

This technique is not limited to simple linear processing of input; we have shown, for example, how it is possible to capture the "butterfly" computations of a Fast Fourier Transform (FFT) quite succinctly in a DCG specification[Sea90]. Again it must be emphasized that such signal processing grammars are several orders of magnitude slower (*e.g.* just over 10 seconds for a 1024-point FFT) than the corresponding operations performed on modern digital signal processing hardware. However, in prototyping novel, *ad hoc* signal processing algorithms, they leave open the possibility of a uniform technical approach down to the lowest levels, which could then be "tuned" as appropriate, while still maintaining the overall grammar as an organizing paradigm. In higher-level SPR applications, not only would the intrinsic contextual nature of grammars add greater discrimination to the recognition process, but the ability to call expensive signal processing subroutines in a more focused and directed manner, *e.g.* on isolated "regions of interest" in the overall image or signal, only as called for by the grammar, may also lead to greater efficiency.

9 Conclusions

Our experience with DCGs in a wide range of SPR applications demonstrates that they are well-suited for rapid prototyping of grammar-based systems. The grammar can be retained at the higher levels of abstraction, as a controlling framework for the overall application, while incorporating other algorithms or reimplementing low-level operations using foreign function calls. For higher-level SPR parsing, DCGs are already quite efficient because of the attention paid by Prolog developers to fast abstract architectures for the basic operations of resolution-based theorem proving. Other opportunities for increasing efficiency may also be facilitated by the use of logic grammars — for example, the ready accessibility of OR-parallel execution, and of techniques such as chart parsing (which is easily implemented due to the ability of Prolog to alter its own rule base dynamically[Sea88]).

Aside from efficiency, the expressive power of logic grammars is a major advantage. The flexibility of logic variables — for instance, their ability to express arbitrary term structure and easily to carry it, even in partially instantiated form, through parses — leads to desirable properties, including the ability to maintain generative power. Combined with parameter attachment, we have found that it is possible to readily implement a wide variety of computational linguistic techniques, including some which are particularly associated with SPR; these include not only stochastic grammars, but also greater-than-context-free formalisms such as *indexed grammars*[Fu82, Sea89], which we have used to good effect in the DNA domain[Sea89]. Based on these experiences, we recommend the DCG formalism as a highly standardized, reasonably efficient, and extremely versatile foundation for SPR applications in general.

Acknowledgements

The database used in Section 5 was part of the "US Postal Service Office of Advanced Technology Handwritten ZIP Code Database (1987)" provided by the Office of Advanced Technology, US Postal Service. The authors thank Tim Finin and Charles Boohar for critical readings of an earlier version of the manuscript, and Adam Goldstein for implementing the original grammar of Section 5.

References

[Abr88]   H. Abramson. Metarules and an approach to conjunction in Definite Clause Translation Grammars: Some aspects of grammatical metaprogramming. In *Logic Programming: Proc. of the Fifth Int. Conf. and Symposium*, pages 233–248, 1988.

[ASM88]   W.H. Abdulla, A.O.M. Salleh, and A.H. Morad. A preprocessing algorithm for hand-written character recognition. *Pattern Recognition*, 7:13–18, 1988.

[Bra86]   I. Bratko. *Prolog Programming for Artificial Intelligence*. Addison-Wesley, 1986.

[BW79]   J.M. Brady and B.J. Wielinga. Reading the writing on the wall. In A.R. Hanson and E. Riseman, editors, *Computer Vision Systems*, pages 283–299. Academic Press, New York, 1979.

[DA84]   V. Dahl and H. Abramson. On Gapping Grammars. *Proc. of the Int. Conf. on Logic Programming*, 2:77–88, 1984.

[Fu82]   K.S. Fu. *Syntactic Pattern Recognition and Applications*. Prentice-Hall, Englewood Cliffs, New Jersey, 1982.

[HHS88]   L. Hirschman, W.C. Hopkins, and R. C. Smith. Or-parallel speed-up in natural language processing: A case study. In *Logic Programming: Proc. of the Fifth International Conf. and Symposium*. MIT Press, 1988.

[Hir86]   L. Hirschman. Conjunction in meta-restriction grammar. *Journal of Logic Programming*, 3:299–328, 1986.

[Hir88]   L. Hirschman. A meta-treatment of wh-constructions in English. *Proc. of META'88, Meta-Programming in Logic Programming*, 1988.

[HP86]   L. Hirschman and K. Puder. Restriction grammar: a Prolog implementation. In M Van Caneghem and DHD Warren, editors, *Logic Programming and Its Applications*, pages 244–261. Ablex Publishing, Norwood NJ, 1986.

[HPD+89]   L. Hirschman, M. Palmer, J. Dowding, M. Linebarger, R. Passonneau, F-M Lang, C. Ball, and C. Weir. The PUNDIT natural language processing system. In *Proc. of the IEEE 1989 AI Systems in Government Conf.*, 1989.

[Hul87]   J.J. Hull. Character recognition: The reading of text by computer. In S.C. Shapiro, editor, *Encyclopedia of Artificial Intelligence*, pages 82–88. Wiley-Interscience, New York, 1987.

[KHB89]   A. Kundu, Y. He, and P. Bahl. Recognition of handwritten word: First and second order hidden Markov model based approach. *Pattern Recognition*, 22(3):283–297, March 1989.

[Kru83]   J.B. Kruskal. An overview of sequence comparison. In D. Sankoff and J.B. Kruskal, editors, *Time Warps, String Edits, and Macromolecules: The Theory and Practice of String Comparison*, pages 1–44. Addison-Wesley, 1983.

[LBD+88] E.L. Lusk, R. Butler, T. Disz, R. Overbeek, R. Stevens, D.H.D. Warren, A. Calderwood, P. Szeredi, S. Haridi, P. Brand, and M. Carlsson. The Aurora OR-parallel Prolog system. *Proc. of the Intl. Conf. on Fifth Generation Computer Systems*, pages 819–830, 1988.

[Per81] F. Pereira. Extraposition Grammars. *Computational Linguistics*, 7:243–256, 1981.

[pos85] Specification for postal numeric encoding technique (POSTNET), August 1985.

[PS87] F. Pereira and S.M. Shieber. *Prolog and Natural Language Analysis*. Center for the Study of Language and Information, Stanford University, Stanford, Ca., 1987.

[PW80] F.C.N. Pereira and D. Warren. Definite Clause Grammars for language analysis – A survey of the fomalism and a comparison with augmented transition networks. *Artificial Intelligence*, 13:231–278, 1980.

[Sea88] D.B. Searls. Representing genetic information with formal grammars. *Proc. of the National Conf. of the American Assoc. for Artificial Intelligence*, 7:386–391, 1988.

[Sea89] D.B. Searls. Investigating the linguistics of DNA with Definite Clause Grammars. *Proc. of the North American Conf. on Logic Programming*, 1:189–208, 1989.

[Sea90] D. Searls. Signal processing with logic grammars. *Intelligent Systems Review*, 1(4):67–88, 1990.

[SN91] D. Searls and M. Noordeweir. Pattern-matching search of DNA sequences using logic grammars. to be published in *Proc. of the 7th IEEE Conf. on Artificial Intelligence Applications*, 1991.

[Sta87] E.P. Stabler, Jr. Restricting logic grammars with government-binding theory. *Computational Linguistics*, 13:1–10, 1987.

[ZS84] T.Y. Zhang and C.U. Suen. A fast parallel algorithm for thinning digital patterns. *Comm. of the ACM*, 27(3):236–239, 1984.

Document Image Defect Models

Henry S. Baird

AT&T Bell Laboratories, Computing Science Research Center,
600 Mountain Avenue, Murray Hill, NJ 07974, USA

A lack of explicit quantitative models of imaging defects due to printing, optics, and digitization has retarded progress in some areas of document image analysis, including syntactic and structural approaches. Establishing the essential properties of such models, such as completeness (expressive power) and calibration (closeness of fit to actual image populations) remain open research problems. Work-in-progress towards a parameterized model of local imaging defects is described, together with a variety of motivating theoretical arguments and empirical evidence. A pseudo-random image generator implementing the model has been built. Applications of the generator are described, including a polyfont classifier for ASCII and a single-font classifier for a large alphabet (Tibetan U-Chen), both of which which were constructed with a minimum of manual effort. Image defect models and their associated generators permit a new kind of image database which is explicitly parameterized and indefinitely extensible, alleviating some drawbacks of existing databases.

1 Introduction

Technical challenges in document image analysis arise, generally speaking, from three sources:

symbols: the set of idealized shapes that can occur, often in a hierarchy where simple symbols are assembled into more complex ones, at several levels of organization;

deformations: a range of shape variations that symbols are permitted to undergo, including geometric transformations (translation, rotation, scaling, stretching, etc.) and more complex or time-dependent distortions (*e.g.* due to the biomechanics of handwriting); and

imaging defects: imperfections in the image due to printing, optics, scanning, spatial quantization, binarization, etc.

This taxonomy, while useful, is somewhat arbitrary and may vary with the context. For example, in some applications a greatly deformed symbol is best regarded as a new symbol altogether: for example, the letter M, deformed by an extraordinarily large rotation, finally approaches W. Less obviously, a geometric transformation may be thought of as a deformation when it is large, but as an imaging defect when it is small: for example, the deformation that "grows" the roman R into its boldface variation **R** can be closely approximated by a small defect in binarization (due to blurring and thresholding). Nevertheless, in most applications there is a clear distinction between symbol formation (without respect to imaging) and image formation (without respect to symbols) — and it is this distinction that is the focus of this study.

Symbols and their deformations are the subjects of virtually all recent published research in document image analysis. Papers routinely exhibit examples of symbols, and often describe their expected deformations, but only rarely discuss the range of image defects that is tolerable. In effect, the great majority of papers assume that image defects can be neglected, or at least need not be analyzed quantitatively. Such an assumption may be justified in some applications: for example, it may permit an uncluttered exposition of the algorithm being studied. However, it is often obvious that there are classes of defects which can occur and will cause failure: and this raises the question of exactly when the method is likely to succeed.

Furthermore, when experimental trials are attempted, image defects are often found to play a critical role. Among symbolic-modeling techniques (including many syntactic and structural (SSPR) methods), image defects can trigger a rapid proliferation of slightly varying models, even when hybrid methods with statistical or Markov characteristics are used. This proliferation of models can have unpleasant effects on the space and time complexity of algorithms for recognition. I believe it is fair to say that if it were not for this problem, accurate and even fast recognition of isolated machine-printed multi-font characters would have been achieved decades ago.

Problems due to image defects often arise quite early, when extracting the most elementary shapes in the symbol hierarchy. It is not surprising that purely syntactic chain-code models (of perfectly digitized lines, squares, etc) are rarely applicable to real images — but on the other hand it is striking that reported vectorization methods are rarely based on an explicit model of imaging defects.

The inference of SSPR models, whether carried out manually or automatically, is complicated by image defects. In exact-match SSPR methods, it is often assumed that an exhaustive set of symbolic models can be specified. If defects were negligible, it might be possible to enumerate these by hand; but often in practice new cases arise throughout a long series of experimental trials.

These observations suggest that imaging defects threaten the effectiveness of many techniques for document image analysis, and that they have not yet been studied as systematically as they deserve. I suggest that an appropriate research program should include at least the following topics:

- *Parameterization:* a defect model should ideally be expressed as a function of a small number of parameters, presumably for the most part real numbers.

I will propose a preliminary model of this kind, suitable for use in studies of text, line-drawings, music, and other classes of documents.

- *Completeness*, or expressive power: this measures the probability that, given any particular defective image, there exists some choice of model parameters (and some randomization) that will duplicate the image. In this study, I will address this point only qualitatively, by exhibiting a characteristic range of effects.

- *Calibration:* the degree to which a distribution defined on the model parameters fits a given population of defective images. I have been able to measure the distribution of a few parameters; for some of the rest, I offer theoretical considerations to motivate a plausible choice.

- *Simulation.* A defect model, together with a distribution on its parameter space, can be used to generate representative sets of image samples pseudo-randomly. In some cases it may be possible to infer models from these sets automatically. This approach may be particularly well suited to SSPR methods that use hybrids of symbolic and statistical matching. I will discuss several exercises of this kind later in the paper.

- *Enumeration.* One interesting potential use of these models is to support the automatic computation of *all possible* symbolic prototypes implied by a given feature-extraction system. I am not aware of any successful effort of this kind: this may be a challenging and rewarding arena for future research. Of course, characterizing the effects of imaging defects using purely analytical means may be a difficult or impossible task. By contrast, deformations are often handled analytically by a variety of efficient and robust normalization algorithms, applied either to isolated symbols or partial structural matches.

2 A Model of Imaging Defects

In this section I describe work in progress towards a parameterized model of local imaging defects. I hope it will serve to stimulate research into more complete and fully calibrated models. It is based on approximations to the physics of the printing and imaging process ([Sch86, Eks84]).

The idealized input symbol can be thought of as a bilevel image at effectively infinite resolution. Illumination intensity is in the range [0.0,1.0], with the convention that white=0 and black=1. The model was developed for use on images of hand-written or machine-printed characters. Some parameters of the model are in typographical units: a *point* equals 1/72 inch; an *em* is equal to the nominal size of the text (usually the closest permissible vertical spacing, in points). It should be clear, however, that the model is adaptable to a wide variety of symbol types.

Resolution: The degraded image will be spatially quantized. In practice, this is the result of both the absolute size of the symbol and the scanning digitizing resolution, which I in fact specify separately as *size* (in points), and *resolution* (in pixels/inch). For experiments in character recognition I use a distribution of sizes that is uniform on [5,14] point, at a resolution of 300 pixels/inch (roughly equivalent to [10,30] pixels/x-height). Here are seven examples from 5 to 11 point, scaled to the same absolute size for clarity.

Blur: The point-spread (or, impulse response) function of the combined printing and imaging process is modeled as a circularly symmetric Gaussian filter with a standard error of *blur* in units of output pixel size. Note that *blur* < 0.7 implies effectively zero cross-talk between non-8-connected pixels: thus 0.7 may be close to the optimal hardware design for bilevel scanners, according to a theoretical study of the trade-off between spatial and intensity quantization [LPW87]. It is often difficult to find a manufacturer who will specify the point-spread function of his document scanner. For experiments in character recognition I assume *blur* is distributed normally with mean $m = 0.7$ and standard error $e = 0.3$. Here are seven images, illustrating the effects of blur parameter values $\{m - 3e, m - 2e, m - e, m, m + em + 2e, m + 3e\}$ (this set of values is also used in other illustrations below, unless noted).

Threshold: Binarization is modeled as a test on each pixel: if its intensity $\geq threshold$, the pixel is black. A threshold of 0.25 guarantees that a stroke that is one output-pixel wide will not be broken under the mean blur of 0.7. For experiments on high-resolution prototypes I let threshold vary, from image to image, normally with mean 0.25 and standard error 0.04. On coarsely quantized input, other choices are appropriate (for an example, see the Applications section).

Sensitivity: Each pixel's photo-receptor sensitivity is randomized in two stages: for each char, *sensitivity* is selected, in units of intensity $\in [0,1]$; then, for each pixel, a sensitivity adjustment is chosen randomly, distributed normally with mean 0 and standard error — *sensitivity*—, and added to each pixel's intensity. For experiments in character recognition I let *sensitivity* vary from image to image, normally with mean 0.125 and standard error 0.04.

R R R R R R R

Jitter: I assume that the arrangement of the output pixel photo-receptors is an only nominally square grid: their actual location is allowed to vary slightly, in two stages: for each symbol, *jitter* is specified, in units of output pixel size; then, for each pixel in the symbol, a vector offset *(x,y)* is chosen (each component independently) from the normal distribution having mean 0 and standard error — *jitter*—. I have not yet been able to measure this directly, but it is clearly unlikely that two pixel centers will touch. Therefore, for experiments in character recognition I let *jitter* vary, from image to image, normally with mean 0.2 and standard error 0.1. The effects are often subtle.

R R R R R R R

Skew: The symbol may rotate (about a given fiducial point) by a *skew* angle (in degrees). In experiments on over 1000 pages of books, magazines, and letters, placed on a flatbed document scanner by hand with ordinary care, I have observed a distribution of angles that is approximately normal with a mean 0 and a standard error 0.7. The actual distribution is somewhat long-tailed: absolute skew angles greater than 2 degrees occur more often than in a true Gaussian. For experiments in character recognition I use a distribution with twice this standard error.

R R R R R R R

Width: Width variations are modeled by a multiplicative parameter *x-scale*, that stretches the image horizontally about the symbol's center. Measurements on low-quality images, such as produced by FAX machines, suggest that this is approximately normal with mean 1.0 and standard error 0.05. However, for experiments in character recognition I use a distribution uniform in the interval [0.85,1.15], for a reason peculiar to the application: I wish to model a range of font deformations (the "condensed" and "expanded" font varieties). Here are samples spaced uniformly across the range.

R R R R R R R

Height: Height variations are modeled by a multiplicative parameter *y-scale*, that stretches the image vertically about the baseline. Measurements on low-quality images, such as produced by FAX machines, suggest that this is approximately normal with mean 1.0 and standard error 0.05. However, for experiments in character recognition I use a normal distribution with mean 0 and standard error 0.02.

R R R R R R R

Baseline: In machine-printed text, the height of a symbol above the conventional baseline (or, in some writing systems, below a top-line) is often significant: this *baseline* parameter is in units of ems. In measurements on over 120,000 characters from letterpress books (printed somewhat more erratically than is usual), a long-tailed normal distribution was again observed, with a mean 0 and a standard error 0.03. For experiments in character recognition I use a distribution with twice this standard error.

R R R R R R R

Kerning: The parameter *kern* varies the horizontal placement of the image with respect to the output pixel grid. Of course, in most writing systems the horizontal position is irrelevant for segmented symbol recognition. The motivation to avoid systematic digitizing artifacts. This is easily accomplished by letting it vary uniformly in [-0.5,0.5], in units of output pixel size; here are examples spaced uniformly across the range. The effects are often subtle.

R R R R R R R

3 A Pseudo-Random Generator

I have built an image generator that simulates this defect model. Given a bilevel image and a set of model parameters, it computes a degraded bilevel image. It can also generate any specified number of images, chosen pseudo-randomly from the defect distribution model; in this case, the parameters are assumed to be independent random variables. For input, I have used high-resolution original typographical descriptions (ideal prototypes at effectively infinite resolution) as well as samples selected from images of printed text. The results are most interesting when the input is an image of a large, cleanly printed original example; the model may require some adjustment on poor-quality input.

For speed, the skew, baseline, height, and width transformations are performed on a boundary representation. Then, it is converted to a high-resolution bitmap, and the point-spread function is applied at each computed pixel center;

this is the most expensive step. Each resulting pixel intensity value is modified by the sensitivity adjustment, and binarized by comparison with the threshold.

The image defect generator is written in the C programming language. The pseudo-random number generator uses an additive-feedback algorithm [Zei69, Mar84] in a portable, machine-independent implementation. Normal distributions are truncated to 0 farther than three standard errors from the mean.

To illustrate the range of defects that can be simulated, we show a set of images at 5 point, in Figure 1. Each line holds images whose Mahalanobis distances (Euclidean distance from the mean, scaled component-wise by standard error) lie in the range shown. Baseline, jitter, and kerning are not included in the Mahalanobis distance.

Fig. 1. Pseudo-randomly generated samples in various ranges of mahalanobis-distance from the mean of the defect distribution.

I invite the reader to judge from the examples in Figure 1 the degree to which the model is complete. It is inevitable that an image defect model will approximate the physics of the many stages of printing and imaging. However, it is essential that it be capable of expressing a wide range of commonly occurring effects. I hope these examples will stimulate discussion of categories of defects that the model cannot yet express.

4 Applications

I now discuss two applications of the generator.

The first is a "uniformly fair" multi-font classifier for machine-printed ASCII. For each of 39 fonts, for each of 10 sizes (from 5 to 14 point), and for each of the 94 symbols in the printable-ASCII set (where available in the font), I generated 25 images, for a total of 804,500. Using half of this database (the odd point sizes), I inferred a classifier using the method of [Bai88a]. This was tested on the other half of the database. Half of the errors are due to confusions that are arguably inevitable in a multi-font environment:

```
11I|!J  OO  ' '   ^~
```

Ignoring these, the success rates were 98.21% top choice and 99.45% within the top 5 choices. If the 6-point test samples are also ignored, the success rates are 99.19% top choice and 99.87% in top 5.

When performance measures such as these are quoted in technical papers, it can be difficult for the reader to judge whether they represent a significant advance over competing methods. In the present case, however, a reader is capable of replicating the test since I have listed the alphabet of symbols, an image defect model has been specified, and the fonts are commercially available (the author will supply their names on request). Only the seeds of the pseudo-random number generator remain unspecified, but the large scale of the test (over 400,000 images) will permit statistically significant comparisons no matter what seed was used.

On another point, high top-5 accuracy scores promise excellent accuracy when contextual constraints can be exploited. In particular, they allow the use of fast data-driven contextual analysis algorithms, which require *uniformly shallow* accuracy: that is, the correct interpretation for all classes must be found with high probability in a short list of alternatives supplied by the classifier. This is a more stringent standard than average top-choice or even average top-k correct. An important factor in achieving uniformly shallow accuracy is the use of training sets that are uniform in a strong sense: they should contain an equal number of samples of all symbols, over all fonts, and distorted by the same distribution of image defects. Such a *uniformly fair* sample set can only be provided by an image defect generator: attempts to collect such a set from actually occurring image populations are futile.

The second example illustrates the use of the generator to read exotic large-alphabet languages with a minimum of manual effort. A 441-page machine-printed Tibetan-to-Tibetan dictionary [R82] has been translated into ASCII with an estimated 95% accuracy, after two weeks of work by one person. The work was performed by Mr. Reid Fossey, a student of the Tibetan language, while visiting Bell Laboratories. Although trained in Tibetan, he had no prior exposure to the OCR system — and the system had received no prior training on Tibetan. I provided the tools used by Mr. Fossey. Only one change in these was required, to accommodate Tibetan's U-chen (top-line) typographic convention.

Mr. Fossey first acquired bilevel images of all the pages in the book, using a flatbed document scanner at 400 pixel/inch resolution. Next, the images were analyzed fully automatically into columns of lines of symbols, using the method of [Bai88b]. Then Mr. Fossey selected sample images of each symbol in each font style. The number of these was held to a minimum, since at most one image of each distinct symbol was required, even if it occurred at more than one size. Dr. Kurt Keutzer, a researcher in computer science at Bell Labs and also a student of the Tibetan language, performed an additional pass of training on the text to correct for oversights in selection and labeling. In Figure 2 we show twelve "original" images of the 'sku' character, selected by Mr. Fossey.

For each of these symbols, 75 distorted images (over a range of three sizes)

Fig. 2. Twelve original Tibetan character images (symbol "sku"), selected from the digitized pages.

were generated to make up the training set. Figure 3 show twelve pseudo-randomly generated training instances, using the first of the images above as the prototype:

Fig. 3. Twelve pseudo-randomly generated images, using as the prototype the first shown in Figure 2.

To compensate for the coarsely quantized input, the *threshold* parameter is Gaussian with mean 0.5 and standard error 0.4. The randomized samples show a somewhat wider range of defects than the originals.

The next few steps were completely automatic: these included the inference of a classifier, the classification of the entire document, and the translation of the symbols into user-specified ASCII (the Wylie transliteration was used). The classifier technology [Bai88a] uses a hybrid of structural shape analysis and statistical decision theory, and requires a large (> 50) and representative training set for good results.

The last step was the manual proofreading of the computer-recognized text. The set of distinct symbols encountered in the dictionary numbered 438, in two slightly different font styles. Altogether, 61,124 symbols were translated, not counting punctuation. Fossey and Keutzer, after proofreading a fraction of the output, report an accuracy of approximately 95% (not counting spacing, punctuation, or special characters used for transliterating Sanskrit).

5 Discussion

There is clearly work to be done to establish the completeness and calibration of this experimental image defect model. Still, it has already proven useful, and may be helpful as a starting point for discussion.

The fact that images generated by the model possess explicit parameterizations opens up interesting new ways to study pattern recognition methods. In principle, it should be possible systematically to explore the limitations of any given pattern recognition algorithm by regression analysis on the parameters of images on which the algorithm fails. In some cases this experience may suggest algorithm improvements; in other cases, it may at least permit *compensatory training*, in which specially designed training sets, with a greater-than-usual occurrence of troublesome defects, are used to reduce the error rate.

Standardized image databases, available to all researchers, have played an important role in driving pattern recognition technology. The existence of image defect generators makes possible an interesting new class of *implicit databases* which are indefinitely extensible. Instead of sharing a finite set of images, researchers would share a model (and its generator), so that while they are experimenting on the same distribution of images, they are not limited by an arbitrarily fixed sample size. This can be a significant advantage. For example, present neural-net learning algorithms require a large number of presentations of training images for convergence, often many times the number of distinct images available, and therefore there is often concern that the networks may be undertrained. More generally, while experienced practitioners are careful to use distinct training and test sets when measuring the performance of an algorithm, they are often forced by lack of data into a subtler but similar methodological trap: while refining the algorithm manually, they reuse the same (training and testing) data repeatedly. Ideally, they should be able to throw away each set and start from scratch: an image defect generator offers a way to do this.

The obstacles to achieving a consensus on the details of image defect models (which may be considerable, and both technical and political) should not discourage the attempt, for several reasons. The present state of affairs, in which image defects are usually ignored, is unrealistic and unwise. Explicit, quantitative models provide a foundation for scientific understanding and may be the only possible basis for reliable engineering. Investigating these models is an essential step towards the goal of mapping the range of applicability of pattern recognition methods as applied to document images.

Acknowledgements

The *jitter* parameter was suggested by George Nagy. I am grateful for stimulating discussions with him, Theo Pavlidis, and Sargur Srihari.

References

[Bai88a] H. S. Baird, "Feature Identification for Hybrid Structural/Statistical Pattern Classification," *Computer Vision, Graphics, & Image Processing* 42, pp. 318–333, 1988.

[Bai88b] H. S. Baird, "Global-to-Local Layout Analysis," *Proc. IAPR Workshop on Syntactic and Structural Pattern Recognition*, Pont-á-Mousson, France, 12–14 September, 1988.

[Eks84] M. P. Ekstrom, *Digital Image Processing Techniques*, Academic Press (Orlando, 1984).

[FL90]   R. Fossey and P. Lofting, "The Typestyle Jockey: Putting the Horse Out Front in Devanagari and Tibetan," *Nordic Institute of Asian Studies Report,* Copenhagen, pp. 5–30, 1990.

[LPW87] D. Lee, T. Pavlidis, and G. W. Wasilkowski, "A Note on the Trade-off between Sampling and Quantization in Signal Processing," *J. of Complexity,* Vol. 3, pp. 359–371, 1987.

[Mar84] G. Marsaglia, "A Current View of Random Number Generators," Keynote address, *Computer Science and Statistics 16th Symp. on the Interface,* Atlanta, March 1984.

[Sch86] W. F. Schreiber, *Fundamentals of Electronic Imaging Systems,* Springer Series Information Science 15, Springer–Verlag (Berlin, 1986).

[R82]   Tshe bDang rNam rGyal, ed., *Dag Yig Ma Nor Lam bZang* (The Excellent Path to Wealth Dictionary). Lhasa: Mi Rigs dPe sKrun Khang (Humanity Publishing House), 1982.

[Zei69] N. Zeirler, "Primitive Trinomials Whose Degree is a Mersenne Exponent," *Inf. Control,* 15, 1969.

IAPR 1990
Workshop on SSPR

SSPR'90 Workshop Report

Henry S. Baird and Lawrence O'Gorman

AT&T Bell Laboratories, 600 Mountain Avenue, Murray Hill, NJ 07974, USA

The International Association for Pattern Recognition (IAPR) Workshop on Syntactic and Structural Pattern Recognition (SSPR), was held in Murray Hill, New Jersey, USA, during 13-15 June 1990. This was the most recent in a bi-yearly series of workshops sponsored by IAPR Technical Committee No. 2 (TC-2) on SSPR, that historically has attracted theoreticians from Europe, Japan, and the U.S. SSPR methods emphasize the use of formal *a priori* models of the symbolic content of images or signals. For many types of complex printed and handwritten documents, SSPR methods are natural and helpful. For this reason, the organizers decided to place special emphasis on applications to document image analysis, and invited IAPR TC-11 on Text Processing to co-sponsor the workshop.

The principal organizer and Program Committee chair was Henry Baird. Lawrence O'Gorman was the local arrangements chair. Alberto Sanfeliu, the chair of IAPR TC-2, and Rejéan Plamondon, the chair of TC-11, helped arrange for IAPR advance funds and scholarship grants. Sargur Srihari and the SUNY Buffalo administration helped apply for and administer a grant from the U. S. National Science Foundation. Roger Mohr, the organizer of SSPR'88, assisted in many ways. Kazuhiko Yamamoto coordinated publicity for the workshop in Japan. The other members of the Program Committee were: Horst Bunke, Robert Haralick, George Nagy, Theo Pavlidis, J. C. Simon, Ching Y. Suen, Ju-Wei Tai, and Eiichi Tanaka. Additional referees included Philip Chou and Karl Tombre. AT&T Bell Laboratories donated secretarial, printing, mailing, and telephone resources.

SSPR'90 was an intensive, 100%-participation, open-call workshop. Every attendee was required to submit a full paper or abstract. Full papers were reviewed by three referees from the Program Committee. Abstracts (restricted to one page) were selected on the basis of relevance, and as evidence that the attendee was actively working in the field. Thirty refereed full papers were accepted for long presentations (often after substantial revisions), and 27 abstracts were accepted for shorter presentations.

The 64 attendees represented 12 countries: about 1/4 from Asia, 1/4 from Europe, and 1/2 from North America. A complete list of the attendees is given at the end of this section. Fully one-third were industrial researchers: this large

industrial participation, somewhat unusual for the SSPR workshop, is evidence
of the commercial growth of document image processing and the relevance of
research to the next generation of industrial systems.

Over half of the schedule was devoted to panel discussions and working
groups. The workshop was organized into morning plenary sessions with talks
and panels, and afternoons for breakouts into smaller working groups. The plenary session topics were: Syntactic Methods, Syntactic Applications, Image Feature Extraction, Handwriting, 2D and 3D Structure, Printed Documents, Graphics and Technical Drawings, and Music Notation. There were ten working group
sessions in total, five held on each of the first and last afternoons. These were parallel sessions, each attended by ten to twenty people, and the topics were similar
to those of the plenary sessions. The working group sessions offered researchers
an opportunity to discuss face-to-face and at length their current research and
directions for the future. Each working group was assigned the task of drawing
up two lists, of open problems and proven methods. Summaries of some of these
discussions are printed in the following chapters of this section.

The morning of the first day consisted of sessions on syntactic pattern recognition. A provocative talk by Kakuma and Tanaka entitled "A pessimistic view of
syntactic pattern recognition" led up to a spirited panel discussion among Theo
Pavlidis, Dov Dori, Horst Bunke, and Eiichi Tanaka. The debate attracted many
comments by the audience. A majority of the panel members seemed to agree
that while in some cases it is undeniably useful, it is by no means a panacea.

The plenary sessions on the second day dealt with extraction of features for
pattern recognition, recognition of symbols, and use of features for handwriting
recognition and 2D and 3D structure. On that afternoon, attendees were invited
to visit the Murray Hill facility of AT&T Bell Laboratories, for four demonstrations: printed page reading (Henry Baird), handwritten numeral recognition by
neural networks (Yann Le Cun), equation recognition (Philip Chou), and page
layout analysis for an electronic library system (Larry O'Gorman).

The invited speaker that evening at the workshop banquet was Gary Herring,
Director of the Office of Advanced Technology of the U.S. Postal Service. He
described the large scale and great difficulty of the document-image analysis
tasks facing the world's postal services, and challenged the audience to tackle
them.

On the final day, plenary sessions focused on systems-level pattern recognition
problems, including printed-document, technical-drawing, and music-notation
recognition. This latter topic was new to many of the attendees and proved to be
especially interesting since it brought together many issues discussed in isolation
earlier. This was the first time that representatives of as many as four research
teams working on music recognition had met together. The final five working
groups met in the afternoon; then, in a general plenary session, a representative
of each of the ten working groups summarized their discussions.

SSPR'90 gave its attendees an excellent opportunity to meet and share ideas
with their counterparts, and to become acquainted with new work. In addition
to the full daily program, there was ample opportunity for informal socializing.
It was generally agreed that the fields of syntactic and structural pattern recog-

nition are healthy and making steady progress on important problems, and that document image analysis is an important and growing application area for these methods. The next SSPR workshop will be held in France in the fall of 1992.

Many of the attendees were assisted by grants to the workshop from the IAPR and the U.S. National Science Foundation. A total of $1800 in IAPR funds was granted to attendees as scholarships. The U.S. National Science Foundation provided $7185 for travel and administrative expenses. All scholarship requests from students were satisfied before any from principal investigators. The workshop recovered all of its advance funds and operating costs, and was able to pass on a small profit ($275) to the 1992 SSPR Workshop.

SSPR'90 appears to have been the first international technical meeting devoted predominantly to research into document image analysis, in the broad modern definition of the field. In view of the breadth of topics represented, it may seem remarkable that most of the papers strongly interested most attendees. Several people commented, with a sense of discovery, that the document image analysis field seems to offer a coherent set of interrelated problems.

Towards the end of the workshop, the idea of an full-scale international conference on the subject was floated. The following week, at the 10th ICPR in Atlantic City, NJ, a formal proposal to this effect was presented to the IAPR Board by Robert Haralick and Ching Y. Suen: after discussion, it was voted on and carried. Later, TC-PAMI of the IEEE Computer Society agreed to co-sponsor the conference. It will be known as the *First Int'l Conf. on Document Analysis and Recognition (ICDAR'91)*, and will be held in September 1991 in St. Malo, France, and again in 1993 in Japan.

Document Analysis: SSPR'90 Working Group Report

Junichi Kanai[1] and Andreas Dengel[2]

[1] Department of Electrical, Computer, and Systems Engineering,[3]
Rensselaer Polytechnic Institute, Troy, NY 12180-3590, USA
[2] German Research Center for Artificial Intelligence (DFKI),
Kaiserslautern Site, P.O. Box 20 80, D–6750 Kaiserslautern, Germany

This report summarizes the discussions of the Working Group on the Document Analysis of the IAPR 1990 Workshop on Syntactic and Structural Pattern Recognition, Murray Hill, NJ, 13-15 June 1990. Thirteen researchers from three countries participated: T. Bayer, S. C. Chennubhotla, A. Dengel, H. Fujisawa, J. Kanai, R. Kasturi, G. Nagy, L. O'Gorman, M. Okamoto, L. Spitz, S. Tsujimoto, M. Viswanathan, and M. Yamada. Andreas Dengel moderated the discussion, and Junichi Kanai served as scribe.

The participants were divided almost evenly between private industry and universities (and one non-profit laboratory). The group first spent a few minutes identifying mature research topics and the remaining time was spent discussing knowledge acquisition and representation schemes in document analysis.

1 Mature Research Topics

In the 80's, research in document analysis has concentrated on discrimination of text regions from non-text regions on a page. Some techniques further segment text regions into text-lines and characters. The members of this working group agreed that many of these techniques were mature enough to be used in commercial products. However, the extraction of characters in graphic regions, such as technical drawings and maps, needs more work.

Another mature area is the Optical Character Recognition (OCR) of detached (isolated) printed symbols. Many systems are already commercially available for this. But the recognition of hand-written characters and printed symbols in graphic regions is still difficult to solve. This problem arises in the field of address block location and recognition on structured documents, such as commercial printings on flats or parcels.

2 Knowledge Acquisition and Representation

The discussion focused mainly on knowledge acquisition and representation for the analysis of the logical structure of a document. It was assumed that the

---

[3] Presently with ISRI, University of Nevada, Las Vegas, Nevada 89154, USA

domain of knowledge is limited to a narrow class of document, such as business letters and technical reports. The knowledge acquisition process consists of two tasks: to identify features of logical objects, and to recognize relationships among logical objects, such as the arrangement of logical objects. The domain knowledge can be obtained from the following sources:

1. International standards, style manuals, author's kit, and printer's guidelines.
2. Macros (ms and me for troff and LaTeX) and style sheets in word processing and typesetting programs.
3. Training (sample) data.

However, some members were skeptical about the usefulness of "standard styles" because writers and typesetters have considerable artistic freedom and often ignore guidelines. Thus, one very important question is how to acquire all different layouts to direct feature adjustment. In addition, it is not clear how much knowledge is needed for a layout analysis of documents.

Almost all the members of the working group had studied general cases first and then used exceptions to improve the performance of their systems. A member pointed out that this approach may not improve the performance of a system because new knowledge may conflict with old knowledge.

The members agreed that parametric knowledge, such as type sizes and line spacings used to typeset a logical object, can be interactively or automatically obtained from sources, such as sample pages. On the other hand, generalization of the knowledge of logical objects and structures is extremely difficult. Therefore, machine learning that induces structures of documents is an open problem.

Pros and cons of some knowledge representation methods were discussed, including:

1. The declarative approach is an ideal way to represent the domain knowledge. However, backtracking in the inference process is computationally too costly to implement in a practical system.
2. The procedural approach and the heuristic approach are computationally effective ways to represent the domain knowledge. However, these approaches may not clearly separate the domain knowledge from the inference mechanism.
3. To represent a variety of formats of document objects, such as table of contents of different journals, the syntactic approach is theoretically effective. The effectiveness of this approach has not yet been confirmed.

Finally, the members agree that the knowledge of documents is not enough to solve some problems. For example, the reading order of an article typeset in multicolumn format may not be uniquely determined without understanding the text, and the semantic analysis of portions of a document, such as section titles, simplifies the classification process. The roles of natural language understanding techniques must be examined.

3 New Areas of Interest

Besides problems related to the knowledge of documents, the following problems were identified as new areas of interest. Current research has concentrated on extraction and classification of documents objects, but has neglected to develop user-interfaces that let users access digitized documents (document objects). To develop document retrieval systems and document browsing systems, the following problems must be solved.

1. A document representation scheme must be developed.
2. The reading order of a document must be preserved.
3. Logical relationships among document objects must be represented. For example, a citation and the corresponding entries in a bibliography must be connected.
4. External connections may be needed. For example, an entry in a bibliography may be connected with the document itself.

Another area is analysis of pages printed in color. Documents are traditionally printed using black ink on a sheet of white paper, so that most of the research treats a page as a binary image. Color photos in magazines and news papers, and colored graphs and charts in business reports are becoming more common every day. Furthermore, color laser printers and color digital copiers increase the use of color in documents. Hence, document analysis techniques must be extended to color images.

4 Summary

The working group concluded that layout analysis techniques have matured to the point where they are commercially usable. The research interest has shifted from extraction and classification of layout objects to the analysis of logical structures of printed documents. Since a document object can be typeset in a variety of formats (styles), knowledge acquisition and representation schemes are currently the main interest in research.

Character Recognition: SSPR'90 Working Group Report

Thomas Bayer[1], Jonathan Hull[2], and George Nagy[3]

[1] Daimler-Benz Research Center, Wilhelm-Runge-Strasse 11, D-7900 Ulm, Germany
[2] Department of Computer Science, 226 Bell Hall, SUNY at Buffalo, Amherst, NY 14260, USA
[3] Department of Electrical, Computer, and Systems Engineering, Rensselaer Polytechnic Institute, Troy, NY 12180-3590, USA

This report summarizes the discussions of the Working Group on Character Recognition of the IAPR 1990 Workshop on Syntactic and Structural Pattern Recognition, Murray Hill, NJ, 13-15 June 1990. The participants were: H. Baird, T. Bayer, H. Fujisawa, T. K. Ho, J. Hull, T. Itagaki, D. Lee, S. Liebowitz, O. Matan, G. Nagy, T. Pavlidis, and S. Srihari. George Nagy moderated the discussion and Thomas Bayer prepared this report based on notes by Nagy, Jonathan Hull, and himself.

It was not easy to agree that any problem in this field is definitely solved. Perhaps this is one: on a small number of known fonts of the printed Latin alphabet, at bodytext sizes (≥ 8 point), under moderate distortions, and in a controlled environment, it should be possible to achieve better than 99.9% top-choice accuracy using a variety of well-understood techniques including dictionary context. However, it's important not to forget that even a 99.99% recognition rate is still unacceptably low for many applications.

It was considerably easier to draw up a list of open problems.

1 Digitizing Resolution

Postal OCR systems use a resolution of 200 ppi; however, 300 ppi seems to have become the standard in office applications. Quite obviously, you need more pixels per inch (ppi), if you change to smaller fonts. Some participants felt that to read 8 point type very well, at least 400 ppi is necessary. In addition to distortions that occur at low resolution, characters will also tend to merge more often, triggering a cascade of problems for later stages. According to studies by Prof. Pavlidis [CVPR'86] OCR recognition rates increase up to 500 ppi, depending of course somewhat on the type of recognition algorithm. When using template matching, performance can actually decrease with increasing resolution, since the high resolution exaggerates features that are detrimental to matching.

2 Sample Image Databases

OCR research is strongly influenced by the availability of large databases of scanned text. It was pointed out that the IEEE has recently begun a pilot project to disseminate their publications in electronic form. This is done by scanning pages at 300 ppi and storing the binarized image in compressed form on CD-Rom. This database may provide an important experimental environment as well as an application domain for OCR research.

3 Distortion Modeling

A common technique for adapting recognition algorithms to distorted patterns is to train the system on large sample sets. However, this technique is time consuming and expensive since the patterns must be collected and each pattern must be labeled. An alternative technique is to analytically model noise so that, starting from a prototype of each class, an arbitrarily large set of samples can be inferred automatically. The advantage is obvious: no time consuming collection of a sample set and a very easy labeling process. However, both techniques have to model a truly representative set of actual samples, else the methodology is suspect — and it is often difficult to make convincing arguments that any given set is or is not representative.

4 Non-zero Skew Angles

The existence of even small amounts of skew (rotation) can be troublesome to text recognition algorithms. In commercial systems this is currently a severe problem. In handwriting recognition skew normalization is as necessary as normalization of size and aspect ratio. Some approaches are available to de-skew a complete document. However, they only work successfully in specialized applications, such as accurately printed documents where there a single dominant skew orientation.

5 Style Consistency

The detection of the font style, point size, etc. of a text is an obvious way to improve the capabilities of text recognition algorithms. This would allow for hundreds of fonts to be used for training but retain the recognition accuracy and potential speed of a system that uses a small number of fonts. This appears to be a promising but hitherto almost neglected topic.

6 Locally Adaptive Algorithms

Text recognition algorithms that can be readily (ideally fully automatically) adapted to specific constraints are interesting. For example, say you have a recognition system trained on three fonts. If a fourth font is added to the system, recognition performance should not decrease. So far, there is little to nothing published on this issue.

7 Contextual Information

This subject has attracted attention for quite some time, and many useful techniques have been developed. However, specific techniques may require information not provided by current methods. For example, syntactic analysis of languages has been shown useful in some domains. However, only a few syntactic models have been exploited for OCR. The utilization of semantics of languages has been even more limited.

8 Feature Selection

The general problem of feature subset selection is well known in pattern recognition. An area of current interest not covered by most classic techniques is the dynamic selection of the most useful features based on the characteristics of an image.

9 Combination of Recognition Techniques

It has been observed that a series of classifiers each based on a specific limited feature set can be applied in parallel to yield performance that is potentially better than using one classifier based on all the features. An open problem is how to effect the combination to achieve performance consistently superior to all the individual classifiers, for any sufficiently rich mixture of classifiers.

10 Should 100% Top-Choice Accuracy Be The Goal?

On isolated characters, it may not be possible efficiently to achieve close to 100% correct recognition rate if noise introduced by scanning and preprocessing is too great. Such noise can degrade even human performance to 80%. However, under the same conditions, people can achieve 100% correct when word context is provided. Therefore, it might be sufficient for isolated-character recognition algorithms to exhibit a peak correct recognition rate of only, say, 80% on such data, so long as it achieves much higher accuracy *in top k*, for small $k > 1$ (or some similar measure), so that the remaining errors can be corrected by contextual postprocessing.

Line Drawings, Feature Extraction, and Symbol Recognition: SSPR'90 Working Group Report

Patrick S. P. Wang[1] and Dov Dori[2]

[1] MIT AI Lab, Room NE 4-815, 545 Technology Square, Cambridge, MA 02139, USA
[2] Department of Computer Science, The University of Kansas, Lawrence, Kansas 66045, USA

This report summarizes the discussions of the Working Group on the Line Drawing, Feature Extraction, and Symbol Recognition, of the IAPR 1990 Workshop on Syntactic and Structural Pattern Recognition, Murray Hill, NJ, 13-15 June 1990. The somewhat awkward mix of topics was, nevertheless, very popular: nineteen people attended, six from Japan, three from the UK, two from Germany, two from France, one from Korea, and the rest from the USA. The discussion moderator was Dov Dori, and Patrick Wang served as scribe.

First, we drew up a list of problems involving line-drawing analysis, from our own experience:

- Engineering drawing recognition;
- Music notation recognition: broken lines, overlapping symbols;
- Symbol recognition, including printed and handwritten characters, zipcodes, check courtesy amounts;
- Diagram analysis;
- Map and facilities-drawing understanding;
- Geometry conversion;
- Flow-chart recognition;
- Signature and fingerprint identification;
- 3D image reconstruction from 2D drawings; and
- Mathematical morphology applications.

There was broad agreement that, for a variety of reasons, most researchers thought of the problems as occurring a series of "levels" of representation, starting with the raw image (purely iconic) and ending with the final interpretation (largely or entirely symbolic).

There was general agreement that most line-drawing analysis still occurs in two "classical" stages: some kind of skeletonization, followed by some kind of vectorization. This raised many questions:

- Is there a "best" method?
- Are there any robust methods?
- What information should be extracted at each stage?
- How should "non-straight" lines be treated?
- What is the most efficient method for extracting arcs?

- When will vectorization attain "industrial" quality?

It was felt, not always unanimously, that the literature contains some reliable, proven methods for these key problems:

- Thinning (there exist some 250 algorithms, with no one significantly superior to all the others);
- Contour-following, under a variety of heuristic error-norms;
- Edge-detection;
- Collinearity detection (the Hough transform); and
- Line and arc segmentation.

The general opinion was, that though many of these methods are reasonably good in practice, that many of them are in no sense optimal, and more basic research is needed to bring the field to maturity.

Our list of open problems tended to be rather vaguer:

- How to choose the best knowledge representation at various levels?
- Binarization (conversion of a grey image into a bilevel image): is local dynamic thresholding always best?
- Must one state an explicit noise model?
- When should application-specific knowledge be introduced?

These last two items provoked extended debate.

Since the raw image is almost invariably distorted by noise, a debate developed as to whether a theoretical model for noise should be sought. Some, especially those working on "practical" systems for handwriting or printed document analysis, argued that such a search was futile. How could you hope to model a spilled-coffee stain on smudged ink, next to a grease spot? Others argued, on methodological grounds, that, even if *all* available models were imperfect, it is helpful to evaluate a proposed method by reference to *some* explicit front-end noise model.

Another debate arose about the appropriate level at which domain-specific knowledge should be exploited. According to some, it should be deferred late into high-level processing, until it is impossible to proceed without it. One potentially important advantage of this approach is that it might lead to the development of methods with broad applicability (*e.g.* O'Gorman's "thin-line code" (TLC) datastructure). The opposite opinion was also voiced, that it should be used as early as possible. The advantage of this was said to be that it will permit particularly high-speed processing in the early, most-expensive stages of processing, without loss of accuracy in the specific application. An intermediate "pragmatic" engineering strategy, favored by others, is to employ known, general-purpose methods as a first cut, and then specialize them gradually, at whatever level gives the best results, using domain-specific knowledge or through experimental calibration.

Technical Drawing Analysis: SSPR'90 Working Group Report

Eric Saund[1] and Steven H. Joseph[2]

[1] Xerox Palo Alto Research Center,
   3333 Coyote Hill Rd, Palo Alto, CA 94304, USA
[2] Department of Mechanical Engineering, Sheffield University,
   Mappin Street, Sheffield S1 3JD, U.K.

This report summarizes the discussions of the Working Group on Technical Drawing Analysis of the IAPR 1990 Workshop on Syntactic and Structural Pattern Recognition, Murray Hill, NJ, 13-15 June 1990. Approximately twelve persons attended this session. We were charged with the task of identifying sound methods and open problems in computer-based or computer-assisted analysis of technical drawings. The discussion was moderated by Stephen Joseph and recorded by Eric Saund.

The discussion began with a review of applications for computer-based technical drawing analysis, and of the limitations of current technology. Applications include:

- redrawing/cleanup of drawings currently existing on paper.
- storage of drawings in electronic form for purposes of data compression, ease of modification, and distributed access.
- indexing into databases of drawings on the basis of graphical and symbolic content.
- integration of drawing and design processes including use of CAD models, fault diagnosis, and automated reasoning methods.
- incorporation of maps into automated navigational aids.

Shortcomings of current technology include:

- uneven quality of results (current techniques make many mistakes).
- limitations on image complexity.
- limitations on tolerable image degradation.
- limited domains of applicability; for example, even seemingly basic operations such as vectorizing are in many cases tailored to a certain type of drawing (*e.g.* engineering drawings) and don't work on other types (*e.g.* maps).
- poor interpretation of symbols and annotation.
- narrow range of feature types (lines, regions designators, symbols and notation, etc.).

Some effort was devoted to exploring what it means for a technique to be considered a "sound method." General consensus was reached that a sound method cannot be required to *never* make what would be regarded as mistakes by later processing stages. Instead a method is sound when its behavior is well character-ized, and when it is well understood under what circumstances "mistakes" will be made. Finer distinctions can be drawn between: (1) methods which are sound because system designers understand their behavior and therefore understand how and when to use them; and, (2) methods which are sound because the al-gorithm itself reports the degree to which its output is stable and reliable. Very few algorithms in current use satisfy criterion (2). One participant observed that even algorithms that are well-understood scientifically (and therefore are sound by criterion (1)) may be of no practical value in industry.

Most present agreed that several classes of techniques in widespread use today may serve as foundation stones for further developments in technical drawing analysis, and may be considered sound to some degree, even as these techniques are refined and improved. These include:

- binarization methods including adaptive thresholding;
- the line adjacency graph data structure;
- chain coding of contours;
- image preprocessing techniques such as salt-and-pepper noise removal;
- thinning and skeletonizing methods;
- connected components analysis;
- vectorization; and
- the Hough transform.

However, it was noted that techniques currently regarded as standard procedure may ultimately be revealed as temporary way-stations on the route to more powerful approaches. For example, image thresholding may become obsolete as memory costs decline and more powerful grey-level-based processing evolves.

Although the discussion of *open problems* pinpointed a few issues ripe for a directed research effort, most of the discussion was devoted to exploring broader issues reflecting the research pursuits of the working group participants. Goals for future research in technical drawing analysis include:

- techniques for segmenting different semantic entities on drawings, for exam-ple, extracting the contours of a part from the surrounding dimensioning lines, or extracting lines denoting roads from those denoting contour lines on a map;
- developments of the approach of successively stripping away different kinds of information on a drawing, for example, removing all pixels which it is hypothesized belong to regions of text — this procedure is nontrivial when many different kinds of information are present;
- user interface tools to facilitate verification of image processing output and for recovery from mistakes;
- technology for recognition of arbitrary symbols (as opposed to the standard alpha-numeric symbols), and for one-shot learning of novel symbols;
- techniques for indexing into databases of drawings on the basis of partial descriptions derived from symbols or from shape analysis; and

– methods for building 3D shape models from different 2D views present in a drawing.

Some discussion revolved around the role of *knowledge* in document image analysis. Knowledge of the properties of particular drawing domains may play roles at various levels in a document analysis system. This can include lexical knowledge about primitive graphical and symbolic elements, syntactic knowledge of rules governing the ways in which these elements may be arranged spatially, and semantic knowledge concerning interpretations in terms of the real-world domain to which the drawing refers (the shapes of physical objects, logical wiring of electronic components, systems of roads, etc.) Participants expressed concern that algorithms dependent on domain-specific idiosyncrasies can become a form of knowledge that makes systems brittle and unmodular. This can be especially true in low-level algorithms such as line tracing and text/graphics separation.

Much research remains to be done on the relationship between the knowledge of human experts and knowledge incorporated in computer programs for drawing analysis. In what sense can a program be said to have technical expertise about, say, mechanical parts assemblies? One answer is that a computer program should have the following property: the program should embody data structures, statements, and symbolic assertions that closely reflect the sorts of observations or comments that a human engineer would generate when shown a technical drawing. Workshop participants concluded that in order for knowledge to be incorporated effectively it must be modular, and it must be easily addressed, examined, and modified by human experts, these not being necessarily the program builders. The issue of knowledge also comes into play in the use of feedback between various levels of processing to correct mistakes and ambiguities of previous stages, and in the integration of symbolic and graphic information, as when using notated dimensions to refine spatial measurements made on line art.

Finally, participants touched on several broader directions in which progress would benefit the field. First, it would be beneficial to have a more thorough framework in which to understand the purpose of technical drawings for accomplishing work. What do different document domains have in common about the ways in which they use line art, region designators, symbols, spaces, etc., and how do different domains differ along these dimensions? Second, it would be useful to better understand how drawings are produced and visually interpreted by people. What sorts of motor errors are committed or avoided by draftsmen, what sorts of visual events are confusing or salient to the eye? Finally, machines need a counterpart to what in humans might be called, "perceptual common sense," for today's machine vision programs commit glaring errors obvious to any person. Ultimately, computer analysis of technical drawings must be grounded in a science of visual perception.

Recognition of Music Notation: SSPR'90 Working Group Report

Dorothea Blostein[1] and Nicholas P. Carter[2]

[1] Department of Computing and Information Science,
Queen's University, Kingston, Ontario, Canada K7L 3N6
[2] Department of Physics, University of Surrey,
Guildford, Surrey GU2 5XH, U.K.

This report summarizes the discussions of the Working Group on the Recognition of Music Notation, of the IAPR 1990 Workshop on Syntactic and Structural Pattern Recognition, Murray Hill, NJ, 13-15 June 1990. The participants were: D. Blostein, N. Carter, R. Haralick, T. Itagaki, H. Kato, H. Nishida, and R. Siromoney. The discussion was moderated by Nicholas Carter and recorded by Dorothea Blostein.

Music recognition is a rather new field with many open problems. To begin with, the term "music recognition" is not very well defined, since the goals of recognition vary depending on the application. Consider, for example, these applications:

1. generate an audio performance from the written score;
2. create a library database to permit more effective music indexing and searching than is possible from a card catalogue;
3. capture and analyze the typesetter's personality; and
4. read in a score and generate parts or *vice versa*.

Researchers who have different applications in mind find it difficult to agree on questions such as "what is successful recognition?," "should page coordinates be part of the music representation?," and "what does 90% recognition rate mean?." The development of a series of clearly specified music recognition problems will assist this communication process. As a start, we can distinguish at least the following three levels:

A. recognition of characters, symbols, and lines (analogous to vectorization);
B. recognition of parallel sequences of notes with pitch and duration; and
C. complete recognition and interpretation of all symbols.

Applications 1. and 2. require recognition at level B, application 3. may be served by recognition at level A, and application 4. requires recognition close to level C. Recognition at level C involves difficult grouping problems: it is necessary to recognize which note(s) to associate with an annotation such as a slur, a crescendo, a dynamic marking, a lyric etc.

An orthogonal classification for the music recognition problem is based on what types of music are covered. For example, the recognition process may assume:

- piano music only;
- orchestra scores;
- one voice per staff;
- percussion music;
- baroque music; or
- modern music (very little relation to standard notation).

A closely related open problem is how to explain the results of recognition. There is no standard for expressing results, and the desired results vary with the application. Researchers need a standard music language in which to represent recognition results. There was some discussion about whether this music language should be tied to locations on the page; for many applications page-coordinates are undesirable, but for typographical analysis they are necessary. It was suggested that "extraction" could denote extraction of music representations that are tied to physical page coordinates, and "recognition" could denote recognition of music representations that are independent of the physical page coordinates. ANSI committee X3V1.8M on Music in Information Processing Standards is reported to be making steady progress and a standard is within sight: the current acronym is SMDL (Standard Music Description Language). The music printing software community has pledged some support for SMDL and it would seem to be the answer to a few prayers of music-OCR people.

Standard terminology is needed for definition of the error rate. This terminology relates to the different levels of recognition alluded to above. For recognition at level A, error rates can be reported as a fraction of the number of symbols recognized. At level B, error rates can be expressed as a fraction of note-pitches and note-durations correctly recognized.

We briefly discussed the problem of representing the conventions of music notation. A large number of notational rules are used, but these rules interact in subtle ways, and, worst of all, there are exceptions to almost any rule.

While the field of music recognition is too new to have many "sound methods," the following research approach was suggested. We should establish a database of digitized sheet-music with correct interpretations. This database could permit us to compare the performance of various systems. In addition, the database provides the necessary information for constructing a noise model for a music recognizer. Nicholas Carter is currently building up a small database of 20+ pages in order to develop robust models for a reasonable range of symbols; as part of this, he may develop some sort of noise model. Such an effort might pave the way for a methodology to automatically construct a robust recognizer from a database of music input.

Syntactic Methods:
SSPR'90 Working Group Report

Rani Siromoney[1] and Alberto Sanfeliu[2]

[1] Department of Mathematics, Madras Christian College,
Tambaram, Madras 600 059, India
[2] Instituto de Cibernética, Universidad Politécnica de Cataluña
Diagonal 647, 2, 08028 Barcelona, Spain

This report summarizes the discussions of the Working Group on Syntactic Methods of the IAPR 1990 Workshop on Syntactic and Structural Pattern Recognition, Murray Hill, NJ, 13-15 June 1990. The group broadened its discussion somewhat to embrace structural as well as syntactic models, and placed particular emphasis on the inference of models. The members of the group were M. Chandrasekaran, S. Collin, A. Huq, O. V. Larsen, N. S. V. Rao, A. Sanfeliu, R. Siromoney, and E. Tanaka. The discussion moderator was A. Sanfeliu, and R. Siromoney served as scribe.

The field is motivated by the example of the success of the analysis of 1-D patterns (that is, strings), where a great deal is now known about matching (parsing) and error-correction; there has even been some limited success in inferring regular sets from examples. But extensions to higher dimensions have come slowly. For example, almost nothing firm is known about inferring two dimensional models. One member of the working group suggested that there is a sense in which the "topology" of strings does not extend in the ways that we expect.

Learning should concern itself not only with combinatorial structure but also with continuous variables. Problems of matching perfect, noiseless patterns, although they may involve daunting combinatorics, nevertheless often yield to analysis, but this is seldom true for noisy patterns. We should look seriously at parallel computation and parallel algorithms to solve certain open problems in pattern matching.

One participant suggested, pessimistically, that in natural scenes there little or no recursive structure, and so syntactic models are not likely to be helpful — of course, as several papers in this workshop illustrate, recursive structure is not unknown in artificial scenes such as technical drawings. Nevertheless, the pessimistic view should be taken to heart: even when we attempt to understand English sentences, we do not construct parse trees in our brain. We should abandon Chomsky's approach, and find new models for natural languages; and, in image pattern recognition, we must be even more innovative, and try to discover "human-like" pattern models.

There are a lot of different tools for matching information: why should any one be proposed, on any grounds, as the best? The pressing question in the field is not so much "Which method is best?" but "How should we evaluate whether or not a method is sound?" One aspect of this, often ignored in theoretical discussions, is robustness under noise: thus, models of noise may be more important than models of structure.

In the engineering of pattern recognition systems, we often work with a large number of models of various types, so that a single matching paradigm may not be enough. We have to "reason" in a variety of ways, perhaps differently at different levels: sometimes from a geometric point of view, sometimes symbolically, sometimes based frankly on heuristics.

For example, if a specific structure is expected, it then may be possible to extract the relationship between its parts — a goal which is meaningless without the structure. Additional information should be obtained that will help in concluding certain things which could not be done from the syntactic and semantic structures alone. Heuristics might be useful in achieving this objective. For example, knowing that the object in the scene is a glass is to know far more than any syntactic model can tell.

A good approach might be to combine simple syntactic models, *e.g.* regular grammars or equal matrix grammars, with some functional information. Inferring functional properties along with syntactic properties might then be easier as well as more useful. The idea is to attempt to adapt deliberately simple frameworks and tools to applications.

One of the more specific open problems mentioned was to construct an information retrieval system for chemical compounds, using three-dimensional shape, to help define and extract similarity among chemical structures.

We also discussed some broader open problems:

1. What kind of structural representation should we have, to help in matching, reasoning and inference?
2. Given a problem, how do we choose a matching method?
3. When can we use syntactic approaches in image processing and document analysis, and when should we use knowledge representation; when can they be mixed?
4. Does there exist any method of evaluation, to say that one method is better than the other?
5. There are no known polynomial-time algorithms for matching general (sub-)graphs. But what is the case for restricted graphs such as those which are embedded in 3D, which characteristically occur in pictures, 1-skeletons, 3D-skeleton graphs, planar graphs, etc? Cases occurring in biology, vision, chemistry, molecular biology, etc., may have special structure which we can exploit.

SSPR'90 Participants List

Participants in the IAPR 1990 Workshop on SSPR, Murray Hill, NJ, USA, 13–15 June, 1990, are listed below with their affiliations, addresses, etc, as of June 15, 1990.

Dominique Antoine
INRIA Lorraine — CRIN
Campus Scientifique, B.P. 239
54506 Vandœuvre CEDEX France
TEL +33 83.91.80.00 x3027
EMAIL antoine@loria.crin.fr
TELEX NANCYUN 960 646F

Dr. Henry S. Baird
Computing Science Research Ctr
AT&T Bell Laboratories
600 Mountain Ave, Room 2C-557
Murray Hill, NJ 07974-2072 USA
TEL +1 (908) 582-5744
FAX +1 (908) 582-5857
EMAIL hsb@research.att.com
TELEX 219348

Dipl.-Inform. Thomas Bayer
Daimler-Benz Research Center
Wilhelm-Runge-Strasse 11
D-7900 Ulm Germany
TEL +49 731-505-4113
FAX +49 731-505-4106

Prof. Dorothea Blostein
Dept Computing & Inf. Science
Queen's University
Kingston, Ontario
Canada K7L 3N6
TEL +1 (613) 545-6537
FAX +1 (613) 545-6513
EMAIL blostein@qucis.queensu.ca

Prof. Horst Bunke
Universität Bern
Institut für Informatik
   und Angewandte Mathematik
Länggassstrasse 51
CH-3012 Bern Switzerland
TEL +41 31-65-44-51
FAX +41 31-65-39-65
EMAIL bunke@iam.unibe.ch

Dr. Nicholas P. Carter
Physics Dept
Univ. Surrey
Guildford, Surrey GU2 5XH U.K.
TEL +44 (0483) 571281 x2732
FAX +44 (0483) 304212
EMAIL npc@ph.surrey.ac.uk

M. Chandrasekaran
Dept Statistics
Madras Christian College
Tambaram, Madras 600 059
India
TEL 401875

S. C. Chennubhotla
Dept Computer Engineering
113-K EE West
The Pennsylvania State Univ.
University Park, PA 16802 USA
TEL +1 (814) 863-1047
FAX +1 (814) 865-7065
EMAIL s4c@ecl.psu.edu

Dr. Philip A. Chou
AT&T Bell Laboratories
600 Mountain Ave, Room 2C-479
Murray Hill, NJ 07974 USA
TEL +1 (908) 582-5022
FAX +1 (908) 582-7308
EMAIL chou@research.att.com

Suzanne Collin
INRIA Lorraine–CRIN
Campus scientifique, B.P. 239
54506 Vandœuvre CEDEX France
TEL +33 83.91.21.25
EMAIL collin@loria.crin.fr
TELEX NANCYUN 960 646F

Dr. Andreas Dengel
German Research Ctr for AI
P. O. Box 2080
D-6750 Kaiserslauten Germany
TEL +49 631-205-3215
FAX +49 631-205-3210
EMAIL dengel@informatik.uni-kl.de

Prof. Dov Dori
Dept Computer Science
University of Kansas
Lawrence, Kansas 66045-2192 USA
TEL +1 (913) 864-4482
EMAIL dori@ukanvm.bitnet

Dr. Hiromichi Fujisawa
Hitachi Central Research Lab.
1-280 Higashi-koigakubo
Kokubunji
Tokyo 185 Japan
TEL +81 423-23-1111
FAX +81 423-23-1900
EMAIL fujisawa@crl.hitachi.co.jp
TELEX 2832522 CHUKEN J

Prof. Robert E. Haralick
Dept Electrical Engineering
Univ. of Washington
Seattle, WA 98105 USA
TEL +1 (206) 545-4974
FAX +1 (206) 543-3842
EMAIL haralick@cs.washington.edu

Gary P. Herring
Technology Resource Dept
United States Postal Service
475 L'Enfant Plaza, Room 2140
Washington, DC 20260-8118 USA
TEL +1 (202) 268-3864
FAX +1 (202) 268-4980

Tin Kam Ho
Dept Computer Science
226 Bell Hall
SUNY at Buffalo
Amherst, NY 14260 USA
TEL +1 (716) 636-3450
FAX +1 (716) 636-3464
EMAIL hotin@cs.buffalo.edu

Osamu Hori
Information Systems Lab
Toshiba Res. and Dev. Ctr
1, Komukai Toshiba-cho,
Saiwai-ku, Kawasaki 210
Japan
TEL +81 44-549-2242
FAX +81 44-549-2263
EMAIL hori@isl.rdc.toshiba.co.jp
TELEX J22587

Dr. Jonathan J. Hull
Dept Computer Science
226 Bell Hall
SUNY at Buffalo
Amherst, NY 14260 USA
TEL +1 (716) 636-3195
FAX +1 (716) 636-3464
EMAIL hull@cs.buffalo.edu

Dr. Abdul Huq
Dept Statistics
Madras Christian College
Tambaram, Madras 600 059
India
TEL 401875

Takebumi Itagaki
Dept Applied Physics
Waseda University
3-4-1 Okubo, Shinjuku-ku
Tokyo 169 Japan
TEL +81 3-203-4141
FAX +81 3-200-2567
EMAIL sohteru@jpnwas00.waseda.ac.jp
TELEX 2325115 WARIKOJ

Dr. Stephen H. Joseph
Dept Mech. Eng.
Sheffield University
Mappin Street
Sheffield, S1 3JD U.K.
TEL +44 (0)742 768555
FAX +44 (0)742 753671
EMAIL meishj@primec.sheff.ac.uk
TELEX 547216 UGSHEF G

Junichi Kanai
ECSE Dept
Rensselaer Polytechnic Institute
Troy, NY 12180-3590 USA
TEL +1 (518) 276-8229
FAX +1 (518) 276-6261
EMAIL kanaij@ecse.rpi.edu

Prof. Rangachar Kasturi
Dept EE, Computer Engineering
The Pennsylvania State Univ.
University Park, PA 16802 USA
TEL +1 (814) 863-4254
FAX +1 (814) 865-7065
EMAIL r1k@ecl.psu.edu

Hirokazu Kato
Dept Control Engineering
Faculty of Engineering Science
Osaka University
Toyonaka, Osaka 560 Japan
TEL +81 6-844-1151 x4628
FAX +81 6-857-7664
EMAIL inolab@inolab.ce.osaka-u.ac.jp
TELEX 5286110 OUFES J

Stephen Lam
Dept Computer Science
226 Bell Hall
SUNY at Buffalo
Amherst, NY 14260 USA
TEL +1 (716) 636-3450
EMAIL lam@cs.buffalo.edu

Ole Vilhelm Larsen
Institute for Electronic Systems
Aalborg University
Badehusvej 23
DK-9000 Aalborg Denmark
TEL +45 98 — 13 87 88
FAX +45 98 — 16 61 50
EMAIL ovl@vaxa.aud.auc.dk

Dr. Yann LeCun
AT&T Bell Laboratories
Crawfords Corner Rd, Rm 4G-332
Holmdel, NJ 07733-1988 USA
TEL +1 (908) 949-4038
EMAIL yann@neural.att.com

Dar-Shyang Lee
Dept Computer Science
226 Bell Hall
SUNY at Buffalo
Amherst, NY 14260 USA
TEL +1 (716) 636-3843
EMAIL dslee@cs.buffalo.edu

Seong-Whan Lee
Dept Computer Science
Chungbuk National University
Cheongju, Chungbuk 360-763
Republic of Korea
TEL (0431) 61-2263
FAX (0431) 63-0612

Dr. Suzanne A. Liebowitz
Ctr for Advanced Information Tech.
Unisys Corporation
P. O. Box 517
Paoli, PA 19301 USA
TEL +1 (215) 648-2756
FAX +1 (215) 648-2288
EMAIL suzanne@prc.unisys.com

Dr. Guy Lorette
IRISA
Campus de Beaulieu
35042 Rennes Cedex France
TEL +33 99.36.20.00
FAX +33 99.38.38.32
EMAIL lorette@irisa.fr
TELEX +33 84950473 F

Dr. Gerd Maderlechner
Siemens AG
Corporate R&D, ZFE 15 INF1
Otto-Hahn-Ring 6
D-8000 München 83 Germany
TEL +49 (089) 636-3389
FAX +49 (089) 636-2393
EMAIL gm%bvax4@ztivax.uucp

Ofer Matan
AT&T Bell Laboratories
Crawfords Corner Rd, 2G-231A
Holmdel, NJ 07733 USA
TEL +1 (908) 949-9423
FAX +1 (908) 949-1045
EMAIL ofer@irazu.att.com

Prof. Roger Mohr
LIFIA - IMAG
46 av. Félix Viallet
38031 GRENOBLE Cedex France
TEL +33 76.57.46.53
FAX +33 76.57.46.02
EMAIL mohr@lifia.imag.fr

Prof. George Nagy
ECSE Dept
Rensselaer Polytechnic Institute
Troy, NY 12180-3590 USA
TEL +1 (518) 276-6078
EMAIL userewyt@rpitsmts.bitnet

Hirobumi Nishida
Artificial Intelligence Division
RICOH Res. and Dev. Center
16-1 Shin-ei-cho, Kohoku-ku
Yokohama, Kanagawa, 223 Japan
TEL +81 45-593-3411
FAX +81 45-593-3489
EMAIL nishida@rdc.ricoh.co.jp

Dr. Lawrence O'Gorman
AT&T Bell Laboratories
600 Mountain Ave, Rm 3D-455
Murray Hill, NJ 07974 USA
TEL +1 (908) 582-7262
FAX +1 (908) 582-5192
EMAIL log@allegra.att.com

Prof. Masayuki Okamoto
Dept Information Engineering
Faculty of Engineering
Shinshu University
500 Wakasato Nagano 380 Japan
TEL +81 262-26-4101
FAX +81 262-23-4723
EMAIL okamoto@wakasato.cs.shinshu-
u.ac.jp

Prof. Theo Pavlidis
Dept Computer Science
SUNY at Stony Brook
Stony Brook, NY 11794-4400 USA
TEL +1 (516) 632-8465
FAX +1 (516) 632-8334
EMAIL theo@sbcs.sunysb.edu

Ming-Chien Peng
Dept CIS
NJ Institute of Technology
Newark, NJ 07102 USA
TEL +1 (908) 997-7187

Prof. Réjean Plamondon
Dept of Electrical Engineering
Ecole Polytechnique de Montréal
C.P. 6079, Succ. "A"
Montréal, QC Canada H3C 3A7
TEL +1 (514) 340-4539
FAX +1 (514) 340-4147
EMAIL ha03@polytec1.bitnet

Rajesh Raman
Dept Computer Engineering
113-K EE West
The Pennsylvania State Univ.
University Park, PA 16802 USA
TEL +1 (814) 865-2729
FAX +1 (814) 865-7065
EMAIL rzr@ecl.psu.edu

Prof. Nageswara S. V. Rao
Dept Computer Science
Old Dominion Univ.
Norfolk, VA 23529-0162 USA
TEL +1 (804) 683-4414
FAX +1 (804) 683-4900
EMAIL rao@cs.odu.edu

Prof. Alberto Sanfeliu
Institut de Cibernetica
University of Barcelona
Diagonal 646,2 planta
08028 Barcelona Spain
TEL +34 3-334-7704
FAX +34 3-401-6605
EMAIL easan%top.upc.es
    @cunyvm.cuny.edu

Dr. Eric Saund
Xerox Palo Alto Res. Ctr
3333 Coyote Hill Rd
Palo Alto, CA 94304 USA
TEL +1 (415) 494-4474
FAX +1 (415) 494-4241
EMAIL saund.pa@xerox.com

Dr. David B. Searls
Ctr for Advanced Information Tech.
Unisys Corporation
70 E. Swedesford Rd
Paoli, PA 19301 USA
TEL +1 (215) 648-2146
FAX +1 (215) 648-2288
EMAIL dbs@prc.unisys.com

Prof. Linda Shapiro
Dept Electrical Engineering
Univ. of Washington
Seattle, WA 98105 USA
TEL +1 (206) 543-2196

Prof. Jean C. Simon
10 Rue de l'Université
75007 Paris France
TEL +33 1.42.60.79.36
FAX +33 1.42.60.58.01

Prof. Rani Siromoney
Dept Mathematics
Madras Christian College
Tambaram, Madras 600 059
India
TEL 401875

Dr. A. Lawrence Spitz
Xerox Palo Alto Res. Ctr
3333 Coyote Hill Road
Palo Alto, CA 94304 USA
TEL +1 (415) 494-4216
FAX +1 (415) 494-4241
EMAIL spitz.pa@xerox.com

Prof. Sargur N. Srihari
Dept Computer Science
226 Bell Hall
SUNY at Buffalo
Amherst, NY 14260 USA
TEL +1 (716) 636-3191
FAX +1 (716) 636-3464
EMAIL srihari@cs.buffalo.edu

Prof. Ching Y. Suen
Dept Computer Science, CENPARMI
Concordia University
1455 de Maisonneuve West
Montreal, Quebec Canada H3G
    1M8
TEL +1 (514) 848-3006
FAX +1 (514) 848-3494

Prof. JuWei Tai
Institute of Automation
Academia Sinica, PO Box 2728
Beijing 100080 P. R. China
TEL 2564980 Beijing
FAX 2561266 Beijing

Prof. Eiichi Tanaka
Dept Electronics
Kobe University
1-1 Rokkodai, Nada-ku
Kobe 657 Japan
TEL +81 78-881-1212 x5093

Dr. Wiley E. Thompson
Dept Electrical and Comp. Engr.
New Mexico State University
Las Cruces, NM 88003 USA

TEL +1 (505) 646-3811
FAX +1 (505) 646-3549

Dr. Karl Tombre
INRIA Lorraine — CRIN
Campus Scientifique B. P. 239
54506 Vandœuvre Cedex France

TEL +33 83.91.21.25
FAX +33 83.41.30.79
EMAIL tombre@loria.crin.fr

Shuichi Tsujimoto
Information Systems Lab.
Toshiba R&D Center
1, Komukai Toshiba-cho, Saiwai-
ku
Kawasaki 210 Japan

TEL +81 44-549-2244
FAX +81 44-549-2263
EMAIL tsuji@isl.rdc.toshiba.co.jp
TELEX J22587

Mahesh Viswanathan
ECS Engineering Dept
Rensselaer Polytechnic Institute
Troy, NY 12180-3590 USA

TEL +1 (518) 276-8229
EMAIL mahesh@doc.ecse.rpi.edu

Prof. David T. Wang
Dept Computer & Inf. Science
New Jersey Inst. of Tech.
323 Dr. M. L. King Blvd
Newark, NJ 07102 USA

TEL +1 (908) 596-5776
FAX +1 (908) 596-5777

Dr. Patrick S. P. Wang
MIT AI Lab, Room NE 4-815
545 Technology Square
Cambridge, MA 02139 USA

TEL +1 (617) 253-6247
FAX +1 (617) 258-8682
EMAIL pwang@ai.mit.edu

Ynjiun P. Wang
Symbol Technologies
116 Wilbur Drive
Bohemia, NY 11716 USA

TEL +1 (516) 563-2400 x497

Mitsuru Yamada
KDD R&D Labs (Telmatics)
2-1-15, Ohara 2-Chome
Kamifufuoka-shi
Saitama 356 Japan

TEL +81 492-66 7406
FAX +81 492-66 7510
EMAIL yamada@kddsun.kddlabs.co.jp
TELEX J22500 KDD TOKYO

Dr. Kazuhiko Yamamoto
Information Sciences Division
Electrotechnical Laboratory
1-1-4, Umezono
Tsukuba Science City
Ibaraki 305 Japan

TEL +81 298-54-5491
FAX +81 298-58-5949
EMAIL yamamoto@etl.go.jp
TELEX 3652570 AISTJ

Karim Zerhouni
8 Rue Jean Dolent
75014 Paris France